REFLECTIONS ON THE CLIOMETRICS REVOLUTION

This volume marks 50 years of an innovative approach to writing economic history often called "The Cliometrics Revolution," a revolution that brought formal economic theory and advanced quantitative methods to the historical study of economic development in North America, the British Isles, continental Europe and elsewhere. In conversation with cliometricians of the next generation, 25 pioneering scholars reflect on changes in the practice of economic history they have observed and have helped to bring about.

The book presents memoirs of personal development, intellectual lives and influences, new lines of historical research, long-standing debates, a growing international scholarly community, and the contingencies that guide and re-direct academic careers. These scholars' achievements include having found ways to estimate levels and growth rates of national income for the USA, Canada and the UK back to the eighteenth century; they have contributed to numerous debates, for example on the influence of slavery in the American economy, the role of railroads in economic growth and change, the sources and patterns of technological progress, and the effects of early industrialization on material welfare. In personally distinctive fashion, some have taken a longer view, examining the rise of Western economies and their economic interrelationships, and the impact of modern economic growth on human health, mortality and even happiness.

The conversations presented here are engaging, informative and – more often than one might expect – humorous. Together with a framework provided by the editors, they tell a tale of how cliometricians, their allies and their critics, have helped to transform what we know about the economic past. This book will be of interest to researchers, teachers, and students in the history of economics. Likewise, anyone interested in modern economic development will find it a useful guide to how economic historians have come to understand our path to the twenty-first century world economy.

John S. Lyons teaches at the Department of Economics at Miami University.
Louis P. Cain is Professor of Economics at Loyola University Chicago.
Samuel H. Williamson is Professor of Economics, Emeritus, at Miami University.

ROUTLEDGE EXPLORATIONS IN ECONOMIC HISTORY

1 ECONOMIC IDEAS AND GOVERNMENT POLICY
Contributions to contemporary economic history
Sir Alec Cairncross

2 THE ORGANIZATION OF LABOUR MARKETS
Modernity, culture and governance in Germany, Sweden, Britain and Japan
Bo Stråth

3 CURRENCY CONVERTIBILITY
The gold standard and beyond
Edited by Jorge Braga de Macedo, Barry Eichengreen and Jaime Reis

4 BRITAIN'S PLACE IN THE WORLD
A historical enquiry into import controls 1945–1960
Alan S. Milward and George Brennan

5 FRANCE AND THE INTERNATIONAL ECONOMY
From Vichy to the Treaty of Rome
Frances M. B. Lynch

6 MONETARY STANDARDS AND EXCHANGE RATES
M.C. Marcuzzo, L. Officer, A. Rosselli

7 PRODUCTION EFFICIENCY IN DOMESDAY ENGLAND, 1086
John McDonald

8 FREE TRADE AND ITS RECEPTION 1815–1960
Freedom and trade: Volume I
Edited by Andrew Marrison

9 CONCEIVING COMPANIES
Joint-stock politics in Victorian England
Timothy L. Alborn

10 THE BRITISH INDUSTRIAL DECLINE RECONSIDERED
Edited by Jean-Pierre Dormois and Michael Dintenfass

11 THE CONSERVATIVES AND INDUSTRIAL EFFICIENCY, 1951–1964
Thirteen wasted years?
Nick Tiratsoo and Jim Tomlinson

12 PACIFIC CENTURIES
Pacific and Pacific Rim economic history since the 16th century
Edited by Dennis O. Flynn, Lionel Frost and A.J.H. Latham

13 THE PREMODERN CHINESE ECONOMY
Structural equilibrium and capitalist sterility
Gang Deng

14 THE ROLE OF BANKS IN MONITORING FIRMS
The case of the crédit mobilier
Elisabeth Paulet

15 MANAGEMENT OF THE NATIONAL DEBT IN THE UNITED KINGDOM, 1900–1932
Jeremy Wormell

16 AN ECONOMIC HISTORY OF SWEDEN
Lars Magnusson

17 FREEDOM AND GROWTH
The rise of states and markets in Europe, 1300–1750
S. R. Epstein

18 THE MEDITERRANEAN RESPONSE TO GLOBALIZATION BEFORE 1950
Sevket Pamuk and Jeffrey G Williamson

19 PRODUCTION AND CONSUMPTION IN ENGLISH HOUSEHOLDS 1600–1750
Mark Overton, Jane Whittle, Darron Dean and Andrew Hann

20 GOVERNANCE, THE STATE, REGULATION AND INDUSTRIAL RELATIONS
Ian Clark

21 EARLY MODERN CAPITALISM
Economic and social change in Europe 1400–1800
Edited by Maarten Prak

22 AN ECONOMIC HISTORY OF LONDON, 1800–1914
Michael Ball and David Sunderland

23 THE ORIGINS OF NATIONAL FINANCIAL SYSTEMS
Alexander Gerschenkron reconsidered
Edited by Douglas J. Forsyth and Daniel Verdier

24 THE RUSSIAN REVOLUTIONARY ECONOMY, 1890–1940
Ideas, debates and alternatives
Vincent Barnett

25 LAND RIGHTS, ETHNO NATIONALITY AND SOVEREIGNTY IN HISTORY
Edited by Stanley L. Engerman and Jacob Metzer

26 AN ECONOMIC HISTORY OF FILM
Edited by John Sedgwick and Mike Pokorny

27 THE FOREIGN EXCHANGE MARKET OF LONDON
Development since 1900
John Atkin

28 RETHINKING ECONOMIC CHANGE IN INDIA
Labour and livelihood
Tirthankar Roy

29 THE MECHANICS OF MODERNITY IN EUROPE AND EAST ASIA
The institutional origins of social change and stagnation
Erik Ringmar

30 INTERNATIONAL ECONOMIC INTEGRATION IN HISTORICAL PERSPECTIVE
Dennis M. P. McCarthy

31 THEORIES OF INTERNATIONAL TRADE
Adam Klug
Edited by Warren Young and Michael Bordo

32 CLASSICAL TRADE PROTECTIONISM 1815–1914
Edited by Jean Pierre Dormois and Pedro Lains

33 ECONOMY AND ECONOMICS OF ANCIENT GREECE
Takeshi Amemiya

34 SOCIAL CAPITAL, TRUST AND THE INDUSTRIAL REVOLUTION: 1780–1880
David Sunderland

35 PRICING THEORY, FINANCING OF INTERNATIONAL ORGANISATIONS AND MONETARY HISTORY
Lawrence H. Officer

36 POLITICAL COMPETITION AND ECONOMIC REGULATION
Edited by Peter Bernholz and Roland Vaubel

37 INDUSTRIAL DEVELOPMENT IN POSTWAR JAPAN
Hirohisa Kohama

38 REFLECTIONS ON THE CLIOMETRICS REVOLUTION
Conversations with economic historians
Edited by John S. Lyons, Louis P. Cain and Samuel H. Williamson

REFLECTIONS ON THE CLIOMETRICS REVOLUTION

Conversations with economic historians

Edited by
John S. Lyons,
Louis P. Cain
and
Samuel H. Williamson

Routledge
Taylor & Francis Group
LONDON AND NEW YORK

First published 2008
by Routledge
2 Park Square, Milton Park, Abingdon, Oxon OX14 4RN

Simultaneously published in the USA and Canada
by Routledge
711 Madison Avenue, New York, NY 10017

Routledge is an imprint of the Taylor & Francis Group, an informa business

Reprinted 2008

Typeset in Baskerville by
RefineCatch Limited, Bungay, Suffolk

First issued in paperback in 2013

British Library Cataloguing in Publication Data
A catalogue record for this book is available from the British Library

Library of Congress Cataloging in Publication Data
A catalog record for this book has been requested

ISBN13: 978–0–415–74838–4 (pbk)
ISBN13: 978–0–415–70091–7 (hbk)
ISBN13: 978–0–203–79963–5 (ebk)

CONTENTS

PREFACE

This book presents interviews with 25 scholars who participated, directly or indirectly, in the development of an intellectual movement – often called a revolution – that in the past half-century has transformed the economic historiography of North America, the United Kingdom and elsewhere. Excepting the interview with Robin Matthews, which was conducted for this volume, the conversations published here appeared initially in *The Newsletter of the Cliometric Society (NCS)*. The editors thank the Society for permission to republish those materials.

The "cliometrics revolution" began – it is generally thought – when American and Canadian economic historians met in Williamstown, Massachusetts in the autumn of 1957 under the *aegis* of the Conference on Research in Income and Wealth (CRIW). Their subject was *Trends in the American Economy in the Nineteenth Century*, also the title of the conference volume published in 1960. The meeting was the first organized stirring of a movement to "modernize" traditional economic historiography by applying more formal styles of economic analysis and more up-to-date quantitative methods to historical data and problems. Yet, as William Parker wrote in the introduction to *Trends*,

> As an economic historian the editor cannot forbear a . . . caveat against the misinterpretation of all this work. The statistical method, and particularly its use to animate . . . large concepts . . ., has the faults of its virtues. The worst fault is that it imposes a severe strain on the accuracy and completeness of an imperfect historical record. It requires figures, as the Minotaur required maidens, and it requires them exactly and on time.[1]

The second initiative came three years later, in December 1960, when about a dozen economic historians, along with some interested colleagues and students, assembled at Purdue University for the first of a series of economic history seminars that soon was

1 CRIW (1960: 8). The CRIW, established in 1936, is an arm of the National Bureau of Economic Research (NBER). Its members often refer to it as the "Income and Wealth" group, as in several interviews below. A second such conference was held in Chapel Hill, North Carolina, in 1963; most of its papers were published in *Output, Employment, and Productivity in the United States after 1800*, edited by Dorothy Brady (CRIW 1966).

called "Clio," or the "Cliometrics Conference."[2] It was held annually at Purdue for a decade, serving as the locus for presentation of many ground-breaking papers in the "New Economic History." In 1970 it moved to the University of Wisconsin and has continued to the present at a series of other venues.

An offshoot of the first two decades of Cliometrics Conferences is the Cliometric Society, which was founded in 1983 by Deirdre McCloskey and Sam Williamson when they and the Conference were based at the University of Iowa.[3] Formation of the Society was ratified, in effect, by an international group of scholars who attended the first World Congress of Cliometrics at Northwestern University in the late Spring of 1985. Among its other activities, since 1985 the Society has published a *Newsletter*, which includes reports of conference proceedings throughout the world and a series of interviews with major contributors to cliometrics and economic history generally, beginning with Lance Davis in February 1990, and continuing more recently with interviews with scholars of younger generations and of differing scholarly styles.

The interviews contained in this volume were mostly commissioned by the *Newsletter's* editors from pioneering contributors to the field – from one group who organized or participated in the earliest of the CRIW and Purdue Conferences and from a second group educated or based at British universities. Each of our subjects was born before the outbreak of the Second World War (a few before or during the First), and completed academic training at some time between the mid-1930s and the early 1960s. Several were students of elders in these groups. All have had long and intellectually fruitful academic lives, as illustrated by their published work and the work of the students they have taught and supervised. Indeed, the research output of many of our interviewees after they reached normal retirement age could easily constitute the whole of a productive scholarly career.

Most of our subjects would or do admit to being, or having been at one time, a "cliometrician," but a few others demur, either firmly or with some diffidence. We think that such ambivalence about being so labeled derives from the wide variety of meanings and connotations linked to "cliometrics" in the past five decades. What at least some of our interviewees were doing in the 1950s and 1960s was called "The New Economic History" for a quarter-century, but that phrase has fallen out of favor as both the movement and its champions have aged. The term "cliometrics" (with its variants) has not only entered the language of academia, but can be found in dictionaries and discussed in encyclopedias.[4]

2 "Cliometrics" was coined by Stanley Reiter and was first published in Davis, Hughes & Reiter (1960: 540). The term is a play on the words Clio, the Muse of History, and metrics, from econometrics, a field emerging at the time.

3 Before 1996 Deirdre McCloskey was known as Donald and published her work under that name. She was "Donald" or "Don" when the interviews mentioning her were conducted, and we have retained the usage in those interviews.

4 "New Economic History" as a phrase describing the field appeared first in print in M. Morris (1959: 569); other than in Davis, Hughes & Reiter (1960) and in *Explorations in Entrepreneurial History*, "cliometrics" was not used until Unger (1967: 1241). "Cliometrics" appears in such works as *The Oxford English Dictionary* and *Merriam–Webster's Collegiate Dictionary* and was defined as early as 1983 in the *Chambers 20th Century Dictionary*. For encyclopedia discussions see Floud (1987), Engerman (1996) and S. Williamson & Whaples (2003).

Dictionaries often define "cliometrics" in ways sufficiently off the mark to make even a diehard quantitative-analytical economic historian squirm. As McCloskey remarks in *A Bibliography of Historical Economics to 1980* (1990: *ix–x*),

> I have avoided the word "cliometrics." Despite its loony charm . . . and its appearance in recent dictionaries (misdefined as "quantitative history" *tout court*), the word "cliometrics" has given the field more trouble than pleasure. . . . Even my own pamphlet for the Economic History Society, which shows how simple is the economics in historical economics and how workaday are its statistical tools, carries forward the confusion, by its title: *Econometric History*.

We prefer a liberal and encompassing interpretation of "cliometrics," in contrast to those economic historians who have embraced neither the word nor the style of research they have tended to infer from it. Our view of the cliometrics and quantitative economic history undertaken by the scholars whose interviews appear here is that it is best characterized by its diversity. Cliometrics, or historical economics, calls upon much more than technique, examines much more than markets and, willy-nilly, has dragged itself from the early days of quantitative and theoretical revisionism to consider a wide range of historical experience, to develop and apply novel theoretical approaches, and to ask a variety of new questions. One can see in much of this work the rigorous economic analysis and careful measurement that characterize the best of cliometrics, as well as the assiduous unearthing of sources and their cautious evaluation, the clarity of exposition, and the sensitivity to time, place and chance that are the hallmarks of the best of history, whatever its sub-field. And, we would add, as in any other field the worst of this work will be ignored, while the middle range will be judged by and employed for its virtues.

The significance of the cliometric approach was recognized in 1993 with the award of the Nobel Memorial Prize in Economics to Robert W. Fogel and Douglass C. North "for having renewed research in economic history by applying economic theory and quantitative methods in order to explain economic and institutional change." In the citation, the Nobel Committee defined the field in compact language:

> [T]he "new economic history" or cliometrics, i.e., research that combines economic theory, quantitative methods, hypothesis testing, counterfactual alternatives and traditional techniques of economic history, to explain economic growth and decline.[5]

That this Nobel award recognized work in economics reflects the tensions that have beset economic history from its origins in the late nineteenth century in university

5 As quoted in *NCS* 8:3 (October 1993: 4), from URL: <http://nobelprize.org/nobel_prizes/economics/laureates/1993/press.html>. The formal title of the award is "The Sveriges Riksbank (Bank of Sweden) Prize in Economic Sciences in Memory of Alfred Nobel." Fortuitously, the interview with Douglass North was scheduled to appear in that issue of the *Newsletter*.

faculties of history and economics. As the interviews reveal, economic history, even the cliometrics variety, includes a broad array of subjects, questions, approaches and techniques. Careers in economic history – even, or perhaps especially, influential ones – have often involved major changes of direction in scholarly focus, both within the field and toward related but separate disciplines or concerns. The interviews likewise reveal the formation of an international network of social and intellectual ties important to the development of the profession. For this volume several interviewees responded to our invitation to contribute "Further Reflections," which are appended to the interviews, while one regretted that he was "plumb out" of afterthoughts. The book closes with an overview of the New Economic History and cliometrics. Patrick Karl O'Brien, Centennial Professor in the London School of Economics and Political Science and Convenor of the "Global Economic History Network," has been a contributor to and commentator on the field, as in his book with Çaglar Keyder on British and French economic growth (1978) and his article "In praise of New Economic History" (1982). He uses the perspective derived from a long career in quantitative and more traditional history and economic history in an "Afterword" written for this volume.

The interviews reflect the graciousness of our subjects, and we thank them. The interviews also reflect the thoughtful preparation and considerable effort undertaken by the interviewers, whom we thank here collectively. During our tenure at the *Newsletter* (1985–99), with Williamson as Editor and Lyons and Cain as Associates, we were aided by the Assistant Editors who transcribed, checked, proofed, edited and prepared copy for publication: we thank Lois Nelson, Elizabeth Lokon, Leslie Smith, Cynthia Stromgren, and Margaret Voyles; in particular, we thank Debra Morner for her nearly eight years of help and collegiality from 1992 to 1999, when two-thirds of the interviews were published. Our successors at the *Newsletter* (2000–7), Michael Haupert, Mary Beth Combs, Pamela Nickless and Jean Bonde, continued to produce the interview series, including the interviews with Stanley Engerman, Max Hartwell and Charles Feinstein.

We are grateful to The Farmer School of Business, Miami University, which provided funds for research assistance, and to Heather McIntosh, Jennifer Naberhaus, Gina Mussalem and Brenna Finkbeiner, who did the work. Also, Lyons thanks Miami University for funding a period of research leave. The volume was commissioned by Rob Langham at Routledge, who helped us through and beyond the proposal stage. He was succeeded by Terry Clague and Tom Sutton, whose continuing advice has been invaluable.

During production of this collection we incurred many debts: we acknowledge them here, but they can hardly be discharged. The advisers we consulted are responsible for numerous improvements to the work; the editors are responsible for defects that remain. For having read the general introduction and offering their comments we thank Lee Craig, Ron Denham, J. W. Drukker, Naomi Lamoreaux, Patrick O'Brien, Barry Supple and Peter Wardley. On multiple other matters we have benefited from advice, assistance and information; for their help we thank George Akerlof, Bill Burkhart, Marilyn Coopersmith, Nicholas Dawidoff, Alex Field, Sir Roderick Floud, Matt Gallman, Claudia Goldin, Tony Gómez-Ibáñez, Dorothy Hahn, Frank Hahn, Will Hausman, Alison Hoddell, Jane Humphries, Bill Hutchinson, Peter Kilby, John Latham, Deirdre McCloskey, Judy McQuiston, Morris Morris, Marinella Moscheni,

Ed Nelson, Jarrett Parker, Dan Raff, Elspeth Davies Rostow, Sharon Squyres, Dick Sylla, Nicole Tateosian, Mark Thomas, Nick von Tunzelmann, John Wallis, Gavin Wright, and Sir Tony Wrigley. Finally, we are especially grateful to Patrick O'Brien for reading the interviews and our editorial matter and for writing the concluding words.

Oxford, Ohio
Glenview, Illinois
Charlevoix, Michigan *2007*

SOURCES AND CONVENTIONS

The interviews in this volume are a partial oral history of more than a half-century of scholarly activity, and the editors are aware of the sorts of problems of memory and myopia discussed by Tribe (1997) and Weintraub (2007): for example, reading the set of interviews as a group revealed a number of inconsistent statements. These have been corrected to the extent possible with the aid of several interviewees augmented by the documentary record. The biographical introductions to the interviews are based on published information, as in Mark Blaug's *Who's Who in Economics* (ed. 1999), on materials such as *curricula vitae*, and on responses to our queries.

Both editorial matter and interviews refer to numerous sources. Works mentioned only once are provided with publisher's name and year of publication in text or notes and are not otherwise listed. Citation in the editors' contributions is by the author-date method. In the interviews most references are implicit, except where the name of the first author might not be evident or where useful information is contained in the year of publication. In some cases, our interviewees mention work in progress by themselves or others; the references in this volume list the published versions of those books and articles. Where the name of the (first) author is obvious the citation, when explicit, is simply by year. Works cited are listed in full in the "references" section, which is preceded by a list of abbreviations commonly used in the text or reference list. Where allusion is made to the body of publications of a particular person, rather than to a given work, there is no reference listing.

INTRODUCTION

Economic History and Cliometrics

It is likely that certain sins against reasonableness have been committed in some . . . recent works. It would be equally unreasonable, however, to judge them too severely. The introduction into economic history of serious economic and statistical analysis is still at its early stages. Much has been and much will be learned. . . . But whatever the present shortcomings of "New Economic History," there is no doubt that important things have been accomplished and that, at least for some time to come, this is the area in which the most rewarding contributions to economic history can be expected. . . . [T]his afternoon it was intimated that analytical tools are increasingly applied simply because they are there. I believe that suggestions of this sort do not begin to do justice to what motivates, what inspires our graduate students. What attracts them is the thrill of asking new and exciting questions and of obtaining answers which in turn give rise to new questions . . . Very rightly, the feeling is abroad that here lies the still untouched soil which will repay the effort in research with a rich harvest. Periods like this are the star hours in the history of a discipline, and no dogmatic criticism . . . should be allowed to interfere with the work or to dim its promise. Nothing, of course, lasts forever. . . . The innovators of today may well become the conservators of tomorrow. But this is *their day, and its splendor should be neither beclouded nor begrudged.*

Alexander Gerschenkron (1967)

The guild of economic historians sets no rigid qualifications for membership within its ranks; it welcomes and, indeed, must draw extensively on the contributions offered by students and scholars of the most diverse interests and talents. It asks of its fellows only that they remember the main objective of their association: to promote a clearer understanding of how man's struggle for material existence has been carried on through time. By this standard the economic historian's claim to journeyman's or master's status will be judged.

Harold F. Williamson (1944)

A half-century ago a small group of scholars adopted a revolutionary approach to investigating the economic past. This approach originated in North America, but soon it traveled to Great Britain and Ireland, the European mainland, Australia, New Zealand, and Japan. The revolution had roots dating to the 1920s and in the years following the Second World War was an element of a much wider intellectual transformation that affected history, economics and the other social sciences. In the United States, at least, it was a self-conscious and loosely organized social movement fired with missionary zeal. What came to be called "The New Economic History" or "Cliometrics" was impelled by the promise of significant achievement, by the novelties of the recent (mathematical) formalization of economic theory, by the rapid spread of econometric methods, and by the introduction of computers into academia. In the early years, cliometricians developed a research program with mutual support and encouragement, conducted an unusually large proportion of collaborative work, and were much criticized from without and within. The movement was marked also by methodological disputes, considerable dissent, and some acrimony.

Since the 1950s the cliometric approach to economic history has spread widely, coming to dominate the American *Journal of Economic History (JEH)* and contributing more than a third of the articles in the British *Economic History Review (EHR)*. In the 1960s *Explorations in Entrepreneurial History (EEH)*, the "house publication" of cliometricians, was the locus of debate about the new approach.[1] Later diffusion of the approach provided the *raison d'être* for founding the European Historical Economics Society (EHES) in 1990; its *European Review of Economic History (EREH)* was established a few years later. At the level of pedagogy, textbook authors and teachers of economic history, beginning in the US and moving elsewhere, have incorporated progressively more cliometrics into their presentations.

Over the past five decades, economic history, whatever its style, has been subjected to forces of specialization within its parent and related disciplines. In the US, economic historians and "mainstream" historians have grown apart in method and perspective, as have economic and social historians in Britain (even when housed in the same department). Business history, once integral to the work of economic historians, has become

1 Whaples (1991) is a quantitative study of the rising incidence of such work in the *JEH*. *EEH* became *Explorations in Economic History* in 1969; for further background, see Neal (1994).

more independent, despite considerable overlap in personnel. Historians of technology, with a few striking exceptions, have separated themselves from their marriage of convenience to economic historians with overlapping interests. In economics itself, economic history has come to be treated as one of many standard "fields" of applied economics, rather than as, in Joseph Schumpeter's view, the primary leg of a tripod supporting the entire profession.[2]

Cliometrics arose with the spring tide of post-war American university expansion, driven by the demographic bulge of the baby boom and the democratic impulse of the states to increase participation rates in post-secondary education.[3] Financial support for study and research in economic history, long forthcoming from the great private foundations (dominantly American), was multiplied by government funds in the United States in the early 1960s and not long thereafter in Canada and the United Kingdom. In Britain, Australia and New Zealand, new departments of economic history were established, several in entirely new universities. Rising real salaries and falling real travel costs aided temporary academic migration, fostering cross-fertilization of minds for a year, a semester, a term, even a weekend of conversation. Those were the days! As Barry Supple (appropriating Wordsworth) declared,

> Bliss was it in that dawn to be alive,
> But to be young [and numerate] was very heaven!

What marked those days has faded into memory, as the circumstances giving rise to them have changed. The academic boom of the 1960s has yielded to periods of retrenchment in state-funded higher education accompanied by shifts of interest toward "practical" subjects among university undergraduates. In the United States both history (dramatically) and economics (less so) have suffered from declines in their shares of undergraduate degrees granted, with consequent effects on academic recruitment and employment security. Such changes in educational preferences, in part, have driven the number of higher degrees earned and the number of positions available.[4] Likewise, in the UK and in some relicts in its former *Imperium*, the once free-standing Economic History departments have all but disappeared – retaining nonetheless some vigor in other faculties into which they have been absorbed. By contrast, since the early 1990s on the European mainland, economic history has been stimulated by the initiatives of the EHES and various national and regional organizations, often supported by generous funding from the European Union.

This tale might suggest a climacteric reached some time ago, but (perhaps because we teach in the United States and he in England) we are rather more sanguine than Patrick O'Brien, author of the "Afterword" to this volume, in thinking there are grounds for optimism. Undergraduate students of economic history, although less numerous

2 Romer (1994); Schumpeter (1954: 12–13).

3 This paragraph and the next draw on Hughes (1971), Supple (1971: poetry 423), Hartwell (1971b), Harte (1971), Coats (1980), A. Field (1987), Nicholas (1997), Rouvray (2004), and the editors' recollections.

4 See Easterlin (1995) on degrees and career choices. On history and economics degrees, see A. Field (1987: 9, 13) and US Department of Education, National Center for Education Statistics, *Digest of Education Statistics*.

than 30 years ago, still find it an intriguing subject. A steady flow of academic economic historians continues to emerge from graduate study in faculties of economics and history – and they find employment. The scholarly output of economic historians of all descriptions appears in a rising number of journals of high quality. Accordingly, our subjects' reflections presented here are not a series of elegies; they are memoirs of the development of a vital subject.

I ANGLO-AMERICAN ECONOMIC HISTORY TO WORLD WAR II

> Let it be acknowledged that for a long time to come there are likely to be many honest and hard-working and intelligent men who will be interested in economic theory; let it be acknowledged, likewise, that there are likely to be a number, – small, indeed, in America and England, but still noticeable, – who also are honest and hard-working and not altogether unintelligent, who will be interested in economic history. Let us try for the next twenty years to leave one another severely alone, and see what will come of it . . . if we cannot agree, let us be silent.
>
> W. J. Ashley (1893)

> The besetting sin of the economic historian is antiquarianism; it is creditable to him that he largely escapes it. And yet – though I realize the dangers of my prescription – I think he will find a course of Economic Theory a useful tonic . . . It is a good thing that courses in Economic History are now offered in many universities . . . Yet there is some ground for anxiety. That Economic Theory and Economic History should be treated, as in some places they are, as quite separate *Fächer*, as if they were unconcerned with one another, and could be kept in watertight compartments of the brain – this is not a satisfactory state of affairs.
>
> William [J.] Ashley (1927)

Our story opens in 1893, when the Englishman William Ashley delivered his inaugural lecture at Harvard as the first Professor of Economic History in the English-speaking world.[5] On that January day the young Ashley (*aetat.* 32) advised the theorists and the historians to occupy separate spheres, thereby to finesse a methodological divide in British economics that recently had re-emerged. The rift was a dispute between the theoretically and scientifically oriented Alfred Marshall, Professor of Political Economy in the University of Cambridge, and the empirically oriented William Cunningham, then also of Cambridge, who in 1884 had tried and failed to be elected to the Chair won by Marshall. Their struggle was between the formal and deductive neo-classical economics championed by Marshall and a loosely defined inductivist "British historical school." It was also, despite being an inherently English dispute, an echo of more

5 Ashley is given global priority by Gras (1927: 26) and Harte (1971: *xxiii*). Barker (1977: 5) limits the claim to Anglophone nations; on the Continent there were such Professors in fact if not in name (see Drukker 2006: 48).

strident battles on the Continent – the *Methodenstreit* between the "German School of Historical Economics" of Gustav Schmoller and the "Austrian" marginalist school of Carl Menger. The German endeavor was historical, seeking empirical laws of economic progress; the Austrian was universal, seeking theoretical laws of economic behavior.[6]

At Cambridge, where economic history had been offered as an option in the History degree since 1875, Marshall prevailed and led the successful campaign to establish (neoclassical) economics as a discipline, with a separate degree initiated in 1903. At a succession of other British universities economic history developed into a distinct degree course much influenced by the empirical style of Cunningham. The German Historical School had an impact on the field, coming largely through Ashley, who had studied with Schmoller in the 1880s. Ashley returned to England in 1901 to lead the newly founded Faculty of Commerce at the University of Birmingham. He later wrote, according to J. H. Clapham, the "best introduction to economic history in the language," *The Economic Organisation of England* (1914).[7]

In the 1870s, on the Atlantic's western shore, scholars had begun teaching the "economic history" of both Europe and the United States. To the American legal–institutional approach, Ashley added the social conscience of his late Oxford friend Arnold Toynbee, the institutional historicism of Schmoller, and his own skill in the "application of scientific historical methods" (Scott 1928: 319). The influence of the institutional and comparative economic history favored by Ashley was only intensified in 1902 when Edwin F. Gay succeeded him at Harvard. Gay had spent a decade in Germany, some of that time with Schmoller; Herbert Heaton calls him "America's first native-born thoroughly trained economic historian." Gay became the founding Dean of the Harvard Business School in 1908 and was a progenitor of business history as an academic field.[8]

By the 1920s economic history had become well-established in both Britain and North America, each with its own methodological bent as well as predominant subject matter. Yet, there was no professional association nor a specialized journal (in English) for economic historians. Although a growing number of monographs and textbooks was being published on both sides of the Atlantic, some British economic historians grew restive at the difficulties they encountered with publication in journals. The American Economic Association (AEA) had been founded in 1885, part of a wave of disciplinary professionalization in history and the social sciences. Almost from the beginning, the AEA's *Publications* (succeeded in 1911 by *The American Economic Review*) had included historical work (*e.g.*, Ashley's paper on the early "English woollen industry" in 1887). The Royal Economic Society (RES), founded as the British Economic Association, published the *Economic Journal* (*EJ*) beginning in 1891. Its very first number contains an

6 On Cunningham *v* Marshall, see Maloney (1976), Matthews & Supple (1991) and Hodgson (2001: 104–9 esp.). Broader discussions of economic history and (its separation from) economics in England are provided by Koot (1987), Coleman (1987) and Kadish (1989). On the Germans, see Tribe (*e.g.*, 1995) and Hodgson (2001: Part II).

7 See Tribe (2000) and Deane (2001: 234–48) on the Cambridge Economics Tripos; also Harte (1971: *xxiv–xxvi*). Barker (1977: 5) quotes from Clapham's obituary of Ashley in *EJ* 37:148 (1927: 678–84).

8 See Heaton (1949: quoted 1) and the biography, Heaton (1952) on Gay. His students dispersed over North America; see Cole (1968) and Rouvray (2004).

historical analysis of French peasant landholding patterns (Seebohm 1891). On the British side, however, the Cambridge editorship of the *EJ* maintained a hammerlock on the style of article they would publish, and only certain types of work in economic history were thought acceptable. Accordingly, a group of British scholars founded the Economic History Society in 1926 (with Americans on the Council from day one), and *The Economic History Review* had its premiere in January 1927.[9] The first 11 pages of the *Review* are taken up by William Ashley's address, "The place of economic history in university studies," containing his plea that economic historians take a small tonic of theory, along with a further note of concern:

> The theoretical economists are ready to keep us economic historians quiet by giving us a little garden plot of our own; and we humble historians are so thankful for a little undisputed territory that we are inclined to leave the economists to their own devices (1927: 4).

Before 1940 the (North) Americans had no equivalent society. They published books, or published articles in the economics and history journals; some joined the Economic History Society; some published in the *Review* itself. Business historians were served by the *Bulletin of the Business Historical Society*, published from 1926 at the Harvard Business School (renamed *The Business History Review* in 1954).[10] Although an abortive move to organize had been made in the mid-1930s, as Heaton writes, the onset of war in Europe gave "the advocates of an American society . . . the signal for action." If economic history was "doomed to be blacked out in Europe, the lights must burn more brightly in America." A committee was formed at the American Economic Association meetings in December 1939. A year later, with the historians meeting in New York *and* the economists in New Orleans, the Economic History Association was founded. On April 26th, 1941, 16 weeks, six days and six hours after the initial Editorial Board meeting, the first "copy of *The Journal of Economic History* was placed in the hands of the chairman" of the EHA Council.[11] In his retrospective at the EHA's 25th anniversary Herbert Heaton, a Yorkshireman and immigrant to the US *via* Australia, spoke with pride of the Association's cosmopolitan values: "There has never been the least desire

9 These points taken from Barker (1977: 6–13). It is alleged that Keynes and the RES tried to subvert this group's initiative with its own publication, hiving the *EJ*'s historical articles off into an annual supplement ("issued to Fellows free of charge") called *Economic History*, which appeared from 1926 to 1939. The diversion failed. The first journal of economic history, the *Vierteljahrschrift für Social- und Wirtschaftsgeschichte*, began publication in Leipzig in 1903.

10 Another HBS initiative was the *Journal of Economic and Business History*, founded by Gay and his student N. S. B. Gras, which appeared in only four volumes from 1928 to 1932, failing both because of a sharp decline in business funding during the Depression and severe editorial disagreements about the nature and quality of work it should publish. See Gras (1962: 24, 186); Sass (1986: 43); Redlich (1962: 63–4).

11 See Heaton (1941: 107, 109), who relates the short version of these events. The longer version tells of the roles of several of Gay's students in promoting the organization, the assistance provided by Joseph H. Willits, late Dean of the Wharton School of the University of Pennsylvania and then at the Rockefeller Foundation, and the leadership of Anne Bezanson, Professor at Penn and consultant to Willits (see Rouvray 2004).

to make the *Journal* all-American in theme or authorship, or to suggest that economic history began with the Industrial or American Revolution" (1965: 474).

In 1920 the National Bureau of Economic Research (NBER) was founded to produce research firmly based on facts, quantitative if possible, scientific and impartial, and neutral with respect to policy. During the interwar period, the Bureau added substantially to the statistical infrastructure for examining American economic development. Its first President was the ubiquitous Edwin Gay, who had retired from the Harvard Business School deanship. Much of the NBER's initial focus was contemporary, guided by the experience of its Director of Research, Wesley Clair Mitchell, whose early writings nonetheless had placed considerable weight on historical developments. The Bureau's work in the 1920s concentrated on the size, industrial composition and distribution of US national income, and, most importantly for Mitchell, income fluctuations. A major initiative occurred in 1930, as Solomon Fabricant (1984: 14) relates,

> The big step forward in the scale and quality of the Bureau's work on national income came . . . when Simon Kuznets, a student of Mitchell's and already on the Bureau's staff, was asked to take charge of the area. After some hesitation he agreed – a momentous decision – and began the preliminary work for what proved to be a notable series, extended over the next three decades, of studies of the nation's income, savings, and expenditures.

Kuznets was to have great influence not only on developing a preliminary version of the United States national income and product accounts (1934), but also in producing, or encouraging others to produce, long runs of historical national accounting data for the US and elsewhere. In the UK, financial and institutional support for historical work was slim, and much of the external funding for British social science research before the war came from the Rockefeller Foundation, as it did for some time after the Allied victory. The closest British analogues to the NBER are the Oxford Institute of Economics and Statistics, founded in 1935, and the National Institute for Economic and Social Research (NIESR), established in 1938 (partly funded by Rockefeller) with a focus on contemporary policy issues.[12]

At the opening of the post-war era, British economic historians carried on their research along familiar lines, as they had during the adversities of depression and war, while the Americans began to turn their historical lens on problems of economic development and growth.[13] Nevertheless there were notes of discord; much of the

12 See Middleton (1998: 198–9); on the NIESR, see K. Jones (1998). Some American research was financed by the Committee on Research in Economic History, a unit of the (US) SSRC funded by the Rockefeller Foundation. On its activities, see Cole (1944; 1953; 1970). Rouvray (2004; 2005: Ch. 3) examines the links between founding of the Committee, which received Rockefeller support, and of the EHA, which did not.

13 The American interest in growth and development is reflected in the rising number of regular articles on these subjects in the *JEH* over the 1940s, in the papers presented at the 1947 EHA meetings, on "Economic Growth," and at the 1950 meetings, on "Government and Business Enterprise in the Promotion of Economic Development." By contrast, we can detect no sea-change in the nature of topics dealt with in *EHR* in the five years after war's end.

Anglo-American band of economic historians was what the Left called "bourgeois," despite the presence in Britain of Fabian socialists like Beatrice and Sidney Webb and R. H. Tawney of the LSE and the presence of historically-minded critics of American capitalism like Leo Rogin and Robert A. Brady at Berkeley. A new Marxian critique of capitalism had been spearheaded in the 1940s by Paul Sweezy (1942) in the US and by Maurice Dobb (1946) in Britain. Dobb was senior in a group of "British Marxist Historians" who challenged the "new positivism" of the "economic statisticians" and much of traditional economic history, which in their view was "unable to deal with any but the simplest forms of historical change."[14] The Marxists confronted their bourgeois rivals soon and directly, with Eric Hobsbawm carrying the banner against the earlier-massed forces of Friedrich Hayek, W. H. Hutt, T. S. Ashton and their allies. Max Hartwell responded, and the two debated. Thus they revived the grand and venerable "Standard of Living Controversy" (discussed in Section V).

Before that external engagement, however, was another, internal to Marxian historiography. Dobb and Sweezy became embroiled in a dispute about prime movers in the "transition from feudalism to capitalism," mostly in the pages of the American Marxist journal *Science & Society*.[15] Sweezy later turned to critiques of American capitalist society, but, as a graduate student at Harvard in the 1930s, he cut his eyeteeth on Marxian analysis and – harbinger of things to come – on an economist's style of doing economic history.

II BEFORE THE NEW ECONOMIC HISTORY

> This is an unusual book. The writing of economic history has been left in the main to historians, trained in the techniques of historical research and applying them to the special field of economic history. There have always been exceptions; monetary history in particular has owed much to economists. But the greater part of our knowledge of industrial history we owe to the historians. Mr. Sweezy would, I think, call himself primarily an economist. He has tackled the problem of the limitation of the Vend with the same apparatus of thought that a competent economist might be expected to use on some contemporary problem. I am old-fashioned enough, however, to feel a slight shock at meeting marginal revenue curves in a book on economic history, and I pray that all who come after him will not find it necessary to litter their pages with the bleaching bones of all the analytical camels which have carried them to their destinations.
>
> Austin Robinson (1941)

In 1997 John Meyer contributed some thoughts to a panel at the annual meeting of the American Economic Association; the subject was "Cliometrics after 40 Years." He

14 Quotations from the editors' "Introduction," p. *ii*, in the first number of *Past & Present*, February 1952, a journal founded by the Marxist historians group.

15 For the first phase of the debate, see *Science & Society*, 1950–5. These and later contributions are collected in Hilton, ed. (1976).

expressed some bemusement at his inclusion with a group of "distinguished economists and historians," and attributed his presence to a "youthful folly" which had led him early in his career to do some research in economic history. In his remarks Meyer quoted Austin Robinson's words, which come from a review of *Monopoly and Competition in the English Coal Trade, 1550–1850* (1938), an expanded version of Paul Sweezy's Wells Prize-winning Harvard Ph.D. dissertation of 1937.

John Meyer is one of the earliest cliometricians; he quoted Robinson both because littering his pages with analytical camels is "much of the fun of cliometrics" and because he was assuring the audience that *he* knew he was not the first. He called Sweezy's book "a bit of cliometrics done well before the term was invented," thus appealing to the principle of continuity in historiography, and acknowledging that a quantitative–analytical approach to economic history had developed in the interwar years (Meyer 1997: 409, 10). Characteristic elements of "cliometrics" were further stimulated by events, by changes in economics, and by an intensification of what might be called the statistical impulse.

First, depression, war, the dissolution of empires, a renewal of widespread and more rapid growth in the Western world, and the challenge of Soviet-style economic planning combined to focus attention on the sources and mechanisms of economic growth and development.

Second, new intellectual currents in economics, spurred in part by contemporary economic problems, arose to dominate the profession. In the 1930s, and especially during the war, theoretical approaches to the aggregate economy and its capabilities grew out of the new Keynesian macroeconomics and the development of national income accounting. Explicit techniques for analyzing resource allocation in detail were introduced and employed in wartime planning. Econometrics, the statistical analysis of economic data, continued to grow apace.

Third, the gathering of facts – with an emphasis on systematic arrays of quantitative facts – became more important. By the nineteenth century, governments, citizens and scholars had become preoccupied with fact-gathering, but their collations were ordinarily *ad hoc* and unsystematic. Thoroughness and system became the *desideratum* of scholarly fact-gathering in the twentieth century. American efforts in this direction combined the interest and expertise of academics with a smidgen of the funds amassed by the wealthy of the Gilded Age and dispensed by their philanthropic offspring.

The Carnegie Institution supported scholarly monographs in American economic history, commissioned an extensive bibliography of economic materials in American state documents, and initiated a series of sectoral studies of the economy that appeared from 1915 to 1933. The Rockefeller Foundation helped to institutionalize the collection and interpretation of economic data at the NBER, which, according to Arthur H. Cole, was "an institution pulsating with the belief that, if only adequate scientifically dehydrated facts could be assembled, the major problems of the world could be put on the road to solution, if indeed not resolved immediately." At the request of Edwin Gay (American) and William Beveridge (British), Rockefeller money helped to establish the International Committee on Price History in 1929, and financed both the Committee on Research in Economic History in 1940 and the Research Center in Entrepreneurial

History at Harvard in 1948.[16] On the side of technique, Alfred Cowles, Jr. helped finance the creation of the Econometric Society in 1930, and the Cowles Commission for Research in Economics supported many contemporary econometric studies.[17] Thus the analytically minded economic historians already at work by the 1930s had funds, data, new methods and new theory near at hand, and were beginning to tie their investigations of old and current problems to others that would emerge full-blown after the war.

Harvard was only one institution fostering the early quantitative–analytical historical enterprise. When Arthur D. Gayer moved from Oxford to Columbia in 1930, he was unsatisfied that he "had exhausted the fruitful possibilities" of his doctoral research, "Industrial Fluctuation and Unemployment in England, 1815–1850." In 1936 he organized a "broader research project in the same field" with funds from Columbia, and was joined by Anna Jacobson (later Schwartz) of Columbia, shortly thereafter by Isaiah Frank of Columbia, and in 1938 by Walt Rostow of Yale and Oxford. Their efforts produced the two-volume study *The Growth and Fluctuation of the British Economy, 1790–1850.* It was essentially complete in 1941 but was not published until after Gayer's death a decade later.[18] They presented a massive compilation of data on British prices and output, provided a narrative of economic events organized into major and minor trade cycles, supplied new indices of share and commodity prices, and essayed a theoretical explanation of the cyclical patterns they had found. They used the NBER's method of characterizing the cycle that would be attacked as "Measurement without Theory," but Gayer and co-authors were careful to base their discussion on theories of business investment and of the impact of changes in exports. Their book received stringent criticism, notably from R. C. O. Matthews, who pointed to numerous inconsistencies in the theoretical argument and to omission of some extensive data sources.[19]

Forrest Capie and Geoffrey Wood stress the book's priority:

> [Gayer, Rostow and Schwartz] deserves to stand as perhaps *the* pioneering work in British, and possibly any, econometric history . . . It is the kind of blend of history, statistics, and economic analysis that is still aimed for by those who think of themselves as "new" economic historians (1989: 87).

Still, *Growth and Fluctuation* was a transitional work, a forerunner that did not establish the mold. It was a product of the institutional and empirical tradition encouraged by

16 The Carnegie studies are rich in data, and have been used extensively by quantitative economic historians. See Heaton (1965); Cole (1968: quotation 573); Aitken (1967); Cole & Crandall (1964). The Harvard Center founded and published *Explorations in Entrepreneurial History* (1948–58). The journal was revived by Ralph Andreano as *EEH/Second series* for 1962–9.

17 Ambirajan (1995: 199); Landreth & Colander (2002: Ch. 16).

18 See Gayer's "Director's Preface" in Gayer, Rostow & Schwartz (1953: *v*) and Postan (1982: 3–4).

19 While not recanting his substantive critique, Matthews later expressed regret for the "ungenerous" tone of his review, adding "More tribute should have been paid to what was without question a major and pioneering contribution to the application of economics to economic history." His comment appears in a "Postscript" to his review (1954a), as reprinted in 1972, p. 130. Tjalling Koopmans (1947), a leading econometrician, used the quoted phrase to title his review of Burns & Mitchell (1946).

Mitchell and the NBER, with theoretical components not much affected by the more formal or mathematical approaches just emerging in economics.

In the 1950s, the economic history written by those trained as economists was a blend of different ingredients. The economic analysis was deliberately more general, as Robert Solow states: "a set of analytical tools to be applied quite directly to observable situations." The statistics – as numerical data – were similar, but the statistics – as data manipulation – was no longer primarily descriptive. Both differences reflect a change in the character of economics during and after World War II that continues to the present, a shift to "model-building" where the stress is to focus on "one or two causal or conditioning factors, exclude everything else, and hope to understand how just those aspects of reality work and interact." Model-building was stimulated by access to larger quantities of economic data and by the "explosion of econometrics" which became an "essential part" of an economist's professional training.[20]

Added to this new style of doing economics were new or renewed fields of inquiry. The wartime years, Moses Abramovitz observes, "turned economists' thoughts to the long-term growth of national productive capabilities," sparking articulation of the economics of development and a resurgence of work on economic growth.[21] Growth needed measurement (and encouragement, given widespread apprehension that depression conditions might well recur after the war) and, among others, economic historians shouldered these tasks. A leading figure in amassing facts – facts carefully derived and consistently defined – was Simon Kuznets, who published the first of his works on historical US national income in 1946, who presented a paper on economic measurement at the EHA Growth symposium the following year, and who later led an international effort to compile historical data on national income and output.

The point of this new wave of fact-gathering was to explain growth as well as to measure it. Following his move to Stanford from the NBER in 1949, Moses Abramovitz contributed a chapter on the "Economics of Growth" to a set of surveys sponsored by the AEA (1952). When Walt Rostow went to MIT in 1951, part of his remit was to teach a course on the subject, leading to his book, *The Process of Economic Growth* (1952). Writing from a development policy and historical perspective, W. Arthur Lewis characterized his *The Theory of Economic Growth* (1955) as neither *the* theory nor a survey, but as a map at a relatively large scale. Alexander Gerschenkron (1952) developed a suggestive model of "relative economic backwardness," linking the timing, nature, and speed of economic growth to institutional structures and past development patterns. The literary and theoretically informal style of these works, and their wide-ranging discussions of likely causal factors, contrast strikingly with the formal economic models of limited compass that had been propounded from the 1930s. Similarly striking is their stress on physical capital formation as a source of rising income per person, in large part because such an emphasis "reflected an outlook common to the [Keynesian] economic thought of the time" (Abramovitz 1989: *xii*). Their focus on investment changed radically – and soon.

20 Solow (1998: quotations 60, 61, 65). See also Landreth & Colander (2002: Ch. 16) and Backhouse (2002: Ch. 11).

21 Abramovitz (1989: *xii*). On the influence of wartime and post-war defense activities on economics, see Bernstein (2001: Chs 3, 4).

Abramovitz states in his survey (1952: 91), "It is probably safe to say that only the discovery and exploitation of new knowledge rivals capital formation as a cause of economic progress." He later accepted a "modest assignment to summarize US economic development since the Civil War" for an AEA session on economic history, and turned "in some desperation" to the national income figures of Kuznets and to a method of productivity analysis developed by John Kendrick of the NBER. Here is Abramovitz writing in retrospect (1989: *xii–xiii*):

> If real national product had risen between two dates, the increase could be attributed partly to an increase in factor inputs . . . and partly to an increase in output per unit of input. An index of the first would be given by the factor input quantities of each year multiplied by their base year earnings. What remained of national product increase would be a measure of the change . . . of the productivity of employed resources . . . What could be simpler? The exciting thing was the lopsided result. . . . Productivity growth . . . had been the apparent source of virtually the whole increase of per capita income for nearly a century.

At that session Abramovitz (1956) announced that the proximate source of economic growth in the United States was the roughly 85 per cent of the outcome that could not be attributed to resource accumulation, a massive "residual" that he was careful to call a "measure of our ignorance." In a celebrated article published the next year, Robert Solow (1957) replicated Abramovitz's result and placed it in the context of a formal growth model.[22]

Not long after World War II, then, North American economic historians had novelties to work with: a method incorporating the economists' model-building style, a capacity to deal with statistics (in both senses of the term) deriving from developments in econometrics combined with the first generation of digital computers, and a new and extensive historical *problematik* – measuring and accounting for the economic growth of nations. By the mid-1950s, as Herbert Heaton noted, they were climbing onto "The Economic Growth Bandwagon."[23]

III NEW ECONOMIC HISTORY IN NORTH AMERICA

> [T]he method of making an economic historian and the ingredients used have depended on the time, as well as the place, of his production, upon the generation to which he belonged.
>
> Herbert Heaton (1949)

22 Abramovitz (1956: 133) for quotation. Despite the startling upshot of his own calculations, Abramovitz credited his predecessors and colleagues in detail, both at the time (1956: *passim*) and later (1989: *xiii n*). The measure is usually called the "Solow residual;" it is sometimes solely and incorrectly identified with the effects of technological change.

23 Heaton (1965: 495); Walt Rostow commented (1957: 519) ". . . articles on economic growth – in fact or in name – have hit the economic journals like a biblical plague." The "new economic historical" treatments of economic growth supply the theme of Drukker's (2006) study of post-WW II quantitative economic history.

> . . . the real answer to those who shrink from the suggestion that modern economic theory should be applied to the earlier forms of society is that they misunderstand the nature of Economics. For, whatever may have been its origin, the subject has ceased (or almost ceased) to be a set of conclusions and has become an apparatus of thought: no longer a doctrine, it has become a method.
>
> T. S. Ashton (1946)

> Economic historians have always rested heavily on economic arithmetic. They will doubtless learn, perhaps with some lag, to make use of economic algebra and economic calculus. But I trust they will also continue to use their wits, like Sir John Clapham, when they need answers that the quantitative methods do not supply.
>
> Carter Goodrich (1960)

Amid the new emphasis on economic growth and development, cliometrics was unveiled formally in Williamstown, Massachusetts, in the autumn of 1957 at an unusual gathering sponsored by the Economic History Association and the Conference on Research in Income and Wealth. Unlike the EHA's normal two-day affairs, this conference lasted four days and was attended by about 150 people, rather more than normal. Most of the program was designed to showcase recent work by economists who had ventured into history. The joint sessions were suggested by Solomon Fabricant of the NBER and were arranged for the CRIW by Harold Williamson, Stanley Lebergott and John Sawyer, and for the EHA by program chairman Alexander Gerschenkron.[24]

Young scholars in the Income and Wealth group presented their contributions to the historical national accounts of the United States and Canada, spearheaded by Robert Gallman's estimates of US commodity output, 1839–1899. He was joined by a group of academic and government economic historians who investigated related topics. William Parker, impresario of the 1957 conference and editor of its proceedings (CRIW 1960), characterized their efforts this way:

> We are working to develop . . . the record of the quantities that have constituted the outward manifestation of American economic change. By itself no single series of such quantities has much strength. Its sources are thin and limits of error wide. . . . But a bundle of such statistics, bound roughly together with a bit of theory may, like a divining rod, direct further search in the details of society's history to points where hidden springs of economic change may lie (1962: 233).

A pair of headline sessions dealt with method. The one on comparative economic history was staffed by two senior figures, Sylvia Thrupp, medievalist, founder of *Comparative Studies in Society and History*, and later President of the EHA, and W. T.

24 See Rouvray (2005: 246–8) for intent and attendance. See Parker (1987: 4), CRIW (1960: *vii*) and *JEH* 17:2 (1957: unnumbered back page) for organizers and session titles.

Easterbrook, co-author of the then standard textbook in Canadian economic history.[25] The other session, on economic theory and economic history, was also opened by a senior figure, Walt Rostow, then only 40 years of age but for two decades a leading scholar in economic history. In "The interrelation of theory and economic history," Rostow recalled his undergraduate years at Yale, where he had been led to ask himself "why not see what happened if the machinery of economic theory was brought to bear on modern economic history?" In England, at age 21, Rostow saw what happened, in his influential article about "Investment and the Great Depression" of the late nineteenth century (1938). Following his service in World War II, he returned to academia, entrancing his British audiences at Cambridge and Oxford with an analytical style of historical economics and, at MIT in the 1950s, applying this new mode of teaching and writing to the problem of economic growth. At Williamstown he said, "economic history is a less interesting field than it could be, because we do not remain sufficiently loyal to the problem approach, which in fact underlies and directs our efforts."[26]

Joining Rostow in the theory and history session were two newcomers, both then Assistant Professors at Harvard – each influenced by Alexander Gerschenkron and on the platform at his urging – John R. Meyer and Alfred H. Conrad, who presented "Economic Theory, Statistical Inference, and Economic History" (1957), a manifesto for using formal theory and econometric methods to examine historical questions. They adopted the social-scientific perspective that particular historical circumstances are instances of more general phenomena, and thus suitable for theoretical analysis. They argued further that quantitative historical evidence, although relatively scarce, is much more abundant than many historians had asserted and can be analyzed using formal statistical methods.

A day earlier Conrad and Meyer presented "The Economics of Slavery in the Antebellum South" (1958), which incorporated their methodological views to refute a long-standing proposition that the slave system in the southern United States had become moribund by the 1850s and would have died out had there been no Civil War. Such views of the nature of American slavery had been attacked earlier from the "new" anthropological perspective by revisionist historians, notably Kenneth Stampp.[27] Conrad and Meyer buttressed the point by showing that slaveholding, viewed as a business activity, had been at least as remunerative as other uses of financial and physical capital. They estimated the profitability of slavery using economist's concepts and modern theory, while more broadly illustrating "the ways in which economic theory might be used in ordering and organizing historical facts" (1958: 44).

Two decades later Robert Gallman recalled that the Williamstown "conference did more than put the ball in motion . . . It also set the tone and style of the new economic history and even forecast the chief methodological and substantive interests that were

25 For Thrupp, see "In memoriam," AHA *Perspectives* (March 2000); for Easterbrook, see Ian Parker, "Introduction" to Easterbrook (1990).

26 Quotations from Rostow (1957: 510); for Rostow's impact in post-war England, see the Matthews interview, Mathias (2001) and Saville (2001).

27 For discussion of Stampp (1956) and others, see Fogel (2003: 1, 8–12).

to occupy cliometricians for the next twenty-one years" (1979: 1007). What began in the late 1950s as a trickle of work in the new style grew to a freshet and then a flood, incorporating new methods, examining bodies of data previously too difficult to analyze without the aid of computers, and investigating a variety of questions of traditional importance, mostly in American economic history. The watershed was continent-wide, collecting the work of small clusters of scholars bound together in a ramifying intellectual and social network.

An important and continuing node in this network was at Purdue University in West Lafayette, Indiana. In the late 1950s, a group of young historical economists assembled there, among whom the cross-pollination of historical interests and technical expertise was exceptional. In this group were Lance Davis and Jonathan Hughes (joined later by Nathan Rosenberg) and several others known primarily for their work in other fields. One was Stanley Reiter, a mathematical economist who traveled with Davis and Hughes to the EHA meetings in September 1960 to present their paper explaining the new quantitative historical research being undertaken at Purdue – and to introduce the term "cliometrics" to the profession. To build on the enthusiasm aroused by that presentation, and to "consolidate Purdue's position as the leader in this country of quantitative research in economic history," Davis and Hughes (with Reiter's aid) sought and received funds from Purdue's Quantitative Research Institute for a meeting of about a dozen like-minded economic historians in December 1960. They gave it the imposing title of "Conference on the Application of Economic Theory and Quantitative Methods to the Study of Problems of Economic History." This title remained official until the late 1970s, but the meetings were soon called "Clio" or the "Cliometrics Conference" by their familiars. Sessions were renowned from Clio's early days as occasions for engaging in sharp debate and asking probing (and occasionally unanswerable) questions.[28] There were six presentations at the first meeting, none more engaging than Robert Fogel's estimates of the "social saving" accruing from the expansion of the American railroad network to 1890, a paper taking hours to present. Hughes later wrote (1971: 411–12), "Fogel's 1960 paper was a real watershed. One reason the paper took so long to read was the intense and almost tortuous grilling Fogel underwent at the hands of the other participants in defending his work."[29]

Those who attended the first "Clio" conference established a tradition of rigorous and detailed analysis of the presenters' work, as well as a requirement that papers be made available in advance so sessions would focus on discussion. In the Purdue years (1960–69) the Conference gradually expanded to include about a dozen papers. About the meeting at which he presented his first Clio paper (1969), Richard Sylla comments (2002: 4), "There was a lot of dedication to the cause, and the discussions were exciting

28 The EHA paper is Davis, Hughes & Reiter (1960). See S. Williamson (1991: 20, 23–4) on the Clio Conferences; quotation, p. 29.

29 Other papers were by James H. McRandle & James P. Quirk, William Parker, Gordon W. Bertram, George G. S. Murphy, and John W. Snyder. Those by Fogel, McRandle & Quirk, and Parker were presented at the Econometric Society meetings later that month; abstracts appear in *Econometrica* 29:3 (1961: 475–77). Papers at the first six Purdue seminars are listed in *PFP*, pp. *vii–viii*. The Cliometric Society website lists the papers from meeting one to the present, via URL: <http://eh.net/Clio/Conferences/index.htm>.

and constructive. We had the feeling that if we could make it to West Lafayette in the winter, survive the discussions of our papers, and make it home again, then we could do almost anything."

Much early cliometric work was refined in Purdue's crucible – unveiled, picked apart and reassembled. Although about two-thirds of the presentations in the 1960s were on American economic history, topical coverage was diverse, with papers on methodology, output and investment, international trade and finance, price history, and wealth distribution interspersed with the more frequent papers on agriculture, manufacturing and technological change. Many papers in the new vein, and many of those first tested at the Clio meetings, were published in journals whose freshly appointed editors were sympathetic to the quantitative–analytical style: Ralph Andreano at the revived *Explorations in Entrepreneurial History*, and Douglass North and William Parker at *The Journal of Economic History*. Cliometricians became a continental, then a global, community. As Parker has written, "a collection of quantifiers grew up, with the strength of a pack," who felt

> the reinforcement of inner strength that comes from family life. When the number of scholars grew to a certain point, they produced their own conferences, became one another's reviewers and critics, established a private language and tradition . . . the corporate life grew through students and through friendly attachments. They formed an example of the social equivalent of what in atomic physics is known as a critical – or in this case, some would say, uncritical – mass (1987: 7).

During the 1960s, the mass became supercritical. Young historical economists, encouraged by sympathetic members of the older generation, engaged in a proselytizing mission, enticing students to investigate historical questions using economists' expertise, publishing textbooks and monographs for the enlightenment of undergraduates (and others), and preaching to their neighbors in economics and history. The revisionists were reacting – some would say overreacting – to the dominantly descriptive and institutional approach of earlier scholarship. Walt Rostow, dissatisfied with this older tradition, had pointed to a paucity of synthetic work in American economic historiography, which he thought "a peculiarly shapeless affair . . . It is, indeed, possible to criticize much of conventional economic history as too political and social and not sufficiently economic." Leading senior figures in a more traditional vein, such as Fritz Redlich and Harold Williamson, also argued that their colleagues in American business history had been reluctant to generalize and seemed too intent on gathering data for their own sake.[30] In the later 1950s, both William Parker and Alexander Gerschenkron sought funding to bring new blood into the field, "first rate young economists who have developed an abiding interest in economic history . . ." because, as Gerschenkron observed privately

30 See Rostow (1957: 520, 2), Redlich (1962) and H. Williamson (1966). As cliometricians began to use theory and econometrics more intensively in analyzing markets and sectors, business historians moved towards behavioral and structural explanations of individual firm behavior. See, *e.g*, the influential works of Alfred D. Chandler (1966; 1977; 1990). Parker (1991), John (1997) and Landes (2001) are assessments of Chandler's approach.

to Simon Kuznets, "Economic history is in a poor way. It is unable to attract good students, mainly because the discipline does not present any intellectual challenge . . ."[31]

Some cliometric young Turks were not so mild. While often relying heavily on the wealth of detail amassed in earlier research, they asserted a distinctive identity. Parker notes (1973: 20), "Among the self-styled new economic historians . . . criticism of the elders became a ritual to be practiced in the advance of any new constructive undertaking," and Albert Fishlow asks (1974: 463), "Where would the new economic history be without [its] benighted forbears?" The old economic history, it was said, was riddled with errors in economic reasoning and embodied an inadequate approach to causal explanation. The most vocal proponents declared a new order. Douglass North proclaimed that a "revolution is taking place in economic history in the United States . . . initiated by a new generation of economic historians" intent on reappraising "traditional interpretations of US economic history" (1963: 128). Robert Fogel said that the "novel element in the work of the new economic historians is their approach to measurement and theory," especially in their ability to find "methods of measuring economic phenomena that cannot be measured directly" (1965: 92). The cliometricians insisted on a scientific approach to economic–historical questions, on careful specification of explicit models of the phenomena they were investigating. By implication and by declaration they said that much of conventional wisdom was based on unscientific and unsystematic historical scholarship, on occasion employing language not calculated to endear them to outsiders.

The hallmark of the top rung of work done by the new economic historians was its integration of fact with theory. As Deirdre McCloskey observed in a series of surveys (1976; 1978; 1987), the theory was often simple. The facts, when not conveniently available, were dug up from surviving sources, whether published or not. Indeed, the discipline imposed by the need to measure usually requires more data than would serve for a qualitative argument. Many new economic historians expended considerable effort in the 1960s to expand the American quantitative record. Thus, with eyebrow raised, so to speak, Albert Fishlow remarked in 1970, "It is ironic . . . to read that 'most of the "New Economic History" only applies its ingenuity to analyzing convenient (usually published) data.' " Similar views have proven quite durable; for example, B. W. Alford observes, "Some practitioners of the new approach – unencumbered by the need for archival research – frequently overreached themselves as they sought to graft selective historical evidence onto the latest fashion in economic theory and sell it as economic history."[32] To the contrary, many cliometricians worked their magic not merely by relying on their predecessors' compilations; they went to archives and obscure publications to collect their data, some never before available, others not extensively used. Early in the computer age they put them into form suitable for tabulation and statistical analysis.

William Parker and Robert Gallman, with their students, were pioneers in analyzing individual-level data from the United States census manuscripts, a project arising from

31 See Rouvray (2005: Ch. 6): Parker's views are summarized, p. 263; on Gerschenkron, see pp. 253–61; Gerschenkron quoted, pp. 254–5, from a letter to Kuznets of September 23rd, 1957, written after the Williamstown meeting.

32 In Fishlow & Fogel (1971: 19), quoting a review of Soltow, ed. (1969); Alford (2004: 640).

Parker's previous study of Southern plantations. From the 1860 agricultural census schedule they drew a carefully constructed sample of over 5,000 farms in the cotton counties of the American South and matched those farms with the two separate schedules for the free and slave populations. They used information from this sample of farms and the more than 70,000 people inhabiting them to analyze the structure of the ante-bellum cotton economy, addressing questions about such issues as slave labor productivity, wealth distribution and regional self-sufficiency in food production. The Parker–Gallman sample was followed by census samples for northern agriculture and for the post-bellum South.[33] Paul McGouldrick's study (1968) of the larger New England cotton textile firms was built upon a foundation of manuscript business records to assess profits, dividends and investment spending; Gavin Wright (1971: 440) called this book "the most 'vertically integrated' study of econometric history to date."

The early practitioners of cliometrics applied their theoretical and quantitative skills to some issues well-established in the more "traditional" economic historiography, none more important than asking when and how rapidly the North American economy began to experience "modern economic growth." In the nineteenth century, economic growth in both the US and Canada was punctuated by booms, recessions and financial crises, but the new work provided a better picture of the path of GNP and its components, revealing steady upward trends in aggregate output and in incomes per person and per worker. The latter, it seemed clear from the work of Abramovitz and Solow, must have derived significantly from the introduction of new techniques, as well as from expansion of the scale and penetration of the market. Several scholars thus established a related objective, understanding – or at least accounting for – productivity growth.

Walt Rostow incorporated rapid economic expansion and productivity increase into his concept of "take-off into self-sustained growth," asserting that "The introduction of the railroad has been historically the most powerful single initiator of take-offs" (1956, 45; 1960, 55). In their detailed studies of large-scale introduction of railroads, Robert Fogel (1964) and Albert Fishlow (1965) estimated the extent of resource saving that had accrued from adoption of a transport system with costs lower than those of canals, in the process confronting and refuting many of Rostow's views. Both estimates suggest a relatively small effect, about 5 per cent of GNP, but a recurring question asks whether 5 per cent should be seen as "large" or "small." Fishlow's estimates for 1859 compare railroads with the existing system of water transport; Fogel's for 1890 compare railroads with a hypothetical system of canals that would substitute for the actual railroad system of that date. Measuring the consequent "social saving" involves estimating resource costs of an existing method of production (rail transport services) and contrasting the result with the costs of a "counterfactual" alternative (canals only).[34] Fogel argued in effect

33 See Parker, ed. (1970); Bateman & Foust (1974) and Atack & Bateman (1987); Ransom & Sutch (1977).

34 Fishlow (1965: 57–62) is dubious of Fogel's 5 per cent for 1890; he argues that "realized gains in 1890 . . . probably go beyond 10 per cent of income rather than falling below 5" (p. 61); by 1860 railroads were "on the threshold of a significant and increasing influence . . ." (p. 62). Use of an hypothetical alternative is an application of the economist's concept of opportunity cost. A similar method would apply, say, to calculating damages in an antitrust case, where the actual world is compared to a hypothetical world without the alleged violation. Both require theory to characterize the alternative state of affairs and data to determine its quantitative significance. Fishlow's and Fogel's measures of social saving differ somewhat,

that it is unwise to think that any *single* technical innovation, even one of as massive a scale as rail transport in the US and elsewhere, would be crucial to economic growth.

The combined application of economic reasoning, employment of (usually) appropriate statistical methods, and the unearthing or estimation of new data was a joint objective of the new economic historians. But even the simplest and most straightforward contributions raised substantially the technical level of "new" economic history papers over the more "traditional." Since most new economic historians resided in economics departments and had to conform to economists' standards of professional quality, the method and style of the new economic history (and the more emphatic assertions of its virtues) tended to alienate historians and "traditional" economic historians rather than to entice them into joining the movement. The injection of formal economics and statistics into the realm of history – coupled with a diminution of such putatively major historical forces as railroad construction and operation, or with taking an allegedly socially insensitive view of the slave plantation merely as a business proposition – inevitably led to resistance by those with more humanistic training. By the early 1960s, members of the wider historical profession were lamenting, as did American Historical Association President Carl Bridenbaugh, that some colleagues had succumbed "to the dehumanizing methods of social sciences." He warned against worshiping "at the shrine of that Bitch–goddess, QUANTIFICATION. History concerns itself with the 'mutable, rank-scented many,' but it fails if it does not show them as individuals whenever it can" (1963: 326).

Nevertheless, the attribution of cause or significance to a given factor in the unfolding of history is central to the work of historians who wish to interpret rather than simply to list or describe, who insist "that history should explain something" (Parker 1973: 21). It is almost impossible to assess the importance of such a factor without supposing its absence in alternative circumstances, and it is not at all difficult to point to work by traditional, humanistic historians who ask similar questions. Fogel (1967), for example, pointed with apparent relish to many implicitly counterfactual arguments in a paper, by his friend and colleague Eugene Genovese, on the impact of slave plantations on Southern economic development (1962). Fogel argued that the cliometricians differed, by their attempts to make counterfactual arguments explicit, measurable, and therefore more readily testable.

Distinguishing between explicit and implicit hypothetical alternatives reflects only one element of a divide that grew up in the 1960s between practitioners of the new and the old economic history. Fogel praised the economist's formal, well-specified counterfactuals because, he argued, they would yield better answers to both traditional and novel questions. Such formulations nonetheless involve building economic models and analyzing quantitative evidence in ways foreign to the historian. Robert Riegel, for example, said in a review of Fogel's book on railroads, "For historians [it] raises very interesting questions of the importance and utility of many mathematical procedures, which at present are almost completely incomprehensible to most of us" (1965: 636).

as Summerhill (2003: 215–6) shows succinctly. Early critics of Fogel are Nerlove (1966), McClelland (1968) and David (1969), as well as Fenoaltea (1973), who takes on both Fogel and others. For retrospective reviews, see Davis (2000) on Fogel and Majewski (2006) on Fishlow.

Some new economic historians may have been bedazzled by their own technical abilities, but they could also use those skills for vigorous defense and intimidation. Harold Woodman (1976: 231) remembered that when historians had been brave enough to raise objections to cliometric results, they were met with "a barrage of counter-argument bristling with hard data . . . unfamiliar formulae, bewildering jargon, and esoteric mathematics."

By the early 1970s, the cliometricians felt themselves ready to present their work in two textbooks of multiple authorship. One, *American Economic Growth*, was a clear manifest of the community that had developed, assembling a dozen authors under the direction of Lance Davis, Richard Easterlin and William Parker (1972); it has a telling subtitle, *An Economist's History of the United States.* The other text, *The Reinterpretation of American Economic History* (1971), consisted mostly of reprinted essays, compiled and introduced extensively by its editors, Robert Fogel and Stanley Engerman. These volumes – important milestones in the advance of cliometrics in the US – covered much the same ground but in different ways. *American Economic Growth* is organized around the macroeconomic–sectoral approach pioneered by Kuznets, while many of the chapters of *Reinterpretation* reflect the new quantitative–analytical style of addressing largely microeconomic problems of economic development. Contributors to both books took care to explain theoretical concepts and quantitative methods to the uninitiated, and their chapters present results from the wide variety of issues that were taken on by the new movement. Today a large share of the economic history profession in North America consists of the intellectual children and grandchildren of the first generation of cliometricians who reported on their pioneering accomplishments in these volumes. But the influence of the pioneers is not limited to that continent alone, nor are the questions now being asked – and the answers given – merely the old issues discussed in more detail. The economist's style in the practice of economic history has diffused worldwide. Novel historical issues have arisen, and new modes of analysis have developed that extend beyond both the limitations and the ambitions of early cliometrics.

IV HISTORICAL ECONOMICS IN BRITAIN

> I intend to . . . argue that both as an intellectual and a real phenomenon, this particular permutation of economic history is based upon institutional factors that probably cannot be duplicated elsewhere . . . Why are the techniques of modern quantitative work so little used by the "mainstream" *economic historians* who work and teach in universities in the United Kingdom, compared to the situation here? It has to be a matter of choice, and the vote has apparently gone against computers, economic theory, econometrics and all the rest.
>
> Jonathan R. T. Hughes (1971)

> . . . as long as the tide of interest in British economic history is running in the direction of what (for want of a better phrase) can be called "analytical–economic" topics and questions, the appropriate methodological adjustment will follow as night follows the day – albeit in a more

> uncertain and lagged fashion as befits the unreliable British climate ... The new techniques will be institutionalized, and perhaps civilized, in one arm of British economic history. For in the last resort they reflect a range of analytical concerns that cannot be ignored.
>
> Barry Supple (1971)

Cliometrics arrived relatively slowly among British economic historians, but it did arrive. Some was homegrown; some was imported – borne east by a succession of visitors from West Lafayette, Indiana, Rochester, New York and the like. When Jonathan Hughes expressed his doubts that the American style of cliometrics could ever be an "export product," he was already wrong, as Barry Supple suggests. Admittedly, by 1970 the new style had been employed by only a tiny minority of those writing economic history in Britain. The homegrown, in fact, goes back to the 1920s, when George T. Jones studied post-1850 British and American industrial history and invented the product- and factor-price method of calculating productivity growth. His work, however, had little immediate impact.[35] The more dominant style of British quantitative economic history of the inter-war and early post-war periods is represented in the writings of two men, J. H. Clapham of Cambridge and T. S. Ashton of the LSE. Clapham adduced a wide variety of facts in his own work but cautioned economic historians that they should "have acquired the statistical sense" – of asking of their evidence – "how large? how long? how often? how representative?" He accomplished his ends by careful use of evidence combined with basic arithmetic and native wit. Ashton, Clapham's intellectual successor, infused plenty of neoclassical economic reasoning into his writings.[36]

In Britain, however, there was no equivalent to the National Bureau or Simon Kuznets. A welcoming home for historical work was the Department of Applied Economics (DAE) at Cambridge, inaugurated in 1945 at J. M. Keynes's earlier suggestion. The closest British analogue to Kuznets was Colin Clark of Cambridge, statistician and researcher for Keynes in the 1930s. Clark pioneered the compilation of national income measures for multiple countries in successive editions of his book, *The Conditions of Economic Progress* (1940 [1951; 1957]), and developed a method of international real income comparison similar to that now in common use.[37] Yet at mid-century the sort of broad comparison pioneered by Clark was alien to most British economic historians.

Introduction of a more formal style, in Britain as in North America, fell to those trained as economists, initially to Alec Cairncross, Brinley Thomas and Robin Matthews. Cairncross's book on home and foreign investment (1953) and Thomas's on migration

35 Perhaps because of Jones's death at age 26 in 1929; his thesis of 1928 was edited by Colin Clark for publication as *Increasing Return* (1933). McCloskey (1976: 441 *n*9) stresses Jones's early discovery of "the residual."

36 Clapham's major work is *An Economic History of Modern Britain* (3 vols, 1926–38); quotation from his essay on "economic history" (1931: 328). Ashton, prior to works on the Industrial Revolution (1948) and the eighteenth-century British economy (1955), used business archives to examine the iron industry (1924) and studied the "statistical movement" in Manchester (1934).

37 The current comparative measure is of "purchasing power parity," refined by Kravis *et al.* (1978) and widely used in historical (*e.g.*, Maddison (2001)) or contemporary comparisons (*e.g.*, by the World Bank in *World Development Indicators*). Clark had earlier written on British national income. For Clark's career, see Maddison (2004), our source for some details cited here.

and growth (1954) developed, or collected into one place, a great deal of quantitative information for theoretical analysis; their method, as David Landes noted, was "in the tradition of historical economics, as opposed to economic history."[38] Matthews's *Study in Trade Cycle History* (1954b) which examines the trade cycle of 1833–42, was written, he said, in a "quantitative–historical" mode, and contains theoretical reasoning, economic models, and statistical estimates. The *Study* is economist's history, prefaced by what may have been a pre-emptive half-apology to disciplinary colleagues for its reliance on " 'literary' sources." The book elicited from Professor Usher the observation that it "displays the full power of analysis that combines historical and theoretical methods."[39]

Systematic use of national accounting methods to study British economic development was undertaken by Phyllis Deane in the DAE at Cambridge. Her work resulted in two early papers on British income growth and capital formation (1955; 1956), then in two books of major importance and lasting value: the study of *British Economic Growth, 1688–1959* written with W. A. Cole (Deane & Cole 1962) and the compendium of underlying data assembled with Brian Mitchell (Mitchell & Deane 1962). Despite skeptical reviews, the basics of the Deane–Cole estimates of eighteenth- and early nineteenth-century aggregate growth were broadly accepted for two decades and provided a quantitative basis for discussing living standards and the dispersion of technical progress in the new industrial era. Also at the DAE, Charles Feinstein estimated the composition and magnitude of British investment flows (1961) and produced detailed national income estimates for the nineteenth and twentieth centuries (1972), augmenting, refining and revising, as well as extending, the work of Deane and Cole.

All these studies belong to a decidedly British empirical tradition, despite the use of contemporary theoretical constructs, and contain nothing like the later claims of some American cliometricians about the virtues of using formal theory and statistical methods. Research in a consciously cliometric style was strongly encouraged in the 1960s at Oxford by Hrothgar Habakkuk and Max Hartwell, although neither saw himself as a cliometrician. Separately and together, they supported the movement, encouraging students to absorb both quantitative and formal analytical elements into their work. They supervised, or proffered advice about, the research of Jonathan Hughes, Eric Jones, Patrick O'Brien, Gary Hawke, Roderick Floud, and Nick von Tunzelmann.[40]

The incursion of cliometrics into British economic history was – and has remained – neither so widespread nor so dominant as in North America, partly for reasons suggested by Hughes. Although economic history had been taught and practiced in

38 Landes (1955: 327). Further, in the 1950s Henry Phelps Brown was compiler and analyst, with Sheila Hopkins, of long-period series of wages and prices and of a famous and still-used price index; their papers are collected in Brown and Hopkins (1981). Likewise, Alec Ford, promoter of cliometric work at the University of Warwick in the 1970s, was working on international capital flows and the Gold Standard at the time. See Ford (1962) and Sadler (1992).

39 Matthews (1954b: quoted *xiii*). On the "apology," see Goodrich (1960: 531); A. P. Usher, review of Matthews (1954b) in *REStat* 37: 3 (1955: 317).

40 The resulting theses in cliometrics style from this group, as subsequently published, are Hawke (1970), Floud (1976), and von Tunzelmann (1978). Floud (2001) relates how he received a bit of imported advice in 1965. On hearing about the massive set of business records Floud had just acquired, Lance Davis advised him to "use a computer" to process the information. Floud tells us he had to learn how to do so at the summer quantitative institute at the University of Michigan.

British universities since the 1870s, after World War I most faculty members were housed in separate departments of economic (and social) history that tended to require of their students only a modicum of economics and little of quantitative methods.[41] With the establishment of new British universities and the rapid expansion of others in the 1960s, a dozen new departments of economic history were founded, staffed largely by people taught in history and economic history departments. The limited presence of cliometric types in Britain at the turn of the 1970s, as Supple and Hartwell (1971b) observed, did not come from deficient demand, nor was it due to hostility or indifference. It was due to limited supply, as Robin Matthews (1971) argued, stemming from the small scale of the British academic labor market and an aversion among young economists to excessive specialization. Yet the situation was then being rectified. On the demand side, British faculties of economics began to welcome more economic historians as colleagues, and on the side of supply, advanced students were aided by postgraduate stipends and research support provided by the new Social Science Research Council.[42]

During the 1970s, a British version of new historical economics began to take shape. Its practitioners expanded their informal networks into formal institutional structures and scholarly ventures; their style was merged into undergraduate pedagogy and postgraduate training. Roderick Floud published two books (1973; ed. 1974) intended to assist "humanistic" students to cross the threshold into numeracy, and Clive Lee (1977) explicated the new quantitative literature. Some students seeking economic history degrees dealt with technical material even earlier. Quantitative methods courses explicitly geared to analyzing historical data and issues began to appear in the early 1970s: at Exeter, Nicholas Crafts offered one newly required for the economic history degree in 1971, and Lee and Richard Perren were teaching such a course, also compulsory, by 1973 at Aberdeen.[43]

The organized British movement opened in September 1970, more-or-less officially at an Anglo-American "Conference on the New Economic History of Britain" in Cambridge – the one in Massachusetts. The proceedings were published as *Essays on a Mature Economy: Britain after 1840* (McCloskey, ed. 1971). Following presentation of papers that addressed "problems" of economic maturity, the views of Hughes, Supple, Hartwell and Matthews on the "exportability" of the new economic history were aired.[44] Several of those present formed the core of an alliance of new (and some old) economic historians of Britain intent on disseminating the quantitative–analytical style, notably

41 For discussion of institutional and structural change in British academic economic history, see Harte (1971; 1977; 2001) and Coleman (1987).

42 The British SSRC, established by the first Labour Government of Harold Wilson in 1965, was the long-delayed equivalent of the American organization of the same name. Political opposition to government aid to the social sciences was overcome only with Wilson's election; the SSRC was challenged during the first Thatcher government, surviving in 1985 with a new name, the Economic and Social Research Council (ESRC). The American SSRC was founded in 1923 and supported research at the National Bureau, as well as Kuznets's international historical accounts project. See Gaber (2005a; 2005b) and Worcester (2001) on the two Councils.

43 For Exeter, personal knowledge (Lyons); for Aberdeen, Lee (1983: 29).

44 The 1970 conference was attended by nearly half the scholars interviewed for these *Reflections*. Two further "Anglo-American" conferences were held, one at Cambridge (England) in 1972 and another again in Massachusetts in 1973; many of the papers appeared in *EEH* 10:4 (1973) and 11:4 (1974).

Roderick Floud and Deirdre McCloskey, who initiated an ambitious project to apply the new approach more widely in British economic historiography. Aided by funding from the SSRC (UK), they assembled a group of British and American authors to write *The Economic History of Britain since 1700*.[45] Their collection, published in 1981, was a milestone for British "new economic history," not without fault, but on balance favorably received by the critics. It was a very different textbook from the usual run, raising problems rather than solving them and providing a "positive minefield of debating issues," wrote Phyllis Deane. Brinley Thomas was a bit chary of "the cult of the measurable," yet he conceded that "Cliometrics has made significant advances" while not granting it superior authority. Nonetheless, despite sometimes grudging kudos, criticisms of detail and perspective, the consensus was, as François Crouzet wrote, that "this is an important and useful, but not a revolutionary work."[46]

Equally ground breaking, probably more so, was the outcome of parallel developments in English historical demography, whose practitioners had become progressively more quantitatively and theoretically adept since the 1950s, and for whom 1981 was also a banner year.[47] Although portions of the book had been circulating as the British academic equivalent of *samizdat* for some time, E. A. Wrigley's and R. S. Schofield's *Population History of England, 1541–1871: A Reconstruction* and its striking revisions of English demographic history were now available in one massive document. This book and many others were produced by the Cambridge Group for the History of Population and Social Structure, founded in 1964 by Peter Laslett and Tony Wrigley, with Roger Schofield as an important early member. Their work revealed the "modernity" of household structure and the ferment of migration (especially through London) in pre-industrial England (Laslett 1965; ed. 1972; Wrigley 1967). In the mid-1970s the Group's ability to commit to long-term and large-scale projects was bolstered when it became a directly funded unit of the SSRC, providing "a most welcome additional impetus to the work" (Wrigley & Schofield 1981: *xiv*). The Group produced its detailed results using a nominal record-linkage technique called "family reconstitution," pioneered in France in the 1950s by Louis Henry and Alfred Sauvy, and a computational technique, "back projection,"

45 Floud & McCloskey, eds; 2 vols (1981). Volume I covers Britain's economic "rise" to 1860 – the Industrial Revolution and preceding developments; volume II Britain's steady (relative) economic decline from the 1860s to the 1970s. Only a quarter of the contributors were US-trained and based. The SSRC and ESRC also funded an annual Quantitative Economic History Workshop modeled on the American Cliometrics Conference. The Workshop was intended to draw together those engaged in quantitative economic history, especially younger scholars and "those working in near isolation," as von Tunzelmann reported about the first meeting in 1978 (1980: 219).

46 Quotations from reviews by Deane, *EJ* 92:367 (1982: 720); Thomas, *JEL* 20:4 (1982: 1573, 2); and Crouzet, *J Modern History* 56:2 (1984: 339). The book was successful enough to generate a second edition, of three volumes, in 1994. A new and expanded venture, *The Cambridge Economic History of Modern Britain*, edited by Roderick Floud and Paul Johnson, was published in 2004 in three volumes. Alford (2004) compares this work favorably with the cliometrics of the 1960s and 1970s.

47 This and succeeding paragraphs are distilled from Wrigley & Schofield (1981) and Wrigley (1983; 2002); Wrigley (2002) includes a compact discussion of the development of methods in historical demography. Wrigley, Davis, Oeppen & Schofield (1997) is a second major volume revising details but not the broad conclusions of 1981. Results are summarized in Wrigley (2004). Early critics are Lindert (1983), Olney (1983), Weir (1984) and Goldstone (1986); for responses and extensions, see Schofield (1985; 2000).

developed by Ronald Lee and Jim Oeppen and later further developed by Oeppen as "inverse projection." This method made it possible to convert flows of vital events (periodic counts of births, marriages, deaths) into population stocks, thereby enabling the Group to calculate the vital rates (fertility, nuptiality, mortality) – the lodestones of demography. The flow data were collected from over 400 usable Anglican parish registers by a regiment of amateur population historians, part of an army of devotees of British local history.

Almost at a stroke, Wrigley–Schofield confuted Michael Flinn's (1970) earlier dismissal of parish registers as potentially useful data sources and showed that the conventional wisdom of "demographic transition," where population first grew more rapidly as mortality declined and then less rapidly as fertility declined, at least for England, was incorrect. The book provided evidence supporting Hrothgar Habakkuk's "percipience" in postulating quite the reverse in 1953: that rising fertility was the source of the higher English population growth rate of the later eighteenth century. Indeed, the Wrigley–Schofield results attributed more than two-thirds of that demographic increase to fertility change and the remainder to mortality improvements. Because marriage and household formation are intimately linked with economic fortunes and social convention, the short-period cycles and longer-term trends in population size and vital rates delineated in the *Population History* are of major import in understanding and even revealing economic and social change.

Wrigley and Schofield offered their own explanation, linking marriage rates to (much) earlier changes in the "real wage," as measured by the fascinating but rather limited Phelps Brown–Hopkins price index. Other economic historians and historical sociologists, however, were unhappy – either with the procedures leading to the estimates of annual vital events or with the socio-economic model.[48] The precise modes of economic-demographic interaction in seventeenth- and eighteenth-century England (or elsewhere) are still not settled, but as Wrigley (2002: 160) observes, we now know more in detail about pre-industrial demographic change than we are ever likely to know about the economy. A central conclusion almost certain to withstand further scrutiny is the late eighteenth-century disappearance of a previous inverse relationship between real income and population growth rates.

As in North America, after the first wave of "quantifiers" invaded parts of British economic and demographic historiography, cliometrics was refined in the heat of scholarly debate.

V CONTROVERSY: OR ONE THING LEADS TO ANOTHER

> [T]he feature I find noteworthy – and unhappily symptomatic of more widespread tendencies in the recent writing of quantitative economic history – is that in neither [of these two cases] has an effort been made to

48 Later work suggests that the apparent "lag" between economic change and demographic response disappears when better real wage data are used; see Wrigley (2004: 78, fig. 3.7).

> reconcile the obvious empirical implications of the "simplifying" premises with anything else that happens to be known about the economy under examination. . . . It used to be the vogue for champions of "the new economic history" to belabor their more "traditional" brethren for passing off, under cover of literary license, all sorts of unfounded statements about the past. An uncharitable observer might conclude that it will be the peculiar achievement of the new economic historians to have demonstrated that this can also be managed without benefit of a readable prose style.
>
> Paul David (1971a)

> In common with street crime, political purges, and scholarly controversy in other fields, the violence is greatest among the closest neighbors . . . the cliometrician reserves his foulest eye-gougings . . . for his closest colleagues, not – as the non-cliometric victims sometimes mistakenly believe – for the non-cliometric historian or economist. The cliometrician embraces the nonsense of the fact-blinded historian and, still more commonly, of the theory-crazed economist the better to assail . . . the cliometrician next door.
>
> Deirdre McCloskey (1978)

Cliometrics was molded gradually from a mix of curiosity and possibility, but it was fired in the kilns of controversy, ranging from a slow bake to white hot. Cliometricians started or continued a series of debates about the nature and sources of economic growth and its welfare consequences that decidedly have altered the picture of modern economic history. Our interviewees played central roles in most of these engagements. The first – perhaps the most fundamental – was initiated by Walt Rostow, who argued that modern economic growth begins with a brief and well-defined period of "take-off," with the necessary "preconditions" having already become the normal condition of a given national economy or society. The "take-off" metaphor first appeared in a journal article (1956), and was popularized in Rostow's famous book, *The Stages of Economic Growth* (1960). The International Economic Association (IEA) in 1960 summoned a group of scholars to examine the arguments in *Stages*, the only time it has sponsored a conference devoted to a single work. By and large, Rostow's formulations were found wanting; like other stage theories, his model offered no clear link from one stage of growth to the next. Nevertheless, along with Simon Kuznets, Colin Clark, Alexander Gerschenkron and Arthur Lewis, Walt Rostow is praised as a scholar who tried to view modern economic growth from an economist's perspective and who saw it as the outcome of history's complexities.[49]

The nineteenth-century expansion of the American railroad network was long

49 On Rostow and the IEA, see Dacey *et al.* (2004: 3334). The presumed doubling in capital formation as a share of GDP associated with "take-off" was not to be found and not all preconditions were present. See Rostow, ed. (1963), his introduction, and contributions of Kuznets, Habakkuk & Deane, and Gerschenkron. Rostow responded further to critics in later editions of *Stages* (1971; 1990). He edited the 1963 volume while engaged in policy planning at the State Department. Later, during the height of the Vietnam War, he was President Johnson's National Security Adviser before returning to academia in 1969. On Rostow and the profession, see Mancur Olson's review (1985) of Kindleberger & di Tella, eds (1982).

regarded as a major force in the development of the US economy, as argued by Leland Jenks, George Rogers Taylor and especially Paul Cootner.[50] Rostow's "take-off" stage of growth incorporated this view, with railroads acting as "leading sector," both as source of industrial demand and supplier of cheaper transport. In their books both Fishlow and Fogel tested these propositions – finding many of them wanting – by means of deeper examination of sources of quantitative data and explicit use of counterfactuals. Their work, in turn, sparked other investigations and debates about social saving calculations and about the use of counterfactuals. Fritz Redlich, for example, complained that the hypothetical alternatives used in making counterfactual arguments were mere "figments," not history at all (1965: 485), while others have defended the method. Stanley Engerman attempted to dispel some misunderstandings by observing, "Not all debates and disagreements in the new economic history have been about counterfactual issues. . . . debates that appear to be about the implementation of counterfactuals frequently really concern the nature of the questions which the scholars consider to be of interest and importance."[51]

Until the cliometricians made a pair of disputatious incursions, the economic history of the American South was largely the province of regional historians – almost a footnote to the story of US economic development. In the antebellum period, the South produced the nation's most important export, cotton, but after the Civil War its retarded economy contributed little to the nation's massive economic growth. Sparked by Conrad and Meyer (1958) and Easterlin (1960; 1961), for two decades cliometricians focused intently on the place of the South in the national economy, and of slavery in the Southern economy.

To what extent was early national economic growth driven by Southern cotton exports; how self-sufficient was the South as an economic region? Douglass North (1961) argued that the key to American economic development before 1860 was regional specialization, that Southern cotton was the economy's staple product, and that much of Western and Northern economic growth derived from Southern demand for food and manufactures. Critics systematically examined North's underlying model, which "is simple yet powerful, internally consistent, and apparently supported by contemporary evidence. It's also probably wrong." Cotton did not displace food production, the strong regional complementarity was between the West and the North, and the national significance of cotton was as the major credit entry in the international accounts.[52]

Contention about Southern self-sufficiency was vigorous, but emotions were low. Not so in the slavery debate. John Meyer recalls that both he and Alfred Conrad thought that examining the profitability of slavery in their undergraduate courses was "particularly suitable for illustrating the role of economics in analyzing historical issues" and

50 Jenks (1944), Taylor (1951) and Cootner's Ph.D. dissertation (1953); Cootner published his views, somewhat revised, in 1963.

51 Engerman (1980: 164, 5). Fishlow observed that any theoretical approach to history is "inherently in the conditional mode" (1974: 455). Fogel, in his Presidential address to the EHA (1979), vigorously defended the counterfactual method. See also McClelland (1975: Ch. 4).

52 Quotation from Atack & Passell (1994: 161). The supporting observations are given by, among others, Fishlow (1964), Gallman (1970) and Hutchinson & Williamson (1971). See also Hughes & Cain (2007: 178–80).

that their students "took it as an objective exercise with none of the emotional reaction we later encountered with more senior reviewers." Indeed, their two early papers were presented as "simple extensions of the teachings to which we had been exposed," and the "most shocked people at Williamstown . . . were Conrad and myself as we beheld the storm o[f] 'reaction' that we generated."[53] They had touched a nerve. It appeared in 1957 that their methodological prescriptions about integrating history and theory were the more provocative, but their paper on slavery sparked a series of critiques in the 1960s. Their demonstration of profitability did not imply the slave system was viable in the long run; Yasuba (1961) was able to fill that gap, and others tested and refined these early results. As a system of organizing production, American slavery was found to have been thriving on the eve of the Civil War; the sources of that prosperity, however, needed deeper examination.

Time on the Cross (1974), by Robert Fogel and Stanley Engerman, not only reaffirmed the profitability and viability of Southern slavery, but also made claims about superior productivity in Southern versus Midwestern agriculture and about the relatively generous material comforts afforded to the slave population. Their book sparked a long-running controversy that extended beyond academia and prompted critical examinations and rebuttals by political and social historians and, above all, by their fellow cliometricians. A major critique was *Reckoning with Slavery* (David *et al.* 1976), as much a defense of cliometric method as a catalogue of what its authors saw as the method's improper or incomplete application in *Time on the Cross*. Fogel subsequently published *Without Consent or Contract* (1989a), a defense and extension of his and Engerman's earlier work.[54]

The remarkable antebellum prosperity of the Southern slave economy was followed by an equally remarkable relative decline in Southern income per capita after the war. While the remainder of the American economy grew rapidly, the South stagnated, with a distinctively low-wage, low-productivity economy and a poorly educated labor force, both black and white. The next generation of cliometricians asked "Why?" Was it the legacy of the slave system, of the virtual absence of industrial development in the antebellum South, of post-Civil War reconstruction and backlash, of continued reliance on cotton, of Jim Crow, or of racism and discrimination? Roger Ransom and Richard Sutch (1977) investigated share–tenancy, debt peonage and labor effort in maintaining cotton cultivation, using individual level data, some derived *à la* Parker and Gallman from a sample of the manuscript US censuses. Gavin Wright (1986) focused on an effective separation of the Southern from the national labor market, and Robert Margo (1990) examined the region's low level of educational investment and its consequences.

53 The first two quotations are from the interview with Meyer; the latter pair from a 1977 letter to A. W. Coats, quoted in Coats (1980: 187).

54 Fogel's 1989 book was followed by two others, one discussing evidence and methods (Fogel *et al.* 1992), and a two-volume work containing technical papers (Fogel & Engerman, eds 1992). For a retrospective review and appreciation of *Time on the Cross*, and of the disputes it generated, see Weiss (2001). Some of Fogel's and Engerman's conclusions have become part of a consensus but their "benign" view of slave welfare remains controversial. Likewise, disagreements continue about their finding of higher productivity in the plantation South than on Midwestern farms. *Cf.* Fogel's *Slavery Debates* (2003: 29–45) and Wright's *Slavery and American Economic Development* (2006b: 94–122); the two books provide numerous references.

An entirely new line of investigation derived from the research on slavery, measuring the "biological standard of living" using anthropometric data.[55] Their use in cliometrics resulted from a conversation between Robert Fogel and the demographer James Trussell in 1975 (Fogel interview). Fogel enlisted a talented team of graduate students to bring such evidence to bear on questions in economic history, particularly those related to slavery. Richard Steckel's paper on slave height profiles (1979) led directly to the discussion of "Anthropometric Indexes of Malnutrition" in *Without Consent or Contract* (1989: 138–42). In a corrective to the Fogel–Engerman interpretation of the slave diet, Steckel (1986) showed how stunted (and thus how poorly fed) slave children were before they came of working age. John Komlos (1987) discovered that heights (of West Point cadets) were declining even as American per capita income was rising in the years before the Civil War, what he called the "Antebellum Puzzle." Anthropometric techniques have found many applications in the US and elsewhere. Roderick Floud led a project employing anthropometric data from records of British military recruits, while records for male and female transportees to Australia have been examined by Nicholas, Steckel and Oxley.[56] A related project initiated by Fogel, "Early indicators of later work levels, disease and death," documents the history and prospects of human health and mortality using anthropometric and many other data for Union Army veterans.[57]

Industrialization and its new technologies in the US pre-date the Civil War. In writing about technological progress, economic historians before the 1960s had tended to concentrate on single industries or economies.[58] Yet distinctive "national" technologies emerged in the early nineteenth century (*e.g.*, contemporary British observers distinguished "The American System of Manufactures" from their own). Amid the early ferment of quantitative economic history in the United States, Hrothgar Habakkuk published *American and British Technology in the Nineteenth Century: The Search for Labour-Saving Inventions*, a truly comparative study. It was 1962, when, as Paul David writes, "economic historians' interests in Anglo-American technological divergences were suddenly raised from a quiet simmer to a furious boil by the publication of . . . Habakkuk's now celebrated book on the subject" (1975: *ix*). Habakkuk expanded on an earlier postulate by Erwin Rothbarth (1946) that an apparent labor-saving bias of American manufacturing techniques was due to land so abundant that American workers were paid (relative to other factors) much more than what their British counterparts received,

55 Anthropometrics is measurement of human physical characteristics by age and sex, such as height, weight, or girth. Such data were used by the World Health Organization in the 1970s to assess the nutritional status of populations in developing countries.

56 Floud, Wachter and Gregory (1990); Nicholas and Steckel (1991); Nicholas and Oxley (1993). For a survey, see Steckel (1995); for multiple countries, see Komlos, ed. (1994) and Steckel & Floud, eds (1997). On augmenting the written record with skeletal data, see, *e.g.*, Steckel & Rose, eds (2002), Koepke & Baten (2005) and Steckel (2005).

57 Fogel summarizes his work in his Nobel lecture (1994a) and in *The Escape from Hunger and Premature Death* (2004a). The veterans' project is discussed below in Fogel's "Further Reflections" (with Mark Guglielmo).

58 The exception proving the rule is A. P. Usher's *A History of Mechanical Inventions* (1929), ranging widely in space and time but even then avoiding detailed examination of the economic implications of the inventions discussed, as Usher himself observed in the second edition of 1954 (p. *ix*).

but he did not resolve whether the bias was due to more machines per worker, better machines, or more inventiveness.[59]

One strand of the debate over what Peter Temin (1966a) called Habakkuk's "labor-scarcity paradox" left to one side the question of "better machines." It fell to Nathan Rosenberg and Paul David to explore the distinctive technological trajectories of different economies. Rosenberg's work is largely empirical, combining careful examination of particular technological systems with a dose of appreciative theorizing; in this context he pointed to the emergence of "technologically convergent" production processes and to the importance of very low relative materials costs in American manufacturing (1963; 1967a). Paul David (1975: Ch. 2) reviewed the debate and put a distinctive stamp on the discussion, beginning to formulate a theoretical approach to explain sources of technical change (and divergence). He argued that an economy's trajectory of technological development is conditioned, perhaps only initially, by relative factor prices, but then by opportunities for further progress based on localized learning from, or constrained by, existing techniques and their histories. The concept David developed is defined thus: "A dynamic process whose evolution is governed by its own history is 'path dependent'." W. Brian Arthur (1989) developed a similar perspective concerning the impact of increasing returns to adoption of competing technologies, what he called technological "lock-in by historical small events." The views of both authors contradict received wisdom in equilibrium economic analysis and provoked a continuing debate with economists, such as Stanley Liebowitz and Stephen Margolis, who insist that globally optimal technical choices exist and that market processes will seek them out and ensure their dominance.[60]

The first systematic cliometric debate involving European economic history took place at the 1970 Anglo-American conference at Harvard. It involved an alleged British technological and economic failure in the late nineteenth century, when the Germans threatened to overtake Britain and the United States bade fair to overtake them both. The slower growth of income and exports, the loss of markets even in the Empire, and an "invasion" of foreign manufactures (many American) alarmed British businessmen and policy makers alike and led to opposition to a half-century of "Free Trade."[61] Who

59 The issue is akin to the "factor proportions" or "choice-of-technique" problem already extant in the economic development literature (*e.g.*, Eckaus 1955, Sen 1960). The related literature includes Fogel (1967), Rosenberg (1967b), Ames & Rosenberg (1968), Asher (1972), Cain & Paterson (1981), Lazonick (1981), A. Field (1983), James & Skinner (1985) and Leunig (2003). For compact discussions of the Habakkuk hypothesis, see Hughes & Cain (2007: 211–13), Atack & Passell (1994: 201–5) and Crafts (1987: 178–81).

60 Quotation from David (2005: 1). The idea that (some) economic–historical processes are irreversible is an early element of this view, and was part of David's (1969) critique of Fogel's railroad social saving calculations. A useful example is the QWERTY typewriter keyboard, which in the late nineteenth century emerged as the standard owing to "positive feedbacks" arising from "network externalities." That is, wider use of a given technique or form, no matter the reason for its initial diffusion, conveys to new adopters advantages unavailable to those opting for alternatives (David 1985). Liebowitz and Margolis (2002) reprints their first assault of 1990, "The fable of the keys," and later writings.

61 A campaign for tariff reform and Imperial Preference early in the twentieth century was headed by Joseph Chamberlain, leading light in founding the University of Birmingham, where William Ashley was a vocal ally. See Barker (1977) and Koot (1987: Chs 5, 7 esp.); also Semmell (1957) on Ashley's "conversion" while at Harvard from free-trade liberal to "fair trade" tariff reformer.

was to blame for loss of competitiveness? Although some scholars attributed Britain's 'climacteric' to the maturation of the technologies underpinning her success during the Industrial Revolution, others attributed it to "entrepreneurial failure" and cited the inability or refusal of British business leaders to adopt the best available technologies. At the Harvard conference a vigorous (and heavily American) defense of the British was mounted against some of their own descendants. The papers argued, by and large, that British businessmen made their investment and production decisions in a sensible, economically rational fashion, given the constraints they faced; they had made the best of a bad situation. As subsequent research has demonstrated, the problem is more complex and is yet to be resolved.[62]

A parallel cliometric exercise, again with trans-Atlantic contributors, has revised the story told by earlier quantitative revisionists of the British rise to a summit from which the economy later "declined." The economic changes that began in Britain sometime in the late eighteenth century have long been called an "Industrial Revolution." Much ink has been spilled debating the applicability of that metaphor, but more to the point has been the ink devoted to measuring the phenomenon. Quantitative economic historians, following Clapham's admonition to "offer dimensions in place of blurred masses of unspecified size," have been at the forefront in delineating the timing and magnitudes of economic growth, the loci and impact of technical progress, and the distribution of costs and benefits of early industrial change in Britain. This last issue is the question of the standard of living during the Industrial Revolution, or "the condition of England." It has a venerable history – beginning as a debate between contemporary "optimists" like Andrew Ure and "pessimists" like Friedrich Engels and Karl Marx.[63]

Into this continuing ideological dispute between free-market liberals and Marxian critics about the nature of industrialization, Eric Hobsbawm fired another salvo in 1957, questioning both evidence and argument that recently had been deployed by defenders of capitalism.[64] The liberal riposte from Max Hartwell (1961) was that British workers had experienced a "*rising* standard of living" in the first half of the nineteenth century. Hartwell injected "a measure of theory into a debate from which it ha[d] hitherto been largely absent" (Taylor 1975: *xiv*). Hartwell's optimistic case appealed to evidence about the relatively rapid rate of British economic growth after 1780 recently revealed by Phyllis Deane (reported in full in Deane & Cole 1962). Following a direct confrontation

62 See Brown & Handfield-Jones (1952) on the "climacteric" and Aldcroft (1964) for a summary indictment of British business of the period. McCloskey (1970) and McCloskey & Sandberg (1971) review the "failure" literature and offer a defense; papers on specific industries appear in the conference volume, McCloskey, ed. (1971). T. Nicholas (2004) reviews the debate overall, and raises the still outstanding question of "entrepreneurial failure compared to what?"

63 Cameron (1982) argues that thinking of British industrialization as "revolutionary" is a bad thing; Fores (1981) argues that an historiographic focus on "industry" is even worse; see also Coleman (1992). Clapham is quoted in Heaton (1938: 599). See Ure (1835), Engels (1845 [1891]), and Marx (1976: Ch. 15.4; 15.5 esp. [1867]).

64 Hayek, ed., *Capitalism and the Historians* (1954), responded to Fabian views of industrialization as social catastrophe. The book reprinted an article by T. S. Ashton (1949) demonstrating improved living standards for British workers and an optimistic view of factories by W. H. Hutt (1926). New contributions were from a set of meliorist papers presented at the 1951 meetings of the Mont Pelerin Society, an organization founded by Hayek in 1947 to further the cause of classical liberalism. See Hartwell (1995: 39, 66, 93–4).

(Hobsbawm & Hartwell 1963), the two combatants largely left the field to others.[65] In concert with more traditional economic historians, young cliometricians jumped into the fray – many remain there in middle age – marshalling additional evidence with rather mixed results. Peter Lindert and Jeffrey Williamson thought in 1983 they had settled the dispute on the side of the optimists. They used a broad-ranging assembly of (men's) wage data and a new price index to generate a measure of real wages that from 1760 to 1820 grew only slowly, but nearly doubled in the ensuing three decades. Their results were in fact "super-optimistic," falling outside the bounds of previous estimates. Their colleagues were astonished and suspicious, and their "bourgeois" meliorism was quickly attacked from the Left by R. S. Neale (1985).

Contemporaneously, cliometricians were chipping away at the Deane–Cole estimates of British growth, particularly for the eighteenth century. In a series of publications beginning in the 1970s, Nick Crafts and Knick Harley outlined a new picture of British aggregate economic performance. In brief, they argue that before about 1760 the level of income, especially in agriculture, was much higher than had been believed; likewise, previously estimated rates of industrial output growth were too high. Consequently, economic growth rates per capita in the central decades of the Industrial Revolution (1780–1830) were barely a third of those reported in *British Economic Growth*. Critics, both traditional and cliometric, have been unwilling to allow Crafts and Harley seemingly to revise the Industrial Revolution out of existence, and their view has itself instigated a continuing debate. With the sharp downward revision of post-1780 growth rates and with overall population growth rates well established, the early decades of economic expansion during the Industrial Revolution were being viewed through a new lens.[66]

Similarly, there was much less output increase to benefit British workers; support for super-optimism about rising living standards simply had been cut away. In the past two decades the tide has turned further against the optimists and in favor of a redefined "pessimism," but in disputes less ideologically contentious than the old left–right face-off. For assessing "the condition of England" a remark made long ago (in another context) by Charles Babbage is apposite: "the errors which arise from the absence of facts are far more numerous and more durable than those which result from unsound reasoning respecting true data."[67]

Lindert and Williamson tried to rectify that absence of facts, but their surprising results led to criticisms of their procedures and to searches for yet more information. The most assiduous of these searches was conducted by Charles Feinstein, who was not persuaded by Williamson's later work (1985) on British income inequality. He published a detailed critique in 1988, adding new information about occupations and incomes.

65 Including, notably, a slightly younger member of the British Marxist historians' group, Edward P. Thompson, whose *The Making of the British Working Class* (V. Gollancz; Pantheon 1964) contains an eloquent and elegiac chapter on "Standards and Experiences."

66 The primary contributions are Crafts (1976; 1985), Harley (1982; 1999), and Crafts & Harley (1992). Notable critics are Hoppitt (1990), Berg & Hudson (1992) and Cuenca (1994). A careful synthesis is supplied by Mokyr (2004). Revising the growth estimates downward has led also to a disputed picture of a (more limited) extent of British "inventiveness" during the industrial revolution. Compare McCloskey (1981b), Crafts (1994), Temin (1997a) and Harley & Crafts (2000).

67 From Babbage (1963 [1835]: 156), quoted by Rosenberg (1992), as reprinted 1994: 27.

Over the ensuing decade he expanded the wage and salary database and constructed a price index more detailed than any previously available. The upshot was Feinstein's "Pessimism Perpetuated," which concludes, "For the majority of the working class the historical reality was that they had to endure almost a century of hard toil with little or no advance from a low base before they really began to share in any of the benefits of the economic transformation they had helped to create" (1998: 652). His estimates of changes in material income standards, although not unassailable and as he admits containing the occasional "heroic assumption," seem sound enough to allow Joachim Voth, author of the most recent survey of the controversy, to deal with the real wage question in only two pages before turning to other indicators of economic welfare (2004: 271–3). What remains after all this quantitative revisionism is still an "Industrial Revolution" – a profound and even precocious change in economic structure, but with neither abrupt take-off nor exceptionally rapid growth.[68]

Many results of the cliometrics revolution come from application of theory and measurement in the service of history; a converse case comes from the macroeconomists. Monetarists, in particular, have placed economic history in the service of theory, prominently in analyzing the Great Depression of the 1930s. Milton Friedman and Anna Schwartz, in *A Monetary History of the United States, 1867–1960* (1963), opened a discussion that has led to widespread, but not universal, acceptance among economists of a sophisticated version of the "quantity theory of money." As Hugh Rockoff (2000) points out, their detailed examination of several episodes in American monetary development under varying institutional regimes allowed them to use a set of "natural experiments" to assess the economic impact of exogenous changes in the stock of money. The Friedman–Schwartz enterprise sought support for the general proposition that money is not simply a veil over real transactions – that money does matter. Their demonstration of that point for the Great Depression initiated an entire scholarly literature involving not only economic historians but also monetary and macroeconomists. Peter Temin was among the first of the economic historians to question the Friedman–Schwartz argument, in *Did Monetary Forces Cause the Great Depression?* (1976). His answer was essentially "No," stressing declines in consumer spending and in investment in the late 1920s as initiating factors and discounting money stock reductions for the continued downturn. In a later book, *Lessons from the Great Depression* (1989) Temin, in effect, recanted his earlier position, impelled by a good deal of further research, especially on international finance.[69] The present consensus is that what Friedman and Schwartz call "The Great Contraction, 1929–1933" may have been initiated by real factors in the late 1920s, but it was faulty public policy and adherence to the Gold Standard that played major roles in turning an economic downturn into "The Great Depression."

The debate about the Depression, among both theorists and historians, is only the most prominent element of a flowering of historical research about money, banking,

68 See Crafts (1994: 59 esp.), Crafts & Harley (2004), and Crafts (2005) for their perspective on how the nature of the "revolution" has been revised.

69 See, *e.g.*, Eichengreen's work leading to his *Golden Fetters* (1992). In reviews of Temin (1989), both Richard Grossman (*JEH* 52:1, 1992: 244–6) and Anna Schwartz herself (*Economica n.s.* 58:232, 1991: 535–6), the latter rather acerbically, noted Temin's change of perspective.

and financial systems. Lance Davis devoted much of his early career to studies of the financial sector, tapping and analyzing previously little-used sources of quantitative data from the business archives. He also raised more general questions about finance and the economy, arguing, for example, that integrated capital markets were long delayed in the US, given evidence of high regional interest rate differentials. He also argued that sources of industrial finance developed in radically divergent ways in the US and the UK, leading to "investment banking" in America and nothing like it in Britain. Ascertaining the extent and timing of American capital market integration has been a preoccupation of financial historians of the US ever since, and recent work argues that capital markets were more integrated than Davis thought.[70]

A broad new approach to economic change over time has emerged from the mind of Douglass North, Lance Davis's sometime co-author. Confronted in the later 1960s with European economic development in its variety and antiquity, North became dissatisfied with the limited modes of analysis that he had applied fruitfully to the American case and concluded that "we couldn't make sense out of European economic history without explicitly modeling institutions, property rights, and government" (North interview). For that matter, making sense of a wider view of American economic history was similarly difficult, as exemplified in the Davis-North venture, *Institutional Change and American Economic Growth* (1971).[71] The core of North's model, conceptual rather than formal, is that when changes in underlying circumstances alter the cost–benefit calculus of existing arrangements new institutions will arise if there is a net benefit to be realized.[72] Although their approach arose from dissatisfaction with the static nature of economic theory in the 1960s, still North and his colleagues followed what most other economists would do in arguing that optimal institutional forms will arise dynamically from a "profit-maximizing" response to changes in incentives. As Davis and North were quick to admit, their effort was "a first (and very primitive) attempt" at formulating a theory of institutional change and applying that theory to American institutional development. It was, as Cynthia Taft Morris notes, little more than "telling vivid stories," effectively on a *post hoc* basis; it did not compare US developments with other cases where apparent net benefits did not lead to growth-enhancing institutional change. A striking commonality among the critics, however, is their stress on the progress made: "we should not dismiss the questions raised by the new institutional economics merely because we are not always satisfied by the answers so far obtained."[73] North recognized the limitations of his early work on institutional change and has endeavored to develop a more subtle

70 See Davis (1960) on textile finance and Davis (1963; 1965; 1966a) on capital markets; also Sylla (1969). Davis's investment banking hypothesis has withstood further examination: see Bodenhorn & Rockoff (1992) and Calomiris (2000). For discussion of similar issues in Britain, see Edelstein (2004) and Cottrell (2004).

71 North's incursion into European developments was undertaken with Robert Paul Thomas in works about the manorial system and *The Rise of the Western World* (North and Thomas 1971; 1973). For an appreciation and critique of *The Rise*, see Coelho (2001).

72 Benefits realized by whom is not specified; critics of the European work, like Fenoaltea (1975) and A. Field (1981), were not persuaded by the process described, for this and other reasons. The underlying premise is that an efficient regime of property rights is the basis of an economy's capacity to grow; and thus that the key question is how property rights come to be defined, enforced, limited and altered.

73 Quotations from Davis & North (1971: 4), C. Morris (2000), and Basu, Jones & Schlicht (1987: 19).

and articulated approach; for example, in an analysis with Barry Weingast of the impact of the Glorious Revolution in England (1989). In *Understanding the Process of Economic Change*, North again stresses that modeling institutional change is less than straightforward, and continues to examine the persistence of "institutions that provided incentives for stagnation and decline" (2005: *viii*).

The initial investigations of the cliometricians, the consequent debates and controversies, and the new directions taken by the field's pioneers clearly have led to substantial changes in cliometrics. Other forces have led also to major changes in the parent disciplines, history and economics, and to the place of economic history as an element of those broader scholarly enterprises.

VI CLIOMETRICS OVER 50 YEARS: RETROSPECT AND PROSPECT

> To be sure, the claims of our early revolutionaries taxed the patience of historians who understood that history is at bottom an art and could never be transformed into an exact science. But, in the hands of its ablest practitioners, [cliometrics] has devised methods that compel all honest historians to quantify the quantifiable and to bring unprecedented rigor to the study of that range of human experience amenable to measurement. The revolution has been real and irreversible, even if it has disappointed the youthful hopes of those who thought it could introduce the Kingdom of Heaven here on earth.
>
> Eugene Genovese (1994)

> Ultimately we economic historians have nowhere firm and distinctive to stand if we do not stand shoulder to shoulder with the economists; it is less of a comfort to have them riding like sometimes mischievous monkeys on our backs.
>
> Eric Jones (1990)

> One man cannot think in two ways.
>
> [Hrothgar] John Habakkuk (1971a)

In the 1960s, when the first cliometricians began to group themselves into a distinct intellectual and social movement, buoyed by their revisionist achievements, they (at least many of them) thought they could use their scientific approach to rewrite history. This hope may not have been a vain one, but it is yet to be realized. The same kind of optimism had infected Edwin Gay, Wesley Mitchell, and their supporters in founding the NBER. That organization did not change the world either, but its projects have added a good deal to our understanding of modern economies. Similarly, the best efforts of cliometricians have merged with those in other traditions to develop a rather different understanding of the economic past from views maintained half a century ago.

As economic history has evolved, so have the environs economic historians inhabit. In the Anglophone world, economic history – and cliometrics within it – burgeoned with the growth of higher education, but it has recently suffered the effects of retrenchment in that sector. Elsewhere a new multilingual generation of enthusiastic economic historians and historical economists has arisen, with English as the language of international discourse. Both history and economics have been transformed by dissatisfaction with old verities and values, by adoption of new methods and points of view, and by posing new or revived questions. Economic history has been beneficiary of and contributor to such changes.

Whatever favorable movements there have been, however, economic history as a corporate enterprise will always struggle with the tension of having been spawned by parents who think in not-quite-compatible ways. Economists, from Marxians to free-market fundamentalists, have sought to reveal general "laws of motion" of economic society, or simply have applied the "laws" available to them at the time. Historians have seen broad patterns of change as contingent, where generalization is strictly limited by details of time and place, or they have been content to contribute a few dots of color to paintings from the studios of *pointillist* masters. The divide is between nomothetic economics and idiographic history; any economic historian who takes seriously both sides of her heritage is liable to a career-long bout of cognitive dissonance. Yet, if any form of history is to be more than "one damned thing after another," then an urge to explain must be satisfied, and, as Meghnad Desai says (2001: 59) – echoing Marshall – "There is no escape from theorising."

Even before the explicitly theorizing cliometricians arrived on the scene, tensions had been felt between close neighbors, business history and economic history. While their intellectual currents overlap, and while a business historian and an economic historian can be found often in the same person, the two fields have followed separate paths. In North America, despite a modest overlap in membership of the Business History Conference and the Economic History Association, historians predominate in the one and economists in the other. Likewise the style of article in the BHC's journal *Enterprise & Society* differs distinctively from that in *The Journal of Economic History*.[74] A similar partial divide has grown in the UK with publication beginning in 1959 of *Business History* and formalized by the Association of Business Historians, whose annual conference began in the early 1990s. There have been attempts in the US to reconcile alternative disciplinary approaches, but with only modest success.[75] British business historians commonly have used more economic theory in their work than have the Americans, but divergences of interest and approach among those trained in economics, history, or economic history remain.[76]

Although this introduction focuses on the development of historical economics in the

74 *Enterprise & Society* began publication in 2000, succeeding the BHC's annual conference proceedings, *Business and Economic History* (1972–99).

75 Peter Temin, Naomi Lamoreaux and Daniel Raff edited three essay collections attempting to merge the structuralist approach of American business history with the economic analysis of cliometric historians: Temin, ed. (1991), Lamoreaux & Raff, eds (1995) and Lamoreaux, Raff & Temin, eds (1999). This project has had limited impact, according to Galambos (2003: 21), because it has yet to develop a "dynamic synthesis that would be an alternative to the Chandlerian context." For further commentary on this project, see the Temin interview; see also Lamoreaux *et al.* (2003).

76 On British *v* American business history, see Honeyman (2005: 177). For the British style, see Hannah (1999).

United States and the United Kingdom, we note that the cliometric approach has diffused well beyond their boundaries. In France the economist's quantitative approach was fostered when Kuznets's historical national accounts project recruited scholars in the 1950s to amass and organize the agricultural, output and population data available, in a new *histoire quantitative*. Still, that movement was overshadowed by the *Annales* school, whose *histoire totale* involved much data collection but limited economic analysis. As George Grantham (1997) observes, economist's economic history of France, written by scholars trained there, did not arrive in force until the mid-1980s. French cliometrics was written at first by economic historians from (or trained in) North America or Britain; the Gallic cliometrics revolution occurred gradually, for "peculiarly French" institutional and ideological reasons.[77] In Germany similar institutional barriers were breached partially in the 1960s with the arrival of a "turnkey" cliometrics operation in the form of an American-trained American scholar, Richard Tilly, who went from Wisconsin to Münster; Tilly was joined later by a few central Europeans who received American degrees, and all have since taught younger German cliometricians. Leading cliometric scholars from Italy, Spain and Portugal likewise received their postgraduate educations in Britain or America. The foremost Japanese cliometrician, Yasukichi Yasuba, received his Ph.D. from Johns Hopkins, supervised by Simon Kuznets.[78]

If cliometrics in and of continental Europe could trace its roots to North America and Britain, by the 1980s it had developed indigenous strength and identity. At the Tenth International Economic History Congress in Leuven, Belgium (1990), a new association of analytical economic historians was founded at an *ad hoc* meeting. Rejecting the use of "cliometrics" as descriptor, the participants endorsed the nascent European Historical Economics Society. In July 1991 at Copenhagen, Rolf Dumke declared with some pride at the first formal gathering of the EHES that this was a "new era for *real* European historical economists" – that at this conference "one could in fact find European historical economists discussing European historical economics."[79] Subsequently national associations and seminars have grown up under the umbrella of the EHES – for example, French historical economists have the *Association Française de Cliométrie* and a new international journal, *Cliometrica* (2007–), while Portuguese and Spanish economic historians have sponsored a series of "Iberometrics" conferences. Other long-standing economic history organizations have experienced an incursion of historical economists, as in Scandinavia, Ireland, and Italy.

A major social revolution over the past four decades has brought a substantial number of women into academic life, accompanied by an efflorescence of scholarly work

77 Pioneering quantitative studies of France include Toutain (1961) and Marczewski (1965). Other surveys of recent work in French economic history are Crouzet & Lescent-Giles (1998) and Hoffman & Rosenthal (2000). The institutional peculiarities of the French economic-historical enterprise in the 1950s and 1960s alluded to by Grantham (pp. 354*ff*) are examined in Rouvray (2005: Ch. 5). Two brief surveys of *Annaliste* economic history are Forster (1978) and Drukker (2006: Ch. 3).

78 On cliometric studies of Germany, see Tilly (1997), the introduction to Komlos & Eddie, eds (1997), and Tilly (2001) and accompanying articles. For Yasuba (1930–2005) see his conversation (2005) with John Latham.

79 From recollections of Lyons and J. W. Drukker, who participated in the EHES founding meeting. Quotations from Dumke (1992: 3), emphasis added.

on contemporary and historical issues of sex and gender. Historians of female professionals stress that women virtually disappeared from academia in the English-speaking world for the generation born between the wars. Only two interviews in this volume could be conducted with pioneering women in quantitative economic history, assuredly because of a generational phenomenon influenced by changing social currents. Both Anna Schwartz and Phyllis Deane were educated in the 1930s and were preceded by a distinguished company of female scholars. In the United States these include a founder and President of the EHA, Anne Bezanson, and the first woman cliometrician, Dorothy Brady. Maxine Berg has documented the work and lives of women economic historians flourishing in Britain before the Second World War, especially Eileen Power, an LSE professor who was a driving force behind the success of the EHS and its *Review* in the 1920s and 1930s. However, aside from Schwartz and Deane, there were effectively no women in quantitative economic history for a quarter-century. Their prominent contemporaries, like Sylvia Thrupp and Joan Thirsk, took non-quantitative approaches, and most other leading female cliometricians of the present and recent past did not acquire their final degrees before the 1960s.[80]

This later generation of women (with some male counterparts) has brought to the fore many issues previously given inadequate treatment in the history of developed economies. Women as well as men operated farms, retail and manufacturing enterprises, made independent economic lives, contributed to families' material welfare via household production and formal and informal market activity, and have been integral to the structural changes accompanying economic development, all in the face of powerful legal and social impediments. New cliometric work has extended earlier scholarship about women in past economies and parallels studies conducted by social historians and historical sociologists.[81]

For general history, when Carl Bridenbaugh warned his colleagues in 1963 against the seductive appeal of quantification, the profession was absorbing new practitioners with new styles of inquiry, notably the collective history of the "new" political historians and the "new" social historians. They were writing "history from below" – the history of ordinary people as revealed in their countable leavings. In a survey written for an audience of American historians, Naomi Lamoreaux (1998) remarks on a lamentable fragmentation since the 1960s of the body of historians into sets of sub-specialists. She sees each group inhabiting an "intellectual ghetto" and focuses on "the wall that . . . divides economic history from the rest of the historical profession . . ." resulting from of the advent of the sub-specialists of cliometrics. Until the mid-1970s, the cliometricians presented an image of solidarity, but their apparent subjectivity, their internal disagreements, and the potential fallibility of their method were exposed to the outside world with the controversy about *Time on the Cross*, even though pioneer cliometricians had been aware of such problems from day one. Consequently, she argues, historians

80 On Bezanson: Rouvray (2004); Brady: Easterlin (1978); Power and others: Berg (1992; 1996) and Harte (1971). See Scott (1987) and Goggin (1992) on women in the US history profession, and Dimand (1995) and Hammond (1999) on women in American economics.

81 For surveys of the economic–historical literature on women in the US see, *e.g.*, Costa (2000) and Goldin (1990; 2006); for Europe and Britain see, *e.g.*, Honeyman & Goodman (1991) and Honeyman (2000).

felt that "cliometrics had little to offer them . . . and stopped following developments in the field." The upshot is that the resulting "gulf . . . between economic history and history proper has clearly been detrimental to scholarship." She notes in closing some encouraging efforts to bridge the divide.[82]

Despite Bridenbaugh's warning, some historians and others in the 1960s campaigned to put quantification and social science theory into the standard toolkit of the historian.[83] The presence of quantitative work in American mainstream historical journals grew steadily to the mid-1980s, but it has fallen off sharply since then (Reynolds 1998). A powerful reason for the recent decline in quantitative work has been a two-fold reaction to histories of people *en masse*: first, a "revival of narrative," and second, use of anthropological or cultural analysis and linguistic theory, known as "postmodernism" or "the new cultural history." In its moderate form this "linguistic turn" has improved historians' sensibilities in interpreting the language and context of sources as well as the meaning of what their historical subjects have said or written. Although postmodernism has not swept the field entirely, history departments have experienced a loss of interest in matters measurable. Jan deVries, a historian and arguably a card-carrying cliometrician, has said that changing curricular needs in history would make the kind of work presented in his own dissertation appear "simply as too far afield from the interests of [a history] department's members to fit with the needs of the graduate program. . . . the historical questions that interest us [as economic historians] can't be pursued within history departments now."[84] Given a partial withdrawal of history from either "objectivity" or "hard" numerical evidence, one wonders what the chances are that *economic* history can engage many young professional historians.

A related question is whether it can continue to engage economists. Almost a quarter-century ago William Parker organized a symposium at the economists' annual meetings, entitled "Economic History: A Necessary though not Sufficient Condition for an Economist." At that forum Robert Solow expressed disappointment at the nature of some works he recently had been reading: ". . . this sort of economic history gives back to the theorist the same routine gruel that the economic theorist gives to the historian." Solow was stressing the inadequacies of economics as reflected in the history mirror; he thought economics would benefit from being "less mechanical and more opportunistic," and from seeing that "the validity of an economic model may depend on the social context." Years earlier the theorist Robert Clower regarded economic history as an "oasis" that had been invaded by theoretical "academic bedouins who not only gabble

82 Lamoreaux (1998); quotations and allusion from pp. 77, 76, 72–5, 75. On "problems," see Davis (1966b; 1968), who delights in relating how both named and unnamed cliometricians could go amazingly off-base.

83 The campaign resulted in several books showcasing quantitative work or discussing methods and sources: *e.g.*, Rowney and Graham, eds (1969), Swierenga, ed. (1970), Aydelotte, Bogue & Fogel, eds (1972), and Lorwin & Price, eds (1972). New journals appeared: the *Journal of Interdisciplinary History* (1970), and *Social Science History* (1976), on which see Ross (1998).

84 See deVries (1974); quotation from an interview with Alan Taylor (deVries 2005: 11). William Sewell, a quantitative "new social historian" who turned to postmodernism, observes that a focus on language need not imply rejection of hard quantitative data, but notes regretfully: "At the University of Chicago, at least, most history graduate students would count it an insult to their intelligence and dignity if their professors so much as intimated that they might . . ." engage in quantitative work (2001: 209).

incessantly and muddy the local springs but also trail sand across the grass. . . . It is easy to see what the oasis has to offer the bedouins, but what have the bedouins to offer the oasis?"[85] Developments that might gratify Clower, however, have begun to transform economics with the advent of a new breed of academic bedouin intent on modifying or questioning earlier restrictive assumptions, with the rise of the economics of information asymmetries, behavioral economics, the strategic sparring of the economic theory of games, the "new" growth theory, and institutional or evolutionary approaches. These augment what William Baumol sees as the premier accomplishment of economics in the twentieth century, transforming even conventional practice, bringing "to a far higher level, the integration of theory, empirical investigation, and application." Likewise, empirical investigation, in the hands of an economist like George Akerlof willing to break free of the *a priorism* built into the economics of the older style, can be "opportunistic" so that models can be based on a connection "between the telling incident and the nature of economic structure." The defining characteristic of the contemporary economist – building models – thus remains, but the models (some of them anyway) emerge from the facts of the case, not the reverse.[86]

Cliometricians wrestled to generate this sort of synergy between fact and theory from the outset with, perhaps, too much initial emphasis on technique. Traditional economic historians thought these "new" economic historians tried, as Shepard Clough wrote, to "intimidate the rest of us . . . to get control of everything concerned with the discipline" and, as David Landes recalled, they "proclaimed explicitly or implicitly the obsolescence of their teachers and elders." Landes's Presidential address to the EHA in 1977, entitled "On avoiding Babel," was a call for comity between the humanists and the quantifiers. He acknowledged that "Cliometrics is clearly here to stay . . ." but he pointed to a distressing asymmetry: cliometricians could read with ease the work of their historical colleagues (if written in English), but "historians, at least of the older generation, cannot read the more sophisticated cliometric work." He argued nonetheless that the profession would benefit from cooperation among members trained in either of its parent traditions.[87]

Landes's ecumenical appeal has been answered in part, not least by many of those whose interviews appear in this volume. Although critics of historical economics still grumble about a residuum of old-style economics in recent work, well-informed students recognize that much recent cliometrics is not characterized by old-style economics. British economic and business historian Pat Hudson, who has surveyed the development of "econometric history," stresses the widespread use of and the limitations imposed by neoclassical theory in the early years of the "New Economic History." In

85 Papers from this symposium of December 1984 in Dallas, Texas, including Solow's essay, appeared in *AER: P&P* 75:2 (1985: 320–37). Quotations: Solow (1986: 26, 28) in a volume expanding on the session, Parker, ed. (1986); Clower (1973: 4).

86 Baumol (2000: 30); Akerlof, in the introduction to (2005: 3). Concepts that would have been considered by economists entirely off limits some years ago are now common in the literature: *e.g.*, procrastination, fairness, self-control, caste, reciprocity, and happiness; see the works cited by Akerlof (2005: 22–4) and Rabin (2004: 98–102).

87 From Clough's memoir (1981: 198) and from Landes (1978: 3, 10, 4).

contrast, she notes that recent changes in economics "suggest that the future might be brighter" for economic history.[88]

Cliometrics has transformed itself over the past half-century, forging important links with other disciplines. Yet cliometrics in its middle-age lacks the full vigor of its youth, when it was the "New Economic History." As Patrick O'Brien comments in the "Afterword," there is a sense that the parents have "rejected" the child – that cliometrics remains too theoretical for the majority of historians and not rigorous enough for the majority of economists. This may be inevitable for a field constantly balancing fact and theory, the particular and the general. Its scholars are not making such startling discoveries as "American chattel slavery was viable" or "railroads were not *the* engine of growth." Rather they are showing that the "new" phenomenon of "globalization" has origins and manifestations going back half a millennium and, given the recent experience of the formerly Socialist "transitional" economies, they are showing that the deep historical roots of institutions, organizations, values and behavior in the developed economies cannot be duplicated by following simple formulae.[89] Affluent societies in general seem less concerned about why and how they acquired their capacity for almost continuous economic growth; today it is merely a fact of life. There are fashions in scholarship and always there will be competition for the public imagination while public interest in major issues waxes and wanes. The research, however, does not stop because it cannot; the issues are too important and there is the constant "pleasure of finding things out" (Feynman 1999). Despite the presentism of contemporary society, economic history will continue to address essential questions of origins and consequences, and it seems likely that cliometricians will complement and sometimes lead their colleagues in providing the answers. How that further research is to be conducted will be deeply influenced by the contributions of the pioneering economic historians and cliometricians whose interviews appear in this book.

88 Hudson (2003: 232–3); (2000: 208). A non-technical and appreciative survey of developments in economics in the past two decades, giving due attention to historical work, is Coyle, *The Soulful Science* (2007).

89 For approaches to long-term changes in global living standards and to the history of globalization, see Allen *et al.*, eds (2005), Bordo *et al.*, eds (2003), O'Rourke & J. Williamson (1999), and J. Williamson (1996). Issues of transition are mentioned in this volume in the North and Meyer interviews and in the "Further Reflections" of Fogel and of Temin.

Part I

BEFORE THE NEW ECONOMIC HISTORY

North America

Moses Abramovitz

M. C. Urquhart

Anna J. Schwartz

Walt W. Rostow

Stanley Lebergott

The most influential precursor to cliometrics is undoubtedly the research inspired and supported by the National Bureau of Economic Research. From its inception in 1920, the NBER insisted on careful measurement, a defining characteristic of the research of Wesley Clair Mitchell, the Bureau's first Director. The NBER thereby provided a foundation for the work of the pioneering American quantitative economic historians and some of their successors. Mitchell's continued study of business cycles (1927) led, in the 1920s, to a deeper examination of national income and its components, and in the early 1930s, to Simon Kuznets's two-year secondment to the Federal Government to prepare the first set of National Income and Product Accounts for the United States.[1]

In 1936, the Council for Research in the Social Sciences at Columbia University had been persuaded by Mitchell to fund a "British study" proposed and supervised by Arthur D. Gayer, on growth and fluctuation of the nineteenth-century British economy, and to finance fellowships for Anna Jacobson (Schwartz) and Walt Rostow. Although this study by Gayer, Rostow and Schwartz (1953) was not an official project of the NBER, the collaborators benefited from what Gayer called "the privilege of unlimited consultation" with Bureau staff, and were able to employ the full array of the Bureau's business cycle analysis techniques. Likewise, by the late 1930s, the American national income project had grown so that new staff were needed. Moses Abramovitz was recruited in 1938 to revise the 65-page "chapter" on inventories, work that later became his 600-page book, *Inventories and Business Cycles, with Special Reference to Manufacturers' Inventories* (1950). Stanley Lebergott was never formally associated with the NBER, but nonetheless found its methods useful at the US Bureau of the Budget in the late 1940s and 1950s. Even the Canadian M. C. (Mac) Urquhart went to the Bureau, participating in its Financial Research Program in 1942–43 while teaching at MIT. The NBER, along with related organizations such as the Conference on Research in Income and Wealth (founded in 1936), has continued to be an important institution for cliometricians. Anna Schwartz joined the Bureau in 1941 and in 1948 was encouraged by Arthur Burns, Mitchell's successor, to work with Milton Friedman, resulting over the next three decades in

1 We draw on Abramovitz (2000, 2001), Bernstein (2001: Ch. 3), Bordo (introduction to Bordo ed. 1989), Edelstein (2001), Fabricant (1984), Fogel (2000), Gayer, Rostow & Schwartz (1953 [1975]: prefaces), Green & Lewis (2002), Katz (1989), Kilby (1987), Kindleberger (1991: Chs 8, 12–15), Schwartz (2002), and Rostow (2003: Chs 1, 2, 6, 10).

their monumental monetary histories of the United States and the United Kingdom (Friedman & Schwartz 1963, 1970, 1982). In the late 1970s, the Bureau began to support a program, initiated by Robert Fogel, on "The Development of the American Economy," which, through its working paper series, has sponsored a substantial portion of the cliometric research on the US and international economies undertaken in the past quarter-century.

As Anna Schwartz observes, the connecting link is measurement: Mitchell and Burns encouraged the search for data, historical as well as contemporary. Kuznets, whose influence pervades the careers of many of our interviewees, sparked an international effort to construct historical national accounts for the developed economies. The Bureau's impact is obvious in the comments of Abramovitz, Schwartz and Lebergott, while Rostow stresses his use of the Bureau's methods. Urquhart remarks that there was nothing in Canada comparable to the work Kuznets had done at the NBER for the United States (until Urquhart himself nurtured a quest for Canadian historical data).

The Great Depression and World War II deeply affected the lives, scholarly interests and outlook of our subjects, working their ways into these interviews and other recollections. Urquhart's education was slowed by the collapse of wheat prices in the 1930s. Rostow, early in his undergraduate career at Yale, chose to study economic fluctuations in other times and places. Schwartz became accustomed during the Depression to living with a modest income and developed life-long habits of frugality. Lebergott, because of poor prospects for an academic position after taking his M.A. in 1939, abandoned his pursuit of a Ph.D. and took a job as a Junior Economist with the Bureau of Labor Statistics. Abramovitz felt able to marry (in 1937) only because he was able to secure a position as an Instructor at Harvard (in 1936).[2]

During World War II economics came of age as a policy-oriented discipline both in the United States and the United Kingdom, and economic historians were full participants, including several of our subjects. Urquhart's stint at the NBER was brief because in 1943 he was called home to serve in the Civil Service, in part to aid in developing a new system of Canadian National Accounts. Stanley Lebergott spent the entire war at the Department of Labor. In his interview he stresses the importance of knowing "the size of the pie;" as the war was ending he investigated unemployment because of the widespread fear that depression conditions would return after an Allied victory.

Both Abramovitz and Rostow had more direct involvements with the war effort. In 1942 Abramovitz and Kuznets went to the War Production Board, where their estimates of American productive capacity and allocation patterns helped to reveal the enormous capabilities of an economy still recovering from depression, but also to rein in the excessive optimism of military planners. The next year Abramovitz was drawn to the Office of Strategic Services (OSS) by his old Harvard economics tutor, Edward S. Mason, the Deputy Director of the Research and Analysis Branch. As head of the German Industrial Intelligence Section, he investigated the capabilities of the German economy. In 1945, even before the end of the war in Europe, he engaged in

2 The American academic labor market in the 1930s was exceedingly thin, and any position was welcome; see, *e.g.*, Kindleberger (1991: 43).

an on-the-ground survey of German economic conditions for the Allied Reparations Commission and helped modify the punitive and potentially disastrous Morgenthau Plan for post-war Germany.

Mason recruited widely from American universities for the OSS, and chose Rostow to work as his assistant for a year, and then sent him to London in late 1942 for an assignment with the Enemy Objectives Unit in the Economic Warfare Division of the US Embassy. There Rostow and the others in the Unit helped to select bombing targets, based on Allied intelligence and the vulnerabilities uncovered by Mason and his staff in Washington.[3] At the end of the war Rostow was invited to join the US Strategic Bombing Survey to help evaluate the effects of the EOU's target selection and the Army Air Force's bombing. He declined, returning instead to Washington and the State Department for a year. Participants in the Bombing Survey emerged with a negative assessment, but Rostow maintained throughout his life that elements of the bombing campaign were undervalued in the Survey's report.[4]

Moses Abramovitz returned to the NBER in 1946 to complete his book on inventories. Given his wartime and early post-war concerns, he was also eager to begin research on the nature of economic growth. Arthur Burns, by then Director of Research at the Bureau, objected to such a project and insisted on more work in business cycles. Abramovitz worked out a compromise, beginning his investigation of Kuznetsian "long swings," but was sufficiently disenchanted with Burns's rigidity that he soon sought an academic position. He moved to Stanford in 1948 where he was free to do the research on economic growth that cemented his reputation. He collected much of this work in a book, *Thinking about Growth* (1989), which illustrates the development of his approach (and also of the field of growth analysis) from the early 1950s. Of that book, Alec Cairncross commented, "The cumulative effect [of Abramovitz's essays] is impressive. The treatment is systematic, comprehensive and magisterial . . . and there is a breadth of approach that takes in aspects of growth insufficiently discussed by economists" (1991: 392). One such aspect was what Abramovitz called "social capability," a concept he introduced at a conference in the 1970s (1979) and on which he elaborated in later work, including a highly cited *JEH* paper, "Catching up, forging ahead, and falling behind" (1986b) and the chapter completing his long collaboration with colleague Paul David, "American economic growth in the era of knowledge-based progress: the long-run perspective" in the *Cambridge Economic History of the United States, volume III* (2000).

In 1945 Mac Urquhart went to Queen's University for the remainder of his academic career. His early publications were on the contemporary Canadian and international economies, but he was soon engaged in the historical work for which he is best known. First, was the *Historical Statistics of Canada* which he edited with Kenneth Buckley (1965); second, came the estimates of Canadian GNP from the Confederation to

3 Nicholas de B. Katzenbach, President Johnson's Attorney General, remarked "I finally understand the difference between Walt and me. I was the navigator who was shot down and spent two years in a German prison camp, and Walt was the guy picking my targets." Quoted in obituary of Rostow by Todd S. Purdom, *New York Times*, 15 February 2003.

4 See Rostow (2003: 52–8). For other participants' viewpoints, see Kindleberger (1991: 74–89), Abramovitz (2001: 114–25), and R. Parker's biography of J. K. Galbraith (2005: 172–90).

the interwar period, reported in aggregate at an NBER–Income and Wealth conference (1986) and in fine detail in *Gross National Product, Canada, 1870–1926: The Derivation of the Estimates* (Urquhart 1993). These volumes are "the two bibles of Canadian economic historians" (Green & Lewis 2002: 249). The earlier book was a breakthrough in providing past quantitative data for the Canadian economy, similar in scale to the first edition of *Historical Statistics of the United States* (US Bureau of the Census 1949), but with some obvious gaps for the later nineteenth and early twentieth centuries. (See Chambers 1966.) Aside from filling many of these gaps, the later book substantially revised the picture of Canadian growth in the two decades before World War I. (See Inwood 1994.) The book "is a rich and rewarding reference source" and "one of the best-documented historical national accounts in the world" (van Ark 1994: 1927).

Anna Schwartz became Research Associate Emerita at the NBER in 1985 but that nominal change in status has made no difference to her work habits; she is now well into her seventh decade of research at the Bureau, still going to her office daily. She said recently, "I had no interest in retirement . . . having something to think about is a much better life" (Schwartz 2004: 409). Her research ranges over historical and contemporary issues in monetary and financial economics, from the history of private banking institutions through the role of central banks to international monetary arrangements and financial crises. The books and articles resulting from her collaboration with Milton Friedman on American and British monetary history and policy have led to widespread acceptance of what began as a decidedly heterodox view – that variations in the quantity of money in an economy can play an independent role in generating economic fluctuations – an acceptance deriving in large part from Schwartz's careful compilation and estimation of monetary and other financial data. She has also worked alone and with others on such topics as the operation of the Gold Standard, including a collaboration with Michael Bordo, with whom she has written 25 papers since 1977. (See, *e.g.*, Schwartz 1996; Bordo & Schwartz, eds 1984.) Her current research, with Bordo and Owen Humpage as co-authors, will result in a book on the history of US official intervention in the foreign exchange market. Barry Eichengreen (1990: 260) identifies the basic qualities of her research: "attention to the characteristics of historical data, fastidious empirical work, and rich historical narrative, all superimposed upon a coherent theoretical framework."

Walt Rostow joined the economics faculty at MIT in 1951, following a year at the State Department and four more in Europe after the war; at MIT he taught economic history and developed the ideas that ultimately appeared in *The Stages of Economic Growth* (1960). Simultaneously he continued his engagement with contemporary political affairs, helped to found the Center for International Studies at MIT and wrote books and articles on the USSR, China and on US foreign policy. John F. Kennedy asked Rostow to join what the press called his "Brain Trust" for the 1960 Presidential campaign and invited him to Washington in 1961, where Rostow served initially as deputy special assistant for national security affairs. He moved to the State Department as Director of Policy Planning (1962–66), and returned to the White House as National Security Advisor to President Johnson during the height of American involvement in the Vietnam War (1966–69). Rostow moved to the University of Texas in 1969 after those years of controversy and "went back to his academic work as if he had never left it in the first place."[5] He continued research in economic history, as ever with an eye to taking the long view. His repeated riposte to J. M. Keynes's maxim about the long run was "The long period is with us every day of our lives" (*e.g.*, 2001). In Austin he wrote 19 of his 34 books, including the two "big" books discussed in the interview, *The World Economy: History and Prospect* (1978) and *Theorists of Economic Growth from David Hume to the Present* (1990a). While criticizing Rostow for a continuing devotion to nation states and stages, William Parker (1978: 1041) thought of *The World Economy* as a mature work in which Rostow "has got his act together . . . [his] incursions into theory and politics have troubled many of his peers, but there is no question that he is a closer approximation to an economic historian *type pur* than perhaps anyone of his generation."

In 1945 Stanley Lebergott left the Department of Labor and worked for three years at the Montreal office of the International Labor Organization. He returned to the US in 1948 to work at the Bureau of the Budget, where he rose to Assistant Division Chief of the Office of Statistical Standards, with responsibility for improving the compatibility of statistics generated by various Federal agencies. During his years at the Budget Bureau (he left in 1961), Lebergott combined his service as government bureaucrat with a role as a scholar, publishing about 20 articles on such topics as historical unemployment, wage trends, labor supply and income distribution. By the time he joined the Wesleyan faculty in 1963, he was ready to publish a synthesis of his two decades of research on American labor markets, *Manpower in Economic Growth: The American Record since 1800* (1964). The core of the book presents, as Robert Margo (2006) stresses, "absolutely fundamental data – estimates of the labor force, industrial composition, unemployment, real wages, self-employment, and the like." Margo concludes, "There are few activities that economic historians can engage in of greater consequence than reconstructing the hard numbers. In this line of work Lebergott had few peers." His later work illustrates his mastery of sources – obvious and obscure – and his ingenuity in assembling the data, publishing estimates of wealth-holding, living standards, and income distribution (1975), nineteenth-century US government land sales in his EHA Presidential Address (1985) and, notably, his very detailed estimates of twentieth-century American consumption expenditures (1996). His numbers are accompanied by prose spiced with literary tags and historical anecdotes, with telling quantitative comparisons capturing the essential answer to a question (its "quiddity"), and a wit by turns dry, puckish, facetious or sardonic. One of us ended his review of the 1996 book thus: "Lebergott's consumption data, like his employment data, will endure long after his words have been forgotten. They are an important, valuable, and much appreciated legacy" (Cain 1997: 775).

The members of this group do not think of themselves as cliometricians. Neither Abramovitz nor Lebergott even mentions the term in his interview, although both contributed extensively to the cliometric canon. Anna Schwartz sees herself as both empirical economist and economic historian, remarking, "If Cliometrics is a combination of measurement and history, Rostow was an early practitioner. Burns, Mitchell and Gayer can also claim that distinction." All are thus "of the ilk" in a broad sense,

5 On Vietnam, see Rostow (2003: Ch. 10) and the sources cited therein. Quotation from Dacey *et al.* (2004: 3336).

even if, like Rostow, one feels "very warmly" towards cliometricians but considers oneself an entirely independent scholar.

Whether or not they fit the definition, it is quite clear that these five scholars have had a great influence on cliometrics. Their work has been, and continues to be, an important input to the major issues investigated in the field. Rostow's *Stages of Economic Growth* in its various editions is still cited frequently as inspiration or foil. Schwartz's work on monetary history, with Friedman and with others, and Lebergott's on manpower, are basic references for further research as well as stalking horses for younger scholars. Urquhart's carefully compiled historical statistics and GNP estimates have provided foundation for the work of generations of Canadian cliometricians. Abramovitz's contributions to understanding economic growth, convergence and social capability are enduring. Cliometrics is therefore much in their debt and has been fortunate to call them friends.

MOSES ABRAMOVITZ

Interviewed by
Alexander J. Field

Moses Abramovitz was William Robertson Coe Professor of American Economic History, Emeritus, at Stanford University, Stanford, California. He was born in New York City in 1912 and died in Stanford in 2000. He was educated at Harvard College (B.A., 1932) and Columbia University (Ph.D., 1939), and began his long association with the National Bureau of Economic Research in 1938. During World War II he served at the War Production Board and at the Office of Strategic Services. After two more years at the NBER, he was professor of American Economic History at Stanford University from 1948 until his retirement in 1977. Abramovitz was elected Fellow of The American Statistical Association and Fellow of the American Academy of Arts & Sciences, both in 1960, was named Distinguished Fellow of the American Economic Association in 1976, and was elected Foreign Member of the Academia Nazionale dei Lincei (Roma) in 1991. He was President of the American Economic Association (1980), of the Western Economic Association (1989), and of the Economic History Association (1992). From 1981 through 1985 he was Managing Editor of *The Journal of Economic Literature* and continued as its Associate Editor through 1993. He was honored with a *Festschrift* edited by Paul David and Melvin Reder, *Nations and Households in Economic Growth* (Academic Press, 1974). He completed *Days Gone By: A Memoir for my Family* (2001) only a few months before his death. ALEXANDER J. FIELD, of Santa Clara University, conducted the interview at the offices of the *JEL* at Stanford on December 9th and 16th, 1992. Field writes:

Moses Abramovitz was one of a select group of scholars whose path-breaking empirical work has vastly expanded our understanding of the dimensions and determinants of economic growth and fluctuations in the industrializing and industrialized countries of the nineteenth and twentieth centuries. He is best known for his work on inventories, which identified the critical role of fluctuations in inventory investment in short-term cycles in output, for his studies of long swings of growth in the nineteenth and early twentieth centuries, for his work separating the relative contributions of technical change and capital accumulation to economic growth in the nineteenth and twentieth centuries, and for his research on catch-up and convergence: the closing of the productivity gap between the United States and its competitors in Western Europe and Japan.

How did you first get interested in economics?

It was during my first year at Harvard, I intended to concentrate in history and literature. Two courses that I took during my first year, however, proved to be quite uninteresting. In English literature of the seventeenth and eighteenth centuries, the professor talked only about the authors' styles and those of the earlier writers from whom they derived; the substance of the literature, what was being said, was of little or no concern. And the course in history was the great survey course, which all the undergraduates at that time took. I thought it fairly shallow. But I took a very good beginning course in economics, and I had a very good instructor. His reading list offered us the opportunity to read a short book by H. D. Henderson in the old Cambridge Economic Handbook Series called simply *Supply and Demand* (Harcourt, Brace 1922). That proved to be a formative, almost aesthetic, experience. It provided in utterly lucid terms a summary of the neoclassical theory of that time. It showed you how from people's tastes, the state of technology, and people's feelings about the relative costs of different kinds of jobs one could derive the prices of finished goods, the relative quantities of output of different kinds of goods, and factor prices, and the whole thing hung together. It seemed a lovely structure. It fascinated me and I could see its practical applications, so I decided to concentrate in economics. This was in my freshman year. When I came back in the fall for my sophomore year, I was assigned a tutor, Edward S. Mason, then a young assistant professor. When I paid him my first visit in the witching month of September 1929, I asked him, "Well, Professor, when is the stock market going to break?" He answered without hesitation, "Almost immediately." When I came back for my second meeting two weeks later it had happened. And then I learned something about economists. I said, "Well, Professor, you must have made a mint of money." He laughed, "Are you crazy? I've never owned a share of stock in my life."

I had another very good tutor later on, Douglas Vincent Brown, the man who later taught labor economics at MIT for many years. And there was a talented group of economics students in Dunster House where I lived. We saw each other often and talked at great length; all of us became economics professors or writers. Paul Sweezy was there, Spencer Pollard, John Perry Miller and still others. We were a self-reinforcing support group.

Besides Professor Mason and Professor Brown, were there others at Harvard who particularly impressed you as an undergraduate?

Frank Taussig was surely one. He taught price theory to both undergraduates and graduates. I took both courses, and I owe my knowledge of the classical writers and even more of Alfred Marshall to him. But the man who impressed me the most as an undergraduate was Schumpeter, who was a visiting professor in 1931. I came to know Schumpeter much better later when I returned to Harvard in 1936.

How did the graduate training you received at Columbia compare with what you received at Harvard?

If I hadn't been to Harvard, Columbia would have been a poor preparation. But I had a good preparation at Harvard. I have mentioned Taussig's courses. This was important because Columbia, at the time, offered no course in price theory for graduate students. It was regarded by the faculty as theology, and they refused to teach it. The result was that graduate students, who knew better, organized themselves into study groups that were led by Milton Friedman and me because we were among the few students with some prior theoretical training. The neglect of price theory went on at Columbia for years.

Was this antipathy to micro theory due to Columbia's greater concern for aggregative, more macro aspects of the economy?

Yes. Also, there was Columbia's institutional flavor. As between Harvard, Chicago and Columbia, which were the leading schools at the time, Columbia was the one with an institutional flavor and an empirical bent.

Whom did you work with ultimately?

I worked with J. M. Clark mostly, so far as anybody could work with that brilliant but reclusive man. He rarely answered a question orally. Instead, he went away to think it over and responded by letter. Perhaps that was better.

Before we go further, I wanted to ask you about your government service during the war as an economist for the War Production Board and the OSS, and later as an advisor to the US delegation to the Allied Commission on Reparations. Were there ways that government service enriched your understanding of economics or suggested certain problems?

I'm not sure whether it was government service in itself or simply the subjects with which I was concerned during the war, which later became important for me. At the War Production Board I was an assistant to Simon Kuznets. We were attempting to put together estimates of the production capabilities of the US economy as a basis for major decisions about such matters as the size of the armaments program that was feasible, given the requirements for civilian consumption. We made estimates of potential GNP at full employment for past years and tried to extend them, having regard to the growth of the labor force, the numbers of men who were being pulled out to serve in the armed forces, the number of women coming into the labor force to replace them, and the amount of capital accumulation, adding an allowance, as well as we could, for the growth of productivity. We were, in effect, formulating a forward-looking picture of what our aggregate economic capabilities might be and what that implied for the armaments production program and for the allocation of resources between the armed forces and civilian production.

There were two great controversies to which all this applied. The first one, however, was largely resolved by the time I came to Washington in early 1942. That had to do with the country's production capabilities when our first great armaments program was being planned in 1940 and 1941. When the early plans were being put together, the only clear evidence of the country's capacity to produce went back to 1929 because the intervening years were those of the Great Depression. Absurd estimates were proposed that put our production capacity at perhaps ten percent more than we had done in 1929. But the group around Kuznets and, in particular, Robert Nathan, became convinced that our economic capabilities were vastly greater, making allowance for the growth in the labor force and for the increase in productivity and, of course, for the recovery in the intensity of use of the resources we had. Well, Nathan and a few others like Richard Gilbert managed to sell the view that we could have a huge armaments production program, and I think that may have been the most important strategic decision made in Washington during the war. When the contracts for numbers of airplanes, larger than anybody had ever conceived of before, were awarded, and similarly for tanks and for ships and so on, it turned out that we did have the capacity to produce them along with a flow of civilian goods which was at least as plentiful as anybody had expected. And, in the end, the Axis was overwhelmed by Allied men and materiel. When this production success became apparent, however, the ambition of the military knew no bounds, and they formulated armaments programs which, in the opinion of our group at the War Production Board, could never be handled. If contracts on that scale had been awarded, competition among producers for the limited supplies of labor and crude materials would have caused great misallocations of resources. That was the second fight about war production. It was a very difficult one indeed because the Army strongly resisted having to cut their programs. But we were largely successful.

But to answer your question, in what way was this experience formative? After a year at the War Production Board I was drafted into the Army and assigned to the OSS (Office of Strategic Services). There I was put in charge of the section on German industrial intelligence. The problem here was the same: What were Germany's economic capabilities; what was bombing doing to Germany's economic capabilities? So I worked on Germany for a couple of years, and that is how I came to work with the Reparations Commission. These experiences did more than make me appreciate the importance of GNP for the outcome of the war, a war that was won by GNP. The question that lingered in my mind was this: How did the different countries – the United States, France, Germany, Britain, Japan, the USSR – come to have the economic capabilities which, in fact, they did have? In short, I was thinking about economic development. That was the formative influence of my wartime experience.

But your dissertation was on inventories?

Why, no. My dissertation was a theoretical essay. It was called "Price Theory for a Changing Economy." The question that I posed was: If supply curves and demand curves are in process of change, what effect does this have on the allocation of resources and on the way prices are set? Obviously, the old static theory had a kind of answer to this question, but I was asking whether there was something more. And it was in the course of answering that question that I came to consider inventories as one of the ways in which the economy responded to prospects of change. So I suppose it was in part because of that that I was eventually recruited by Mitchell to come to the Bureau to work on inventory cycles.

The thesis itself was largely theoretical.

It was completely theoretical. My Harvard training had, after all, made a lasting impression.

So it was only after you joined the Bureau that you began to do empirical work?

That's right, only after I joined the Bureau in 1938. I worked there for four years before I went to Washington. You should know, first, about the state of business cycles research at the Bureau. When the Bureau started in 1920, their first project was national income. That produced Wilford I. King's book. The second project was business cycles. That was Mitchell's undertaking to extend the work – limited work, as he saw it – that he had been able to report in his classic 1913 volume. His conception of the project was that he should repeat what he had done for the 1913 volume, only in a more elaborate form, with some more extensive data, covering a longer time period. Mitchell's 1927 book, *Business Cycles: The Problem and its Setting*, was an elaboration of Part I of the 1913 volume. Then he went on to study the cycles in production, prices, construction, marketing, inventories, credit and banking, the money supply, and so on. Working essentially single-handedly at first, later with much help from Kuznets and later still with much help from Arthur Burns, he had completed almost the entire cycle of these studies. It was a remarkable achievement. But when Mitchell and Burns came to review these chapters, they decided they were not adequate. They would have to be redone, and it was hopeless to think that Mitchell could do the job by himself. So they decided to enlarge the staff by adding research associates to each of whom one of these chapters could be assigned. These associates would do still more extensive empirical work and perhaps contribute a deeper understanding. Finally, Mitchell and Burns would put the whole thing together. That was the state of affairs when I came in. There was a "chapter" on production of 850 pages. There was a "chapter" on prices of 450 pages. There was a "chapter" on construction of 350 pages. I was given a short chapter on inventories; it was only 60 pages long.

Who else was on the research staff at the Bureau at the time?

Well, if you are talking about the major members, there were, of course, Mitchell, Kuznets, and Burns. Leo Wolman worked on unions, wages and labor markets. Fred Mills was working on prices. There was Fred Macaulay, who studied the securities markets and who published that very good book on stock prices, bond yields, and interest rates. Sol Fabricant was doing his path-breaking work on production and productivity. Milton Friedman was there for a while working with Kuznets on incomes from professional practice. He largely took over that work from Kuznets and made it his own. Alan Wallis, Geoff Moore, Ruth Mack and Thor Hultgren were other younger people in the business cycles program. So we were a goodly group.

The genesis of your book on inventories was essentially an assignment to complete work that Mitchell had started . . .

Yes. But you should know that the Bureau's collection of data on inventories was quite small, and it referred to the most diverse and often insignificant commodities. That is what Mitchell's chapter was based upon. The collection was in itself altogether inadequate to provide any useful picture of aggregate inventories and inventory investment. Fortunately, Kuznets was then completing his book on national product from the expenditure side (1946). In that connection, he had made crude estimates of aggregate inventory investment that were one component of total investment and product.

So I spent some months finding out how he had arrived at his numbers. He had a wonderful set of workbooks. You could trace every figure. I went through his work sheets carefully, asking him lots of questions, and that's how I really became acquainted with Simon. His inventory figures were another example of Kuznets' ability to use the most imperfect kinds of materials and proxies to make valuable estimates. His judgment about the construction and use of these materials was so good that the results turned out in the end to be quite consistent with the measures that the Department of Commerce later made on the basis of surveys of manufacturing, wholesaling, retailing and other sectors. Kuznets' data yielded very striking results. They suggested that some 85 percent of the change in aggregate output from the peaks to the troughs of short recessions consisted of changes in the volume of inventory investment, and similarly, but not quite so strikingly, in the longer expansion phases of business cycles. So in the minor fluctuations, which were the larger part of the cycles identified in the Bureau's chronology of business cycles, it was not investment in durable equipment or structures that was the major proximate source of the fluctuations in output, it was fluctuations in the rate of inventory investment. This finding was the most important thing reported in the book. It was a result yielded by Kuznets' estimates and, indeed, one he had anticipated in an earlier paper. Then I used Mitchell's miscellaneous collection of time series to formulate views about the very different behavior of finished goods, goods in process, and purchased materials inventories.

What notable advances have occurred in our understanding of inventory behavior since you wrote?

There have been very important advances. The theoretical model, which relates inventory investment to business cycles, was given an enormous push forward by Lloyd Metzler and Ragnar Nurkse. Before they wrote, J. M. Clark and Kuznets had proposed speculative hypotheses about inventory investment based on the acceleration principle. But in their models, the movements of sales were taken as given and inventory investment was a response. I got no further in my book. Metzler and Nurkse worked out models in which income and sales responded to inventory investment and vice versa, and they showed how cycles of output could be generated from this interaction. That was one great forward movement.

Beyond that, there have been very considerable advances in our notions about what constitutes rational inventory policy and, therefore, what expectations we can hold about the way inventories would behave during cyclical fluctuations. So really a great deal has been done since my book.

It seems that after the war your interests moved beyond cyclical fluctuations to issues of long-run growth.

That's right. I explained that to you when you asked about my experience in Washington. That's where the seed was really planted. My interests did shift to long-term growth. I could not get to the new subject, however, until the inventory book was completed, and that stretched until almost 1950. Then, when I proposed to Arthur Burns that I begin working on issues having to do with long-term growth, I met considerable opposition. Burns had been against involving the Bureau in work on long-term growth for some time past. He had been reluctant to have the Bureau support Simon Kuznets' proposals to work on long-term growth and to extend his estimates of national product back into the mid-nineteenth century. He distrusted the data. So Burns was hardly enthusiastic about my proposal. That was apart from the fact that he wanted me to continue to work on business cycles. We compromised. The compromise, which was interesting for me and which engaged me for some years, was to work on long swings. And I still think that the work on long swings is a useful way in which to study the manner in which the longer-term movements of the economy assume a cyclical shape and generate alternating periods of fast and slow growth, as well as major depressions. I worked on those subjects off and on for most of the 1950s. But I really got into the work on long-term growth itself when I came to Stanford. Bernard Haley asked me to prepare a survey article on economic growth for the *Survey of Contemporary Economics.* That was my first growth project. My second was the result of an invitation to contribute a paper to the AEA meetings of 1955 in which the economic growth of the United States since the mid-nineteenth century was being reviewed. That was the article that was published as "Resource and Output Trends Since 1870." And that was how I got into the early work on growth accounting and encountered the big "Residual."

You continued, didn't you, in this same vein with work you did with Paul David?

That was later, of course. We began in the middle sixties, and we continued working into the early seventies. The general objective was to gain a better understanding of American post-war growth in the light of the longer-term record. Our plan was to compare economic growth in the nineteenth and twentieth centuries, emphasizing the post-war experience. The framework of the comparison was, at least initially, the growth accounting framework. We built growth accounts for the twentieth century based on the very considerable number of publications that existed by that time, particularly those of Kendrick, Denison, and later Jorgenson. Paul put together the data for the nineteenth century. This rested partly on his own original studies of output and inputs before 1840 and partly on the work of Gallman and his collaborators on output, investment, and capital accumulation in the later part of the century.

That led us to a great puzzle, one that I tried to talk about to the Economic History Association this past September [1992]. The growth accounting results for the nineteenth century were, on their face, completely at variance with the growth accounts for the twentieth century. In the nineteenth century, capital accumulation was a far more important source than total factor productivity, whereas the reverse was true in the twentieth century. Indeed, total factor productivity growth appeared to have been so slow in the nineteenth century that one had to ask oneself whether one can possibly believe that technological progress was as unimportant as the figures suggested. Our answer was that no, it was really very important, but it took a form that created a great demand for capital. Technological progress in the nineteenth century was strongly physical capital-using. It raised the rate of return to investments in physical capital much more than to labor and therefore supported a rapid accumulation of capital relative to labor. In the growth accounts, therefore, capital accumulation per worker was very large, and little was left over to represent technological progress.

This taught us something important about the limitations of growth accounting. The various sources of growth are interdependent and interactive: Technological progress supports capital accumulation and, in various ways, capital accumulation supports technological progress. The supposed measures of the proximate sources of growth that appear in standard growth accounts or in regression analyses that are based upon the same growth model are, therefore, inaccurate. It is much more difficult to work out the relative contributions of the different sources of growth than the growth accounts suggest. The major "sources" are jointly responsible for growth.

Let's return to long swings. You also wrote about the monetary side of long swings; would you tell us what particularly interested you about the international aspects of infrastructural and other lending?

The notion I had starts from some simple considerations. Kuznets had focused on the physical manifestations of long swings: immigration, population growth, construction, aggregate output. Presumably, there were also monetary requirements. When you look at the figures, you find that the long swings in real output growth are matched by long swings in nominal output growth, which are of greater amplitude, and by long swings in the growth rate of the money supply. Those three curves run in a beautifully parallel relationship to one another. If one takes the price fluctuations as given, then it's clear that long swings in real output imply similar swings in money supply or velocity. The fluctuations in the growth rate of prices mean that nominal income fluctuates with a greater amplitude than physical output, and this demands concomitant large movements in money supply or velocity. It turns out that the velocity movements were relatively small, and virtually the whole of the fluctuation in the difference between real output and nominal output takes the form of variation in the growth rate of the money supply.

Operating under a fixed exchange rate, as we did for so long, the question is how that came about. My hypothesis is that it happened because of swings in what I call the exogenous components of the balance of payments. "Exogenous" here should not be taken to mean truly independent of the whole process of adjustment and response. I use the term in the same preliminary way that Keynes does when he treats investment as "exogenous." I identified exports and capital imports as the exogenous components of the balance of payments. I argued that an increase in the sum of exports plus capital imports leads to growth of high-powered money and this to an increase in money supply and nominal income, which results partly in a rise of output and partly in prices. I treated imports, on the other hand, as a lagged response to the swings in nominal income. The hypothesis is at least consistent with experience, in that a graph of the growth rate of exports plus capital imports displays long swings essentially parallel with those of the money stock and nominal income for the century between the mid-1820s and the early 1930s.

In any event, the long swings in nominal income growth involved some kind of alternating degree of enthusiasm for lending, some changing impetus from the European side which swelled the surpluses on capital account during an expansionary phase, financing some of those huge peaks of railroad construction?

Not necessarily. I traced it primarily to the fact that the long swings in output were essentially based on long swings in railroad building and earlier in canals. I tried to explain the characteristics of railroads that produced long swings in railroad construction and how that bore on capital imports. The point is that when railroads became profitable after a period of depression, they could market their bonds. Their bonds were very attractive to the British and to other foreign investors as well. The general underlying idea was that there was a long-term need for additional railway capacity. The pace at which this could be satisfied, however, depended upon the ability of railway companies to obtain finance. Railway bonds were treated by the market somewhat like equities. Their value rose and fell together with stock market prices in general and for railroads in particular.

Reflecting the probability that they would indeed be serviced?

Exactly. So that's the sort of direction the argument took. Now you realize that Simon Kuznets, who really brought long swings to the fore, had a quite different sort of theory. He had no money in his theory. Indeed, he treated the long swings as divorced from ordinary business cycle considerations. It was fluctuations in productivity growth and accompanying movements in immigration, labor force growth, and in the allocation of investment that generated fluctuations in the growth rate of productivity and total output without any contribution from a fluctuation in the intensity of use of existing equipment. My own view was quite different. I regarded serious depression as the culminating (or originating) episode in each swing, and I attributed the spurt in productivity growth that was characteristic of the opening phase of long-swing expansion to a rise in the intensity of use of employed resources.

What about the long swings in immigration?

My notion about the immigration waves is that a long-term condition drew people to the United States. It lay in the different levels of wages in Europe and America. But the timing of immigration depended upon the levels of unemployment. There's lots of evidence that there was very good communication between older immigrants who were already established in America and intending immigrants in Europe. The letters from here would say, "Now is not a good time, wait until next year, employment is difficult," and then later letters would say, "Come ahead, we can get you a job when you get here." So when the unemployment situation improved in the course of a period of long-swing expansion, when we had come out of a period of persistent stagnation or depression, then we had a big flow of immigrants. Indeed, the waves of immigration lagged behind the growth rate of total output, just as the employment rate does. Kuznets had a different view. It turned on the rate of growth of real consumption per head, which he attributed to shifts in the allocation of investment between equipment and structures, that is in housing and railroad building.

Your story would certainly be consistent with the story that Brinley Thomas tells about the alternations in the pace of domestic capital accumulation in the UK and overseas.

It is consistent in that it takes account of the origins of waves of capital imports and their significance for the growth rate of the money supply.

Your *Economica* article of 1968 was entitled "The Passing of the Kuznets Cycle . . ."

Yes. That had to do with a number of developments after World War I that together changed the process from which present-day intermediate-term fluctuations in growth rates arise. One was immigration restriction. Immigration declined sharply during the war, but the old mechanism didn't start up again in the 1920s because of the new restrictive legislation.

The old waves of immigration that rose and fell with employment conditions gave way to a more stable rate governed by the immigration quotas. That, in turn, changed the mechanism of residential building cycles. Whereas in the past, residential construction had followed the waves in immigration and population growth, it now became more responsive to changes in the ratio of households to population, the relation of which to long swings in output growth was far more complex. Then, beginning in the thirties, came the expansion of the Federal budget with its built-in stabilizers. In the fifties, the dollar-exchange standard replaced the gold-based, fixed-rate regime that had ruled for so long before the Depression, and that shift altered the old balance-of-payments money-supply mechanism. And a more sophisticated Federal Reserve policy and deposit insurance did away with the recurrent monetary crises that had been such prominent concomitants of the older long swings. The moral of my article was not that long swings were a thing of the past, but that their notable features and the mechanism that had produced them had changed in decisive ways.

How did you get interested in comparative growth?

That arose from the same project in which Paul David and I were engaged with respect to the United States. When John Kennedy came into office, he became disturbed by the fact that the dollar was under pressure in the foreign exchange markets and that we were losing gold. He attributed this, correctly in my view, to the fact that our growth rate, as he would have put it, or our productivity growth rate, as I would have put it, although high by our own historical standards, was now much lower than productivity growth rates in western Europe and Japan. He wanted studies made of the causes of these difficulties, and the SSRC at the behest of the Ford Foundation undertook to organize them. Denison conducted one of these projects and reported his results in *Why Growth Rates Differ*. Another was entrusted to Simon Kuznets. He planned a comparative study in which the central question would be: How can we understand the post-war experience of the advanced countries in the light of their longer-term experience? It was decided that there should be studies of five European countries in addition to the United States and Japan. I happened to be in Paris when these plans were being formulated, and Kuznets asked me to find the European collaborators. I undertook to do that and, in addition, Kuznets and I agreed that when the seven national studies were completed, the two of us would prepare a synthesis. So I came to feel that I had a measure of responsibility for developing a general view of the post-war growth boom in the industrialized countries. As often happens, the national studies came along very slowly, and some of them never were completed. Kuznets was drawn off to other work. I was left with a sense of lack of completion. I finally did something about it at the Tokyo meeting of the International Economic Association in 1977. The program included a section devoted to growth for which I was invited to present a paper (1979).

I was able to undertake the job because several years earlier I had finally hit on a view of what had been happening, which enabled me to talk in general about the experience of the industrialized countries. I'd been casting around for a long time for some sort of hypothesis that would have a wide application, that would bring out what was common in the post-war experience of the industrialized countries and serve to explain them.

My hypothesis was that the great growth boom of the fifties and sixties was a boom of catch-up and convergence, the central feature of which was a transfer of technology from the leading country, the USA, to those that were behind, with an effect on their growth roughly inversely proportional to their initial productivity levels. This would account for America's relatively slow growth and for the systematic pattern of relative advance among the "followers."

The notion of rapid growth based on technological borrowing and catch-up was not unfamiliar. But its cogency as a generalization was borne in on me only when I came to look closely at the early Denison and Maddison estimates of productivity levels and growth rates. In these, the productivity levels had been rendered comparable across countries by purchasing power parity conversion rates derived from the pioneering work of Milton Gilbert and Irving Kravis. When I lined up the countries by their productivity levels, two things stood out. One applied to the fifties and sixties. In this period, the variance of the productivity levels declined rapidly, and there was a close inverse association between countries' initial productivity levels and their subsequent growth rates. The second, which the longer Maddison series revealed, was that in earlier decades, the inverse association was much weaker and the rate of convergence of levels much slower. The failure of less-developed countries to catch up was also in my mind.

I had to think of an hypothesis which was consistent with both observations. I argued that catch-up and convergence were a general tendency but that their operation and strength depended on the satisfaction of other conditions. As stated in 1977, these were of two sorts. One was a set of conditions that I summarized under the heading of "Social Capability." These constrained the potential for rapid growth that was otherwise created by the possibility of technological modernization. The other sort had to do with what I called the "factors supporting the realization of potential." The macroeconomic conditions of a period are one such factor, but there are others. The catch-up and convergence boom of the post-war period arose from a favorable conjuncture of strong potential, adequate social capability, and macroeconomic and other conditions supporting rapid realization. With some refinements and supplements, these are the central ideas that have concerned me ever since.

A final question: what of the future and current state of economic history as a profession

That's a deep question, Alex. I'm afraid I don't have any clear thoughts. My notion is that we now have built into economic history – indeed into economics in general, but economic history in particular – a respect both for work that is close to formal theory and work that is distant from formal theory but still informed by it. It's surely true that both kinds of work are useful provided they're pursued seriously. I do think both are being pursued seriously and that economic history, therefore, is in a flourishing condition. I think it's going to continue to be valuable, particularly because economists at large have become more interested in questions of economic development and in international comparisons. For both purposes, historical work is essential. I think there has already been a revival of interest in economic history within economics departments, and I look forward to that continuing.

M. C. URQUHART

Interviewed by
R. Marvin McInnis

Malcolm Charles (Mac) Urquhart was the Sir John A. Macdonald Professor of Political and Economic Science at Queen's University, Kingston, Ontario. He was born in Alberta in 1913 and died in Kingston in 2002. He was educated at the University of Alberta, completing a B.A. degree in honours economics in 1940, after some years as a part-time and correspondence student while teaching at a rural school. From this he proceeded to the graduate program at the University of Chicago. After completing his coursework at Chicago he taught for a year at MIT, but World War II interrupted his academic life; he was summoned to Ottawa in 1943 to work in the Canadian Ministries of Finance and of Reconstruction. He moved to Kingston in 1945 to join the faculty at Queen's. MARVIN McINNIS, a long-time colleague at Queen's, conducted the interview in two sessions a couple of weeks apart in February 1995. The site was Urquhart's office, which the University kindly permitted him to use for more than two decades of post-retirement research. McInnis adds:

Mac Urquhart's academic career at Queen's was punctuated only by a development mission to Pakistan and sabbaticals at Berkeley and the LSE. As Head of Department in the 1960s he was instrumental in establishing a highly regarded Ph.D. program and in building up a modern faculty in Economics. He was elected Fellow of the Royal Society of Canada in 1966, was President of the Canadian Economics Association in 1969, and was awarded the Royal Society's Innis-Gérin Medal in 1983. His two monumental contributions to Canadian economic history are the *Historical Statistics of Canada* (1965) and *Gross National Product Canada, 1870–1926* (1993). Although both were collaborative efforts, they were strongly shaped by his sure hand as manager and editor. He also published an article on "Capital Accumulation, Technological Change, and Economic Growth" in 1959 in the old *Canadian Journal of Economics and Political Science*, pursuing the line of thought widely associated with Solow, Swan and Abramovitz. The article was part of what would have been Mac's doctoral dissertation. The ideas were formulated in the late 1940s at the University of Chicago and presented at a workshop there in 1953, so he was in on the ground floor of modern growth accounting. Mac Urquhart exhibited a rate of scholarly output that seemed to accelerate with age and continued to show up at his office until 2001.

You were at the first meeting of the group at Purdue that eventually came to designate itself "The Cliometric Society." Can you tell me why you thought you were invited to participate in that first get-together? Were you the only Canadian?

No, there were two of us. The other was Gideon Rosenbluth, who was also at Queen's at that time, and I'll mention some of the relevance, perhaps, of both of us being asked. I'm not quite sure why we were asked, but there were possibly a couple of reasons. The first was that there had been established a Committee on Statistics of the Canadian Economic Association some years earlier, on the initiative of the younger members of the profession who wanted to get more quantitative data for analytical purposes. For one reason, having quantitative data was for a more rigorous testing of economic theories and for a better understanding of historical developments; for another, it was to develop models, mostly macroeconomic models, dealing with the performance of the Canadian economy.

So that was not necessarily about economic history, but just a general quantitative data and empirical economics matter?

Yes, and that related to the Committee on Statistics. Perhaps the second possible reason is that there was an Institute for Economics Research at Queen's University which had been established, I think in 1953, on Frank Knox's entrepreneurship.

Frank Knox is not well known to non-Canadians, I suppose, but he had a long connection with the historical side of things and he taught a quite famous course in economic history at Queen's.

Yes, he did, and he also had quite an interest in public policy matters and analysis of economic development. There had been, during his career, a number of Royal Commissions dealing with either Dominion–Provincial relations or other things of that sort, and a good deal of quantitative data had been developed in connection with them. If I could just carry on with that – the function of the Institute for Economic Research, headed initially by Knox, was to bring to Queen's University anywhere from seven to eight, perhaps 10 people – young economists from other universities – to spend eight to 10 weeks at Queen's during the summers. The Institute's function in part was to keep these people from taking jobs outside economics in order to supplement their university incomes, which were then very low and had not recovered to anything like an equilibrium level. The people who came received research assistance and a small monthly salary. I've forgotten just how much it was – perhaps $600 or $800 – but it was enough to keep them carrying on with their research work. Well, through its life and up until the time of the Purdue Conference (there had been seven years of its existence), the Institute for Economic Research brought to Queen's University a very high proportion of the younger economists of the country who were active in research, and so there developed a community of these younger economists which had, I might add, quite fruitful consequences, not only at that time but in subsequent years. Well, in any event, Gideon Rosenbluth had quite a lot to do with the Institute for Economic Research. I had become head of the Institute in about 1958–59, and I think just from the nature of its operation, our Institute might have had some bearing upon our invitations to go to Purdue.

Had you had much prior contact with any of the people involved with the Purdue meeting?

No, not directly with most of them. I'd had quite a lot of participation in American conferences, National Bureau of Economic Research Conferences, and the American Economic Association, but I don't recall being acquainted with most of the people who were at this conference, except perhaps Dunc McDougall, a graduate of Queen's.

What were your first impressions of that conference? What do you remember as most notable?

Well, my general recollection is that there was great enthusiasm for using quantitative data in dealing with historical analysis. There had not been all that much done previously in the way of rigorous application of quantitative data. Although one needs to be careful in making that statement because in Canada people like W. A. MacIntosh, who was an economist at Queen's and later became Principal of the University, had been responsible for developing data on Canadian foreign trade and on prices running back as far as 1867. But I think economic history had not used quantitative data in the way that cliometricians came to use it. One got the feeling of general enthusiasm for this, and it fitted in with the attitude of Gideon Rosenbluth and myself. Later, we both had quite a bit of experience in the use of quantitative data in that way.

Did you have a sense that at that first meeting something new – a new kind of venture and new direction – was under way? Or was it just much in line with the kinds of things that you and Gideon and others had been doing on the Canadian scene?

Well, I think it was new in the United States – for instance, relative to the work that had been done in the National Bureau of Economic Research. Now, the National Bureau had been producing large quantities of statistical data for a great many years prior to that, but the approach at Purdue was more to developing and, of course, using data for specific purposes.

To test specific propositions?

Yes, yes – and looking at particular episodes.

People have often spoken of being impressed by the "heat" of discussion in some of the early Clio meetings. Was that true right from the onset?

No, I don't recall that it was. I think there was a general enthusiasm for trying to develop along the line of what later became known as cliometrics. Perhaps the one big episode of the conference was the emergence from obscurity of Robert Fogel in connection with his research on railroads and canals in the United States. He presented this in a substantial amount of detail, as he did with most of his projects, and it was quite amazing that when one asked whether he had looked at this particular piece of evidence or that – oh, yes, yes, he had, and here was the answer to it. That was the emergence of Fogel and, of course, the development of the use of the counterfactual method, although I'm not sure that this latter way of looking at things has proven as useful as some believe it has.

Did you go back to any other cliometrics meetings?

I think I went to one or two of the later ones, but then one of the things that happened with me was that, first, I got very heavily involved in the historical statistics project through the early years of the 1960s, and then from 1964–68 I was Head of the Department here at Queen's. In consequence, I got myself up to my ears in taking care of them both. That was because, you see, the great expansion in the number of students came at this time and, unfortunately, the availability of finance wasn't as great as it became later. I think it wasn't until the late sixties – say, 1967–1968 – that academic salaries had returned to what one might call an equilibrium level.

There has been a Canadian group in Quantitative Economic History meeting for almost as long as the American cliometrics group. You were there (as I was) at their first meeting. Could you tell us a bit about their beginnings?

Well, I didn't have so much directly to do with that. An interest among Canadians probably arose out of what had happened at the Purdue conferences. Both Gideon Rosenbluth and I had been there. Ken Buckley and some others knew about it and were interested. John Dales of the University of Toronto had a fairly early involvement with the Purdue group. It was Dales, I believe, and his colleague Ed Safarian at Toronto, who organized that first Canadian meeting.

What I remember most about that first Canadian meeting was the paper

by Chambers and Gordon, on primary products and economic growth, which stirred up quite a bit of controversy and seemed to take up much of the conference. Do you recall your reaction to it?

I think we all found it a bit much to absorb fully at first pass, and there was a lot of concern that all of the general equilibrium effects had been adequately accounted for. I thought it was encouraging, though, to see them using quantitative evidence to evaluate an important historical issue. I still think they went a bit overboard in trying to interpret the staples model as merely dealing with per capita income growth.

You mentioned the *Historical Statistics of Canada*; you would have been well into work on that project from the time you went to that first Clio meeting. Was that so?

Yes, the Historical Statistics project developed as a consequence of the existence of the Committee on Statistics. At the Committee on Statistics there was an interest in seeing whether we could have a publication of the *Historical Statistics of Canada* similar to what had just emerged with the publication of the United States data [1949]. Ken Buckley had been asked by the committee to look into that to see if there were enough data to justify such an enterprise, and he came back with the recommendation that it should be done and then . . . I became the editor, and pretty much the manager of the project, and he was assistant editor.

I'm interested particularly in the contrast with the US. The US *Historical Statistics* volume had been a product of their Census Bureau, and ours was a kind of private initiative, by a group of scholars who said, let's get on with something like this.

Yes, it was entirely private.

Did you have any special funds? Were you able to get a grant?

Perhaps I might come back to that, but I should mention that the US volume had involved a lot of people from outside the Census Bureau itself, but the Census Bureau did the managing of the appointment of the people and the publication and all that kind of thing. Yes, we in Canada received a small grant from the Social Science Research Council, more or less to get ourselves started. We needed some help – secretarial help and that kind of thing – and part of the undertaking was to arrange for the financing of the project. Now, this involved using a great many sources. One source was the Canada Council which provided us with some money, but not a large amount.[1] We used all kinds of other sources. We got help from the Bank of Canada, from

1 The Canada Council, established in 1957, was the Canadian federal government funding agency for arts, humanities and social sciences. In later years, the funding of economics research was passed to the Social Sciences and Humanities Research Council of Canada.

the Dominion Bureau of Statistics, from the Department of Agriculture, from the Department of Labour – much of it in kind – but in some cases, posts were provided that paid the modest emoluments for the section chiefs. I would like to mention especially one person who helped us a lot, Ken Taylor, who was the Deputy Minister of Finance at the time. As you know, Taylor had been an academic economist prior to World War II and had been responsible for developing the foreign trade statistics.

He was the Taylor of Taylor and Michell, *Statistical Contributions* . . .?

Yes, that's correct, and he had gone to Ottawa during the war, I think with the Wartime Prices and Trade Board, but in any event he stayed after the end of the war and had become Deputy Minister of Finance. Ken Buckley and I went in to see him and he understood right from the beginning what we were trying to do, and he was most sympathetic. He arranged, for instance, directly for the statistics on the federal public finances to be prepared from the basic records right in the Department of Finance. He also helped in seeing that posts were provided in the Dominion Bureau of Statistics and I think perhaps in the Departments of Agriculture and Labour. Well, this helped us in getting financial support, but it took a good deal of time, of course, to arrange for these things. Fortunately, I had been connected with, well, the federal civil service, from 1943 to 1945, and I knew most of the people who were engaged in economic research or in obtaining economic data at the federal level, especially in the Dominion Bureau of Statistics. I should mention also the Bank of Canada, especially because they had collected a fine group of young economists who were keen on the developments in the monetary and other aspects of the performance of the economy at the time, and I knew these people in the Bank of Canada very well.

I have often thought, Mac, that it must have been a pretty daunting task to think of putting together a *Historical Statistics* for Canada. In the US there had been so much prior work done by the NBER and various other agencies. They seemed to have a lot to go on. It is my impression that, at the time, we had fewer things to go on. Did you see it that way – that you faced a pretty formidable challenge?

Well, it was true that we had considerably less data than the US, but we did have more than might have been thought. I already mentioned two of the sources of data, the Dominion Bureau of Statistics and the Department of Finance. There was also a series that had been developed in the Department of Labour under the influence of R. H. Coats, who later became Chief Statistician in the Dominion Bureau of Statistics. The Department of Agriculture also had developed considerable statistics, and quite a bit had been done on the development of municipal statistics by Harvey Perry. Nevertheless, you are right, we had quite a bit less, and one of the functions of the project itself was to develop new statistical series.

You had quite a list of contributors, with section chiefs and others helping, but it seems to me that in a project like that, the person who puts it all

together and is responsible for seeing it through finally ends up with an awful lot to do. And that was you. Am I correct?

Yes, although not perhaps in the way that you are describing. Perhaps I just might mention the matter of the appointment of the section chiefs, who all had panels, as we called it, advisory panels. Well, that was quite a large job in itself, which Ken and I managed. And our knowledge of the people in the economics community, from our experience with the Institute for Economics Research and the federal government, came in very handy. I think we knew people right across the country who would take part in it. Nevertheless, it did involve getting in touch with them, seeing whether they had the time and enthusiasm to undertake the work, and we got that done. By and large, they were quite good in getting the work to us. To begin with, of course, we had to decide how the different areas of statistics were to be divided among the sections of the publication. I think that there were 21 sections altogether, and we had set out these divisions and collated the material. The section chiefs would come back to us with proposals of what they would include and we would then see if that worked out satisfactorily. In most cases, they got on with their work, though, in explaining how the data were obtained. There were some instances where we had to make up the introductory parts to the sections themselves but, aside from our own sections – Ken had three and I had two – we didn't have a lot of work to do in getting the statistical data itself, except in one or two cases.

Looking back on it, what is your judgment of the impact of the *Historical Statistics* volume? I'm thinking particularly of how it may have induced scholars to take a bit of a longer view of things or make use of longer spans of historical evidence.

Oh, I think it did – just as the *Historical Statistics* of the US had that effect – I think it encouraged academic research workers, in particular, to undertake projects that they wouldn't have done otherwise, to take on projects that involved the use of quantitative data, and it may actually have led to some of them trying to develop data that were not yet available, and hadn't been available for the *Historical Statistics* volume.

What do you think of the importance of the longer view and of economic history in the education and work of economists? Should economics graduate students have an exposure to economic history as a matter of course?

Well, I'm not sure whether it should be a requirement for everyone. I think, however, that a good course that stresses quantitative information can be very helpful to most people who are going to do economic work. Now, there are some specialties where perhaps that's not so relevant – for instance, when one gets into econometrics that require the use of substantial data in the detail that wasn't available for the earlier period, but is for the more recent period. But, I think, for anyone who is trying to deal with the development of the Canadian economy, it would be essential that they have the knowledge of much of the economic history.

Some issues just keep coming back around, again and again.

Well, one of the things that's interesting now is that there are a number of people who are looking at the 1990s slow-down (if that's the right word to use) in our recovery and wondering if there are perhaps some similarities to what happened in the 1930s and earlier in the way of downturns.

Yes, I sometimes ask students if it's any coincidence that the early 1990s and the early 1890s should have been slow, depressed periods. Now, let's turn to the beginnings of Mac Urquhart as a scholar. I think I'm correct, am I not, in saying that your roots are very much in the farming community of the prairies, and your life was strongly shaped by the depression of the 1930s. How did you get started on this journey?

Well, it's true, I was brought up on a farm which my father had homesteaded in virgin country at the turn of the century. I went to a one-room rural school from grades 1 to 9 and set off to Edmonton for two years in grades 10 and 11, but the end of the 1920s came then, and at that time wheat prices declined enormously. So I couldn't be sent off for the final year of high school, and I worked for a year on the farm – I was too young at that time to be admitted to Normal School.

You were going to be a school teacher?

Yes, I was – that was my father's plan, because it was a way of leaving the farm and getting a start on something else and earning enough money, perhaps, to go on to other things. Well, after working for a year on the farm in which my final experience was handling a stook wagon on a threshing crew in the fall, I went to . . .

Did that convince you that farming was perhaps a less preferable occupation?

Not really. I liked the farming and I enjoyed – you know, when you are young and have all kinds of time, energy, and so forth . . .

Pitching bundles is a good way to work it off?

Yes. In any event, I went to Normal School. There's one thing that I would like to mention that follows from that – incidentally, I borrowed $300 to go to Normal School, which I paid back later, but it was sufficient to support me during my school years. When my Normal School terminated, I had an experience, a most helpful experience, that shows how a particular person can shape one's life in many ways. It followed from a suggestion by the principal of the Normal School, G. S. Lord, that I should go to summer school in the six weeks before starting teaching in the autumn and take, oh, perhaps five of the eight subjects that would make up Grade 12, the final year of high school.[2] Well, for a six-week course he knew that the registrar of the summer school would never permit me to take that number of courses. So, on his own, he walked up with me from the Normal School several blocks to where the registration for the summer school was taking place, and interceded with the registrar, persuaded him to allow me to take the three mathematics courses and a science course, which I think had a lab to it . . . and I've forgotten the other course, maybe history.

You're not supposed to say that history was the forgettable one!

No, no. Well, I always remembered that kindness on his part. He incidentally also managed to lend me $20 to help tide me over, a little loan funded from the Normal School. In any event, following that I taught for five years.

So you really started off as a school teacher?

Yes, I started off as a school teacher in a one-room school: I had all the grades from 1 to 11 – not all at the same time, as there would be some gaps – but different times for those grades. Also during that period, as well as finishing my final year of high school, I got the first year of university done, by correspondence and summer school.

Then you went to university.

Yes. I finished the degree in honours economics at the University of Alberta.

Did you still have in mind being a teacher? When you went into honours economics, you must have decided that economics was going to be the thing.

No, I didn't intend to continue on as a teacher, and I think that there were a number of things that led me into economics. One was that my father had been active politically with the United Farmers of Alberta – who had formed the provincial government, incidentally, from 1921 to 1935 – and so I'd always had an interest in that. It was what now would be called a prairie populist party. My father was also a member of the wheat pool – a farmer-owned wheat marketing agency and a co-op kind of thing that ran their own elevator system as well as attending to the marketing. Well, it was, of course, with the onset of the Depression in the prairies, a very, very bad time. The price of wheat fell to a small fraction of what it had been in the 1920s and it was a combination of those things, I think, that made me interested in economics.

2 In most of Canada in 1930 it was still possible to enter teacher training college with only three years of secondary schooling.

After economics at Alberta, was it directly off to graduate school?

Well, not quite. Canada was already at war and I volunteered to join the Royal Canadian Air Force but was not accepted. I had been accepted for graduate work at the University of Chicago, so off I went in the fall of 1940 and I put in three-quarters there in each of the next two years.

Why Chicago?

I would hazard that my admission there resulted from my having studied with G. A. Elliott, who was highly regarded by Jacob Viner. Elliott had actually been a colleague of Viner for a year as an assistant professor. I just took it from Elliott that I should go to Chicago. This was a time at Chicago when the bright lights were, besides Viner, Frank Knight, Theodore Yntema, Henry Simons, Oscar Lange, and Gregg Lewis. Paul Douglas was already involved in political life by this time. I should just note that it was Oscar Lange who received most attention from the students. He taught macroeconomics, especially the theories of Keynes, microeconomics and mathematical economics, and, despite his strong left-wing stance politically, he was quite objective and very systematic in his lecture presentations.

But you didn't finish the Ph.D. at Chicago. What happened?

Well, I completed my comprehensive exams at Chicago in the spring of 1942, then participated in the Financial Research Program of the National Bureau of Economic Research, and taught at MIT in 1942–43. Then in the spring of 1943, before the end of the academic year, I received an urgent call from W. A. Mackintosh to join him in Ottawa, where he was full-time special assistant to the Deputy Minister of Finance, W. C. Clark. I agreed, but with the stipulation that the Air Force, which I would be joining, would take the responsibility for seconding me to a civilian post in the Department of Finance. So I joined Mackintosh as his assistant. Among other things, Mackintosh was made responsible for much of the planning for the post-war period. The memories of the 1930s and its devastation were very strong and there was great concern that another depression might follow the war. My work turned out to be making plans for the post-war.

What did that involve?

I should like to make three points about the circumstances in Ottawa at the time. First, at the intermediate level in the Department of Finance, the Bank of Canada and External Affairs, a small but highly competent group had been assembled. There were also many young executives from private business – "dollar a year men" – who held posts in wartime production, the Wartime Prices and Trade Board, and the like, and contact with them was very fruitful. Second, as part of our need to gain an understanding of the working of the economy and also of the Keynesian developments, measurement of national income and related aggregates became very prominent. Our national income work was greatly stimulated by the work of Richard Stone and James Meade in Britain in setting up a whole system of national accounts, which became the system worldwide. Third, I became intimately involved with a wide range of persons engaged in the analysis and application of an extensive range of provisions for the post-war period.

Such as . . .?

One part of my work was as a member of an interdepartmental committee to plan for the full national accounts for Canada. That led to the establishment of the national accounts section in the Dominion Bureau of Statistics. There was also great interest in providing for the data needed to implement post-war policy. Two things might illustrate my work in that direction. First, I prepared the first estimates for Canada of private sector, fixed capital formation and both private and public sector public utilities for 1926 to 1941, and O. J. Firestone did the estimates for direct government capital formation. Second, I was given the responsibility of developing a macro forecasting model for the Canadian economy. One element of that was to develop an annual survey of business investment intentions, which was, and still is in fact, carried out by Statistics Canada.

But then, Mac, you put all that behind you and moved into the academic world at Queen's.

I hadn't intended to remain in government employment after the war, and so I did not. As the war's end appeared in sight, I arranged to take up an appointment at Queen's University, beginning in the spring of 1946. As it turned out, the numbers of servicemen attending the university in the fall of 1945 was so great that there was an urgent request for me to join the university that fall. I only managed to come here in late November of 1945, to teach three courses without any time to prepare. Then there were special full sessions in the summer of 1946, so I taught steadily, without any break, from the autumn of 1945 to the spring of 1947, and I continued to contribute to the development of the forecasting model in Ottawa until well into 1946. I have to admit that this burden taxed my health in a way that took nearly ten years for a full, robust recovery.

So it was hard to get back on the track of the research you had begun in graduate school . . .

I did have one major break in 1948–49, when I spent the year back at the University of Chicago as an invited fellow. It was most stimulating and it was then I laid the main foundations for one big component of my later work on capital formation, technological change, and economic growth.

This was the study that was ultimately published in the *Canadian Journal* in 1959?[3]

3 The 1959 paper had among its findings that capital accumulation played a larger role in total factor productivity growth and a correspondingly smaller role in US economic growth in the latter half of the nineteenth century than in the first half of the twentieth – a point that was re-established and given considerable emphasis several years later by Abramovitz and David (1973).

Yes, although that was only one part of what I had done. I had put a lot of work into collecting data for the 1800 to 1850 period, but eventually felt that only the 1850 to 1950 material could be used. The approach to measuring the effects of technological change was pretty much worked out in 1948–49.

And by 1953 you had presented that material to a seminar at the University of Chicago. I always thought it a bit of a shame, given all the attention received by Solow, Swan, and Abramovitz, that your early exploration of that field did not get more recognition.

Well, I'm not sure I would put it that way, but my heavy teaching schedule at Queen's and the interlude of 15 months in Pakistan did have the unfortunate effect of delaying the completion of that work.

Recently your big project was to produce historical national income estimates for Canada. It must have been a great pleasure to see that project completed. Would you tell us a bit about the origins?

Well, there was a real recognition among the Canadian group that something along these lines was needed. We were aware that we didn't have anything comparable to the work that had been done by Simon Kuznets, Solomon Fabricant, and others on measuring national income and such for the United States, as far back as 1869. Also, there was a lot of dissatisfaction with the pioneer decadal estimates that had been published by Firestone. A group of economic historians then thought it was time we in Canada should do something about that.

Do you recall who made the initiative?

It was discussed in the group, but there was no collective agreement to carry it forward. I picked it up as something that I could do as a sort of general manager, and since I had some experience . . .

With the national accounts?

Yes, and with assembling a collaborative group.

As it turned out, you did the largest part of this yourself?

Well, yes, but . . .

So we now have this substantial volume of Canadian national income material that takes us almost back to Canadian Confederation in 1870. I have thought that, in many ways, the new material might set an agenda for the next few years. About when did you get started on the project?

I think we really got started around 1974–5, but all of us who were involved were busy on other things, so it was a part-time activity.

A long time in the making, but it seems to be pretty worthwhile.

Yes. I think it's proven to be worthwhile – it's being used a good deal in analytical work and, of course, there is a great interest now in quantitative developments in Canadian history, partly, I think, arising from some unease about the present circumstances, about what's happened with there being a lag in recovery from the downturn not only in Canada and the US, but almost . . .

The productivity slowdown?

Yes, yes.

What are you up to now, Mac? You just finished this large volume on national income and you are still as active as ever it seems – so tell us about where you are headed.

Well, I'm not quite as active as I used to be, but I'd like to make one comment about the thing that I think should happen – should have high priority – and that is to develop a decent cost of living index for Canada from 1900 backwards. That can be done. It would be a project of considerable size but the data can be found, I think, without question. I think that should have the highest priority. To come back to the question that you raised about what I am doing now: Frank Lewis and I are looking at what life might have been like in the early days of the settlement of Upper Canada (Lewis & Urquhart 1999). We are quite fortunate in that there are quite a lot of data that were gathered and might be used to estimate at least a substantial part of total production.

So we may be able to do some considerable filling in of what the picture before 1870 – maybe even well before 1870 – looked like in this country?

Oh, I think that is true. We do have some work that already has been done for 1850 – Firestone made an estimate for that year – and we need to look more carefully at that, but Frank and I are now looking back into the 1820s, which is quite an early time in the settlement of Upper Canada.

ANNA J. SCHWARTZ

Interviewed by
Eugene N. White

Anna Jacobson Schwartz is Research Associate Emerita of the National Bureau of Economic Research and Adjunct Professor of Economics in the Graduate School of The City University of New York. She was born in New York City in 1915 and was educated at Barnard College (B.A., 1934) and Columbia University (M.A., 1935; Ph.D., 1964). Schwartz was President of the Western Economic Association in 1988 and was named Distinguished Fellow of the American Economic Association for 1993. She was honored in 1989 with a *Festschrift* edited by Michael D. Bordo, *Money, History, and International Finance*. The interview took place at the New York offices of the NBER in April, 1995, and was conducted by EUGENE N. WHITE of Rutgers University, who writes:

After receiving her M.A., Anna Schwartz spent a year at the US Department of Agriculture before returning to Columbia to collaborate with A. D. Gayer and W. W. Rostow on *The Growth and Fluctuation of the British Economy, 1790–1850* (1953), a classic of British economic history. Her renowned collaboration with Milton Friedman produced a trio of books: *A Monetary History of the United States, 1867–1960* (1963), *Monetary Statistics of the United States* (1970) and *Monetary Trends in the United States and the United Kingdom* (1982). In addition to having taught at Brooklyn College, Baruch College, Hunter College and New York University, she is a founding member of the Shadow Open Market Committee (1973), and served as staff director of the US Gold Commission (1981–2). Characteristic of her large *oeuvre* of articles and books is the scrupulous compilation of statistical data to test her interpretations of history. It is fair to say that without Anna Schwartz modern macroeconomic history would be very different from what it is today, perhaps unrecognizable.

What led you to become an economist?[1]

From the time I had a high school course in economics at Walton High School, an all girls public school in the Bronx, I have never ceased to find the subject matter challenging. I majored in economics at Barnard, and economics was my choice for graduate school.

How did you become interested in monetary and financial history?

Possibly it was from the influence of Arthur Gayer, known as "Archie" Gayer, who was one of my teachers at Barnard. He was the author of an article on the Banking Act of 1935, which I didn't understand well enough at the time to see that it moved the Federal Reserve in a direction that I would not now support. He edited a collection of essays in honor of Irving Fisher in the mid-1930s that introduced me to the work of noted international financial economists of the period. I was a research assistant to James W. Angell who taught money at Columbia, during a brief period when he was associated with the NBER, and started the project that eventually became the estimated money stock numbers.

Who else had an early effect on your career?

[Wesley] Mitchell certainly was an influence. He was a supporter of the study that I worked on with Gayer and Rostow, the study of British business cycles and growth from 1790 to 1850. Mitchell's interest influenced our adoption of the NBER method of cyclical analysis. Periodically, we would meet with him to report on what we were doing. Mitchell's integrity and commitment to research that was thorough made a lasting impression on me. What [Arthur] Burns achieved was indoctrinating me to insist on checking not only numerical data but every statement in a manuscript. Rostow, at the time we were colleagues, already had fully formed views, which I believe he still entertains. He was a lot of fun to be with, but didn't have a permanent influence on my intellectual development. Friedman's influence on me has been profound, but it came later than the influence of the others I've mentioned.

Doug North says that Walt Rostow was a major contributor to the early development of cliometrics. What do you think of his influence, or the influence of Mitchell, Gayer, Burns, and yourself?

If cliometrics is a combination of measurement and history, Rostow was an early practitioner. Burns, Mitchell and Gayer can also claim that distinction.

1 An earlier interview with Anna Schwartz was conducted by David Fettig of the Federal Reserve Bank of Minneapolis (Schwartz 1993). Eugene White thus did not repeat Fettig's questions and focused on Dr Schwartz's general views on financial and monetary history. By permission, we reproduce portions of Fettig's interview, denoted by * at the head of his questions.

How did your work with Gayer and Rostow arise?

Well, Gayer had written his dissertation at Oxford on British unemployment, 1815 to 1850. Although his dissertation was never published he was interested in expanding that work. I think that he proposed the project to Mitchell, who thought it was worthwhile. And because of Mitchell, the Columbia Council for the Social Sciences was ready to make a grant. I was probably the student most interested in economics in all the classes that he [Gayer] taught at Barnard. Rostow appeared after we had gotten started, but he became the center of the project.

I thought that the book was ignored because, by the time it was published in 1953, the denigration of the Bureau's method of cyclical analysis was already firmly in place. Although there was a lot in the book that was Keynesian, the fact was that the technique we used was just copied from how the Bureau handled its time series. I thought that limited the influence that the book had at the time. But, on the other hand, it seems to have lived. It hasn't died out and it's been republished. R. C. O. Matthews gave it a rather negative review, but said many years later he hadn't been just in his evaluation. Maybe that helped. But, you know, in general, business cycle analysis lost luster until quite recently. It was not the key kind of subject that economists discussed. Even though the Bureau's technique hasn't been revived, dating business cycles is [now] a big deal.

How did you and Milton Friedman come to work together?

I met him at the National Bureau. He had been in New York during the war when he was working on a mathematical project at Columbia. I might have run into him, but I didn't really get to know him until he returned to the Bureau in the early 1950s. It was Burns who made the arrangement and decided we should work together. And he was right.

***What inspired [*A Monetary History*] and what did you hope to accomplish through the work?**

What inspired the book was the National Bureau's program to study the cyclical behavior of different economic processes – transportation, inventories, consumption and so on. We had constructed estimates of the US money stock from 1867 to 1960; annual estimates before 1875, semi-annual until 1881, annual again through 1906 and monthly from May 1907 on. It was our assignment at the National Bureau to study the cyclical behavior of the money estimates. Our plan was to begin with a narrative describing fluctuations in the growth rate of the money stock, organized in accordance with the NBER dates at which business activity reached a cyclical peak or trough. We wanted to examine the factors that accounted for the fluctuations in money growth and how the changes in money affected the course of events. We initially proposed to prepare another study dealing with trends and cycles in the stock of money. We published the study of trends, which appeared 19 years after *A Monetary History*, relating the trends not only in the US but also in the UK money estimates to income, prices and interest rates. In between those two dates, we published *Monetary Statistics*, describing in detail how the US money estimates were constructed.

When *A Monetary History* was first published, did you feel that it would have the impact it has had?

I was highly uncertain that *A Monetary History* would have a favorable reception. Our views were so distant from mainstream macroeconomics in the importance we accorded money. It took years for our views to have an impact. (Incidentally, *A Monetary History* served as my [Ph.D.] dissertation at Columbia.)

You describe the book as part of a larger research program, but there's a sustained passion in the volume which makes it good reading. Did you feel that you were laying down a challenge or a new foundation?

Both, I suppose. We presented empirical research that investigated the channels by which changes in monetary growth were transmitted to the economy. That was a controversial view that challenged prevailing macroeconomic approaches. But the study also laid the foundations for the proliferation of econometric work on money demand and theoretical developments like rational expectations.

***Have new treatments of monetary history caused you to rethink any of the book's suppositions?**

New treatments of monetary history have usually challenged our interpretations of particular events, such as the failure of the Bank of the United States in December 1930, why national banks didn't fully exploit profit opportunities that the issue of national bank notes afforded, whether it is news or fundamentals that explained the behavior of variables like the exchange rate. These challenges don't really cause me to rethink the book's suppositions.

The Romers (1989) have challenged the monetary shocks we identified in *A Monetary History* as actions of the monetary authority that were independent of contemporary changes in output and that were followed by cyclical declines. They allege possible bias in our selection, and in their view only two qualify as a monetary disturbance – the discount rate hikes in 1920 and 1931. However, they conclude that bias does not account for the contractionary effect of the monetary shocks.

We ourselves have modified two interpretations we offered in *A Monetary History*. One was a reference to the permanent income elasticity of demand for money as much higher than unity, that money was a luxury good, the percentage change in demand for which increased by more than the percentage change in income. Comparison with velocity in the UK convinced us that we had overestimated the income elasticity for the decades before 1903 because we did not allow for the effect of the changing financial structure of the US economy . . .

The other interpretation in *A Monetary History* that we have since modified relates to deposit insurance, which we celebrated in the book as the greatest success of the New Deal. We attributed the absence of bank failures to deposit insurance. Yet, there were no bank failures in other industrialized countries that had never adopted deposit insurance. Bank failures emerged in the mid-1970s both here and abroad. The explanation seems to be that a relatively stable world price level until the mid-1960s contributed to sound banking. Sound credit analysis depends on the assumption of price stability. Unexpected price change can invalidate the assumptions underlying bank lending and investing. We associated sound banking with deposit insurance, when the explanation we now believe was price level stability.

The "cliometrics revolution" began approximately the same time as you and Friedman were working on the *Monetary History*. A key event in the development of cliometrics that many point to is the meeting in Williamstown in 1957. Were there any connections between the two projects?

Both involved measurement. I contributed a chapter (1960) on gross dividend and interest payments by corporations at selected nineteenth-century dates to the "Income and Wealth" volume. For the monetary history we needed a measure of the money stock among other variables. The NBER sponsored both, but one, the Income and Wealth Conference, was an annual project in which improved measurement was the objective, but each year different dimensions of income and wealth were examined. The other was part of the business cycles program with the time of gestation of the project determined by the authors. Measurement is the only link.

Economic historians find a big divide before and after the cliometrics revolution. Is there a similar divide for monetary history?

Monetary history before the publication of our book applied a credit history approach to the subject. Our approach was to study changes in money supply and the effects of these changes. So it might be said that there was a big divide before and after our book appeared, but the credit approach did not disappear. We added something to the mix, but we haven't displaced anything.

***You have [also] written extensively about Great Britain over the years. What lessons does that country's economic history hold for the United States?**

With respect to the lessons the UK's economic history holds for the US, the importance of the difference in institutional structures of the two countries is clearly dominant. The Great Depression was far more catastrophic in the US than in the UK. One reason is the ineptness of the Federal Reserve compared to the Bank of England's performance. Banking panics in the US occurred in the nineteenth and twentieth centuries, whereas the last one to occur in the UK was in 1866. The banking system in the

UK has been much more stable than in the US. I'll leave the comparison to that dimension – the difference in institutional structures.

Do you think that economic history has been downplayed by the economics profession?

My impression is that it was downplayed in the post-war period by the emphasis on econometrics, but in recent years it has recovered ground. History for most beginning economists seems to begin in 1945. How to imbue students with an interest in the past – a thirst to learn how the present relates to the past – is not obvious.

How has it recently "recovered ground?"

American economic history is one of the areas that has attained prominence in the work of Fogel and his students. I'm not sure that the economic history of other areas of the world has been the focus of equal concentration.

You have often criticized the treatment and use of data, especially historical data, in economic research. Do you think the economics profession has in recent years improved its use of data?

No. The main disincentive to improve the handling and use of data is that the profession withholds recognition to those who devote their energies to measurement. Someone who introduces an innovation in econometrics, by contrast, will win plaudits. The fact that it is so easy to access data stored in a computer has discouraged familiarity with the problems in the data, let alone an interest in the construction of data. Users are unaware of the large margins of error surrounding statistics that they take at face value and happily apply in the econometric exercises they conduct.

I recently reviewed (1994) *Studies in Income and Wealth, Volume 55*, on measuring international economic transactions, where exposing all the problems, all the deficiencies, all the shortcomings of one series after another leads Ed Leamer, a discussant, to ask why we are so hyped on the latest fad in econometrics, instead of devoting our energies to improving the data we plug in.

Do you think that financial and monetary historians have adequately treated the role of institutions? And what about financial and monetary economists?

My impression is that historians are more likely to treat the role of institutions than are financial and monetary economists. Having said this, let me add that, whether identified as a historian or as an economist, indubitably one cannot discuss basic issues underlying finance and money (such as what determines output) without concern for the institutional environment, including prevailing organizational forms, contractual arrangements, and the structure of property rights. Similarly, one cannot discuss labor markets without concern for the institutional environment, including the role of unions, welfare provision and so on. With respect to finance and money proper, economists tend to take institutions for granted, while historians tend to explore the development of institutions.

What do you consider the most important recent advances in monetary and financial history?

I'm not sure that recent developments should be described as advances. They represent new directions. One direction is the focus on finance, the behavior of asset prices and credit rationing. A problem I find with all these new – I'll call them fads – is that the people generating the fads don't bother to see if there is anything in the past in economics that anticipated what they want to say. This problem fits in exactly with a paper I discussed at a conference on the interest rate spread between high grade and low grade securities. There is a big literature about it that pre-dates what's going on now. Did the authors ever look at what Braddock Hickman had done for the Bureau on just that subject? I know they didn't. So maybe it wouldn't have altered one iota of what they wanted to do with this concept, but it should at least have had the feeling it was grounded in something, and that this did not start *de novo* the day they began work in that area. I think that the profession is poverty stricken in that sense. It doesn't really take advantage of past work that the common phrase, "standing on the shoulders of giants," suggests.

Have macroeconomists and monetary economists absorbed enough history?

The role of history as a testing ground for theoretical propositions has won wide acceptance in many areas of economics, including labor economics, petroleum economics, the economics of fertility, and monetary reform, to name only a few areas. It's not a matter of absorbing history but exercising imagination to see how historical evidence can enrich one's understanding of economic relationships.

Do you consider yourself an empirical economist or an economic historian?

I suppose I'm both. I don't know that we can make it "either/or."

WALT W. ROSTOW

Interviewed by
John V. C. Nye

Walt Whitman Rostow was Rex G. Baker, Jr. Professor of Political Economy at the University of Texas at Austin. He was born in New York City in 1916 and died in Austin in 2003. He was educated at Yale University (B. A., 1936; Ph.D., 1940) and was a Rhodes Scholar at Oxford in 1936–38. During the 1940s he alternated academic with public service. He taught at Columbia in 1940–41 and worked in the Office of Strategic Services in Washington and London during the war years. In 1946–47 he was Harmsworth Professor of American History at Oxford, went to Geneva to work at the United Nations Economic Commission for Europe in 1947–49, and was Pitt Professor of American History at Cambridge in 1949–50. He was a member of the humanities faculty at the Massachusetts Institute of Technology from 1951 to 1961. During the Kennedy and Johnson administrations he worked at the White House and at the Department of State, returning to academic life at Texas in 1969. He was honored both for public service and for scholarship. In 1945 Rostow received an honorary Order of the British Empire and from the United States a Legion of Merit, and was awarded with The Presidential Medal of Freedom in 1969. He was elected Fellow of the American Academy of Arts & Sciences in 1957 and Fellow of the American Philosophical Society in 1983; in 1982 he was presented with *Economics in the Long View*, a three-volume *Festschrift* edited by Charles P. Kindleberger and Guido di Tella (New York University Press). The interview took place in March 1994 at Rostow's home in Austin, and was conducted by JOHN V. C. NYE, then of Washington University in St. Louis, who writes:

Walt Rostow was one of the most influential, imposing and controversial figures in the fields of economic history and development for over half a century. He is best known for *The Stages of Economic Growth* (1960), which popularized the term "take-off into sustained growth" and which had an enormous impact on the economic development policy literature. His first works on the growth and development of early industrial Britain, partly in collaboration with A. D. Gayer and Anna Schwartz, served as pioneering works of cliometrics even before the term was invented. Despite his early interest in quantification, Rostow remained outside the cliometrics movement of the late 1950s and early 1960s. He often referred to himself as a maverick in the profession.

Walt Rostow continued to teach his two-term course, "The World Economy: 1750–present" until only a month before his death in February, 2003, and added to his extensive writings, publishing *The Great Population Spike and After: Reflections on the 21st Century* (OUP 1998) and *Concept and Controversy: Sixty Years of Taking Ideas to Market* (2003), an "eclectic memoir," published posthumously.

You were an early exponent of a quantitative approach to economic history, particularly in your work on the Industrial Revolution. How did you become interested in that subject, and also in your joint work with Gayer and Schwartz?

It began while I was an undergraduate at Yale. I did my freshman work on a scurrilous journalist of the French revolution, [Jacques René] Hébert, and his newspaper *Le Père Duschene*; the files were in the library. During my second year I worked on the character of the English revolution of the seventeenth century, centered on Winstanley and the Diggers. At just this time, I took a black market seminar in economic theory with Dick Bissell and three others. The seminar took place on Thursday nights. Dick was fresh back from a year at the London School of Economics where he read Wicksell, Marshall, Wicksteed and the Austrian theorists of capital. And so did we. Bissell had one of the greatest gifts of exposition of anyone I have ever known. He was doing a thesis at Yale on the theory of capital. My first introduction to theory was mathematical and both micro, and macro, as we now call it; and out of that seminar I posed for myself two questions. One, suppose you were to take economic history, which was at that time a rather descriptive and institutional field, and apply to it modern economic theory and modern statistics. Two, there was a larger question, in effect the Marxist question. That was the relationship between the economy and the society, the social structure and political culture. I had already decided they were interactive rather than linear, as in Marx's formulation. Those are the two questions that have interested me ever since I formulated them at age 17.

The first work I did was in 1934, on the inflation during the Napoleonic wars and the deflation afterwards. I found that the major characters in monetary history all wrote about that episode. But I also read Tooke. I found that the monetary theorists explained only a very small part of the process that affected prices during and after the Napoleonic wars. You had to look at the supply side and you had to take Tooke very seriously. In fact, Tooke was much more careful about monetary analysis than the monetarists. They were quite content to deal with the process by making a correlation between the rise in discounts and country bank notes, on the one hand, and prices, on the other. Ricardo's analysis was superficial: why prices rose at that time and then fell afterwards from 1812. This was a desperate part of the war. You couldn't understand what happened except in the context of the Continental System and the Orders in Council, the closing off of Hamburg, and the routes to the Mediterranean and Scandinavia, and so on. It was out of desperation they started the boom in Latin America at the same time. This was the kind of a war it was. By throwing myself into the whole process, I learned a great deal.

Did you feel you were making a break with traditional economic history, or that you were doing a better job?

I didn't think of a job – I didn't think of it. This was what I wanted to do. I viewed the British economy as part of the whole society of Europe and the Americas. Well, I was conscious I was breaking away, but that was not nearly as important as following my own bent. I wrote three essays in economic history as an undergraduate. In my sophomore year I did "Inflation and Deflation: A Chronicle of the Napoleonic Wars in England." That was in 1934. Then as a junior I did "1873: The Study of a Crisis." Then as a senior in 1936 I did "Outline for an Economic History of England: 1896–1914." In each of those cases I devised a method which I ultimately used in my thesis. I told the story of a whole economy in motion by doing it year by year, cycle by cycle. I think I differ from a great many economists in that, from the beginning, the questions I posed demanded that I look at the whole economy and not some part of the economy.

Now what happened on the Gayer study was that I had finished my Yale thesis, which was largely written at Oxford.[1] Gayer, it must be said, had done at Oxford a very good thesis about this period, 1815–1850. In New York he conceived of doing this same period with the full techniques of the NBER. He had Anna Schwartz and Isaiah Frank working with him. He had collected a good many of the series, and he put them through the National Bureau method. Meanwhile, Anna did a price index, the best there is, with good careful weights. Isaiah Frank was doing the stock exchange and related institutions. But they had no method for putting together the price index, the stock exchange index, and the statistical data which they had put through the NBER cyclical and trend analysis. Gayer called me down from Yale where I had just finished my thesis. So in 1939–40 I did Volume One, the history, and began work on Volume Two with Anna Schwartz. I used the NBER method which I took apart in the light of history. The reason that I could take apart the average figures and the deviations from the average was I that knew every case in these 60 years. The econometricians who work with averages do not know what they're talking about. I mean that not in the cheap sense, but that they don't know what the deviations mean. Part Two fulfilled Wesley Mitchell's dream. We had the history, the theory and the numbers. There is only one other book like that. (Well, there is one for the 1830s, which Robin Matthews

1 The thesis was published in 1981 in the Arno Press Ph.D. series: *British Trade Fluctuations, 1868–1896: A Chronicle and a Commentary*. It contains introductory remarks written some four decades after the event.

did, and one for the 1850s, which Jon Hughes did.) But the only other first-rate study of that kind is Svennilson's study (1954) of the interwar years. It is a beautiful book, but it was not popular after the war.

The link between the Gayer study and my past was that I'd been doing these finger exercises as an undergraduate and graduate. By 1939, I was ready to play my part in the Gayer study. I was able to do it in a year plus because I taught 1940–41 at Columbia. Anna Jacobson Schwartz was a splendid statistician – I liked her. But she defected to Friedman. And she defected away from the explanation of the price increases and price decreases we used in the Gayer study. So you will find in the Harvester edition of the Gayer study (1975), in the Preface, a good summary which brought together the literature on the period 1790–1850, since we'd finished the study before the war. And there she takes her distance from our explanation of the price fluctuations. I stick with the "old time religion."

Did you see a link between your work and the cliometrics movement when it came around in the 1950s?

I gave a paper at Williamstown in 1957 which still is my final word on this subject: "The Interrelation of Theory and Economic History." I urge you to read that because I talk of that relationship exactly.

Could you state in a nutshell what you thought?

I took it for granted that other people have the right to make their own decisions about what they do their research on and how they do it. My own view of the different kinds of cycles concerns concurrent interactions, which is my view of how history unfolds. For example, long demographic cycles, the short demographic cycles, Kondratieff cycles and trend periods, housing cycles, major cycles, inventory cycles. The problem that the historian faces is dealing with all the forces in play, not a mono-causal world.

Among the cliometricians there was a feeling they were doing something different, that there wasn't enough systematic use of economic theory. Did you agree, or did you feel that the body of historians writing at the time were doing a pretty good job?

I felt very warmly towards them, and I wrote, I forget where I wrote it, but I wrote in favor of cliometrics. The only thing I held against them was that, with the exception of Landes – and David, who broke out of it – they were victims of the reigning neoclassical economists.

You mean David Landes and Paul David?

Yes, they broke out, especially Paul David in his criticism of Fogel's slavery book.

What did you think, for instance, of Conrad, Meyer, North, Davis, Hughes, Parker . . .?

I liked them. I just took a different tack. I did my own thing. Meyer and Conrad did the first work on slavery, for example; North has worked on institutional influences, and Hughes did the 1850s, and for Parker it was productivity. I felt in my bones that cliometricians in general, Fogel particularly (whom I like very much and who has done so well by his students), were too much in the grip of the neoclassical economists, and this mainly accounted for their failure to deal with the issue of technology.

Let me give you a simple example. In *The World Economy* I take apart the Fogel analysis of railroads.[2] Fogel says if anything was a big factor it was the nail industry, which meant more in the 1840s and the 1850s than the volume of output of iron for the railways. But the point was not at all quantitative. The point was that the railways induced both France and the United States to get out of the farmer's iron business and to bring in the blast furnaces and then the modern methods of making iron from coke. Steel came along in the late 1860s and 1870s. But the iron came first. It was not a question of the quantities of iron used by the railroads, but the fact that technological change came about through the railroads and the iron industry. The same thing happened to Russia. Up in Siberia they gave up making iron with timber, which was plentiful, and took to modern iron and steel manufacture when the railways united Donets coal and Krivoi Rog iron.

The new commitment to neoclassical economics was what kept cliometricians from doing what they should have done. They should have done the economic history of the United States when we did the Gayer study. There was no successor to Smith and Cole (1935), the pioneer book on the early American economy. They were kept from dealing with the American economy as a whole because they were in the hands of the mathematical economists. In his book, *Unbound Prometheus*, Landes deals with the question of technology head on.

But does he really deal with it? If I might push you on this: it seems that he just asserts things. He doesn't check for alternate theses; he asserts, and judges success by use of what he feels were the leading technologies.

There is no way to deal with technology except by description, which Landes did. Why is it that technology came in four batches? In the 1780s, the steam engine, Cort's method of making iron, and the factory method of making cotton textiles – these all came together. The railways came concurrently in Britain and the United States, with Germany and France only a little behind, and they induced the steel revolution at the end of the 1860s. Electricity was spread about, but it explains the rise of France. They were poor in iron and coal as compared to the Germans, but the Alps were a great source of hydro power. Due to hydro power, the French had a higher rate of growth

2 Rostow (1978: 746–7 *n* 53).

than the Germans or Americans before the First World War. So first you had the textiles, then you had the railways and the iron revolution and steel, then you had the electricity and the internal combustion engine and chemicals. You really didn't have another technological revolution until the 1970s. In the middle of that decade you began to get microelectronics, the new genetic engineering, the laser, and the new methods of producing physical objects with plastics or ceramics.

Towards the end of *Theorists* I go through the mystery of why it is these technologies come in bunches; why they come about every 60 or 70 years. Now, Schumpeter made a decisive error by linking the Kondratieff cycles, which are cycles in relative prices, to the technological cycles. To this day it [has] shocked me that he made that mistake. He was a fascinating figure, Schumpeter. He was absolutely right in making his pitch about entrepreneurship, but he had no theory of growth. In his youthful volume (1912), he didn't deal with population, technology and investment, and the late-comers and the early-comers . . . This bunching issue has stirred a considerable literature. But to this day I don't know of a conventional theorist who has contributed to that literature.

To return to the question of theory, I have six variables which I ask my students to use. Now if you wish to characterize my work compared to conventional economics, here it is. Conventional economics evades these six variables: population; technology and investment; relative prices, which embrace the Kondratieff cycles; business cycles, but seen as a form which growth took – not abstracted from the whole system; the stages of growth, which repeat in a sense the technological revolutions, but from a different perspective – the perspective of a single country; and the non-economic variables which affect the world economy. Among these are perfectly obvious ones like the traumatic effects of wars – the Napoleonic Wars, the Civil War, and the World Wars. But the economy is also affected, for example, by how the ruler disposes of his limited resources . . . There are three directions that rulers could take: they could dispose of resources to redress old wrongs; to build up the center versus the regions; and there was the question of welfare . . . It's very important to be clear about the primacy of politics, generally, notably in modern economic development.

Yes. The work of the 1950s, particularly yours, but also Gerschenkron's, was often self-conscious about communism as a tempting alternative model for developing nations. Can you comment on the relevance of your "non-communist manifesto" to the eventual economic and social collapse of the East?

That's the title *The Economist* gave to the book.[3] I didn't mind at all; but it was a "non-communist manifesto" in the sense that it was an alternative to Marx's theory of

3 In the autumn of 1958 Rostow gave a series of undergraduate lectures on "The process of industrialization" while on leave at Cambridge University. He was persuaded to publish the lectures in abridged form in two numbers of *The Economist*, August 15, 1959, pp. 409–16, and August 22, 1959, pp. 524–31. The articles were called "Rostow on Growth; A Non-Communist Manifesto," thereby providing the subtitle for *The Stages of Economic Growth.*

development. It was not a polemical book except at the very end where I state my assumptions about human beings and the process of growth, as opposed to the communist view.

I think that I should tell you, though, that I was anti-communist from a very early time. My father came over in 1904 from Russia. He had already been in the Social Democratic movement, and he had fought the communists over the issue of "What is to be Done" in 1902. And he didn't like the communists because they wanted to seize power even though they were a minority. I remember we had at our house a visitor from the Soviet Union. He was charming, wearing a leather jacket in the early 1920s. I couldn't have been more than six. Afterwards, Father was asked what our visitor's view was. And he said no good would come of them. They took over the czarists' police, but they made them tougher. The czarists at least did not go after the families. They only sent off to Siberia the political dissidents. These fellows took the families. My father taught us from that early time: in politics the methods used were as important as the aims you nominally sought. I never forgot that lesson. I dealt with it in the *Theorists* book in the analysis of Marx.

I had the great pleasure in Moscow in 1958 of quoting Charlie Curtis (a Boston lawyer). I said in the Institute of World Politics the problem with Marx was that he did not understand Charlie Curtis's Law. Charlie Curtis's Law was that the end of a discussion was not "By golly, you're right," but "I've got to live with the S. O. B., don't I?" And that's what Marx did not understand. He had a blood lust in him. He was very harsh to his wife and daughters and indeed, in the end, with Engels. He was a troubled man. He had never built a theoretical structure out of his Manifesto. He spent his whole life trying. Now Gerschenkron and I were anti-communists, but I dealt with the Soviet system and with Soviet diplomacy in an unemotional way. But I did take the Cold War seriously.

Although you and Gerschenkron seemed aware of the human cost of the communist system, my impression is that you overestimated their industrial success.

This should interest you as a historian: even their own experts had predicted the key sectors of the 1950s and 1960s would decline. Read over the passage in *Stages* that begins: "Beware of linear projections!" The theory of the demise of the Soviet Union, which I put at the beginning of the third edition of *Stages* (1990), details their failure to pick up the automobile revolution, but they were terrorized by their failure to pick up the computer revolution in the mid-1970s. So they missed two technological revolutions in a tragic effort to dominate the world and to behave like a superpower. After the Second World War they fell off their growth curve, but you can't understand the process unless you look at the sectors. At the end of the analysis of Russia and the Soviet Union in *The World Economy* I describe the deceleration of the economy as early as 1978, and I give the major reasons for it. They diverted their best scientists and engineers to military purposes. I visited the Soviet Union in 1990, and I observed that they were still, on the whole, palpably tied to the technology of the 1950s.

The Soviets were clearly unable to catch up with the technological wave, but to what extent did they not even take full advantage of technology of the 1950s? How much did we overestimate their success even in the earliest periods?

Well, you've got to be very careful about that. They kept a high rate of growth in the steel industry, they allocated 30 percent of their output to military production, to which they allocated their best engineers and scientists, and they produced a hell of a lot of bombs. They were very dangerous. They lagged us in the quality of their aircraft by two or three years. Their tanks were very good. But they came unstuck out of a mixture of a fall in their rate of growth, which the experts predicted to be on the way in the 1950s, and in Afghanistan they took on problems they couldn't handle, militarily, given the opposition of the Muslim world – in fact, the whole non-communist world. Then they were hit by an absolutely new phenomenon – the success of China under Deng Xiao Ping in the late 1970s.

Yes, shouldn't we talk about that? Because China seems to be a contradiction – they missed more of the technological breakthroughs than the Russians.

No, no. The biggest thing the Chinese under Deng Xiao Ping had going for them . . .

Agriculture is what developed the industry . . .

That's the point. Family responsibility is the key thing in the late 1970s under Deng Xiao Ping. From the families you could lift off the communes, the bosses, the cadres – families had to turn over a certain amount as taxes and rents, and the rest they could keep for themselves. When I visited China in 1983 people in the cities – for the first time in Chinese history – were outraged that people in the countryside were doing better than they were.

But isn't that a purely market phenomenon – not a technological one?

It's not technological at all.

So it's the market, right? It's institutional . . .

Wait a minute. Wait a minute. It's institutional, but it's not market. Because the Russians had treated their peasants like animals – they killed off 10 million – they set up a system of collective farms and the best people on those collective farms went to the cities, where they did better. So on the collective farms were the old people and children. This was well-captured in a cartoon that came my way when I did a book on Soviet society.[4]

4 The cartoon depicted a sturdy family at the gate, waving to the frail grandmother, and saying, "Goodbye, grandmother. Do the family's work on the *kolkhoz*."

They had these garden plots which were terribly inefficient, but they got 30 percent of the food for the cities from these garden plots. They were caught between the market gardening of this kind and the slovenliness of the state farms. They threw tremendous amounts of capital into agriculture. A vast number of tractors were down for lack of spare parts, because their factories were measured, and given their instructions, in terms of complete units, not spare parts. So they cannibalized their farm machinery. On collective farms machinery belonged to everybody; therefore, it belonged to nobody. Nobody felt responsible.

Now in China, on the other hand, they still had the family – intact. They still had the small farms except in Manchuria, where there were collective farms. But the reason that China has done very well is that it was an agricultural country; they freed up agriculture, and then they went into light industry, which was easy to do. And so the south grew and industry moved inland from the coastal areas. The south is alive with construction and light industry. They jumped from textiles to computers. Now the biggest problem that the Chinese face is what the hell are they going to do with the old factories which they got from the Russians in the 1950s? The Party still gives them subsidies. They are gradually going to bring in the Japanese and others to modernize their old factories. That's the policy the Russians ought to pursue, but they haven't been able to do it. They can't bring their 1950s factories up-to-date except by bringing in foreign firms. They ought to bring them in for 20 years – and make profits and try to sell abroad – and then at 20 years they would have the right to buy the foreigners out.

Let's go back to a subject you mentioned earlier: your abiding interest in long cycles. How much emphasis should economic historians place on such work, and what suggestions do you have for questions worth pursuing?

Relative price movements – of foodstuffs and raw materials relative to manufactures – play a very large part in the multiple forces that enter economic history. You have the upswing, 1790 to 1813. There's a fall again when Napoleon was forced to reform his army after the debacle in Russia, and he re-opened foreign trade. The downswing continues after the war and extends to the shortage of grain in the 1840s and 1850s. Then you have the upswing until 1873. You have the downswing until 1896, which is not a depression in terms of employment, if you do it cycle by cycle and measure it carefully, but it was a depression of prices. Then you have the upswing to 1920, and the downswing to 1933. You have the upswing until 1951. The subsequent downswing plays a very important part in the 1950s and 1960s. All the industrial countries benefited from the downswing in the prices of foodstuffs and raw materials. And then stocks begin to attenuate in grain as well as energy, and you have the upswing in the 1970s.

These long cycles were an important part of the story from 1790 to the 1980s; but I reiterate, they are among the key variables you have to track. They don't stand alone in economic history. In my first post-war book, actually my first published book, *The British Economy of the Nineteenth Century* (1948), I said at the beginning that the long cycles of fairly uniform time sequence were a product of the nineteenth century. I did not predict they would continue into the second half of the twentieth century. I said that improvements in agricultural productivity would be more even than the opening up of new territories, which was the method used in the nineteenth century to deal with shortages of grain. I reckoned without the switch to oil, or that it would take 10 years to open up the Norwegian and British reserves, and 10 years to get the North Slope going. I don't think there is any reason for the rhythm to continue. But you can't understand history without understanding these long movements of relative prices. I did a mathematical model of the Kondratieff cycle, quite different from the one that appears in the *Business Cycles* (1939) of Schumpeter, and quite similar to Arthur Lewis's explanation. Long movements of commodity prices, raw material prices, have had a lot to do with the contours of economic history. But as I say, I don't deal with them alone. I tell my students to look at population movements, technology and investment, relative prices, business cycles as part of growth. The thing that's so much fun about economic history, and what's so interesting about the Ricardo–Malthus debate, is that Malthus was aware there were so many things operating at the same time . . .

Is that what you called in an earlier essay "the problem of economic history" – the debate between your sort of real-world theory and abstract theory?[5] You pose Malthus as representing the real world to some extent and Ricardo as representing abstraction.

Yes, I do indeed. Milton Friedman asserted flatly, in one of his books or one of his essays, that he's going to stick with his theoretical view dominated by one variable. Some people are gifted that way; some are gifted to look at the whole of reality. What I would assert is that a historian is bound, by his profession, to deal with multiple variables. In that sense, I'm a historian. But, for each of my variables, I have a theory: a theory of demographic cycles, a theory of innovations and investment. I keep saying it very politely, but the proportion of income invested isn't at all the product of a Keynesian system. It isn't at all the product of the consumption function. It's a product of how much of the backlog of technology you missed and are as a society willing to make up.

Would you elaborate on that notion – of a backlog of technology?

After the war the Japanese ran a 30 percent investment rate. After the war the Europeans ran a 22 to 24 percent investment rate. In the United States it hovered around 15 to 17 percent, and the rates of growth accommodate themselves to the investment rates. Well, the Japanese were furthest behind. The Japanese were impoverished; they had a broken society. But they came up like a rocket. They set about acquiring every type of technology. Along the way they started with cameras. The cameras arose out of their expertise at making bomb sights, and they were very good at it. And they went right up. They planned a technological chain. They were a well-educated people. They climbed

5 See Rostow (1992: 224–5) and Rostow (1986).

a chain right up to the 1990s crisis. And they ran, in so doing, a 30 percent investment rate for most of that period, although it fell off towards the end. The Europeans also came up. They had the war damage to make up, and they hadn't had the mass automobile age or the age of consumer durables. The automobile age came in the 1950s and 1960s. It was interesting to see the British and the Continental factories where the bicycle racks gave way to the parking lots. They didn't have American automobiles at the time. They had smaller automobiles and they had a big tax on petrol. But they had the automobile age, and they had refrigerators, and they used oil instead of coal, and they got rid of smog. In other words, the investment rate is a function of how close you are to the technological frontier and how acquisitive your entrepreneurs are.

This sounds very Gerschenkronian. Is it like his idea of backwardness?

No, it isn't backwardness. You're assuming that the stage of education of the populace is the same; you're assuming that the entrepreneurial acquisitiveness is the same. If that were the case, the advantages of being late would be uniform. In Russia you had not only the backlog of technology, but a population that was not very well-educated and a system that was counterproductive entrepreneurially. But if you assume other things are the same – which an economist normally assumes – then indeed Gerschenkron falls apart. He said something important about Russia, Germany, France, Britain. But let's take the Swedes and the Italians. They had takeoffs about the same time as Russia. The Swedes moved right up in the 1930s to the technological frontier; the Russians didn't. So you have to factor in other variables, along with the size of the technological backlog. The Japanese were very well-educated people; so are the Koreans. The Koreans are the real miracle. They were the poorest kids on the block. A recent issue of the *Korean Business Review* reports the six major industries for export, and they all have a high rate of growth. All are high-tech industries. That's what you can do if you've got an entrepreneurial system that works, and well-educated people, and an organization of society that gives them their head.

Since your interest is very strong both in cycles and in trying to fit technology into economic history, what do you think of attempts to introduce evolutionary elements into economic history? I think specifically of Paul David's work, Doug North's work, and Joel Mokyr's work. Three very different approaches, but all three have recently tried to come to grips with technology, with evolution rather than mechanical notions, and learning and change.

I think that's the only way you can go and make progress. The only one of those books that I've kept up with is Mokyr's book on the Industrial Revolution. It has a long introduction (1985), which I thought was very good. I have sympathy for people who approach history this way, who take into account the institutions, the technology, and other things which lend themselves only to treatment by historical methods. Now you can formalize that by bunching together the technologies. I do that towards the end of *Theorists*, in the mathematical appendix. But I have great sympathy with a broader approach to economics, and I think that those who cut economics down to the size of the differential calculus lose an awful lot.

Since we've started on the education of an economist, can you comment on the role of economic history in that education? What should it be? How has its influence varied over the past half century or so, and what about the future of the profession?

I can say no more than I did in the preface to this book, *Theorists*. It is dedicated to the next generation. It's the way I feel about the next generation, that they're missing so much.

> To the Economists of the Next Generation: in the hope that, without abandoning modern tools of analysis, they may bridge the chasm of 1870 and reestablish continuity with the humane, spacious, principled tradition of classical political economy.

That's what I think they ought to do. I don't feel sore at anybody. I think that, at the moment, a lot of talent is wasted. The economists are sidelining themselves, but that is what I hope for the next generation. You see, I've put the appendix in the *Theorists* book to show what mathematics is good for. Mathematics is good for isolating certain forces at work. But if you're going to tell the whole story of an economy in motion, which is what I've tried to do in my lifetime as an economic historian, you have to remember Malthus and Ricardo. The historian is bound to deal with many variables operating at the same time. And that's what Malthus and Ricardo split over. I want the economist to deal in an orderly, logical way with each of the variables. He then deals with the unfolding of history. And history is never linear. I'm undogmatic with my students. I make them the greatest living experts on the critics of Rostow. I tell them that this isn't at all to score off them – my critics. I tell them to read the critics because that's the way to expose the problems in economic history: the conflicts between economists.

Why do you think there was this change? You suggest that, in your youth, there was a co-existence of both the narrow and rigorous with the broader, wide-ranging views. Why was there a split so people feel that economic history – to quote *Science* magazine – became a "backwater field" in the profession?[6]

That's simply the triumph of Samuelson and *The Foundations of Economic Analysis* (Harvard UP 1947). The triumph of that kind of economics took the whole profession out of the game.

But why?

6 Commentary on Economics Nobel Awards to Robert W. Fogel and Douglass C. North; *Science* 262 (22 October 1993), p. 508.

Why? Because the differential calculus could not deal with these factors that matter: with population, with technology and investment, with relative prices, business cycles as an aspect of growth. So economics became everything you could deal with through the calculus.

Isn't that odd? If economics couldn't deal with them, that should have created a greater demand for historical work. What is it about the university system? You, yourself, were a colleague of Samuelson . . .

I like Samuelson. I regard him as a friend. I would never, never question his right to deal with economics his way. I wish wistfully that he'd understood not only that "mathematics is a language" – which is a direct quote – but also the wonderful wisdom that "nature is much more complex than could be dreamt of by a single mind," or revealed by a single technique or variable. Despite what Keynes said about bridging the gap in economics between micro- and macro-analysis of prices, he didn't bridge it. His was a Marshallian short-period analysis in *The General Theory* (1936). What is missing from the way we teach economics is the sector. It's the sector in which technology comes. It's the sector you must study to understand high prices of raw materials and the low prices of raw materials. There is no theory of the sectors. Think about it.

Tell us some more about that. What should the theory of the sector be about?

The theory of the sector should be the rise of a technology. Kuznets's early book, *Secular Movements in Production and Prices* (1930), caught the sectors very, very well – the life of the sector is a life of deceleration, and he specifies the reason for the deceleration in that book, and the counterpoint to this in prices – acceleration, deceleration, and the leveling off of prices. And growth consists . . . that's what section 5 of *The World Economy* tells: that there are aggregate figures of industrial production, GNP and population – and underneath the smooth aggregate curves you have the coming in of the new technologies. That you can only catch by looking at the sectors.

From time to time you have referred to yourself as something of a maverick. Yet, you've obviously been a successful maverick within the profession. How did that work?

I don't know whether I was successful or not; I've had a lot of fun. When I wanted to take the time off to do something else, I did. For example, I thought even before the war I would write, someday, a book on the world economy, because you couldn't understand Britain without understanding the world economy. After I left the government in 1969, I caught up with economic history. I felt I knew as much as I was likely to absorb. I planned a 700-page book and I suddenly decided that 1790 was a curious year, because the Industrial Revolution was underway. So, I'll take some time off to write a chapter on how it all began. And that became a book. I found that there was no satisfactory theory of the Industrial Revolution. I worked it like a detective story. I took traditional societies first and asked why didn't they experience sustained growth. They had odd inventions scattered through their history. Then at last came the breakthrough in the eighteenth century. And when I was finished with *How It All Began*, I felt I had done enough on the Industrial Revolution and I was ready for *The World Economy*, which occupied me from 1973 to 1978.

Going back to being a maverick: Landes has written about my pleasure, my easiness, at the Konstanz conference when Kuznets mounted the attack on *The Stages of Economic Growth.*[7] And the answer is that I never was sore at anybody. I just had fun doing my own thing; and if I wanted to take time off to do this series of books on "Ideas and Action" after 1978, I did it.[8] It was in 1985 that I was ready to do another 700-page book – *Theorists of Economic Growth.* When I was finished with it in 1989, my wife said to me, "You don't look pregnant with another 700-page book." That started something we called the joint venture. There it is. [He points to a box.] JV – we had a whole seven boxes on JV, joint venture. We thought of a number of things we might look at in the post-Cold War world and did an essay or two.

And who is this "we?"

My wife and myself. We looked at the American economy and finally we decided on the problem of the cities. We spent five years on that, two years of study, a year of writing and clarifying the operational hypothesis, four months of planning and then 15 months of making it work and bringing it to scale, and going to the foundations. But why did we take five years off at this stage of our lives to study the cities? Because we felt it was a very serious problem. We wanted to make as much of a contribution to it as we could, even though we are both over 70.[9]

So I treasure my colleagues and am delighted that they did what they wanted to do and I've done what I wanted to do. I wouldn't ask for anything else. The reply, which I wrote while I was in government, that's in the opening pages of the Konstanz book, says that it is true that economists are like other people. It's not a monopolistic market, but it's not a free market either. The coming in of a new vocabulary which I used in *The Stages* cuts into the attention paid other people. There is a hard test of the usefulness to others of the views which are put forth in there. This and the other original views I've fostered must look after themselves . . .

I have a theory about Ph.D. theses. They ought to be done soon. The bad thing is to stretch out the time, hang around graduate school. The Ph.D. thesis should be a great

7 See Rostow, ed. (1963), the proceedings of a conference convened to examine Rostow's concepts of stages and the "take-off".

8 A series of six monographs intended to "explore the relationship between ideas and action," where ideas are "the abstract concepts that public officials and their advisers bring to bear in making decisions." Quotation from Rostow (1981: *ix*).

9 Walt Rostow and Elspeth Rostow established "The Austin Project" in 1992 as their "joint venture." See Rostow (2003: Ch. 11).

book because you will be satelliting off it for years to come: You have a wife and child, and the child has its teeth straightened, etc., and so you want to state your goal in the world. There's something in Schumpeter's emphasis on your 20s being the critical decade. I have a table in the *Theorists* book as to the time when ideas were formed. And it was, almost without exception, before they were 30; Marx, John Stuart Mill and so on. It's a shame to waste that great period on a trivial subject, and therefore, I discourage students from being disciples – my disciples or anyone else's. M. M. Postan felt the same way about his students; he did not want them to be disciples of his.

Yes . . . I understand that Postan spent a good portion of his last years visiting you here in Texas. Would you tell us something about that interchange, and about his influence on your thought and work.

Well, he didn't have a great influence on my thought and work. I knew him from the time in 1938, when I sent him an article based on my Oxford thesis. I was asked by Postan to come to Wiltshire and visit him and his then wife, Eileen Power, a wonderful woman, and a great Medieval scholar. She died in 1940, suddenly. Postan was an authentic scholar, but he was also much involved in the current world. He did the official history of the aircraft industry, one of the series of books Hancock edited. He understood exactly what I was trying to do. He didn't try to influence me at all. But we liked each other, we enjoyed each other, we enjoyed each other's company. And he was a friend. He came three times to Texas in the 1970s before his death. He was marvelously productive in the 15 years after age 65. Until then, he ran economic history at Cambridge. He also ran the International Economic History Association and much else. Then he retired and he had time to write, and he wrote about the medieval period; that was his thing. We differed about the modern economy somewhat, but he may have been right. I didn't disagree with him. But I pointed out that it was not inevitable. He feared we were going to have a period of chronic, high unemployment. He feared the new technology. He felt we wouldn't be fast enough in training people in the technology. And he was right.

So he felt there was a transition problem caused by the technology.

I said the major danger lay elsewhere. Computers didn't worry me so much because I'd studied the logistical chain of computers à la Leontief. There are jobs all the way up and down the chain. But robots might put people out of work. I talked to him about where the workforce should be employed: in the infrastructure, which is poor in Europe, poorer still in the United States. It took longer to get from the Charles DeGaulle airport to my hotel than it did to fly in from Luxembourg to Paris. He worried about the *Lumpenproletariat* who would be unemployed. My answer was that there was no reason for them to be unemployed, that there were ample jobs to make a decent infrastructure. But I didn't wholly rule out his anxiety. Postan was a friend and we enjoyed each other. We didn't influence each other, but I took him very seriously, indeed.

What would you say is the biggest change in emphasis in your thinking

about the stages of growth in the last 30 years? That is, what had you not quite anticipated when *The Stages* first came out?

The Stages proved a salutary method for giving shape to the foreign aid field. The consortium method focused around a country plan, buying time through the preconditions, getting them into take-off. And then we say good-bye as they were far enough advanced to get their loans from the private market. I said at the White House the other day, March 4th [1994] – I said there are very few of us who remember the year 1958. A junior senator from Massachusetts, who was John Kennedy, and a Republican senator from Kentucky, John Sherman Cooper, made common cause to pass the resolution in the Senate in favor of the support for the Indian Second Five Year Plan. Three bankers were sent abroad. Herman Abs of West Germany, Alan Sproule from the United States and Oliver Franks from Britain went out to India and Pakistan. From their report came the first World Bank consortium. It brought everyone together in a unified way around a country plan: the Japanese, the West Europeans, and the Americans. The Indians had been thought to be fit subjects for triage (*i.e.*, aid could not help them). Now, they have a middle class of 200 million. They surely still have people sleeping on the streets of Calcutta, but that's because of the excessive birth rate, although it's falling. So the take-off hypothesis served its purpose in its time.

What you ask is a good question though: what is it that I hadn't anticipated, that we have learned? In *The Stages* I didn't write enough about the differences in the length of time of the preconditions. It was something I taught, but I didn't put it into the book. It took the Mexicans from their independence, let's say in 1820, until 1940 before they took off. It took so long because they had to go through the political problems and define the law of the land, and decide what color they were, and who would rule, etc. It took the Chinese from, let's say, Hong Kong and the Opium Wars of 1842–43, and they didn't get going until the 1950s. The Japanese were intruded upon in 1851–53, and they took off in 1885. Why did the Japanese take off promptly and the Chinese have such a hard time? Why are the Africans having such a hard time?

One of the two best questions put to me on a trip around the world we took in 1983–84 was at a World Bank agricultural technicians' college in India. They had an African there. He stood up and said, "We black Africans obtained our independence in 1960. We still haven't taken off. What's wrong with your theory?" I laughed at a good question, and took him through the length of time people take for the preconditions. Africa is peculiarly difficult because they've been divided up by the map, not by tribe. It will take a long time before they work through the generations and eventually pull their countries together in growth. I don't think they'll take as long as the Chinese or the Mexicans, but it will take a few more generations before they square themselves away. I would have given more weight in *The Stages* to the difference in the length of time of the preconditions, the cultural and political problems people face. I do spend some time at the end of the *Theorists* book on this problem.

The World Bank and the IMF – to judge from their recent pronouncements – seem to think that they have a very mixed record of helping out in development. How sanguine are you that development assistance can be undertaken properly in the future? Can we learn lessons from what we have done well, and from what we have done badly?

I wouldn't dogmatically draw conclusions. The different parts of the world vary a great deal. It started off in East Asia. We did very well. We bought time for the Koreans to find their feet and to find a generation which really wanted to develop, and we found that generation in the 1960s. One of the two times that I spoke up as an agent of the President in opposition to cabinet level people was on Korea in 1961. I asked permission from the President to speak as a development economist rather than as an aide to the President. And I said that everyone – military, civilian – was predicting that at the end of the 1960s they'd be in as much trouble economically and politically as they were in 1961. They would not expand their exports. They wouldn't increase their GNP. There would be political turmoil. I said no, that's too pessimistic; it's a question of the generations. A new generation was coming to life, represented by Park and his people. They were going to do things. We see a very different South Korea today. The President came around to my side of the table afterwards and said quietly to me in his usual humorous style, "You were one of the only ones who predicted last year that I'd beat Nixon, so I'll take you seriously."

But it's interesting in Asia, because it started off well. The usual argument was that the Chinese are behind all of this ferment in Thailand, and the other Confucians, the Japanese, the Koreans are doing well. But now Malaysia has taken off. Now Indonesia's taken off, and India is far down the road. Bangalore is one of the great international centers for software, with satellite hook-ups to big companies in America and elsewhere. It isn't simply overseas Chinese, although they played a big part in this story. The Middle East is much more troubling. They've made a lot of progress in education and technology. It's partly the political problem posed by Israel, but it's not only that. You can see that in Iran and in Egypt, which don't really take the Israeli issue very seriously. They've had trouble finding their way into the modern world. I think the Egyptian case is baffling. They've had excessive birth rates. Yet anyone can go to the universities. They have overwhelming bureaucracies. And they stultify their own development. Turkey, on the other hand, has done well. So East Asia's a success; the Middle East has cultural problems they'll have to overcome; Africa will have to wait several generations; Latin America is finding its feet now. The middle-size and smaller countries worry me a lot, because they are not big enough to be a critical mass and to have an MIT. Brazil, Mexico, barely Argentina, are big enough to become part of the modern world, but for the others I think the technological issue will do better than trade in bringing them together. They're on their way. They're going to be somebody. In short, it's not helpful to generalize. One must look at each region. But on the whole, by an economic historian's standards, the late-comers have done well.

Now let's move back to the West. In discussing America's future you've

focused on the need to shift from an emphasis on zero-sum pie-sharing to cooperative growth promotion. How can we do that, given the expectations developed by decades of the welfare state, especially in Europe and Japan?

It's a serious problem. You see the 1950s and 1960s – and partly the economists are to blame for this: Swan, Tobin and Solow didn't understand the 1960s. They thought that the contemporary three times the average rate of growth since 1820 was permanent, when it was the product of a convergence of the factors I cited earlier, that neoclassical economists didn't take into account. That was when, with a certain *noblesse oblige*, governments piled up welfare state guarantees. In the long run, they will have to make accommodations. The welfare state has to be taken apart. Certain things can be guaranteed, like education. Education is a tremendous factor on the Continent and in the United States, but that involves, only in part, the welfare state. You've got to link the private sector and the education system to educate people for the new jobs in the modern high-tech world. You could bring the people up from the South, for example, from sharecropper farming to work on the assembly line for Ford or Chevrolet. And they could make that transition. You can't do that any longer. There are more chips in an automobile than there are in a computer and you need education. Education is sluggish because it hasn't been subjected to Japanese competition. We owe the Japanese a great deal. They've forced a revolution in administration in the United States. But the instruments of government have not been subjected to that kind of competition and they're still way out-of-date. That's one of the things we're fighting for in dealing with the urban problem. But one problem worries me.

One problem . . .?

Yes, it worries me more than any other: the fall in the birth rate in Japan and Russia and Germany. This means that these countries will hollow themselves out. Now improvement in medical science gives, in part, an out. We can extend the age of retirement from 60–65, which is arbitrary, to 75. These people can improve the workforce. We can improve the productivity of the workforce, as we're doing now in the United States. We also need to improve education. Eighty percent of the people in our public school system do not go to college for four years. They must be trained for the modern workforce. Higher productivity of labor will help solve the problem. But still I fear for the older industrial countries versus the younger industrial countries on demographic grounds. The Russians are terrified, for example, that the Chinese will take Siberia one day. That played a part in the revisions of foreign policy of Gorbachev. I worry a lot about people not being aware of the implications of the demographic revolution for the social security network we now have. Older people take a tremendous share of medical expenses. And the medical expenses will increase as the population ages. You're right to raise the social welfare gap. Because social welfare immediately comes under pressure, if you don't have a high rate of growth and people then are caught between cutting down on investment in infrastructure and cutting down on their allocations to social welfare. The social welfare system is wrong in that most of it goes to deal with remedial damage control. You want to get the causes of it, and our whole program addresses the causes – to prevent problems.

I think that somewhere along the line, there will be another surprising surge in the population growth rate of the kind there was after the Second World War till about 1960. But you asked me what worries me most: it's the demographic issue. The other thing that worries me is that we use APEC well, so that China and India don't repeat the German and French folly.

APEC?

The organization of Asian–Pacific Economic Cooperation. It was founded at the same time the Berlin Wall fell, but it surfaced in Seattle. That will be the instrument for making the Pacific Basin really peaceful. The twentieth century is a dreadful century. It's dominated by the First World War, the interwar bad period, then the Second World War and then the Cold War. We can't afford to have that happen again, given weapons of mass destruction. Therefore, I worry a lot about the twenty-first century. At the same time, it was the era of the end of colonialism, and of diffusion of technology to Asia, the Middle East, Africa in time, but Asia particularly. Asia and the United States will have to work this out. Let the Chinese come forward and join the collectivity and the Indians; let them remember that in the twentieth century we spent the bulk of our time beating the Germans and the Japanese and the Russians into some reasonable proportion to their real places in the society of nations. And that was a hell of a way to spend a century, and I don't want to see that happen again.

Is there any possibility that political problems might lead to reversal of "The Stages," so large portions of the world fall into war and revert to a traditional economy?

You can't say no and never. Look at Yugoslavia. But that will burn itself out in time, this phase of nationalism, and parts of the world will go on. But the Nations are quite right to hold a summit on unemployment. Europe worries me a great deal. Nationalism is rising in Europe and it's a new version of the interwar period. The central question is: how do we get that machine going? You don't want to blame it entirely on Reagan. From the mid-1970s on, the tendency to cut social welfare expenditures is worldwide, but it was also because of political pressure, a time of reduction in investment in infrastructure. This period of stagnation means you can't employ people who can work on the social infrastructure.

Would you like to sum up, or give advice to the younger generation?

The younger generation – I've given them all the advice that I want to give in expressing the hope I did at the beginning of *Theorists of Growth*.

STANLEY LEBERGOTT

Interviewed by
Fred Carstensen

Stanley Lebergott is Chester Hubbard Professor of Economics, Emeritus, at Wesleyan University in Middletown, Connecticut. He was born in Detroit, Michigan in 1918 and was educated at the University of Michigan (B.A., 1938; M.A., 1939). He taught at Wesleyan from 1963, following 20 years in the Federal Government, at the Department of Labor during the war years and at the Bureau of the Budget from 1948 to 1961, and a year as Visiting Professor at Stanford. He was President of the Economic History Association in 1984 and was honored with *Quantity and Quiddity: Essays in U. S. Economic History* (1987), a *Festschrift* edited by his colleague, Peter Kilby. The interview took place in Lebergott's office in June 1992, and was conducted by FRED CARSTENSEN of the University of Connecticut, who writes:

Sometimes we don't do the obvious thing until circumstance forces it on us; then we realize how much we have missed. I had circled Stan Lebergott for nearly three decades without having had much of a conversation with him before the interview. Some of my ancestors were involved with founding Wesleyan, and a forebear was an early president, but my brother and I were the first men (it was until recently, remember, a men's college) not to go there; if I had, Stan and I would have arrived together, and I would probably have been his student. I got closer when I went to Yale for graduate work, but Yale's global vision (*i.e.*, its insularity) somehow didn't include Middletown. And then after a decade, I returned to Connecticut, now to the north and east of Wesleyan. Though I am a bit of a seminar groupie, my trips to Cambridge, New Haven, and Manhattan didn't bring me together with Stan. So when I was asked to do this interview, I was delighted. It would give me the opportunity to do something very interesting and the excuse to open up a conversation with what – based on his public persona and those marvelous quotations with which he so often opens his chapters and articles – must be one of the most engaging of scholarly minds. Indeed. What a wonderful conversation. I got excited about economic history all over again.

Since his conversation with Carstensen, Stanley Lebergott has published *Pursuing Happiness: American Consumers in the Twentieth Century* (Princeton UP 1993) and the study mentioned in the interview, *Consumer Expenditures: New Measures and Old Motives* (1996). He still lives in Middletown.

Two of the questions you sent me focus on how I got involved in economic history and what I am engaged in. During my work in the government, the primary motivation for a whole variety of projects was one question: "What is par for the course?" The first major project that comes to mind was in the post-war division of the BLS [Bureau of Labor Statistics], which had heady ambitions. They were going to plan the labor market after the war. My first assignment – perfectly appropriate for someone fresh out of college – was to take all the programs lying around that proposed to get the economy out of the Depression. I was to assess what would be possible after the war. Lunatic, of course, but appropriate if you are in your 20s. I will never understand why Davenport, who was then in charge of operations in that division, wanted this. He came from the Harvard Business School and had dreams of a bureaucratic empire. So I spent about nine months writing a book summarizing all the programs, assessing all their virtues and limitations, and thinking about this issue. It was very instructive; I learned a lot. What the taxpayers got is another matter.

I then spent some time assessing schemes for chasing money around the economy, primitive anti-recessionary schemes, like time-dated currency. One scheme was supported by a guy of some importance in the agency, and two of us had great fun trying to tell how this proposal might fail to work as desired. This led me to learn more about statistics. We didn't make any friends because this was a superior officer, but we learned a lot. I think we stopped him from making much more trouble with his scheme. Then John Pierson, who had been a Yale assistant professor, became assistant division chief. He had a scheme for expanding consumption, so we put that in our net. At the end of it, it became clear that we didn't know a helluva lot about all this.

My next assignment turned out to be orthogonal to much of that. Chuck Stewart, my immediate superior, sensibly said, "Well, one of the things the Labor Department has got to deal with after the war is unemployment." Those were the days when everyone, except Woytinsky, knew there was going to be a great crash. Stalin's favorite economist, Varga, was writing that it was going to be the end of the world. Samuelson and Hagen published something for the NRPB (National Resources Planning Board) which said we were probably going to have massive unemployment after the war, and I was no less ignorant in a lead article in *Harper's* in 1945. So that was the central economic problem for the Labor Department. Chuck said, "We don't know how much unemployment there was in the Depression." We had conflicting estimates, including NICB's (National

Industrial Conference Board) negative employment, but didn't have "par for the course." What could we hope to return to? Our concern eventually became labeled "normal unemployment."

Does that mean the "natural rate," as some would have it?

Well, I don't believe in "normal unemployment," but there *is* an average or median historical unemployment. We didn't even have that, so I spent about nine months working on unemployment estimates for the Depression, and I continued thereafter on and off. When I got pretty well finished with those at the BLS, I was offered a job at the ILO (International Labor Organization). I continued to work on the estimates on my own. Then, for whatever reason, I decided that there was an antecedent period; the world didn't start in 1929 on Wall Street, so I pushed my estimates back to 1900. Much of our orientation, at least in the generation I came from, was the Depression. But, what came before the Depression? America, as a major economic leader with tremendous confidence, had no history behind it; the national accounts start in 1929. Not that there aren't data before it, but we didn't have anything that gave us a run. (For quite separate reasons, I am now running consumption back to 1900 in that gory 103-item detail the PC permits.) What did the period of earlier prosperity accomplish; what did it look like? That ought to be studied if we are trying to establish a reasonable policy goal.

Now, there was a related inquiry. The Joint Economic Committee asked me, Moe Abramovitz and Ray Goldsmith to testify, partly, I imagine, because Paul Douglas was on the committee. The JEC wasn't interested in writing history; they wanted to use history to get some sense of par for the course on mobility (my topic), growth (Abramovitz) and capital (Goldsmith). This goes to the second aspect of why we're interested in economic history. They wanted some sort of broad model of reality. What are the variables and the variances? I remember emphasizing that we had a sea-change with the GI Bill and federal subsidies to housing. When somebody has planted his crabgrass, he's going to want to hang around to see how it came out. Now that was partly a graphic illustration for them, but it was partly because we had just bought a house, and I was trying to grow grass in the damn Maryland clay. The Lord did not mean grass to be grown there, but I was trying. I remember Senator Sparkman laughing and taking it up for a couple minutes in the hearing. What the policy guys were asking for was a sense of a relevant model with its constituent variables, with a hunch as to the variance.

Somewhat earlier, while I was still at the Budget Bureau, my boss became the American representative to the UN contributions committee; they were trying to establish how much each nation should kick in to the UN. The League [of Nations] had used industrial production, which was not very helpful if you're talking about all those then new states in Africa. So we moved to national income; Simon [Kuznets] was the key adviser to that operation. During the late years of the war there was a lot of work over at the War Production Board on what was national income. Why were they interested in national income? Very simple. The military and Congress (representing the civilians) were struggling over the size of the pie. The first thing you have to do is make some statement as to what the size of the pie is.

I don't want to get us too far off base, but you've told an extraordinarily interesting tale about how a concern for intelligent policy means you must have some understanding of history, of what "par for the course" is. I'm curious: where do you think we stand now? Have policy makers become less or more aware of the importance of continuing that effort?

It's done both. Fortunately, young economic historians are filling in pieces that strike them as of intellectual interest. There is enough sheer intellectual curiosity among people who came out of the 1960s, and, like those of us who came out of the 1930s, they see acute problems in this society they think ought to be fixed. They want to inquire in ways that are relevant to that orientation. The new social history is motivated, as the Marxist historiography was, by "I'll show you what the bastards were really like." Fine. Look at what Marx dredged up, what he put together. You need a fire in your belly to move you through the archives and all the dull documents.

So I take it you agree with McCloskey's recommendation that we ought to pay more attention to the new social history.

They're working in the vineyard; anybody who is doing honest work in the vineyard, whatever his motivation, is someone from whom we can learn. I once read a Wisconsin editor named Pomeroy, who was a leading Copperhead, his autobiography; it was the most touching piece. Now Lincoln is the only person in American history that I think of as really special – John Adams is close – and there was Pomeroy saying, "Kill Lincoln." As historians, we want to know why was he taking that attitude. Original sin is just the starting point. Pomeroy, this impoverished kid from the Midwest, at the age of six or seven, walks – you know what walking in a Midwestern winter can mean – from farm to farm with a pail. He collects ashes from the farmers to supplement the family income. He shows up at one farm – apparently in a Methodist area – where the housewife looks at him and says, "Go away, you damned Presbyterian." Such differences burn into the soul and shape behavior. Mere money maximization is a long way from what is going on. I didn't feel I fully understood Pomeroy after that, but I felt I had a bit more comprehension about him. I've never had the altruism to figure out what motivated Joe McCarthy, or Richard Nixon, but they had reasons, obviously.

As historians, we have to look around at anybody who has a piece of information and a loud voice – or, like the new social historians, every one of them has done homework. Since they are young enough, much of it is honest work. They tracked sources; they made discoveries. Indeed, one of them showed a flyer from the Lowell Mills; just printed the flyer. All he was interested in was that hours were long and life was miserable. But there was a line in the flyer about vaccinations. I began to think about why the Lowell Mills took an interest in vaccinations. After a while it fitted into a piece I am writing. There it was. I wouldn't have had it without this social historian. Bright young people have bees in their bonnets. If you don't have a bee in your bonnet, you're not interested in anything. They give the field vitality; they give us an endless vision of understanding.

I guess I distracted you.

No, that was a couple of questions. There are only two other things on the model of reality. After summarizing all those recovery plans, and finding it was stimulating but very frustrating, I moved on to a more systematic look. Having recently labored through Tinbergen, I felt Tinbergen as well as Keynes was part of the new revelation – Tinbergen even more so. Obviously copying him, with some changes, I developed a small-scale econometric model to forecast national income. It appeared in the *AER* (1945b). I was very pleased; it was a big thing for me. I looked back a few years ago, and it seemed to me a sort of sensible model.

Many years later I got involved with the Brookings model. It was a group effort by very good people. Lawry Klein and Jim Duesenberry were co-directors of the project. Among others, we had Frank Fisher, Dale Jorgenson, Bob Eisner, Ed Kuh, Danny Suits. The model may have had 260+ behavioral equations, plus how many identities I hesitate to think. We had, I guess, three summer sessions of two weeks apiece. Boy, it was the fastest, hardest learning I've ever done; it was marvelous. When you have X offering his views about what determines the short rate, and Y immediately saying, "Hell, no, it's another" and everybody then piling in, you learn.

For all the proposals and programs, one asked "What variables count?" It's the whole quantitative emphasis that we economic historians live with, variables. Sherm Maisel said, "I can give you residential investment, if somebody develops a marriage model." (Vacancy rates are affected by marriages, of course.) Lawry asked me, "Why don't you do the marriage model, too?" So I did a marriage model, and I had to have Vietnam conscription and avoidance in it, as well as crossing status and caste and age lines. You clearly get into sociology's domain, but that was what made things go . . . Remember Charlie Wilson's wonderful book on Unilever? How do you understand that company if you don't understand these two crazy sets of people trying to work together, each with their own separate orientations? You've got to understand this firm. Talking about maximizing money income or present value doesn't explain it. So, when I had this pseudo-sociology in the marriage model (outside customary age lines for marriage and moving outside the customary groups), that was a revelation of what happens when you really try to model behavior. There are great opportunities to tackle what we don't now know, as long as it's only these two or three variables.

You remind me of the *caveats* of Adam Smith at the end of *Wealth of Nations* about the dangers of specialization – that doing really good scholarship means that you must not respect the putative barriers between fields.

Well, I don't remember that, but I agree you must not. I will add that we can only do so much. I am prepared to say, "That's sociology." I don't know of anything in our training that gives us any great competence for it, but I am not prepared to say that it's superficial. But someone like Gary Becker comes along, fine. Let's hope the next young guy or gal who comes along will be as good, or better.

Were you at Williamstown?

Yes. I was on the committee, perhaps because I had been in the Income Conference. It was a delight to meet Hal Williamson. Simon had surpassing virtues, is still a superb idol. But Hal had that grace. And, of course, he was a tremendous honest workman. The high point of that meeting was unquestionably the Conrad–Meyer piece. Their discussants could not accept the idea these guys would fit their simple model to a reality like slavery. Granted they were cocky, but if John Meyer didn't have the right to be cocky, then who does?

But I must add, about a year or so before I had been wandering through *Agricultural History* and came across an article by Robert Worthington Smith. Smith, bless his modest heart, was "just a historian." But he had laid out all the elements correctly. There they were. Same elements, not with the pizzazz, not with the clear understanding of the economic factors, and not with the heartiness of "Look what we've done, guys." But there it was. Now, had the profession, had the historians, the wit to take the article to heart, we would have had fewer forensic results over the next half century. Conrad and Meyer started with an observation that only economists would make and Smith did not – why is the ratio of male to female prices so different from the ratio of male to female hire rates? That is an absolutely critical question, of course. That isn't why there has been so much attention since; that's one reason why it is a superb article.

It's one of those things that screws up wealth, welfare-maximization . . .

It'll do it every time. Macroeconomists are all economic historians, but they do it on the cheap. If it's the last ten years, that's their history. The real difference between them and economic historians is we say there is a world longer than the last three recessions. In principle, I don't think they disagree, but they are still taking the last five or ten years.

The historians for a long while were far too respectful of cliometric history. I remember an article by Vann Woodward, that great gentleman. Apropos one of the real noisy presentations he said, in sort of a quiet way, this seems to be the wave of the future. Most good historians are very ambivalent about having an explicit model of anything; largely a fear of God, because they know in their guts there are too many variables, too many that are hard to observe. Wallerstein and whatnot can explain everything by throwing words around. But most historians are being cautious, leaning over backwards. Sometimes their humility turns to aggression, but, you know, they may not hate economists any more than others do.

You have a question here about "new directions." How has the attitude evolved in the past 30 years? I don't think the sparring has changed much. You can look at something like Bill Parker's conference volume (1986) with Arrow and Solow. Had you asked Arrow or Solow 30 years ago, they would have said the same thing, I think. These guys have such broad perspectives that you wouldn't have caught them being negative about the worst idiocies of what we did at Williamstown or at some of the cliometric sessions. They would not have said "this is immoral," the way poor Redlich did.

I want to push you a little on this. There are people, historians, traditional historians, who – I'm aware of this partly because I came into the field in the midst of questions about *Time on the Cross* – withdrew in some ways from taking economic history seriously because they felt cliometricians had an attitude that "we are going to come and help you."

Well, you have to parcel this out. I spent maybe 15 years in Washington at the Budget Bureau, working on income distribution and national income. In that time there was Simon Kuznets, a glorious, dedicated scholar. Now, Simon Kuznets was not the field of national income. He oriented the rest of us; he energized us; but he wasn't the field. *Time on the Cross* is not the field. That historians treated it as "the field," I can understand.

Remember that session in Rochester?[1] Robert Silber from *The New York Review of Books* called me up before it. He wanted to get a line on a silly rebuttal he had from a historian. I remember futilely trying to tell him, you don't have to agree with their work. I can tell you eight reasons why it is inadequate, but you have to understand what it does achieve before you can start cutting away. But I couldn't get through to him. If historians have pulled away because of the noise, so much the worse for them. Do you think the younger guys have done that?

My perspective is that history departments seem to have pulled away from economic history in particular, but also more broadly from social science. I have been struck – as during your comments on the new social history – by an absence of a clear conceptual framework. It's an attempt to do social science history without the social science. If you don't make clear what your framework is and what your assumptions are, you're not going to be able to make much real sense. Your example is perfect. I think it says a lot about an enterprise when they [Fogel & Engerman] have a line in there that says something about vaccinations. Now, you might want to argue the slave-owners just want to take advantage of you by keeping you healthy . . .

That's right. For an economist it is sort of "so what?" It depends on the terms of trade and what is involved. I once read a book where the author recreated Angers, a tiny

1 A conference, "*Time on the Cross*: A First Appraisal," sponsored by the Mathematical Social Sciences Board and the University of Rochester, October 24–26, 1974.

French city in the eighteenth century, lovingly dealing with it, a chapter on the church, on the markets. It was like one of those Japanese paper flowers that opens out in water. You don't understand the town, but you are overwhelmed, living for a while in that rich reality. That is an historian's great accomplishment. Economists can do other, good things; historians can benefit from all that but they shy away from an analytic structure. Too bad.

There has been a resurgence of interest in labor-historical issues, in the work of Margo, Sutch, and Goldin. A lot of this flows from exciting theoretical developments in labor economics, but it brings us back to what we think was the large role played by spot markets for labor in the 1850s or 1870s. Now we have a much different kind of labor market. What do you think is going on?

These are creative economists who are moving things forward. As for spot markets, I guess William Julius Wilson is one of the commanding figures in the field. But he doesn't seem to know much about spot markets. You can't allocate labor unless they all have automobiles – that seems to be one of his central assertions. But that's not so in economic history – in the 1940s in Washington at the head of Georgia Avenue, a spot market functioned every morning. Domestic servants appeared. They took the trolley car; friends gave them a lift; taxi drivers, because many were black, dropped them off there. The ladies from the suburbs would drive up and take them to clean in their homes. Or the construction boys would say I need three men; three men would climb on. The market was allocating. And they *were* spot markets. If you need more examples, go back to the rolling harvests across the Midwest, in the 1870s, 1880s, 1890s; who the hell had cars? The guys didn't even have horses. The people on the demand side picked them up, moved them to the locus of production and moved them back. This technical imperfection sounds like a kinked-demand curve, everything works except at one critical point. Well, is there a kink? This is where economic history comes in. You can say we've had millions of people who had no facilities for transportation who have been moved decade after decade in all sorts of conditions that were far more difficult than those for people in Chicago today. Either you really have to explain why it is not being done, or you have to give up that nifty little kink.

History is a discipline on economics.

History should be a discipline on every new policy choice. All countries experiment. It must have been decades ago, I heard [Maurice] Allais describe time-of-day pricing in the French electric system. It was marvelous. Of all places, in France. Maybe the ghost of Cournot was involved. For policy in Washington, or in Hartford, you want to understand what other people have done. And you have two choices: you've got history and time, and you've got space. Then you can discover how spot markets work.

Given the recent labor economics work, I would say we're going through some sort of cyclical process. The last ten years I've thought economic

history was more exciting, more interesting, because we'd gotten back to doing what the early cliometricians did, which is to get back to the archives and do the primary research. We had gone through a period when we were trying to use the technical power of economics to beat up on old data sets . . .

Not doing our homework.

We were trying to do our history on the cheap.

That's right. So data had been around already. "Now we'll take an interest in economic history, and we know economics. Therefore, all we have to do is pick a few observations, and we can solve the problems." You're right, there was and there is still some of that, of course. But Margo and the others, these are people who are going back and thinking. Last week, I finally picked up Thorold Rogers, *History of Agriculture and Prices*. This guy spent a life turning up data for the rest of us. Among other things, this is why we should always be respectful of the historians. Especially younger people, who learn by grubbing and learn by getting their hands dirty. How much is temperament and so on? These young people are doing it. They are using their drive to get the relevant data, in some cases to go to the archives. They then try to fit it into some kind of analytic model. It works. It's a marvelous combination.

That reminds me of the kind of energy you have given to empirical work. Like the recent work on the 1920s, or going back to early income survey data, which nobody had used because – I think – they had been intimidated by the size of the data sets. I've been gratified, maybe because economists when they get to work seriously aren't intimidated by looking at a 100,000 . . .

With computers, it's a different world.

I know Bob Fogel commented in his interview about this incredible productivity enhancement. You go in with a little laptop, and you can enter the data directly and go through enormous data sets and really construct a far more complex . . .

Far richer, far safer to work with. I remember when I was working at the Budget Bureau, I would go down on Saturdays because there was a hand-crank calculating machine. It was great because it didn't have the rounding problem that the slide-rule did. You know, I can't bear to throw away this beautiful . . . [SL pulls out a magnificent 24-inch slide-rule he keeps in his desk drawer.]

On a Saturday it took me virtually one whole day to run a regression with five explanatory variables. Worse still, to get five variables, I had to throw out 40 that I considered. When we first started on this consumption job, we were entering all the work sheets in pencil, so you could erase. You had to do the arithmetic twice to check what you had. Now, I can even check estimates for errors by regression – nearby states, nearby patterns, or a larger group. I'm not trying to analyze; I'm just trying to check. It's easy to pick up gross errors. Then there's the gray area where you say, "Maybe it's an error, but maybe it's the truth." In which case, I leave it in. The estimates may be bum, but I haven't fiddled with them.

Then someone else can figure out a better way to make the estimate.

Sure. The computer makes that editing possible. Of course, for 1900, my estimates, alas, differ from Dick Easterlin's.

Well, it's a whole new field for someone to sort out: resolving the Easterlin–Lebergott conundrum . . . On another matter, I was really struck by and enjoyed your article on why the South lost the Civil War, and your persuasive argument that it was because they weren't paying attention (1983; see also 1981).

Glad someone read it.

How did you get into it? It was a striking article and a little unexpected, in terms of its authorship.

As a depository library, Wesleyan has that marvelous serials set, thousands of wonderful volumes. A large hunk of that is called *The War of the Rebellion*. After surgery, I was at home and had several volumes around. Well, as you know, they can be thirteen hundred pages each, with an enormous amount of documentation. So, just turning over the pages, reading all these wonderful despatches one occasionally sees something. I came across long discussions about international law: What's an effective blockade? I began to wonder how much cotton was exported, what the blockade amounted to. Later, I went into the National Archives, got into that wonderful Confederate document collection, and began to piece out average tonnage. Then I came upon, I guess this was in the 1866 Report of the Secretary of the Navy, lists of all the vessels captured. And that wonderful piece by the glorious antiquarians on itemizing every ship that slipped through the blockade. When that was sort of put together, I began wondering what the hell did it mean? When I saw the orders of magnitude, I began to consider the opportunity cost. Why are they *growing* cotton? Eventually I came to Tyler's 1861 address to the Virginia legislature, "King Cotton will have the monopoly of the world."

I was struck by it too because, when asking about current policy implications, there is a lot of discussion now about G & A in the 1980s – greed and avarice – and the degree to which we undercut ourselves in the long term: investments in education; corporate strategy. The new book, *Merchants of Debt* (Anders 1992), asks how much damage the leveraged buyouts really did. It struck me as having some very powerful parallels . . . [SL turns around and reaches for his marvelous collection – hundreds of copied articles in loose leaf binders.]

Just read the little insert.

" 'It was an extraordinary thing to see our squires and poorer people split the bellies of those dead Saracens so that they might pick out the gold coins from their intestines, which they had swallowed down their horrible gullets while still alive.' Abbott Fulcher at the siege of Jerusalem." Where *do* you find these things? That is wonderful.

I would say that somebody in Wall Street M&A is pretty moderate compared to that. And he doesn't pretend to be carrying the Gospel.

Right! I admire your paying attention to interesting questions and pursuing them, which I think all of us ought to do . . . In closing, do you have any broad, sweeping insights that you want to share with the profession?

I am just optimistic about economic history.

Good.

There are three areas that would repay work. One is war. I mean, war as an overwhelming fact in human existence. Whether it is a small scale (like the headhunters in the Philippines) and it gets confounded by religion or values, or large scale (like World War II), there are enormous impacts on the economy, on supply, relative prices, production. I don't just mean nifty innovations. There is a great future for economic historians, young historians, looking at that. There are many wars, all over the world, all through time. Many of them have records. There are military historians. They must have miles of records just for the US. Charlie Schultze had a marvelous piece on the effect of El Niño on the price of anchovies, hence the price of grain, hence inflation under Carter. Well, if El Niño can do something like that, what about war?

Well, of course, the huge Soviet casualties fundamentally changed the structure of their labor market for two generations.

Sure. Number two is a real oddity. Consider a group of earnest, youngish economic historians setting to work. Then, imagine an area with an immense set of publications, pretty well indexed, of all kinds, in English. Would you be interested in studying that world? Well, *they* ain't. Why, I don't know. Scots history! [Bangs the desk.] Who developed the British Empire? A few Brits, including incompetent second sons. But the Scots were all over the British Empire. Who do we think of as the father of economics? And David Hume and Hutchinson, the real visions of the enlightenment. Our library has records for Edinburgh going back to the fifteenth century. So here you have a language, you have events, brilliant minds, aggressive entrepreneurs, not to mention the

Darien Company or clearing the highlands or the beginnings of modern industry. Robert Owen began in Scotland as a young guy. So I think Scots history is a natural because the stuff is there, it's in English, it's indexed, it's relevant to the development of the industrial revolution, and they have some of the most wonderful ballads.

That's a comment on welfare functions.

Yes, indeed. The third is the change in the public health in the last century in various countries. Preston and Haines have recently done something for the US, but I don't think we have any understanding of what brought about changes in mortality rates. For many of the countries, we have cause of death. Which means you don't have to talk vaguely about cleanliness, and rats, and cleaning up the Thames; you have particular causes. Granting problems with diagnosis, changing patterns of diagnostics, and all that, you have an enormous set of coherent, consistent data on major phenomena. When life expectation doubles, you get a major impact, not merely on welfare, but on all the economic processes. What is bringing this about? There's a great project!

Part II

BEFORE THE NEW ECONOMIC HISTORY

Great Britain

H. J. Habakkuk

Phyllis Deane

W. A. Cole

R. C. O. Matthews

In Britain the usual designation for the style of research on which this volume focuses is "quantitative economic history," reflecting a tradition of quantitative investigation extending back to the time of Gregory King and others in the seventeenth century. The four scholars whose interviews appear in this Part belong to that tradition, yet – aware of this continuity and entirely without declaration of revolutionary intent – they all were pioneers in melding a more systematic use of economic concepts and principles with historical quantification. None came from a Department of Economic History: Phyllis Deane and Robin Matthews were trained as economists; Hrothgar Habakkuk was an historian who had been exposed to the "high theory" of Cambridge economics in the 1930s; Max Cole's background was in intellectual and social history but after 1955 he was transformed into a quantitative economic historian. Their body of scholarship was produced largely at the ancient universities of Cambridge or Oxford, or both, and can be divided into two strands. One is the direct analysis and estimation of the quantitative dimensions of British economic development to be found in the work of Deane, Cole, and Matthews on growth, capital formation, prices, incomes and welfare. The other is the theoretically informed but less systematically quantitative approach to be found in the work of Habakkuk on population dynamics, technical change and industrialization.

The senior member of this group, H. J. Habakkuk, who became "Sir John" in 1976 when he was knighted for his services to education, was known throughout his life as Hrothgar to a wide circle of friends and colleagues. His studies at Cambridge in the 1930s produced his only works published before 1950, a venture into imperial history (1940a) and a paper on "English Landownership, 1680–1740" (1940b). The landownership paper is a classic, establishing a field of enquiry productive for many other scholars and to which Habakkuk returned after half a century in his *magnum opus, Marriage, Debt, and the Estates System: English Landownership, 1650–1950* (1994). Like his American counterparts of the same generation, Habakkuk was diverted from scholarship by being drawn into the war effort in a professional capacity as both historian and economist. In 1950, he was elected a youthful Chichele Professor of Economic History at Oxford, "largely on the basis of one published article" on landownership. He was already known for his "keen intellect" and was later to become "internationally acknowledged as one of the most incisive minds ever in the field of economic history." His work on population change and economic growth (1953, 1958, 1971b) was insightful, even prescient, but he gained trans-Atlantic fame with *American and British Technology in the Nineteenth Century* (1962), a carefully qualified and nuanced theoretical approach that sparked the continuing debate on the "Habakkuk hypothesis." In 1962–3 Habakkuk held a visiting professorship at The University of California, meeting the new breed of American cliometricians in full force both at Berkeley and at the third cliometrics conference at Purdue. He writes, ". . . it was only in 1963 when I met [Albert] Fishlow and Bob Fogel that I came into contact with econometric history and realized that my mixture of economic theory and casual empiricism was obsolete."[1] That realization, however, did not prevent Sir John from encouraging new and more quantitative work by the research students whose work he singles out in his interview.

The names of Phyllis Deane and W. A. (Max) Cole will always be linked because of their "congenial" partnership in writing *British Economic Growth, 1688–1959* (1962 [2nd edn, 1967]). Deane's early work contributed to developing national income (or social) accounting, a field then in its infancy. The first (1948a) of her two books on social accounting in several African and Caribbean colonies was based on records available in war-time London; the second book (1953) was based additionally on fieldwork in Central Africa in 1946–47, including writing and conducting her own surveys of village economies. To Deane this research was perhaps the ideal preparation for the task of assembling and interpreting the quantitative record of a "pre-industrial" and modernizing economy that appears in the Deane–Cole volume. It was certainly what drew her to the attention of Simon Kuznets, who was responsible for initiating her investigation. As Max Cole relates, he was drawn into the project fortuitously from his recently completed studies of seventeenth-century Quaker politics. Their ground-breaking joint work for the first time essayed to provide a "measured" and inclusive portrait of British economic development over several centuries. Deane and Cole took pains to inform their readers just how tentative and provisional some of their conclusions were; their early critics, in turn, took pains to point out defects of evidence or analysis; numerous scholars have since mounted frontal attacks on their work. Despite those revisions, the Deane–Cole "estimates continue to be important building-blocks in on-going research," as one of their most serious critics, Knick Harley, has written (2001). In this retrospective assessment of *British Economic Growth*, Harley concludes, "It is hard to think of greater praise for a book than to note that it stimulated research for over a generation and that it remains a fundamental source after nearly half a century."

During a further two decades of teaching at Cambridge, Phyllis Deane wrote a standard text, *The First Industrial Revolution* (1965), and moved to the history of economic thought with two additional books, *The Evolution of Economic Ideas* (CUP 1978) and *The State and the Economic System* (OUP 1989). After a period at Bristol, Max Cole went to Swansea to establish a new degree program as founding Professor of Economic History. In the 1970s, both contributed to expansion of the quantitative approach in Britain, for example at the Second Anglo-American Conference on New Economic History at Cambridge (England) in 1972, by reconsidering elements of *British Economic Growth.* Deane discussed capital and industrialization (1973) and Cole revisited British growth

1 Quotations from Nick von Tunzelmann's obituary notice (2003) and from a narrative *curriculum vitae* written by Sir John after 1994 and kindly supplied to us by his daughter, Ms. Alison Hoddell.

in the eighteenth century (1973). Cole also contributed the chapter on "Factors in demand 1700–1780" to the "new" economic history of Britain edited by Floud and McCloskey (1981).

By inclination and his intellectual–political environment, Robin Matthews was drawn for most of his career into theoretical and policy-oriented economics, but much of this work was colored by his background in economic history. The "quantitative–historical" approach of *A Study in Trade-Cycle History* (1954b) was inspired by the novel mix of history and theory he heard in Walt Rostow's Oxford lectures of 1947 and by his teacher J. R. Hicks's theoretical analysis. When Matthews later turned from economic fluctuations to economic growth in his work with Charles Feinstein and John Odling-Smee, *British Economic Growth, 1856–1973* (1982), he and his co-authors adopted the "quantitative–historical" style, continuing to apply theory (but not *a* theory) to the historical record. In a conversation with George Feiwel about the role of economic theory some 20 years ago he observed, "I think there are two things about being an economic historian: one is that you see matters as continually evolving from one thing to the next, so that you are not particularly interested in concepts of stationary equilibrium. Quite separate from that, however, you become a little bit suspicious of general models" (1987: 614–5). The "unconventional" papers he wrote in the 1980s and early 1990s, mentioned briefly in the interview, reflect a restiveness with the limited orbit of standard economics, a response not uncommon among scholars with the economic historian's temperament, as other interviewees reveal. In particular, regarding his work with Feinstein and Odling-Smee, Robin Matthews comments (in Blaug, ed. 1999: 746), "I came to feel that straightforward economic analysis, applied in conjunction with careful and wide-ranging scrutiny of the statistical and other evidence, is capable of explaining a great deal about the course of economic change . . ." Their volume was the British element of a larger project of international comparisons proposed by Simon Kuznets and Moses Abramovitz; Matthews, on the evidence of only partial completion of the project and the delayed appearance of his own contribution, says the project as a whole was probably a "mistake." If, however, multiple citations in the journals and recurrent references in volume II of *The Cambridge Economic History of Modern Britain* (Floud & Johnson, eds 2004) are anything to go by, we can argue that Matthews's assessment of his book tends to undue modesty about what has proven to be an important work.

As the cliometrics revolution was taking hold in North America, these four British scholars made judicious (and in some cases tentative) applications of economic theory to the quantitative record, contributing to the advance of economic history and historical economics, even if cliometrics is not the apposite term. As their works demonstrate, scholarship that builds upon and remodels an existing edifice, that investigates new sources, offers new interpretations and corrects for each other's errors, and that inspires colleagues and students to extend the investigation, is scholarship that truly contributes to progress in understanding historical change. It has transformed British economic history and paved the way for those in the next generation for whom cliometrician is an apt description.

H. J. HABAKKUK

Interviewed by
Mark Thomas

Hrothgar John (Sir John) Habakkuk was Distinguished Fellow of All Souls College, Oxford. He was born in Barry, Glamorgan in 1915 and died in Somerset in 2002. The interviewer was Mark Thomas of the University of Virginia, whose B.A. degree was conferred officially by Habakkuk himself, but who did not get to know Sir John well until this interview, which took place in Habakkuk's study at All Souls, July 4, 1997. Mark Thomas writes:

Sir John Habakkuk was one of the most important figures of the past century in economic history in Britain, and had a major influence not only through his own work but also via his training of many graduate students. He took first-class honours in Modern History at Cambridge in 1936 and was elected to a Fellowship at Pembroke College, Cambridge in 1938. During World War II, Habakkuk was seconded to the Civil Service, serving first in the (then secret) code-breaking operation at Bletchley Park, in the Ministry of War Transport (official historian) and finally in the Commercial Relations and Treaties Department of the Board of Trade. He returned to Cambridge in 1946, taking on additional responsibilities as University Lecturer in Economics. In 1950 he was elected Fellow of All Souls and Chichele Professor in Economic History at Oxford. He spent two academic years in the US; in 1954–55 he replaced Alexander Gerschenkron at Harvard but declined an invitation to join the faculty permanently, and in 1962–63 he was Ford Research Professor at Berkeley. He vacated the Chichele Professorship in 1967 when he was elected Principal of Jesus College, Oxford, a position he retained until his retirement in 1984. Professor Habakkuk also served as Vice Chancellor of Oxford during the difficult years of 1973–7, and was President of University College, Swansea (1975–84). He received his Knighthood in 1976 and was elected Fellow of the British Academy (1965) and Foreign Member of both the American Philosophical Society (1966) and the American Academy of Arts and Sciences (1969). Among his many contributions to the profession were his co-editorship with M. M. Postan of *The Economic History Review* (1950–60), and his Presidency of the Royal Historical Society (1976–80). He also served with Postan as a general editor of the *Cambridge Economic History of Europe*. In 1994 Professor Habakkuk was honored with a splendid *Festschrift* edited by F. M. L. Thompson, *Landowners, Capitalists, and Entrepreneurs*.

Let me start by asking you about your background and how it influenced your intellectual development.

Coming from South Wales turns one to social and economic rather than political history because Wales is not a state, it doesn't have a central government, it doesn't have a central government policy. It was an area of very rapid economic and social change and these become objects of study and curiosity. I was born in South Wales in 1915, in a town [Barry] which hadn't existed 30 years earlier. It was just a collection of small villages and was then developed as a dock by the great entrepreneur, David Davies, to export coal from the South Welsh valleys. This was an extraordinary economic phenomenon and stimulated one's curiosity about how such things happen. And the school I went to was one which aroused one's intellectual curiosity. I read some economics at school and in the Sixth Form I was given Usher's *Industrial History of England* (Houghton, Mifflin 1920), which was then very *avant garde*, and which I still think is rather a splendid book. And I also read sections of Adam Smith, including Book Three, "Of the Progress of Opulence in different Nations," which is economic history of a sort.

Where were you an undergraduate?

I went up to Cambridge in 1933 to read history.

Did economic history have much impact on the syllabus at Cambridge?

I think quite a marked impact. When the History Tripos was invented, they were very anxious it shouldn't become a soft option and so great emphasis was laid on the study of structure. Great emphasis was laid on constitutional history and economic history, and in the first year there was a general paper in economic history and I attended Clapham's lectures on the subject. But my main interests as an undergraduate were not in economic history, they were in medieval European history – largely because it was all fresh to me.

And what led you to move from medieval to economic history?

Accident. There were very few research students in my day. You could hardly take a topic which didn't appear promising and if one had a truant disposition and a number of intellectual interests, one started on a large number of topics. My first research subject was the influence of Dutch theologians on political thought in the seventeenth century and I remember going in 1935 to see G. N. Clark who was then, curiously enough, Professor of Economic History at Oxford – he gave me introductions to a large number of Dutch theologians. I moved from that into William Paley because Harold Laski thought it would be an interesting subject; he also suggested Arthur Young and I dabbled in Arthur Young. And Clapham suggested to me that really I ought to write the history of the Industrial Revolution in South Wales, and I very much regret I didn't take his suggestion. I was at that time, I suspect, rather anxious to get away from South Wales. It was Postan who suggested that I should do eighteenth-century landowners. I think he had just come back from looking at the archives in Northamptonshire and was very much impressed by their abundance. And I was very anxious to have a subject which wouldn't run out because of lack of sources. So I decided to do Northamptonshire and added Bedfordshire for safety. So my transition to economic history was very circuitous, with a lot of accidental twists and turns.

What was it like being a research student in the 1930s? Were you closely supervised, or allowed a free run of the subject?

I think by modern standards it was all very casual. I was never registered for a doctorate; very few people in my situation were. I was loosely assigned to John Clapham, and I used to go along to him once a fortnight. He used to sit at his desk opening his correspondence and I would talk and he would comment, and comment very shrewdly. Land ownership wasn't his subject, but he found a lot of interesting things to say about it and he gave me good advice. He recommended taking a single family, doing it thoroughly and surrounding it with a penumbra of suggestions – another of his ideas which I wish I had acted on. He didn't profess to guide me to the sources on land ownership and he knew very little about the legal arrangements of the landowners, in which I became rapidly submerged. But he was a great man and I think that, in so far as I was sustained in research, it was by his example and his general personality and character, and by the fact that each fortnight he was very interested in what I said.

How were you influenced by having Clapham as a supervisor?

Clapham liked talking about problems. He liked historical anecdotes. He was a wonderful lecturer because, although there was no general scheme and a complete absence of analysis, there were some wonderful vignettes. So, at his lectures on England before 1066, you felt as though you were living in an Anglo-Saxon village. And he was as good on the Middle Ages as on the nineteenth century. And he brought nineteenth-century industrialists to life. He knew an enormous amount about them and it all flowed out. Why he wasn't interested in theoretical systematic explanation, I don't know. I think it was partly a judgement that this was what the subject needed at the time. It needed a large number of raw facts, not linked to any theory at all, just raw material. But I think that Usher's criticism of him was justified. He ought to have made more attempt to pull the bits together. But then again, his output was enormous and the range was enormous. He wrote from the horsing of the Danes to the current history of the Bank of

England. And I think that he wouldn't have done it if he had been interested in analysis.

You published your first article on land ownership in 1940, and you are still pursuing issues in this area almost 60 years later. How have you maintained your interest and enthusiasm for so long?

Because of a liking for the English countryside – and vested academic interest. I have deserted the field at various times and in one period, immediately after the war, thought I was going to desert it forever. In 1939 I was asked by my old tutor, who was editing the *Cambridge History of the Empire*, to write a chapter on the economic history of Empire from 1853 to 1870 as a matter of urgency because the original contributor of the chapter had let them down. I think it is an indication of the extraordinarily casual and unprofessional nature of the research community before the war that someone who was deeply immersed in family settlements in the eighteenth century could be expected to turn aside and apply himself to a different period and a very different set of problems and with, even then, a very considerable set of literature. So I worked like hell for a year and eventually produced the chapter, which was published in 1940. And that gave me an interest in nineteenth-century history and in the sort of history which contemporary economists wrote. And then during the war I was for some years in the Board of Trade, immersed in economic questions, which raised a lot of sticky points and interests which diverted my research into more recent periods and into more strictly economic subjects.

One of your wartime duties put you in contact with Keynes, did it not?

Yes. I was one of the Secretariat at the talks on post-war financial reconstruction, which I suppose took place in the early part of 1943, before Bretton Woods. The talks were attended by delegations from the Commonwealth countries and they discussed Keynes's plan for an IMF – as well as plans for an International Trade Organization and the plans for international commodity agreements. I suppose they lasted about four months. Keynes was one of the dominating figures in the discussions and much the most magical of the protagonists. But the talks brought me into contact with someone who had much more influence over me – Dennis Robertson, an economist with very strong historical interests, whose first book had been on industrial fluctuations, and I suspect my later interest in the trade cycle of the nineteenth century arose in part from knowing him and getting to read his book.

Did this experience alter your approach to economic history?

I think so. I think that those three or four months, in which I listened to Keynes, Robbins and Robertson and T. E. Gregory and [James] Meade and Hubert Henderson and a splendid Canadian economic historian, W. A. MacIntosh, were very influential. They were discussing in a sense an episode of history – their discussion of the plans for the post-war was overshadowed by their ideas about pre-war problems – all the plans were revised to prevent a repetition of the 1930s. That made one analyse the 1930s in a quite different way. I think it was a crucial episode for me. When I went back to Cambridge in 1946 and had rapidly to prepare lectures for second-year economists, what was meant to be a general course on world economic history since 1750 became two terms of comparative study of industrialization followed by a third term on international and economic relations since 1850, using economic theory throughout, however primitive. And, of course, one mixed with economists. I spent the summer of 1947 on a working party of dons who were ex-civil servants giving advice on what attitude the British Government should adopt to moves towards a European Customs Union. There was very strong pressure from the Americans as part of the Marshall Aid package, and the Treasury and the Board of Trade appointed the group of us who used to meet at frequent intervals. That was another immensely formative episode.

You mentioned your interest in the nineteenth-century trade cycle earlier. Later, you had a student, a very famous student, work on the topic, did you not?

Yes. Well, when I came to Oxford, I set such pupils as were amenable to suggestions, and some who were not, on two fields. One was trade cycles. I set someone onto the 1820s. W. A. Sinclair, the Australian economic historian, was set onto the period after 1886 and the recovery from that. John Wright [Trinity College, Oxford] did a later nineteenth century cycle, and J. R. T. Hughes did the 1850s. I think the argument was partly that there was a body of theory, partly that it at least provided safe subjects. That is to say they were limited in time and limited in sources and if you worked hard, you finished your thesis. Jonathan Hughes worked harder than anyone I have ever met and he finished it in two years – a very remarkable achievement. The other set of research topics I thought were suitable, again for a similar reason, was English industry – so Roderick Floud did the machine tool industry and Ian Byatt, the electrical industry. And again, the reasoning was that no-one had done these industries, they were relatively well defined and an industrious student couldn't fail to finish.

Do you feel that those dissertation topics were perhaps a little restrictive in terms of the possibilities for ingenuity and inference that they allowed?

Jonathan Hughes was very kind and said that that piece of detailed work occurred at the right time in his career. But looking back it was absurd to set a man of his range into such a Procrustean bed. But I think as a first piece of research, the cycle is a useful field to work in. It gives you some of the tools of the trade. It gives you some sense of the complexity of the interconnections between the various sectors of the economy.

You have had strong connections with the US and American academics. When did that begin?

My first visit to the United States was in 1952. I went as a member of a committee set up to examine the retention and choice of records for permanent preservation, and

I went with a man called Paul Chambers, who eventually became Chairman of ICI, to the States to see how they did it. So I saw a lot of records but not much of American academics. My first academic visit was in 1954–5, when I took Alexander Gerschenkron's place at Harvard for the year. I was then at Berkeley in 1962–3.

You must have noticed a difference in the academic dialogue between those visits!

The difference between the two was enormous. When I went to Harvard, the seminar was enormously stimulating. There was Henry Rosovsky. I suppose he was then a young research student. There was Goran Ohlin. There was Alfred Conrad, who sometimes used to come, and, of course, John Meyer. Then there were a number of people from the entrepreneurial research centre – Hugh Aitken and, of the older generation, Arthur Cole. But I think there was nothing either in the theory or in the statistics in the seminar which I felt was beyond me. The most advanced statistics I remember being used were by Goran Ohlin, who did a thesis on population in the eighteenth century. Now he did employ what I think were very sophisticated statistical methods but I don't remember statistical methods being applied to other problems. I knew Conrad quite well, I was a good friend of his, I think we talked poetry![1] Now when I went to Berkeley, I was taken to a conference of cliometricians – I don't remember where. And I saw a great deal of Fishlow in Berkeley, and I remember thinking that he was a different sort of historian. I did sense an enormous divergence between what many of the Americans historians were doing and what I did.

Did you come into contact with Fogel at all?

I think I must have done because I've been looking at my papers, and Fogel used to send me the early editions of some of his papers. And when I had a New Zealand research student who had been well equipped in statistical methods [Gary Hawke], I did explicitly put him onto Fogel's problem in relation to British railways, which was very rewarding.

Coming from Cambridge, what struck you most forcibly about this new breed of economic historian?

Looking back, before 1939, there were people who did the statistics of national production – stocks and things like that. I had a colleague in Cambridge who was a close friend of mine, J. W. F. Rowe, who in the 1920s was doing national production figures. But I never remember thinking that what he was doing had any relevance to what I was doing. There was a curious hiatus between the statisticians and the theorists and between the theorists and the historians. I think it is partly a matter of the English intellectual tradition – the tradition is that you do things on your own, that you're a handyman; particularly if you're an historian, you're a craftsman. You write a carefully

1 Conrad was married to the poet Adrienne Rich.

crafted book and it's yours. It's partly, I think, a matter of the production of statisticians, and I suspect they were more abundant in the United States than they were here. So there wasn't the spill-over into other subjects. It's also partly that economic history, more often than not, was not in economics departments. It is partly that the background to the development of the subject in England owes much to German legal studies and the German historical economists. [Alfred] Marshall set off a great tradition of applying theory to actual situations. But if you look at his history, there is very little theory in it. Indeed, in some senses he was *avant garde*. When I read Temin's presidential address (1997b) in the *Journal of Economic History* on culture, I immediately thought of Marshall. When Marshall wants to explain the recovery from the depression of 1873, he does it in terms of national character and the distinguishing ability of Englishmen to rise to the occasion – no nonsense about interest rates and production functions. So he believed in the influence of culture. And Clapham, who helped Marshall with his historical chapters, although a Professor of Economics, ostentatiously eschewed theoretical speculation. I once acquired a volume of Clapham's. It is Cassel's *The Nature and Necessity of Interest*, and it is full of underlinings and little notes in the margin and he was obviously fascinated by this highly theoretical subject. Nothing at all of this appears in his works. He wrote the classic article on "Empty Economic Boxes," which foreshadowed Joan Robinson and imperfect competition, but none of it is in his history.

But you did get interested in the interplay between economic theorizing and historical change. How did you get interested in the themes of American and British technology?

The accident was knowing a German refugee called Erwin Rothbarth who had been trained at the LSE and was evacuated with the LSE to Cambridge in 1939. We were introduced by an old college friend, and he was a highly intelligent, highly analytical person with a passion for history and a passion for speculating and I would provide facts and he would tell me what they meant. A sort of *histoire raisonée*. We would have talks about the Black Death and its effect on the ratio of the population to the land, and he would develop theories and he would ask me if these were plausible hypotheses. Among the things we discussed was the ratio of land to labour in America. And he published a paper on this, although posthumously. Now Rothbarth was a very brilliant man and a very admirable man, too. He helped Pigou and Keynes with their statistics but then volunteered for the armed services – I think on the grounds that he had a special obligation as a German and a Jew to do so. He was killed at Arnhem [actually, near Venray] – a great tragedy because he really was extraordinarily clever and a very nice person. He laid a lot of seeds, intellectual seeds, and when I came back after the war and had to do lectures on comparative industrialization, the four lectures on America were grouped around the ideas of labour scarcity. I developed the ideas further at Harvard, where I met a lot of economists so that, when I was asked to lecture at Columbia in 1958, this topic seemed the most appropriate. Labour scarcity hadn't figured very largely in my lectures in 1946, but by 1958 they were a major preoccupation. So, I spent a semester at Columbia, developing the ideas into formal lectures. They were published as the book in 1962.

That book unleashed what has been one of the longest-running intellectual debates in economic history. It has been going for 35 years, and there are still people thinking about it and discussing it. What's your reaction to this longevity?

Well, I kept up with the literature on labour scarcity after a fashion until 1978, and I delivered some lectures at Princeton, the Jane Lectures, which were revised thoughts, which have never been published because after that I was overwhelmed. I supposed that if culture as an explanation really takes over, I shall end up by thinking that it is all due to the fact that the Americans were democrats, egalitarians, enterprising people living in an enterprising culture. We needn't go further than that!

You're not an adherent of the idea that culture was shaped by labour scarcity and factor availability!

Oh, I am. I am just overwhelmed by recent evidence to the contrary. At least recent evidence by historians I respect, who have taken a different view.

The technology book was in some ways a major departure for you. Indeed, I suspect that a reason that the labour scarcity debate has had such stamina is because it raises some important theoretical questions, rather than just being limited to historical issues.

Yes. I think there were some terrible muddles there. I realized that when I first read Peter Temin's first critique (1966a). And there obviously was a body of theory which was considerably more complicated than I had supposed. And I think if I were to do the subject justice, I would have had to devote the rest of my life to it, which I didn't really want to do! Indeed, in the end, I decided not to publish the Princeton lectures because there was so much literature appearing. Partly I wasn't really competent to assess it, and partly it went against the grain and the prejudices of an historian. I think that an historian never loses the sense of the individual and the circumstance, and generalizes over large categories with a great deal of diffidence. I find I quite like doing parochial work – the enclosure movement in Little Biggleswade – and I quite enjoy large speculations of the kind which started off with labour scarcity. What I am disconcerted by is the middle ground which involves the hard work, when you take a body of evidence and apply a theory and use the theory to get from the known to the unknown. And that seems to me to involve so many assumptions on the way that it is difficult to take any other person's work without going through the pain and labour of the whole procedure, and it is difficult to do it oneself unless one has a firmer grasp of econometrics than I have. So it is partly a lack of technical training, and it is partly a certain emotional resistance to the emphasis on system, which I think is involved in most forms of cliometrics in the strict sense. I think that the mere presentation of statistics, like the article on the first 2,000 steamships, doesn't really count as cliometrics, although I suspect that it was in relation to that exercise that the word was devised (Hughes & Reiter 1958). Now that seems to me something one could do without any interest in theory, just an interest in quantitative history. But I think that is quite different from the exercises in American slavery, which do involve a simplified version of economic theory and data, known data, to get to the unknowns and which interpret the links by reference to the theoretical model. That is something which I think doesn't come easy to an historian and wouldn't come easy to an historian even if he were a better master of the tricks of the trade than I am. But until 1978 I did try to be. And I do find Fogel and Engerman enormously fruitful, partly because the prose is lucid, even though some of the calculations are beyond me and also because they do throw out problems. And also because they make one realize the extent to which when one writes qualitatively, one is implying quantitative estimates which one couldn't in fact defend.

More recently, you have returned, as it were, to your academic starting point – the land. Would you tell us about your current work?

I have finished landowners for the moment. I am interested in the rate of interest and the price of land in the Middle Ages. This is a subject which I was interested in as an undergraduate, after a fashion, and I have taken it up again. I think it is the sort of subject where a person with my rather primitive theoretical apparatus can ask questions which a well-trained medieval historian wouldn't necessarily ask but which would be commonplace to any student of asset markets at any later period. And the hope is to say something which is interesting in new ways and which will raise new problems, which will enable people to interpret evidence in a different way.

And is there is one particular overriding problem which you have been trying to straighten out?

Yes. What set off the problem was what set off my problem in 1935 – that land was valued at ten years' purchase in 13th-century England and 20 years' purchase by the mid-15th century. And one might suppose that so marked a change in the valuation of the major asset must have deep causes and possibly deep consequences. Or at any rate, that an attempt to explain why it happened would shed interesting light on the main economic variables. This is a major change, and I hope to compare it with similar transactions on the Continent. There was a very large body of literature produced by the German historical economists and by the German historical lawyers in the 1880s and 1890s on the return on the sale of rent charges. They were interested in the problems of usury in the canonist doctrine and they were not interested in the economics of it, but the raw material lends itself to asking economic questions.

You have not yet reached a resolution to this particular paradox?

I have, but it is so complicated that it is not suitable for verbal explanation!

Let me ask about your 1994 study of land ownership. Am I right in thinking that you consider this your *magnum opus*, the most important of your books?

Yes, most certainly.

Would you like to explain what you think its significance is?

No, I'd like to defend it! My candid friends say, why the hell are there so many examples and why are there so few statistical tables? And this is a charge I can't rebut. The formal defence is that landed families differ enormously in their history. And it takes a great deal of time to get the history of even one family – its financial history, its legal history, its demographic history – straight. When you have studied a number of families in detail, you get hunches. It's a process of subconscious inference. You get a hunch as to how things happen. You don't feel that you know enough about a sufficiently large number of families to use them as units in a table, so the writing becomes essentially descriptive, with illustration. And I don't think it is possible at this stage to do anything else. But it must be said that my choice of evidence is partly dictated by a dislike of statistical tables. There is information available about land ownership in the eighteenth century which does lend itself to statistical tables. There is all the land tax evidence. And I did look at land tax evidence when I started in the 1930s. That can be put into tabular form and deductions drawn and indeed a splendid Canadian historian, [Donald] Ginter, has done just that. He has produced an enormous work. And he has done it no doubt partly because he had research assistance in the way someone working in England, certainly before 1940, would not have. But partly also because he is not deterred by statistical tables. I went and looked at the archives of the individual family rather than the aggregate statistics and that is partly a matter of my training as an historian, but it is partly a cultural matter.

Particularism of this sort surely doesn't preclude your coming to general conclusions.

Oh, no, I've drawn general conclusions. What it does preclude is a really satisfactory demonstration that they are the right conclusions. This is not merely a matter of historical training. It is true of English economics and particularly of Cambridge economics in the period when it influenced me. The most influential economists were not interested in large-scale empirical research on the National Bureau model. And allegedly Keynes was not sympathetic to Tinbergen's econometric work. They concerned themselves with a relatively limited range of established facts, and devoted a considerable amount of intellectual effort to discovering and analysing why on this basis the system worked as it did. The intellectual habits which my Labour Scarcity essays betray are much more those of Cambridge economics than they are of Cambridge history.

The Cambridge applied tradition has always been more macroeconomic rather than microeconomic and I suppose that the cliometrics revolution when it began was essentially microeconomic rather than macroeconomic in orientation, though it did later change. You earlier mentioned Dennis Robertson's study on industrial fluctuations, and that was a fairly broad piece of applied work and so, too, was Pigou's book on industrial

fluctuations. So there is a case that some Cambridge economists were prepared to take a broader brush, but once again from a macroeconomic or trade-cycle perspective, rather than a microeconomic.

And also there is an absence of the formal statement of propositions and then the statistical proof of their truth. Robertson's book is enormously detailed and extremely useful to an historian. But the conclusions are suggested by theory rather than formally demonstrated. His methods of argument were literary and qualitative, not theoretical and quantitative.

So this aspect of the "new economic history" was not especially new to you?

No, I think that what is new is not the use of statistics and not even the use of theory. I think the real intellectual revolution was this association of very high-powered models being used to deduce the unknown from the known, or to measure the unknown, and I don't know what the origin of this is. But these ideas are certainly the main change in my lifetime. And I was 50 when it really hit me and it hit me too late to do anything about it.

Ah, now that raises an interesting question. If you had been born 25 years later, do you think that your career might have unfolded differently?

No, because I think that three years doing history at Cambridge shapes one so. Even when Postan, who was a great systematizer and enormously stimulating, was lecturing, the approach was fundamentally narrative – in terms of the development of institutions or of constitutional change, or in terms of political episodes. And that does produce an emotional reluctance to exert the effort necessary to acquire the tools to do cliometrics in the Fogel–Engerman tradition, or even to understand them fully. My impression is that I followed the cliometricians reasonably well for the first ten years and then lacked the appetite and the capacity to continue. I certainly recognized while reading them that they had altered the world, dramatically. And they had the enormous advantage in having as their sort of leader, Fogel, who writes in a very attractive way and does his best to be intelligible to people like myself who don't practice, and manages to reach out. Just look at *Time on the Cross* – the enormous impact this had on general American history.

I think, too, that my choice of original research subject confirmed my disabilities because it is not a subject which lends itself very easily to models based upon rational choice and because it is bound up with social prestige. It's hard to escape the conclusion that land is the most uneconomic of all commodities, at least when it is in the hands of an aristocracy. So it is the furthest removed from rational calculation. If I had gone to do banking, I think I might have felt differently. At the end of 1938 I applied for a Henry Fellowship to go to Harvard to study railways. My instinct was right and the project was killed by John Clapham, who being a very honest man said, "I am one of the electors, I am not going to support you. I think that this is infirmity of purpose. I think you ought to sit in one place and finish your work on Northampton landowners. That is what you were elected to do and it is what you ought to do." And, of course, he was perfectly right. It was frivolous of me. But it was the right instinct. And my thinking would no doubt have been very different today if it had happened. But there it is.

Indeed.

PHYLLIS DEANE

Interviewed by
Nicholas F. R. Crafts

Phyllis Mary Deane is Professor Emerita of Economic History in the University of Cambridge. She was born in 1918 in Hong Kong and was educated at the University of Glasgow (M.A. 1940). She served as Research Officer in The National Institute of Economic and Social Research (1941–5), and in the UK Colonial Office (1947–9). She has resided in Cambridge since 1950, when she joined the University's Department of Applied Economics as Senior Research Officer (1950–61); from 1961 until her retirement in 1983 she was a member of the Cambridge Faculty of Economics as Lecturer, Reader, and Professor of Economic History. She went to North America as a Visiting Fellow at Johns Hopkins University (1956), and as Visiting Professor at the University of Pittsburgh (1969) and at Queen's University, Ontario (1975). She was editor of *The Economic Journal* (1969–75), President of the Royal Economic Society (1980–2) and was elected Fellow of the British Academy in 1980. Her biographical study, *The Life and Times of J. Neville Keynes*, discussed in the interview, was published in 2001. The interview was commissioned by the Institute of Historical Research, University of London, as one of their video-taped series, "Conversations with Historians" and was transcribed for publication in the *Newsletter*. The interview was conducted in Cambridge in the Spring of 1993 by Nicholas Crafts, then of the London School of Economics.

Before we talk about your scholarly work, I think it might be useful to find out how you started out in life and consider the period before you went into academic research. I believe that you spent a nomadic childhood, ending up in Scotland.

Yes. My father was an employee of the Admiralty and his job took him to Glasgow just at the point at which I could spend the last two years of my schooling at Glasgow, and that put a bit of discipline into my education. From there I went to the university. I originally intended just to study history, but it was a four-year course starting with a fairly wide first year, and my horizons were opened up to economics. I decided to do a degree in what was called Economic Science and was actually a mixture of political economy and history.

You became more of an economist than a historian?

I did, as it happens. I think I was influenced greatly by the economics teachers. I certainly had some very good history teachers. I can remember G. O. Sales as a rather splendid lecturer whom I always tried to emulate when I got onto the rostrum. I was also taught by William Robert Scott, who of course was not only an economist but a historian, author of a famous three-volume textbook on joint stock companies at the beginning of the eighteenth century, and also by Alec Cairncross, who then was very young and fresh from Cambridge with *The General Theory* clutched in his hand, which he introduced to us at a fairly early stage. This was in 1938–39. My interest was stimulated by this, and so I did more economics and economic history, although there was a steady stream of political and constitutional history in the course.

So there was a strong influence of the new Keynesian economics?

Indeed, yes.

Was your degree more theoretical or institutional?

It was fairly theoretical. Not greatly institutional.

But by today's standards not very mathematical?

No, not mathematical. I did statistics, but it was a relatively un-mathematical statistics.

Did you do graduate work, in the sense of formal graduate training?

Well, no graduate training, but I went on for a year after my first degree to do research into economic reconstruction. I took my finals when the retreat from Dunkirk was happening, and it really produces a very relaxed attitude to one's own career prospects when that kind of event is happening! Then I went straight into a research project run by Professor J. R. Bellerby on post-war economic reconstruction.

We all believed at the time that the end of the war was just a year or two away, and we ought to be ready for economic reconstruction after the war. And then a year after that, I was invited to London to join the National Institute of Economic and Social Research, where I undertook a project inspired by Keynes and by Richard Stone and James Meade who had just set up a system of social accounts for the UK. What Keynes wanted was to apply this system to a completely different economy than the UK, for example, to colonial territories. So I sat in London through most of the War using the Colonial Office library and other such sources trying to work out national income for Northern Rhodesia and Jamaica and to see whether I could set the results into a system of social accounts. I was very fortunate in having Austin Robinson as a supervisor. Many well-known economists were working in Whitehall for the war effort, including Austin Robinson, Richard Stone, James Meade, and Arthur Lewis, the last three of whom subsequently became Nobel Prize winners. They used regularly to come over to the National Institute to have a sandwich lunch with me and advise me on my work. So I started out with an advantage that very few research students have. I had interested attention from people who found it a break from their daily grind and were glad to assist me. At the end of the War, as soon as the seas were open again, I wanted to go to developing countries to find out what it was like on the ground because I had so far worked with documentary evidence only. So in 1946–7 I went to Northern Rhodesia and Nyasaland and produced national income accounts for them.

Do you think that those national income accounts were actually reliable?

Well, of course, it was what one of my colleagues once called the "perpetual invention" method. I had to make estimates all along the line on the basis of rather little data, experimenting all the time with the kind of data I could find. It ranged from actually sitting down in African villages and taking family budget studies to visiting copper companies, finding out what their accounts meant, and getting the latest details from them. I was also fortunate enough to be allowed into the census office in Lusaka – this would never be permitted nowadays – where there had recently been a census of the European population. The returns included income data, and I was allowed to work through the originals. There wasn't a large European population, but I was allowed to make use of the great variety of data in the returns. I did not know how accurate the information was. What was quite clear was that most of Northern Rhodesia's national income was generated by the copper companies. It was also clear that for most people their standard of living depended on agricultural yields; it was an eye-opener as to how uninformative such aggregates are and how important it is to analyse the components. There were a lot of interesting questions that arose as to what the concept of national income meant in a country like that and what uses it might serve.

So in your early career you really did get your hands dirty?

Yes, very dirty! [laughs]

You got a grounding in national income accounting and an exposure to development economics, where Arthur Lewis would have been an important influence at the time.

Indeed, yes. This was a period when everybody was interested in the conditions of economic progress. In the early 1940s Colin Clark had produced his book on *The*

Conditions of Economic Progress; economists were already looking forward to economic reconstruction and to stimulating economic progress in developing countries.

This brings economic growth very much to the centre of the stage; that has been a big feature of your intellectual activities since. But before we pursue your work after this experience, going back to the earlier years, did living through the 1930s – quite a traumatic period in economic and political terms – did that have any serious influence on your later career?

I think living through the 1930s made one much more receptive to the sort of economic policy which was emerging from, say, *The General Theory*, and made one understand what the high level of unemployment meant for a place like Glasgow, where in some areas something like 60 per cent of the people – in Clydebank, for example – were out of work and you actually saw it happening. So I suppose it gave me a rather strong interest in the importance of income distribution as well as growth, and of the importance of economic policy and the influence of ideas on policy.

At the end of your spell doing colonial national income accounting, you moved to Cambridge?

Yes, I spent a brief period in the Colonial Office in a department which was said to be a research department, but it did not turn out to be academic research, and so I escaped! I was invited to come to Cambridge to join the Department of Applied Economics, which Richard Stone had just set up. My task was research into regional social accounts of the United Kingdom. I was applying a social accounting system which would show the structural characteristics of the regions.

Was that research published?

It was. But this was a relatively short phase. Meanwhile, I got involved early on in an international research organization called the International Association for Research in Income and Wealth, which was designed to bring economists in government service and in universities throughout the world in touch with each other, to share problems of estimating national incomes and applying the results. Simon Kuznets was one of the initiators and founders of this organization. It was instructive to bring a great many academic economists in contact with their counterparts in government. We were all learning from each other all the time. With this organization behind him, Simon Kuznets – who had already been doing national income research in the United States from the 1930s onwards – set out to initiate inquiries into long-term growth, not just national income studies as a basis for current policy, but historical national income studies in all countries of the world.

The purpose of studying national accounts historically or taking the long view was what?

Well, it was to analyse the conditions of economic growth and the reasons for the differences in rates of economic growth the world over.

So this might inform economic development policy?

Yes.

And so it was natural to try to push things back towards early industrialization?

Yes.

And you then got involved in the project to examine British national income historically?

That's right, yes.

Going back to 1688?

That's right. To the Glorious Revolution! To Gregory King!

Now that work was published in the form of various articles as you built it up and it eventually formed the backbone of perhaps your best known research monograph, *British Economic Growth, 1688–1959*. Looking back at the work, what's your main memory of how you actually put it together? It seems a monumental task; certainly everyone who's researched afterwards has always used that work as the starting point. It must have looked like an absolute mountain before you started.

Well, it did seem a mountain because only two of us were involved in it in the first instance.

Yourself and Max Cole?

Myself and Max Cole, yes.

Seems strange in a way. We normally think of a big team these days.

You do nowadays. We were, of course, really skimming across the surface of the information. We could not collect a great deal of primary data. We used data which had already been either processed or published in some sense.

Would you say the thrust was description as opposed to analysis, description in an analytic framework?

Yes, it was. Yet *British Economic Growth* threw up a lot of analytical problems as we went along.

So you were setting an agenda for future research rather than a definitive set of estimates?

That's right. We were trying to see how far we could develop a set of estimates which were sensible and plausible on the basis of the data we had. But they could at best be only hypotheses.

You set out those hypotheses – I think it would be fair to say – in a not particularly formal way. Was that a deliberate choice, or did you just think that actually they were not capable of being formalized?

I think we approached it piecemeal, as it were. Nobody else had done quite that sort of thing before, and we just beavered away at trying to produce useful results.

By the time *British Economic Growth* was published in 1962, the big news in this area of economic history and development was the arrival of Walt Rostow. Certainly when I was a student his ideas on take-off, leading sectors, and the stage theory of growth very much ruled the roost.

Indeed, yes. And it was a very important new set of ideas, very striking, very dramatic, with almost a political rather than an economic kind of motivation behind it. By the time he published his 1956 article in the *Economic Journal*, estimates were being produced not only in Britain but in other countries, and Rostow stimulated comparative studies and fresh research.

At the time he was actually writing that article, and then the book, which came out in 1960, was there a lot of interaction between you, or you and Max Cole, and Rostow?

No. We did meet him, but the big interaction came in the early 1960s when there was a conference of the International Economic Association – again something set up by Simon Kuznets – which had brought together economists of all degrees of theoretical or empirical bias, economic historians, sociologists, to sit round a table and attack Walt Rostow. Of course, he absolutely flourished under this, and it led to the International Economics Association publication, *The Economics of Take-off into Sustained Growth* (Rostow, ed. 1963). What the round-table did was to make some of those involved in Simon Kuznets's international project combine to fight the more implausible parts of the Rostow thesis and to engage in new research in order to prove their point.

That is, you were engaged in asking the question: Do Rostow's ideas match the evidence? And you concluded perhaps that they didn't?

They didn't. But these were questions that were really worth asking and, more important still, they were worth answering in detail.

So you thought it important to throw the stones. Do you still think there's any value in the notion of take-off, which was indeed the *leitmotif* of that work?

Not really. I don't think there is any country in the world in which his particular model could be justified.

It was too revolutionary and too dramatic?

Yes. Much too dramatic.

Growth is generally a more evolutionary process?

I would go back to Ashton, who believed that there was evolution and continuity about the business of an industrial revolution, for example, and that it is distorting to try to turn it into a revolutionary process.

Is this one of those cases where the average conceals?

Yes.

So you ended up thinking that the Rostovian programme was misguided but had been fruitful?

I think it was fruitful partly because it was flamboyant. You couldn't avoid taking notice of it.

Do you think Kuznets's contribution is more convincing than Rostow's, then?

Yes, I do. I think it was more careful, less designed to create an instant impression. But perhaps Kuznets's project didn't stimulate discussion so much as Rostow's.

***British Economic Growth* comprised in a sense a new view of the British industrial revolution – certainly different from some of the earlier strands in the literature which had emphasized revolution. In compiling this work and thinking about it, what were you able to draw from people like Clapham and Ashton, who probably were the most famous of the relatively recent writers at the time you were doing your work?**

I think we got more out of Ashton, although I'm not sure how far we expressed it in *British Economic Growth*. What one got out of Ashton was a feeling for the fact that there are institutional, social, and other factors to be taken into account which are left out of our aggregates.

And from Clapham?

Well, there's a great deal of detail in his work. But I'm not sure that we got more than a mine of information out of Clapham.

Perhaps it's not very exciting to read, either.

It's not just that. He had a descriptive rather than analytical approach to statistics.

Then you came to Cambridge to work in the DAE. I imagine that was very much a research post.

To begin with just a research post. I had no desire to do any teaching. When I left university I thought that there were two things I didn't want to do: I didn't want to enter the Civil Service and I didn't want to teach. Well, I was quite right about the Civil Service. I did go into it for two years, and it was not satisfying. But teaching in Cambridge I found rather attractive because I started by supervising, which involves an exchange between equals, rather than pontificating. Eventually I was appointed to a faculty post in teaching.

That would have been about 1960? Did you find the transition from research to teaching difficult?

I started lecturing in the 1960s. It was not difficult, but it was an advantage to have done research because it gave one something to communicate. Lecturing was a different game, but if you're not lecturing to the first year in economic theory – and I never was – you are lecturing to small groups of people and you can create a discussion.

Did you find the process of writing your lectures helped your research or was it a distraction?

I think it helped the research. It certainly forced me to concentrate on putting my findings into an interesting form.

The lectures led to *The First Industrial Revolution?*

Yes.

In writing that book what did you seek to achieve?

What I wanted to do most of all was to introduce the economist's approach into economic history – much more than had so far characterized existing texts. I wanted to use economists' methods of analysis and bring in enough economic theory to fit economic history into a first-year course for students working towards a degree in economics.

So you were trying to make links to things like development economics?

Yes, I was currently teaching development economics to graduate students.

Yet, at the same time, in reading that book I detect an attempt to adjudicate on the well known arguments of the day. You do have a view on the standard of living or on the population growth controversy. And yet I don't think you published very much in the way of research articles on those questions. May I ask why?

Well, I did not actually do original research in that sphere; my lectures were largely a synthesis of my own and other people's researches.

There has been an enormous amount of work done subsequently. Do you find your views have changed very much? Do you take a view on the renewed debate on gradual versus somewhat more dramatic growth experience in the late eighteenth and early nineteenth centuries?

I still hold the view that it was a fairly gradual experience. The reason why the opposite result looked plausible was that much of one's information at that time was based on the trade statistics. These were misleading because in 1783 the War of American Independence ended and trade suddenly soared.

So there's a tendency to create an artificial view of explosive growth. What you just said raises an interesting question. You mentioned construction of index numbers. I suppose the first version of national income accounting was done in current prices. In looking at the long-run picture, the index number problem looms very large. Do you think economic historians in general handle that well?

I think they still haven't solved the problem. In the last analysis, the fact that the values of consumers and governments change through time creates difficulties of weighting. I'm not sure that it makes much sense to try to construct index numbers that stretch over very long periods of time.

And yet you yourself were engaged in a very long-run view. Is there a contradiction?

No, it's just a lesson learned about the difficulties of interpreting statistical aggregates in a context of radical structural change!

To finish off on the industrial revolution, the main thing that I got from

your work was not to overvalue the importance of cotton. That does seem to be a message which has been resilient and robust in the subsequent period.

Yes, I think it has.

Now let me move away from the industrial revolution and back to working in Cambridge at that time. My recollection as a student is that 1960s Cambridge was a pretty Keynesian kind of environment. That obviously influenced your work. Do you think it limited it?

Yes, it probably did.

Did you spend much time in America or working with Americans who, on balance, took perhaps a more neoclassical view of things?

I taught in America for a couple of short periods. I probably was limited by my Keynesian preconceptions. You have to remember that I started work in what seemed the brave new world of Keynesian macroeconomic analysis in the early 1940s. It would have been rather difficult to get that out of my system.

And it inspired a lot of very interesting work in British economic history, much of which was around the idea of the trade cycle or economic fluctuations. One thinks of Cairncross, one thinks of Ford, of that generation. Different probably from what was starting to develop on the other side of the Atlantic. In the early 1960s we started to confront the so-called New Economic History – Fogel, the railroad, social saving. How did you react to that? Did it affect your own research programme at all? Did you approve of it?

I approved of it in the sense that I thought these were interesting new questions which produced surprising answers! But it wasn't the sort of activity that I was tempted to imitate.

Let's think how your work progressed in the 1960s. You tended to move more towards the history of economic thought?

Yes, from the late 1960s onwards, I found myself stimulated by the recent work that had been done in the history of ideas. It was also relevant that if one was not prepared to set up a research team in the sort of work that I had been doing so far, it was not possible to make much impression on the subject as an individual.

The natural follow-up to your work was, I suppose, the Matthews, Feinstein and Odling-Smee volume. You didn't want to participate in that team?

I felt that I had done what I wanted to do in that area, and I was glad that the task was being picked up and moved further, as it were, but I'm somewhat a lone ranger!

You prefer to work on your own?

I prefer on the whole to work on my own, except when, as with Max Cole, I find myself with a very congenial collaborator who is also in a sense working on his own. We worked side-by-side rather than as a team.

So you chose to work on your own more in the history of economic thought?

To begin with, I was invited to give a course of lectures in the history of economic thought. Partly as a result of being in a faculty which was deeply involved in these controversies, I became interested in trying to analyse the debates and see how they had developed through time.

One of the better-known histories of economic thought was written by Mark Blaug [*Economic Theory in Retrospect*; 1st edn 1962]. How would you differentiate your work from his?

Well, my work was more descriptive and less critical. I was more interested in the way the ideas evolved than in discussing their analytical deficiencies.

So in a sense it is more historical?

It is more historical. I would regard my work as not at all competitive with Mark Blaug's but as complementary – another way of looking at it.

In both your recent books, *The Evolution of Economic Ideas* and *The State and the Economic System*, there seems to be quite an emphasis on the world prior to 1914. Is that an unfair reading?

I don't think it's unfair. Do you think it's an undue emphasis?

Well, it's a matter of choice, but clearly figures like Ricardo have a considerable interest for you. That might be part of the Cambridge environment, of course. And yet another part of the Cambridge environment would be to dwell rather more on Keynes than I think you did in those books.

What I was trying to do was to write about subjects which I thought had been inadequately dealt with, and perhaps I was satisfied that there were more competent people to talk about Keynes in Cambridge than I.

What should the history of economic thought contribute to a study of

economic history? I think many economic historians neglect history of thought. I'm certainly guilty of that neglect myself!

I'm not sure what history of thought should do for economic history, but there's no doubt that economic history has made a great contribution to the development of economic ideas. People have generally tried to answer questions which reflect the spirit of their age. Economists have tended to produce theories which they find acceptable to current policy-making authorities. That is the sort of thing that I was really interested in when I developed my latest book, *The State and the Economic System*. I was interested in the way economists' theories and researches were defined by problems of policy as they arose and by the political attitudes of the authorities that might make use of economic conclusions.

The most obvious example I suppose is Keynes responding to the unemployment of the interwar period, and perhaps the demise of Keynesian influence during the inflation of the 1970s. Were you trying to suggest that policy makers set the agenda for economists?

I think they do. I think that economists in government service, for example, who are most directly in touch with the policy makers, need to be aware of the fact that only certain kinds of advice and certain kinds of research will be acceptable to policy makers. If you're really serious about having an influence on policy, then you have to recognize those constraints.

Is that what makes the nineteenth century more interesting – there were more mavericks because there was less pressure from the government of the day or financial pressure? Despite that greater freedom, the intriguing feature of the writings of people like Smith and Malthus is that they failed to foresee in large part the economic growth which was just materializing. Economists were clearly poor forecasters, then as now!

They're always poor forecasters!

Do you have a view as to why these eminent writers failed to see what was happening?

I think because all the evidence which lay behind their researches is historical evidence.

Backward looking?

And the world changes. It doesn't change totally, but it changes all the time and the changes are often themselves unpredictable. Who would have predicted what has happened in Eastern Europe, for example, in the past few years?

So economists are better at solving the problems of the past than the future.

Well, yes.

I think the biggest continuing debate is about whether it is better to have rules or to allow policy makers a lot of discretion. My generation would have interpreted Keynes as suggesting that more discretion should be given to policy makers than the nineteenth century had thought wise. Would you share that view?

Yes, I think I would. If you fix very tough rules in a changing world you have no flexibility.

That, I think, is definitely a Keynesian view. You said when you started out in the 1940s you saw yourself as very much influenced by the new Keynesian economics. Are you now a "neo-Keynesian?" How have the passing years changed the youthful Keynesianism which was very optimistic and confident that there were better ways of running the world?

I'm not so confident nor as optimistic. I'm not so confident that one can be sure that economists will produce the right answers or even that the policy makers will. I think it is still important to allow a fair amount of flexibility to economic policy making. It is also important that there should be a rather large expenditure on research on the way the system works and is changing. I'm not sure that this need was recognized in the original Keynesian project because it was rather assumed that the economists knew how the system worked.

Would that research be econometric?

Also institutional and sociological, I'm afraid. I mean what one is trying to describe is economic behaviour and how economic behaviour changes, not only in response to shocks to the system but in response to the constraints that are imposed on the system by policies.

I know you're still researching actively. Could you tell me what you're doing now?

Well, as usual I want to do something different, and I have decided to write a biography. I'm not sure that I know exactly the shape it'll take. I just know what kind of material I want to embody. I want to write a biography of John Neville Keynes, who was the father of Maynard Keynes. John Neville lived from 1852 to 1949. He came up to Cambridge as a student in the early 1870s and became a Fellow of Pembroke. Later he became Registrary of the University. So his career fell in what was a revolutionary phase in the history of the University. There were terrific changes in his time in the nature of the University, which was almost a clerical enclave at the beginning of the story.

John Neville came from a dissenting family at a point of time when it was possible for dissenters to take degrees and eventually to become members of its governing body. He was an economist and a logician. He took the moral sciences Tripos, which was a combination of moral philosophy, psychology, logic, and political economy. It was a broad area of study, and he wrote a famous treatise on *The Scope and Method of Political Economy*, published the same year as Marshall's *Principles* [1890]. He was closely associated with both Marshall and Henry Sidgwick.

A few years ago I was invited to write an introduction to an Italian edition of *Scope and Method*, which represented the final word on methodology of economics until the 1930s, and I found myself skimming through his diaries to analyse his relations with his colleagues, for example, Marshall, Foxwell, Sidgwick, and Pigou. Many people have skimmed through these diaries with aims which are not associated with Neville Keynes as much as with his son Maynard Keynes, or with Marshall and others with whom he associated. Having read some of these references to the diaries, I decided that they had misinterpreted John Neville Keynes, and that I would let him speak for himself by basing my biography largely on his diaries. So this for me is a new sphere of writing, but it's an interesting challenge.

The modern way would be to take a serious training course before doing this.

I'm too old for serious training courses, so I'm just going to learn the hard way! This is really a chance for John Neville Keynes to vindicate himself (or to be vindicated), and an attempt to bring out the different kind of environment and the different kinds of forces acting on academics in the nineteenth century.

That prompts a final question. Cambridge University must have changed a lot in the many years you have been associated with it. On balance, have those changes been for the good?

When I first came to Cambridge in 1950, the typical undergraduate was not a schoolboy but an ex-serviceman, and in that period it was really very exciting talking with these young men because they were not blank sheets to be written on. They were people who already had questions pouring out of them. Of course the servicemen went, and one came to the schoolboys and schoolgirls again. I think it is still true that the undergraduate in Cambridge gets much more attention and personal tuition than is true of most other universities, and that the research student is relatively neglected.

So by the 1980s a return to your first love – research – seemed the order of the day?

That's right.

W. A. COLE

Interviewed by

A. J. H. Latham

William Alan (Max) Cole retired as Professor and Head of the Department of Economic History at University College Swansea in 1986, and now lives in Somerset. He was born in Buckinghamshire in 1926 to parents who were both Quakers "by convincement;" his father was proprietor of a small family grocery, and his mother was daughter of a south London baker and confectioner. After schooling at The Friends School, Sibford and Leighton Park, Reading, he arrived at Peterhouse, Cambridge, in 1943. Owing to wartime and post-war National Service, he did not complete his undergraduate work until 1950, and then remained at Cambridge for a Ph.D. in History (1955). He was Research Officer in the Department of Applied Economics, Cambridge, 1955–9, taught at Bristol, 1959–66, and became Professor of Economic History at Swansea in 1966. The interview took place on 17th April, 1998, at what is now (since 1995) The University of Wales Swansea. The interviewer was A. J. H. (John) Latham, who writes:

After Max had been appointed Professor, I was his first appointment, taking up my job in Autumn 1967. I remained at Swansea until my own retirement in 2003, apart from two semesters with Larry Neal at Champaign–Urbana (1979 and 1988). I look on the years when Max was my "boss" as happy and productive, and we turned out some good students, including Professor Richard Griffiths (Rijksuniversiteit Leiden), Dr Peter Wardley (University of the West of England, Bristol), and Dr Katherine Watson (University of Birmingham). The Department was particularly interested in the history and process of economic development. Max's political philosophy was very different to my own – by ethos and ethnicity I'm basically a Manchester School Free Trader – but these political differences were mutually acknowledged and tolerated. We were always on friendly terms.

Max, your work with Phyllis Deane, *British Economic Growth*, was a milestone in British economic history, and indeed in economic history in general. Phyllis Deane has spoken warmly of your collaboration with her. What were you hoping to achieve with this project and how far do you think you were successful?

Our objective was to establish the main quantitative features of British economic growth over as long a period as the available evidence would permit. Given the fragile basis of many of the estimates, the results of the enterprise were a pretty mixed bag, although if it is judged by the reception it received and the influence it has had, we seem to have succeeded beyond our wildest dreams.

How did you become involved?

By being in the right place at the right time. In the autumn of 1954, my Ph.D. thesis was in draft, and I was looking for a job. My wife at the time was a Research Officer at the Department of Applied Economics, and in consequence I knew most members of it, including Phyllis Deane, who was already working on *British Economic Growth* and who wanted a historian to work with her on the inquiry. When I was interviewed for the post, it was not my first choice because at the time I was also a candidate for a permanent lectureship at the University of Keele in the Midlands, in seventeenth-century history which I had come to regard as my special field. But perhaps fortunately for my subsequent career, I was runner-up at Keele, so I published two articles based on my thesis and went to the Department of Applied Economics at Cambridge instead.

Phyllis Deane says that the pair of you worked independently on your sections of the book and then the sections were put together. Which sections were you responsible for?

I was responsible for Chapter 2, the section dealing with the eighteenth-century origins of (modern) economic growth. But I must also accept responsibility for Chapter 3 on industrialization and population change, which, though it was not part of my original remit, I undertook during my last three months in Cambridge because the topic happened to interest me.

What do you think were your key findings?

This was not quite how I put it at the time, but looking back, I think that my key findings were that after what proved to be a false start in the middle of the eighteenth century, the take-off in Britain (i.e., a substantial increase in the overall rate of economic growth, as a result of which it consistently outstrips the growth of population) dates from the 1780s – although, as now seems clear, the acceleration was fairly gradual, and it was not until about 1830 that the long-term rates of growth of both total output and output per head were stabilized at about three times the level prevailing before 1780.

This was in the days before computers. How did you tackle the manipulation of the statistical material on which the study depends?

Fairly easily, given that the volume of material was much less than that which can be dealt with very rapidly on a modern computer. If I wanted to do a relatively large amount of number crunching, I prepared my own programme and gave it to a young woman in the computing room who, incidentally, was called a computer, and she did all the calculations on an electrically operated calculating machine.

Your original Ph.D. was, I understand, on the Quakers; perhaps you can tell us something of this?

Yes. The thesis attempted to analyse and explain the evolution of the early Friends' political standpoint between 1652 and 1660, and the genesis of Quaker pacifism. For the early Quakers were by no means consistent pacifists, and it was not until January, 1661, after the Restoration of Charles II, that they adopted the famous Quaker Peace Testimony from which the movement as a whole has never since departed. My reasons for choosing this topic were twofold. I had earlier made an abortive start on a subject in late medieval economic history, and as a result I was obliged to switch to a clearly defined and more manageable topic which I could hope to tackle effectively within the space of two years. But secondly, and perhaps more important, in my own boyhood in the mid-1930s, no doubt because of my Quaker upbringing, I was an ardent pacifist and keen supporter of the Peace Pledge Union. Yet when war came a few years later, I felt compelled to abandon my pacifism and became a reluctant, but nevertheless fully committed, supporter of the war against German and Italian fascism. The decision was not an easy one, and partly for that reason, I never became a member of the Society of Friends. So I was naturally concerned to understand the considerations which had prompted my spiritual forbears to make a similar *volte-face*, albeit in the opposite direction. As so often happens in history and life, the explanation in both cases appears to have been that circumstances alter cases.

Can you tell us something of your days in Cambridge, both as an undergraduate and as a postgraduate researcher? Who were your friends, who were the notables of the day, who were your influences?

Although I had a wide circle of friends and acquaintances in Cambridge, few of them were economists, apart from my colleagues at the Department. Nor were many of my close friends economic historians, although I did, of course, rub shoulders with Peter Mathias from time to time and, rather later, with Tony Wrigley. My own college, Peterhouse, was bursting with historians in those days, and, indeed my reasons for choosing it were that it had an excellent reputation for history – at one time the Professors of Modern History, Medieval History, Economic History and Political Theory and Government were all Fellows of Peterhouse.[1] In addition, it was the only college in

1 Herbert Butterfield, David Knowles, M. M. Postan and D. W. Brogan.

Cambridge whose kitchens were endowed, and which had an excellent kitchen garden, not inconsiderable recommendations in wartime! I suppose that the senior members of the University who influenced me most were Postan, who first aroused my interest in economic history as an undergraduate, and who continued to take a fatherly interest in my subsequent career almost until his death, in, if I remember correctly, 1981; Brian Wormald, who was my supervisor for two of my three years as an undergraduate and for my Ph. D. thesis, and who introduced me to the work of the American theologian, Reinhold Niebuhr, whose Gifford Lectures on *The Nature and Destiny of Man* exercised a major influence on my intellectual development; and Maurice Dobb, the most distinguished Marxist economist in Britain and perhaps the world at that time, a foundation member of the British Communist Party, and an old-fashioned English gentleman to boot!

And finally, a visiting notable, Walt Rostow, whose earlier work on the British economy of the nineteenth century had both stimulated and provoked me in my final year as an undergraduate, and who spent a sabbatical year in Cambridge in 1958 when he delivered his famous lectures on the "Stages of Economic Growth" which I, together with many other gob-smacked youngsters, was privileged to attend. Incidentally, I attended a party for Rostow at that time at which I was introduced to him by Postan as "our resident cliometrician." That was, I think, the first time that I had heard the term, and, I should add, it is not a title I would claim for myself either then or now.[2]

Your wartime experience split up your days in Cambridge and involved both working in a coal mine as a "Bevin Boy" and later service in RAF Pay Accounts. Can you tell us a little of those days?

Well, technically, I wasn't a Bevin Boy because I wasn't conscripted into the mines but volunteered for underground service when I registered for National Service in August 1944 because at that juncture it seemed the most useful thing to do. I was called up almost immediately and sent to the government training centre at Creswell in Derbyshire and from there to Gedling colliery near Nottingham. I started work at the pit bottom and thence worked my way up the roads to the coal face (it was a conventional long wall pit) where I worked for a time under the supervision of an experienced collier who taught me the tricks of the trade and how to cope with potentially threatening situations before going it alone. Eventually, I had a "real" Bevin Boy working under me, but in November 1945 I was discharged from the mines on medical grounds. A month later, I was given another medical, graded 2 and pronounced fit for "non-combatant" duties in the RAF where I served for two years as a pay clerk and was eventually released at Easter 1948, in time to do a term's supply teaching before returning to Cambridge to complete my course for a "straight" history degree.

2 In 1958 Postan could not have used "cliometrician," since the term was invented in 1960. Professor Cole does not recall the related term that Postan used.

My time in the RAF was more or less uneventful and certainly less interesting than my 15 months underground; but it was nonetheless very valuable, as two years in Pay Accounts made me reasonably proficient in mental arithmetic which was to stand me in good stead in my research work in later years!

You were a member of the Communist Party for many years; can you tell us something of that?

That's rather a tall order, but I'll do my best. I joined the student branch of the Communist Party almost immediately after my arrival in Cambridge in October 1943 and remained a member for 15 years. I had been a communist in all but name for two or three years before I became eligible for party membership and a socialist of sorts ever since I was old enough to think about the world around me. For socialism, as another former Communist (Denis Healey) has put it, is based on a belief in the brotherhood of man which it seeks to realize through political action, and as such it has a good deal in common with Christianity, especially Christianity of the kind I took in with my mother's milk. But there were, I think, two major influences which prompted my move from this idealistic, and sometimes rather woolly, form of socialism to communism. First, in the spring or summer of 1941, I acquired a copy of John Strachey's 1936 volume, *The Theory and Practice of Socialism*, which so impressed me that in the years which followed, I immersed myself in the classics of Marxism, particularly the historical and philosophical works of Marx and Engels. (*Capital*, I'm afraid, only came later, towards the end of my undergraduate career.) But meanwhile, of course, the Germans had also invaded Russia in the summer of 1941, and the titanic struggle which followed, which Churchill dubbed "the Russian glory," had such a profound effect on a highly impressionable teenager (I was 15 at the time) that I became determined to join the Communist Party as soon as I was eligible to do so.

Once inside the Party, however, though outwardly a disciplined and belligerent Communist (much to the chagrin of my first-year Director of Studies, Herbert Butterfield), I frequently managed to incur the displeasure of the Party hierarchy, either for my deviations from the Party line, or for the manner in which I often made fun of the tendency of some of my comrades to treat the Party as some kind of secular substitute for the Church of Rome. But I did not consider leaving it until after the events of 1956 [the Soviet invasion of Hungary] demonstrated beyond a doubt that the Party to which I belonged had, to put it mildly, feet of clay. The problem then was not so much the actions of the Soviet Party in Hungary or even the misdeeds of Stalin in the past, neither of which by that time came as a complete surprise, but the reaction to them of the British Party which made me doubt whether that organization, as then constituted, had any useful role to play in a democratic society. And so after two years prevarication, I resigned from the CP and a little later joined the Labour Party instead. I should perhaps add, however, that this was not in my case a matter of a God that failed, because the Communist Party was never my God, nor did I ever regard the writings of Marx and Engels as Holy Writ. But a Marxian socialist I became early in life, and a Marxian socialist I remain.

After Cambridge, you went to Bristol where you were in William Ashworth's Department. Can you tell us something of your days in Bristol? How did you get on with him?

Bill Ashworth, or William as he preferred to be called, arrived in Bristol the year before me as the first Professor of Economic History within the History Department. His major effort was directed towards the development of a Joint Honours Degree in History and Economics, the centrepiece of which was a group of four or five courses in international economic history leading to a discussion class in the final year at which students were invited to consider issues in the economics of development in the light of their historical knowledge.

My experience in Bristol proved to be a very useful interlude in my career partly because the demands of a teaching appointment provided me with the opportunity to extend my own reading in areas of the subject which had perforce been rather neglected in earlier years, and partly because the fact that I was involved at the birth of a new degree scheme in Bristol meant that I already had a clear idea of where I wanted the subject to go when the time came for me to develop my own department.

You asked how I got on with Bill Ashworth. I have always been very fortunate in the course of my academic career with my academic superiors, with Phyllis of course, but also with William Ashworth who showed great forbearance and understanding during a rather traumatic interlude in my private life and who also indulged my wish to teach a special subject course on the industrialization of the USSR.

You then moved to Swansea in 1966 as Professor of Economic History to establish a new Department of Economic History there. You retired I think in 1986, although as an Emeritus Professor, you are still a member of the College Court of Governors. Can you tell us something of your days in Swansea?

Yes, although when I went to Swansea, it was not envisaged I would seek to establish a new Department of Economic History. This was because the chair was established in the Faculty of Economic and Social Studies, which had been set up the previous year to provide a broad range of inter-disciplinary degree schemes in the social sciences leading to a BScEcon degree. And since there were no single-subject courses in the faculty, and students were not required to decide the subjects in which they wished to specialize until the end of their first year, all applications for admission were dealt with by the faculty and not by individual departments.

These arrangements, however, did not last long. For at that time social science degrees were becoming very fashionable, with the result that the number of students in the faculty rapidly increased despite attempts to regulate the influx by imposing above-average admission requirements. Moreover, the set-up in Swansea was calculated to appeal to prospective applicants who wished to read for a social science degree but who were undecided about the area in which they wished to specialize. This obviously created opportunities for expansion for economic history, which was not a mainstream school subject, and this meant that we were soon bursting at the seams; new members of staff had to be appointed who provided a wider range of courses, which in turn promoted a demand for opportunities for a greater degree of specialization in the subject. To some extent we met that demand by persuading the Faculty to treat economic and social history as separate subjects within the BScEcon degree scheme, which meant we could offer single honours in economic and social history masquerading as a joint honours degree. Other successful manouevres on our part ultimately led the Faculty of Economic and Social Studies to amend its regulations so we could offer a complete range of Single, Joint and Combined Honours courses for the BScEcon degree. Throughout these manoeuvres, however, we sought to ensure that the basic structure of the courses we offered was consistent with the objectives which had first taken shape in my mind in Bristol and which I sought to explain in my inaugural lecture, *Economic History as a Social Science*, 12 months after my arrival in Swansea. The last innovation during my time in Swansea was the introduction, in cooperation with the Centre for Development Studies, of a Joint Honours degree in Economic History and Development Studies, a development which would surely have appealed to development economists from Adam Smith onwards.

I was sometimes asked whether I ever experienced a desire to move to a department elsewhere, but my answer was always "no" because Swansea had provided me with the opportunity to do from scratch what I wanted to achieve and to build a department in which, though we sometimes quarreled amongst ourselves as academics are often wont to do, we were never divided about our fundamental objectives. But after 20 years at the helm, I was acutely aware that the competing demands of the job meant that I had done very little of my own work and my teaching was beginning to suffer; and so, when the question of early retirement arose, since there was little more that I could hope to do in Swansea, I decided that perhaps the time had come to move on.

Can you tell us about your visit to Brazil in the 1970s?

Yes, a little. I spent about three months in Brazil between the end of July and the beginning of November 1974 at the invitation of Professor Canabrava, the Professor of Economic History at the University of São Paulo. I was asked to go at very short notice, apparently to deputize for a French economic historian who had been obliged to cancel at the last minute. I was asked to give a weekly lecture about British Economic Growth to the postgraduate students in the Faculty. The visit was both interesting and enjoyable, since although I had traveled widely in Europe, this was the first and only time that I have had to visit a developing country on the other side of the world (and at the same time to sample the delights of Rio).

You gave a paper at the Leningrad International Economic History Congress in, I think, 1982. Can you tell us something of this?

The Fifth Congress at Leningrad was actually in 1970, and on that occasion my paper was based on an attempt to measure the variations in the rate of change of British industrial structure since 1850, in order to test the oft-repeated charge of a failure of British entrepreneurship in the period between 1870 and 1914. Since the exercise suggested that the rate of change was not significantly different in that period from that prevailing in earlier and later periods, and there were alternative explanations, in the economic circumstances of the time, for the delay in exploiting some of the major technological innovations of the late nineteenth century, I came to the conclusion that the charge of entrepreneurial failure was misplaced, or at least greatly exaggerated.

I also gave a paper at the Eighth Congress in Budapest which was held in 1982. This paper, which was entitled "Long-Term Trends in the Economy of Pre-Industrial England," was a preliminary attempt to explore the possibility of using probate inventories to push back the study of British economic growth to the early sixteenth century. Although it was based on a very small sample of 706 inventories drawn from four readily-available published series, the exercise sufficed to convince me that such a study might indeed be feasible and could be expected to yield worthwhile results.

You are still engaged in research in economic history. What are you working on these days?

My current research arose directly from the Budapest paper, but for various reasons, although I was able to make a preliminary survey of the field in 1984–5, it was not until 1991 that I was able to get down to serious work on it. My aim is to produce estimates of the long-term trends in the level, distribution and structure of the household wealth of the probate population of middle England in the two and a half centuries between 1530 and 1780. The study is based on a sample of approximately 7,000 inventories drawn from the records of seven probate courts whose jurisdiction extended over ten counties in Midland and Southern England and whose combined population accounted for nearly a fifth of that of the country as a whole. The amount of information contained in these documents is enormous, but before it is possible to make use of them, it is necessary to produce classified abstracts of the data in machine-readable form which are appropriate for the purpose of analysis. This is a laborious and time-consuming task which has kept me busy for most of the past six years and is not yet complete. But the end is now in sight. When that point has been reached, I hope to begin to analyse the data myself, in order to see what conclusions can be drawn from them, but in the meantime all I can say is this. At the end of my Budapest paper, I ventured to remark that the process of "self-sustained growth in a pre-industrial context," as I had once half-jestingly described it in a mildly provocative dig at Rostow, was by no means confined to the early part of the eighteenth century; and it seems most unlikely that this broad conclusion will be contradicted by the outcome of the present research.

You are universally and affectionately called "Max" Cole, although your initials are W. A., which stand for William Alan. Wasn't it something to do with your fondness for Maxim Gorky's works in your schooldays?

Yes, more or less. In the Autumn of 1941, during my first term at Leighton Park, the school Literary, Historical and Archaeological Society decided to hold a symposium on Russian Literature to commemorate our new ally's entry into the war, and I was asked to produce a short paper on a Soviet writer. I chose to talk about Gorky and became known thereafter as Maxim, or Max for short, mainly, I must confess, because at that time he was the only Soviet writer I had even heard of, although I did become quite interested in him as a result of the work I had to do in preparing my paper.

R. C. O. MATTHEWS

Interviewed by
Nicholas von Tunzelmann
and Mark Thomas

Robert Charles Oliver (Robin) Matthews was born in Edinburgh in 1927, son of a solicitor who was a Writer to the Signet.[1] He attended Corpus Christi College, Oxford (1944–47), graduating with First Class Honours in Politics, Philosophy and Economics. He remained at Oxford for the ensuing two years, first as a postgraduate student at Nuffield College and then as Lecturer in Economics at Merton College. In 1949 he moved to Cambridge as Assistant Lecturer in Economics, became Lecturer in 1951 and Fellow of St John's College in 1950. He returned to Oxford in 1965 when he was elected as Drummond Professor of Political Economy, succeeding his former supervisor, Sir John Hicks, and also became Fellow of All Souls College. Again at Cambridge, from 1975 to 1993 he was Master of Clare College, and also Professor of Political Economy from 1980 until 1991. Robin Matthews has devoted a good deal of his career to academic public service. Among other appointments, he has served as Chair of the Social Science Research Council (1972–5), President of the Royal Economic Society (1984–6) and as Chairman of the Bank of England Panel of Academic Consultants (1977–93). He was elected Fellow of the British Academy in 1968, was made CBE (Commander of the Order of the British Empire) in 1975, was elected Honorary Fellow of the American Academy of Arts and Sciences in 1985, and was made Foreign Honorary Member of the American Economic Association in 1993. Matthews is less well known for his achievements in chess composition: he is author of two books on the subject (1963, 1995) and was named International Master of Chess Composition in 1965 by the World Chess Federation (Fédération Internationale des Échecs – FIDE). He retired in 1993 and now lives in Norfolk. The interview took place at the British Academy in London, 25th August 2004, and was conducted by a former student and colleague,

1 The Society of Writers to Her Majesty's Signet is an organization of Scottish lawyers founded in the sixteenth century.

Nick von Tunzelmann of the University of Sussex, and by Mark Thomas of the University of Virginia.

We would like to begin with your background and your introduction to economics and economic history. You were born in Scotland, were schooled in Edinburgh, and in early 1944, at age 16, went to Corpus Christi College, Oxford where you read PPE (Politics, Philosophy, and Economics).

I came to Oxford at an unusually early age, because I thought that I was likely to be called up. That didn't actually happen because I was exempted from military service when the time came because of my bad eyesight. And so I stayed straight on.

I understand that Corpus in those days did not have an economist; how did you cope with learning the subject?

I didn't start off by doing economics. Although I was young and immature, I was mature enough to know that I wasn't sufficiently acquainted with what the alternatives were to be able to decide what I wanted to read. So I went on with my school subjects, Latin and Greek, for the first four terms – the so-called Classical Mods (Honour Classical Moderations) – with the intention of looking around and seeing what other people were doing and what it amounted to. I didn't specifically come up with the intention to do PPE.

So what attracted you to economics?

I had various friends who were doing PPE, including David Henderson (later Professor of Political Economy at the University of London), who was a close friend. I looked at what he was doing and what he was writing and I thought that this was very interesting. I came up with a quite open mind as to what I was going to read. I very seriously considered reading Russian, because I was interested in that and it has remained an interest ever since. But I decided, and I think rightly, that there were so few people around who were reading Russian and even fewer who were teaching the subject that I wouldn't be getting the best out of Oxford if I did Russian. I looked around at the other things I was interested in and PPE was what I decided to do. And I didn't particularly plan to do Politics, Philosophy, or Economics as a major. So it wasn't a case of how I *chose* Economics. I was very ignorant about the social sciences. I am amazed now at how ignorant I was. My classical work had been essentially linguistic and although in retrospect I think it was quite a good discipline to know about language, in the social sciences linguistic skills are not the only thing that you need. You need other sorts of skills and you also need imagination, which wasn't called for very much in what I did in the first stage of my Oxford career.

The analytical component of economics, however, must have come to you quite quickly, because after you finished at Corpus in 1947 you went

immediately to Nuffield to do postgraduate work in economics. How many economics papers did you take altogether as an undergraduate?

I took four, and one semi-compulsory paper in economic history, my first exposure to that field. (The alternative was international relations.)

And on the basis of that you discovered that you had both a talent and a liking for economics?

It was all a matter of comparative advantage. I don't know that I was marvelous at it, but I was quite sure I didn't want to do Philosophy, which was rather a specialized taste, or Politics, which I did not find interesting. I have to say that although I was very happy at Corpus, the lectures in Oxford in wartime were not very good. I did have two pieces of good fortune. I was sent out of college to John Hicks, a Fellow of Nuffield, who served as my "outside tutor." He taught me for the Special Theory paper and amongst other things called my attention to the lectures that were being delivered by that year's Harmsworth Professor, Walt Rostow. These were a preliminary version of the book that Rostow later published called *The British Economy of the Nineteenth Century* (1948).

That was in the winter of 1947 – the famous lectures he gave in the Hall at The Queen's College, where he stood in front of a blazing fire and mesmerized his audience.

Yes. I remember Walt Rostow standing there with his hands in his pockets, warming his bottom in front of the fire. He was much better than most of the Oxford lecturers we had – he was relaxed and jovial. He was, I would say, the second best lecturer I had when I was at Oxford (the best was E. D. M. Fraenkel, Professor of Latin, a German who inspired a generation of Oxford students).

Who taught you for your economic history paper?

[Neville] Ward-Perkins was my tutor in economic history. Dear old Ward-Perkins, he was quite jolly, he had a lovely map of the railway system . . . But his approach wasn't very intellectual. And that was the difference with Rostow. In retrospect, I have criticisms to make of Rostow, but it was a good performance and very interesting. I'd been discussing with Hicks what subject I would take as a postgraduate student. We agreed that it would be economic history. Hicks had just written his little theory book on the trade cycle and it seemed a good idea to try to write up one particular nineteenth-century trade cycle. I looked up the annals and the most interesting one seemed to be the one with its peak in 1836. So I settled down and did that. And I must say, with all respect to my teachers and to the great general encouragement I had from Hicks, I really did this entirely on my own. This is not a criticism of anybody. Obviously, Hicks wasn't an expert on this and there was nobody else who was in the least bit interested in it. Rostow's lectures were the only instruction I had in this sort of thing.

Yet, the trade cycle was a big topic at the time. Of the people you mentioned, Hicks wrote on trade cycle theory, Ward-Perkins worked on the trade cycle of the 1840s, Rostow's dissertation focused on the cycles of the late nineteenth century, and, of an older generation of scholars, both D. H. Robertson and Sir William Beveridge had written on the trade cycle. There was also the work of the NBER – Mitchell and Burns, and so on. How did you fit into this intellectual framework?

When I was working on *A Study in Trade Cycle History* (1954b), I didn't think I was doing anything particularly new or original methodologically. I thought I was just trying to explain the course and causes of this cycle, by looking at the data carefully, in the light of broadly accepted theory. Precedents were provided not only by previous business cycle studies but also by some League of Nations books on international monetary movements.

One of the virtues of the book is that you don't force the facts into a single theory. You make the point in the introduction that "what we seek to apply in analysis of these events is theory rather than *a* theory."

My theoretical framework was Keynesian, mainly in the sense that the central focus of attention was fluctuations in *real national income*. The lack of such a central focus was the weakness in the National Bureau's interwar work on business cycles and also of Robertson's early book. I think that the *practical* use of the income and expenditure approach owed more to Keynes's 1940 pamphlet *How to pay for the war* rather than to the *General Theory*, though of course I spent many hours a week teaching the *General Theory* to students.

However, this income-and-expenditure approach is a house with many mansions. Schumpeter as well as Keynes influenced me. Micro considerations about the relations between price and quantity, notably in the cotton industry, were also relevant. The approach was not Keynesian in the sense of having anything to do with stabilization policy, nor did I engage in any formal model-building. I did occasionally pause to ask myself what would have happened in the 1830s if the authorities had adopted a post-World War II combination of fiscal and monetary policy, but I didn't pause for long, because it seemed such a silly question (what "authorities," for a start?).

We wanted to ask you about the "quantitative–historical" approach you took in the book, because what you did was an early form of what we might think of as historical economics. It seems that what you were doing then was different from what most British historians would have conceived as economic history and yet it was very much in a British tradition, in the same mold as other pioneers of applied economics of the past – Alec Cairncross, Dennis Robertson, even Pigou wrote in this style. Yet, this was long before cliometrics became recognized as a distinctive approach.

When Bob Fogel published his book, *Without Consent or Contract* (1989a), he kindly gave me a copy and he inscribed in a way which I thought was very flattering – "To Robin Matthews, pioneer Cliometrician." I was rather surprised at that, because I hadn't regarded myself as a cliometrician, certainly not in the same sense as Fogel, who was considering an actual striking hypothesis – did slavery pay? I wasn't asking myself any question like that, because I was not trying to draw any general conclusions about cycles in the nineteenth century. I was drawing conclusions rather like a historian – working out what happened in 1839. In so far that there was anything good about that, it was that I tried to look rather hard at the statistics, and to work out if what they say about the movement of the prices is consistent with the movement of the quantities and, if not, what is the explanation. And I did give quite a lot of thought to trying to make sense of the statistics; that was really what I was trying to do, but not in the econometric sense, not applying a lot of correlations, but just focusing on one event. Why was there a crisis or not a crisis? How did it come about that they all said there was such a frightful slump but the figures show that output went up?

In the book, you seem to be able to move very easily between the statistics, on the one hand, and the theory, on the other.

It didn't seem to me to be particularly difficult. You had to get the statistics, obviously. There was rather a lot of statistical material for this period, quite a lot of statistics in the Parliamentary papers mainly related to prices, but also quite a lot on material on output – Shannon's brick index, for example – statistics about railway building, and of course a great deal in the way of statistics on foreign trade. You had essentially price data, quantity data, a certain amount of wage data, and a great deal of chat, questions of the sort, "Tell me, Mr. Horner, do you regard the workpeople as having been worse off in this period than they had been in 1825?" followed by an interesting reply. There was also a great deal of material about money in the Parliamentary papers, because all this was leading up to the Bank Charter Act [of 1844]. There were other sources too – Gayer, Rostow and Schwartz (1953), for example, which was not yet published, but Rostow kindly allowed me to see the pages, or at least some of the pages. Working through all these statistics took a lot of sweat, because it was all done by hand – it is really quite extraordinary, I didn't even have a calculating machine!

In the preface to the trade cycle history book, you observe that anecdote is a very important part of understanding the past. Do you still feel that is true about economics today?

I think less true, because after all the British economy was very small at that time and the industrial part was even smaller. One of the things that I enjoyed about taking this very short period, you really got to know the economy, you almost felt you knew the principal characters – if you'd gone into the dining room at the Bank of England you would have recognized some of the Directors. And now, goodness knows, there are hundreds of industries, but at that time, if you covered textiles and building and one or two others, you'd more or less done it. That wouldn't be true now. Moreover, it now matters rather a lot what is happening in Germany, and France, and Italy, and China, whereas the geographical range of the trade cycle book was limited mainly to the UK and the US.

How important do you think a historical perspective is to an understanding of contemporary economics? Is it that you need a long-run perspective, or that you need to understand where today is relative to the past, or is the historical method itself also important?

These are very good questions. And I'm not too sure that I can answer them. I had a look at my book in preparation for this interview and I was struck in some ways by the extent to which issues that have become modern already presented themselves then, *e.g.*, that the supply of money is responsive to the demand for money. This is exactly what we discussed in connection with the revival of monetarism under Margaret Thatcher. It was the same issue, and it was not by accident, because it was all connected with the Bank Charter Act. Interesting how the same issues seem to come up again and again.

Are you an advocate of path dependence?

Well, there is a class of people like Paul David who tend to think that there are theories or theoretical approaches which are somehow particularly appropriate to history. I am a bit sceptical about that. OK, you can have path dependence, sometimes that will be important, and sometimes it won't be important. I don't know whether wars should be described as path dependent, but they are certainly important for economic history.

If we could take you back to the narrative: you started the trade cycle project in Oxford and finished it in Cambridge.

Yes, I moved in 1949 from an unsatisfactory job as Lecturer [in Economics] in Merton in Oxford – I had hoped that it would lead by the usual Oxford *cursus honorum* to a Fellowship, but it turned out that, at that time, Merton had not even decided to create a Fellowship in Economics, far less give it to me. So when I was offered an appointment as University Assistant Lecturer in Cambridge, through the good offices of my supervisor John Hicks and his friend Dennis Robertson, I accepted it. Hicks warned me that I would find Cambridge very different from Oxford. I found that this was true, but the move was a great success and I have never regretted it. I moved to what was for me a much more stimulating intellectual environment than Merton had been.

My duties at Cambridge were to devote half my lecturing time to a newly created special subject, the British economy, 1875–1900, and half to some other subject to be determined. But it soon became apparent to me that economic history was not highly esteemed by the most influential people in the Economics Faculty, like Richard Kahn. For example, they made no effort, as far as I know, to keep Habakkuk when he was thinking of leaving Cambridge in 1955. Dennis Robertson did have a good awareness of the historical approach, and I got on well with him from the first, but he had lost the battle for power in Cambridge. The subjects rated highest in Cambridge were theory and policy, especially macro-policy. After my disappointing experience at Merton, career considerations were bound to play some part in my choice of which way to move after finishing the book on the 1830s. A move away from economic history did not involve any intellectual sacrifice, because the standards of work on economic theory and economic policy were so high. My Cambridge Economic Handbook, *The Trade Cycle*, published in 1958, was primarily theoretical, but had strong historical underpinnings. The Cambridge Economics Faculty was a wonderful place for a young economist to be in the 1950s, at least for one who was *persona grata*. The seniors included Richard Kahn and Joan Robinson, Nicholas Kaldor (a genius who was the most brilliant economist never to have won a Nobel Prize), and there were also Dick Goodwin, Harry Johnson and soon Robin Marris and Frank Hahn – a marvelous array. Kahn took great trouble in recruiting new talent and cultivating it.

An opportunity did occur a little later to go back to Oxford as an economic historian, but I was not much tempted. Much later I was again invited to go back to Oxford, this time as Drummond Professor. This was too large a promotion to be turned down, though I left Cambridge with regret. I stayed in Oxford as Drummond for ten years, before moving back to Cambridge again as Master of Clare in 1975.

You have mentioned teaching. Would you like to tell us a bit about that?

When I first went to Cambridge, my seniors were very kind to me, I must say. For my non-History lecture course, they said you can teach more or less any subject that you choose except International Trade which Harry Johnson lectured on. I thought about it a bit and I hadn't reached any conclusion, when I received a card from Richard Kahn which said "What about the trade cycle?" and that seemed rather a good idea. I gave those lectures and they were a great success – much more successful and had a much larger audience than the History lectures.

Most people tend to regard undergraduate teaching as a great chore, and so it is if you do too much. When I was at Merton I did 18 hours a week, not a thing anybody would require now and I think it was scandalous expecting me to do that, frankly, looking back on it. Looking over my career in undergraduate teaching, I have no doubt whatsoever that the best undergraduate student I ever had – I thought so at the time and I think so now – is the current Prime Minister of India, Manmohan Singh. He was a marvelous student; every essay was alpha. If you asked him to make a case for some bad policy like rent controls, he would make a list of all the possible arguments. He was a wise man, even at such a young age. And what so pleases me is that here was a man who had no particular advantages as far I know; he didn't have personal influence or connections, he had done a degree at a minor Indian university and then came to Cambridge. From then his career went from strength to strength, and he was considered a great success as Finance Minister and now he is Prime Minister. I must say that I can't help feeling very proud at having had Manmohan Singh as my student.

You supervised a number of Ph.D.s in economic history, including that of Charles Feinstein.

Yes, that was in the early days. I didn't so much supervise Charles as simply observe his progress; he was very professional and self-motivating.

Some years later, you collaborated with Charles, and with John Odling-Smee, on your other major contribution to British economic history, namely *British Economic Growth, 1856–1973*. Would you tell us about that experience?

I am conscious of the fact that most of the major things I've done were done on someone else's suggestion. Moe Abramovitz and Simon Kuznets had the idea of commissioning a series of books which would take a historical–economic growth approach, one for each country. I am obliged to say that I think in retrospect this was a bad idea. One reason, apart from anything else, for saying that is that the majority of the people who were commissioned never delivered, and of those who did deliver, two of them – Malinvaud and Carré on France (Carré, Dubois & Malinvaud 1975), and Ohkawa and Rosovsky (1973) on Japan – stopped the story much too early – sometime in the 1950s or early 1960s, which meant that they didn't have a long-run perspective on the post-war period. Feinstein, Odling-Smee and I sweated away for far too long – 20 years – and it eventually became an absolute misery. It nearly gave me a Casaubon complex – "My book, my book, I shall never finish my book" (George Eliot, *Middlemarch*). One reason why it took so long was that a lot of my time in those years was taken up in non-research activities. Abramovitz and Kuznets chose for their country authors people who had already become eminent, so they were liable to be distracted into becoming Vice-Chancellors or such like. I shall mention presently some of the distractions in my own case.

Bombach on Germany and Fuà on Italy produced some occasional papers, but never put them together in a book; Moe's book on the United States, to be written with Paul David, was never completed.[2] Moe felt terribly guilty about this; as general editor he would write you letters every now and then nagging you for not having finished your book, but he was obviously in an extremely weak position. The fact that so many of these people never finished does suggest to me that it was a bad idea. And I think I understand why it was a bad idea. It became apparent to us because of the difficulties that we were experiencing as we got closer and closer to the end, and that was where to stop. You wanted to get a decent period after 1945 for analysis, and it was very difficult to find one. If you took 1979 as the end of history that would be quite wrong because we had a great Thatcherite slump and it took a long time to recover from that, so where do you call a halt? Maybe the idea of writing a long-term "decline and fall" while it is going on is not sensible.

2 Some 40 years later Abramovitz and David, in their contribution to *The Cambridge Economic History of the United States, Volume III* (2000), presented work that met to some extent the project's original purpose.

One of your most influential papers on British economic history was not originally written for this purpose, but was rather aimed at a contemporary issue, namely why Britain had achieved full employment since 1945. When you wrote this, it was quite controversial.

The article that I wrote in the *Economic Journal* (1968) said that we didn't actually practice Keynesian economics in the post-war period. This did attract a certain amount of attention. People are very crude; if there is a crude conclusion, that is the one they remember.

This was exactly the case of where you had probably been thought of by most people as a Keynesian of some kind, and here you appear to be knocking away the basic prop.

Perhaps. But saying that the government didn't actually do a lot of deficit spending in the 1950s and 1960s is more of an empirical point. Some people have argued that I anticipated the Friedmanite critique. Not at all. The paper wasn't in the least bit Friedmanite.

It wasn't a rejection of Keynesian fine-tuning as a concept, but a statement that it had not been implemented?

Yes, though that conclusion was a bit qualified in our *Growth* book.

Let us turn to the paper that you wrote with Frank Hahn on "The Theory of Economic Growth" (Hahn & Matthews *EJ* 1964), which is a masterful synthesis of the literature. How did it come about?

This is another case where the suggestion was put to us by somebody else. Austin [Robinson] was organizing a series of survey articles for the [Royal Economic] Society and he said, what about you doing a survey article on growth? I said yes, if I could have Frank Hahn as collaborator. And we found that we got on better than we had expected and Frank said to me, my opinion of your IQ went up! I think Frank quite liked to see that some of the things that he thought were rather clever and highbrow mathematically could in fact be expressed quite well in words. I said that there is no point in torturing the students by putting it into algebra when you can put it into prose. And if they want to put it into algebra, they can.

Section II on technical progress really has worn very well – a lot of the issues you raise there continue to be live issues, in a way that perhaps is less true of the more formal parts.

There was a section that I wrote which I've always regretted did not have more impact, on the subject of population. I thought it was quite interesting, but nobody has taken it up at all. I'm not sure if it is valid; I hadn't done very much empirical work on population at the time. I did much more empirical research on population when it came to working on *British Economic Growth*, and for that I was helped quite a lot by Roger Schofield, who of course knew a great deal more than me.

Why do you think that economists ignored population economics?

Well they had no excuse for it, because the Royal Commission on Population of 1945 had a very good historical section – short, but very good – and you could learn nearly all that you needed to be told.

I was going to suggest that a reason that people avoid population economics is because they got it so wrong in the 1930s, with the focus on depopulation and how the British population was going to dwindle to next to nothing by 1960 – a widespread belief at the time in many countries and one which, in the end, was so wrong that it betrayed the frailties of forecasting.

But it came more nearly true in the former Soviet Union in the 1990s.

There are fears again today, of course; countries like Italy have very low reproduction rates.

I'm not really sure; but there are things that I didn't understand and that I never succeeded in understanding. For example, you get turning points in mortality at almost the same date in countries of vastly differing levels of income. What on earth can be the explanation? I don't know. But it is a good subject; it has always seemed to me to be a good subject. One problem with economics is that one is dealing with concepts which, let's face it, are a bit phony – output as measured by index numbers, for example, is a slightly shadowy concept. But fertility and mortality are very plain, so I rather envy people who work on that sort of subject.

Unlike many academics, you also had a flourishing career in public service. Could you tell us something about that?

I have referred to the outside activities that took up so much of my time when we were finishing *British Economic Growth*. These included not only being Master of Clare and involvement in central Cambridge University affairs, but also Chairmanship of the Social Science Research Council (SSRC), Chairmanship of the Bank of England's panel of economic consultants, founding and chairing the CLARE group, and at one time activity at the edge of national politics. I found that having been appointed to a prominent position like the Drummond Professorship in Oxford made one a prominent general personage, and one thing led to another. They were all interesting activities, most of them worthwhile, but time-consuming.

Perhaps the most notable was becoming Chairman of the SSRC, which was more or less a full-time job for five years and was extremely stressful. I took it on because I thought I would learn about the other social sciences. That wasn't quite what happened – I didn't learn more than a little about the other social sciences. What I learned a lot about was the public expenditure and how you control it, and how you survive with it being continually cut. And I learned how to work with Margaret Thatcher, who appointed me to the job (she was then Secretary of State for Education and Science in Edward Heath's government). When I took it on, I went and talked to a member of the Council – a senior lady in the Conservative party, Dame Kathleen Ollerenshaw, who was a big person in Manchester local government – and I asked her if she would give me a tutorial on how to handle Margaret Thatcher. She was very helpful. She said, well, you should think of Margaret as a good student with strong prejudices. If she has done her homework, she will give you an alpha essay; if she hasn't done her homework, you will get the standard prejudices of a Tory lady in a hat.

I took that into account and I also took into account the fact that it was no point making suggestions to Margaret Thatcher that would obviously be uncongenial to her. As a result, I got on with her extremely well for practical day-to-day purposes. I remember one of the civil servants at the Department of Education and Science saying, "Marvelous meeting of minds," and I was surprised at that because I didn't share her political views at all. But I took great pains not to put mine forward. I knew that my job was to be Chairman of the SSRC and she was the Secretary of State and she had the statutory legitimacy – she was the boss, in the last resort. I have surprised many of my left-wing friends by praising Margaret Thatcher and saying that I found her a very good person to work with; surprisingly, I found her much less difficult to deal with than her Labour successor, [Reg] Prentice. But she became much more right-wing after she became leader of the Conservative opposition; she was much influenced by Keith Joseph, whom I knew at All Souls, and she became much more doctrinaire altogether.

You later founded the CLARE Group, which became a major critic of Thatcherite policy making after she became Prime Minister.

Yes, but this was criticism from the outside – it was quite different from seeing how politics worked, as I did at the SSRC. In a way, what I learned at the SSRC was more interesting. I learned that if budget cuts were imposed when most funds are already committed in three-year tranches, the only thing that could be reduced were year-to-year expenditures, such as studentships [one-year grants to individual postgraduate students]. Nobody would understand why the studentships seemed to have been reduced so much in proportion. That is public finance, it is economics, and I tried to convince economics students that, in practice, this sort of consideration is important in public finance, but they weren't interested in that, they wanted to draw curves tangential to each other.

Some time later, the Bank of England set up a panel of economic consultants of which I was asked to be the Chairman. My job was to decide what was a suitable thing to discuss and to extract what was the common ground among the panelists and what were the underlying differences between their positions. This could be difficult because in many cases there was no common ground. This was at the time when the monetarist controversy was at its worst. I expect you remember the letter in *The Times* in 1981, signed by the 364 economists opposing government policy. I declined to sign the letter, despite much pressure to do so, because I said I think that if you do write this letter, that will be 364 economists that Margaret Thatcher will decide to pay no attention to in future; also we don't want to exaggerate the esteem with which economists as such are held. Moreover, I don't altogether agree with all that was said in the letter, for instance, that you can never recover from a recession except by means of government action. I think that's not historically correct. They said, well you must sign it – it would be awful if you don't sign it. I didn't, but I don't think I got any credit for not signing it. Everything was terribly contentious in the 1980s.

There is no doubt that when Margaret Thatcher came into power, academics came to be held in less esteem, whether they were right-wing or left-wing. Right-wing economists thought that they were going to get a lot of preferment. They didn't. Preferment went to the businessmen. Look at the statistics of relative salaries of academics; they just went down and down. I don't know that any leadership could necessarily have reversed that. That was a difficulty we had with Margaret Thatcher. She respected scientists but not other academics. She had read chemistry, and she remembered that when she was a student in Oxford the chemistry professor, Sir Robert Robinson, knew more about chemistry than she did. She was prepared to defer to the expertise of scientists; she was not prepared to admit that social scientists had similar expertise. When I was at the SSRC I tried to persuade her that what we were doing was of practical importance for jobs or labour relations, that it was an important economic issue and it was therefore right and proper that we should devote a lot of money to studying labour relations. But she thought that everybody who studies trade unions is a left-winger, and I couldn't get her out of that. Curiously, although I didn't agree with Margaret Thatcher, I admired her in a way because she did lead firmly. On non-political issues she took an independent view and could be a staunch ally.

Over time, I became very much more concerned with politics in one way or another. I feel more strongly about things politically than I used to. I was very active as a member of the Social Democratic Party (SDP) when it was first founded in 1981. I was a member of its policy committee for a year. I was very disillusioned by the break-up of the SDP–Liberal Alliance (1987). I thought my leaders were not showing themselves in a good light – I thought that they were behaving in a childish, self-interested manner and I rather dropped politics after that. I had, for a moment, considered going into politics myself as so many people did as the SDP was first founded. Then better sense prevailed.

One of your comments in Mark Blaug's *Who's Who in Economics* is that your conception of how economics works has been influenced by your "personal experiences of practical administration and decision-making, academic and other." Can you elaborate a little on that?

They did lead me to reflect on elements in decision making other than textbook utility maximization. This led to publication of a series of papers in the 1980s and a little later on subjects that would now come broadly under the heading of behavioural economics. They included papers on animal spirits and investment, morality and efficiency, professional ethics, endogenous changes in human nature, charities, the relevance of institutional change to economic growth, competitive selection as a source of economic change, and the relation between political and economic competition. Some of these were closer to economic history than others, but few of them could have been written by someone without a historical background. I did think of putting them together as a book, under some title such as *Economic Psychology and Institutions*, but they needed a capstone essay, and it took a long time to find a suitable subject for one. I contemplated writing one on institutional changes brought about by the fall of the Soviet Union, since I had long had an interest in Russian economic history and could read Russian. I was taken aback by the huge amount of the literature, even just in English. The substance of the subject kept changing from year-to-year and the literature expanded rapidly with it. Meanwhile, new literature kept accumulating on the subjects I had already written about in published papers. The book I had contemplated was becoming out-of-date and a less attractive proposition to a publisher. So I called it a day. But my friends Geoff and Gay Meeks kindly bound up the essays to put as a volume for use by students and placed it in the Marshall Library in Cambridge.[3] I regard it as a significant part of my work.

Let us change the conversation to something else completely. You were a Visiting Professor at Berkeley in 1961–2; while there you were invited to attend a Cliometrics meeting at Purdue – the second ever, in fact. We would be interested to hear your recollections of the meeting.

First of all, I was impressed by how many people were there, and what good work they were doing. Bob Gallman was there, so too was Bob Fogel. I also remember Bill Parker, Richard Easterlin, Lance Davis, Peter Temin. I already knew Al Fishlow in Berkeley, Paul David, who was on the other side of the bay in Stanford, and Jonathan Hughes, who had been at Oxford and who had worked on the trade cycle of the 1850s. I remember Hughes wrote to me in about 1953 telling me he was working on it for his dissertation and asking me if I had any suggestions. I said that the most useful thing I could do was to send him the page proofs of my forthcoming book. I think he said that he more or less started again after that.[4]

If you look at the list of papers at that meeting, it is an interesting mix. Paul David gave a paper on British domestic investment in the 1860s . . .

3 They also reprinted the "animal spirits" paper in an edited volume, *Thoughtful Economic Man: Essays on Rationality, Moral Rules, and Benevolence* (CUP 1991).

4 In the preface to *Fluctuations in Trade, Industry, and Finance* (1960: *vii*), Hughes states that "the plan and specific method of the present work owe much to Matthews." In particular, after reading Matthews's page proofs, "With great relief, Jon pushed a pile of now-superfluous manuscript off his desk into the wastebasket" (Cain *et al.* 1991: 2).

Yes, he thought of it as a possible dissertation but it was never finished.

Overall, the papers seem quite representative of the flavour of the cliometrics revolution. Out of the seven papers that were presented at the meeting, two of them have in their title, "a simulation model," which reflects the counterfactual style with which people were approaching economic history, setting up a model and then shocking it by applying different parameters to see what the effects would be. This must have seemed to be a very intellectually engaging field.

Oh yes, certainly. And there was a great *esprit de corps* among those there – all part of a movement.

Did you feel this to be a particularly American research project?

Yes. I thought that it was easier to have this in America, a) because the academic profession in America is larger, and b) because the United States is larger and the history of the United States is a larger topic. A lot of the history of the UK, which is what people would start off with in this country, is rather a twice-told tale.

Yet, of the seven papers, three of them are on British topics. Clearly, the cliometricians were quite happy to take their techniques and tools and assumptions and attempt to model the British economy in that fashion. Indeed, many of the most important papers to come out of the 1970s and 1980s were on British topics. We said earlier that there was this long tradition of historical–economic work in Britain, from Robertson through Cairncross to yourself and Feinstein, and yet despite the fact of that long tradition (or perhaps because of it) there was not the revolutionary ferment that existed in the United States.

Coming from Cambridge, although I was impressed by the American economic historians whom I met at Purdue, I was privately a little surprised that they made such a song and dance about the novelty of the cliometric approach. Of course I knew that they were asking themselves some rather different questions from mine, but I was not entirely convinced even so. I couldn't help discerning an element of self-advertisement. (*cf.* elderly Cambridge economist Claude Guillebaud on Walt Rostow: "There goes a man with all his goods in the shop-window.") When some cliometricians went on to draw Panglossian conclusions about the virtues of the market economy, I definitely parted company from them. I think that it is a less a Panglossian movement now but it did have that character at one stage.

It may seem ironic that Britain had the institutional apparatus for there to be more application of historical economics in the 1960s and 1970s, given the large number of departments of economic history in the UK, yet those departments never lent themselves to this sort of this

approach. Did you regret the general absence of a cliometric approach in Britain?

It would not have been feasible. A very large proportion of our graduate students in Britain were not British. They were interested in working on development problems; that was the favourite topic for research.

Do you have any closing thoughts?

One question: am I an economic historian? The four years or so that I spent on the trade cycle book are the only part of my long working life that have been devoted full-time (apart from teaching) to research on economic history! I can't include under this heading the many years when Charles and John and I were trying to finish *British Economic Growth*, because so much time in those years was spent on non-research tasks. Moreover, the field of the trade cycle project was narrow, both geographically and in period. The field of *British Economic Growth* is wider, but still limited. So I have always felt myself a bit of impostor as an economic historian. I am awed by the range of some of my colleagues.

In one respect the passage of time has increased my historical awareness. Now that my personal recollections cover what is quite a substantial chunk of history – from the 1930s to the 2000s – I am increasingly conscious of and curious about the relation between my own memories and the trends familiar to me from the books.

Part III

NEW ECONOMIC HISTORIANS

The Elders

William N. Parker

Douglass C. North

William Parker and Douglass North were the senior members of the youthful clan of cliometricians that began to coalesce in North America in the 1950s. By the 1960s, Parker was known as "the oldest New Economic Historian;" North was only a year younger. They are linked here not simply because they are contemporaries, but because they were partners in promoting the new field. Both contributed to the first organized stirring of the movement at the Williamstown NBER–EHA conference in 1957, with Parker as editor of the proceedings (CRIW 1960). Together they edited *The Journal of Economic History* from 1961 to 1966, accepting a rising number of articles written in the new vein. Their evident enthusiasm for "new economic history" sufficiently alarmed some members of The Economic History Association that they were called on the carpet by the Trustees – impeached, as North recounts, but not convicted, and allowed to finish off their term. Another joint venture, in concert with ten others, was a synthesis of the findings of the new economic history in a textbook written for undergraduates, *American Economic Growth: An Economist's History of the United States* (Davis, Easterlin & Parker 1972), about which Parker ruefully recalls, "it was a damn good collection, which nobody bought."

Before and after their collaborative efforts, North and Parker produced a variety of research, from finely detailed studies to broad-ranging syntheses, and regularly taught both American and European economic history. Their legacy lies not only in their writings but also in the minds and work of their students, and now of several more generations of intellectual descendants in economic history and other fields. North, in his teaching debut in 1950 in a graduate seminar at the University of Washington, was fortunate to have two other first-generation cliometricians among his students, Lance Davis and Jonathan Hughes, just as they and numerous successors were fortunate to have North as teacher, critic and *provocateur*. Some 30 years later, Hughes wrote "To have been in his seminar was a once-and-for-all experience . . . It was not a slick and well-planned 'course of study.' North's interests changed, the subject matter changed, the arguments changed . . . But the critical attitude was a constant, like the drive for focus and creativity." Parker was just as inspiring; his lectures were "noteworthy for their wit and humanity." His effect as a teacher, Parker felt, lay less in "the information conveyed through lectures or readings," but in his attempt to "[reveal] a network of physical and social relationships that underlies and overlays any sample of historical experience . . . a phantom model of the social structure in its historical movement."

This "grand schema" influenced the thinking of many of his students but, to Parker's regret, none subscribed to it fully. A former student, Gavin Wright, explains: "The reason . . . was very simple . . . Bill understood that a vital part of scholarship was bringing out the creativity and individuality of each student, and he gave this goal high priority in his advising. He never saw his students as extensions of his own ego, much less assigned them to confirm some favored thesis of his or refute some adversary" (2006a: 6). Fittingly, in 1994 and 1995 the Economic History Association awarded North and Parker the first two prizes for excellence in teaching economic history, established to honor the late Jonathan Hughes.

Parker was from Columbus, Ohio, a child of the Midwest, with "much of its small-town and small-city culture bred in [his] bones." Yet, by way of Harvard, Williams College and Yale he became an Easterner, low-key, literate, ironic and urbane, an adoptive Yankee. North was born a Yankee but had a cosmopolitan youth in Canada and Switzerland as well as in New England. Rather than attend Harvard, North went to Berkeley in 1938 and remained on the West Coast until the 1980s. To his students in 1950 he was an enigma – a diffident Easterner – but he became, by stages, a Westerner, direct, quietly assertive and always skeptical. His "unwillingness to be convinced" is an apt trait for one who, on moving to the Midwest, chose to live in Missouri, the "Show Me State." Parker and North differ in temperament and upbringing; throughout an association of more than 40 years they were not only comrades and sometime collaborators but were always ready to doubt as well as to praise each other. At Parker's retirement conference North "observed that though they had had many strong disagreements and though Bill had been a relentless critic of Doug's work they had . . . maintained a friendly relationship through it all."[1]

Their formal educations were interrupted (and broadened) by the war service expected of their generation. After two years in the graduate economics program at Harvard, Parker cut his professional eyeteeth at the Office of Production Management in the summer of 1941, and then was drafted into the Army Ordnance Corps. From late 1943 he worked at the US Embassy in London in the Enemy Objectives Unit of the OSS, with Charles Kindleberger, Walt Rostow, and Richard Ruggles (college classmate and later Yale colleague). There Ruggles and Parker refined the OSS's "numbers racket," a statistical procedure for estimating German productive capacity from captured equipment; Parker also went into the field to perform the often grim task of data collection. Following further (civilian) government service, Parker returned to Harvard, where Abbott Payson Usher became his mentor, and settled on a dissertation about the German coal and steel complex.

After getting his B.A. in 1942, North says, he joined the Merchant Marine "because of the strong feeling that I did not want to kill anybody." He thus spent the next three

1 Quoted by Wright (1989: 6). Autobiographical quotations here and below from Parker (1971: 3, 11), (1991a: Preface, *xiii*), (1996: 457); from North (1994b). For Jonathan Hughes on North see (1982b: 4, 7, 11). We have drawn also on Parker's unpublished memoir, kindly supplied by Jarrett Parker, and on Katz (1989: Ch. 4), Saxonhouse & Wright, eds (1984: *xi*), and Wright (2000: 542). For commentary on the body of North's work, see Sutch (1982), Libecap (1992a), Parker (1993), McCloskey (1994), Myhrman & Weingast (1994) and Fogel (1997); Fine & Milonakis (2003) are among the critics of North and of New Institutional Economics more generally.

years traversing the Pacific, on watch as navigator and off watch as avid reader, especially from a list of Marxist writings. He returned to Berkeley intent on learning more economics, and fell under the influence of three decidedly unorthodox teachers, M. M. Knight (who supervised North's dissertation on the US insurance industry), Leo Rogin and Robert A. Brady.

Although Parker began his career as an economic historian of Europe, he found that "it was the Turneresque story of the continent's agricultural settlement that affected [him] with a true and almost political passion." At North Carolina he began the careful quantitative work on Southern and Northern agriculture that established his eminence: on labor and land productivity, and the pioneering matched the (Parker–Gallman) US Census sample of Southern people and farms for 1859–60, which had grown from his previous study of cotton plantations. After he moved to Yale he reverted to an earlier "humanistic direction" and "began to pull away from quantification in the style of the National Bureau and turned [his] energies almost entirely to some interpretive essays . . ." His later work, renowned for style and breadth, includes surveys of European industry (1979), the American South (1980a), American economic historiography (1980b), and industrial civilization in the American Midwest (1991a). He is also well known for incisive book reviews and probing review essays, which often included evocative extended metaphors.[2] Parker's devotion to a literary style was a constant, but he did make a major change in scholarly direction – not so much in area of research, since from the 1950s he worked on both American and European topics, but in focus – expanding his viewpoint from the technical and material, quantitatively assessed, to an attempt "to formulate (if not to 'model') a structure for the whole field . . ." That is, he believed and taught "that the history of material life could only be understood in the context of society, polity, and culture."

North has made two such changes. Following his years in Berkeley and on the Pacific he arrived at the University of Washington committed not only to understanding the world but to changing it – claiming to be a Marxist (which, as Hughes recalls, North's students thought "hilariously funny") but criticizing Marxian theory at every turn.[3] In Seattle he succumbed to the seductive power of neoclassical price theory and how it might be applied to patterns of economic development, resulting in his first book, *The Economic Growth of the United States, 1790–1860* (1961), with its model of American regional interactions. Shortly thereafter, as he has stated often, North began to question whether neoclassical price theory could deal with the sorts of historical problems he encountered in studying the feudalism and limited markets of the late medieval and early modern economy of Europe. Since that time, in collaboration with several others, North has tried to articulate an explanation of economic change in terms of alteration

2 See, for example, his essay on the then most recent volume of the "great freight train" of *The Cambridge Economic History of Europe*: ". . . bursting out from its dark tunnel, it rattles across our landscape, loaded high with gold and spices, coal and lumber . . . Livestock are terrified and students astonished; but as happy economic historians we line the tracks and wave our greeting . . ." (1966: 99).

3 In Seattle North joined his Berkeley comrade of undergraduate and graduate days, Morris D. Morris, who supplied the list of North's wartime readings. Morris is perhaps the first "new" economic historian of South Asia (see, *e.g.*, M. Morris 1963; 1965). He taught economic history with North, and was Associate Editor of the *JEH* during the Parker–North editorship.

and persistence of "the rules of the game" – of the underlying structures and institutions of economies over time, of property rights regimes and transactions costs, for which the bounds of orthodox economic theory are much too narrow. North has attempted to alter the mode of economic–historical explanation, in the process "float-[ing] up from the concrete, complex experiences of European and American history into the higher world of theory" (Parker 1993: 627). His most recent work, *Understanding the Process of Economic Change* (Cambridge UP 2005), extends into the realms of "social learning," intentionality and cognition to examine institutional origins and adaptations.

Doug North and Bill Parker were important promoters of the quantitative and formally analytical approach of the New Economic Historians, but both have been cognizant of the limits of cliometrics, if narrowly defined as neoclassical economic theory applied to (quantitative) historical data. In the early 1960s, North was among its most vociferous and enthusiastic proponents, for instance in explicating the cliometrics revolution to the economics profession (1965). Yet, he observes in his interview that the revolutionaries were "more successful in demolishing existing explanations than in constructing new ones," and has for almost four decades, by example and exhortation, encouraged economic historians to expand their horizons. Parker was one of the American profession's literate and elegant stylists, as well as advocate for and pioneer in the "new" economic history. He was, however, a "skeptical pioneer," the voice of conscience for the field, prone to critical detachment, cautious in stating claims, well aware of how much of the old was in the new, and not above gentle reminders to his fellows that their movement might have been "at times too conscious of its own virtue" (1971: 3). Nevertheless, the critical and encompassing approach to economic history practiced and taught by both Parker and North provides breadth and, as Parker says, "something to be smart about."

WILLIAM N. PARKER

Interviewed by
Paul Rhode

William Nelson Parker was Phillip Golden Bartlett Professor of Economics and Economic History, Emeritus, and Professor Emeritus of American Studies at Yale University, New Haven, Connecticut. He was born in Columbus, Ohio in 1919 and died in Hamden, Connecticut in 2000. He was educated at Harvard (A.B., 1939; M.A., 1941; Ph.D., 1951). During and after World War II he worked at the Office of Production Management, the Office of Strategic Services, the US Senate and the Department of State. He began his teaching career at Williams College (1951–6), continuing at the University of North Carolina-Chapel Hill (1956–62) and then at Yale from 1962, retiring in 1989. Parker was Editor (with Douglass North) of the *Journal of Economic History* (1961–6), President of the Economic History Association (1969–70) and of the Agricultural History Association (1979–80), and was elected Fellow of the American Academy of Arts & Sciences in 1987. He was honored in 1984 with *Technique, Spirit and Form in the Making of the Modern Economies*, a *Festschrift* edited by Gary Saxonhouse and Gavin Wright.

The interview took place in January 1991 in an office at the University of North Carolina, not far from the one Parker had occupied in earlier days. The interviewer was Paul Rhode, then at UNC, who, through Gavin Wright, is one of Parker's intellectual grandchildren. The two had first met while traveling to Estonia and Russia to attend a conference on a shared interest, agrarian development. Rhode says he has been inspired by the humor and literary quality of Parker's work, but above all by his logical and systematic approach to finding structure in complex phenomena, without losing sight of the humanity involved.

During his retirement, Parker continued his work in economic history, publishing the second volume of his essay collection, *Europe, America and the Wider World* (1991a), contributing to Volume II of *The Cambridge Economic History of the United States* (Engerman & Gallman, eds 1996; 2000) and writing several more in his long series of distinctive book reviews.

To get ready for our talk, I sent you a list of questions . . .

Your questions indicate, in my opinion, certain misunderstandings of my misunderstanding of myself. Then, I can also comment on some of the specific things that you ask about, especially regarding studying and teaching economic history, what is it and how do I think you do it, both individually, like an old-fashioned scholar, and jointly with like-minded, and sometimes rather different-minded, colleagues in the Cliometrics clan.

The questions are good questions, but I almost think they take me too seriously. You may say that that is not for me to judge, but recently I've become conscious that this question of how I take myself, and how I present myself, has been a problem for me all along. I have an instinct to want to seem to underplay things I feel deeply about – including myself. I have wanted to seem to take myself not quite as seriously as one is expected to. A few people have told me this, especially women. Women generally see through a self-deprecating pose, but men, since they view you as a potential competitor, generally are glad to take you at your word. Once, when I was making some irreverent remark, Claudia Goldin said to me, in exasperation, "Don't you ever take *any*thing seriously," and I said, "NO." I mean, what else could I say when directly challenged like that?

My answer may have puzzled her. But at the root of it was a kind of sense of irony, and a self-consciousness that seems to be built in me. I am fascinated with observing myself and observing myself observe myself. I'm doing it right now. Still, of course, one has to learn to carry on simultaneously, on another track of the mind, some objective and impersonal discourse. It is impossible to see one's self as one truly is, or even as others perceive it. But I do think that I am in some sense more personal, more psychological in approach to life than many of my colleagues. I like to look at individual people and really get quite interested in them. I try to learn both about them and about the world and human nature from their viewpoint, and I try to learn to feel empathy. You can only come to know another person, or yourself, through love and sympathy. Certainly, I am immensely interested in learning about myself, and through that, about other people. But whether my sympathy is in the service of my curiosity, or the other way around, I've never been sure.

Has this self-awareness affected the relationships you have had with students? Could you talk a little about that and about them?

Well, some people say to me, "Your real contribution has been your students," and that always nettles me slightly. Of course I'm very proud of my students. But, damn! Their success might also have to do just a little bit with the content of what I have had to teach them. I consider them all my friends, and I have a very high regard and respect for their individual qualities. But they didn't come to all their views and values just by themselves. Still, I do think that Ph.D. students are not only responsible and trustworthy but also much more inspired than they get credit for.

The director of a dissertation mainly has to help a student to find a topic that taps into their own background in some obscure way and draws on what I call the emotional sources of their research energies. After a student had gotten into their work, I would read their drafts carefully, but I hardly ever made any suggestions until the student had the thing in the bag and was ready to tie it up. Then I would jump in. This way I didn't risk the danger of crushing what may have been some precious insight by premature criticism. And I found that by listening, I was capable of learning something myself. It made for an effective, personalized, and respectful teaching and learning experience for us both. And I don't mean this just for the "best" students, because they are all good in some sense, if they survive. (If they don't survive, they are also good, conceivably, in some more important sense.)

Yes, for variety and intrinsic quality, independence, and strength, I think that the body of students I've had, they are just the best, and certainly to me that is indeed a major satisfaction.

It's a compliment that you paid to Frederick Jackson Turner that his impact was so strongly felt on and through his students.

Turner's students were, as I said, like the sons or tenants of a great landowner, spread out over the landscape. But I don't quite see myself as the founder of a school, though on the several occasions when a group of the ex-students has come together to read papers, some of them note some common features, some resemblances in approach, emphases, and attitudes toward the subject. Whether this is the result of teaching or of natural selection, I'll never know.

Let me speak a bit too about other levels of teaching – lectures, and seminars, and small classes, undergraduate and graduate. Some years after I had come to Yale, I learned that one of the letters of recommendation for me had predicted that I would be a better teacher in small seminars than in a large classroom. That shows, I think, just how wide of the mark the recommendations we give one another can fall. I've rather enjoyed lecturing and the bit of showmanship that goes with it. I don't say that I'm one of the great performers, but a lecture can give you a real thrill when you can see that you are getting it across. I like public speaking. When I was a kid, my mother had me given "elocution" lessons, declaiming poetry and purple passages from the great orators. And in high school I was "orating" all the time in the student council or before the school assemblies. But in college I had virtually no opportunity to speak. I can remember only once – the time when I got up on a bench on Boston Common and made an impassioned speech for FDR, in 1936. On the whole, my career as a public speaker died out with the end of high school, until I came later to give lectures in class and papers and comments at professional meetings – oh, and at faculty meetings now and again. Just before I leave a place, I seem to reveal an instinct to go for the jugular of the President.

Of course, Williams, Carolina, and Yale have all been wonderful places to teach. In none of those places were there big 200- to 300-student classes – at least in economic history. The largest was 90 in the undergraduate course at Carolina. Ordinarily, it was 35–50 there, and at Yale. At Carolina and at Yale, at least half of my teaching was in the required graduate economic history course every year. That's a very different ball game from undergraduate teaching. But even in graduate teaching, I am much more comfortable giving a lecture than trying to lead a discussion. I've found it very hard to say "provocative" things – things I don't think are true – just to get a discussion stirred up. In seminar teaching to a small group, I've not been very comfortable either. I've been most comfortable talking to individual students or, in another mode, in making a public address, rather than in that half-formal, half-informal atmosphere of a seminar. If the students aren't prepared or haven't read anything, they just sit there, and I end up lecturing anyway, out of sheer boredom. The trouble is, I think, that I don't like to enforce discipline on other people, making sure students do their reading, quizzing them about it and embarrassing them. That goes against my grain, except in the relative privacy of an oral exam. But my personal approach doesn't always make for an effective class.

The work with the graduate economics students in the required two-term courses in economic history at Carolina and at Yale succeeded, I think, by and large, because it was the students' only exposure to topics with any breadth or much relation to the other social sciences. Some suspicious, ultra-scientific students, carried away by the beauties and rigor of mathematical theory, claimed to find history repellent, loose, and sloppy. No doubt they found real life that way, too. You can't just be smart in economic history; you have to know something, too, so you have something to be smart about. The really strong students liked the freedom it gave them to speculate. It was a kind of therapy for them – a relief from their immersion in theory, especially as the applied courses got more and more *un*applied and more theoretical. I had the support, too, on the faculty, of several other Harvard-trained members of the Yale Department who were sympathetic to economic history in the style we had learned it from A. P. Usher. And Gus Ranis and John Fei in economic development and Joe Peck and Dick Nelson in industrial organization bought my stuff. But I felt that the field also had the respect of the mathematical theorists, and of the "old Europeans" in the Department – Fellner, Triffin, Koopmans, Wallich, Goldsmith – and also Mike Montias, of course.

With the Ph.D. students in economic history itself, the ones who wrote all the good dissertations, I was helped by two especially lucky circumstances. When I took the Yale job, John Perry Miller, the dean, had instituted a special graduate program between economics and history with half a dozen fellowships from an HEW program to support this idea.[1] So right off I got some very good students – George Grantham in economics and Jan deVries in history, for example. There were ten or so of them altogether. That took me through the 1960s. Then as that ran out, a second "wave" came along as a result of the unrest and dissatisfaction with standard economics that many students felt in the late 1960s and early 1970s. Yale had hired one of our own Ph.D.'s to teach the course in the History of Economic Thought – David Levine. He was tough and rigorous, but he explained to students – some of them hearing it for the first time – that there was something out there called Capitalism, whose history could be subjected to analysis. Unfortunately, but inevitably, I suppose, for one whose thought was cast in so Hegelian a mode, he failed to get tenure. When he left, I fell heir to four or five of his students – tough, brilliant, ambitious, independent-minded scholars. I take credit for guiding some of them to some hard-headed, empirical work in their theses. Both these groups, and a number of some of the most able students who came one by one, were wonderful material including the several who found notable careers outside the university. When I retired in 1989, there were still four in the pipeline, of whom two came out with theses and jobs this year, and the other two, who now have excellent jobs, have still only a couple of months' work (I hope and expect) to go. I should mention also at this point the excellent assistant professors whom Yale appointed to work with me in these years. Their names are, I think, well known, and need no boost from me, but only heartfelt thanks and appreciation, both for their labors and for their personal friendship. I feel that I've been a very lucky guy all round.

Out of my 25 years at Yale, I cherish, too, the work I did as Director of Graduate Studies. I held the job off and on for about ten years. It gave me a deeper relationship with all the students, whom, of course, I had already had in class. What a fascinating array of intellectual, social, financial problems they had! And, since no one else wanted the job, nobody would, or could, lay a finger on the graduate Economic History requirement while I was in charge of graduate studies. The relation with all those students, year after year, was very rewarding. Yale seemed to me to be a very happy program in those days.

How did you come to be an economic historian? What attracted you to the field?

Well, I'm afraid you've let yourself in for a little miscellaneous reminiscing concerning the rather tortuous path that my life and ambition took me down in the years between college graduation in 1939 and 1955, at which time I left Williams for Carolina. It was at Carolina that I began the really concentrated work and career in economic history as a life-long "affair."

In college my humanistic bent won out over social science. It was touch and go. My interests were about evenly balanced between history or politics, on the one hand, and literature, on the other. But I did enjoy the aesthetic experience of reading literature. I

1 HEW is the former US Department of Health, Education, and Welfare.

remember a course in seventeenth-century French drama: Corneille and Racine. I'd recite the speeches aloud – probably in an execrable accent – enjoying the music of the language, even on such an imperfect instrument. I suspect that that side of me indulged itself the more because of the almost utterly inactive social and emotional life at Harvard, then a wholly male institution. There were no girls around and I had not gotten to thinking – well . . . THINKING, YES. I think a young guy thinks about girls most of the time, but there were no opportunities to think of what was called in those days the "opposite sex" in any objective, concrete way. I was wholly innocent of all that when I was at Harvard. And I didn't have a radical disposition that might have given me some public emotional outlet. I just shut myself up with books and was a good boy. I would get spells of adolescent melancholy, that kind of sweet romantic sadness that comes, I suppose, from frustration. But that did not give me any concept of rebelling at all. The middle-class format gave me enough leeway to express myself, and it was all I knew. I was a liberal democrat, but in those days that had not come to be considered radical. I have gotten more radical as I've gotten older, while the country has gotten more conservative. I see how society shapes young people and how it can oppress or release them.

In college, then, I had this big dilemma about what to major in – political science or English. I followed my heart, I guess. There was all that literature out there that I wanted to read, and this was the easy way to read it. I also wanted to "write" – essays, creative stories, no poetry. I polished my writing skills in a certain classical style pretty far. Dr. Johnson had advised that to develop a beautiful style, a writer should give his days and nights to the study of Addison. So I read the *Spectator* papers and tried to imitate them. I got up at six one term to write out translations of Cicero, just to dissect his style and develop my own. It worked to a certain degree. I've always had great pleasure in working out expository prose. This well served my interest in politics and history in college. But I had a genuine love for literature as an art form. Still, I finally came to feel that literary analysis was a problem either in sociology or in psychology. I couldn't see any way between these that would give any criteria outside of personal taste. In the end, it was not an aesthetic impulse but a kind of socio-scientific instinct that I couldn't satisfy through literary studies.

In 1939, on graduation, I had my fellowship renewed for any graduate school or department at Harvard that would admit me, even Law or Medicine. I went to the chairman of the English Department, a man of the wealthy, gentle-scholar type of that era. I remember telling him that if I went on in his graduate department, I would eventually want to teach English at the high school level, and get into educational administration. This shocked him, I could see, and he told me coldly that for the Ph.D., I would first have to study Anglo-Saxon. So I went over to the Harvard School of Education and talked to a notable educational psychologist. He told me that before long he would have me in the laboratory, testing rats. I didn't want that either.

But when I went shopping to the Economics Department, I came under the spell of John D. Black, the "dean" of agricultural economists. He was a big, heavy-set, rotund man, from Minnesota, and a Jim Farley type of politician. He saw that I was a skinny, idealistic city boy, and he put his arm around me and painted before my eyes a picture of world agricultural development, and described how I could contribute to it. That hit my weak spot. I had always asked myself, "Where is all the world's poverty?" and had answered, "In India and China, among the teeming masses of peasants." Agricultural economics seemed fundamental to every other world economic problem. Agricultural fundamentalism is very strong in me. It was not the virtues of its way of life, but its basic position in economic development, and in the economic history of earlier ages that attracted my attention. I don't know where in the hell this belief came from, because in Ohio I grew up in a city of 300,000. I had no relatives on the farm except for one uncle. Just maybe I had this impression about farming simply because it is true. Agriculture *is* basic to the problem of poverty and social order in most of the world. This fact came to the surface in my thinking again in the 1950s, after the war and the short-run, post-war concerns had begun to recede from immediate view.

I passed my Ph.D. general exam in the spring of 1941. I did okay for a guy who had been a college English major. With the draft already on, several of us figured we would be drafted soon for a year's service in the army (this was before Pearl Harbor). So, instead of registering to begin my dissertation, I took the civil service exam for junior economist and went to Washington on a government job in the summer and fall of 1941. Jim Tobin and I and some other fledging economists were hired by the Civilian Supply part of the OPM (Office of Production Management). Each of us was given an industry to plan a program to control its output, so as to cut down its demand for steel. I was given the commercial refrigeration and air conditioning industry, and I really had a wonderful time. I was 22. I had the vice presidents of Carrier, Frigidaire, coming in terribly worried, and treating me with great deference. Then one morning in November, 1941, a month before Pearl Harbor, the "Greetings" came from the local draft board back in Columbus. I resisted as best I could, but the chairman of my draft board, who used to live across the street from us when I growing up, said I was an over-educated ass who had had too much Harvard, and the Army would be the best thing for me.

What happened next?

I went in and stayed for four years. But mid-way in 1943, I escaped from the real army through the good offices of my old college buddy, [Richard] Ruggles, who was in the OSS office in London. He had a project to estimate German production of war materials from the serial numbers on the captured equipment. I was in London, then in Paris and Germany, responsible only to Ruggles and General Eisenhower. I traveled all over Normandy and Alsace in a jeep with a couple of enlisted men. Our job was to get to the knocked-out equipment after a battle and copy down the markings. After the war, we went around the factories to see how close we had come. We came very close, within a few percent for individual items – guns, tanks, trucks, even buzz bombs (V-1's) and rockets (V-2's). Of course, we got the information too late to do much good. There is an article about it in the *JASA* (Ruggles & Brodie 1947). But the job gave me some interesting war experiences. They were spiced with an occasional bomb that made me feel like a soldier, but it was a very easy and interesting life.

After the war, for about nine months in 1946, I went to work on Capitol Hill for the Senate Committee on Atomic Energy. That, too, was an exciting year. I was a major by that time and I still had to wear my uniform because you couldn't buy white shirts. It gave a minor advantage in my first effort at really seriously courting girls. Then, the one I became engaged to went off to the United Nations and ditched me. That left me in great despair, and in the fall of 1946 I went back to Harvard to try to write a thesis on the Atomic Energy Act of 1946. But I was too much of an economist by then to take up a political science topic. I just couldn't do it. I'd lie in bed hearing the college bell ring every hour, feeling like a freshman all over again. My morale was just miserable, and it showed in all sorts of ways.

So I gave up and took a research job back in Washington with the State Department in January, 1947, so as to build up to another thesis topic. Stuart Hughes, the intellectual historian, was the chief of the division – a lovely man. The section was also staffed by various émigré scholars – Herbert Marcuse, the famous radical philosopher, was the chief. I always felt that he considered the economics division, which I was in, to be very dull and pedestrian. I wrote some studies on the different Allied zones of Germany – the French zone, and one on the Russian zone on the basis of intelligence reports. I was getting a certain reputation for that in other offices of the Department. But I still felt I wanted to get that thesis done. And when I met this exciting modern dancer with the French name – Yvonne – in the elevator, I really wanted to marry her, and, after a tolerably brief period, I found, amazingly, that she would marry me. At the same time, I used the techniques of economic decision making to take a long look at economics, and decided my comparative advantage lay in economic history, or possibly in industrial organization. I had been very interested in the post-war economic settlements in Germany, both that of Versailles and the one I saw unfolding around me in the State Department. Back at Harvard, Usher encouraged my idea for a study of the German coal and steel complex in the 1920s. So in 1948, I got married and took off on an SSRC fellowship, supplemented later by a Fulbright, to stay in Paris and Essen for two and half years to do a thesis. We lived in Germany practically free on the occupation economy, in the old Krupp hotel, the *Essenerhof*, and were fed on British Army rations – miserable food, but served with great elegance by the German head waiter, in tails and with a sneer on his face, and we had the use of an Army jeep and driver for taxi service. I was able to bank the G. I. Bill stipends for a nest egg for after I got home and so came back several thousand dollars ahead of the game. It must have been one of the few cases when anybody got a bit richer while writing a thesis.

I see in retrospect I really didn't approach the whole job quite right. Usher's teaching had emphasized raw materials, natural resources, technology; he came at things from the ground up. So I spent a lot of research time unraveling the technical details of coal as a commodity and its markets. I worked, too, with the structure of the Syndicate and its relation to the steel combines. But I took too physical, too engineering a view of the whole thing. Looking back, I can see, as one does with one's parents, Usher's decided influence, and – I would say now – not all for the good. I never was a student who worshipped a professor, and Usher was not the sort of professor who sought disciples. He was modest in excess, if anything, and rather dull as a lecturer. His personal relationships were couched in an old-fashioned formality. But there is no discounting the power on me of his ideas and his values. They were absorbed like a dye or a disease for which I suppose I must have had a receptive predisposition. Gerschenkron, who had succeeded Usher in 1948, allowed me to pass my final oral in May 1951.

I went to teach at Williams for five years for Émile Despres, a man who had many of the qualities of greatness. Then, in 1954, I was invited by the geographer, Norman J. G. Pounds, to write the last half of a historical study of the European coal and steel industries. It started me on a long career of writing on invitation. In fact, there are only a very few pieces in my bibliography that were not done more or less at somebody's request, or as part of a larger project, sometimes one of my own devising. I like to develop my own ideas, but within a structure of other scholars. Where such a structure did not already exist, I joined with others to create one. In 1956, when I was invited to North Carolina by that lovely, gentle man, Milton Heath, I was well settled into economic history, with an interest in the long-run history of economic sectors. And when I got to Carolina, I took up my old interest in agriculture as a sector, but now in a historical context. I remained hooked on that cycle of research for the next 15 years.

I would be interested in hearing you and Bob Gallman discourse on the Parker–Gallman sample. There hadn't been a lot of work done previously in gathering together samples of this size. And it certainly has had a huge impact.

Well, so far as I know there hadn't really been an effort before to apply any sort of scientific sampling to the Census materials, except for the population censuses. The historian who came closest was, I suppose, Frank Owsley, but sampling simply wasn't in earlier historians' tool bag.

Did you think it would have such wide use?

I didn't think much about that, one way or the other, but I could see I was on to a good thing. I could see infinite bodies of data that could be exploited in this way. The quantitative study of slavery had gotten a big boost with Conrad and Meyer's paper at the EHA meetings in 1957. Racial integration was just barely beginning, and sociologists were showing a new interest in labor systems in underdeveloped countries. But my interest was simply in the conditions under which cotton was supplied to the world market in the nineteenth century. Tom Cochran had asked me to write a paper on large management units in American agriculture for a session of the International Economic History Association at its first (1960) meeting at Stockholm. Plantations were the only largish scale enterprises, in terms of labor employed, in the American experience.

Some wheat farms in the Red River Valley in Minnesota and in California in the nineteenth century were large land holdings, but not large bodies of year-round labor. Of course, these and the plantations, too, were peanuts as compared to East European estates with serf or hired labor.

But in my paper on the slave plantation in American agriculture, I tried to think out the different aspects that could illuminate, and be illuminated by, the economist's natural questions – demand, regional balance of trade, capital inflow or outflow, internal self-sufficiency, even the bias against industrial development. I think it hit on the main lines along which the treatment of the subject indeed did develop. Certainly, I had in my head an implicit economic model. I did considerable quantitative research before I wrote the paper, though I didn't include any numbers explicitly. But I went over from Chapel Hill to the Duke Library, where the nineteenth-century manuscript census records of Louisiana, Arkansas, North Carolina, and (I believe) Mississippi were held. A very sturdy graduate student, Don Schilling, helped me, and we dug out by hand some of the 1860 records on large farms.

Then we got greedy. I began planning a large sample of the manuscript returns from the Census of Agriculture, matching the farm productions, by name of farm operator, with the farm labor force, as reported for each slaveholder in the Census of slaves and for free family labor in the Census of the white population. We planned to do this for the counties in the Census of 1860 harvesting 1000 bales of cotton or over, with selection from all the major soil-type regions. Before the work could begin, I had to get a grant from the university grants committee at Carolina. The dean of the School of Business wanted to earn respectability with the liberal arts college, and he endorsed the proposal with enthusiasm. The chairman of the grants committee was Fletcher Green, a southern historian who had produced more Ph.D. theses than any man in the world: 500–600, it was said. He didn't know what I could do with all these numbers, but he could see that they concerned farmers, and I suspect he was a bit of an old Populist. In any case, his committee gave me all the money I needed in order to explore. Next Jim Blackman, then gone from Carolina to NSF, helped us to get an NSF grant to get the data filmed from about a dozen state libraries in the South. Franklee Gilbert (now, Whartenby), a very good thesis student at Chapel Hill, was awarded an SSRC grant to go down to South Carolina and several other places to collect data from the plantation records for the 1830s and 1840s for her dissertation. She didn't use the census records themselves, but she tracked down where they were. When we got the films together, we set up three microfilm readers, side by side, to try to match names in the census of agriculture with those of slave holders and the heads of white families.

All of this fitted into a larger structure of the study of American agriculture that was my part of a sizable Ford Foundation grant, shared with Ross Robertson, Moe Abramovitz, and Jack Sawyer – a general grant for the economic study of American economic history. In my portion of the work, I divided agriculture up by crops, and tried to get labor input in each operation on each crop. The work on slave plantations was a by-product of this scheme of measuring the contribution of agriculture to American development overall. After the project got started, I made the move from Chapel Hill to New Haven, and Bob Gallman and his students re-worked the sampling and improved it and then brought out a series of fundamental studies. At Yale, Gavin Wright and Peter Passell drew on it for their dissertations. The recorded result of much of all our work was published in a book, *The Structure of the Cotton Economy of the Ante-Bellum South*, in Wright's beautiful book, *The Political Economy of the Cotton South*, and, supplemented by their own exhausting investigations, in Fogel and Engerman's *Time on the Cross*. Its influence moved out in many directions, both in the study of Southern economic development, and as the predecessor of similar researches in the nineteenth-century census manuscripts of agriculture and manufactures.

Let's move on to look at some more general issues of methodology. You've always had sort of a structure or schema in your teaching and writing. Where do you think that habit of mind comes from? You were saying that you were trying to find a "structure" when you studied literature.

Well, it seems to me to be the way anybody has to think. Idealization is involved in it, a kind of theorizing. A tension or ambivalence is produced between ideal structures – ideal type structures, Parsonian structures – on the one hand, and the facts of a body of history. You try to explain historical change within a structure, as it is observed in operation, but you also have to explain how the behavior at a deeper level of structures creates and alters the economic structures themselves. And so on, *ad infinitum*. That tension between the general and specific is what moves historical and sociological research down into ever deeper levels. If you get pulled too far in one direction, your thinking steams up into clouds of philosophy, and if you go the other way – down toward the particular – you get buried in the dust and don't say anything of general interest. You have to hold steady on a middle ground.

Again, that is a moderate attitude – part of that shying away from radical thought that is in my bones. Perhaps that is an English–American intellectual trait. Usher had it quite strongly and articulated it. He never had much use for "ideal-type structures," as he called the theories of Weber and Marx. But he did deal in large topics – technology and population. He seemed to think that there was a sort of optimal size of topic that could be handled. If you went beyond that, it got too complicated, and if you got below that, the work seemed trivial and antiquarian. That is the name of the game in economic history – to work at an interesting, yet sustainable level. It is an engineering problem really, though, oddly enough, the history of technology with a few well known exceptions, has itself rarely been handled with this kind of balance.

You don't favor some of the structures that people typically use to organize their studies, such as the growth of the national incomes of nation states.

Well, I think the national income framework has been very useful. But I would like to see explorations at both lower and higher levels of aggregation.

As a way of analyzing an economy, you seem to emphasize regions and resources.

Yes, Usher's emphasis on resources, geography, technology produced in my mind a kind of opportunity/response framework. When I came to organize the graduate course in economic history at Carolina, I picked this up as a way of handling the material. Three natural forces combine to create an opportunity framework for an economy: resources, technology, and demand. The response to opportunity is a problem of human organization – a political problem rather an economic one. It is not about wresting a living from the earth's materials, or feeding hungry mouths. It is about power and contrivance and how individuals control one another mutually, how some are better at the game than others, and what are the different economic results of the different combinations of roles and actors. It was only after ten years or so at Yale that I began looking past the "opportunity" part to this other element, where culture, society, and a collection of individual personalities all come into the structure of explanation, piled on top of one another in layers.

But I had no really formal training in the other social sciences to help me. In the early years at Yale I read sociology – the German historians, Weber, Veblen, Sumner, and a few of the more attractive moderns, Riesman, Parsons, Merton, Mills – and, to even more profit, the older anthropologists – Malinowski, Furth, and some of Mead, Benedict, Frazer, Herskovits, and later, Sahlins. I felt great sympathy with the French *Annales* school and their peasant studies, and particularly with the wonderful books of Marc Bloch. I never talked about *histoire totale* much and I never wrote about it, but I soaked it up. My mind and imagination were very receptive to it. I think that that strain of interest goes back partly to college. I remember the sophomoric bull sessions we had about understanding the world. We all aimed at a total comprehension, a totality, a Hegelian "holistic" concept, though we had never heard of Hegel. We had a phrase – "Knowing what it's all about." As Harvard men, we thought we "knew what it was all about." (About the rest of mankind, we were not so sure.) In a way, we were talking in college about a social equilibrium of different character traits affecting every item of behavior and culture. I remember reading Burckhardt's *Civilization of the Renaissance* – the section on the state as a work of art – and Huizinga's *Waning of the Middle Ages* and Eric Erikson's books, especially *Young Man Luther*. Books like these – and there are not very many of them – I really sopped up. Sometimes with these great books it will be a decade or longer before you really realize what you had read.

Then, in US economic history, I had to come to grips at last with the relation of the industrial culture of New England and the Midwest to an underlying ethos or mentality. I read some on the Puritans – not just Weber, but some about the actual doctrines. (The Yale Library is a great place to do that.) I'm really deeply interested in the psychology of all that. I don't have too much respect for historians who ridicule its importance by producing counter-examples from the capitalism of the Mediterranean or Japan. The relevant question is – what is the sum total of factors that are present and how do they interact? There are many factors, but in the Western context, Protestantism is surely one. Just because three and two make five does not mean that four and one also couldn't make five. The economic response to a production or trading opportunity will be organized in one way in one social group and in another way in another. If the opportunity is very wide, then strong individuals pursuing a variety of goals may come to fit together in a market framework. Tidy, bureaucratic social organization of the response may be the most effective response if you already have well-disciplined individuals. But the measured outcomes of two different combinations of individual characteristics and organizational form may be very similar. I had an example of this in the growth of the iron industries in German and French Lorraine after 1870. Lessons like this come from attention to comparative economic history, particularly when, as in Al Chandler's latest book, Germany, with its special organizational and characterological features, is one element of the comparison.[2] So in studying both European and American agrarian structures and industrialization on the two continents, I have tried to suggest, at least a little, how the human side of organization fits with its natural and technological constraints. Consequently, I feel very uncomfortable in bull session talk about individualism and "collectivism." There isn't any simple weighting that fits all cases. It's a day-by-day confrontation, as life develops, between human impulses transmitted in different forms and with differing relative intensities.

So I have remained calling myself an economist. Besides, I have great sympathy with the policy side of economics, the possibility of some really useful contributions to the functioning of a democracy with the limited economic knowledge that we have. It always seemed to me a bit self-indulgent to enjoy reading about primitive tribes simply because their societies could be imagined to form such pleasant, aesthetically pleasing wholes. I suppose you will say that *my* Puritanism is showing.

What do you think about the relationship between economic history and the economics profession?

I am bemused to think that the people who favored the economic history requirement during my years at Yale were not always the traditional applied economists, but rather the development people and the mathematical economists. With a few exceptions, like Joe Peck, applied economists, if they think about history at all, tend to think about it mainly in relation to current issues in their own fields. The fact that history is a synthesis of many areas was something you always had to keep up in front of them.

In my editor's postlude to *Economic History and the Modern Economist* (1986), I claimed that an economics program has many different uses for economic history. But from any view, it is a healthy thing for students to be exposed to. For one thing, it attaches at the ends to all the other social sciences. If you are of a naturalistic, physical-science bent, you still have to see where demography, or politics, or sociology must be brought into economic studies. History leads you out of the strict, narrow economic maximizing paradigms to the rest of God's creation. For economists, it offers all the benefits of foreign travel.

2 Chandler (1990); Parker wrote a review essay (1991b) on Chandler's book for the *JEH*.

Alongside quantification and model-testing, history's narrative techniques still undeniably make some kind of sense, even though you cannot prove every interpretation or calculate the statistical probability of its truth. And for students to get the "feel," the intuitive feel, of the actors in an economy – putting themselves in the place of people in a different culture – this is an exercise of imagination and thought that economists need, both in framing hypotheses and in making policy recommendations. After all, where do hypotheses and assumptions come from? They are impressions arising in the mind from the cursory examination of a record. Narrative economic history is a tissue of untested hypotheses. Sure, most of them are untestable, but they are nevertheless powerful stimuli to the imagination, and to the mind's effort to learn and explore.

Would you call the so-called "new" economic history the result of a "rebellion" against the "old?"

Well, not exactly. I don't think of "new" economic history as really a "rebellion." Except for Carter Goodrich, Hal Williamson, and Chester Wright, the "old" economic historians in American economic history of the 1940s and 1950s had been trained as historians. Kirkland, Shannon, and Faulkner, for example, had written the three principal texts, and they – and their economist counterparts – were all very solid scholars indeed. It is true that a lot of loose talk on capitalism came out of the followers of Veblen. I think Veblen was a great thinker, a great intuitor as well as a great writer. The institutionalists who followed him – Ayres, Brady – tended to be a bit windy. I didn't have much respect for that as a school of careful thought.

I never used the phrase "new economic history," until others took it up. It always made me squirm a little because I was sensitive to the continuity of the effort with the writers of the 1930s – Clapham, Heckscher, Usher, and Bloch. Those earlier scholars had different ways of going about history, but it was all wonderful scholarship. In the United States, certainly, Beard was pretty extreme sometimes in his willingness to paint a big picture. It made your flesh creep a little, but it was inspiring. I didn't want to throw it out. The book in agrarian history I most admired was Webb's *Great Plains*; it is so original, and seems so thorough, so honest, and true. Of course, Webb was a vastly spirited and entertaining writer. Shannon's *Farmers' Last Frontier* at places swings into that mode, but Shannon struck me as probably a narrower man, without Webb's scope. I found the mastery of detail and the sound economic judgment in L.C. Gray's *History of Agriculture in the Southern United States* admirable. Parts of Phillips's books on the South, too, I was affected by. I knew he had his biases, but he had his sympathies as well. I liked Malin's books, too, and I admired greatly Bogue's really fine book, *From Prairie to Corn Belt.* I think Gavin Wright's books on the South carry on in this tradition, with more, and more exciting, technical economics in them. Those older agricultural historians were my heroes, even though I worked in a statistical, "counting" sort of way.

So I felt a great sense of joy to break out from the numbers far enough to write the chapter on agriculture in our 12-author textbook *American Economic Growth* and also the chapter about the American farmer in a book on peasants that Jerry Blum edited. It gave me great satisfaction getting my information and intuitions together and saying it in nice language. With those pieces, and with that chapter in the *New Cambridge Modern History*, Volume 13, on European industry before 1850 – which, being based on my lectures, flowed out of me like a novel – I felt I hit a stride. I felt that with the quantitative work, too – the piece on grain which Judith Klein and I did, for example. When the data – so painfully gathered and sorted – began to fall into place, they outlined a logical puzzle which gave real intellectual satisfaction to work out. But I enjoyed, too, the emotional satisfaction that came out of sticking a little sociology beneath the agricultural history, as I did in the two survey essays. In these ways, work in the field came to satisfy both the intellectual and the emotional sides of my nature.

The second volume of your collected essays (1991a) really forms an outline history of American economic growth. It is dedicated "to Doug and Dick and Lance and Bob and Stan and Bob and Stan and Al and Paul and Peter" and to your joint efforts. Can you say a few words about these people?

You want me to tell you what I think about my colleagues? Incidentally, you must have seen a typescript copy, because in the published version someone at the Cambridge University Press has cut out the second "Bob and Stan" that I had put in the manuscript. But the need for this explanation only serves to emphasize that colleagues are a sensitive matter. Nobody ever completely approves of anyone else's personality and work except his own, and if he is any good, usually not that either. I was moved to make that dedication because I felt – well, it's what you feel when a department is working well, when people are getting along well together. Some joint product was coming out. I really did feel a sense of intellectual communion among that group of guys with their different talents and emphases. I thought that altogether we had really got the subject organized, and I take a good bit of credit for my part in organizing a sub-set of us into a reasonably harmonious group for our textbook, which came out in 1972.

About the textbook?

I had signed up with Irwin to write an economic history textbook when I was still at Williams in 1954. At Carolina in 1958–59, Dean Lee gave me a Ford Faculty Fellowship to spend a whole year in the Library of Congress. I worked pretty hard. I had an outline for 40 chapters and I got two chapters written, one, on geographical discovery, and a second chapter on minerals discovery. By that time the year was up and I had written two out of 40 chapters. I said to myself, "This is not a game you know how to play." Working full-time, I would be another 20 years finishing this outline, and you can't get fellowships for that long a period. So I just put it up on the shelf while various joint efforts began to materialize, especially the National Bureau volumes. Along with Dorothy Brady and all the authors, I put a great deal of thought and effort into both Volumes 24 and 30 of the *Studies in Income and Wealth* [CRIW 1960; 1966].

By 1968, I felt that we really were quite a little group. I had given up writing a textbook by myself, but it did seem we could do a good job working together. Lance Davis had the same sort of idea, and, with Dick Easterlin as critic and consultant, we went down a list of topics and a list of people. Some topics were not covered by anyone in our group. But the two lists corresponded quite closely with one another. It was as if the natural division of labor, enforced by the Invisible Hand, had made us steer clear of one another's areas. Putting everyone together, the fit was quite good. There was Lebergott on labor, Gallman on national income, Easterlin on population, Davis on capital, Fishlow on transportation, Rosenberg on technology; I had resources and agriculture – 12 new economic historians altogether. It was subtitled "An Economist's History of the United States," and it was a damn good collection, which nobody bought. I think it was because professors took their lectures out of it and didn't want their students to read it first.

The famous Purdue seminars, which turned into the Cliometric Society, had been, of course, a looser format. When we were able to squeeze ourselves between the covers of a textbook, we had gone about as far as you could ever go to get these fellows to pull one wagon. That's what I meant when I made that dedication. I think they were all intellectually in the book. Bob Fogel, Stan Engerman, and Paul David did not write chapters, but they were obvious people we all counted on and looked to for intellectual support.

Do you have any closing words of wisdom?

OK, I get the hint. Yes. Let me make one last industrial statesmanly statement – a feeling which I would like to express and to propagate. This has to do with your mention of the nation and the nation state. American economic history is the history of a continent. Why isn't European history the history of a continent? Why do we keep all such heavy emphasis on national histories? It seems to me that over the next 20–30 years, if the study of European economic history is going to be of any use or interest, in much the same way that Kuznets's comparative cases were to students of national development, it is going to have to have a different format, one in line with a common market, a history of transnational trends and development in which the political units were set. That, too, was largely Usher's emphasis.

Even the homogeneity that resonates from one state to another – the general adoption of liberal policies in the mid-nineteenth century, for example – meant that many of those states were abandoning mercantilism for 50 to 80 years, at least until the 1920s, and allowing a freer market and freer trade. World War I messed that all up, and that is what I would gather that the bureaucrats in Brussels, and the liberal-minded intellectuals – as well as some business and banking interests that support them – are trying to restore. Can't historians help this effort in some way? Of course, we talk about Western Europe and "Western Culture" as if those terms were not simply an artificial creation of the Cold War. Europe is really three cultures – North, East, and South; that is, loosely, Germanic, Slavic, and Latin, with enclaves of even older ethnic groups. The *West* of Europe is the United States, with all its ethnic diversity.

But a suitable organization of the world's nations and ethnic groups into a peaceful, prosperous and joyous community is a subject rather larger than what Usher would have considered to be of optimum scale. Still, I'd like to give it a whirl with all that blessed irresponsibility that a scholar can show in his seventies. Maybe I can imitate Scheherazade (or, Shevardnadze) and keep telling my story to put off the day when the Sultan cuts my head off.

Come to think of it, that last remark is a good example of what I meant in my opening remarks as I tried to explain myself to myself, before your questions began.

But this sort of talk takes us beyond even the capacious bounds of economic history, much less of Cliometrics.

DOUGLASS C. NORTH

Interviewed by
Gary D. Libecap,
John S. Lyons and
Samuel H. Williamson

Douglass Cecil North is Spencer T. Olin Professor in Arts and Sciences at Washington University in St. Louis, Missouri, and Senior Fellow at The Hoover Institution, Stanford University, Stanford, California. He was born in Cambridge, Massachusetts in 1920 and was educated at the University of California, Berkeley (B.A., 1942; Ph.D., 1952). He taught at the University of Washington in Seattle from 1950 to 1983. Before moving to St. Louis, he was also Peterkin Professor of Political Economy at Rice University (1979) and Pitt Professor of American Institutions at Cambridge University (1981–2). North was Editor (with William Parker) of the *Journal of Economic History* (1961–6), served as a Director of the National Bureau of Economic Research (1967–86), was President of the Economic History Association (1972–3) and of the Western Economics Association (1975–6), was elected Fellow of the American Academy of Arts & Sciences in 1987, and received the John R. Commons Award in 1991 from the international honor society in economics, Omicron Delta Epsilon. He was awarded the Nobel Memorial Prize in Economic Science, jointly with Robert W. Fogel, in 1993. He has also been honored with a *Festschrift*, edited by his former students Roger Ransom, Richard Sutch and Gary Walton, *Explorations in the New Economic History* (Academic Press 1982) and with *The Frontiers of the New Institutional Economics* (Academic Press 1997), edited by his Washington University colleagues, John Drobak and John Nye.

The interview was conducted in 1993 in two parts, first in a series of telephone calls and letters with GARY LIBECAP, then at the University of Arizona, followed by a conversation with SAMUEL WILLIAMSON and JOHN LYONS on October 2nd at the Economic History Association meetings in Tucson, Arizona. Gary Libecap writes:

My contact with Doug North's work began in the fall of 1972 at the end of my three years in the US Air Force. I was not sure I wanted to return to graduate school at the

University of Pennsylvania, so I decided to read some more economics books to see whether they would spark my interest. Bill Whitney at Penn sent me a reading list which included *Institutional Change and American Economic Growth*, by Lance Davis and Douglass North. I was intrigued by their use of neoclassical theory to analyze the development of important legal and political institutions, and I began to read more on the subject, which remains of central concern to me. In a very real sense, I owe much to the work of Doug North, his colleagues and students. I was thus interviewing someone I greatly admire and whose work has played a vital role in the development of economic history. North has been foremost in insisting that more attention be directed to institutional structures and property rights arrangements to explain differences in economic performance across societies and over time. He has urged us to relax our self-imposed devotion to the constraints of neoclassical economics and to broaden our investigations to include analyses both of the role institutions play in economic growth and of the process of institutional change. More recently, he has called for consideration of the elusive concepts of ideology, fairness, and path dependence in attempting to explain why some societies have been successful in economic development, while for others sustained economic growth remains a distant goal.

Since the interview North has continued an active scholarly life, having published many articles and the recent book on economic change (2005). With John J. Wallis and Barry Weingast he is now at work on another, *A Conceptual Framework for Interpreting Recorded Human History*.

What gave the "New Economic History" its early drive?

The "New Economic History" revolution – and that's what it was – was already in the wind by the second half of the 1950s. Walt Rostow was an early influence but, of course, Simon Kuznets was most influential, as was all the activity going on in the field of development. The NBER also played an important role. I was invited to be a Research Associate at the Bureau in 1956–57, and Solomon Fabricant (then Director of Research) went out of his way to provide encouragement – sending me down once a week to spend the day with Kuznets in Baltimore. Both Dick Easterlin and Bob Gallman were there as well. The culmination of that year, 1957, was the EHA–NBER Income and Wealth Conference at Williams in the fall. At the time we were convinced we could overturn old, obsolete dogmas and remake the field of economic history. But more fundamental was the inspiration we got, not only from Kuznets, but also from a broad array of economists who were deeply interested in what we were up to. Of course, it was Jon Hughes and Lance Davis at Purdue who got us all together in 1960 for what became the annual frozen February trek to Lafayette.

Tell us about those early meetings.

The early Clio meetings were heady affairs, usually with a mixture of economists and econometricians thrown in with us economic historians. They tended to be pretty much no-holds-barred discussions. (One participant got so mauled that he locked himself in his room for a spell and never returned.) It was very exciting. First of all, there wasn't such a distinction in those days between economists and economic historians, so that all of us, the economists included, were really excited about what we economic historians were trying to do. So economists attended the early Clios, providing a powerful encouragement. In fact, they egged us on in a way. That was very important. There were a lot of them – not just at the first meeting, but at most of the meetings. We spent a lot of time arguing – disagreeing – about how we could use our economic theory correctly.

A while back I went through the old Purdue volume where they list the participants, and I was amazed at the people who did attend whom I had forgotten about. What I do remember is that it was exciting; it was fun; we really had a good time. Dick Easterlin came – and I don't know whether it was the first or second session – but part of it was on my first book, *Economic Growth of the United States*. Dick Easterlin had written a 22-page book review for the *Journal of Economic History*, and Bill Parker and I were the editors. He was critical; Dick didn't have a good word to say about my book in 22 pages, so I said, "Well, that's all right, but isn't it a little long?" And I said to Bill, something like. "You handle it, but I think I'd cut it down to about six pages."[1] We really *did* give each other the business, and it was very good as a result. I felt wounded a lot of times, but then we *all* did, and that's the way it should have been. I've never been to a set of meetings that I looked forward to – even including the lousy fare in Lafayette – as much as I did those things; they were really exciting.

There is this story – and I don't know if you've ever put it in print – about you at the airport on the way to the first meeting – how does that story go?

The one about Bob Fogel? Well, that's a true story. Bill Parker and I had met at the airport and we were standing there and I knew everybody else – we were all *old* friends – and I said, "Who's this guy Fogel who's supposed to come to this? I never heard of such a guy." And then this great big bear of a form, you know, turned around and said, "*I'm* Bob Fogel." But that's the way I met Bob Fogel. Sitting there in the airport in Chicago, on our way down to getting snowbound that year. There had been a lot of preparations and we all not only knew who was going, but we'd known a lot about it, we'd had a lot of talk. Since Lance and Jon, you know, were formerly my students, we'd spent a lot of time talking about who should be there and everything. So Fogel was a surprise – I'd never heard of him.

What was the reaction of historians and other economists to the "new" approach?

1 Easterlin presented his critique at the second Purdue seminar in December 1961; it was published as Easterlin (1962) and is little more than three pages in print.

Initially, the reaction of historians was very hostile. Economists were generally enthusiastic; the demand for "new economic historians" by economics departments in the 1960s and early 1970s was ample testimony to that. Surprisingly, I think the long-run effect has been the reverse. Cliometrics has had more influence on historians than on economists. Historians, even while protesting about cliometrics, have become much more self-conscious about quantitative methods and at times even tend to be uncritical in accepting the theory we employ. But economics departments have largely reverted to thinking of economic historians as marginal to department needs. The reason, I believe, is that we do not add any particular dimension to economics. We just use their tools to explain the past.

So cliometrics hasn't lived up to its early billing?

No, I don't think it has. It was a real revolution in the beginning, and everyone in economics was caught up in what was going on. But the limitations of neoclassical theory as a tool kit are today more appreciated by many in economics – where I think a revolution is going on – than in economic history, which tends to be more reactionary in terms of theoretical innovation than economics. And until economic historians break out of the strictures imposed by neoclassical theory, cliometrics will remain a relatively uninteresting field.

With no useful policy implications?

Nothing is a more telling indictment of economic history than its failure to play an important role in understanding economic development and in providing policy guidelines for development of Third World countries and, now, Eastern European economies. We should have been in the very forefront of the development field. I think it is promising that those economic historians who are breaking new ground are in substantial demand because they do have something to contribute to the development field.

Nevertheless, there were some major achievements?

Yes, our primary achievement was the rigor of analysis that came with systematic use of neoclassical theory and quantitative methods – the economic way of reasoning. Equally important was the development of quantitative data on the past performance of economies. The result was to overturn a lot of accepted explanations in economic history, none more spectacular than Bob Fogel's attack on the indispensability of the railroad. But we were more successful at demolishing existing explanations than in constructing new ones.

What we did then was impressive enough to be called a revolution, but the failure to go on to deal with the two major shortcomings of neoclassical theory applied to history have aborted the revolution. One is to model the frictions in economies that result in imperfect markets – political and economic – and produce very diverse performances across economies. The second is that economic history is about *change through time*, and economic historians have simply not addressed that difficult but essential problem. Here and there some work is starting to be done, the exploration of path dependence, for example. I don't mean to sound too bleak because there is an increasing number of very bright younger people (and others like Paul David and Bob Fogel), who are integrating new developments from the social sciences with economic history to produce some exciting results – and the ongoing revolution is much broader than just in economics. It's just that one would have thought that economic historians, with their revolutionary tradition, would have taken the lead instead of being laggards.

Looking back, do you think you all quite realized the significance of what you were doing in those days?

Well, Jon Hughes came to me early on and said, "You know, the new economic history isn't really going to dominate the profession in my lifetime."

Is that so?

Yes. We didn't think it would – it was not the economists, the economists loved it – because in those days, four-fifths of economic history, at least, was being taught in history departments. So the idea that economists would ever come to dominate it, that it would move more into economics departments, seemed to be very, very remote, but then what happened was that economists made room in departments all over the place. In the 1960s, if my students didn't have six job offers, I thought they were really doing terribly. So, it was a great time. But the historians did dominate it then – I don't know quite how we ever really infiltrated into economics; I think mostly it was just that economics departments opened up to economic history in those days. Jon Hughes said that to me, I remember, in 1958, when we were both at the meetings in Toronto. About ten years later, I remember bugging him and saying, "Look! Look what's happened!" and Jon expressed amazement, he couldn't have believed there'd have been such a rapid change. So it was an extraordinarily rapid revolution, and it *was* a revolution, you're darned right it was a revolution.

What led you to become an economic historian?

I finished undergraduate work at Berkeley in 1942 and went into the war. I was going to become a lawyer, and war came along, so I went off to war and had four years in the Merchant Marine, running around the world, doing – well, reading, and by the time I got through – and I was a good radical, I was a Marxist – I'd decided that I'd like to change the world. And I asked myself, "How can I change the world?" And I said, "Well, economics is the way to change the world." And then, "Well, what kind of economics?" And finally, "Understanding how economic change takes place has got to be the key to what you need to do to change the world." I have not changed my view about that in the last 50 years; I'm still trying to figure out how economic–societal change takes place. So, in a way, I've got a single-minded objective. I started out with that view in 1944, and I still have it today; it's a guiding factor that is still shaping the way I'm trying to evolve.

So you went to graduate school . . .

I went back to the only place that would take me – I had about a C– average as an undergraduate because I led this little "left" protest at Sather Gate in Berkeley in 1940–42 – Berkeley took me only as a provisional student. They said, "We'll give you one semester" – I got all A's and then went on.

Who was influential on the faculty?

Well, most of the left wing: Robert Brady, who was a leftist, and M. M. Knight – and Leo Rogin, who was the biggest influence on all of us graduate students at Berkeley, a wonderful influence – very bright guy, taught history of thought. But when I got out, I didn't believe any neoclassical economics. In fact, I got Distinguished in the writtens; then when I went to the oral exam, where somebody asked me a simple sophomore-level question in economic theory, and I couldn't answer it because I'd just memorized all this stuff (which you could do for the writtens). They had a long debate whether to pass me or not. They should have flunked me but they didn't: it's hard to flunk a guy who's gotten Distinguished in the writtens and couldn't answer any of the orals and not to admit that your writtens were all a big mess. So, I didn't learn any economics until I got out of graduate school and went to my first job at the University of Washington with a guy named Don Gordon, who was – is still – one of the best theorists I've ever known in my life. He and I played chess every day from 12 to 2, every single day, and during those four years we fought over economics, and I learned neoclassical economics from Don.

Over a chess board.

Over a chess board! So then I became holier than the Pope, you know; I was a Chicago School neoclassical theorist, and that's when I became one of the founders of cliometrics. And I was gung-ho on neoclassical economics. It wasn't until much later that I began to say, "Huh? This theory can't seem to provide me with tools to deal with a lot of the problems," not so much when I was in American economic history as when I shifted over in the late 1960s to European economic history. And it was clear: the tools weren't there to be able to make sense out of history. Then I began this long evolution that I've been going through ever since.

Some of your first students at Washington have gone on to become –

Yeah, lots of them. Well, I haven't counted them, but I think there are somewhere between 40 and 50 Ph.D.'s that I've turned out.

And undergraduates?

Lance, and Jon – Lance and Jon were in my first class.

Anybody else?

Oh, Willie Wolman who is now editor of *Business Week*, and Irwin Unger – who got the Pulitzer Prize in history. It was an *incredible* first seminar, and they all thought that I was [whistles] – incompetent. They were right; I *was* incompetent. But they were a terrific group. I've never had a seminar like it; it was just by happenstance that I had them. And we had a wonderful time. By the end of the semester, we had all established rapport and afterwards Lance and Jon went on to do their own thing.

And later, Richard Sutch was a student who went on to MIT. Except for those three, all the rest stayed on. Roger [Ransom] stayed on to get his Ph.D. – Roger, Terry Anderson – oh, god, I can't remember all the names – every once in a while, one pops up I've forgotten about. But it's a large number – there must be at least 20 or 25 still active, and a lot of them went off into development. Half a dozen of my students are at the World Bank, and some went into business and so on – so they're all over the place – but a lot are economic historians.

It's hard when you're a starting professor, and you get a class like that, to realize how exceptional it is.

Yeah, I didn't know it at the time. What a class! What a recalcitrant bunch of bastards they were! There's a wonderful story: Irwin Unger, in about our fourth session when I was talking about the Mechanics' Lien Law, asked me a question about it and I didn't know the answer. Unger leaned over and said, "Anybody who doesn't know *that* about the Mechanics' Lien Law is incompetent to teach a graduate seminar in economic history." How would you like to have a class that began like that? Whew! It was a tough class.

When you and Bill Parker were editors of the *JEH* in the 1960s, do you think that you were drawing the "new economic history" out and presenting it to the world, or were you overseeing something that was happening anyway – just selecting what you saw as most worthy at the time?

In a way, we were sort of pawns in a big game that we didn't really quite know. Did you know that we got impeached?

I hadn't heard *that*.

I'm not sure that many people did – but midway through Bill's and my tenure as editors, why, the Trustees voted to impeach us; that is, they voted to examine whether we should stay on as editors. The basis was complaints (by some people I'll leave nameless) that we were incompetent. So the Trustees then demanded that we explain ourselves. Well, Bill was very nice and cooperative and went before them – and I wrote them a nasty letter saying, "Go jump in the lake. I won't have anything to do with it." I said, "You've made us editors; I think we're doing a good job, and that's that." Now

Bill and I disagree about *everything*, you understand – in fact, Bill and I almost came to blows over Bob Fogel's railroad article, which he didn't want to publish as Bob had framed it and I did. But we did compromise – we tried very hard to take account of all the criticism. But we were pawns in a big game: economic history was changing, we were starting to get articles that mirrored this, like Bob's article, and at the same time, why, there was lots of tugging that this was a terrible thing. Fritz Redlich was denouncing us and lots of other people were, too – and there we were, trying to walk this tightrope, which we didn't walk well – I didn't walk it as well as Bill. Bill was much more diplomatic and very good about it, and I tended to say, "damn the torpedoes and let's go on." Between us, however, I think what we did was a landmark for the *Journal*. It's true people complained about things, but the fight was over – that is, that this sort of economic history had an important place and was really part of what economic history was going to be. What proportion it should be, and how it should be done, and things like that, were still controversial, but not that it shouldn't be done and that it shouldn't be a part of the profession. I might add, we got impeached but we didn't get fired; finally, they went back and agreed to continue us, even though with some reluctance on quite a number of the Trustees' parts.

How did you get interested in the study of institutions?

In 1966–67, I went to Geneva on a Ford Fellowship and decided to retool and become a European economic historian. It didn't take me very long to become persuaded that we couldn't make sense out of European economic history without explicitly modeling institutions, property rights, and government. The studies with Lance Davis (Davis & North 1971) and Bob Thomas (North & Thomas 1973) were both pioneering efforts to apply an institutional framework to American and European history. The underlying assumptions were from neoclassical theory, but there were too many obvious loose ends that didn't make sense, such as the notion of institutions being "efficient," however defined. Ignoring polities and the consequences of politics for economic performance was an enormous hole in our research. Moreover, it just wasn't possible to explain long-run persistent poor performance of some economies in a neoclassical model. So I gradually began to explore what was wrong. Individual beliefs are obviously important to the choices people make, and it is only the extreme myopia of economists that prevents them from understanding that ideas, ideologies, prejudices matter. Once you recognize that, you are forced to examine the rationality postulate critically. In turn, that leads to the very exciting field (in terms of its implications for social science theory) of cognitive science. Political economy research has finally become an accepted sub-discipline. The notion of path dependence was developed by Brian Arthur and Paul David to explain technological change, but it seemed to me that it has important applicability to institutional change, although the explanation I have is somewhat different from Brian's and Paul's. But I should emphasize that I still consider myself a neoclassical economist. What I want to do is modify the discipline, not to start all over again. The economic way of reasoning is a very powerful tool of analysis.

Our ability to address and come to grips with the central problems of economic history will continue to improve, I think; not only will this provide fundamental new insights, but it will make economic history a vital and essential part of economics. Our job is to model economic and other kinds of change through time – not just institutional change, but also demographic and technological change. The difficulties are to develop useful theory in these areas and then do the empirical work to demonstrate the usefulness or limitations of the theory. It's nice to be able to note that exciting work is going on now in all three areas; for example, your [Gary Libecap's] work on institutional change; Bob Fogel's on demographic change; Nate Rosenberg's on technological change.

Just now you mentioned your work with Lance Davis and Bob Thomas; recently, you've done some work with others. Tell me, how do you collaborate?

Well, collaboration is a very personal psychological thing, and I don't collaborate well with a lot of people. Lance and I, for example, had some difficulties collaborating. On the other hand, Bob Thomas was a bit easier to collaborate with: we were very different, but we complemented each other. Barry Weingast and I collaborate very well. I'm working now with Art Denzau, who is a very smart guy and a very good theorist (Denzau & North 1994). It's another difficult collaboration, because he gets an idea a minute and he goes in all directions, and my job is doing the reverse of what I usually do: often I'm the idea person but now I'm always constraining him just because we can only write one article at a time. So, collaborating is hard, but I like to collaborate because I'm not a high-powered theorist; in fact, I flunked plane geometry in high school and that's the last math I ever had. I don't know – I'd flunk every prelim now that we give in our field. On the other hand, I think I have good instincts for issues and good intuition, and I have a solid sound sense about economic theory. But these days, if you're going to do a lot of work, you really need to collaborate with people who are better trained and better organized and know the modern discipline and all that jazz. Or game theory: I did some work with Paul Milgrom and Barry, and that's been wonderful, and terribly important (Milgrom, North & Weingast 1990). In fact, you can't be my age and be able to keep up with all the new stuff. So, if you're really going to keep up with things, to say something interesting, you do need to collaborate on occasion.

How did you and Lance get together to write your book on institutions and manage to overcome those "difficulties?"

Lance and I just got talking when I got back from Geneva in 1967, and with my dissatisfaction with the state of economics – I had just begun to get interested in institutions and transactions costs. Lance was interested, too, and so we started collaborating. I think it was a good book that came out of it, but it wasn't all that simple to get it done. That's probably as much an indictment of me as anything – it's just that Lance and I didn't find it easy to integrate the ways we think about problems.

But there was some positive feedback?

Oh, yes, I think it we had strong positive feedback, and all that, and despite our struggles at the time, why, we're still best friends. I guess I'm as close to Lance as I am to anybody in the field at this point in my life. And I have been for, well, 40, 43 years – since we started in 1950.

To some people it appears that you have moved well away from the old "new economic history" as you have moved into institutional economic history.

Right! Now I'm sometimes looked on as a traitor to my cause, you know, because I'm attacking cliometrics in many ways.

What do you mean by that?

I think the tools that we get out of neoclassical economics are inadequate to do what we ought to be doing as economic historians. There are two critical things here: one, economic history is about why markets *don't* work, and two, economic history is about time. I think those are both missing from the theory. Neoclassical theory isn't about time – neoclassical theory is statics, comparative statics, and there is no way time gets incorporated into the argument at all. If you really wanted to be hubristic, you'd say what we're trying to do is evolve a dynamic theory of change, but that has escaped our profession as economists. We certainly want to be so self-critical that our models attempt to do that, but we haven't – we really futz around, and most of the program today futzes around, with looking at little details at a moment in time. If we look over time, we can make the connection from one time to the other.

You seem to be defining cliometrics rather narrowly. Is "cliometrics" the wrong word? Don McCloskey wants to call us historical economists, and Phil Mirowsky prefers "bad econometricians." Yet the comment you, perhaps more than anyone, originated, was that cliometricians were going to bring some economic theory to historical questions and see if that could add to the story. For example, you said "How can you talk about the Navigation Acts without knowing something about the elasticity of demand?"

I wouldn't change that at all. I heartily agree. Look, I'm still a neoclassical economist; I think of myself first, last, and always as a neoclassical economist so, unlike Mirowsky, who thinks it's all physics or whatever, I think that price theory and opportunity cost – the economic way of reasoning – is the most powerful tool of analysis in all the social sciences, and you don't give that up. It's the essential tool. It's what makes any of us able to walk into a room of other scholars – and I've done this so many times in my life now that it's ridiculous – and after a while we always dominate the conversation, not necessarily because we're loud, but because as a way of reasoning, we have a very powerful tool. You get to focus on the core of a problem right away, and that's the heart of what we ought to be doing. It's just that it's an inadequate tool unless you radically modify some of the assumptions of neoclassical theory. One is the rationality assumption, and the other one is that you've got to think about time, and that's a tough subject. It's what I'm working on now – I'm trying to work on time conceived as a theory of learning. What we should mean by "time," I think, is how individuals and groups and societies evolve in terms of the way they perceive the world. That's really where time comes in. And then you're able to start to plug that into models which then can evolve and provide some context for why we're changing. The most exciting question in economic history is "How do we get from there to here?" And we don't do a good job of answering that question.

Why can't cliometrics be seen also as including path dependence and . . .

Oh, no, I think it should be. No, that's why I say I'm *still* a neoclassical economist; I don't want to abandon it – a lot of cliometricians think I've deserted them, but I don't think I've deserted them. I'm trying to drag them off into doing these things.

As is Paul David.

Yes, that's exactly what we want to do. We don't want to abandon all the things that made the cliometric revolution a revolution, which it *really* was. What we want to do now is to keep on extending its horizons to encompass problems that we didn't think of before. What's made me really change my view of the world has been the last six years, when I've become deeply involved in problems of development, where I've wandered around in the formerly socialist economies. I've gone to Moscow for the Soviet Academy of Science; I advised Vaclav Klaus in the Czech Republic at the time of privatization. I've just learned that we haven't really come to grips with things we should have had handles on. We should have been able to tell people how economies work over time, which, in turn, would give you a handle on how to make them work better. We have really not done that and, boy, it makes you very self-critical once you become deeply involved in problems of development, at least if you're an economic historian. And that's what – more than anything else – really changed my whole approach to economic history, trying to understand the importance of property rights and other institutions in the countries in Eastern Europe. And a lot of the work I'm doing now is little incremental steps in that direction.

Continuing the cliometric revolution the way you suggest requires not only new questions and theory, but also what we might call continuous time data. Does an excess of comparative statics in economic history come from economizing on data collection?

Well, probably – in small part, it's a problem of getting different data. But even after that, I'd say if we get all the *different* data that I would like to have us gather, there's still a big problem when you talk about time – and the way people learn. Learning is what makes changes in the choices people make, and the choices people make are what determine how economies work and, therefore, how they evolve. So learning is the key. True, you could say, well, it's exogenous forces – you know, earthquakes and so on – that, first of all, work through people's perceptions, but people mostly, to use an old and hackneyed phrase, "make their own history." And they make their own history because they perceive the world differently through time. And why they perceive it differently and how they perceive it differently is what I would like us to get a handle on. Now, that really doesn't answer your question very well, because then what kinds of data really get at that? Well, some can. Here's one that does indirectly, for example: I try to measure, as I'm doing in some Third World countries, transaction costs in particular markets through time, and then you go back and say, "Okay, what made it so that transaction costs changed during this time period?" And then you look at the institutions and the things that changed, and then you ask yourself the still further dirty question, "What made them change?" So it's sort of an infinite regress, but it gets you at the problem. But there's no easy way to answer that; that's a hard question to answer directly, I think.

Aside from yourself, aren't there a lot of people trying to break out of static neoclassical analysis, in addition to people like Paul David and Brian Arthur?

Yes, that's right. In fact, I said earlier that I really wasn't that bleak about it, but I thought that there were signs of younger people coming along who were doing interesting work in addition to old people (well, semi-old), like Paul David and Bob Fogel and Gary Libecap. All of them are doing things that I think are really interesting. No, to name some, I think Jean-Laurent Rosenthal and Avner Greif and my colleague John Nye are real stars coming up in the profession, who have a real grasp of interesting issues and write well and are going really to be major contributors to changing the shape of the field. So I'm really quite optimistic about what's happening. What bothers me is that economics has been changing before economic cliometrics has. Economics is a very exciting place these days, at least wherever I seem to be invited, anyway, which is maybe exotic parts of economics. I was at a conference in Lund on law and economics that was just full of interesting stuff, and two weeks ago I was at a conference in London at which there were several good papers on Third World development problems. So there's a lot of work going on, most of which revolves around trying to deal with the problem of frictions, *i.e.*, the problem of why markets don't work well – political and economic – or they're trying to deal with the issue of rationality or they're trying to develop dynamic models of change, whatever a dynamic model of change is. But something in which you incorporate time – really, what makes economic history economic history, is that we're trying to explain things through time. And we didn't do that for a long while, and now I think we are starting to do it. So, no, I'm really quite optimistic about the field. But it has been very slow. You'd think that since we were the revolutionaries, we'd have stayed revolutionary, but we didn't. We made a revolution and then everybody sat back and spent at least 25 or 30 years saying, "Wasn't this great?" and patting themselves on the back. Now McCloskey and I disagree. He thinks we're still revolutionary. I don't think so; I think we quit being revolutionary some time ago, and I think the proof of the pudding is that in economics departments the demand for economic historians has really dried up. I hope it's coming back again, but it did dry up for a while.

Wasn't the environment of the 1960s so expansive anyway that an economic historian, with all the appropriate econometric and theoretical tools, was a nice "consumption good?" But did the people who hired the economic historians in the 1960s – the economists who did that – really think then it was important to have economic history and have since *lost* that view?

McCloskey would have the latter view; I think that *we* lost, and I think that cliometrics really was a very boring field for a while; there were a just lot of people running around testing hypotheses about the past, with not such good data, and doing the same thing economists were doing. And I think economists said, "Well, that's fine, it's nice to have one around if you don't have anything better to do, but they don't add a new dimension." The dimension we're supposed to add to economics is that we're supposed to do things they *don't* do. And that's looking at the things they hold constant – that's why what Nate does in technology is so important, what Bob and Paul do in demography is so important, and all the institutional work, because it's adding a whole dimension that economists don't have, and I think that's all very exciting stuff.

But a lot of what is exciting in economics, as opposed to economic history, takes an awfully long time to filter down to the ordinary folk teaching economics and . . .

Oh, I think that's right. There's another thing I'm impressed with, too, which is that the other social sciences are becoming really interesting – political science, in particular. Now, political science in a way started to ape economics when they adopted rational choice models and all that jazz, but they are now much more receptive to change, because they don't have a paradigm like economics, where you develop formal mathematical models which are hard to break away from. Some of them have that now, and I think they're exciting – sociology and anthropology are full of interesting people. The Political Economy Center we have in St. Louis is just a very exciting place – we have people in law, business, finance and anthropology and so on – all of whom are doing very interesting work. And that combination makes it exciting. And I think that's another facet of economics – you can't be a good economic historian and just be an economist; all of economic history is really a mixture of political science and sociology and economics and law and anthropology, and you've really got to know your way around those disciplines. And that's asking a lot.

Sure. But can you be a good *economist* without knowing all that stuff, too?

Well, okay, I'd agree with you there, I think you can't be a good economist, either. But it's particularly true in economic history: it's more glaring, there are some things in economics – I can see where you can study financial markets, or other things, where the degree to which you have to go out of the field is quite limited, but in economic history, there's really no major topic you can find that isn't going to take you to the edges of other disciplines. And it should – and that's what makes it really the most fun discipline I think it is; it's much more challenging, it's exciting. *Still* exciting.

Since you've moved into institutional economic history, you've tended to publish your major ideas in a series of books. Which are you most pleased with?

I'm always most pleased with the most recent work, since it does represent an evolutionary development from my earlier work. But if I had to pick one that I think most completely and effectively put it all together at one moment in this evolutionary process, it would be *Structure and Change in Economic History.*

Why do you say that?

Well, I think I did two things there: I tried both to develop some theory and to apply it, to illustrate how useful it was. In my newest book, *Institutions and Institutional Change,* I was most concerned to develop the theory, and there isn't much history in it, even though it's developed because of history. And so *Structure and Change* has been very satisfying on that score. It's not that I don't like my new book – I like it a lot, but it's just that *Structure and Change* satisfied me a great deal at the time. One thing that turned out to be very interesting is that *Structure and Change* is starting to have some impact on economic history – there's always a lag of about eight or ten years with books of mine – but the new book is already having a big influence outside economic history; the new book is now in its fourth printing and is being sold like wildfire amongst economists, political scientists, sociologists. I get stuff from all over the world about the new book, so it has had a completely different effect, but not much amongst economic historians; I don't really think that economic historians have paid much attention to it. But *Structure and Change* is starting to have some impact; even though I think that in *Structure and Change* the theory is very incomplete – it's much better developed later on – but it nevertheless had enough illustrations of the implications for history, so I thought it turned out better.

In *Structure and Change*, and in much of your other work in the past 25 years – wouldn't you say you've specialized in "grand theorizing?"

Yeah, that's certainly the right way to put it. It is grand theorizing . . .

And Eric Jones has tried to do the same thing. Do you see an overlap of your work with his *European Miracle* or *Growth Recurring*?

Well, I like his stuff. I'm more of an economist than Eric, so I tend to think – to try to frame the issues – in economic terms, so that it's congruent to economic theory. I think that if we're to do our job right, we've got to make it so that we can tie in with what economists can do and understand. And Eric is a little less of an economist. On the other hand, in some ways he's more imaginative than I am, he's more creative in the sense that he looks at things that I never would have thought to do, I mean, all this stuff on agriculture and a lot he's played around with are wonderfully exciting things, or on catastrophes. He's very good and a real important addition. You know, we need people like that. We need people who are going to do the grubbing but we also need people to try to provide some vision on the large issues. So I think he's fine.

How should a young person just entering the field begin? What path of research do you recommend?

I think every young economic historian should begin by doing empirical work and making a contribution to our stock of historical data. I would, of course, most like them to contribute data to flesh out the new theoretical developments that are occurring. Second, I'd urge them to carve out an important aspect of historical change, and dig in; that is, to undertake the ongoing and exciting task of the give and take between developing theory, and then empirical work, and so on. There's no substitute for learning by doing. Third, I would try to persuade them that economic history is no better than the theory we possess, and that the theory is so far woefully inadequate. Young scholars should not only be up-to-date on innovations in economic theory that appear useful, but also in the related social sciences as well. As I said, you can't be a good economic historian just by knowing economic theory; you must also have knowledge in depth of the history relevant to your research. That's an awesome set of requirements, but it's an awesomely challenging field of scholarly research.

You recommend knowing a lot – the theory, the related fields, and collecting the data. Should an *economic* historian cut her teeth doing the data grubbing? Perhaps that's not professionally wise these days?

Oh, I think that *is* professionally wise. I think you should get tenure before you go out and do crazy things, and getting tenure means you do things that the discipline, in this case economics, is going to buy and accept in journals. And that's pretty conservative stuff. Avner Greif is probably the most interesting exception that I've seen. I've never seen anybody else who could go out – he's writing about belief systems and culture and all kinds of things – I think they're great but they're also terribly dangerous, but he is smart enough, so I think he'll get away with it. But most young people, you know, should cut their teeth on providing some empirical foundations. That shouldn't be dull: there's no reason they can't be somewhat imaginative, but it's got to be within the frame that can get published.

For empirical work you have to go into the raw materials of history, maybe an expensive proposition in terms of career. When "straight" economists say "empirical" they often mean things (like running regressions) that don't mean anything like that to a historian.

No, I'm very old fashioned here. By "empirical" I mean data-gathering; I mean going to the public records office or whatever, because there is no substitute for getting really queasy about understanding what a number means, and you don't understand what a number means until you've tried to gather them, and, boy, that's a sobering experience. When I did the balance of payments for the United States, I found that just a very tiny change in the initial assumptions I made about the indebtedness of the United States, 70 years later at the end of the period, would have made a change of *astronomical* proportions. So, number-crunching and number-gathering and putting that in historical context is something I think everybody ought to do, just so they see what they're doing. You can't theorize or do anything else grand without first of all understanding some real empirical work, and by that I mean qualitative as well as quantitative.

Counting is useful, but knowing *what* you're counting . . .

Knowing what you're counting – and whether what you're counting is *really* what you're counting – those are all critical parts of the whole story.

That's surely true for economic history, but empirical work, defined as you just did, doesn't cut much ice in some economics departments, does it?

Well, I think that the direction economics has gone, to formal theory and mathematics, is ridiculous: it's become more and more sterile, concerned less and less with anything that has any possibility of being applied to empirical work, and it therefore has become less tied to empirical work. If economics loses sight of that link, it loses sight of everything that's valuable now. Even at MIT or Minnesota or Stanford, where they still have high-powered mathematical theorists, there's still a big blooming of other people who realize you must have close ties to empirical work, to the real world, trying to solve real problems. And I think that's happening and I think that's very salutary. And so I disagree with lots of people who want to go in other directions. I fight about that endlessly in my own department. Lance was grousing to me over dinner the other night about how all the formal game theorists are dominating, and I agree – I like game theory, and I use it – but formal game theory is as sterile as high-powered mathematical economics.

Yes, but it's interesting that the basis of what you like in Avner Greif's work is formal game theory.

Yes, and Avner and I were just arguing about this, and I said, "All right, you show me, I'm perfectly willing – if you can show me, provided that it adds an important dimension to the explanation of how economies evolve, I'll buy it." He thinks he can. I think the power of game theory – and it's the way I've used it – is that it makes you structure the argument in formal terms, in precise terms, so you use it just like neoclassical theory: it's a foil against which to think properly about the issues. But after it's done that, it doesn't seem to me that game theory adds a lot. Now Avner thinks it does add more than that, particularly since I think that it doesn't lend itself to dynamic change, that is, to change through time, and he does. So I said, "Fine, then show me." Since he's doing a book for me, we're going to see (Greif 2006). You know, I've been wrong a lot about this – every once in a while when I tell a good theorist that, well, there's a lot of baloney in what you're doing, they'll show me that in some dimension I'm wrong, that the theory is useful. So I remain open – at least I hope I remain open – to those things. And I think that's important. I think of myself as a good neoclassical economist, but as a neoclassical economist who really wants to widen, open up new boundaries, modify the rationality assumption, introduce transaction costs and imperfect information and all these kinds of things, and then we've got an exciting body of theory.

Learning, too . . .

And particularly learning. That's where I'm going now, trying to figure out how people learn and what that does to our theories. Now I keep quoting Frank Hahn from a 1991 issue of the *Economic Journal* where they asked leading economists to forecast the next hundred years. He said, "This is the end of high-powered theory." He said that the future of economics is going to be less precise; it's not going to make formal mathematical economists happy, but it's going to be more historical, more concerned with, related to the other social sciences – I don't know, he went on and on. When Frank first said this, I was at the Center [for Advanced Studies in the Behavioral Sciences in Palo Alto] – and Frank I know from the days when we were at Cambridge together. He gave a talk to the Stanford Economics Department in 1987 in which he said, "*Mea culpa* – I think I've come to a dead end . . . General equilibrium theory and all this, it has nowhere to go." And he said, "The future rests with institutional economics." He *said* that. And Paul Milgrom in the back of the room asked, "Why don't you talk to Doug North?" and Frank said, "I *have*!" But it's true, I think that that's exactly where it's going – and somebody that bright, like Ken Arrow, sees the same thing. There are a lot of people who are very smart and realize that the future really lies in developing these other areas. The trouble is, of course, that we don't attract economists because we can't develop a lovely and neat body of theory which you can formalize in mathematical terms. We may never be able to do it. And I can see where that would be terribly frustrating – if I had all my human capital invested in a body of theory that I could form into a set of equations, I'd love it. But I can't – and I doubt that we ever will. Now, to the extent we can, we should. And you know, people like Paul David – they might be able to do it, because certainly I'll never be able to do it.

But you know, it's very exciting. Somebody asked me the other day, if I could start all over again, what would I do different? And I said, well, I might like to do it better, but I said I wouldn't change a thing. It's been a very satisfying 40-some-odd years. Very, very satisfying.

Including the Merchant Marine?

Yeah. The Merchant Marine was fun; I couldn't possibly ever have done it if I hadn't had those four years to sit and think about what the hell to do. Oh, no, that was very, very good.

Further reflections

Douglass C. North

In the 60 years since I started graduate school, economic history has come a long way. In 1946 most economic history was taught in history departments. Berkeley was an exception; there it was taught in the economics department. M. M. Knight was my teacher. He was Frank Knight's brother but agnostic about economic theory. His approach could be called "institutional description" – rich in historical detail but devoid of explicit theoretical content. At its best it was excellent story telling and friendly to the historian's approach.

The cliometric revolution that we initiated in the 1950s introduced formal neoclassical economic theory and statistical methods and quickly came to dominate the field in the United States. Economics departments enthusiastically adopted the New Economic History (to the dismay of most historians). The result, inspired by Simon Kuznets's research, was much more rigorous analysis and quantification of past performance. Cliometric students in the late 1950s and the 1960s were in high demand on the economics job market.

By the end of the 1960s, however, two changes began to occur. Economists came to see economic history as a luxury rather than as adding a new dimension to economics, and economic historians found that the tools of economic theory were ill-adapted to the analysis of economic history. The result was that the demand for economic historians decreased and some economic historians (a small minority) began to search for new tools of analysis. The new institutional economics inspired by Ronald Coase's work was a consequence.

What was missing from neoclassical theory? How well did the new institutional economics rectify the deficiencies? Neoclassical economics is a theory of choice in the context of well-developed markets. Absent are how humans make choices, the non-economic dimensions of markets, and time. The first missing ingredient requires an understanding of how, subject to true uncertainty, the mind and brain operate in making choices. The second entails integrating political and social theory with economic theory. The third requires an explicit introduction of time into economic analysis.

We have made progress on the first two missing ingredients. There has been, in recent years, a substantial literature on social norms and political economy and on efforts to integrate that analysis with economic history. In my most recent book, *Understanding the Process of Economic Change* (2005), I deal explicitly (although rather incompletely) with the cognitive foundations of beliefs and the way they are transformed into institutional structures, and with the integration of political and social analysis into economic analysis.

Much less progress has been made on the third issue. Economic history should be about time but it is not. The reason is straightforward: a dynamic theory of change does not exist. Yes, we have game theory models that purport to be dynamic, but they are only superficially so – although Avner Greif's recent book (2006) does have an interesting game theoretic model moving from one equilibrium to another. A dynamic theory of economic change would integrate geographic, climatic, genetic, cognitive, social, political and economic analysis and define their interactions through time. Certainly such a formal theory goes well beyond our present capabilities. Nevertheless, we can do much better – and we should.

The biggest failing of social science theory is its essentially static character, which leads to drastic shortcomings in our understanding of history and society. An analytical framework must inevitably be complex, reflecting the many threads that interact to shape the human condition through time. But such research, at the more informal level of blending theory with descriptive analysis, offers the promise of enormously enriching our knowledge. Just being self-conscious about the temporal interaction of theory and description would yield enormously valuable insights into the overall process of change.

The foregoing is not to be construed as an argument for abandoning theory. Just the reverse: we must use *all* the tools of social science theory that we can (not just the economic), and we must apply them rigorously to confront the complexities of economic history. We can surely go part way in developing theoretical tools to deal with change through time. But then we must go further and employ the comparative advantage we possess as economic historians to explore societal change overall. Economic history would then come into its own by providing a new and exciting dimension to understanding the human condition.

Part IV

LA LOI LAFAYETTE
Cliometrics at Purdue

Lance E. Davis

Jonathan R. T. Hughes

Nathan Rosenberg

In the mid-1950s Purdue University, in West Lafayette, Indiana, was known primarily as the biggest school of engineering in America and home (then, as now) of athletic teams called "The Boilermakers." The times, however, were changing and Purdue was expanding and diversifying in the post-war educational boom, providing a confluence of factors perhaps uniquely favorable in time and place to innovations in economics and economic history. Emanuel T. Weiler, a first-rate economist but self-described as disliking the conventional economics of the period, had been hired in 1953 to head Purdue's newly independent Economics Department, as well as a new Department of Industrial Management. In effect, he was given a blank slate on which he wrote to suit his professional tastes. He recruited an eclectic group of faculty members whose remit was to pursue their own research interests, publish or perish together and forge new and unconventional curricula for undergraduate and graduate students. In these aims Weiler was surprisingly successful; his "procedure was to listen to faculty say what they wanted to do, to order them to do it, and then to hold them responsible for performance;" "he had an intuition that maybe something would emerge out of a process that did not try to prevent things from happening" (Ames 1981: 359; Smith 1981: 369). He therefore "allowed" research and teaching in the "new" economic theory, econometrics, and quantitative economic history to emerge from the interests of the economists he had hired, and, by the early 1960s, Purdue had become famous as the home of "one of the most dynamic young economics departments in the country" (Cain *et al.* 1991: 3).

In time, Purdue also became known as the home of a product of that dynamism, Cliometrics, owing in large part to the enthusiasm and sheer hard work of the economic historians who lived in or regularly visited West Lafayette. These are not limited to the scholars whose interviews appear in this part, Jonathan Hughes, Lance Davis, and Nathan Rosenberg, but also include several Purdue colleagues who were enticed to pursue historical topics, such as macroeconomist Duncan McDougall, mathematical economist Stanley Reiter, and theorist and Soviet specialist Edward Ames.[1] Their distinctive approach to economic history had, by 1960, achieved such notoriety that

1 Others at Purdue who wrote one or more studies in economic history or historiography are Robert Basmann, M. June Flanders, George Horwich, James McRandle and James Quirk, all of whom have work reprinted in *Purdue Faculty Papers* (1967).

Carter Goodrich, a senior American economic historian, called it *La Loi Lafayette* (Davis, Hughes & Reiter 1960: 540; Hughes 1981: 363).

Formulation of *La Loi* fell largely to Davis and Hughes. Weiler had recruited Davis in 1955 directly from his graduate work at Johns Hopkins; the next year Hughes was hired away from 18 months of laboring at the New York Fed on recommendation from Davis, his old friend and fellow student of Douglass North at the University of Washington. They and McDougall offered an introductory course in American economic development for first-year undergraduates, resulting in a textbook organized topically rather than chronologically, and openly intended to be "a revolutionary treatment" (Davis, Hughes & McDougall, *American Economic History*, 1961; 1969, p. *vii*). Simultaneously, they and several colleagues were filling the journals with economic historical research incorporating quantitative or analytical elements. Davis published work on banking and capital formation, while Hughes wrote on British commercial crises, foreign trade and growth, but the strikingly novel publications were collaborative. Hughes and Reiter estimated annual increments to the early nineteenth-century British steam shipping fleet in "The First 1,945 British Steamships" and Davis and Hughes supplied an entirely new and consistent series of exchange rates in "A Dollar–Sterling Exchange, 1803–95."[2]

Such work in economic history was then an oddity, so unusual that Davis's paper on "The New England Textile Mills and the Capital Markets" (1960), filled with tables and diagrams and originally submitted in 1957, was rejected outright by the editors of *The Journal of Economic History* whose "temporary limitationist resistance" resulted in a "minor *cause célèbre*." It was eventually published in the final year of the editorship of George Rogers Taylor, a distinguished "traditional" economic historian. (See Hughes 1971: 411.) Perhaps that *contretemps* led to the invitation that Davis, Hughes and Reiter explain themselves at the EHA meetings in the autumn of 1960. Carter Goodrich, the convener, opened the session with a query: "Economic History – One Field or Two?" (1960); the Purdue trio replied by discussing quantitative research in economic history, in the process introducing Reiter's whimsical neologism, "Cliometrics," to the profession. They said "If we are successfully to relate our work to the main body of economic history, we must be able to show the fundamental relationship between quantitative analysis and more conventional methods of economic historians" (Davis, Hughes & Reiter 1960: 539). This they did, but they were also dissatisfied with "conventional methods," as reflected in the preface to the ensuing textbook: "If the result of our labors is a sharp break with tradition, we can only say that, as teachers of economics as well as of economic history, tradition has not served us well" (Davis, Hughes & McDougall 1961: *viii*).

Not content merely with declaring their interest in quantitative work, Davis and Hughes had already arranged for a small conference of like-minded economic historians to be held at Purdue in December 1960, with the deliberately imposing title of "Conference on the Application of Economic Theory and Quantitative Methods to the Study of Problems of Economic History." For obvious reasons this continuing annual conference was soon referred to as "Clio," retaining its full title for funding purposes until the late 1970s, when it became officially the "Cliometrics Conference." Although

2 See Davis & Payne (1958); Davis (1958); Hughes (1956, 1959); Hughes & Reiter (1958); Davis & Hughes (1960). All were reprinted in *Purdue Faculty Papers* (1967).

in recent years this gathering has often been conducted in the polite and measured tones of academic discourse, it began with spirit and vigorous dispute, where participants usually went at each other's new ideas and approaches with hammer and tongs. Nonetheless, as Hughes recalls, "I never again saw anything in the academic world quite like it: the candor, warmth, enthusiasm, intellectual generosity, and comradeship of young men who found themselves to be pioneers" (1981: 364).[3] The camaraderie already established in Purdue's young economics department then served in the conference to build a small community of "new" economic historians, a community that expanded rapidly as freshly minted recruits were drawn into the fold.

Emanuel Weiler's ambitious plans for his Department of Economics were only too successful. In his introduction to *Purdue Faculty Papers in Economic History, 1956–1966* (1967: *v*), Weiler wrote, "Believing that, to some extent, history is the laboratory of economics, the faculty developed a Ph.D. program in quantitative economics that was unique in its emphasis upon the role of economic history in the training of the professional economist. Economic history advanced hand-in-hand with applied mathematics in the general development of modern economics on our campus." So it did, but Weiler had chosen so well that his recruits nearly simultaneously acquired tenure and promotion, and became famous. Purdue simply did not have the resources to meet all the offers its economics faculty were receiving and in the later 1960s they left one by one for pastures less isolated and perhaps greener than those of West Lafayette: Davis was off to Caltech, Hughes and Reiter went to Northwestern, and Rosenberg went via Harvard to join the cluster of economic historians at Wisconsin before moving to Stanford. They departed but retained fond memories and life-long friendships.

Lance Davis is best known for his studies of financial development. His first publication was a book, written with the British business historian Peter L. Payne, on *The Savings Bank of Baltimore* (Payne & Davis 1956). In his early work he focused on the uses and the sources of investment funds in the New England cotton textile industry (1958; Davis & Stettler 1966), the development of capital markets including an important paper on the evolution of a national investment market in the United States (1965), and on comparisons of British and American financial institutions (1966a). Later, with Robert Huttenback, he studied the long-standing issue of links between capital flows and British imperialism in a series of works that led to *Mammon and the Pursuit of Empire* (1987). Meanwhile he and Robert Gallman, once a fellow student at Johns Hopkins, merged their interests in economic growth and financial development in work on American capital formation and global capital mobility. This research led to their extensive study of Britain, the Americas and Australia, *Evolving Financial Markets and International Capital Flows* (1999). In all this work Davis's "central characteristic" is to specify carefully the basic question and to address it with economic theory and new data, often in a massive volume (*cf.* Engerman *et al.* 2003: 319). As he has written recently (2001: 56), Davis saw that his lifetime research agenda has been to build up a set of case studies that would contribute to addressing a fundamental problem: the "gradually emerging systematic analysis of the process of institutional change." Not only have financial institutions engaged him, but more generally government and legal institutions, as in the joint quest

3 Hughes says "young men" advisedly, since only four of the 81 papers presented at Purdue were by women.

with Douglass North to formulate a theoretical model, in their *Institutional Change and American Economic Growth* (1971). The epitome of his quest may reside in a collaboration with Gallman and Karin Gleiter, *In Pursuit of Leviathan* (1997), a study of the rise and decline of American whaling. It is mature cliometrics at its best, containing not only the characteristic quantitative testing of specific hypotheses about productivity and profits but also thoughtful and broad-ranging discussions of technical changes within and without the industry and their institutional consequences. "It is the model study of its kind" (Engerman *et al.* 2003: 325). In his most recent book Davis continues his seafaring, this time with Stanley Engerman, in *Naval Blockades in Peace and War: An Economic History since 1750* (Cambridge UP 2006).

It may appear that Jonathan Hughes abandoned his youthful romance with cliometrics not long after presenting the "Purdue Manifesto" with Davis and Reiter at the 1960 EHA meetings. After all, biography is not part of the economist's standard tool kit, and Hughes's big book of the 1960s was *The Vital Few* (1966a), telling his story of American economic development through the lives and environment of a small group of entrepreneurs ranging from William Penn to Henry Ford. But appearances can deceive. His use of eight central figures (and ten in 1986) – surrogates for legions of the more obscure – was a device for examining the development of the private market economy of the United States, bringing to bear, he hoped, "the precision of the historian, the logic of economic analysis and the art of the biographer" (1966a: *v*). In the preface to the paperback re-issue of 1973, Hughes noted with some acerbity the sharp increase in government's presence in the US economy occasioned by the Great Society and the Vietnam War. Soon thereafter he wrote *Social Control in the Colonial Economy* (1976), followed by *The Governmental Habit* (1977), which appears to be a thorough documentation and indictment of government intervention in the market. Nevertheless, Hughes's bottom line is that the American people in fact got just what they wanted, although the piecemeal and *ad hoc* character of the resulting "non-system" has tended to produce undesirable consequences. While the bulk of Hughes's work was on the United States, he began at Oxford with a thesis on the mid nineteenth-century British economy, published as *Fluctuations in Trade, Industry and Finance* (1960) and returned often to British topics. His last publication (appearing posthumously in 1994) was "A world elsewhere: The importance of starting English," his contribution to the *Festschrift* for Sir John Habakkuk, his Oxford mentor. Jon Hughes's devotion to teaching was manifest in person and in print. In addition to the Purdue textbook with Davis and McDougall, he produced a solo effort, *American Economic History* (1983) which necessarily incorporated the expanding flood of cliometric work on the US economy; it has continued into its seventh edition (Hughes & Cain 2007). His provocative synthesis of nineteenth-century international developments, *Industrialization and Economic History: Theses and Conjectures* (1970), includes stimulating discussion of the economic historian's method and occasionally caustic critiques of the (mis)application of economic theory when oblivious of the relevant facts. In person Hughes was not at all self-effacing: he was opinionated, self-assured, larger than life, a combination of storyteller, scholar and Renaissance man and, with both students and colleagues, possessed of an impish proclivity to make outrageous pronouncements just to see what would happen. Yet, he treated his students as equals, all as scholars in the same boat, each with something to contribute. He was, above all, a vital presence. Such was his distinction as a teacher that the Economic History Association established in his memory The Jonathan Hughes Prize for Excellence in Teaching Economic History.

Nathan Rosenberg entered the Purdue milieu in 1961, joining Jon Hughes, his old friend from Oxford days. During his six years in West Lafayette, Rosenberg continued his pioneering studies of American technology, participated in Clio conferences, and was drawn into the local collaborative style, writing papers on the US business cycle with Hughes (Hughes & Rosenberg 1963) and on technological change and growth with Edward Ames (*e.g.*, Ames & Rosenberg 1963, 1968). He contributed the chapter on technical change to the 12-author textbook edited by Davis, Easterlin and Parker (1972). By then he was well on the road to becoming, arguably, the pre-eminent economic historian of modern and contemporary technology. Unlike the (stereo)typical economist interested in values or volumes of inputs and outputs, Rosenberg has asked how production processes actually work and – the historian's basic question – how they came to develop as they did. In his essay collection *Perspectives on Technology* (1976) and in two subsequent collections (1982, 1994), he has ventured "inside" or gone "exploring" the "black box" of technology, and has re-emerged with important stories to tell about the technical and economic forces affecting the path of technological change. His paper on technical interrelatedness, "Technological change in the machine tool industry" (1963) "remains to this day perhaps the single most influential essay ever written" in the history of technology (Hounshell 1997: 723). His collaborations extend beyond those with other economists to publications with an aeronautical engineer, Walter Vincenti, on the technological implications of building *The Britannia Bridge* (1978) and with chemical engineers, such as the entrepreneur-academic Ralph Landau (Landau & Rosenberg 1992). In 1997 he presented the Graz Schumpeter Lectures, *Schumpeter and the Endogeneity of Technology* (2000), where he summarized his general views: on the dynamism of historical economic change and the role of economic signals in focusing the path of technology, on the historically crucial role of "imitators" in multiplying the productivity results of an initial innovation, on the modern system of universities as generators of useful knowledge, and on the mutually reinforcing interactions of scientific and technological progress. In 1996 the Society for the History of Technology presented him with the Leonardo da Vinci Medal, the highest honor they bestow. In the citation for that award, David Hounshell writes "Nathan Rosenberg has opened the black box . . . [he] has almost single-handedly changed the way economists and economic historians think about technology and the nature of economic change" (1997: 721). Yet, technical progress does not occur simply in its own sphere. It is part of the wider realm of economy, polity and society, a view Rosenberg discusses with great flair in *How the West Grew Rich* (1986), a venture into "big think" history with the legal historian L. E. Birdzell, Jr. They stress the sheer diversity of politics and law, the absence of dominant central authority, the freedom to experiment, succeed or fail which resulted in the "West's" ability to develop new institutions and to adopt and test innovations in economic organization, trade and technology.[4]

Despite the distinctiveness of the Purdue economics program and the role of West

4 For an analysis of Rosenberg's work, see A. Field (1996).

Lafayette as a node for the emergence of the New Economic History, there was never a "Purdue School" of cliometrics dictating some canonical mode of economic–historical enquiry. Each of these three scholars has approached in a variety of ways a range of important questions in economic, social, institutional and technological history; their work has informed or sparked the work of many others, imitators and critics alike, and the relevant literatures are replete with citations to their work. All have brought economic theory and, where relevant, quantitative techniques to bear on their chosen topics. Economics students of the present, who routinely expect to see game-theoretic models and econometric estimations, should be surprised to see how basic – and how powerful – are the methods employed in these works, just as their authors themselves were surprised to learn that what they were doing was considered in some circles to be "revolutionary." The large body of scholarship these three have produced shows that the influence of their experiences at Purdue was maintained long after they departed West Lafayette.

LANCE E. DAVIS

Interviewed by
Samuel H. Williamson
and John S. Lyons

Lance Edwin Davis is the Mary Stillman Harkness Professor of Social Science, Emeritus, at the California Institute of Technology, Pasadena, California, and Research Associate of the National Bureau of Economic Research. He was born in Seattle, Washington in 1928 and was educated at the University of Washington (B.A., 1950) and The Johns Hopkins University (Ph.D., 1956). He taught at Purdue University from 1956 until he moved to Caltech in 1968, has been Visiting Fellow at Nuffield College, Oxford (1964–5) and at The Australian National University (1996), and was Fellow of the Center for Advanced Study in the Behavioral Sciences in Stanford (1985–6). Davis was President of the Economic History Association in 1978–9 and was elected Fellow of the American Academy of Arts & Sciences in 1991. He now lives in Arkansas. The interview was conducted by fax and telephone in late 1989 and early 1990 by Samuel Williamson and John Lyons. Sam Williamson writes:

I first met Lance Davis while I was a student at Purdue. My first class with him was the second course of the two-semester sequence in economic history required in Purdue's economics graduate program at the time. I don't think any of us thought that his approach was "revolutionary" or "new" – after all it was history. As a seminar project for Lance, I was running a linear programming model of the 1820 US economy which tested Doug North's model. It seemed like a reasonable approach to me. Little did I know how foreign this was to many then in the field. One of my early impressions of Lance was about his frankness. If you wanted advice, he would give his honest opinion. If he thought something was lousy, he would tell you. And he had this way of asking "Why not?" when you were not sure you could do something, but he was. And he was usually right.

Lance Davis is both a pioneer of cliometrics and a friendly critic of the field, as in his

1968 paper "And it will never be literature." In 1979 Davis tried to educate his colleagues about the importance of the political in economic history in his address as President of the EHA. A predecessor, Frederick C. Lane, had spoken of the power of governments in an address Davis thought both important and too-long neglected. In his review of developments in the "New Political History," Davis asserted "If we are to understand economic history we must be able to understand and explain the behavior of the government sector" (1980: 2). The interview began with that issue.

Has Fred Lane's piece on "The Economic Consequences of Organized Violence" (1958) had the influence you expected (and wished for)? Or is the relevant long run still far in the future?

I am not certain what I expected, but certainly there has been no massive rush to the barricades. However, there has been a substantial amount of excellent work in the area that could loosely be termed "historical political economy." Let me suggest at least three different strands to that work:

Work Largely in the Original Spirit of Economic History:[1] One cannot fail to mention Gary Libecap's work. Of particular interest are his two recent pieces, one on the regulation of oil prices (and the Texas Railroad Commission) and the other on food and drug regulation and the growth of the meat packing industry (1989, 1992b). In a similar vein, David Feeny's work on Thai development (*e.g.*, 1989) is very much in the spirit of the 1979 talk.

Historical Work by Political Scientists: In the same way that it was the economists who led the so-called "Cliometrics Revolution," I expected the political scientists to lead the "Polymetrics" revolution. While there has been less work than I would have predicted, David Brady, whose work is precisely the kind I called for, is a full professor at Stanford, and even Michigan (the flagship of traditional political science) has turned out a brilliant young scholar, Doug Dion. Dion, even more than Brady, makes specific use of formal models in his historical research.

A Really New Field: Here I would like to cite two quite different efforts. On the one hand, the cooperative venture by two of the most modern historical quantifiers (Al Bogue and Joel Silbey), with the maverick Brady, and the voice of the political science establishment, Nelson Polsby has proved quite fruitful. On the other hand, there are young scholars who have in fact begun to create a new field. I cite only two – Jeff Friedan's student, Lawrence Broz, who works on the politics of the Federal Reserve Act, and Morgan Kousser's student, Shawn Kantor, who has produced a really path-breaking methodological study of the economics and politics of the Georgia fence laws (1991).

1 Davis makes general reference to many authors. Only those works for which he supplied a specific citation are listed in the combined references; works unpublished at the time of the interview are cited in their published form, in both cases by (year).

Have we economic historians become more sophisticated, or not, in the following areas:

a) understanding government behavior?

Some progress has been made, but mostly not by economic historians, and what progress there is has been spotty (*i.e.*, some valuable; some of, at best, negative value). Politicians certainly want to get elected, and some work (*e.g.*, by Alesina *et al.* 1989, on political business cycles) has produced very useful results. Closer to home, Bob Fogel's work on the 1850s, in *Without Consent or Contract*, has been hailed by both Al Bogue and Morgan Kousser as the most successful attempt to explain that political realignment.

On the question of bureaucratic behavior there has been lots of smoke but little fire. Inclusion of income in a bureaucrat's utility function may have been a step forward, but certainly the attempts to test that *assumption* fly in the face of all we know about the scientific method. Analysis based on the assumption that the source of a bureaucrat's power rests in the asymmetry of information (he is a monopolist) in games with the politicians has not proved fruitful (it really assumes a corner solution). Work in that vein but extended to include an analysis of constitutional constraints (that is, initial conditions) by Romer and Rosenthal on Oregon school boards (1979), however, suggests that there may be some hope in sorting out the cases marked by asymmetry from those without. Work on bureaucrats' discretionary income is probably more suggestive, but the concept has proved very difficult to operationalize successfully. On a more hopeful note, Kiewiet's work on committees and their relations with the bureaucracy has provided some clues about the relationship between electoral events and bureaucratic behavior (Kiewiet & McCubbins 1985). Although much criticized, work by Vern Ruttan (*e.g.*, 1980) on the Department of Agriculture seems to me to provide a potentially very useful methodology.

b) understanding human motivation ("beyond greed")?

There has been a decided unwillingness by economists to look for other motives. The bitterness of Paul Schultz's attack on Easterlin gives you some feeling of the opposition (1986). I admit I find it difficult to believe that they really view such research as a mortal threat to the discipline. There are, however, some notable exceptions. First, of course, there is Dick's work on international welfare comparisons (1974) and, with Eileen Crimmins, on fertility, and, more recently, on American youth (1985, 1991). These are all clearly attempts to explore both economic and non-economic motivations. Second, Bob Fogel's *Without Consent or Contract* makes a specific attempt to relate cultural and religious values to politics (and thus, of course, to economics). Third, on a slightly different tack, Naomi Lamoreaux's studies of kinship networks in New England banking is an obvious attempt to extend the traditional list of motives; and she is very effective in linking economic with more anthropological motives (1994).

c) applying useful and relevant theory to empirical historical issues; *i.e.*, using a better mix of theory and fact?

As I have said before, I think the discipline lost a decade to the "I'd rather be clever than right" boys, and we still haven't entirely escaped the application of clever but hopelessly mis-specified models. We are, however, gradually emerging from that ethos (only one item on my mis-specification reading list is less than five years old), and there is a real hope that we will produce work with a better mix of fact and theory. Although I could cite a number of examples of "better mix," I can think of none that captures the spirit more than Eugene White's piece on the causes of the depression of the 1930s – it is a particularly neat attempt to specify alternative theories and then confront them with the facts (1984). In a similar, although less formal, vein, I also call your attention to Price Fishback's study of company towns and company stores in the early twentieth-century coal mining industry (1986) and to Ken Snowden's work on nineteenth-century capital markets (*e.g.*, 1987).

Are we still, as you earlier feared, economizing too often by choosing subjects to match up with readily accessible sources?

I am afraid in this regard I remain quite pessimistic; and I think there are two related problems, not just one. The first is the one to which you allude directly – *i.e.*, bias in the choice of projects. For example, developments in finance coupled with the availability of some stock market tapes have produced a spate of studies on the behavior of security prices that, as far as I can tell, contribute little to our understanding of anything. In a more general sense, as important as monetary developments are, I think it is the availability of data that at least partly explains the relative fascination for financial as opposed to "real" studies.

The second problem deals with the relative rewards for data collection, particularly collection from archival sources. The Legler–Sylla–Wallis enterprise is a notable exception (and can you guess how many economic historians will make their reputations off those efforts), and, perhaps, it proves the rule.[2] Economic historians have generally displayed a marked unwillingness to devote the requisite resources to such activity both because the rewards tend to have gone to the chap with a model and a couple of stylized facts and because it is very difficult to maintain a proprietary interest in a data set for the time needed really to capture a reasonable return from the investment expended in collecting and cleaning. In my 35 years in the profession I have noticed few publications that granted the scholar who developed the data equal billing with the person who analyzed it.[3]

2 They were collecting a consistent data set on US "state" and local revenues and expenditures for the late colonial period through 1906. See, *e.g.*, Legler *et al.* (1988).

3 Davis has told us recently that this sentence could now begin "In my more than 50 years . . ." but would otherwise be unchanged.

This second point brings up another issue that ought to be touched on. Funding for economic history has gotten much more difficult to come by, and funding for archival research almost impossible to obtain. By my last count (no accuracy guaranteed), only one new economic history project (a study of Russian development) has been funded by the NSF over the past three years. The rejected submissions included an excellent proposal by [David] Galenson and [Clayne] Pope that would, as a by-product, have yielded an important data set on interregional mobility and income. The extent of the problem becomes apparent when one examines a book like Baumol, Blackman, and Wolff's *Productivity and American Leadership* (MIT Press 1989). The authors are interested in problems of long-term growth, but the quality of much of the data on which their argument depends is, at best, suspect. And it is not that the authors did not attempt to utilize the best numbers available – as a profession we have failed to provide those basic series. As an aside, I might add that it is not really surprising that the authors did not feel obligated to fill the gap either.

Has any progress been made in our understanding of the "big questions" – of long-term economic change? Is there anything to learn from recent "big think" works of, say, Eric Jones, Immanuel Wallerstein, or Tony Wrigley?

Thus far, I have not achieved much in a way of an understanding of the Big Picture, but of course I am still young – in spirit if not in the flesh. In the case of both the Jones and the Wrigley books, what I have found useful is not the big but the little pictures – the evidence the authors have adduced to support their more general arguments. In the case of Wallerstein, I admit I haven't found anything very useful, but that is probably only the result of my visceral reaction to the methodology.

Is there a new and brightly illuminated focus on fundamental work in economic history emerging from the 1980s? Or is the light dim and diffuse?

I guess I believe we are still using the light bulbs of the 1970s rather than the halogen lights of the 1980s, but that there is substantially more illumination than in the days when we had to depend on whale oil lamps.

In the United States, a substantial amount of work has been underwritten by the NBER's program in the Development of the American Economy (DAE). I make no attempt to provide a complete enumeration, but important work (including the assembly of a number of data sets based on primary sources) has been done by Goldin and by Weiss in labor history; on nutrition, welfare and productivity by Fogel and by Floud and Wachter; on savings and the capital stock by Gallman and by Pope and Kearl; on productivity by Sokoloff and by Davis, Gallman, and Hutchins; and on the government by Rockoff and, most importantly, by Legler, Sylla, and Wallis.[4] While it is

4 Chapters on these subjects by most of the authors mentioned can be found in Engerman & Gallman, eds (1986), Gallman & Wallis, eds (1992), and in Weiss & Schaefer, eds (1994).

Robert Fogel who has taken the lead in this enterprise (as an aside, I note that Claudia Goldin has agreed to pick up the mantle in a couple of years), and while the steering committee (Davis, Engerman, Gallman, Goldin, and Pope) has devoted time and resources to the activity, special mention should be made of the efforts of Clayne Pope. Without his dedication much less would have been accomplished.

I am less familiar with the work abroad, but let me mention a couple of indications of recent wattage. Up north, Mac Urquhart's massive compilation of Canadian development is all but complete; and that empirical exercise should be grist for the mills of unborn generations of historians who don't want to get their hands dirty with original sources. I have just finished reading Sydney Pollard's *Britain's Prime and Britain's Decline*, and while not commenting on the work, I can say that the bibliography indicates the extent to which the Cliometrics "Revolution" (and I mean that in the best sense of the word) has affected British historiography. Finally, it does not take a genius to recognize that George Grantham, Phil Hoffman, and David Weir are in the process of rewriting the history of French development.[5]

Striking the appropriate balance between modesty and conceit, can you comment on how well your work on the British Raj has met the goals and heeded the cautions you set out in 1979 for us all? [*Mammon and the Pursuit of Empire* 1986 with Robert Huttenback & Susan Davis.]

This question is really impossible to answer. Personally, I feel that the economic chapters of the book are as good as Bob and I could make them. Perhaps with unlimited funding we could have added more firms to the sample (the period 1860 to 1880 is not covered as well as it might be), but I don't really think we would have changed the conclusions. I am not so sanguine about the political analysis. The results are inconclusive and they scream for micro studies of the relationship between the business sectors (finance, agriculture, and industry), the social elites, political parties, parliament, and the bureaucracy. Unfortunately the project had already taken from 1971 to 1985, and how much time does anyone have? Also, of course, there were financial constraints – even the cost of pulling the wills of the 3900+ MPs in order to get a handle on wealth and asset holdings proved prohibitive given the financial constraints. These are, of course, not valid excuses, and the political section of the work could, and probably should, have been better. In terms of the reception the book has received, it leaves you with a feeling that all you have done is preach to the converted. If you do a 2 × 2 matrix with US and UK the horizontal designators, and economists and historians the vertical ones, the upper left-hand box is full of enthusiasts, the upper-right and the lower-left representatives appear to like and probably accept the findings, and the lower right-hand box is full of academics who both hate and reject everything about the enterprise. I might add that some members of each set have probably never read the book.

5 See, *e.g.*, Grantham (1989) on agricultural progress, Hoffman (1986) on agrarian society and finance, and Weir (1984) on demography.

What about your having been a pioneer in Cliometrics in the 1950s and 1960s? Were there clearly defined "enemies;" what happened to them, were they converted, or didn't they care?

Looking back at the period (and remembering that the mind tends to block out unpleasant experiences – I sometimes catch myself thinking that my years in the Navy were not really that bad), I don't remember ever feeling that there ever were any real enemies, although there were certainly lots of skeptics. There was direct lineal descent and much affection between the older growth scholars (Simon Kuznets, Moe Abramovitz, and Irv Kravis) and the representatives of the younger generation like Easterlin, Gallman, and Parker. As for the more historiographically inclined, perhaps it was just the extreme arrogance of the young economists, but how could you really believe that anyone who argued that "it's immoral therefore it must have been unprofitable" could be treated as a serious intellectual threat let alone an enemy? Moreover, even the older generation had its share of excellent scholars. For example, Kenneth Stampp, using strictly traditional historical methods, had come to the same conclusion as Conrad and Meyer well before they did.

It certainly was difficult to get quantitative work published; and I had my share of losing bouts with George Rogers Taylor. Looking back on it now, however, I can't help feeling that some of that early research may not have been as good as we were convinced it was, and it is just possible (although of course not likely) that it might well not have been published, even if the editing had been unbiased. Moreover, we should not forget that Henry Rosovsky was editing the old *Explorations* in 1955 and John Meyer took over in 1957; moreover, North and Parker became editors of *The Journal* in 1961.

There were, of course, both skeptics and critics. Since the debate was at its peak some 30 to 35 years ago, some have died and all have retired. Some were converted, some still refuse to acknowledge that there ever was a revolution, and some moved into different fields. Economic history has largely been taken over by economists, and they don't much care what anybody else says, sometimes, it seems, even when their critics are correct. Moreover, since most of the practitioners have appointments in economics departments, they have never been forced to confront more traditional historians.

Outside economic history, and despite heroic efforts by the likes of Al Bogue and Jerry Clubb, QUASSH (QUAntitative Social Science History) has not fared so well – there aren't many jobs and the work has had substantially less impact in social and political history than the work of Fogel, Gallman and the boys had on the economic side. Recently I spoke to a now not-so-junior scholar who had been a post-doc at Caltech. In explaining why he had been such a success as "the quantitative historian" in a well known history department he said, "I've got just the mix of skills they want: some quantitative interest – but not too much quantitative interest." Similarly, some of the new labor historians clearly don't care. They have a message to peddle, and neither facts nor analysis are allowed to get in the way.

However, the entire intellectual landscape is not so bleak. Let me suggest you read Gene Genovese's review of *Without Consent or Contract* in today's *Los Angeles Times* (Sunday, February 18, 1990). Gene, a very distinguished left-wing historian of the Old South, was among the most strident critics of the entire Conrad–Meyer to Fogel–Engerman line of thought. Now he writes that *Consent* should be added to the list of the five most important books about the South and slavery. Clearly, there has been some give, and maybe some take, on both sides.

Would you comment on the direction that studies of financial markets have taken since your early work on the US? In retrospect, do you think that the "different" path you took has been a good guide to fruitful later work by others?

First, let me say, and only partly in jest, that, given the fact that my most recent work on financial markets is more than two decades old (and some of it goes back 15 years before that), I sometimes find myself both amazed and appalled that anybody has ever read it, let alone is still writing about it. On a more serious level, I think we now know considerably more about the evolution of financial markets now than we did in 1955. Whether you want to enter the dispute about transactions costs versus market segmentation or not (and I think it's a silly dispute), most everyone is more or less convinced that efficient well-functioning markets are not always there – even the Soviets have begun to realize that, while economists know a great deal about how mature markets work, they know very little about how markets grow and develop. I think that most of the research that has followed my initial forays has been productive, and even some of the conjectures that have later been partly disproved, have provided fruitful insights. I still believe that economic growth and development involve both capital accumulation and capital mobilization, and mobilization can be effective in a decentralized economy only after financial institutions are invented and innovated.

Moreover, I had always viewed my work on capital markets as research that, while focused on an important substantive area, also raised questions of institutional change and analysis in general. I am probably an old fogey, but it is still an article of my faith that for questions of long-term change, at least, economists who take institutions as fixed are engaged in a practice that is about as likely to produce useful insights as masturbation is to produce children. Old economic historians had long been aware of the effects of institutions, but cliometricians, with training rooted in comparative statics, were often more than willing to ignore that aspect of the economic environment – it was, after all, difficult to model. Thus, like my belief that my contributions to the capital market literature had no net negative effect on human welfare, I believe that my attempts to call attention to questions of institutional change and analysis have not measurably reduced the intellectual output of the profession and may even have increased it somewhat.

To continue, has our historical insight anything to tell current policy makers? Would they listen if we told them, or have we been addressing

too narrow an audience, so that the policy makers haven't gotten the word? Specifically, could historians have helped avoid the S&L disaster of the 1980s if we had thought about the deregulation business or could we have provided better policy advice than others might have done (or did)?

On the one hand, as far as I know, only Peter McClelland has ever attempted to use economic history explicitly as a vehicle for policy analysis, but he was certainly successful enough to make further exploration productive (McClelland & Magdowitz 1981). On the other hand, I think it not unlikely that, although thoughtful economic historians might well have raised some flags about the deregulation of the S&L's, those flags would not have been raised very high, and it seems highly unlikely anyone would have responded to the danger signals.

It seems to me, however, that economic historians do have a potential contribution to make to policy analysis. As a group they are particularly well equipped to make three points: (1) the study of institutional technology may be at least as important to any understanding of economic growth and development as the study of technical change more traditionally defined; (2) when considering alterations of existing institutions, or the innovation of new ones, a policy maker should always attempt to assess the potential long-run implications, even if the change is thought to be nothing more than a short-term adjustment; and (3) that institutions, unlike traditional machines or processes, have an amazing ability to resist the scrap heap (McClelland makes this point very well in his story of Robert Moses and the Triborough Bridge Authority).

Moreover, the present appears to be a particularly propitious time to turn some fraction of the discipline's attention to these policy-related questions. Recent work by economic theorists in mechanism design, by experimentalists in the study of alternative institutional structures, and by political scientists on the political basis for alternative market structures (*e.g.*, is it possible to have a market economy in the absence of property rights?) have opened up a new field of research. Moreover, economic historians are particularly well placed to play a major role in this endeavor, since, Charlie Plott aside, history provides the only effective laboratory for the study of long-term institutional change.

Where exactly did you expect it to end when you turned down the hall in Stanley Coulter Annex [in 1961 at Purdue] to present Ron Stuckey with the Hughes–Davis (or Davis–Hughes or McDougall–Hughes–Davis) manifesto?

Memory fails me, but here it goes. Jon Hughes and I had observed at first hand the first of Stan Reiter's Midwest math–econ symposia, and we concluded that the seminar had achieved at least four worthy goals: (1) it had provided a format that permitted the few high-tech economists who then graced the halls of the Midwest campuses to carry on a productive intellectual interchange (if memory serves me, Minnesota and Purdue aside, no university was represented by more than one of this strange new breed of scholar, if scholar is the right word); (2) it gave Purdue, its dean, and its new program both intellectual stature and fine PR – at least within math–econ circles; (3) it made it possible for these few scholars to spend a substantial amount of free time together to discuss mutual problems in a very informal way (Oz Brownlee always organized a "high" stakes poker game); (4) and it gave hangers-on like Jon and me the chance to drink a great deal of "free" beer while observing the practitioners of this strange new discipline.

I really don't remember whose idea it was, but it appeared to one or both of us that some of these same goals (particularly #4) would aid our efforts to establish the New Economic History at Purdue (if Stan and his buddies got all the recognition and press, there were going to be few dollars left for the likes of us) and maybe elsewhere as well. On a more serious note, it was the chance to break out of the relative isolation of West Lafayette and talk with other like-minded economic historians that we saw as the most important potential contribution of the enterprise. I had been much impressed by the group of scholars who had collected at the Williamstown Conference on Income and Wealth and by those who had attended a seminar I had given in Alex Gerschenkron's Harvard workshop. Jon still retained pleasant memories of his work with colleagues at the New York Fed and the work then going on at Columbia (my memory is weak, but I think maybe he had recently been on leave teaching David Landes's classes at that University or maybe he had just been there to give a paper).

Anyway, partly in defense of the local economic history establishment and partly to see what the rest of the world had to offer in terms of the new history, we approached Emanuel T. Weiler and then, with his blessing, Associate Dean Ron Stuckey. Our pitch was straightforward. Ours was a new "hot" field. With three scholars in residence we had a leg up, but we were not alone and the opposition was gaining: Penn had established a joint history–economics Ph.D. program, Gerschenkron had produced Al Conrad, John Meyer, and the two Henrys (Rosovsky and Broude), and rumor had it that the seminar was now full of young potential hotshots (since that group included Al Fishlow, Paul David, and Peter Temin, the rumor was apparently correct). Ron bought the story (with Em's blessing there was probably no way he could refuse), and we got the go-ahead.

There was only one more problem: Who should be invited? Clearly we could not let ourselves be limited to the Midwest (it would have become obvious that there were far fewer economic historians than mathematical economists and there weren't many of the latter); and we opted for a "national" meeting. It's not clear how any group of 12 or 13 could be truly national, but we did entice Doug [North] from Seattle, Bill [Parker] from Yale, Bob [Gallman] from either Ohio State or North Carolina (I can't remember which), Bob [Fogel] from Rochester, and a few others. Although that first meeting was exciting (and a lot of beer was drunk), it was not until we saw the potential list of invitees for the second and third years (we had picked up Fishlow, David, Temin, Easterlin, to name only a few) that I became convinced that we were really onto something. Jon probably recognized it earlier.

Finally, do you still think, after another 20 years or so of reading cliometric work, that "it will never be literature?"

[Chuckle] With the possible exception of Bob Fogel's latest book, which I have not yet read, the answer is yes.

JONATHAN R. T. HUGHES

Interviewed by
Charles Calomiris

Jonathan Roberts Tyson Hughes was Professor of Economics and the first Robert E. and Emily King Professor of Business Institutions at Northwestern University, Evanston, Illinois. He was born in Wenatchee, Washington in 1928, grew up in Twin Falls, Idaho, and was educated at Utah State Agricultural College (B.S., 1950), in the graduate economics program at the University of Washington, and at the University of Oxford (D. Phil., 1955) on a Rhodes Scholarship. After a time at the New York Federal Reserve Bank he joined the Economics Department at Purdue in 1956 and moved to Northwestern in 1966, where he was based until his death in Evanston in 1992. Hughes returned to Oxford as a Visiting Fellow on two occasions, in 1962–3 at Nuffield College and in 1971–2 at All Souls College. He was President of the Economic History Association in 1981.

The interview was conducted in the winter and early spring of 1991 by Charles Calomiris, then of the Wharton School at the University of Pennsylvania, who had been Hughes's colleague at Northwestern. Calomiris writes:

Before I met Jon Hughes, Max Hartwell spoke of him in glowing terms as friend and colleague, but warned me that I should expect to find a remarkable difference between Hughes as writer and Hughes in person. Having previously read much of the written work, which is characterized by great erudition and close argument, I was delighted to find that his conversational style is discursive, expansive – as big as the West. In the interview, I have tried to preserve in print as much as I could of Jon Hughes talking, and the text transcribes how he responded to my questions and prompting. It's important to do this, I think, because to know Jon through his writings alone is to know only half of him, and at least a morsel of the other half is presented here. In the past half-dozen years I have had many such conversations with him, and more than once he was moved from talk to characteristically generous action. A few years ago he simply gave me his notes and materials from his D.Phil. research. I was in fact receiving all the secondary and primary materials on the period to date, neatly sorted and evaluated, and ready to put in a filing cabinet without even going to the archives. I'm still working through it all, and it is a mark of Jon's thoroughness as a scholar that I figure it will take me another ten years to finish with it.

Was the Cliometrics revolution a *bona fide* revolution or just a word applied to a slight change in technique? People like Wesley Mitchell and Simon Kuznets pre-date it. If it was a revolution, who reacted negatively to it and why?

We didn't think the work we did at Purdue was a revolution at first. We thought only of doing something new. We had this data-processing machinery. Purdue being the way it was, as Lance used to point out, we had computers but no library books. The steamship data were ordered from the New York Public Library. At Purdue, we had no Parliamentary papers or anything like that. If we wanted to do any kind of conventional research in those days, we had to drive to Urbana [Illinois]. Lance used to do that. I was told stories of him parking at a meter in front the U. of I. library and putting a nickel in every hour. I think there were 250,000 books at the Purdue library when we arrived. The library expanded when the Krannert money came in and Rosenberg showed up. It was then developed into a very fancy research library in certain areas. Given the initial scarce library resources, we had to innovate, to do something with our time. We could process masses of data; the question was, what kind of data? Our idea was that we could do historical data, time series primarily, which involved calculations that were beyond the reach of manual techniques. The steamship paper had about a million computations in it. You couldn't do it on a desk calculator. As I pointed out in my "Fact and Theory" paper years ago, other people in the past had become involved in exactly the same kinds of problems. I mentioned a number of older economists going back a hundred years or so. I gave the example of William Newmarch and his bill-of-exchange survey in 1851. So we didn't think our work was revolutionary except we were using electronic machinery. It was make-work – something to do – a way of doing things that we could do there at Purdue. We only became notorious, and then "revolutionary," when Carter Goodrich asked us to talk about what we were doing at the Philadelphia meeting of the EHA in 1960. That was when Stanley Reiter coined the word "cliometrics," to put a name on our work – heavy-duty quantitative work and data processing that hadn't been done before in economic history. I had been an accountant, and my D.Phil. thesis was filled with data that I had compiled. So I had a lively interest in the new computing machinery; I knew what drudgery we were leaving behind.

It seems to me that bringing computers to economic history wasn't the same kind of transformation of the discipline as bringing computers to industrial organization or to labor economics.

The problem was to have the confidence to jump across the unknown. You had to know enough collateral historical information to give you the confidence to interpret and generalize. Old J. R. Hicks told me that he wanted to be an economic historian, but he feared the amount of unknown you had to deal with, and he preferred to be more conservative – to define his own unknowns. The problem in the early Cliometrics papers was how to go from an intuitive understanding based on theory and history to those outcomes on the print-outs. I think we did provide examples, probably very imperfect ones, but examples of how you could go from what was a conventional way of thinking and take economic history into a new area. That wasn't exactly revolutionary.

Were you confident there was already an audience for that paper?

You mean "The First 1,945 British Steamships?" No, we weren't.

Who was the implied audience?

We didn't have an audience beyond Purdue. When Stan and I finished with the steamship paper, I couldn't imagine who would want to read something like that, and Stan said he wanted to try the *Journal of the American Statistical Association* because there were some things we had done in the paper which would be novel to statisticians. And that's why we went to that journal. We didn't ever send the paper around to be criticized by economic historians. What would they say? What could they have to say? They could never have seen anything like it before. I hadn't either. We didn't know how to do any parts of it at first.

I can remember when Lance and I got the output back for the exchange rate paper. We had no idea at all what it would look like. But we got the output back and stretched it out on tables and stared at it. We realized that we had set up a machine, a bunch of equations through which these values had been fed, and they had produced this outcome. What did it mean? At that point the economic historian had to come into play because there was no way of understanding those numbers at all without the broader conception – what the economy looked like in the period that had produced those numbers. The first bunch of numbers, as is well known now, didn't make any sense. We printed them but did not comment on them. We had no explanation. The bad numbers turned out to have been the result of a setting-up error.

Do you think the newer generation of economic historians – because they are more skilled in quantitative methods and econometrics, fields that have become so much more complex – are missing some of those other skills?

I am optimistic about the profession's future.

Do you think economic history is becoming dull, less daring, less original?

I think it's too early to reach conclusions like that. You only have so much time in life to learn things. You guys can't imagine what it was like when we were graduate students, and there was no econometrics. You didn't even study mathematical statistics in most places. We had time to read history books. We had time to read the history of economic thought. We had time to think about big ideas. If you looked at Assistant Professor Morrie Morris and Instructor Douggie North, the gurus of economic history at the University of Washington in those days, that was Big Idea City. There wasn't anything else to think about. Once you get into our contemporary world, where the graduate students are thoroughly trained in modern quantitative methods, they have the hardware readily available. You have data sets of all sorts. It's only natural that people will follow the line of highest payout, and so at first a majority of your work would look sort of picayune. Unfortunately, from the reader's point of view, many of the papers are about sets of equations and data sets. So some of the older guys of my generation are still kingpins in the world of big ideas.

I wouldn't expect this to last forever. I was terribly intrigued by the recent evidence that this country had somehow or other been malnourished between 1820 and 1860. That didn't come from anybody's big idea. I don't even think the Marxists ever claimed that. Did any contemporary ever say that in the 1880s? I don't think so. Mrs Trollope complained Americans drank too much whiskey, ate too much hot bread, and chewed too much tobacco. The evidence for malnutrition appears first in the work of Komlos and Fogel. Now there's something there to explain, and I'm sure explanations will be forthcoming. The work seems to me to be a good example of the validity of Cliometric work; you could produce this kind of serendipity. I mean you have a big result, after all, that covered large portions of populations which nobody had ever asked about before.

If you had to guess where the $1,000 bills are buried, what sorts of ideas, what sorts of subfields of economic history, what sorts of questions, do you think are likely to produce the next revolution?

I predicted some 15 years ago, in print, that the Great Depression of the 1930s would become the next gold mine. Apart from that kind of thing, I think modern history will force economic historians to ask questions which are not data-based in nature, but are certainly to be explained by economic theory. The largest example is the difference between the notion of freedom and fulfillment for individuals in the West compared to other parts of the world. We have just gone through a huge laboratory experiment in the application of different ideologies to economic endeavor. There has been an enormous apparent victory for the world of Western values, those bourgeois values which had been so denigrated by Marxist theorists for so long. I should think that a great area for big payoffs. The history of philosophy will become important again.

I was listening to two of our graduate students (one was from China and one was from Japan) talking about what was unique about the United States. They both agreed, talking only to each other with me sort of listening in, that what seemed odd at first about the United States, and then so wonderful, was freedom. Freedom from all kinds of pressures – from the family, from the society around them, not to mention from the government or from the university. Of course, this goes back to basic stuff. This has always been a big issue in the philosophy and history of political thought: Why it was that Western countries had this notion that their ideal social system was one in which the maximum number of people could do as they pleased? It is not an obvious way for anybody to think of a social system. Most social systems, now and in history, are not based on such ideas. The biggest thing that's happened in the twentieth century is, as the man said, "We won." The question now is why? I would foresee that at first people will say it's because we have the highest per capita incomes. But that's an obvious answer, puts the cart before the horse, and wouldn't even begin to go to the root of it.

Do you think economic historians will or should focus more on the big questions of economic development?

Yes, over huge blocks of time. You know, it's perfectly clear by now there really was something acquired, say from the Greeks and the Hebrews, that made a big difference between our society and others. And the other thing, of course, is the possibility of changing the economics metaphor from physics to biology, as Mokyr has already shown. To consider human societies in a very different way and to realize that they're not necessarily going to converge at all, that they're not heading necessarily for any kind of a common end in time. Some societies will make it farther in time, some have evolved as far as they're going to, and others contain within them possibilities for a great deal of evolution toward a longer and unique social existence.

Does history have lessons for the future?

For a long time the notion of mainstream economic development was that everybody should try to be like us. Progress was defined as Western economic structures and technology, allied with liberal democracy. That was the nineteenth-century ideal Karl Polanyi described as utopian. One of the first papers I ever published, in the *AER*, back in 1958 (something like that), was a paper in which I argued that it was not possible, even with the kind of information available then. If you just used your head you could see it was not really possible for other countries to be just like us, because we were changing every day ourselves. We weren't a finished product. It was like trying to shoot at a moving target from a long distance: you try to be just like us, and maybe you'll get blue jeans, Coca-Cola, and nothing else. One of the points Joel made in his book is very impressive: as far as he can tell, if you want technological development, human improvement based on technological development, to be the outcome, then it's diversity you want in social organization and not uniformity.

Would you say the relationship between economic historians and other economists has changed over the last 30 years or so? And how would you describe the change?

I don't think it's changed much. The issue has always been a very simple thing: people who do economic history have an investment in the study of the past, which then becomes part of their capital, and they insist upon using it. If you don't have that investment, you don't think history is important, and obviously you're not going to use it. You don't use what you don't have. I remember, as a graduate student, some took economic history courses, and some did not. At that point a difference emerged, right there, among the graduate students in how they thought about economic problems. Suddenly a homogeneous collection of graduate students seemed to have divided themselves up between humanists and "engineers." Suddenly there were areas in which we no longer could talk to each other very well because there was silence from those who took something else besides economic history in the program. In my case, at the University of Washington, some students opted for urban planning instead of economic history, and our paths separated forevermore. We all had exactly the same training in theory, but if you had this different experience that entered into your hard disk as part of your thinking material, then you were not the same as those who didn't know anything about it, and this made a difference. Later on, those who had stuck with theory, and only theory, developed an interest in techniques that went beyond matrix algebra, differential calculus, and mathematical statistics, and that then became a very heavy specialization on their part which was the equivalent of the specialization of economic historians on the historical side. So this made the range of information much larger between the two groups of people, but I don't think at the intersection it made any difference.

It always was very valuable to me, and at times very amusing, that Stanley Reiter and I always worked so well together on specific problems. The intersect was always the same, the tangency was always the same, and yet we were always bringing material from vast distances in each of our universes to bear on problems. In one case, we came up with a paper on the law and using the law to study regulated economies (Reiter & Hughes 1981). It has been argued that no one single living person would be able to read our paper except Leo Hurwicz. I always thought of that paper as a duet. Each of us brought our own skills to the music. It is like the Bach "Two Part Inventions" which sum up to three distinct pieces of music: A, B, and C, the blending of A and B.

This brings me to my "Purdue questions." Is that part of what made the group of people at Purdue unusual in comparison to other departments? A sort of willingness to find tangencies? If not, what did make that group so special?

Purdue was an example of the rule of a benevolent despot. The man who ran Purdue was E. T. Weiler. He was a student of Arthur Marget at Minnesota. Weiler had been in the Federal Reserve System; he'd been at the University of Illinois. He didn't like the economics profession. He thought the economics profession was a fraud and irrelevant, and so he began building Purdue, which had no real tradition of its own. Weiler had remarkable taste for talent and hired the group which became so famous. He was very explicit about not wanting to see economics with a capital "E" reappear at Purdue University. For a long time macroeconomics was not even taught there because it was thought to be too prosaic. We had no one doing public policy because Weiler didn't want that around. Weiler hired people by himself for a long time; all those famous people at Purdue were hired as young assistant professors or even instructors by Weiler on the basis of his own intuition. That kind of success rate is fairly unbelievable. Weiler believed people who were trained in theory and did empirical work were going to advance the discipline. We developed a certain perverse pride in doing things differently, and a number of novelties came out of there because of that. Because of that atmosphere of "anything goes," there were no holds barred. Nothing was going to be illegal.

This relates to your point about Western economic development and diversity.

Well, yes. You thought of that, I didn't, but that's what Weiler was after. He told me once, "You know, Jon, I have a recurrent nightmare, and the nightmare is that I will end up running a good Midwest economics department."

I remember when I told him about writing *The Vital Few*. He had heard about my activities. In those days the idea of writing about entrepreneurship seemed incomprehensible. I had only recently become a full professor. He invited me out to his house one Saturday in the winter, and we had some drinks in front of the fire. He asked me what I was doing. I explained it to him, and he stared at me for a minute when I finished talking and then said, "Well, Jon, you're a full professor now and you can do anything you want." When *The Vital Few* came out, he bought 85 copies of it to give to his friends. That was the way he was, you know.

I had this bee in my bonnet. Right after we had launched Cliometrics in 1960, I was already thinking about *The Vital Few*, and I was no longer thinking about Cliometrics. We had made the first big steps in Cliometrica. They were great fun, but I hadn't left the world of finance and gone into academic life to do the same damned thing over and over the rest of my life. I had this new idea. I remember telling Doug North about it at the first Clio meeting, and him saying, "What a neat idea for a book." Doug was another person who would do almost anything to avoid having to hear the same story twice.

Is it possible to have Weiler's kind of entrepreneurship at a major university today?

You couldn't do it where there was already a bunch of full professors or where there was already a tradition. Purdue was a big university, a lot of resources, and a very small and insignificant economics department, so Weiler was able to just set the old profs aside, tell them to enjoy life. He even got them some part-time jobs outside of Purdue so they could make some extra money. He told them they didn't have to play our game, which was publish or perish, up or out.

Purdue became a kind of hothouse. It was so sensational that within three or four years after Weiler started, people from the Ford Foundation came there to investigate. They were convinced there was some secret research technique or organization that was causing this one department to make such a ruckus in the profession. In the end they never could find the reason for it. They gave us a big grant anyway. But I remember them, coming around the offices and wanting information which might explain why there were so many novel and revolutionary contributions at Purdue. Weiler's methods worked. Some guys would score again and again, like Vernon Smith, who was simply an extremely creative guy who had been turned loose and supported. Everything he touched changed the profession. Finally, a whole building was tailored for his experimental economics, once he got going on that.

They built a building?

Partly, the building had rooms built into it for Vernon's experiments, built into the structure of the buildings, one-way mirrors and all kinds of stuff.

The Ph.D. program itself, when you look at the students who were turned out of the Ph.D. program, many are famous people. Why were they like that? Well, again, in part it was that they didn't have to learn anything simply because it had existed for a long time. The major theoretical stuff that existed at Purdue had just been invented, and that's what they were trained in. Purdue became a collection of extraordinary personalities and finally, for reasons which are very diverse indeed, it all fell apart in about two or three years.

Once it started . . .

Everybody left. I've forgotten the number. Something like 19 full professors got out of there in two or three years.

Why couldn't Weiler stop the exodus?

I don't think he wanted to. He had gotten interested in the management school, and he thought the management school had more to contribute, I think. He was happy with the management school. If you talk to people who left Purdue you'll hear all kinds of different reasons. There had been two or three of these places like Purdue in the history of economics, both here and abroad: Iowa State, the University of Birmingham in England. You need a certain combination of things, including the lack of constraining forces, like an old department with a lot of full professors, tradition and stuff, that determines where anything is going to be able to go.

One thing remarkable about your work is the variety of audiences you've written for and the variety of types of books that you've written, from your Oxford product on Britain in the 1850s, to *The Vital Few*, to *The Governmental Habit*, to the work on the Japanese internment camp [unpublished], to Davis and Hughes, Hughes and Rosenberg, and your

work with Stan Reiter. All are very, very different. Having gotten to know you, I think there's a relationship between the variety of styles and variety of lives. You worked at the New York Fed for a while, you worked in a salmon canning factory in Alaska, you were at Oxford, you grew up in Idaho, you helped construct a Japanese internment camp, you traveled all over the place. I would guess that you must have felt like something of a chameleon in your personal life. Do you think that had an effect on your diversity of styles and subjects?

Well, I always thought of my heterogeneousness of social roots a great advantage because I was able to relate to all sorts of people. Some of the work I did that seemed to categorize me, not in one category but in several different categories, represented an overt attempt to do something different. I'll give you two examples. My Oxford thesis was an attempt to satisfy Habakkuk's desire for me to get a D.Phil., and therefore represents stone-fisted research and very careful discussion.

The Vital Few was an overt attempt on my part to correct what I thought had been a bad mistake in the study of entrepreneurship: the absence of the personalities of the entrepreneurs. Because of growing up in Idaho, I was well aware that without entrepreneurs you couldn't have capitalism, and I knew that long before I ever read Schumpeter because I grew up in a town that began rising out of the sagebrush in 1907. So the town was only 25 years old or so when I became cognizant of what was going on around me, and I knew from looking, that businesses were entrepreneurial enterprises that hadn't had time to fossilize into corporations. Where there were people doing things, making things, and hiring others to work for them, there were entrepreneurs. So I had a vivid and lively notion of where the American economy had come from to such an extent that, when I began learning other analyses (like neoclassical economics, Marxism, and so on), to me they were all just fruitless mental exercise. Nothing was said that would cause a man from Mars, say, to understand where this thing came from. So, when I wrote about the entrepreneurs, I wrote about it partly to make a point, and partly to have some fun with my writing. I became an academic because I wanted to write. I wrote *The Vital Few* expressly to reach a large audience.

There again, when you describe these feelings about *The Vital Few*, you're making me think about your presidential address on the Alaskan canning factory where the point, in many ways, is the same. The point is that you have to understand the sort of individual experience of being a worker and an entrepreneur in a particular place to understand what was happening.

That's the trick, isn't it? I was just reading Peter Medawar recently, his book on philosophy of science. There's this problem about induction and deduction. If you rely on deduction alone, you have a general view of the earth and probably no information at all concerning the species on it. Even if you become a great inductivist, on that basis alone you have no idea what the earth looks like overall, although you'd be really great on, say, red ants or termites. And the trick always has been, and it's an art, to go from specific to general knowledge. Either you have to do it, or the specific knowledge just remains in academic journals of interest to those who are interested in red ants and termites. You have to make the jump, and it's a very risky thing. There's some point at which you become convinced you may be wrong, but then you become convinced that, hey, I've got something here that's of general interest. Then you go ahead and produce it. It is a risk, and I don't think you can avoid it.

How did *The Governmental Habit* fit into your plans as an academic entrepreneur?

My book, *The Governmental Habit*, is an overtly polemical effort, but as such it is a failure. I will cause no changes in the real world with this book. I'm glad I did it, and it's been worth doing. It's very interesting to see, in small detail, where the American habits of regulation came from, but I despair of the possibility that the amount of regulation in this country will ever be reduced, whether we know anything about its origins or not. As a historian, of course, I just naturally think that our decision would be wiser if we knew why we were making it. The economy, as it exists, is an artifact. There isn't a thing that doesn't represent the past. All the rules, all the regulations, all the institutions, all the physical capital, the social structure and everything else is nothing but an artifact of the past, and to my mind it is quite pointless to think about regulation and property rights without finding out what were the property rights, where did they come from, what's the origin of our present set of property rights, and where did these methods of regulation come from. All you have to do is live in some other country and you realize that what we do is quite different from what other people do. We have our own way of regulating path dependency: it represents what we did in the past. We could easily improve our system if we would be willing to learn from anybody else, but like others, we don't. We do things mostly as we did in the past.

Does economics provide a foil for economic historians? Do economists provide encouragement because their models often are incomplete or wrong?

Well, they make very easy targets. But, after all, as an economist, in many respects my thinking is just exactly like everyone else's. For example, I always turn off the TV when an economist comes on, and there's a reason for this.

Why?

Because I know he doesn't know what he's talking about. The reason he's there is because he doesn't know what he's talking about, and therefore he can reach a broad audience. But you have to think with economic theory, you haven't got anything else to think with. I've always said theory is like a flashlight in a forest. It's useful for illuminating some points, but only if you know where to look and what you're looking for. When I see economic analysis that is based on not understanding or misunderstanding the historical background of what's being discussed, I feel very sad. There aren't many professions in which the subject's history is of no interest to the practitioners. I mean, medical people are interested in the evolution of mammalian bodies, physicists are interested in geology, astrophysicists are interested, after all, in the most historical thing there is – the origin of the universe. Most serious kinds of study, musicology, for example, are interested in the change in the nature of the thing being studied over time. I think there must not be many professions that are as unchanged in their basic theoretical thinking by changes in the facts as economics is. I don't expect the basic core of thought in economics to ever be changed by any new discoveries about the economy itself.

Is that, in a sense, something that defines economic historians? By virtue of their difference along those lines?

Well, it's been kind of pitiful. You see efforts made again and again to show that what was found in fact was justified in theory. In those cases, one thinks, how sad; as I said long ago in the "Fact and Theory" paper, if I see a six-toed horse I should be interested in that for its own sake. I should not ignore it because theory says there are no six-toed horses. If I find one, I should report it even if there is no explanation at all. A good example of this, return again to Komlos and Fogel, is they have reported this decline in the stature of average American males when no one ever asked them to find that information and we don't know why it happened.

You have just come out with the third edition of your textbook. How did you get started on it and how did it change your views of your colleagues' work?

I had been teaching economic history for 25 years, so I had already assimilated the work. I read the journals to keep up, so I knew before I started writing it how it was going to come out. Not that it's the only way that you could write American economic history, but I had, after all, lived a long time. I had gone through a period when economic history was meant to explain why the American economy was "number one" (as Nixon would say), and, by the end of the 1970s, the question was, "What was it about the American economy that caused it to be something else?" So it seemed to me it was time to examine issues which had been ignored in earlier treatments of American economic history. It wasn't just growth and success we were interested in. It was failure, it was intractable problems, it was decline as well as expansion. We had a lot of things to try to understand, and I'd kept up on all this material.

Do you think you learned anything important just by writing the text?

I learned just how hard it was to keep mistakes out of something that complicated.

I'd like you to talk a little bit about the personal origins of your interest in economic history. How did it happen?

Well, it was very simple for me. As a graduate student I studied more or less the same things the other students studied. I had no more courses in economic history than I had in the history of economic thought or economic theory. I had far more courses in economic theory than I had in history. The two people who had taught me were Morrie and Doug, so that the economic history I had was very vivid in my head. When I got to Oxford I was simply assigned by J. R. Hicks to be the economic historian; he assigned me to Habakkuk and that was that. Then, when I came back to the United States, I didn't do economic history, I went into finance in New York. I was hired at Purdue as a money and banking guy, along with Ed Ames, right out of the Federal Reserve System. But as fate would have it, I ran into Lance again and that was a fateful mixture because, once we got together again, we began discussing the issues that had come up in seminars at the University of Washington. We were joined by Duncan McDougall. We wrote a textbook, and, at that point, we found ourselves faced with the requirement that we teach economic history. It hadn't been taught at Purdue before. When we asked the man responsible for this (why was it we were being forced to teach economic history?), he said the rule at Purdue was that, if you wrote a book on a subject, you had to teach it – God's truth. We introduced American economic history because we had to. So we found ourselves teaching economic history, which we had never intended to teach. It was a lot more difficult to teach than other parts of economics, as you know, and we didn't welcome this new chore.

So you taught it as a team?

No, we would teach it one at a time. We didn't need to be a team because we wrote the book together. McDougall had come there as a macroeconomist, one of the people out of the Kuznets barn. One thing led to another, and pretty soon we found ourselves making reputations for ourselves as economic historians and nothing else. It happened very fast. We had no choice. There was a lot of demand for it. Then came Stanley Reiter and "his word," and the Cliometric Society appeared. We had that first meeting and found the people who were doing this kind of work. Within just two or three years we had a huge development coming out of something which had started without premeditation, totally without premeditation.

I've told the story elsewhere about the paper I did with Lance about the exchange rates (see 1981: 363). That was due to old Arthur Cole. He had seen some of the stuff coming out of Purdue. He approached Lance and said, "I've got the records of these 4,000 bills of exchange. Why don't you and your friends at Purdue see what you can make of these?" So they sent us the records of this company in Philadelphia which they had in the Baker library at Harvard. We sat down across the table from each other and started coding them onto punch cards. That was how we spent days, weeks, months.

If you were putting together a list of people doing significant work on economic history in 1960, how long would the list be?

At that time you had to divide it up between the older people and the younger people, there were very few in between – a topic I took up in the "Fact and Theory" paper. The distinguished senior colleagues, Hal Williamson and Arthur Cole and others, had sort of matured in their subject. Ralph Hidy, Richard Overton, Fritz Redlich, they had a very nice thing they had made that went back to the 1920s, a particular style of economic history which was very mature and was getting to the point where you could use the word historians often use, "magisterial," to describe the output. What then came along was a younger bunch of guys who had been trained in economics whose work could never have been called magisterial and couldn't be to this day because it's a different style. In economics a new theory or a new paper is merely an invitation to an argument. So there is nothing that's finished. No work is finished. I remember one time listening to a discussion about the amount of Cliometrics which had been achieved over the dead bodies of papers that had been proved wrong in the previous meetings. Peter Temin, I think, asked if there wasn't really some virtue in being right the first time? I think that's a big difference between working in economics, economic theory, and quantitative work and other kinds of production of truth which are based on the quality of the argument and how elegant it is. In Cliometrics you no sooner get finished with something than a new bunch of numbers is turned up that may put you in your place, or show that the theory could be improved by dropping a couple of assumptions which would leave your work standing off to one side.

Do economic historians fare better at that than other economists? Does their work live longer?

No, I don't think so. Well, some of it's going to live. Some of the great errors caused some important new departures; important contributions have been made because of big errors. The errors themselves were important. I don't think economic history is any different from economics in this regard. The half-life of most research is not long.

Does it make sense for economic history to be in an economics department necessarily? The British do it a little bit differently.

Yes, well, I've been of two minds. When things are going well, I think it's wonderful to be in the economics department, and, when things are going badly, I think why should we bother with these people. We've got huge enrollments and could have our own department. I think that ideally we should be in both worlds, in history and economics, and some people like Joel Mokyr, for example, have done it. It's very hard to do because the requirements are quite different for superior scholars in economics and in history. There have been people before – David Landes, for example – who have operated always in both economics and in history departments. There have been some, I think, more successful than others. I think that economic history, because it is now mostly Cliometrics, is so thoroughly involved in computery that it must remain either connected to economics departments or to mathematical statistics departments. It wouldn't make much difference, you could do it either way, but you should be somewhere where you know when things change.

It's very easy, as I've discovered already, to become comfortable with your own software and your machine and resist. Old people don't like to change, and tend to resist any further changes in thinking. It is the case that the software used and the hardware used also change the way you think. I was appalled by that when I first came back from Oxford and was shown a roomful of IBM machines at Harvard which had been given by IBM to the Economics Department. The department was trying to think up Ph.D. dissertations that would use those machines. I was just appalled by this because I thought the science should determine the technology used, and not the other way around. But you see that when the technology is so sensational, you can't avoid having some of the technology determine the nature of the science. It's just too bad, maybe, but you can't avoid it.

Did you foresee the direction economic history would take after the Cliometrics revolution?

No, because there was no way to know what the new advances in hardware, software, and theory were going to be. I don't know that I'm surprised by the way it went or even disappointed by the way it went. I alluded earlier to the lack, so far, of big new thinking from the younger people, but then they're younger people. You know, even Eric Jones once worked on small problems. I couldn't have seen 30 years ago how things would be by 1991, obviously no one could. To give you an idea of the extent to which I didn't foresee the future, what I was afraid of, especially after hearing Fogel the first time, was that we might go the route of Oswald Spengler and start developing great algebraic systems of economic history and development that would be bogus. Not that Bob's work was bogus, but it was easy to see how you could go into mechanistic, big systems of, say, difference equations in which you develop mechanistic economic history, and it would be very convincing. On its own terms, it would be irrefutable and would take up time in classrooms beautifully. It would be very popular because the teachers would only have to learn the sets of equations that were being used.

So why didn't it happen?

Rostow once said that the problem about history was that in the end you were stuck with the facts as they are. Truth is that mankind cannot change, so the tendency to try to explain Western civilization, say, in terms of Kondratieff cycles, or whatever, will always fail because of the chorus of laughter from those who know better. I think some other fields are not subject to that discipline. If anybody says that economic history is not scientific, my answer is: Just publish a mistake sometime and see how long it takes to get caught.

Do you think economic historians, as a group, get along better with each other than other disciplines of economics and are more critical of each other openly?

Well, I think of it with a certain sense of humility. After all, a good education tells you the extent of what it is you don't know. I think economic historians have a lively sense of what they don't know about all the tools they use and don't use, and all the areas they want to investigate and are excluded from, for one reason or another. But it was pointed out, back in the Purdue days, that all the best parties took place when the economic historians were in town. This was not pointed out to me by an economic historian, but by a theorist who was very disappointed about a particular group of theorists who seemed to have no fun at all when they came to Lafayette. When the economic historians came to town, it was New Year's Eve for several days. So I think it was on the basis of that observation you could argue that there is some truth to the idea that economic historians tended to be very congenial with each other.

Another thing you notice among economic historians is that there are not many prima donnas. Prima donnaism doesn't pay. I remember several economic historians who began as prima donnas, but it didn't last long. The first time somebody is able to show demonstrably how wrong you are on a particular point, that really blunts the ego and pulls it down. The thing about Cliometrics, as I pointed out before, the terrifying thing about it, was that for the first time a person doing history could be exactly wrong, could be extensively exactly wrong. You could always make little mistakes, but with Cliometrics, when you set up the capital equipment, that is to say the equations you were going to use to feed those numbers through, if you made a mistake then, you would be wrong for a long-time series and a whole analysis based on it. So that kept the egos in check.

I was going to ask you to talk a little bit about "the time of troubles" when *Time on the Cross* was released.

Well, I don't mind talking about that. I was given the responsibility to compare Fogel and Engerman's estimates of slave wages with real wages in England and Europe, which I did at the famous meeting in Rochester [in 1974]. I had studied Gray's *History of Southern Agriculture* under Doug North's fescue at the University of Washington, so it was not news to me that slavery was extremely profitable for those who owned slaves. I was, in fact, astonished there were those who had swallowed the Marxian argument that it wasn't profitable, because it meant you believed a million or so entrepreneurs in the South didn't know what they were doing. The fact that *Time on the Cross* came out in the middle of the civil rights movement didn't add to tranquility at those meetings because a large part of what was being said was, for emotional reasons, based upon various private agendas about the civil rights movement. Had *Time on the Cross* come out at a time when civil rights were not such an issue, there might have been more media light than there was heat. There was a feeling back in the early 1970s that it was almost illegal to apply neoclassical theory to something that was so intensely human and emotional. Then there were the personalities of the contestants. When Conrad and Meyer came out there had been no such emotional outburst.

But their claims were much narrower.

The claims were narrower. *Time on the Cross* was really provocative. If you go back and look at the research on slavery before 1972, then look at it afterwards, you can see the seminal contribution of Fogel and Engerman, whose work caused a total reassessment of the antebellum South and of the North too. People began to ask "Keynesian" questions about what was so profitable in the South? Were there income effects elsewhere, was an economic rent being collected or what? Then it turned out that the English had cleaned up because of slavery, the North benefited because of slavery, and the stain continued to spread. That was the contribution of *Time on the Cross*. There were a certain number of hot-headed things said at various meetings at that time, and I thought Bob Fogel and Stanley Engerman were remarkably thick-skinned to go through that kind of firefight. I'd rather be anonymous than have to go through that. I think there is no long-term enmity because of it. Well, I mean those who made successful arguments against Fogel and Engerman then were up-ended themselves. Which goes back to what I said earlier, that it was impossible to be magisterial where everyone had the weapons and were anxious to use them.

And when you write down specific equations you can't go back and say that wasn't quite the number that I intended.

Thomas Edison once said that he wouldn't patent things because a patent was an invitation to a lawsuit. I think the same thing is true of quantitative economic history. Just as soon as you put a number down or write down an equation or draw a diagram, somebody else is going to be able to advance their own position in life because of it. So you must not suppose that you can get away with anything. And after a while, if you get bruised enough on particular issues, it makes you a very human person.

How would you describe Doug North's influence on your work?

You know, of all of the things that I did, the least original was my thesis, and that was done in a certain way for a certain purpose. After that, after I got my degree and got out of England, and then, in turn, left the Federal Reserve System, I never had any interest, and still don't, in doing anything that somebody else has done just because I see the way to stretch it. I think I got that from Doug North. He used to argue that there's no point in being an economic historian if all you want to do is have small ideas. Economic history is the place where you can have really big ideas. So why get into economic history and not have big ideas? Not explore big things? And God knows that's certainly the way he has lived.

It seems like a lot of students have been influenced by his energy.

Oh, yeah. To be a Doug North student is a very suspicious thing to be.

NATHAN ROSENBERG

Interviewed by
William A. Sundstrom

Nathan Rosenberg is Fairleigh S. Dickinson, Jr., Professor of Public Policy, Emeritus, at Stanford University, Stanford, California. He was born in Passaic, New Jersey in 1927 and was educated at Rutgers University (A.B., 1950) and at the University of Wisconsin (Ph.D., 1955), including two years at Oxford University (1952–4). Before he settled at Stanford in 1974 he taught at Indiana University (1955–7), the University of Pennsylvania (1957–61), Purdue University (1961–7), Harvard University (1967–9), and the University of Wisconsin (1969–74). In 1981 he was elected Fellow of the American Academy of Arts & Sciences. A conference in Rosenberg's honor was held at Stanford in 1992, with the proceedings published as a special issue of *Research Policy* (Mowery, Nelson & Steinmueller, eds 1994).

The interviewer was William Sundstrom of Santa Clara University, who writes:

I spoke with Nate Rosenberg in his office on February 10, 1994. Being there brought back memories of conversations I had with him during the early 1980s, when I was a graduate student studying economic history and history of thought at Stanford. As usual, Nate was open, hospitable, and eager to talk about his many research interests, both past and – especially – present and future. I began by asking him for a brief intellectual autobiography, including his schooling, influential teachers, and how he became interested in issues of economic history and technology.

I came from a very poor working-class background in northern New Jersey, and I was the first and really the only member of my family to go to college. This is partly relevant because my first serious intellectual immersion was in Marxism: my father was a Marxist and a Communist. The early intellectual discussions around the kitchen table during my childhood were all observations on conditions of the working class not in 1844, but in, say, 1934. This shaped a lot of my thinking. I think I unloaded a lot of my Marxist freight by forcing myself to read through all three volumes of *Capital* when I was 18 or 19 years old. That really did it. Volume II was a killer.

Then I went off in the Army and spent a year in Korea. This exposure to an extremely poor country was also a formative influence, leading me to ask questions like: Why are some countries rich and some countries poor? When I went to school – I did my undergraduate work at Rutgers and my graduate work at Wisconsin and Oxford – my interests were primarily on the question of long-term economic growth.

One thing that I carried from my early Marxian exposure, which I still carry, is the notion that technical change is a central part of that long-term growth phenomenon, and that's an element of my intellectual orientation that I have always retained. I found in graduate school, and in reading the economics literature in the mid to late 1950s, that there was really very little if anything that the literature had to say about the origins and the causes of technological change, as opposed to its consequences. And that, I think, is still broadly true even today. There is a great deal of interest in the economic impact of technical change, but there has been precious little done trying to unpack what it is that accounts for technological dynamism – for the rate and direction of inventive activity.

In my younger days I found myself teaching courses on economic development and found very little, still, in the economics literature that shed any light on how technological change came to be the kind of phenomenon it was. That was what really brought me into economic history. As a graduate student I didn't even take a course in economic history, although I did take a wonderful seminar with Abbott Payson Usher one year when he was visiting at the University of Wisconsin.

So, in many ways it was my persisting interest in economic growth and what generates it that really sent me back into economic history, and to the degree that I became an economic historian I became one because I was frustrated with not finding anything useful on the subject of technical change in economic theory. I decided instead to look at it historically. Thirty-odd years later I think that was a very good decision – that a good way to find out about technological change was not to sit down or go to a blackboard and theorize about it, but to look at how it occurred.

How did you begin that "historical look?"

Along the way I was befriended, as a young, non-tenured assistant professor, by two people who came to play a very important role in my own thinking, Bill Parker and Dick Easterlin. And it was really through their encouragement that I did the first kind of systematic study of some important technological change. They invited me to give a paper at an Income and Wealth Conference and we agreed that I would write a paper on machine tools. In the end, the paper was not published in the conference volume, because there were no numbers in it. So, failing that, the article appeared in the *Journal of Economic History*, I guess in 1963. Most of my work, not all, but most of my work since then has involved looking at technological change in particular industries over time.

One thing that has impressed me very strongly is the obvious observation that technological change is really a great many very different kinds of things. It was something very different in the machine tool industry from what it has been, let's say, in agriculture, the aircraft industry, chemicals, forest products, or any number of other industries that I have looked at in particular at one time or another. And so, I guess it would be fair to say, most of my work has been a kind of an inductive search, looking for observations about technological change as an economic phenomenon, but again my primary interest was in looking at the causation more than the consequences, and that is what I am still doing today.

In 1961 I went to Purdue and there I found Jon Hughes, one of my dearest friends. Jon and I had actually been students together and lived together at Oxford. I was not only the best man at his wedding, I was the only man (excepting, of course, the clergyman who officiated). That's true: Jon was a Rhodes scholar, and back in those benighted Neanderthal days, Rhodes scholars were not allowed to marry. So, Jon was married secretly and I was his only man. I found an extremely lively intellectual climate at Purdue: Jon Hughes, Lance Davis, Ed Ames (with whom I did quite a bit of work), and a number of other people; and of course what happened every year was that the cliometrics people would meet, for some strange reason in late January, in West Lafayette.

Often a good part of the meetings were spent at my house. Sometimes the weather got bad; on one occasion, Henry Rosovsky ended up spending the night at O'Hare and Bob Fogel ended up spending an extra three nights at the Rosenbergs', from which we have a large collection of wonderful pictures of our kids that he took. And so, we would get the crowd of Paul David, Al Fishlow, Peter Temin, Bob Fogel, Doug North, Bill Parker, Stan Engerman – which is to say, a group of people that includes some of my oldest and dearest friends. So, I have been very close to the cliometrics movement. Later on, when I ended up at the University of Wisconsin for some years, the Cliometrics meetings gravitated there. And so I learned a great deal of my economic history sitting at the feet of the most innovative members of the cliometrics profession.

Since I came to Stanford, very nearly 20 years ago, my focus has changed in certain ways, but the common theme is still trying to determine the wellspring of technological innovation. I focus now much more than I did on the role of science – on the role of science, but also on the role of research generally. One of the interesting questions that I'm working on right now is, really, when you look at research and development, what is it that you are looking at? In fact, economists tend to make use of the R&D numbers and then frequently talk about it as if what they're talking about is research in basic science. Whereas the fact of the matter is that in the United States, not only today but for the last 30 years, if you look at total R&D spending, only about one-twelfth of it is what the NSF would call basic science; roughly two-thirds is development work. It's not basic science at all. Much of it is product development and testing and revision and further development and testing and so on.

For some time I have been particularly interested in – I use a word I think is appropriate in this context; it's an overused word in some circles – the dialectical relationship between science and technology. And a lot of that involves looking at how technology has shaped and influenced the scientific enterprise as much as science has shaped technology. To a very considerable extent, I regard the causation as being technology generating new science.

How old would you say that dialectic is? I think of science-based technology as something that isn't of much importance in technological progress until the turn of the twentieth century, or the late nineteenth century. Is this a dialectic that goes much farther back than that?

The question you ask is precisely what I am particularly interested in. I think it is increasingly a twentieth-century phenomenon, even though I also believe that even today we still very much exaggerate the extent to which new technology is based upon scientific research. We certainly wildly exaggerate it when we suggest, as it is often suggested by the spokesmen for science in Washington, that technological change depends upon *recent developments* in science. I mean, it is one thing to say that technology is shaped by science, and I would certainly not challenge that proposition, but an observation that I make over and over again is that the science that turns out to be influential is frequently *very old* science. If you look, for example, at the revolution in metallurgy – I think that is a fair term – after Bessemer, say, at post-1856, and if you look at the development of the basic Bessemer process, you are looking at technological developments that indeed draw upon science, but, for the most part, that science was there before the French Revolution.

But has metallurgy ever really been a science?

That's a good question because if you look in college catalogs, as you can here, you will not find "metallurgy." You will find entries under "materials science." So, if science is what universities teach and say are sciences, then the answer would have to be "yes," but, see, I have no difficulty saying metallurgy is a science. I have no difficulty saying that many intellectual pursuits incorporate large elements of basic science, even when the pursuit would today be thought of as an engineering activity.

What about "computer science?" Is that a science? If so, what do you mean by science?

Solid-state physics by definition has certainly underlain the development of the hardware that is made for computers, but if you look at what people who call themselves computer scientists do, they are not scientists in the sense of solid-state physicists, not by a long shot. They are working on questions like the nature of human intelligence, artificial intelligence; in some cases, they are looking at developing algorithms for how human beings as well as machines solve certain kinds of problems. To use a useful term of Herbert Simon, computer science is one of the "sciences of the artificial." It is a science built upon, and in turn contributing to, the building of a discipline which involves the study of human artifacts; but can't the study of the behavior of human artifacts be science?

The dialectic, I think, is [very] pervasive. I mean, consider the fact that much of the progress of science, after all, has depended very heavily upon the development of new techniques of experimentation going back to Galileo's observations, which changed our view of the world. That couldn't have happened without a telescope. Pasteur's work would have been, I think, inconceivable without a microscope, without a pretty powerful one. Much of what has gone on in twentieth-century molecular biology would have been impossible without x-ray crystallography. So, clearly technology influences science in a very profound way by providing its instrumentation. But it does it, I think, in a great many additional ways.

The fact is that technology also leads to anomalous observations which then require explanation. In a certain sense, Thomas Edison discovered the electron but didn't know it. It was of no particular use to him that he could see, so he hardly did anything more than write it up. But if you look at the history of twentieth-century technology you will find time and time again that pushing the technological frontier in one way leads to all sorts of observations, whether it is the collapse of a bridge or the crashing of an airplane or the corrosion of a cable underneath the Atlantic ocean, which in turn led to very serious research, as in the last case it did at Bell Labs, which ultimately resulted in some important breakthroughs in polymer chemistry. So I think that dialectic is really a very complicated one.

Now let me drag you back toward economic history. I was at the 1993 EHA meetings in Tucson, where McCloskey gave a paper asserting we really have not much understanding at all of what brought about the Industrial Revolution and what has been the major set of driving forces in the extraordinary growth of per capita production since then. I wonder if you can give an overall assessment, going back to this early interest of yours in the sources of growth – and putting it in the perspective of Denison's growth accounting: How far along are we now in understanding the process of growth, in particular as it's driven by technological change? That's a big question.

Yes, that's a big question, but a very fair one, of course. I guess I'd be inclined to say that we know a great deal more today than we did, say, 40 or 50 years ago. One thing we know is an increasing awareness of how much we don't know. I think of the work of people like – well, in my own firmament of stars here – Jack Schmookler; I think, of course, of Griliches; I think of Kuznets; I think of my esteemed colleague Moe Abramovitz; it seems to me that we have a much better appreciation for the contribution of technology than we once had.

The economic historians have played a very important role here; our two Nobelists in economic history have each contributed in their own very different ways to an important understanding of the role of technological change. You know, Fogel's book on railroads in American economic growth – it's not very often thought of this way – but when I read that book the most impressive thing to me about it, aside from the extraordinary energy with which he built his counterfactual world, was his successful criticism of what he called in the book the "axiom of indispensability." His basic point was a technological one. He picked what he regarded, and what most economic historians at the time would have regarded, as the most important innovation of the nineteenth century in America – the railroads – and with his huge energetic undertaking he established, to his own satisfaction at least, and to that of a great many others, that by 1890 railroads had made less than a 5 percent difference to GNP.

His general conclusion is that no single innovation was indispensable. I think that was a profoundly important observation. I'm not sure I would have defined the conclusion in exactly the same way that he did, but what he was saying, from my point of view, was that no single innovation is indispensable because a society that has managed, one way or another, to become technologically dynamic therefore has the capability of developing a wide range of substitute technologies for any given technology. So, I've always read Fogel's book as pointing to the impressive ability of advanced industrial societies to develop technologies over a wide range and to provide substitutes when one technology or one particular natural resource base, for example, becomes increasingly scarce.

Going back to the question that you posed from the McCloskey paper, it seems to me that through the works of people like Schmookler, Abramovitz, Kuznets, and Schumpeter, we have in fact learned a great deal. But if you ask what of the growth accounting exercises of, say, someone like Ed Denison, I would have to answer that, first of all, I think it was an enormously important intellectual achievement; it was an attempt to break down the specific components of growth – and in that sense, if nothing else, it gave us a kind of a target to shoot at. It gave us some numbers and that, of course, is in the best spirit of cliometrics. It gave us some numbers and therefore something to chew over and to challenge and to disagree with. My own sense is that the growth-accounting exercises were largely doomed to failure because there was an underlying methodology which strikes me as being somewhat simplistic – that is to say, most basically, the notion that you can take the separate contributions of capital, labor, human capital, make separate estimates for reallocation of resources, separate estimation of economies of scale, attach a value to each and then add it up, until you get to 100 percent, although even Denison still ended up with a rather significant residual.

What strikes me is that you can't simply attach values to each of these separate variables and then add them up. It seems to me that the decisive fact was in the interaction of things. Denison, I don't think, really got very far, nor do I think he ever really tried, to deal with these interaction effects. You know, how can you talk about the contribution of capital to growth without saying something very explicit about technological change?

On the other hand, I guess I have a lot of reservations about some of the other ways of simply playing with or massaging the time-series numbers on capital and labor. If you are allowed to play sufficiently with them, you can exhaust the residual by some appropriate weighting procedure, which has been a kind of a popular intellectual exercise of other people in the profession. So, I think we have learned a lot, but I'm still very much impressed with how much we still do not know.

I take it then, in a sense, one of the reasons that you are not a cliometrician – wouldn't consider yourself one – is that the things that seem most interesting about the process of economic growth may be qualitative processes, often *sui generis*; your emphasis on industry studies and historical specificity suggest that it may be a mistaken presumption to think that you could find something measurable in the same sense you can measure labor force or capital expenditures.

Well, I certainly agree that it's subtle and qualitative and that technological change is very difficult to deal with by the traditional tools of cliometrics. Let me get into a question which isn't readily dealt with in a straightforward cliometric way. A lot of Doug North's work, for example, has been very much in this, if you wish, qualitative, or at least non-quantitative, tradition. Doug has been enormously concerned with questions of institutions and how institutions affect motivation and incentives, and very concerned with legal institutions and political institutions.

Going back to McCloskey's question, "Why did the Industrial Revolution as we know it first occur in Great Britain?," I guess one of the first things that I would like to say is that British society was characterized by a high degree of political stability, as well as a society which had legal institutions and protections of property and contract that were more advanced and more developed than those of other countries. I would take it that one of the most distinctive features of technological innovation if you look at it *ex ante*, not *ex post*, is that it involves decision making under very high degrees of uncertainty. When, on the top of the inherent uncertainty, you pile on political and legal uncertainties, then it seems to me that the willingness of people to make long-term investments in highly uncertain projects is going to be looked at in a very different way. Perhaps economists don't have a great deal to say about political stability in and of itself, but I think an essential consideration is that this is a decisive factor in shaping the environment in which people make decisions that will, or may, lead to new technology.

Now, at the same time, I would characterize much of my own work as really being in a certain sense conceptual in nature. How do you think about technological innovation?

What is it? How does it differ in different sectors of the economy? These questions certainly do not lend themselves readily to quantitative analysis. But yet, at the same time, some of the most important work in the field – again I would cite in particular the work of someone like Jack Schmookler – used quantitative data to shed some very powerful light on what drives inventive activity, both with respect to its rate, its timing and its direction, and I have to think that Schmookler was a very undervalued member of this profession. I think he had a very deep understanding of what drives technical change.

I do think it's short-sighted, in spite of what I've just said about Schmookler's importance and his undervaluation, to concentrate your thinking purely upon activities for which there are readily available measures. And technological change is a peculiarly difficult subject to get a hand hold on directly. So we treat it as a residual or we take proxies like patent data; unfortunately, there are no really good databases on which to draw, and furthermore, it's a very subtle thing.

One reason we have so much difficulty in modeling technological change is that it isn't just one thing, it's not even just one big thing, it's a great many small things. And a lot of my own work has been an attempt to identify what some of those small things are, what some of the more subtle interaction effects are. It's one thing to identify these things; it's another matter to find good proxies or surrogates for them. I'm content to say simply that that has not been my department, but at the same time I think the concerns that have been central to my own work are at least as important as the sort of things that my cliometric colleagues work with. I would make no claim beyond that. That is a very substantial claim.

Let's go back to Marx. You've taught history of thought over the years. How important is it still to study Marx, say, for understanding technological change, or, for that matter, to study other figures in the history of economics? Who are some of the essential characters? What role should studying them have in an economist's education – in particular, an economic historian's education?

Well, I would say everybody should read Chapters 13 through 15 of the first volume of *Capital*, for a variety of reasons. But let me back up. On the question of Marx: Marx was certainly the first major figure in economics who placed the phenomenon of technical change in the very center of his economic analysis. Because Marx was attempting to identify what he called the "laws of motion" of capitalism, I would argue that it is a very common mistake to think of Marx as a technological determinist. I think the real Karl Marx is without question an economic determinist. But he is an economic determinist where economic forces shape technology and create a high degree of technological dynamism. I think Marx captured a very important part of the picture of how capitalism shapes this rapid rate of technological change. And, of course, Marx regarded capitalism as being unique in history as the only social system where the economic interests of the ruling class are apparently tied, not to conservation of the old mode of production, but to change. I think Marx offered, and still does, some very profound insights into the performance of technology.

The problem is, of course, that Marx comes loaded with an awful lot of other freight. Let me tell a little story here. Two years ago I wrote an article for *Scientific American*. In *Scientific American*, the very last page is a one-page essay every month. The editor was out here, I had lunch with him, and made some references to Marx, and he asked me to write a one-page essay, which I did. A large part of what I was saying was, "Look, whatever is going on in Eastern Europe today, Marx had very little to do either with the particular form that the social systems took there or with their present collapse." I went on to argue that Marx still needs to be read as certainly the most important economic historian of the nineteenth century, which is a description of him that I would seriously make. The editors of *Scientific American* gave my little article the title, "Marx wasn't all wrong." Now, as it happens, it was an excellent title. It was not my idea, but it did in fact capture the essence of what I was saying. Marx was not all wrong. In fact, when you think about it, it is hard for anybody to be all wrong. Even a broken clock is correct twice a day. You'd be amazed at the crank mail that I got from that article because there was a large number of people out there for whom Marx had to be all wrong.

I teach courses where I still require the reading of Marx. In terms of my own priorities I think that is an important answer. But you know, if you are as preoccupied as I am with technological change, you're kind of reluctant to lose Marx because there's not an awful lot out there. You've got a page [in Smith] on the pin factory and you've got Charles Babbage. You've got a little bit in John Stuart Mill, but then you've got to jump to the twentieth century. You've got to look at Schumpeter and Kuznets and Schmookler and Abramovitz. I don't even know what to do with Solow, because the so-called neoclassical growth model is peculiar in its handling of technology. In the Solow model technological change is, of course, totally exogenous. It appears as manna from heaven. That's Solow's metaphor, not mine.

Maybe we should take a look at what you've been up to lately. What intrigues me about your career to this point is that you still mix a lot of things that I don't think very many people do: some history of thought and some economic history but also contemporary technological issues. So would you say a bit about that context of your work and where it's headed?

All right, let me say first of all that much of the context of my work has been for some time in the twentieth century. I would also add that the twentieth century is 94 percent history. Everything I do, I do by looking at the phenomena that interest me in the context of history. I guess I differ a lot from some people, many economists, who say, I always think rather patronizingly, economic history is very useful because we go out and test our theories. My view is: What in the world is economics about if it isn't about a process of economic change that takes place over historical time, and it seems to me that the fundamental responsibility of the social scientist is basically to deal with the question, "How did we get here?" How did we get to this present juncture in human and in social affairs? And so, a lot of what I've done, that might qualify as economic history, was done simply because I felt that to understand almost any phenomenon one has to understand it in terms of its history. A fancy term that we use now – we call that path dependence.

As for my present work, much of it deals with the interface between science and technology. Some of it very specifically is concerned with university research as it affects technological advance in industry. I'm very much interested in the economics of science. I believe that not only is technology largely shaped by economic forces but (we touched on this earlier) I think an awful lot of what goes on in the scientific world is shaped by economic forces as well. I'm surprised, given the imperialistic tendencies of modern economics – you know, look at the work of somebody like Gary Becker who has so much expanded the range of problems that can be explained in economic terms – I am surprised that it has taken the economics profession as long as it has to look at science, scientific research, as if it were an economic enterprise or an enterprise which we are willing to finance, at least in considerable measure, because we anticipate there will be economic payoffs drawn from it.

So a lot of my work is concerned with those kinds of interactions between the research community and industrial innovation. At the same time, I've gotten rather heavily into technological change in medicine which, as I hear pointed out at least once a day, accounts for one-seventh of our GNP and will very likely soon be more. And the forces that shape technical change in medicine are, believe me, quite unlike the forces that shape technical change anywhere else in the economy. It is a sector where, until very recently, budgetary constraints were quite simply not important. You know, there is another sector where one can say that that has been so until recently, and that of course is the military sector. But even there at least, there is talk about increasingly tight budgetary constraints.

I'm particularly interested in looking at how useful knowledge grows. In a way, that is my ultimate interest, looking at ways different bodies of knowledge become institutionalized, and how they form new disciplines. The twentieth century has given birth to chemical engineering, aeronautical engineering, computer science, the development of electricity – all that began in the late nineteenth century. These bodies of knowledge then become institutionalized at universities. Universities hire people to teach in these subjects, to do research in these subjects, to certify that students, after they've spent four years in an institution, are in a certain sense professionally qualified.

I try to look at the development of new engineering and applied science disciplines as part of the process by which useful knowledge grows and becomes institutionalized, markets get formed – you don't begin teaching electrical engineering, after all, until you know there are things that people who have EE stamped on their foreheads can go out and do, until there is a market. So one question I'm asking is, how do markets get formed for new professionals? And does that process work very differently in different countries? You almost intuitively know that it does. If you look at the engineering disciplines in Great Britain, and the way they failed to become institutionalized at the great universities there, how does that in turn affect economic performance? Can we get some important insights on the performance of national economies from that particular angle of vision?

I also occasionally go back and write something in the history of economics, Babbage being the most recent. You think of Babbage as the father of the computer, and that's a fair enough label for him, but he was also, I think, a very considerable economist in the specific sense of trying to understand what the Industrial Revolution was all about. And let me come full circle here by pointing out that although Babbage has not been widely read by economists, Babbage had an enormous influence, simply an enormous intellectual influence, upon two people in the nineteenth century: John Stuart Mill and Karl Marx. If you read either of those people, you will find that they quote shamelessly, page after page, from Babbage and I think with good reason.

Well, I always thought his explanation of why the division of labor was efficient was better than all three of Adam Smith's put together.

You're damn right it was. You're damn right it was. And I've written a paper making exactly that point. It's very curious, but if you look at two of the most distinguished books in the history of economics of the twentieth century, which is to say Schumpeter's *History of Economic Analysis* and Mark Blaug's *Economic Theory in Retrospect*, they both have one peculiar feature in common with respect to Babbage: they both describe his book as being a remarkable work, and yet both of them devote no more than one sentence to it. But Babbage was one of the great polymaths that England tends to throw up periodically. I mean, he was a genius. And what he understood about the division of labor was in a way very simple – simple in a sense that many profound observations are simple once somebody has finally made them.

Let me raise one last issue: technology policy. Does history tell us anything . . . you know, since the Clinton years have started, things like industrial and technology policy are back in the public discourse. Any comments you want to make?

I guess the short answer is "No." But don't quote me on that.

Part V

THE EXPATRIATES

R. M. Hartwell

Eric Jones

Charles H. Feinstein

The majority of our interviewees have focused their research on their native countries; an even larger majority have held their primary academic positions at home. For three interviewees, neither is true. Australian Max Hartwell and South African Charles Feinstein spent most of their professional careers in England, writing mostly about the British economy. Englishman Eric Jones, after teaching for a time in England and the United States, spent most of his career in Australia, writing with a global perspective. None has considered himself to be a cliometrician, but each has had a major influence on the field.

Max Hartwell styles himself a "radical liberal of the J. S. Mill and Adam Smith school," a viewpoint nurtured by an Australian outback upbringing and a schoolboy diet of individualism, reinforced by his studies of British industrialization and its consequences for both Britain and Australia. During his tenure at Nuffield College in Oxford (1956–77) he wrote the essays, ran the seminars, and supervised the research which aided in "establishing economic and social history as an independently worthy field of academic inquiry" at that university (Hudson 1994: 611). He is best known for work on the "great discontinuity" of the British Industrial Revolution as an instance of economic growth rather than as the social catastrophe perceived by many others. His optimistic position on the effects of industrialization in the famous "standard of living debate" brought him notoriety in Leftist circles and notice everywhere. Hartwell is both admired and misunderstood for his love of controversy, not for its own sake, but, as he says, because "Argument . . . is the essence of good teaching and controversy enlivens and clarifies thought and understanding."

In the 1960s Hartwell inherited the editorship of *The Economic History Review* from Hrothgar Habakkuk, continuing to strengthen its position as the voice of a "broad church" discipline, while also encouraging contributions from its new and still largely American sect. At Nuffield he became, not a cliometrician (as he stresses in his interview), but certainly a "camp follower," encouraging work in social and economic history in both the "new" and the "old" styles, and providing a home (more welcoming at the time than the remainder of the university) for a series of American visitors: Jon Hughes, Lance Davis, Charles Kindleberger, Stan Engerman, and Bob Gallman among them. He remains firmly committed to his perception of the Industrial Revolution as a watershed in modern history. As Eric Jones, at once student and critic of Hartwell and target of Max's own critique, has written, "He has never thought for an instant that he could be wrong; but this misses the point that what he really did for his part was to stiffen the nature of argument in social and economic history and open the way for the quantifiers."[1]

Eric Jones's initial sojourn abroad was in West Lafayette, Indiana, where he became "a fringe member of the 'Purdue Mafia' " (1990: 159), resulting from Max Hartwell's invitations to the new economic historians to visit Oxford, beginning in the early 1960s with Purdue's Hughes and Davis. Jones visited the Purdue economics faculty in 1965–6 and was later a colleague of Hughes and Stanley Reiter at Northwestern. In the United States Jones contracted only a mild case of "cliometrica," amounting to judicious application of basic economic theory where it proves useful. He has been a life-long naturalist and incorporates into many of his writings a keen awareness of environmental conditions and change. His early work (collected in *Agriculture and the Industrial Revolution* 1974) was part of the virtual re-writing of British agricultural history that began in the 1960s, pushing the so-called "agricultural revolution" of the eighteenth century earlier by nearly a century. In expanding his purview from the details of farming on the Hampshire chalklands (1960) to the links between agrarian and more general economic change (*e.g.*, 1968) Jones began what he perceives as a transformation from the proverbial Hedgehog (who knows one big thing) to Fox (who knows many things); the transformation was complete after he moved to Australia in 1975 and published *The European Miracle* (1981), a work of synthesis and a foray into economic history in the very long run. In that work he makes no attempt to construct a general model, but points to commonalities in (Western) European experience that gave Europe a leg up in achieving modern economic growth compared to contemporary civilizations in Asia.

In *Growth Recurring* (1988) Jones argues that intensive growth (economic expansion *per capita*) is neither an entirely "modern" (post-1750) phenomenon nor peculiar to Europe. Most recently he has tackled the revival of cultural explanations of economic change in *Cultures Merging*, where he is persuaded neither that some fixed set of cultural attributes can account for economic progress or stagnation, nor that culture is merely a manifestation of an economic substructure. Rather, culture has made a tangible but "only ghostly transit through history" (2006: *ix*). Stepping back from global history to his native English countryside, he is at work on a book to be called *Tumbledown People: Family and Environment in Southern England*. Eric Jones has eschewed "limitationist" tendencies, reading voraciously in fields ranging from agriculture and anthropology to sociology and urban studies, always with an eye for treasures that others going in the opposite direction have unwittingly discarded (*cf.* Jones 1981 [2003: *ix*]). In a review of *Growth Recurring*, Barry Supple (1989: 304) wrote what would apply equally well to much of Jones's other work: ". . . the thrust of the argument, the range of conceptual interest and empirical reference, and the exceptional learning remind us of the value of well-informed economic historians departing from specialist byways in order to tackle really important questions."

1 Quotations from Hartwell (2001: 123–6) and prefaces to Hartwell (ed. 1970; 1971a). We have drawn also on introductory matter in O'Brien & Quinault, eds (1993), James & Thomas, eds (1994), and on Jones (1993: quotation 286–7). See Taylor (1997) on Hartwell's role in promoting British social history.

Charles Feinstein left South Africa for a year of studies in economics at Cambridge University in 1954, with a training in accountancy, Marxist sympathies, and a record of active opposition to the Apartheid regime in hand. Four decades later he returned to a now democratic South Africa, resumed his citizenship, and began teaching part-time at the University of Cape Town. As to what happened in the interim, the informed commentary of several Oxford colleagues is revealing. Nicholas Dimsdale writes, "We owe our knowledge of the long-term growth of the British economy mostly to the work of Charles Feinstein . . . He estimated the time series that charts the course of British economic development since the Industrial Revolution . . . Such is the quality of his work that his estimates have not been challenged or bettered." His successor as Chichele Professor, Avner Offer, observes, "Feinstein possessed an austere and supremely disciplined mind, and had an almost magical ability to impose order on the complexity of the past, combined with a scrupulous respect for the smallest detail." Paul David stresses Feinstein's contribution in having ". . . accomplished largely single-handedly the preparation of quantitative foundations for the study of the economic and social history of modern Britain – the construction of enduring platforms that others might extend and revise (as he revised and successively expanded upon the early layers of this structure), and upon which could be erected new and more penetrating interpretive analyses."[2]

At Cambridge in the 1950s, Feinstein's Ph.D. research (1959) focused on late nineteenth-century British investment, domestic and overseas. He wrote recently (in Blaug, ed. 1999: 363), "What began as a brief investigation turned into a thirty-year study," concluding with his extensive contribution to a book he edited with Sidney Pollard, *Studies in Capital Formation in the United Kingdom, 1750–1920* (1988). Along the way he published the classic *National Income, Expenditure and Output of the United Kingdom, 1855–1965* (1972) and other work mentioned in the interview. In addition to building and parsing the components of British national income, both alone and with Robin Matthews and John Odling-Smee, Feinstein extended his research into many other fields, including *The European Economy between the Wars* with Peter Temin and Gianni Toniolo, technology transfer to the USSR (1997) and notably in a series of articles on British prices and real wages culminating in "Pessimism Perpetuated" (1998).[3] As a teacher he was accomplished and warmly regarded by both students and colleagues. In 2003 he received the EHA's Hughes Prize for teaching excellence; an anonymous former student says Charles Feinstein left "no-one untouched by his energy, vision, and the enormous joy of doing economic history."[4]

These three expatriates, as world travelers who have taught and engaged in research on four continents, took part in building the network of cliometricians and other economic and social historians that exists today. Hartwell and Jones have enriched the field

2 Obituaries by Dimsdale in the *Guardian*, 29 December 2004; by Offer in *The Times*, 23 December 2004; and remarks by David at a memorial service in Oxford, 4 June 2005.

3 See Feinstein, Temin & Toniolo (1997); a new edition, revised and expanded by Temin and Toniolo, is forthcoming from Oxford UP.

4 Report by Marcia Frost for the EHA Committee on Education and Teaching, October 10, 2003, accessible at URL: <http://eh.net/>, archive of EH.Teach mailing list.

with their distinctive perspectives and Feinstein's work in the tradition of Kuznets has paralleled the contributions of Urquhart for Canada and of Easterlin and Gallman for the United States. All three have helped to expand the world that economic historians observe and to integrate the international scholarly community in which they have worked.

R. M. HARTWELL

Interviewed by
Mark Thomas

Ronald Max Hartwell is Emeritus Fellow, Nuffield College, Oxford. He was born in 1921 in Glen Innes, nearly 500 miles from Sydney in the northern tablelands of New South Wales, Australia. He began his advanced education in Armidale, NSW, at the Teachers College and at New England University College, where he earned an external degree from the University of Sydney (B.A., 1945). Following Army service he continued at Sydney (M.A., 1948) and at Oxford (D.Phil., 1955; M.A., 1956). From 1950 to 1956 he was Professor of Economic History at the New South Wales University of Technology. He then returned to Oxford, where he was Reader in Recent Social and Economic History in the University and Professorial Fellow in Nuffield College (1956–77). After a further four years at Wolfson College, Oxford, he spent most of the next decade teaching alternately at the Universities of Chicago and Virginia, with occasional forays back to Australia to teach in Sydney at the Australian Graduate School of Management. While at Oxford he served in administrative positions at Nuffield and was a curator of the Bodleian Library. As Assistant Editor and Editor of *The Economic History Review* (1957–68), he encouraged submissions in the newly developing quantitative style while maintaining the journal's breadth and diversity. In keeping with his classical liberal principles, he became a member of The Mont Pelerin Society in 1972, served as its President (1992–4), and published a history of the Society in 1995. He has lived in or near Oxford since his retirement in 1991. The interview took place in Oxford in October 2000 and was conducted by Mark Thomas of the University of Virginia, who writes:

I have known Max Hartwell for more than 30 years. He was my undergraduate tutor for two economic history courses at Oxford. We were later colleagues (Max in economics, I in history) at the University of Virginia. Max has the distinct honor of having been feted with two *Festschriften: The Industrial Revolution and British Society*, edited by Patrick

O'Brien and Roland Quinault (1993) and *Capitalism in Context: Essays on Economic Development and Cultural Change in Honor of R. M. Hartwell*, edited by John A. James and myself (1994).

Please tell us about your background and how it has influenced your intellectual development.

Insofar as I have a world view of the human condition, it was formed when I was growing up in the Australian outback. My family moved to the village of Red Range, New South Wales, when I was about 10, when my father became the schoolteacher there; before that we lived in the neighbouring town of Glen Innes. The interesting thing about Red Range was that you were never aware of the state. The only evidence of the state was the school and the small post office (the mail came three times a week with the newspapers). It was a small rural community, and the attitude was that you got on in the world through your own efforts and hard labour and by being a good neighbour. The idea of community, although not voiced in that word, was very obvious in the village. Sport, dancing, and music were organized on a voluntary basis. It was a happy place, always plenty to do, everyone worked hard; they had to – it was during the Great Depression. Money was scarce, but it was only when I went to teachers' college that I discovered I was born into an exploited colony. It came as a surprise to me. At that time we had the best cricket team in the world, and the idea that we were exploited by the Poms never entered my mind! But that, of course, led to some serious consideration of society and work and what to study.

When you went to university, why did you choose to study economics?

I drifted into economics without any enthusiasm; it was just a subject to be done to get a degree. I began studying at the teachers' college in Armidale, about 60 miles from Red Range. I was fortunate that my first year coincided with the establishment of a branch of the University of Sydney, the first in New South Wales. So when I started, I was a student at both the teachers' college and the university and then transferred to university to begin work on a degree. I never was in the faculty of economics. I graduated with a B.A., specializing in history and economics. Fortunately, I found that I was good at economics, although I never much liked it. My initial job was as a teaching fellow (Assistant Lecturer) in the Department of Economics at Sydney University. The Professor, Sid Butlin, asked me to teach economic history, even though I had never taken a course in it. I remember my maiden lecture – it was just after the war, and the classroom was a bit noisy with ex-servicemen (some of whom had been my colleagues in the army), and I asked them if this was the first economic history lecture they'd ever heard. When they answered yes, I told them to be reassured, because it was the first one I'd ever heard, too.

And it clearly had a profound influence on you!

Let me say that I immediately found it much more interesting than economics. There were certain parts of economics that I quite liked, but on the whole I didn't much enjoy it, because it was more impersonal than history. However, once I started teaching economic history, I realized that I was where I wanted to be, in a subject I liked. My first research was in Australian economic history, and my background in the bush greatly influenced my choice of topic and approach. At the time I became a student, the great classics in Australian economic history were by Brian Fitzpatrick (*The British Empire in Australia* and *British Imperialism in Australia*). But I just could not accept his thesis of imperialist exploitation. It seemed counterintuitive. It was obvious to me that Australians were well off (even during the Depression), and this didn't square with the notion of exploitation. When I began to look more closely at history, I discovered that by 1850 there were three towns in Australia (Hobart, Sydney, and Port Philip [Melbourne]) which were just like well-developed provincial towns in Britain. They had all the paraphernalia of civilization: churches, schools, newspapers, literary societies, etc. And on the whole, I think that they were quite pleasant places in which to live by the standards of the time, which made me highly skeptical about the whole idea of the exploitation of imperialism.

That was my first introduction to historical controversy. So when it came to an M.A. thesis, I thought that I would test the theory of economic exploitation in a micro study of one of the colonies. I picked Van Diemen's Land (Tasmania) because it was separated from the rest of Australia, it was one of the first colonies, and the source material was very good. In my M.A. thesis, I concluded that Van Diemen's Land benefited because it developed during the British industrial revolution. There was a movement towards economic liberalism, which extended to the colonies. Because of the rapid expansion of the Yorkshire woollen industry, there was a demand for fine wool, which Tasmania and New South Wales were eminently suited to produce. So, I saw their relationship with Britain as a highly mutually beneficial relationship.

Your book, *The Economic Development of Van Diemen's Land, 1820–1850*, has been referred to as the first example of New Economic History in the Australian historiography. To what extent do you think that your training in economics shaped your approach to economic history?

Economics has been absolutely vital to my approach to economic history, and *Van Diemen's Land* shows that very much. It was clearly different from anything in Australia that had come before it. I don't think that it has influenced much, but there have been some very fine contributions in the same mold since, such as Noel Butlin's Kuznetsian approach.

What is the source of the economic analysis that went into *Van Diemen's Land*?

It came from courses I had at Sydney University – the first year was Benham, or some such textbook; the second year was public finance and industrial relations; and the third year was the trade cycle, the macroeconomics of the period. I was taught economics well, and although it was Keynesian in the trade cycle and public finance courses, I was only partly seduced by Keynes. The structure of the book followed my understanding of the fundamental structures of economic analysis, most of which had little to do with Keynes. I started out with geography, went on to resources, and then moved on to the trade cycle. Here I was influenced by Rostow's work on Britain in the nineteenth century because I tried to show that peaks of the trade cycle were related to political events. As far as public finance was concerned, there was a simple table in the book in which I tried to calculate the extent of capital flows from Britain. I wanted to emphasize the role of the British commissariat in financing the development of Van Diemen's Land.

You then left for Oxford in 1948 to work on your doctorate. Tell us about your doctoral research.

Wool was the main artery of capital and trade between Britain and Australia. It was the logical topic to explore. But there was more to it than that. There's no doubt that when I arrived in England, the dominant theme in English economic and social history centred on the exploitation of the working classes of England during the Industrial Revolution. Again, I reacted against this. When I wrote my D.Phil. thesis on the Yorkshire woollen industry from 1800 to 1850, I did a lot of archival research on employment and wages, and what I discovered just didn't match up with what historians were saying. So again, when I wrote that thesis, I came to a fairly optimistic conclusion about the condition of the workers, which centred on a whole series of criteria, including wages, education, etc. Consequently, by this stage, I didn't believe in imperialism or what was, in effect, the Marxist theory of history.

Was Oxford an intellectually stimulating place for you?

Not really. Asa Briggs and Neville Ward-Perkins were the people I listened to most often. They ran a seminar and treated me as an equal. But it was the first-year course at Sydney, covering price theory in detail, that did most to shape my thesis. Even when I came back in 1956, the only seminar I went to regularly was run by John Hicks. He was a terrible public speaker, but his seminar on the development of monetary theory from Thornton to his own work was a wonderful experience. Nonetheless, I'm not sure that it influenced me in my published work.

You only stayed in Oxford for two years?

Yes, I went back to Australia in 1950 to a chair in Sydney at the new New South Wales University of Technology (later the University of New South Wales), where I was both the first Dean of Humanities and Social Sciences and the first Professor of Economic History. The university was modeled on MIT and had a similar commitment to teaching humanities and social sciences to students in engineering and other technical disciplines. In the second year, students studied philosophy of science and industrialization, and in the third year, they chose one of the social sciences, normally either psychology or economics. I taught courses on modern economic development. It was a very successful course and programme. I believed that my career was now set firmly on course in Australia until I got into a dreadful row with the Vice Chancellor. As Dean, I appointed a selection committee for a position in the History Department. When the committee recommended the appointment of Russell Ward, the Vice Chancellor refused to appoint him on the grounds of his political beliefs. I said categorically that political tests were unacceptable and put my job on the line. That was probably foolish, because I lost. It went on to become quite a famous case in Australia. After that, I searched unsuccessfully for jobs around Australia. Fortunately and unexpectedly, I got the readership in Economic and Social History in Oxford, so I returned there in 1956.

What sort of work was being done in Britain when you returned?

First, there was a lot of work being done in social history – a rebirth in the post-war period of what people such as the Hammonds had written in the 1920s with a similar ideological perspective. Secondly, industrial history. The Manchester school inspired a number of industrial histories, which were very good discussions of technology, but which never took into account the interplay between supply and demand.

So, the economic perspective was largely missing? Was this what separated you from the generally institutional focus of British economic historians at the time? Would it be fair to say that you brought an antipodean sensibility to the study of the British industrial revolution?

To a great extent, yes. If you look at the idea of growth, for example, my approach was different from most British economic historians and no doubt owed something to my teaching the comparative development course in Sydney. But I would not like to exaggerate the differences.

Two aspects of the Industrial Revolution that I worked on had some influence: the standard of living debate and the causes of the Industrial Revolution in England. When I got to these questions, they planted me firmly in the institutional arena. However, it was not in the way that most economic historians think of institutions. I did not focus on the state as the pivotal element, as Charles Wilson emphasized in his *England's Apprenticeship* (and as Patrick O'Brien has done more recently). Instead, I was much more interested in the role of the common law, which I saw as one of the leading differences between Britain and the rest of Europe. Rather than just examine the institutional structures of the law and how they changed, I wanted to relate this to models of growth. Law and the market, that's the important topic.

You returned to Oxford at the time of the Rostovian controversies over the pace and pattern of economic growth. This formed something of an ideological divide in the British economic historiography between advocates of discontinuity *à la* Rostow and Toynbee and those who adopted

Marshall's emphasis on continuity. Most critics of Rostow have accepted the Marshallian perspective. However, you've referred to the Industrial Revolution as the "great discontinuity." Does this make you an anti-Marshallian, a Rostovian, or something else?

Everyone who is sensible is a Marshallian! The discontinuity is between the world before and after industrializations. Growth in Britain was slow and slowly accelerating; it was also balanced, indeed it had to be. So Rostow's emphasis on leading sectors, on unbalanced growth, was clearly wrong. Indeed, it would be a better generalization to suggest that every sector was undergoing some sort of major change between 1750 and 1850. The growth of skills in the trade and financial sectors, for example, were no less remarkable than the growth of technology in textiles and iron. The demand for navigational skills was burgeoning with the rise of trade, and advertisements began to appear offering training in navigation. Supply responded directly and remarkably quickly to changing demands.

Was this market responsiveness distinctively British? Is this what made the British economy different? Would you see the same sort of behaviour in France, for example?

I'm not sure that you would. But this might reflect the weakness of the market signals more than the weakness of the institutional response. Once Britain had begun the upward movement in growth and development, more challenges and opportunities developed, which created more growth and so on. In France, growth didn't begin as soon; consequently, it didn't accumulate as rapidly.

Your interpretation of the Industrial Revolution is in terms of consequences and impact, rather than process.

Ideally, it should be both, but mostly when I use the term, I'm thinking of the difference between Britain in 1750 and 1850 compared to the change in any similar period before then.

You mentioned earlier the standard of living debate and your role in it. Do you have any retrospective comments?

When I returned to Oxford, it was during an interesting period. There were three primary beliefs that dominated social thinking. The first was that governments could plan to do certain things, and by the manipulation of certain key variables, they could achieve their goals. The second was that civil servants were only interested in public welfare and that they were disinterested vessels of the government's interests. Finally, in so far as the working classes improved their lot, it was entirely due to the actions of government through the welfare state and the pressure of trade unions. Economic growth was never considered. Indeed, economic organization, which was one of the two compulsory subjects in economics for those students taking PPE [Politics, Philosophy, and Economics] in Oxford, was entirely about how to make the intervention of the state work better without ever questioning the basic philosophy of the interventionist state. I remember that John Vaizey and I gave the very first seminar in Public Sector Economics in the university. It was more historical than economic, but we did tackle the central question (as expressed best by John Stuart Mill), "What are the proper functions and agencies of government?" The seminar went very well.

Then came the flowering of social history, largely focusing on the class struggle in the Industrial Revolution, and I thought that it was about time that someone had a go at this sort of stuff. I wrote two articles: a general methodological paper titled, "Interpretations of the Industrial Revolution," published in *The Journal of Economic History* (1959); the second, "The *Rising* Standard of Living," was published in *The Economic History Review* (1961). The emphasis on the word "rising" was intentional and, in fact, the entire purpose of the article. You might say that all hell broke loose! I did not expect that reaction, partly because I believed in the art of civilized discourse and partly because I believed that historians would be persuaded by the weight of evidence and not be particularly influenced by ideology. The controversy was like getting on a nonstop train. It became mixed up with the Marxist theory of capitalism, which focused on the inevitability of revolution and the exploitation of workers.

The great benefit for British historians working in this period was the remarkable literature of the Houses of Parliament, where you find the results of thousands of investigations on all sorts of topics in social and economic history, from drunkenness to prostitution. A wonderful source but a trap for the unwary. If not used properly, the Blue Books can produce worst case history. A good example is the famous investigation of the Health of Towns in 1844. Anyone who reads that will feel sickened by the graphic descriptions of urban living, but you have to remember that this focused on the worst slums and did not report on more positive living arrangements in the towns. You could repeat the same exercise for the 1990s; you would certainly still find some awful places, but you would hardly consider them typical. This was one of the problems with the literature of the Industrial Revolution. The social historians were seduced, on the one hand, by Marx, who used this literature, and, on the other hand, by this wonderful source material. It was only in places like Manchester that great historians such as Ashton and Unwin went beyond the Blue Books to the factory records and actual statistics of work and wages.

Do you consider your work on the standard of living to have been cliometric?

I don't think of myself as a cliometrician at all! I define the characteristics of cliometrics as the specific application of economic tools and the use of quantification to measure what happened and the building up of models to explain what happened. I used some basic tools of economics and used statistics wherever they seemed relevant, but I was never a model-builder and never a user of formal economic theory. There were certain aspects of cliometrics that interested me. But it has its limitations. It's quite obvious that there are many things that cannot be measured. Some people dispute that and say that you should at least be able to rank, but I'm not certain about that. I always say that if I could explain love and hate, I'd be more than satisfied. I suppose these are the extremes of human emotion. But I don't think any sensible economic historian can say that you can measure everything. You measure what you can, and this is common sense. Bob Fogel said to me once that the worse the evidence, the more sophisticated the techniques have to be. The trouble is that you need the techniques. One problem with too much technique is that it reduces the audience. It can also be a dangerous tool for the unwary. History should always determine technique, but too often, the use of technique limits history. I am not and never have been a quantitative historian. I've used figures in my work a great deal, but I have no sophistication in statistical inference at all, except in terms of common sense. Very often common sense and simple arithmetic is enough, but I'm not sure that you would call that cliometrics. I was never a great reader of the econometrics literature.

At the 1970 Anglo-American meeting that Fogel organized at Harvard, you referred to the New Economic History as an import substitute in the British economic historiography (1971b). Were you anticipating that the cliometrics revolution would gradually cross the Atlantic?

I don't think it has. The New Economic History was a bit like a tidal wave, which stirred up a lot, but I don't think that it has transformed much of the landscape in its wake. It has built on various things; it has added precision in various ways. For example, it has slowed down the rate of growth during the Industrial Revolution and has trespassed into the standard of living debate, but I don't think that it has changed very much. An example is the latest article on the standard of living by Charles Feinstein, which is too pessimistic. He does not demonstrate pessimism in the sense that social historians used it in the 1960s, to indicate immiseration.

But to be fair to Charles, his target is earlier cliometricians, who, he argues, exaggerated real wage improvements after 1815 or so. Although he refers to it as a pessimistic interpretation, he essentially states that there was no loss or gain in measurable economic welfare for the average worker and his family but, in effect, stasis up to 1840 or so. The gains were delayed, but there was no immiseration.

Pessimism no longer means decline. Every estimate of industrial activity or other index of macroeconomic activity shows a rise from the late eighteenth century onwards. There's a lower limit to cliometric revisionism.

Why hasn't the New Economic History transformed the British economic historiography?

Partly it reflects the way in which economic history was taught here. It was clearly a mistake to compartmentalize economic and social history into separate departments in the UK. It would have been much better had some economic historians been trained in economics departments, with greater focus on techniques and econometrics, and others in history departments. The institutional structure was unfavourable.

Is it also possible that there were intellectual constraints in operation in Britain? There was no counterpart to slavery as a unifying and defining topic for cliometric analysis in the UK. Is it the case that the major topics of intellectual debate among British economic and social historians (such as the rise of the gentry or the standard of living debate) are either not amenable to cliometric techniques or, alternatively, that there were no counterparts to Ulrich Phillips in Britain who were vulnerable to radical critique?

I think that's right to a degree. I would put it differently. Economic history in Britain is an older subject and was much more advanced at the time of the cliometric revolution. The literature on the big questions was already well established, and the contributions of the Ashtons and the Claphams were not likely to be torn asunder by the use of more up-to-date techniques of model-building and statistical inference. When Gary Hawke applied the Fogel social savings method to the British case, it largely backed up the older interpretation of the role of the railways rather than challenging some ingrained belief in the indispensability of railroads, as Fogel claimed existed in the US. I cannot think of any topic in British economic historiography that has been radically transformed by the application of cliometric techniques.

Where do you see the future of economic history?

Recent work suggests a decline in interest in social history of the Thompson–Hobsbawm variety. New areas of investigation have developed, of which the most important is the role of women. Another which should be much more important is the environment. I would like to see additional emphasis put on economic history as a means to integrate law, culture, custom, and institutions into an overarching interpretation that places economics within the system as a whole (not economics for its own sake). The desire for a broader type of economic history should be extended to the time dimension as well. The work of Eric Jones and others on long-run history is, I think, very important. Of course, studying long-run history is not readily amenable to cliometric approaches. Also its meaning varies from country to country. The Cambridge group has done excellent research on the demographic history of Britain back to the sixteenth century, but that period embraces the entire history of Australia and the US since white settlement!

An ambitious agenda!

ERIC JONES

Interviewed by
Nancy Folbre
and Michael Huberman

Eric Lionel Jones is Emeritus Professor of Economics at La Trobe University, Melbourne, Australia, Professorial Fellow of the Melbourne Business School, University of Melbourne, and Visiting Professor at the University of Exeter, England. He was born in Andover, England in 1936 and was educated at the University of Nottingham (B.A., 1958) and at Oxford (D.Phil., 1962; M.A., 1964) and earned the higher doctorate from Oxford (D.Litt., 1985). He taught in England at Oxford and at the University of Reading, where he was founding Research Director of the Institute for Agricultural History (1968–70), and visited Purdue in 1965–6. He moved to Northwestern University for the period 1970–5 before he became the Foundation Professor of Economic History at La Trobe in 1975. During his tenure in Melbourne he visited the Northern Hemisphere frequently, at Exeter, at Yale, and as a member of the Institute for Advanced Study in Princeton (1985–6). He now lives in Gloucestershire; since going back to England in 2001, he has again taught at Reading and regularly returns to Melbourne to continue his teaching there.

In 1992 he was a Visiting Fellow of the Institute for Comparative Research at the University of California at Davis, where he met two other visitors, Nancy Folbre of the University of Massachusetts–Amherst and Michael Huberman of the Université de Montréal. Eric Jones presented them with a target of opportunity for a relatively impromptu interview, conducted at UC-Davis on March 12th, 1992. Folbre and Huberman write:

We were immediately impressed by Eric. He was most forthcoming with detailed suggestions for our own research. Conversation with him was as rich as it was rapid, moving easily from the trees to the forest. He challenged us never to forget the big picture in our writings. Above all, we found him an unabashed and passionate defender (and practitioner) of economic history in its many traditions.

What do you think of the new work on agriculture and industrialization in light of your own contributions in this area?

I don't find it very interesting. I think that a big opportunity has been missed to generate new evidence from primary sources. Much of the new work is really exemplifying people's command of technique, that is the cliometric type of work, the quantitative work, rather than using some of the big research grants to go round the archives and collect together information from grass-roots primary sources, the kind of source that I was always interested in. The opportunity's been lost. I've still got a lot of cards relating to farmers who had original eighteenth- and nineteenth-century accounts, which we never managed to get a round to collecting at Reading. A few thousands of dollars would have made a big difference there.

What I find is that the new work is constantly churning existing series. Some of the investigators are certainly looking at the archives and collecting samples, but there is too much of a bias towards work on Parliamentary rather than other enclosures. My basic feeling is one of disappointment. Work has become to my mind a display of forensics among people with technical training, which permits them to discuss the implications of various models when, in many cases, the basic series we have aren't worth a damn.

Keeping to agriculture and industrialization, what has been the effect of these "forensics" on the questions asked? Are they any different from what they were 20, 25 years ago?

Yes, we've dropped a major question. We've dropped the question about the causes of the so-called industrial revolution and the agricultural revolution. One of the reasons for this is that the concern with rates of growth over 20-, 30-, and 40-year segments of the eighteenth and nineteenth centuries has produced endless arguments as to where the breaks came. There's been an exhaustion about the original question. What people seem to do when they get exhausted with a question that appears intractable is shift away to discussing aspects of the phenomenon, so that you get case studies by region, by industry, by sector. And yet that would be the place we would have an enormous opportunity, especially with institutionalist types of explanation. We should be looking at the seventeenth century, not the eighteenth and nineteenth, and not remain prisoners of the alleged series of output that seem to exist for the eighteenth and nineteenth centuries.

Does that mean that you don't think it's an intractable problem to ask a question about causes?

I don't think it's intractable. I think there could be exciting new ways to look at it in an institutionalist framework. We need to look at changing political structures, sociological structures, changes in incentives, and things which are messier and require deeper knowledge of social history. (I'm thinking of Britain, of course, and I assume you are in all of this.) This is against the temper of the times. I hold it against the development of so much in the way of technical expertise and the computer, which has drawn attention away from the broader questions. I say it's not intractable, though I don't think it's as tractable as some of the things you can do when you work on the machinery which grinds outputs from inputs in a standard, "engineering" way. Somehow we've lost our way. We're concerned with the dimensions of the problem but not why it happened.

Can you think of any positive ways the new work, the cliometric work, has added to our knowledge?

Well, it's refined our statistical picture of large parts of the dominant mountain ranges of the eighteenth and particularly the nineteenth century, but I'm pretty skeptical about the basis of the information in many cases. It doesn't pay a younger scholar to go off on what would be called a "fishing expedition" – a term I've heard used about people doing work on apparently minor industries or topics. It pays that person better to make clever adjustments to the results made by establishment figures. This is difficult to avoid unless the establishment figures are going to say, "Well, don't refine my work, do something new," and are going to reward that. That's against human nature, I guess.

Your answer, I think, is "no." What are the implications?

One of the unfortunate by-products of the cliometric emphasis is that we've lost our larger audience among historians in general, and also an even broader audience than that – the kind of audience that participates in discussion and debate over general political and economic trends. That audience was once informed by historical research, but has found it increasingly difficult to read, much less understand and debate, the findings that are emerging.

For people in education to say, essentially, "If you're not prepared to go to second-year graduate school in economics you can't expect to read our stuff," is a very curious result. We don't have, in core economic history, the kinds of popularizers one finds in astronomy with Carl Sagan, or in biology with Stephen Jay Gould. I don't see any of our great figures turning aside and grasping for the popular audience, commenting on major trends in the world at the moment, either the faltering growth in this country, the rise of Japan, or what's going on in the Middle East, and saying, "Look, we've got something to say about this. We can ask orderly questions and make sensible responses."

As a result, so many of these broader social and, particularly, international issues (which I am personally more interested in than the British Industrial Revolution), have been left to area specialists, who have very little economics and sometimes very little history. I think we've missed a big market opportunity there and a chance of keeping our audience. I think that economic historians, rather than economists, are the people you should expect to find on the television or in other countries on the radio.

Somehow, we've split into a relatively self-regarding bunch of people doing what I call "follow-my-leader research," that is, doing research on the boot-and-shoe industry somewhere because the professor has done the boot-and-shoe industry somewhere else. The high-tech people are all talking to one another about growth rates, when in fact many of the interesting questions aren't sensitive to a change in locating an inflection point in 1760, 1780, or 1800. That may be heresy from an historian's point of view, but I think it's the case: the interesting questions just aren't sensitive to finding that rates of growth over the late eighteenth, early nineteenth centuries in Britain or the United States varied by plus or minus one per cent from the number you first thought of.

You've taught economic history on three continents. Are there important differences in the way economic history is taught and research conducted?

Yes, there are. There are two aspects to it. One is the institutional and the other the intellectual aspect. Institutionally, having taught in history departments, economics departments, and economic history departments, I think we should be in our own departments because I have a vision of economic history eventually developing as a soft social science. Actually, it's a very hard social science, but you know the conventional terms. This comes from my experience of once being in a history department, where the historians really didn't want to know about even elementary economic reasoning and it was hopeless trying to teach their students, and being in economics departments where people always want one to do fashionable and high-tech things. The difficulty is that separate departments typically become too isolated from economics. But in joint departments one would have thought that, with good will, one could avoid having the economists dictating what's to be done – mainly through pressure on people to do work on recent, developed economies rather than on earlier periods or less-developed economies.

Intellectually, I take an optimistic view. The way the subject is set up may be slightly unfortunate, since the prestige institutions in the US are now very heavily in the hands of high-tech economists. Yet the United States is so big that there's always something else going on. There are loose-knit groups of people interested in all sorts of related topics. There are the area specialists, the women's studies people, anthropologists, comparative historical sociologists, and all sorts of people out there playing around the edges of what we do.

What does this imply for the future of economic history?

These people may capture economic history and the broad audience, and they've got some chance of changing the minds of economic historians. I'm really fairly optimistic. I think we're at the end of a phase, not at its beginning. I was in close to the beginning.

I was at an early cliometrics meeting at Purdue. That's been very powerful; it's drawn in very clever minds and very good debaters. We know what can be done when graduate students in economics get that sort of training. Now is the time to train them more in history, more in area studies, more in the other social sciences. I don't think that an economic historian really needs the full economics Ph.D., but he or she oughtn't to miss out on the main parts of it. We need to trade off some of the high-tech stuff for more work in other social sciences, more work on other cultures, more work on other periods of history, than an economic historian who's taking an economics Ph.D. now gets.

The future, institutionally? It's really difficult for someone who works in Australia to be optimistic institutionally because budgets are being cut. To come to California and find that this land of abundance is also suffering from the first hacks of the axe is fairly depressing.

And future research in economic history?

I would say that economic history of an interesting kind exists to some extent, will go on existing, and will be developed by people who are in adjacent areas or have specialized interests. I'm not sure about labour history, which I don't read, but I sense from the interest here at UC-Davis that women's studies will change things a lot more than labour history has done. Labour history, after all, is only a study of one factor of production, or maybe of how one factor of production didn't get its just desserts, but women's studies is a whole dimension. Environmental studies may well bring back geographical studies, which we've slung out of the window, though I don't find the historical geographers currently very interesting.

There are social scientists – from the historical parts of social sciences – ringing around us and reading some work in economic history – not reading the more difficult economic material, but reading a lot of the conclusions. They're going to incorporate economic history. I've had several comparative historical sociologists tell me that they want to get a better grip of economic history in order to incorporate it in what they do. They don't want to argue in terms of economic models or economic determinism; they simply want to allow for the dimension.

Where will the changes come from?

I think that the changes will come from the outside if we don't bring about changes inside. But I'm actually optimistic about that, too, because we have some very powerful and intellectually outstanding work in economic history. We have seen the big wave of quantification which can answer questions about magnitudes but doesn't in itself tell us much about why things happen. I think that's coming towards its end and will mutate into something else.

Am I allowed to use names at all? I think the most fertile mind in economic history in my lifetime has been Doug North's. You may want to take Alex Field's view (1981) that the new institutional economics is all promise and no performance – you know, "Where's the beef?" But there has got to be something there in the institutional change, institutional analysis, transactions cost approach. And when you consider that North was also a major figure in starting the old New Economic History, there's hope for humanity after all. The other very interesting work is Paul David's. I think if I had to say that there is one person working on the key problem which all the social sciences have failed to address and the historians have failed to address (except by assumption or default), it's Paul David with his work on path dependence.

We need a way of deciding where the writ of history ends and the writ of market forces starts. At the moment we're in economics-style economic history, which is a "structural forces" subject. Although it's supposed to be about change through time, it isn't very interested in history as such. It's interested in the sorts of things you'd expect people in an allocative, equilibria-based science to believe. On the other hand, there are the historians, who believe that everything can be explained by history, by the so-called "genetic" approach, as if I could explain you and why you're sitting here entirely in terms of your pasts. That's as though I could predict that Michael Huberman and Nancy Folbre would be sitting here, as they are, because their parentage somehow led them to this spot, and that all we need to know to understand why you're here today is your histories. Of course, there's some truth in that. There's also some truth that we're held up here in our chairs by anti-gravity or some other structural force. It's putting the two things together that's the issue. I think Paul David may introduce into economic history something we're not going to get from either general history or economics: the start of a line of investigation where we learn how to render at one and the same time unto the God of competitive forces what is that God's, and to the Caesar of the "genetic" approach what is that Caesar's.

In recent work you look at questions of development – why some regions develop and others don't. Why to your mind are Asia and Europe so different?

May I answer that a bit autobiographically, or at least in terms of the two books I've done, because there is a reflection of the nature of our subject in the history of those books? (There are other factors, like the outrageous price asked for the second one in hardcover.) When I wrote *The European Miracle*, I wanted to see what a synthesis of the explanations of what made Europe "first" might look like.[1] I wanted to see whether I could add anything by way of change in emphasis or even originality to that problem, the great problematic of the Rise of the West. And I did it in a conventional way. I put forth special attributes of European economic life, starting with the physical setting and working through a lot of other things by reading as much as possible. I came up with a picture that was a composite. The book is structured so that each chapter partly overlays the next thematically, and also chronologically. It builds up from background

1 Cambridge UP (1981); 2nd edition (1987), with a new introduction; 3rd edition (2003), with a new preface and an afterword.

considerations towards foreground considerations while progressing through time. This seems to have gone quite well, at least judging by the fact that I'm citation rich. Afterwards I started to think that this was the wrong way to approach the question, and certainly the wrong way to explain the divergence between Europe and Asia. You see, all I did in *The European Miracle* that was faintly novel was to play up the environmental aspect and use Asian civilizations as "controls" on European experience. We don't do enough comparative work in economic history or think enough as scientists do in terms of controls. But essentially I assumed that Asian societies lacked a magic ingredient, or rather a recipe, onto which Europe had somehow stumbled. This risks mistaking what are merely European attributes for the general causes of economic growth.

When I came to write *Growth Recurring*, I took a different tack, which I think is far more interesting.[2] This tack sprang from more than one perception. Economic growth does not seem to have a linear history – it seems to have appeared and reappeared more than once, even in the West. Some episodes in the history of major societies in Asia seem to have been ones of real growth. That is where Japan came in. There may have been other cases which are too poorly examined or documented for us to make a guess yet. The argument amounts to asserting that there were early cases of economic growth, though doing so on the basis of development indicators. There simply aren't aggregate statistics on income for early periods. The second perception is that with growth nudging up more than once, it is more interesting to inquire what kept getting in the way than to hypothesize some new historical force as causing it. None of this means that I think growth was, or is, "easy," just that it was a little easier than is suggested by an historiography which traces everything of interest to our profession back to a zero point in the British Industrial Revolution, and no further, or nowhere else. The book perhaps cuts off too early in time to induce people in the profession to read it. It deals too much with faraway places and early periods.

What is your reaction to the reaction to the two books?

The reaction illustrates one of the sociological features of the profession I was talking about when I said that beginning scholars can unfortunately make a bigger splash by providing a clever amendment to the established corpus of work than by doing something original. *The European Miracle* seems to be congenial to a lot of people because it's an ordered compendium which extends by a little bit what they already know, or think they need to know, about the Rise of the West. Plenty of people start their courses with a general introductory topic on the Rise of the West. That's fine. The book gets a good initial run, and people can move on to more serious things.

When the idea of *Growth Recurring* came to me, a lot of things started falling into new places. As Susan Watkins said when she launched the book, it was like shaking a kaleidoscope and getting a completely different pattern out of the same bits and pieces. A

2 Clarendon Press of Oxford UP (1988); paperbound edition, with corrections (1993); 2nd edition, University of Michigan Press (2000), with a new introduction.

student had asked me a question about Japanese growth, and I realized I couldn't assimilate that to the Europeanist, Western conventions about the origins of growth. So I started from the other end, considering the proposition (which I'm sure is congenial to economists) that most people would like to get rich. Providing you can introduce a compositional principle, like the invisible hand, you can go from there to assuming that growth is, in principle, a normal condition. This is based on what's called an Elemental Human Strategy. Admittedly, approaches in that Enlightenment vein are now being eroded by the historical contingencies approach which has invaded the social sciences. There's a book of essays coming out on that topic; Geoff Hawthorn's new book, *Plausible Worlds*, asserts that the Enlightenment programme has ended; and so on.

But supposing one does take the economist's brutal view, that people like to escape from their poverty, then the question is, what's stopping them? I blew this up to the society level. I looked at history in terms of growth. (I didn't look at it in terms of industrialization; I'm not interesting in trainspotting as such, only in whether people get more to eat and shoes for their kids.) As soon as I looked at history, I found that the record strongly suggests there was real growth in at least a couple of East Asian cases, and probably transiently in all sorts of other cases, as well as in the Rise of the West. When I put these two things together, I had the basis for changing the approach from that in *The European Miracle*. I put the emphasis, not on new features which suddenly emerged as laser-beam miracles in modern European history, but on the gradual release of constraints in a number of societies, and the closing down again of those constraints. Working through the constraints suggested in the "obstacles to growth" literature led me to think that the basic problem was rent-seeking – the neurotic compulsion, through the ages, of people with political power to try to take more out of the pot than they put in. In terms of constraining growth, that will do it every time!

There's a great difference between the two books. The fact that the second one hasn't caught on anything like the first, has been kindly reviewed but no more, is an unfortunate reflection of the bias towards reading what will extend the current paradigm, but not toward absorbing a lot of obscure data to challenge it.

Did *Growth Recurring* fail to catch on because we as economic historians don't know very much about countries outside Europe and North America?

You think *I* do? How do *I* know about those places? I went to the library!

Why isn't more work being done on these areas?

Start-up costs are too high.

Is it simply a matter of investment?

Yes, the start-up costs are so high, and the literature is not congenial to people with training in economics because it's so vague. It is difficult to know how you would teach this material, in the sense that you teach undergraduates about Lancashire cotton. Early Asian history, or even early European history, is like trying to pin the clouds down. You don't know anything to start with about the third century BC, you don't know any ancient Greek history and, when you come to read it, you can't find out the things you really want to know. It's hard going. It leaves a lot very speculative, and that's not our mode, is it?

Our mode is to narrow the questions and get determinate answers within a particular intellectual framework. It's not surprising that the bias of the subject is towards modern, Western, national economic history, and even finer slivers than that. But I don't think ours is the way to start teaching people. It doesn't give them a context. You see, our method of teaching, our intention, seems to be to teach people technique and maybe how to debate, but not to give them a broad context. I'm talking about graduate training, or honours level training in Britain and Australia. The assumption is that as undergraduates, or at school, people got all the history and geography and sociology and bits about cultures they could eat, so that all they need are courses which show the cut and thrust of debate about social savings from the railroad or whether or not slavery was efficient.

If it is a matter of incentives, how do we in the discipline change the incentive structure to get more work out on non-Western economic history?

I think, oddly enough, heretical though it may be, that ideas will change the incentive structure. I think you don't change things by telling people what you want them to do, you just notice that bright people coming into a given trade pick up on new ideas. There are some new ideas around. The thing will self-correct. The whole New Economic History revolution was precisely this. It was bright people in economics departments (you couldn't handle it in history departments). It was exciting and new, and the people were highly trained. They were pretty bright people, at first anyhow, so they read the general books too. Many people in the field actually know, not merely more than they write, or more even than they teach, but much, much more. Somehow I think a few people from outside, perhaps from comparative historical sociology, and a few inside, like Doug North or Paul David, will attract more of the bright minds, and things will change in half a generation. There isn't much sign of it at the moment, but I'm relying on a "Quebec Effect" once the change comes.[3]

Further reflections

Eric Jones

In the late 1950s, when I first studied economic history, there were perhaps two main meta-themes. Both were wearing thin. Americans occupied themselves charting and

3 A "Quebec Effect" is a sudden, unheralded social change, as with the slump in marriage, birth rate and church attendance in Quebec in the 1960s.

celebrating the achievements of business and industry in the United States. British economic historians shared a parallel triumphalism but were more concerned with industrialization's failure to wipe out big disparities of income and class. The profession nowhere dealt much with the rest of the world except in "Great Powers" courses covering Britain, the US, France, Germany, the USSR and (the sole non-Western entrant) Meiji Japan. Elsewhere remained in darkness, unless one counts the unhistorical typologies of students of economic development or the musings of area studies specialists, with their distaste for market analysis.

By 1992, when Nancy Folbre and Michael Huberman sprang their interview on me, industrial triumphalism was almost dead, the British profession had lost its moral fervour, and the East Asian Miracle had rendered redundant the statist remedies of economic development. These lamps burned low; illumination came from the beam of cliometrics – which was economic history turned inwards. The broad audience, as I complained, had been surrendered to other professions, with a fair sprinkling of mountebanks to boot.

Likewise in 1992, I was rather despairing about the traditional core of economic history: the question of the Industrial Revolution in Britain and associated changes in agriculture. The British profession continued to grind these topics into ever smaller pieces as – to generalize – it continues to do. Fortunately, something I noted as far back as 1988 has also been happening: "North American scholars of a generation for whom quantitative techniques are second nature are beginning to invade the economic history of early modern Europe."[4] I see no reason to change my mind. The arrival of Bob Allen in Oxford by itself represents a technology transfer of which British agricultural history was in need. In reality, of course, it is not the technology that matters so much as fresh ways of looking at tired problems, or so it has proved. As to the Industrial Revolution, its supposed duration has long been stretched almost to snapping point but I still see few fresh contributions to the old debate about the inception of growth. Occasional nice sidelights, yes, but a central insight, not yet. (There has, however, been an unexpected and welcome return to the subject in a new, edited volume.)[5]

Away from work on national economic histories, which in an integrated world are less compelling than once they were, there luckily has been a revival of energy. This has come, maybe unexpectedly, in the shape of extremely broad comparative work. Since 1992 a straggling complex of studies addressed to the Rise of the West and the fate of Asia has gone on expanding. These studies promise a return of moral fervour because they throw light on the strategies of growth in a world where, despite the marvelous achievements of the West and East Asia, poverty remains the norm. Nothing could be more important.[6]

4 See Jones, *Growth Recurring* (1988 [2000: 25]).

5 Prados, ed., *Exceptionalism and Industrialisation: Britain and its European Rivals, 1688–1815* (2004).

6 As has been recognized by the contributions of Doug North and Bob Fogel to *The Economist's* Copenhagen Consensus project on the priorities for world development.

Less fortunately, as I suggested, the chief driving force of this work has come from the other social sciences, especially Asia specialists, above all Sinologists. What they tend to imply is that Western development was a late-coming, derivative and essentially illegitimate process. Somewhere else, meaning China, was more creative but simply less lucky. At times this thrust is accompanied by anti-Western commentaries that are bitter or downright offensive.[7] Economic historians are playing only a minor part in this work but the austerely technocratic element in our trade, which cost us the leading role, may in the end prove an advantage. This is not only because the techniques are the most coherent in the social sciences but because economics is less overtly politicized than sociology, political science, area studies and the like.[8] If one wants to see economic history justified, by a masterly undermining of the trendy prescriptions of authoritarianism, read Peter Lindert's presidential address to the Economic History Association.[9]

Much economic history nevertheless remains technical, national, recent-period and Western in its focus, and its high-tech nature comes at the cost of being incomprehensible to anyone without appropriate training. Modern Ph.D.s in economics equip their holders with techniques that they think it wasteful not to apply. This, although understandable, tends to restrict the scope of the subject to pre-digested statistical sources. Cheap computing power now makes it possible to decipher and re-arrange bodies of data that hitherto were simply inaccessible. The consequences were already very evident in 1992 and overall little has changed; quite the contrary.

But around the modern core of the subject, people are venturing into soggier territories normally the habitat of practitioners from the other social sciences, general history, geography and so forth. Environmental studies, which has seen a stellar growth already discernible in 1992, has attracted fewer economic historians than it ought, though economists have made a valiant effort at rescuing the area from the ideologues.[10] The intellectual underpinnings of technological change have seen a notable study by Joel Mokyr.[11] Economic institutions have continued to attract an attention they never saw in pre-Northian times, and though I confess that the results have been less dramatic than I anticipated, the topic is of no less importance than it was. Even cultural studies have been readmitted to the canon in high-profile work by Peter Temin and David Landes, and although I am not persuaded by their conclusions this is probably because I have been peering into these cloudy zones for a book of my own.[12]

7 However a number of the anti-Western critiques have now been convincingly refuted by Doyne Dawson, "The Assault on Eurocentric History" (2003).

8 I have commented on such matters as the occasion has arisen: an introduction to the second edition of *Growth Recurring, op. cit.*; *The Record of Global Economic Development* (2002); and an Afterword to the third edition (2003) of *The European Miracle*.

9 Lindert, "Voice and Growth: Was Churchill Right?" (2003).

10 Nevertheless much the most effective voice has been that of a Danish statistician, Bjorn Lomborg.

11 Mokyr, *The Gifts of Athena* (Princeton UP 2002).

12 Temin, "Is it Kosher to Talk about Culture?" (1997b); Landes, *The Wealth and Poverty of Nations* (1998); Jones, *Cultures Merging* (2006).

The output of individual scholars is impossible to predict and the profession as a whole is always drawn hither and thither by unexpected shifts of interest – sometimes by the appearance of an exciting work which catapults a new star into the skies. In general, however, I stick by both of my earlier pronouncements: large and important areas of human knowledge will remain captive to people with fewer skills if economic historians do not explicitly gird themselves to take more intellectual risks *and yet*, despite the counter-attractions, economic history will always succeed in generating a few individuals willing to undertake the risks of synoptic work.

CHARLES H. FEINSTEIN

Interviewed by
Mark Thomas

Charles Hilliard Feinstein was Chichele Professor of Economic History, Emeritus, in the University of Oxford and Emeritus Fellow of All Souls College. He was born in Johannesburg in 1932 and died in Oxford in 2004. In 1950 Feinstein graduated from The University of the Witwatersrand with a B.Com. degree, qualified as a chartered accountant in 1954, and left South Africa for the University of Cambridge, where he completed a doctorate in 1958. He remained in Cambridge until 1978, first as a research officer in the Department of Applied Economics (1958–63), then as a University Lecturer in Economics and Fellow of Clare College (1963–1978). He was Senior Tutor at Clare from 1969 until his departure for the Chair in Economic and Social History at the University of York in 1978. While at York, Feinstein was elected Fellow of the British Academy (1983). In 1987 he moved to Oxford, first as Reader in Recent Economic and Social History and Fellow of Nuffield College and then as Chichele Professor from 1989 until his retirement in 1999. In addition to his many university and college administrative assignments at Cambridge, York and Oxford, Feinstein's service to the academic research community included a term as managing editor of *The Economic Journal* (1980–86), chairmanship of the Economic Affairs Committee of the Social Science Research Council (1985–86), and the Vice-Presidency of the British Academy (1991–93). A collection of essays presented at a conference in Feinstein's honour in 1999, *The Economic Future in Historical Perspective*, edited by Paul A. David and Mark Thomas, was published in 2003 (Oxford UP for the British Academy). His Ellen MacArthur Lectures of 2004, mentioned in the interview, were revised and expanded into a book, *An Economic History of South Africa: Conquest, Discrimination and Development* (Cambridge UP, 2005). The interview was conducted by Mark Thomas, Feinstein's collaborator in writing *Making History Count: A Primer in Quantitative Methods for Historians* (Cambridge UP, 2002). Their conversation took place in Feinstein's rooms at All Souls, 2 August 2002. Mark Thomas (University of Virginia) writes:

Charles Feinstein's influence on British economic history since 1750 has been palpable. It is almost impossible to read a contribution to quantitative economic history over the past 35 years without seeing its debt to Feinstein's canonical statistical reconstructions of national income, capital accumulation, and wages and prices. For those of us working in the field as graduate students and young researchers, Feinstein was a formidable presence, both as a guide to how we should approach quantitative history and as a disinterested, passionate critic of error in the use and application of quantitative data. But Feinstein was more than a simple archaeologist of numbers; he made signal interpretive contributions to such venerable topics as the standard of living in the British Industrial Revolution, the late Victorian climacteric, the origins and diffusion of the Great Depression in Europe, and the reasons for slower economic growth in the British economy after 1945. Towards the end of his life, Feinstein returned to his native roots in South Africa, both physically and intellectually, but he did not abandon his fascination with the contours of British economic development. His last project was a reconstruction of the national accounts for the United Kingdom in 1851, which will appear posthumously under the imprint of Cambridge University Press as *The Mid-Victorian Economy: Making, Earning and Spending in the United Kingdom in 1851*, by Charles H. Feinstein and Mark Thomas.

How did you become interested in economic history?

Well, I suppose the beginning would have been in school, where the subject I found most stimulating was history. But when it was time to think about university courses, history didn't seem to have any career associated with it. The real choice was between taking a B.A., which would lead to a law qualification, or a B.Com. I chose the B.Com. degree, and that was how I was introduced to economics. At the University of the Witwatersrand, the degree involved courses in economics, economic history, and accounting. I do remember that part way through I decided that really this was all a mistake, and I would have been better off doing history and a B.A. I tried to change, but the university wasn't interested, so I persisted with economics and economic history.

I was very fortunate in having two very stimulating lecturers. The first, in South African economic history, was Helen Suzman, who subsequently became very famous as a liberal Member of Parliament. More significantly, perhaps, in my second year the university appointed Lionel Lachmann to the Chair in Economics. He came to South Africa as a refugee in two senses – he had been a refugee from Austria in the 1930s and had come to England. He was very much an Austrian economist, and I think he found the very strong Keynesian climate in England in the early post-war period uncongenial and probably (although I don't know this) was unable to get a job in England. So, he came to South Africa, and I still remember the excitement of this new professor coming from Europe and lecturing to us in his very heavy accent. It completely transformed what I understood by economics and the quality of intellectual thought that went into it. By the time I finished my degree, I was anxious to study economics as a way to contribute to solving the economic problems of South Africa and the world. My parents were very doubtful; they had never met a professional economist. They said that if I would first get a qualification which would enable me to earn a living, they would then support me to go overseas and study economics (there were no grants available in those days). So, I did three years of accountancy and became a qualified chartered accountant. I didn't enjoy that at all, but I think it had a very substantial effect on me, and it was something I was good at. It clearly influenced, although not consciously, what I did subsequently. And, at the end of that period, I came to Cambridge to study economics.

While I was doing accountancy, Lachmann started an Honours Degree in Economics, which three of us elected to do on a part-time basis. The teaching for the course was entirely conducted by Lachmann in a very idiosyncratic way. He chose a book, and we met to discuss it. It was a very detailed exegesis, page by page and line by line. The two books that occupied most of our time were Joan Robinson's *The Rate of Interest and Other Essays* (Macmillan 1952) and Bent Hansen on the *Theory of Inflation* (Allen & Unwin 1951). It wasn't really the importance of these books that mattered as much as the training and the method of taking each sentence and each word and thinking about what it meant. At the end of the course, we had a variety of exams and submitted a dissertation. I did very well in the exams, but my dissertation was a disaster. I chose to write something which reflected my political and Marxist interests at the time and was designed to show that it was quite wrong to reject the labour theory of value as orthodox economics had done. I didn't really understand what I was doing; it was heavily derivative, relying on Maurice Dobb and, more particularly, Ronald Meek. The external examiner was W. H. Hutt of the University of Cape Town, and he found any suggestion that there was merit in the labour theory of value totally unacceptable. As I later came to appreciate with some relief, instead of just giving it a third class mark (which might have destroyed my career), he failed it outright. Although I got first class marks on the exam, I was held to have failed the degree. I had already been accepted to go to Cambridge and wrote in great dismay to Piero Sraffa, who was in charge of graduate admissions. For whatever reason, he said don't worry, just come, and we will evaluate you here. So I came, and it was forgotten.

You went from studying with Lachmann, an arch anti-Keynesian, to Cambridge, the heart of Keynes's territory.

That didn't really concern me. I certainly wasn't an "Austrian," but I didn't think of myself as a Keynesian either. I don't think I would have said I was a Marxist either, since I had doubts about several aspects, but I was very much on that side of the divide. My reason for going to Cambridge was overwhelmingly to study under Maurice Dobb, but the faculty assigned me to be supervised by someone else, Malcolm Fisher. However, I saw Dobb on a regular basis, got to know him well, and edited a *Festschrift* for him.

Your parents had committed to helping finance this Cambridge trip. Was the expectation that you would go for two years and then return to South Africa?

It was fairly open-ended. The initial commitment was for one year, because I was admitted to do the one-year Diploma in Economics. But my parents were very keen that I should not return quickly to South Africa, as I had been heavily involved in what they saw as dangerous political activity, and when I did sufficiently well in the Diploma to be able to stay on to do a doctorate, they were willing to continue to support me.

Before I left for Cambridge, I was asked to review a book by R. Palme Dutt, the leading economist of the British Communist Party, for the South African Communist Party newspaper. It was titled *The Crisis of Britain and the British Empire* (Lawrence & Wishart 1953), in which he argued that the viability of the British economy was entirely dependent on looting the Empire, which would come to an end as the Empire gained its independence. Capitalism in Britain would therefore be undermined, and since this would apply equally to other capitalist countries, the world revolution would come, and we would all be happy.

Given the atmosphere in South Africa at that time and also what was happening in the world economy – the success of the Chinese revolution and the strength of the Communist Party in France and Italy – it wasn't as absurd as it now seems to imagine that capitalism was in serious trouble. I was very taken with this book and saw imperialism as the subject on which I would work at Cambridge. I had realized from my efforts to write a theoretical dissertation that I was never going to do anything worthwhile on theory or the history of thought, but I thought that exploring the Empire historically and in a more scholarly way than Palme Dutt had done would be something I could do well. I still remember very vividly the idea being shot down by a single sentence from Joan Robinson. I met Joan at a meeting of the Cambridge University Socialist Club, and she asked me what I was going to be doing for my doctorate. I told her and she said, in a very brusque and dismissive way, "That's absurd." And when I asked why, she said, "How can you explain the prosperity of the Scandinavian economies if it is all due to Empire?" I went away and wrestled with that for some time and decided that she was right. It fitted in with a whole number of other things happening to me at that stage. Once I got out of the hothouse atmosphere of South Africa and could reflect in the cooler climate of Britain, I remained left wing in my attitudes but came to realize that a lot of what I had believed, particularly about the Soviet Union and about imperialism, was untenable. I didn't abandon the subject, however. Cairncross's *Home and Foreign Investment* had just been published, and I thought there was still room to do a scholarly analysis, although it wouldn't be designed to lead to the conclusion that it was all going to collapse. So that was how I came to my thesis topic.

Can you tell us about the themes of your thesis? [*Home and Foreign Investment . . . 1870–1913*]

I suppose there are two parts to the story. One part involved Prest's national income figures. I wanted to use his profits series as a way of looking at the profitability of the British economy in the period of high imperialism. When I came to do that, I immediately struck a problem: Prest hadn't disaggregated profits from the other components of non-wage income. I started out trying to do that, since it seemed to me to be essential to have that information. But as I got into it, I found some problems in what he had done, which led progressively to reconstructing the national income estimates. That became perhaps the most important chapter in the thesis. It obviously had an enormous influence on what I did afterwards. At the time, I didn't see it as the heart of the thesis. That was meant to be the analysis. A lot of the thesis was devoted to trying to elucidate the interaction between home and foreign investment. One of my arguments, which was novel at the time, was that the critical interaction wasn't between domestic manufacturing investment and overseas investment, but between housing and overseas investment. I remember giving one of the chapters to Postan's seminar, and he was very enthusiastic. He was editor of the *Economic History Review* and said, yes, you must write it up and we'll publish it. But I never had sufficient confidence that what I had done was adequate. It always seemed possible to go on improving the analysis. And so it never appeared. I regret that in some ways. The only part of the thesis that was published was a paper on the national income estimates that was accepted by the *Economic Journal*.

There is a certain path dependence in all things, not least in academic careers. You went on to further work on capital formation and that pivotal period between 1870 and 1914, and the thesis helped shape your future commitment to statistical reconstruction of the British economic historical record. How did things unfold?

The Department of Applied Economics (DAE) at Cambridge advertised two vacancies at about the time I was finishing my thesis, and the two people who were appointed were Brian Mitchell and myself. His appointment was to work with Phyllis Deane and Max Cole on the *Abstract of British Historical Statistics* (Mitchell & Deane 1962); mine was to work with Jack Revell on the National Wealth. I had made one very minor contribution to that, doing some research on shareholding, when Brian Reddaway summoned me. I can still remember very vividly coming into the DAE one morning, when Brian, in characteristic fashion, accosted me from the top of the staircase and said, "Charles, come up here, there is something I want you to do." My task was to complete Maywald's work on domestic capital formation in Britain. Maywald was supposed to finish the book but was unable to do so to Reddaway's satisfaction. There was absolutely no meeting of minds and eventually relationships broke down and I was called in. The original brief was simply to bring the book to a state where it could be published. However, once I started working on it, I found more and more things where I thought revision was essential. After that, I began work on a larger project of reconstruction. Richard Stone had initially launched the project on the retrospective national accounts. The first volume on consumers' expenditure was his own work, and there had been the Prest volume, the Chapman volume, and now the Feinstein-Maywald volume on capital formation. But by the 1960s, he had lost interest in the project and moved on to other things. It seemed to me extremely unfortunate that all this work had been done on the components of the national income but nobody was going to pull it all together and provide the key series for GDP. So I went to Stone and Reddaway and said I would like to do this (1972).

Who were your primary influences while at Cambridge?

Without question, by far the most influential person in shaping the work I did was Brian Reddaway, who had succeeded Stone as Director of the DAE. I learned an enormous amount from him. I obviously couldn't emulate his own skills, his incredibly penetrating critical faculty, but I could learn from his approach, his remarkably clear sense of what was important, and his ability to focus on that without being diverted into less important matters. This was crucial in relation to understanding what one should be doing and in writing it up so that the important points were clearly conveyed to the reader.

You were in a Department of Applied Economics, not an Economic History Department, and were then appointed to a lectureship in the Faculty of Economics. Did you think of yourself as an applied economist rather than as an economic historian?

I certainly did and, I suppose more relevantly, many others did, but I don't any longer. When I was in the DAE, I did a lot of applied economics, for example, writing articles on the current state of the economy. Soon after joining the Department, I was appointed statistician of the London and Cambridge Economic Service, which horrified me, because I didn't think of myself as a statistician. In those days, the London and Cambridge Economic Service produced a lot of statistical tables for which there was no official counterpart. The Service was a pioneer – it produced the first seasonally adjusted series, the first quarterly series of the national income, and so on. And the work of the statistician was to produce the numbers, so I had a crash course in British economic statistics.

Did you have much contact with the economic historians in Cambridge?

The economic historians who were at Cambridge when I was there were mostly in the history faculty with interests that didn't overlap with mine at all, and they very often worked in earlier periods. The initial Professor of Economic History was Postan, from whom I learned a lot, but that had nothing to do with the work I was doing; it was more just the stimulus of his intellect and range and his dynamic personality. His successor for a very brief time was David Joslin, who once again didn't have much overlap with me. And then there was Donald Coleman, with whom I worked closely together on faculty matters, but our approaches to economic history were so very different. More important were the applied economists who had done some economic history, especially Robin Matthews, who had been my thesis supervisor and who invited me to collaborate with him on the study initiated by Simon Kuznets and Moses Abramovitz that became *British Economic Growth, 1856–1973*.

What was it like writing about capital formation in Cambridge at the height of the capital controversies? Did you perceive any tensions with these new theoretical approaches, which seemed to suggest that trying to measure capital was impossible?

Yes, I did. One couldn't be in Cambridge and not be conscious of the intensity and the fervour with which that debate was conducted. And I obviously had to think it through. The resolution I arrived at quite quickly was that although we were both using the word capital, we were really doing different things. They were saying that there was an inherent circularity which couldn't be overcome: you needed a measure of capital in order to estimate future profits, and you needed to estimate future profits in order to have a measure of capital, and there was no way around that. Whereas I was not trying to estimate the future value of the capital stock in that sense; I was trying to estimate how much money had actually been spent in the past on creating the stock of capital.

And was this a point the critics accepted?

I don't think they ever looked beyond the theory. Nothing else mattered.

Your first exposure to American cliometrics and American economic history came in the late 1960s?

Yes. When I was appointed lecturer in the Economics faculty, the expectation was that I would follow the person I was replacing, Frank Thistlethwaite, and teach American economic history. I said that I would rather lecture on Russian economic history. So I was sent to Moscow for two months to learn the language and study Russian economic history.[1] A more exciting consequence was that the choice enabled me to go to America for a year in 1967–68, when I had my first sabbatical leave. Postan had introduced me to Gerschenkron, who was visiting Cambridge, and when I said that I would like to visit the Russian Research Center at Harvard, he offered to arrange that. I spent a lot of time that year reading microfilms in the Harvard Center on pre-war Russian economic history. I did quite a lot of research, but I wasn't very satisfied with the papers I wrote, and nothing really came of it. During that same year, I was also finishing the national income book, so I was moving between the two projects: working with Bergson on the Russian side and also occasionally seeing Kuznets.

You attended the Gerschenkron seminar while you were at Harvard. What was your reaction?

It was tremendously stimulating. There were some remarkable people there, most obviously Gerschenkron himself, who was very warm as a host. I still have very fond memories of our meetings. The seminar used to be held after dinner, and afterwards he would invite me to his room for a brandy. He always began by wanting to discuss baseball, but with a certain amount of effort, I could bring him around to more interesting topics. I also got to know Peter Temin and saw a lot of him that year and some of the others who were in the Gerschenkron seminar, such as Dick Sylla, Peter

1 In 1995 there was a 50th-anniversary conference at the DAE in Cambridge. One of those attending asked Feinstein if he knew he was single-handedly responsible for introducing Russian economic history to most British specialists on the Russian economy.

McClelland, and Bobby Solow. It was perhaps the first time that I felt that I was part of a community of economic historians, because in Cambridge I didn't have a strong sense of an academic community with shared problems and shared interests. In Harvard I did.

And you also went to that hotbed of cliometrics, Purdue, for their annual meeting.

Yes, I didn't know much about it beforehand. It was Peter Temin who suggested I accompany him, so we flew out together. It was my first encounter with people like Bob Gallman and Doug North and others and was a very exciting occasion. I particularly remember a paper by Bob Gallman (1970) criticizing some of the assumptions that underlay Doug North's work on interregional links in the American economy, and I found that really very interesting.

What was the tenor of the sessions? Were they more combative than in Cambridge?

No. I don't know if you have heard the famous quip by Bob Solow – that a Cambridge seminar consisted of Joan Robinson talking for 75 per cent of the time and Nicky Kaldor talking for the other 75 per cent. That was very much Cambridge (it was a very sharp place in those days), so I found America in some ways more restrained.

Were there glimmerings of a similar revolution in Britain?

I've always thought that the Americans needed the cliometric revolution, because their work had lacked quantitative analysis entirely; whereas in Britain, we'd had a very long tradition of it. This was not cliometric in the shiny sense that it developed in America, with neoclassical economics and econometrics at its core, but it was deeply quantitative in terms of measuring what had happened and making the numbers the basis for any analysis. For me, there were three exemplars of that style of work in Britain: Alec Cairncross, Robin Matthews, and W. Arthur Lewis while he was at Manchester. Brinley Thomas was also very influential. So I didn't find what was being claimed in America something that we'd never thought of in Britain. It seemed to me a very well established and significant tradition in Britain, and I saw myself as part of that. The American revolution was also influenced by the personalities of some of the leading figures and their strong desire to proselytize, which was absent in Britain. Apart from personalities, I think there was a sense in America that this way of doing history had to fight against other ways, and that struggle was reflected, for example, in the tensions over slavery. There was no counterpart to this in Britain. After my visit to America and after McCloskey organized the conferences on the British economy (first in America and then here), we were all drawn into the movement. Some of the work that was done then – for example, Sandberg's work on the cotton industry – was, in my view, a very important contribution to British economic history. Some of the other work perhaps less so.

Do you consider yourself a cliometrician?

You would have to define cliometrician.

How about if one defined cliometrics as testing hypotheses with a combination of economic theory and formal quantitative methods?

Then I would have no difficulty with that. I would simply have to say that it is obvious that my own contribution has been primarily in providing the data, not in testing hypotheses.

Have you regretted not having followed that econometric path, if only because others have?

No. I would regret it in the sense that I regret that I am not able to open the batting for England. It would be fine if one could do it, but I've no doubt that I wouldn't do it terribly well.

So, comparative advantage is the correct way to think of it?

It is partly comparative advantage, and it is partly temperament, though you might say that temperament is part of comparative advantage.

The quantitative work that you have been involved with has contributed to two primary historical debates: the first is the debate over the so-called climacteric at the end of the nineteenth century; the second is the debate over industrialization and its consequences. Let's talk about the first. Not everyone believes in the climacteric. Do you?

Yes. But you have to look behind that. I certainly believe that the evidence from the real wage side, showing a pronounced slowdown in the Edwardian period, is very strong, and attempts to wash it away with sophisticated statistical techniques don't persuade me in the least. I believe, as I have for many years, that the root of the problem in the British economy had to do with labour relations and a combination of attitudes on the part of the workforce that were detrimental to productivity, reinforced by employers' refusal to recognize what would have been necessary to overcome those attitudes. I think this class-based attitude of employers towards the working class and workers' response to that was also an extremely powerful factor in Britain's early post-1945 problems, though comparative performance in that period was dominated by the catching-up process in countries like Germany, France, and Japan. I think that it took a long time before Britain saw its way through that legacy.

The early literature that built on the concept of the climacteric emphasized economic decline, while the fashion now is to deny any decline in Britain. Do you subscribe to that?

To a large extent, yes. I joined the catching-up school very early and published a paper in which I argued that most of what happened after 1948 could be explained simply by where the different economies started. Similar arguments would have applied earlier. But because of the way I presented the results, it didn't make the impact it might have done if it had been presented in econometric terms.

To push you. The argument is that Britain didn't decline, yet there is structural impediment to the maintenance of high productivity growth. Are those compatible?

It depends on your measurement of economic satisfaction.

So, you are arguing for a total economic welfare interpretation.

That is implicit, yes.

If we had a holistic view of national income accounting – incorporating welfare elements – then Britain would actually still have been growing?

It is not so much an issue of growth rates but that nineteenth-century Britain wouldn't be seen as a failure. I think that is the right interpretation, and it applies more strongly to the late Victorian or Edwardian period than to the period after World War II. In the early post-1945 period, there were more pronounced problems of arrogance and incompetence and a failure to recognize how the world was changing, which you couldn't simply justify away in wider welfare terms, but in the nineteenth century, yes.

Have you therefore been tempted to try to move towards broader measures of welfare?

No, I doubt whether they could be quantified. What I would like to have done (and have started but left unfinished) is to write a history of the post-war period in which this would be one of the themes.

You have also been drawn in recent years to the period of industrialization.

Yes, this goes back to the completion of the work on capital formation and my second visit to Harvard in 1987–88, where I thought I would go back to my early ideas on imperialism. But then shortly after I arrived, I saw a copy of *Explorations* with an article by David Greasley criticizing my work on wages, and that led me to think about wages. I had found capital formation in the end rather arid. I was dealing with things that had no human interest, whereas once I got started on issues of wages, that opened up questions such as the standard of living. And it also linked up with work which went all the way back to my dissertation on the climacteric. Having started on that project, it seemed desirable and interesting to extend it back to the late eighteenth century. That then overlapped with the debate about the pace of economic growth and the nature of the Industrial Revolution. It seemed to me that all the debate was being focused on the Hoffman index and output data and was ignoring the evidence available on the income side, so I thought I could make a contribution by working on the income estimates. The original project was to start on wages and then extend through into the other elements, and in some ways, I'd still like to do that. But, having completed the work on earnings and the cost of living, which led to contributions to the pessimism debate, I got involved with the issue of the relative size of value added in different sectors of the economy, which in turn led to my current project. It has occupied me for the last three or four years and involves constructing a very detailed social accounting matrix for 1851.

Let me ask you this about the pessimism argument. The combination of slow growth and stagnant real wages has implications for the distribution of income during industrialization. This takes you back to an earlier controversy, perhaps the one most familiar to cliometricians, the "Kuznets curve" debate: the argument that industrialization is accompanied by a rise in inequality, which gradually diminishes over time. You were sharply critical of that argument in your famous review of Jeff Williamson's *Did British Capitalism Breed Inequality?* Would you like to talk a little bit about the origins of the contribution and any new thoughts you've had on that in the last 15 years?

I don't think I've particularly had any second thoughts. I think the thing to be said is that I didn't approach that project, or the one on pessimism or any other controversy I've been involved in, with a strong *a priori* view. This may seem rather surprising for someone who started off with dogmatic Marxist views, but perhaps abandoning those led me to become generally more agnostic. My attitude has typically been to do the research needed to find out what the data can tell us and to report that as faithfully as I can. In the particular case of the inequality debate, I hadn't previously given much thought to the Kuznets curve or to the underlying theory that Jeff Williamson had developed. I was asked by the *Journal of Economic History* to review his book, and I took it with me to the States, thinking it was something I would do during my sabbatical year. When I had agreed to write the review, I thought it was a rather daunting thing to undertake, because I was aware that there was a lot of general equilibrium modeling in the book with which I wasn't familiar. I began by thinking about one of the measures that Jeff had used to produce the results about inequality – the tax data – and became aware that it was flawed. I then got caught up in work on wages and set the review aside.

Nine months later I moved to Stanford for the summer and took up the review as something it was now urgent to get done. I started by looking at the next measure of inequality and found that there were problems with that, and my review went through progressively. As I took up each measure and looked at the procedure that Jeff had adopted or the sources he had used, I found that there was something wrong. I think there were seven measures that Jeff used. He said that some of these may be deficient because the data are uncertain, but they all point in the same direction. I had worked through five of them, thought that was enough for the purposes of the review, and sent a preliminary version to Jeff and also to Peter Lindert. One of the responses I got back was: Well, you haven't said anything critical about the other measures. So I then looked at those and particularly the estimates Williamson had derived from the work of Colquhoun and the other social arithmeticians. I found those too were flawed. Having gone that far, I asked myself this question: If all the estimates that underpin this are seriously flawed, how does the general equilibrium model produce the results that it did? That became the final part of the critique. I should say that I have always greatly admired Jeff's ingenuity and his innovative approaches to economic history and still do, so there was no personal animus in it. I had certainly not set out to do anything destructive. If it ended up being highly critical, that was simply because intellectually that was where the numbers led.

But doesn't the combination of slow but positive growth and stagnant real wages over that crucial period from 1780–1840 point to some movement in the distribution of income? Does this suggest a reconsideration of the legitimacy of the Kuznets curve?

It might, but what it leads me to again is to think that it would be extremely useful if one could get a better grasp of the quantitative record of what happened to the non-wage components of income. If I were going to make any sort of contribution, I could do it more effectively that way rather than by speculating about what might or might not have happened to the components that I hadn't been able to measure. So, what I had in mind when I finished the pessimism paper was that I would try to cover the other components of income. I have collected a lot of evidence towards that, but there is still a long way to go. And some parts, particularly in relation to trading profits, may not be amenable to quantification. I have also been thinking more about the output side, which is how I got diverted into wanting to know more accurately about the composition of value added, sector by sector, and that led to the construction of the 1851 matrix.

So, as part of your philosophical approach, leaving something as a residual is not really good enough.

That's right. And also (perhaps as a result of my work on capital formation), I am very conscious of the length of life of assets. I think that the assets I construct are more likely to prove durable if I do one type of work rather than another. It might be more exciting and more intellectually demanding to try and do more speculative and theoretical research, but I doubt that it would make a lasting or worthwhile contribution.

Do you see yourself as a sort of archaeologist of numbers?

I wouldn't have put it like that, but there is clearly an element of truth in that description. It is partly a matter of knowing where to look and of uncovering "lost" information, but much more of it is seeing that information in perspective, assessing its strengths and weaknesses, knowing how it relates to other evidence and to the historical context, and deciding how it can be used and how it should be interpreted. A palaeontologist who reconstructs an entire species from a single skull or a leg bone is perhaps another apt analogy. I think it comes out most clearly in the social accounting matrix I have compiled for 1851, because it is in many ways the most elaborate project I've ever done. And, because it all relates to only one year, one can spend far more time on each sector than one could afford to when doing a long-run series. Plus, I get a certain satisfaction in finding evidence from disparate sources and establishing that they are in fact consistent and that it is possible to reconstruct how the economy actually functioned, even for a time when there were no censuses of output.

In essence, your comparative advantage is not just patience but also the skill and judgement of being able to discern what is the right number and what is the wrong number.

I would be pleased if my work was evaluated on that basis.

One change associated with the 1990s is your return to South Africa after a gap of over 40 years. You left to go for one year to Cambridge and then for a second year, and as the political situation in South Africa deteriorated, you chose to absent yourself. Now, however, you've revived your connections. What was it like returning?

It was very, very exciting. I was extremely pleased with the success of the transition and am still moderately optimistic about its prospects. There are a lot of things that are enormously worrying, most obviously in relation to the government's response to the HIV/AIDS crisis. But much is happening that is highly encouraging, and I find it an extremely vibrant and interesting society to live in. I get up in the morning and switch on the radio with far more enthusiasm to hear what's happened the previous day than I did in Britain, where politics seem to be incredibly repetitive and usually trivial (though war with Iraq may change that). Most of the time, you go away for three months and you come back and say, "What's happened?" and the answer is, "Nothing." It's not like that in South Africa. I get a lot of pleasure, interest, and stimulus from observing the democratic transition. The fact that I've been able to go back more or less every year now for the last decade and to teach at the University of Capetown has been very fulfilling.

You've not only returned to South Africa to teach, but you are now taking up the challenge of returning to South African economic history.

I am thinking about that. Until recently, I've had so many unfinished projects on Britain that it seemed more sensible to finish them before moving on to something new. But I am near a turning point now where I can see space to do something on South Africa, and I find that a very attractive challenge.

What are your immediate academic plans?

My immediate priorities are to write up the work on the social accounting matrix for 1851. It began as a short paper and has grown inexorably into a large book, and I have several chapters still to write. Then I have to complete the Ellen MacArthur lectures that I have been invited to give in Cambridge. The economic history of South Africa will be the subject for these. Where I go after that depends partly on how the lectures turn out. If it seems fruitful, I may do more work on South Africa. Almost certainly, I will also undertake projects based on the results of the social accounting matrix. Using the estimates of value added, for example, may allow us to resolve some of these issues we've talked about. We can look backwards from 1851 to analyse growth patterns and issues of income distribution over the Industrial Revolution and look forward over the period of the climacteric.

What about the future of economic history in Britain?

It is clearly in a contraction phase at the moment, but even in this period of depression, the students who have come in have been very good, and some outstanding recruits to the profession have emerged. My fundamental conviction is that the intrinsic interest in economic history, the importance of the problems it addresses, and its ability to draw on the strengths of both history and economics to create something which, in its sphere, is stronger than either of them alone ensures that it will remain viable and that it will always attract good students.

Where will its home be? Those who have a more pessimistic view argue that economists are becoming increasingly intolerant of applied economics and that they are becoming much more interested in pure theory or econometrics, while among historians, the cultural climate has turned empiricism into a dirty word.

I think that both of those are yesterday's attitudes. In economics, the evidence is very strong that people are already moving away from that approach. Obviously, there is still a profound interest in theory, but there is also a strong and growing interest in more relevant practical applications. There's a lot of evidence that economists, either voluntarily or under duress, are being forced to take notice of the real economy. And similarly, I think the cultural turn has largely run its course. It never was of much consequence in Oxford, but even in places where it was more important, its standing is no longer what it was. I am not suggesting that economic history will go back to the glory days of the 1960s, but I don't doubt that it will continue to thrive.

Any final thoughts on your own career and the contributions you have made?

I think I've made a contribution in three areas. The first is in research, which we have discussed at some length. The second is as an administrator, where I think I was moderately influential on a number of occasions. For instance, while I was Senior Tutor at Clare College, Cambridge, the College was in the vanguard in admitting women. I also played quite a large part in the transformation of the College, introducing a whole web of changes in the rather archaic regulations that I inherited. That was a long, slow, diplomatic task. More recently, when I was appointed to the Oxford chair, the history faculty was overwhelmingly dominated by undergraduate teaching. There was no serious commitment to graduate teaching. I found that very unsatisfactory and initiated one-year and two-year taught courses in Economic History. These were quickly influential in improving graduate studies in our subject and ultimately in persuading other areas in the history faculty that this was the right way to go. My third contribution was in lecturing, something I've always found rewarding. I put a lot of effort into preparing lectures, and although I would never say that I was an inspiring teacher, a very large number of students who completed the annual course evaluation forms reported that I was the best lecturer that they had encountered in their time at Oxford. It was particularly pleasing when this aspect of my contribution was recognized in 2003 by the award of the Economic History Association's Jonathan Hughes Prize for Excellence in Teaching Economic History.[2]

2 The concluding sentence was appended to the interview at Charles Feinstein's request in 2004.

Part VI

FROM THE WORKSHOP OF SIMON KUZNETS, ECONOMIST

Richard A. Easterlin

Robert E. Gallman

Robert W. Fogel

Stanley L. Engerman

Simon Kuznets contributed extensively to our knowledge of historical patterns of economic change, but he called himself neither an historical economist nor an economic historian – just "an economist."[1] Kuznets was "soft spoken and of moderate stature;" he "usually looked as though the wind would blow him over," but he strode like a Titan through his profession. He was a man of "towering intellect;" "a giant in 20th century economics . . . He was the founder of national income measurement, and he created quantitative economic history;" he was "an economic historian's economist . . . the *exemplar economic empiricist* of the century and possibly of all previous centuries."[2] His role at the NBER, in developing the American national accounts, his impact on American economic planning during World War II, and his efforts to produce historical national accounts for a range of countries are described in the editors' introduction. Here we focus on the values Kuznets transmitted to four of his students: Richard Easterlin and Robert Gallman at the University of Pennsylvania in Philadelphia, and Robert Fogel and Stanley Engerman at The Johns Hopkins University in Baltimore, Maryland. They all took his courses and all but Engerman wrote dissertations under his supervision.

Kuznets was born in 1901 in Pinsk, then in Russia, and died in Cambridge, Massachusetts in 1985. His professional career spanned more than six decades, beginning in Kharkov, where he wrote his first published paper (1921). His last publication, a collection of essays called *Economic development, the family, and income distribution* (1989), appeared posthumously.[3] The Russian Civil War interrupted his studies at the University of Kharkov and in 1922 he migrated with his father and brothers to the United States. He continued his education at Columbia University (B.A., 1923; M.A., 1924; Ph.D., 1926) where he met Wesley Clair Mitchell, his teacher and future collaborator at the NBER.

Kuznets's scholarly work was not only "prodigious" in volume, but "by any quality-

1 *E.g.*, Kuznets (1957: 552). Kuznets disliked the term "cliometrician" and "stoutly denied" being one himself; see McCloskey & Hersh (1990: *x*).

2 See Abramovitz (1986a), Easterlin (1989), Fogel (1989b; 1994b; 1996; 2000), and Kapuria-Foreman & Perlman (1995) [K-F&P below]. Quotations are from Fogel (1994b: 2); K-F&P (p. 1545); Fogel (1994b: 2); Paul Samuelson as quoted in the *New York Times*, July 11, 1985, p. B6; K-F&P (p. 1524, original emphasis).

3 The collection was edited by Louis Galambos and Robert Gallman; Richard Easterlin contributed the Foreword and Robert Fogel the Afterword.

adjusted measure it is awe-inspiring" (Easterlin 1989: 1). He was awarded the third Nobel Memorial Prize in Economic Science in 1971, in part for the research on comparative patterns of economic growth, development and structural change he summarized and integrated in *Modern Economic Growth: Rate, Structure, and Spread* (1966). In concluding her review of that book, Phyllis Deane wrote, "Where else could one find the essential concepts and theoretical arguments so clearly and operationally defined, the main statistics so carefully probed and reduced to comparative consistency, the tenable conclusions so enterprisingly yet so cautiously drawn and the consequent questions so pointedly posed?"[4] Kuznets had little use for economic theory not motivated by nor connected directly with empirical reality; by the same token he had little use for sophisticated manipulation of economic statistics not based on clearly defined and well-founded theoretical concepts. He insisted on establishing facts before engaging in theoretical analysis; as Easterlin notes, this view made Kuznets something of an "intellectual maverick."[5] Easterlin applied this lesson in his own early work, but also learned its inverse: that "there is no measurement without theory" (1997: 14). Kuznets, in his lectures on economic growth, taught the substance of historical technical change, population theory, and comparative national income aggregates; in Robert Fogel's view, equally importantly he taught "the art of measurement. He repeatedly demonstrated that the central statistical problem in economics was not random error but systematic biases in the data" (1996: 6). Robert Gallman recalls that in the mid-1950s "[my] conversations with Kuznets were at that time handicapped – from my side – by my sense that when I spoke with him I was talking with God," but that "[his] lectures on economic development finally settled my course" as an economic historian (1994: 24; 1977: 4). Kuznets's teaching and example deeply affected the scholarly lives of his students, but the profession in general rather less so; Easterlin writes, "One can only feel that economics today is poorer for its lack of tolerance of approaches more like Kuznets's."[6]

Kuznets taught statistics and economics at the University of Pennsylvania from 1930 to 1954, excluding interruptions for government service in the 1930s and 1940s. At Penn Richard Easterlin and Robert Gallman were recruited in the early 1950s into the American portion of Kuznets's ambitious project to document historical national accounts and patterns of development for a range of countries.

A decade ago Richard Easterlin styled himself a "reluctant economist," largely because the values he learned from Kuznets and the Kuznetsian flavor of his own work

4 In *EJ* 77: 308 (1967: 882–3). In a review of a companion volume of essays (Kuznets 1965; UK edition 1966) Deane says Kuznets "provides a number of object lessons in research method," notably his "way with figures. Most of the statistical data he has to hand are extremely crude and sketchy. Kuznets sifts this rough material with the delicate patience of an archaeologist. By a process combining remorseless logic, indefatigable cross-checking and bold judgment he extracts the evidence for a coherent and consistent picture out of what often seems the most unlikely material" (in *EJ* 77: 305 (1967: 112)). See also Easterlin (2001) for a retrospective review of *Modern Economic Growth*.

5 Easterlin (1989: 6). Likewise, Abramovitz says, "As a matter of research strategy [Kuznets] was convinced that until much work had been done to establish the factual outlines of past experience, any detailed and specific theories of growth would be of little use" (1986a: 244).

6 Easterlin (1989: 6). Kuznets was not without critics; some are discussed in K-F&P (pp. 1538–9).

are at odds with the model-building approach of contemporary economics. He sees the typical economist as averse to engaging seriously with the other social sciences, putting the economist's myopia down to the profession's exaltation of theory. "It is hard to overcome the preconceptions indoctrinated by graduate economics training . . . It was years before I could shake off some of [those] tastes . . . and begin to think for myself" (1997: 16, 13). On completing his dissertation in 1953, "Some conceptual aspects of the comparative measurement of economic growth," he joined the Penn economics faculty and was drawn into a project (*Population redistribution and economic growth* 1957; 1960; 1964) supervised by Kuznets and Dorothy Swaine Thomas, a distinguished sociologist and demographer at Penn. Easterlin's contribution to this project led to a paper on regional economies (1960) for the 1957 Williamstown NBER–EHA conference, where he showed that the antebellum South was a dynamic part of the US economy. His results complemented the slavery paper of Conrad and Meyer in drawing attention to the sorts of revisionist answers being produced by the earliest cliometricians. By broadening his horizons Easterlin has shaken off the tastes "inculcated" in graduate economics training. Under the influence of Dorothy Thomas he mastered demography, in which he has become as well known as in economic history. Likewise, he has expanded his knowledge of, and respect for, political science and social psychology and has integrated them into his work. His important contributions include *Population, Labor Force, and Long Swings in Economic Growth* (NBER 1968), *Birth and Fortune* (Basic Books 1980); *The Fertility Revolution* (1985) was written with his wife, the demographer Eileen Crimmins. In his Presidential address to the Economic History Association he asked, "Why isn't the whole world developed?" (1981), a question engaged by many other economic historians in the years since. Recently he has pointed to the importance of "public entrepreneurship" in the health and sanitation initiatives that played a major role in the nineteenth-century "mortality revolution," questioning the devotion to the free market economy of (some of) his colleagues, economists and cliometricians alike. For Easterlin's fruitful transgressions beyond disciplinary boundaries, the sociologist Charles Tilly would prefer to call him, not the reluctant, but "the Thoughtful Economist." On his own philosophy, Easterlin concludes, "it is good to be an economist; it is better to be a social scientist."[7]

Robert Gallman also forged himself as a Kuznetsian historical economist with his dissertation "Value-added by agriculture, mining, and manufacturing in the United States, 1840–1880" (1956), and with his first conference presentation (at the 1957 Williamstown meetings), the related paper on "Commodity output, 1839–1899" (1960). Not quite two decades later, as President of the EHA in 1976, he stood before a not entirely different group, instructing his audience in an area he thought too often ignored by economic historians, the "New Social History." In that address he appealed to his colleagues for multidisciplinarity and a more cosmopolitan outlook. But before the pedagogy and the appeal, Gallman mused on the roads he had traveled: "Certainly I have journeyed often and long with as fine a collection of affable and intelligent eccentrics as I thought the world possessed and can report that there is considerable

7 See Easterlin (2004: Chs 6, 7); Tilly is quoted in the 2006 paperbound edition of that book; the final quotation is from Easterlin (1997: 20).

entertainment value in being an economic historian and thus having to consort with economic historians. Educational value as well" (1977: 3). To that point, and for the next 20 years, his friends, colleagues and students could say no less of him, for his careful scholarship, for his generosity as colleague and teacher, and for the clarity and elegance of his expression. Gallman's work on American commodity output, his estimates of US GNP for 1834–1909 (1966) and his later discussions of American nineteenth-century growth (1980; 2000) are basic to our knowledge. Thomas Weiss and Donald Schaefer observe, "No study of the pace and pattern of American economic growth . . . can proceed without making use of Gallman's research" (1994: *v*). Gallman was a highly productive collaborator, with William Parker in assembling and analyzing the Parker–Gallman Census sample, and with Lance Davis in their considerable body of joint work. As co-author and editor, he also forged a partnership with Stanley Engerman, notably in their supervision of *The Cambridge Economic History of the United States* (Engerman & Gallman eds 1996; 2000). As a teacher he was gently demanding and challenging, "showing a quiet but genuine enthusiasm for the material," as Thomas Weiss (1998) recalls, and "none [was] more deserving" of the Hughes Teaching Prize of the EHA, awarded to Robert Gallman in 1998.

In 1954 Kuznets moved from Penn to Johns Hopkins and soon met several more people who would become "new economic historians."[8] Lance Davis was then a Hopkins graduate student; Douglass North and Kenneth Buckley made a pilgrimage to Baltimore in 1956 to consult with Kuznets, coming from New York where they were associates at the NBER (Gallman interview & 1994: 24). Not long thereafter Robert Fogel and Stanley Engerman became students at Hopkins and were deeply influenced by Simon Kuznets's immense knowledge and scholarly values.

When Robert Fogel's "great bear of a form" (Doug North's words) appeared at the inaugural Purdue seminar in December, 1960, he had already published his first book, on the Union Pacific Railroad and, inspired by a point in one of Kuznets's lectures, he was working on his second.[9] Fogel is not only physically but also intellectually imposing, and without peer in debate. He had entered graduate school in 1956, following nearly a decade of Leftist labor and community organizing, and had shifted his allegiance to what would soon be seen as a revolutionary approach to historical research. His paper at Purdue was called "The social savings attributable to American railroads in the interregional distribution of agricultural products in 1890: an application of mathematical models to a problem of history." Although Fogel brought "econometric history" to the small assemblage at Purdue, Jon Hughes says "It was not the econometrics that impressed us, but the great patience and care involved in the historical research that lay behind Fogel's numbers" (1971: 407). That paper became part of Fogel's Ph.D. thesis, published in 1964 as *Railroads and American Economic Growth: Essays in Econometric History*. A startling demonstration of the relatively small impact on US growth of this major innovation, the book helped to spark a long-running debate about "counterfactual"

8 In 1960 Kuznets moved to Harvard. Until his retirement in 1971 he taught economic growth and development and supervised 15 Ph.D. dissertations, including a few on historical topics.

9 For biographical detail, we draw on Fogel (1994b, 1996). For other points not quoted directly we rely on Engerman (1992), McCloskey (1992b), Gallman (1994), and Genovese (1994).

analysis in history. The thesis was first in a series of projects in which Fogel has applied, refined and extended the "art of measurement" he learned from Simon Kuznets. In later work on American slavery, much written with Stanley Engerman, and on the history of human mortality and physical well-being, he has posed important problems, and has sought and found masses of data to clarify the questions and propose their answers. He says, ". . . the major obstacle to the resolution of [most issues in history and economics] . . . is the absence of data rather than the absence of analytical ingenuity or credible theories" (quoted, McCloskey 1992b: 22).

Fogel's and Engerman's book on slavery, *Time on the Cross* (1974), generated considerable public controversy, but with an ultimately productive outcome. They made all their data available, even to their harshest critics. About their subsequent treatment of slavery, Eugene Genovese says, "They refined their calculations and defended the essentials of their scientific work, but also took to heart a broad spectrum of criticism that transcended the technical problems . . . In *Without Consent or Contract* . . . [Fogel] wrote a splendid work of integrated history that gave economics its full due without succumbing to economic determinism." The later work, as Gallman sees it, was possible because of "a fundamental feature of Bob [Fogel's] personality and character. He has, in a sense, grasped us all by our shirt fronts and made us think about and debate the issues in which he was interested . . . he always finds ways of drawing worthy opponents into serious exchanges with him."[10] The ensuing mortality project – derived, as Fogel relates in his interview, from some of the work on slavery – is less controversial (perhaps) and has enlisted the collaboration of students and colleagues from many fields. Throughout his scholarly career Fogel has adhered to a belief that a scientific approach to history can unearth historical questions of enduring significance and begin to reveal their answers.[11]

Stanley Engerman's reputation as an economic historian of the first order would be secure even without the many publications that bear his name as author or co-author, on the American iron industry, on slavery, on living standards worldwide, on British income distribution or foreign trade, or on factor endowments, institutions and economic development. In a field where leading scholars are notable for providing ample advice and encouragement to colleagues and students, Stanley Engerman stands out. He is renowned for the breadth and depth of commentary he supplies to all who seek his assistance. His office and home in Rochester have "functioned as a crossroads and clearinghouse" for many "new ideas" and for many scholars. Much of their subsequent work has passed again through the Engerman filter, receiving "informed and, above all, generous advice and, more specifically, a bundle of new references that its author had missed."[12] There are scores – even hundreds – of articles, chapters and books which acknowledge his help, merely intimating his deep influence in improving the quality of published work in economics and history. Likewise, Stanley Engerman has been collaborator and intellectual companion *extraordinaire*, having written or edited with 30 other scholars.

10 Genovese (1994: 17) and Gallman (1994: 25). Although the summary volume of *Without Consent or Contract* has a single author (Fogel 1989a), it is dedicated in part to Stanley Engerman.

11 For appreciations of Fogel's work see McCloskey (1994) and Eichengreen (1994).

12 Quoted phrases from introduction to Eltis *et al.*, eds (2004: *viii*).

Within his extensive interests, Engerman for decades has been a premier historian of slavery and more generally of systems of coerced and free labor, ancient and modern. Particularly during the *contretemps* over *Time on the Cross*, he has been involved in scholarly dispute to an unusual degree, but remains dispassionate about such controversy: ". . . the questions raised in debate, even in disagreement, were ones that could (and should) be studied and examined, and . . . it was only by these steps that scholarly knowledge could be advanced" (1992: 13). In his Presidential address to the EHA in 1985, "Slavery and emancipation in comparative perspective," Engerman stressed the lessons one can learn from wide-ranging study of the history of labor institutions: "One point that emerges is the conflict that seemed to belie any easy, universal equations among moral, social, and economic progress . . . for many of the broader concerns of economic historians we can get only so far without a consideration of political, cultural, and ideological factors and, correspondingly, for many of the broader issues of political, cultural, and intellectual history, there remains a major contribution to be made by the study of economic history . . . That is, there is much to be gained by regarding different approaches and methods as complements, rather than to see them only as substitutes" (1986: 339).

The National Bureau has for many years encouraged the variety of work favored by Engerman through its program in "The Development of the American Economy." In 1978 Martin Feldstein, the Bureau's new Director, invited Robert Fogel to initiate the program. The DAE has fostered and disseminated a substantial proportion of the cliometric research on the US and international economies undertaken in the past three decades. Thus it has been home to the revival of a research effort focused on economic growth first proposed in the 1940s by Moses Abramovitz and Simon Kuznets.

RICHARD A. EASTERLIN

Interviewed by
Kenneth L. Sokoloff

Richard Ainley Easterlin is University Professor and Professor of Economics at the University of Southern California, where he has taught since 1982. He was born in 1926 in Ridgefield Park, New Jersey and was educated in mechanical engineering at the Stevens Institute of Technology (M.E., 1945) and in economics at the University of Pennsylvania (A.M., 1949; Ph.D., 1953). He taught at Penn from 1948 to 1982, first as an instructor and in his final four years as William R. Kenan, Jr. Professor of Economics; he was also a Research Associate of the National Bureau of Economic Research (1956–66). In keeping with his wide range of interests, he has been President of the Population Association of America (1977–8) and of the Economic History Association (1979–80), and has since the 1960s served on editorial or advisory boards of multiple journals in economics, economic history and demography. He was elected Fellow of The American Academy of Arts & Sciences in 1978, Member of the National Academy of Sciences in 2002, and was named Distinguished Fellow of the American Economic Association for 2006. The interview took place in the autumn of 1992 at USC, with a few additional responses elicited in early 1993. The interviewer was the late Kenneth Sokoloff of the University of California-Los Angeles, who writes:

With three of the last four Cole Prizes for best article in the *JEH* having been awarded to members of its community, Southern California definitely has come of age as a center for economic history. Lance Davis and Richard Easterlin preside over the local economic history group, and the two close friends are enthusiastic boosters of life in this part of the world. Both are deeply serious about scholarship, applying high standards to their own work as well as to that of others. They differ dramatically, however, in personal style. Lance is intense and social, empathetically drawing from strangers the intimate details of their data and their love lives. With Lance, what you see is what you get. Dick maintains more distance, makes every word count, and exercises quiet charm and dry wit. There is always an air of mystery about him. I have long admired Dick for the originality of his ideas and the fundamental importance of the issues he tackles. Despite his interests having shifted to other fields in recent years, he still matches Bob Fogel, another student of Simon Kuznets, in having the greatest number of individual items on my undergraduate reading list in the American economic history course.

As a scholar who began his career studying the process of economic growth with Simon Kuznets, what observations would you make about the recent [1991–2] slowdown in US economic growth? Are we in the midst of a cycle, or has there been a change in the secular trend?

Well, I think I'm more optimistic than many currently are. I think you want to distinguish the secular forces at work from the cyclical. The moving force behind long-term economic growth is productivity growth. Behind that is technological change, and behind technological change is basically the advancement of scientific knowledge – primarily natural sciences knowledge but also certain types of business knowledge like organizational techniques. So if we go back to the level of basic science, I don't see that our potential has leveled off. I see basic science as continuing to expand, and by implication our technological potential is continuing to expand over the long term. Looking 30 years down the road, I expect we'll see an economy in which productivity expands at rates commensurate with the long-term rate we have observed in historical experience.

Turning to the question of swings, we know that in the past there have been long-term swings in productivity growth connected with aggregate demand movements. I think we are still experiencing something of the same sort. In the past two decades we have obviously had a substantial retreat from the post-World War II policy of stimulating long-term growth of aggregate demand via monetary and fiscal policy, and connected with this we have had a decline of productivity growth. At the same time, there have been major changes of an adverse nature in the international economy. The OPEC changes, the shift from fixed to fluctuating exchange rates, reduced international cooperation – all of these have combined to produce a more adverse environment for economic growth. But I don't anticipate that the bulk of these developments will persist.

What government policies, if any, do you think would be desirable?

I am sympathetic to policies of the traditional sort to maintain economic stability and a high growth of aggregate demand – that is, a combination of monetary and fiscal policy that will promote high employment. I think international economic cooperation in the state of the world today is an essential prerequisite of rapid economic growth. And I think a desirable emphasis is on policies that promote investment and education as opposed to consumption, coupled with a reduction in military spending.

There has been increasing concern recently about a shift in the distribution

of income in the US and to a lesser extent in other industrial countries, perhaps driven by changes in international environment or technology. Do you have any strong feelings about these recent developments – whether they are permanent or transitory, or whether there might be policy changes capable of offsetting these trends?

Again, I think this is a temporary rather than a lasting phenomenon. Most of the work I am familiar with suggests that it's connected with technological developments, probably things like computerization, that have raised the relative demand for more educated workers and increased the wage differential by level of education. The international argument has to do with the adverse impact of international competition on the manufacturing sector, and the evidence, at least for the US, doesn't seem so persuasive for that hypothesis.

The movement in wage differentials by level of education is ultimately a function both of supply and demand developments, and I think experience suggests that the supply of young persons responds to earnings differentials, or at least to awareness of job opportunities if not earnings differentials *per se*. (The exact mechanism is debatable.) And so I anticipate that supply-side changes are going to operate to reduce the wage differential substantially, as has occurred in the past when we have had disproportionately big influxes of college graduates. So I don't see that development as a long-term one.

The other element in the picture, it seems to me, has to do with the relative supply of young persons in the labor force. Young persons are typically low-income people, and the age distribution is going to be changing in a way that will have a favorable impact on the income distribution. We are moving into a period where the baby bust cohorts are coming into the labor market, and that's going to reverse the labor market conditions that existed for the baby boomers. We're going to find shortages of younger, less-experienced workers, and that's also going to contribute to lessening relative wage differences, in this case among age groups.

If I read your hypothesis correctly, you also predict rising fertility and perhaps fewer two-income families from the baby bust generation. Do you think that's happening or are there other factors?

Well, fertility is definitely moving upward, from about 1986, 1987 to about 1990, 1991. Certainly the recession [1991] has set it back, but my basic reason for expecting those developments to materialize or resume is that the size of the young cohorts reaching the family-forming age is continuing to decline and will decline through this decade. So, assuming we get this economy going again, my expectation is that in the next few years we should see resumption of these developments. I don't anticipate a decline in two-worker families but a leveling off in the phenomenon among younger adults, rather than the continued uptrend that has been occurring.

You and Eileen Crimmins have recently been working on value formation

among American youth. In particular, what accounted for the rise in materialism and corresponding decline in social consciousness during the 1970s and 1980s? My understanding is that your explanation is focused on unmet economic expectations on the parts of their parents, due both to cohort size considerations and to a slowdown in economic growth. Since economic growth has continued to be slow and a variety of factors seems to be driving a widening of income distribution, how confident are you of a return to less emphasis on material success? Do you think that changes in values have an independent effect on growth?

As far as income distribution is concerned, as I've just indicated, I don't see that as a persistent secular problem. It's a serious problem, but not a persistent secular one. Again, I want to distinguish in my answer between long-term secular trends in relation to values and shorter-term movements. I think over the longer term values do exert an independent effect on economic growth, and that's the sort of thing I talked about to some extent in my Presidential address because I think education can influence aspirations. It has the effect of developing rational attitudes and producing a set of values more commensurate with the attainment of long-term economic growth. I think the evidence from studies done by sociologists like Alex Inkeles is consistent with the notion that there is an independent impact of values on economic growth.

With regard to fluctuations in values, our work, based on data since the 1960s, has stressed that there is some evidence of swings which occur between more purely materialistic goals of making money and public interest values – the importance of helping others, racial integration, greater equality, environmental concerns, and so on. It's very clear that from, say, around 1973 to about the late 1980s there was a substantial shift toward private materialism and away from the public goals, as far as youth were concerned, and I think also for the adult population. It's less clear how much this has persisted in the last few years, although obviously there has not been a substantial swing back. Our explanation for the value shift is that basically it's a reflection of the slowdown in economic growth, which has left a shortfall between aspirations and the realization of desires. The result has been to make adults more concerned about making a living and passing that sort of emphasis on to their offspring. With the resumption of a more normal rate of productivity growth, I feel that there will be a swing back towards public concerns. So I see education and its impact on values as having a substantial independent long-term secular effect on economic growth, but I see the swing back and forth as being induced by changes in the state of the economy as productivity advances and slows.

What are your thoughts about the outlook for fertility and the stability of the family in our society, or industrialized societies, more generally?

Well, the theme of what I say always seems to be secular versus cyclical. From the secular point of view, I don't see evidence of a decline in the nuclear family as a value. When you look at the concerns and goals that young people express in surveys running back over the past two decades or so, the persistence of the notion of forming a nuclear family, staying with one spouse, and of having at least two children, prevails in 80 percent to 90 percent of the population. These are the people who will be in the family formation ages over the next 30 years. So I think the notion that the family is in decline is not really supported by the evidence. Turning to the cyclical aspect, it's very clear, however, that the ability of young people to realize their aspirations has been adversely affected as the baby boom generation has come of age. The baby boom generation has been under severe labor market pressure by virtue of its size as well as from adverse changes in aggregate demand conditions. As a result, baby boomers made a lot of adaptations to economic circumstances by postponing marriage, postponing childbearing, and increasing mother's labor force participation while they had pre-school children. But the boomers are going to be succeeded now by the oncoming baby bust generation and I think there will be a reversal of these conditions and a return to less problematic family circumstances.

Sam Preston, a former colleague of yours, has made a great deal of increasing numbers of births outside marriage in European societies as well as in the US. Would your analysis of European cases be similar to that for the US?

Yes, if you look at the demographic history of the developed European countries – the leading ones in the northwestern and central sectors of Europe (the ones that went through the demographic transition by the 1930s) – the pattern is very similar to the US. They had very low fertility in the 1930s, then they had a post-World War II baby boom, and since around 1960 they have had a baby bust. So in all these countries there was a young adult generation after World War II that was relatively small in size, followed by a young adult generation that was relatively large, and now a new generation that will be relatively small. So I see this phenomenon as occurring fairly commonly across the spectrum of countries, though with individual variations. Since the mid-1980s fertility has moved upward in the US and these European countries. For some the increase is negligible, but for others it is very sizable. And the US is one with a sizable increase. The Census Bureau projections published in 1989 based on data through 1987 were already below actual fertility in 1989. In 1990 and 1991, even though 1991 was a recession year, the actual number of births in the US was above the high projection of the Census, and was 12 percent above the middle projection, the one that everyone adopts for long-term projections. So I think recent evidence is favorable to the hypothesis that fertility will go up.

Given the pattern of fertility across income class and the widening distribution of income we discussed, do you think the evidence is consistent with the hypothesis?

Well, we don't have the evidence yet on recent fertility by income class. We do know that fertility seems to be edging up among people in their 20s. Now, whether that's true of those at the lower end of the income distribution, we just don't know. Heretofore swings in fertility have been widely diffused among all income classes, education groups, and racial and ethnic groups. It would be unusual if any new sizable upswing were not participated in by every group. But of course the recent growth in income inequality may mean less participation by the low income group – we'll see.

Probably because of slow economic growth, there is increasing concern about immigration into the United States. Would you favor any change in immigration policy?

No, I think the existing policies are satisfactory. If you compare rates of immigration – that is, immigration in relation to the size of the adult labor force – we are considerably below the rates of immigration that we had back before World War I. I don't see present rates as a serious negative in the picture. I think the concern arises when the economy slows down and, as a result, all sorts of anti-immigration and anti-free trade types of attitudes are fomented.

Some observers would claim that despite their high material welfare, the populations of western countries have become an increasingly surly lot, with many segments of those populations preoccupied with their relative rather than absolute position. Is this your take on the current situation? If you were writing an addendum to "Does Economic Growth Improve the Human Lot?" what would you say?[1]

As I suggested earlier, what we are observing is, I believe, a phenomenon linked to the slowing of economic growth and the disappointed aspirations this has produced in the population at large. If I were writing an addendum to that article, I don't think I'd change anything. I think the basic idea is still correct. Put simply, it is an extension of the idea that you have to deflate the money value of national product to get real national product. If, in addition, you want to evaluate happiness, then you have to deflate real national product by aspirations, which are themselves a function of real national product. So aspirations are going up commensurately with real national product, leaving happiness unchanged over the long run.

Has relative happiness declined for the people of less-developed countries as they have become more aware of conditions in the developed countries?

No. I think that material aspirations that people form are a function of the living conditions they experience in their own country as they age. Indians, in India, are exposed through numerous movies to the consumption levels that prevail in the United States. But they don't identify with what they observe on the screen. And so when they are asked about what they need to make themselves perfectly happy, it's not a Mercedes – it's a transistor radio or something that is a realistic element of their own experience.

1 A series of addenda includes Easterlin (2001) and (2006).

Some of your recent work [published 1995] has dealt with long-term projected population change in industrialized countries. Is the prospect as dismal as some suggest? I gather, probably not.

Correct. I think this is a good example of how important it is to look at historical experience. The arguments about the dire implications of population change in developed countries have to do with the adverse effect of dependency on productivity growth as the population ages. Also, to some extent, with slowing growth of aggregate demand connected with slower population growth. As I have already indicated, I think that projections based upon persistent low fertility are highly dubious. But even if one accepts projections of low fertility, they compare prospective dependency 60 or 70 years down the road with conditions at the present time or, at best, with conditions in the last couple of decades rather than with past periods of comparable length, let alone longer periods. If you take a longer historical perspective, say over the past century, the kinds of dependency burdens we are looking at are not out of line with historical experience in any of the countries. Moreover, there is a caricature of the aged that has presented them as low-educated or illiterate people. But the aged who are now coming along are typically people who are much better educated than the aged used to be. They are people who, in many cases, have completed secondary school or higher and compared with the past the differentials in education from the young are small. One issue of some relevance is whether the tax burden will be disproportionately great as the population ages. OECD projections, however, suggest that very modest rates of growth of real wages would result in no increase in the tax burden. By modest, I mean 0.5 percent per year.

How about environmental stress? Does that concern you?

Well, I think environmental issues are serious in certain areas – much more serious in third world areas than in developed areas that are more attentive to them and can afford to be more attentive to them. But the critical environmental problems have to do not with the fact that there are more people, but that there are people able to afford goods like automobiles. It is modern technology that creates the environmental problem, not population growth.

To my knowledge Simon Kuznets did not outline any systematic patterns of how political development progressed with economic growth. Should his followers be working on such patterns? If so, what issues should they focus on?

Well, Kuznets did try to look a little bit at political conditions, but his major work was on economic growth. The data that he used were purely cross-sectional and fairly rudimentary. I think it was the lack of time series evidence that was responsible for his not pushing that line of inquiry. In contrast, the availability of so much demographic data led to that being the line of research that he pursued more intensively himself. Certainly the linkage between political and economic change is a key matter. I think that one way to look at it more intensively is to focus on the role of developments in universal education and how those are connected with political change in a society. And there has been a recent growth in political science research of a quantitative nature that's generated a lot of historical evidence, as well as in quantitative research on education. However, exploring links between economic growth and political change via education may be asking too much of economic historians.

Speaking again of Kuznets . . . how did you become an economic historian?

It was Kuznets's influence in a couple of ways. Partly, he introduced me to economic history and economic development, and Bob Gallman and I were classmates in Kuznets's courses.

You just went to Penn and found Kuznets – you hadn't gone because he was there?

No, no. But, clearly, he was a towering intellect, and all the students were somewhat in awe of him. I think I was interested . . . most people who end up in economic history start with some sort of predilection toward the study of history and so, you know, Kuznets's approach fits in. Also, for part of my thesis, he had me read a lot of the earlier literature of the British economic historians, the German historical school and more, so that, I think, served as additional fuel to stimulate my interest.

He certainly has had a big influence – not just in his own work, but on the economic historians – you, and Gallman, and Schmookler . . . Was there a seminar at Penn?

No. Kuznets gave two courses and supervised theses. One course was in statistics and one was a course he called "Economic Development." A lot of that course was really traditional economic history, going back and reading people like Usher. I read his proposals for the study of economic growth when he was trying to get the National Bureau to develop a program in this area, which involved the systematic measurement of national income over long periods of time and a variety of things, and I think that was of considerable appeal to somebody who was coming from economics as I was, because it was a little bit like he was doing what the German historical school aspired to do, namely, comparative economic history. But he had put his finger on a quantitative technique that provided for a much more systematic study than the German historical school had worked out.

So he was one of the fathers of cliometrics, then?

Well, I would say, definitely, from the point of view of quite a few of us who were involved.

What in your view have been the most important advances in knowledge in economic history? The most serious shortcomings?

By far, the most significant advance has been in the area of measurement. Thanks to the work of Kuznets, and many others whom he inspired, we now have quantitative records about long-term economic growth in many countries, developed and less developed. These records encompass not only overall rates of growth, but allocation of resources, distribution of income, and international relationships. Compared with what was available when I studied economic history in graduate school, a vast void has been filled, increasing our knowledge of the facts of economic growth as well as our ability to test hypotheses and generalizations.

The shortcomings stem, it seems to me, from a tension in the field of economic history that has prevailed throughout my career, a tension of the following sort. On the one hand, there is a set of questions that were traditionally the focus of concern in economic history, questions set very largely by people who came from the discipline of history. Then, starting with the emergence of economic development as a field in economics after World War II, a new set of questions arose, put by economists like Simon Kuznets. These had to do with the sources and measurement of technological change, and its role in raising productivity growth, with population growth, with capital accumulation, with education, in short, with an application of the economist's production function framework.

Unfortunately, much of economic history since its takeover by economists has continued to focus on the first rather than second type of question. Take the subject of technology, one dear to your own heart. If we go back to Schmookler's work with US patent data, almost nobody did anything further with those data for the next two or three decades. And yet here is something that would really provide insight into the way technology spread and grew in our society – quantitative insight.

I think education is another example. The number of economic historians who have done serious quantitative research on education is very limited. To my mind some of the fundamental questions of economic growth have to do with technology and education. So from my point of view, many important issues in economic history have shown relatively little progress. One might, perhaps, point to recent work on institutional change as a hopeful sign – certainly I feel that way. But even those interested in institutions tend not to look at education, a most fundamental institution. In addition, one could hope for more attention to quantification in the study of institutions.

The development approach to economic history leads to a concern with the worldwide experience of economic change. This contrasts again with the traditional emphasis in economic history which has been on the national experience of a handful of Western countries, plus Japan and Russia. We need to know more about how development in Western countries had an effect on the developing ones – a few people like Lance Davis and Bob Hanson have done important work in this respect. But the history of international trade, migration, and capital flows is viewed by most economic historians as at the margin of the subject. We also need to know much more about historical experience of developing countries. Indeed, they currently provide a laboratory to observe the process of economic growth, and most economic historians are not taking advantage of this opportunity.

To sum up, I feel we have made enormous progress on the facts of economic growth. When it comes to improving understanding of economic growth, however, there needs to be more attention to questions of technological change and institutional change, including education, as well as to international relations and the experience of less-developed areas.

Technological change was already identified by the 1960s as a major contributor to modern economic growth. Have cliometricians failed to take on the challenge of explaining technological change?

Well, my answer is in two parts. When you say technological change was identified as an important factor in economic growth, I think the primary basis for that would be Solow's work, which essentially said that the main source of growth was an upward shift in the production function; he called that technological change without identifying it as technological change substantively, and a lot of work subsequent to Solow's, such as that by Denison, and to some extent by Griliches and Jorgenson, moved in the direction of diminishing the role of technological change and replacing it with things like education and economies of scale. So, in the substantive sense of major inventions and patenting, I don't think that there had been acceptance of the importance of technological change. And, I think the cliometricians were not particularly attuned to that.

Since we're talking about cliometrics, my first participation was in 1961 at the second meeting, as a reviewer of Doug North's new book (the name of which I now forget because he's written lots since then, much to the benefit of the profession). The thesis of that book (1961) was essentially the staple thesis of Harold Innis, that international trade was the great genesis of economic growth. In my review at the meetings and in my review published in the *Journal of Economic History* (1962), I argued that I thought that was wrong, that the critical basis for understanding American economic growth was the transfer of technology from Great Britain and the indigenous development of technology in the United States and its interplay with the high level of education in the United States, compared to other areas. To judge from the small amount of subsequent work on such topics, I don't think that line of reasoning had any widespread acceptance among the cliometricians. The tendency was to focus on shorter-term factors rather than substantive technology.

How did Rostow and Habakkuk influence cliometricians' approach to growth?

Well, you know, it's a little hard to go back and recreate the circumstances of the time.

Let's take Rostow first. Rostow basically never argued about the importance of the transfer of technology. His emphasis in the take-off was a rise in the savings rate. So I think his argument was more consistent with a traditional emphasis like Harrod–Domar models, rather than looking at concrete technological change. Habakkuk, on the other hand, was certainly much more attuned to the importance of technological change, and interested in the issue of transfer of technology and the role that factor prices played in that. His work was, in my view, moving in the right direction. But very little was done among the cliometricians to pursue that; maybe Paul David was an early exception when he, as I recall, did an analysis of the introduction of the reaper. Among the American cliometricians, I felt that there was very little attention to technological change, in terms of trying to do a systematic study of it quantitatively. I remember I thought another interesting line of work was by a Swedish geographer, Torsten Hägerstrand (1967), who was studying the diffusion of technology, quantitatively. I set up a session at the 1965 International Economic History conference in Munich; what he had to say there seemed to fall on deaf ears. So I was discouraged with the kinds of things cliometricians tended to focus on, which ignored the central role of technological growth and transfer.

Do you think that's changing now?

Yes, moderately, but not a great deal. I certainly think that your own work is on exactly the kind of thing that I'm interested in (*e.g.*, Sokoloff 1988), and Nate Rosenberg was of course the exception. But Nate, as you know, never did things quantitatively, and I think that made his work not very amenable to cliometric approaches. Although there has been greater attention to technological change, for Clio I still feel it's pretty minimal. Let me add that Ed Mansfield's work in economics is another example of relevant analysis of technological change, and Dick Nelson's work and to some extent, Zvi Griliches' work: I just attended a conference in Nate's honor a couple of months ago at Stanford, and the papers there represent a major advance over the state of research on technology of 20 or 30 years ago (see Mowery *et al.*, eds 1994). But I didn't see the economic historians very well represented there.

Given the record of economic historians, are you surprised at the importance of economic history within economics departments – within the discipline of economics?

It's a little hard to say. I would like to think that if economic historians had paid more attention to these concerns – if, for example, productivity change and its substantive interplay with technology and scientific development had been a more central concern of the discipline – that economics departments would feel that economic historians have a lot more to say that is relevant to today's circumstances. But it's also true that many economists tend to have a black box view of technological change and are much more preoccupied with short-term issues.

Would you say there is more of a short-term orientation in the younger

generation of scholars in economics and economic history compared to your generation?

No, I wouldn't say that. I hesitate to generalize about how one generation compares with the next. But it seems to me there are younger economic historians who are working on more important problems. But there is valuable new work going on, on technological change, on education, on international economic relations. So I would hesitate to generalize about the merits of research in the current generation versus the last. I'd like to see more of the current generation working on the problems I've talked about and with a broader perspective. But there weren't a lot of people who ever did that.

We may have passed sort of a local peak with respect to attention to technique over the substance, or to technical aspects as opposed to the substance – where do you think the discipline stands in this regard? Have we gone too far, at least this time, in emphasizing technical purity?

I guess what concerns me is the lack of attention to data versus technique. Much of the discipline of demography involves techniques for evaluating data, for improving comparability and continuity, and so on. I see no counterpart to this in economics or economic history regarding economic data.

I'm also concerned about the extent to which technique serves to establish the questions that one researches. I need hardly point out that time series analysis is in disfavor. The kinds of econometric techniques that predominate are oriented primarily toward the short-term issues on which one can get a substantial body of relevant data. The techniques are valuable for that purpose, but a lot of the analysis of historical experience involves the use of fragmentary data for which econometric techniques are not well suited – using complementary types of series to piece together the clues that you get, to see whether you can find a consistent pattern. One reason I was persuaded that long swings in economic growth were a real phenomenon was that when you look at series on production, wage rates, the composition of output, occupational change, and so on, you get a very consistent pattern. In terms of economic analysis, this pattern told a plausible story about what was going on. It seems to me that today there are often historical studies where one gets a one-shot body of cross-sectional data and runs regressions on it, without much insight regarding historical change. The preoccupation with econometrics tends to predispose work in that direction. I do think that technique is becoming more a matter of routine, and there is more interest in substantive concerns. But it still remains the case that sometimes technique prevails, and important questions are left unresearched.

One last question which is, I suppose, of personal interest. How would you say that the life and experience of someone in the university, of an academic, has changed over the years?

Well, it's very much a generational phenomenon. My generation was a small cohort and had the advantage of being in academia when it was expanding very rapidly during the 1950s and 1960s. There was a scarcity of faculty, research money was readily available, and there was no serious competition. That situation has clearly turned around both on the supply and demand sides. I see today's young faculty as being under much more pressure than our generation to get funding and to publish. I don't feel that it's a very desirable thing. It forces people to work on the current fad and on what will lead to quick publication. I don't see any solution to that until people get their tenure and by then, they may be so committed to a certain line of work that they're not going to turn to more basic research. I wish I had a solution to this problem, but I don't.

ROBERT E. GALLMAN

Interviewed by
William K. Hutchinson

Robert Emil Gallman was Kenan Professor of Economics and History at the University of North Carolina at Chapel Hill. He was born in 1926 in Bloomfield, New Jersey and died in Chapel Hill in 1998. He was educated at Cornell University (B.A., 1948) and at the University of Pennsylvania (M.A., 1949; Ph.D., 1956). Before moving to UNC in 1962 he taught at The Ohio State University (1954–1962); he held visiting positions at several other institutions, including a fellowship at Nuffield College, Oxford (1972–3). He was President of the Economic History Association (1976) and of the Southern Economic Association (1978). A conference held in his honor in 1990 resulted in a *Festschrift* edited by Thomas Weiss and Donald Schaefer, *American Economic Development in Historical Perspective* (Stanford, 1994). In 1998 he was awarded the EHA's Hughes Prize for excellence in teaching economic history. Gallman's interlocutor for this "interview" was WILLIAM HUTCHINSON who, over the course of a visiting year at UNC in 1990–1, discussed with Gallman a variety of issues and questions. Bob Gallman responded to Bill in the form of a letter, which we reproduce as his interview. Hutchinson adds:

Bob Gallman is the kindest and one of the most helpful people I have ever met. Most conversations with Bob are peppered with stories that he relates with great care and detail, usually ending with a surprise or impact that was not totally expected by the listener. These stories are often drawn from the vast stock of mystery novels that Bob has read. Having previously read his work, I first met Bob at the joint EHA and World Congress of Economic History meetings at Bloomington, Indiana in September of 1968. (For many cliometricians, that conference generated its share of interesting tales.) That was the first of many times that Bob's encouragement would serve as an incentive for me in my own work. In his letter Bob relates many situations where he has either collaborated with others or enabled them to generate first-rate research of their own.

His extensive service in a variety of editorial capacities is further evidence of his willingness to assist other scholars in their efforts.

Dear Bill,

Instead of an interview, how about a letter dealing with some of the issues you mention in your list of questions? Jon Hughes wrote many of us a number of years ago and said we should set down our recollections of the early days of cliometrics, before all that history was lost. That is the plan I propose to follow.

As everyone has said, there were three events that got cliometrics going: the joint meetings of EHA and the Conference on Research in Income and Wealth (Williamstown and Chapel Hill), on the one hand, and the early Purdue sessions of the Seminar on the Application of Economic Theory and Quantitative Methods to the Study of [Problems of] Economic History. I was lucky enough to be present at all three. The Williamstown meeting came first – fall of 1957 – and I got advance word of it by way of an invitation from Raymond Goldsmith to do a paper. Raymond was chairman of the Income and Wealth Executive Committee at the time. It may be that he was one of the moving spirits for Williamstown – certainly he always had an interest in historical topics and was the first person to propose the [1963] Chapel Hill meeting, to my knowledge. He was an encouraging, open-minded kind of man, in my dealings with him. He must have got my name from Simon Kuznets, or perhaps from Raymond Bowman, who was also on the executive committee and whom I knew when I was a graduate student at Penn.

I agreed to do the paper, and the next thing I knew one William N. Parker descended on me.[1] I was then at Ohio State and Parker turned up, partly to visit his family in Columbus and partly to work out something about the sessions with me. There comes to my mind as I think of this meeting – and many other meetings with Bill – a line from an old scat song: "scheming schemes and dreaming dreams." That seemed to be what we were always up to.

In 1956 I went off for a year to visit at Hopkins, where I met three other cliometricians. The first was Lance Davis. I described that meeting in my introduction to Lance's presidential address to the EHA. Lance was part of a group discussing the Democratic Presidential Convention, which was then in progress. The discussion displeased Lance, who after bearing up in silence for some time, finally spoke. I did not know Lance at that point and he was not addressing me, but his performance had a big effect on me, anyway. Here's a piece of that description.

His speech was decisive and authoritative; it demolished all previously expressed

1 The paper is Gallman (1960). As with Lance Davis's interview, the references section lists only those works specified by (year).

> opinions; it was brief and energetic; it was delivered at a scarcely credible speed. What it reminded me of most was a burst from a sub-machine gun. I was tempted to look at my chest to see if his words were spelled out there in bullet holes.

Lance was in Baltimore for part of the summer and then returned to Purdue. The next cliometricians to turn up were Doug North and Ken Buckley, who came down from New York to talk with Kuznets about their research. Simon asked me to sit in. North, Buckley, and Dick Easterlin were visiting at the National Bureau in New York that year, and Dick had filled me in on Ken and Doug and what they were up to and the adventure of putting in time with them. Doug was then writing his first book, and Ken was working his way into the population data for Quebec. Both were interested in long swings. Doug spoke first and in standard Doug style. In a minute or two the enthusiasm had filled the room, about up to our necks, and we were in danger of floating up to the ceiling. Kuznets was charmed. Now it was Buckley's turn. He gulped once or twice and then started off in the most modest, shyest manner one could imagine. This was not what I had expected of him, or what, on other meetings, he delivered. He was a dashing fellow. But meeting Kuznets seemed to have completely unnerved him. Or maybe it was the prospect of trying to get anyone to pay attention to him, after Doug had had the floor for half an hour.

You ask how the cliometric approach sat with my more traditional colleagues in economics and history. The exchanges at Williamstown between Conrad and Meyer, on the one hand, and the discussant of their slavery paper, Douglas Dowd, on the other, have fixed the notion of early conflict firmly in the history of the period. My own recollection of the Williamstown and Chapel Hill meetings, however, is somewhat different. Conrad and Meyer were very young and very cocky at the time, and they infuriated Dowd, partly for ideological reasons. Dowd ranted and they grinned. The rest of the discussion of that paper, and a second on methodology, which Conrad and Meyer presented was lively, but I do not recall a general division between cliometricians and traditionalists throughout the meeting. The quantifiers were warmly welcomed by people such as Hal Williamson, that marvelous man, and I do not remember that the Income and Wealth papers upset the traditionalists in any way. Three of them gave very thoughtful and friendly reviews of these papers. But, of course, there is probably some selection bias here; those people who attended the meetings presumably had interest in the topics and lots of tolerance to begin with.

The exchanges between cliometricians and historical traditionalists were sharper in other settings, and they became sharper still after the publication of Bob Fogel's work on the railroads. I remember a meeting at Hagley – Bob was not there – at which a railroads paper was given that contained no mention of Bob's work.[2] In the discussion, I mildly asked why not, and got a reasonable response. After the session, however, a

2 "Hagley" is shorthand for the industrial museum, library and archive at Eleutherian Mills, near Wilmington, Delaware, operated by the Eleutherian Mills–Hagley Foundation.

wrathful Fritz Redlich descended on me. That madman Fogel, he said, plans to build canals across the Appalachian Mountains!

Years later I attended a *Time on the Cross* conference in South Carolina, at which Bob, who was there, and Stan, who was not, were smitten hip and thigh by all the panelists but me. I made one point: Bob has always had the knack of obliging everyone to talk about what he wants to discuss. He did it with railroads, and Stan and he did it with slavery. Those panelists had each devoted God knows how much time to sifting *TOTC* in search of errors of fact or inference. Stan and Bob got the advantage of all that criticism; they had recruited the profession as their research assistants. And now I find myself drafting, with John Wallis, an introduction to a volume that deals, among other things, with height-by-age measurements (eds, 1992). Bob Fogel has struck again.

The conflict that occurred during the early period was all between cliometricians and traditional historians. Economists had no loud complaints about us. They seemed to be pleased that economic history was making more use of theory and quantitative methods, and they were quite encouraging, when they paid any attention at all. I don't quite have that feeling now. Don McCloskey (*e.g.*, 1976) has been warning us for years that we must make our case to economics, if we are to survive, and we have been encouraged by others to draw the policy implications of what we are finding out, for the same reason. I am sure this is good advice, if we want to prosper, but it does seem to call for designing our research programs to suit the preoccupations of others, rather than our own.

In my Presidential address to the EHA I took a somewhat different tack from Don's. I pointed out the interesting work that was going on in the new social history and suggested that we read it and that we begin talking seriously to the people who were doing it. I think Don was not then happy with that advice, since he preferred that we turn toward economics, not history. But I think it was good advice (and he has certainly since followed it). I continue to be impressed by the new social history – and the new political history, the subject of Lance's Presidential address – and I find the Social Science History Association meetings lively and stimulating. I do wish that the powers that be in history would pay more attention to this work, as I wish the powers in economics paid more attention to our work. But there have been some recent movements in this direction. Stan Engerman reminds me that the findings of the new social history have made their way into the history texts. So far as economics is concerned, the revival of interest in long-term growth, such as in the work of Paul Romer, Christina Romer, and Robert Gordon, is certainly encouraging, and the recent NSF initiative with respect to environmental issues seems to represent, among other things, an opening to the economic historians.

Let me return to the beginnings of cliometrics, for a moment. The Income and Wealth meetings were certainly successful – and the one at Chapel Hill was also a lot of fun – but I do not believe that they created the *esprit de corps* that developed among cliometricians, the sense of revolutionary adventure. For one thing, those of us who did the Income and Wealth papers for volumes 24 and 30 were contributing to an existing literature and joining an established group of scholars drawn from many cohorts.[3] Measurement, after all, was not new to the Income and Wealth people – Abramovitz, Kuznets, Goldsmith, Denison, the Ruggles, Brady – or to the NBER people or to Arthur Cole or George Taylor or Tom Berry or Anne Bezanson – the scholars who had been assembling price index series. There was an audience for such work and there were people to talk with.

The creation of a special cliometrics group with a sense of identity came from the Purdue meetings. These meetings brought the young Income and Wealth types together with other young people who were doing good analytical empirical work, but were not essentially in the Income and Wealth mold. Before I went to the first Purdue meeting, I thought of myself as a development economist of a Kuznetsian variety. After a couple of Clio meetings it was clear to me that, in view of what I wanted to do by way of research, I could find a congenial home among cliometricians. There was plenty of room among them for Kuznetsian historians. Discovering that there was a group of scholars who were interested in the full range of issues that had captured my imagination and who were at work on really creative, useful research along these lines was the most exciting discovery of my scholarly career. Here were people to talk with and exchange papers with. Each year there were new people, most with good ideas. I remember distinctly the first time that Al Fishlow and Paul David came and dazzled us all, and I remember with great pleasure my first long talk with Stan Engerman, on a Lake Central plane on the way back to Chicago. Then there was Dick Easterlin – whom I had known in graduate school – administering the third degree to North, and Ed Ames and Joe Stiglitz, all of whom gave as good as they got.

Early in the game there developed the unwritten rule that one could be as frank and free in discussion as one wished, but that eventually one ought to come up with some constructive suggestions. Reputation went to those who could show how to repair a flawed paper, which is one reason why Engerman's and Fishlow's reputations are so exalted. Good constructive criticism is one of the things that made the meetings so valuable.

At Ohio State I had been teaching development, public finance, and money and banking (my graduate major, until I took Simon Kuznets's class and went through my conversion experience, was finance) and had been researching nineteenth-century US growth. When I went to Chapel Hill, I shifted over to teaching economic history and, while I continued researching the nineteenth century, took up a new piece of work in collaboration with Bill Parker. But first let me tell you that at Chapel Hill I inherited Bill's desk, which contained his grade book. The latter I looked through with wonder. Here I found that one Jones got on his mid-term a grade of B ++–+, while Smith got B–+–+. Could I be so scrupulous as that? Not likely.

Bill had been very active, indeed, during his few years at Chapel Hill – years, incidentally,

3 Volume 24 is CRIW (1960); Volume 30 is CRIW (1966).

in which he spent enough time in Washington to warrant acquiring a house there. (When I was being recruited by UNC, Bill wrote me that Chapel Hill was a great place to get some work done. How he knew that, I do not know, in view of the fact that he was so rarely there.) He had caused to be assembled in the UNC library microfilms of the manuscript censuses of agriculture, slave population, and free population for the South at mid-century. Together with a first-rate graduate student, Don Schilling, now at the University of Missouri, he drew samples from the Louisiana and Georgia agricultural schedules for 1860 and matched them to the two population schedules. The sampling and matching were done in blocks of 50 farms.

Schilling stayed on for a year or so after Bill left and worked with the sample. Bill and I then put in to NSF for a grant to create a more comprehensive sample and to analyze it. We got the grant in 1964, two years after Bill had left Chapel Hill, and I remember Bill's letter to me about it, straight from *The Child's Garden of Verses*: "The world is so full of a number of things I'm sure we should all be as happy as kings." The grant was for $55,000 or $65,000 – some mountainous sum.

The new sample was organized by Jim Foust and Dale Swan, graduate students at Chapel Hill. They decided that we could sample and match in blocks of five and get better results, which we did. The sample was to describe what we called the cotton South, and it was to represent every county in the US in 1860 that produced at least 1,000 bales of cotton. To give you an idea about that cutoff, if we had made it a little lower, we would have had to include a county in Illinois. The task of putting together that sample was onerous. I will not describe the routine of choosing counties, manuscript pages, etc. (Jim and Dale wrote up accounts of the sampling and testing processes, mimeographed copies of which are still extant.) Parts appear in Jim's dissertation and in the *Agricultural History* volume devoted chiefly to the project (Parker, ed. 1970). The people gathering the data had their heads inside microfilm readers – they couldn't read the films, otherwise – and they took down data by punching keys on an adding machine, blind. Foust worked out a system of check-totals that worked quite well. Those miserable tapes then had to be converted to computer cards, and the cards were then put on computer tape – each transition opening the opportunity for error. The computer was a Univac; it took up the whole basement of Phillips Hall and was apparently a little less powerful than the PC on which I am typing these ramblings. Foust and Swan should be memorialized – say with plaques on the wall of the current meeting room for cliometrics. They are heroes of cliometrics.

Foust went on to add a smaller sample for 1850 and to write a good dissertation on yeoman farmers in the cotton South; Swan created a very comprehensive sample for the rice counties and also wrote a first-rate dissertation based on this material. Later, Mark Schmitz and I put together samples for the Louisiana sugar regions and the parts of Kentucky and Tennessee that concentrated on the production of provisions and tobacco. Mark did a good dissertation on the basis of the sugar data, and Don Schaefer has used the Kentucky and Tennessee samples in his very exciting work on migration. Finally, Ralph Anderson did a fine dissertation on self-sufficiency, based chiefly on his research in the plantation records of the Southern collection of the UNC library. Anderson's work nicely rounded out the project on self-sufficiency, which pursued one of the major topics originally laid out in the Parker–Gallman proposal to the NSF. There were also some papers on the distribution of wealth in the South and in the rest of the country, and one by Foust and Swan on productivity. So for a while, a fair amount of work on the Southern economy went on at Chapel Hill. For me, the capstone of the project came at a joint meeting of the Agricultural History Association and the American Historical Association in New York toward the end of the 1960s. A session was devoted to the project; Bill and I were immensely flattered to find the place packed when we arrived. Our joy was dissipated some when we learned that the *Times* had published a story that day concerning threats issued against one member of the party – remember, this was the end of the 1960s and protest was the order of the day. Violence was by no means unknown. Bill and I began to wonder whether all those people had come to hear us or to see us shot. If the latter, they were disappointed. There was no violence, even between paper-givers and discussants. Bill, Stan, and I then went off to dinner with Rina Rosenberg and Bill's mother and aunt, three lively women. I remember the dinner as hilarious, although it probably did not seem so to the *maitre d'* and the other clients of the place.

You have asked about the criticisms of the sample made by Frederick Bode and Donald Ginter (1986). Bode and Ginter very kindly got in touch with me as soon as they had opened up their project and found themselves questioning our work. I talked with Bill about the matter, and he pointed out that the sample, had it been human, would have been old enough to vote at that time and he therefore thought it ought to be able to take care of itself. He proposed to stay clear of further discussion. Bill, you will remember, once said that Doug North never responded to criticism because he was too anxious to get on to his next mistake. Bill and I could be characterized in the same way, for our failure to respond formally to Bode and Ginter, but you must remember that many years had passed since we had helped build the sample and returning to those records was a little bit like exhuming a former intimate, long ago interred. I did correspond with Bode and Ginter, and I think the exchanges were very useful. Certainly, I learned from the exchanges, and I enjoyed coming to know Bode and Ginter (although we have never met in person). One could not have fairer critics.

It seemed to me initially that Bode and Ginter were setting excessively high standards for evidence. That is, they had found errors and ambiguities in the Georgia census data for 1860 and were initially inclined to write off the census as a source. I argued that all of the data used by historians are flawed in one way or another, and that we had no choice but to use these data – carefully and cautiously, of course. I think that by the end of the correspondence we were much nearer agreement than at the beginning, although I think they remained more pessimistic than I.

As to the Parker–Gallman sample, I agreed that it would be of very limited value for them, since they wanted to study land tenure, and the sample was not designed for that purpose. But it seemed to me then – and does now – that the sample had other important uses. For example, I do not think that the weaknesses that Bode and Ginter identified are important so far as the self-sufficiency studies conducted at Chapel Hill are concerned. The sample is not perfectly designed for the study of wealth-holdings; nonetheless, I believe that all of the major conclusions reached by Gavin Wright and me in our papers on this subject have held up very well indeed. And that does not surprise me at all. The sample also has served well in the efficiency studies conducted by Stan and Bob, Don and Mark, and in the very impressive work of Betsy Field.[4]

As to the matter of land tenure, I have wondered if the Georgia findings can be generalized to the rest of the South. I have not kept up with this topic and therefore do not know if a Bode–Ginter style of attack has been launched on the data for other Southern states. But at the time that I was corresponding with them I did go back to our original code sheets for the other states and looked for clues of the kinds of phenomena unearthed by Bode and Ginter in the Georgia data. I got the impression that the Georgia returns might be unique. If so, I do not know whether this is because tenancy was less widespread elsewhere, or because enumerators handled the problem differently in other states – perhaps associating all inputs and outputs and the value of the farm with the farm, rather than splitting responses between owner and farm. To settle these questions would be a very big job, I think.

Some features of the sample that have proved troublesome to subsequent users would not have done so if we had explained our procedures with greater clarity and in more detail, a point made in a good paper in *EEH* by Schaefer and Schmitz (1985). For example, the census population schedules list occupations. Sometimes ditto marks appear below an occupational designation. In some instances this probably means that, indeed, the two or three people against whose names the ditto marks appear shared the same occupation; in other cases, it is clear that the ditto marks simply identify the members of the family of the person whose occupation is given. We did not plan to make use of the occupational data, but we gathered them, in case others might need them, and we told the coders to list exactly the data given by the census, even if it occasionally seemed obviously in error (a two-year-old female overseer). We preferred to leave to the users of the data the task of setting out criteria for distinguishing real from erroneous data. But we apparently did not make this decision clear to subsequent users, which caused some of them some grief.

So much for my memories of early cliometrics – a small sample of a large universe of memories, with probably very much too much weight given to the Parker–Gallman sample. I have had to leave out any account of work on nineteenth-century growth, in which I was fortunate to have collaborated with Lance, Stan, Tom Weiss, and Ed Howle. One could not have better collaborators.

I have spent so much space on the Parker–Gallman sample partly because of the

4 Wright (1970), Gallman (1969), Fogel & Engerman (1974: 191–209), Schaefer & Schmitz (1982), E. Field (*e.g.*, 1988).

questions you asked, and partly because Bill devoted little attention to the project in his interview and it seemed to me that more information should be provided. For my part, I think the project was worth doing, but I am not sure that I would not have done better to let someone else do it. It was a very difficult, frustrating project.

You have asked me questions about my own work, two surprisingly technical, but I am game. The technical questions are, "How do we deal with the problem of capital goods pricing in longitudinal studies of investment/capital accumulation – should we use historical or replacement cost? How do we interpret considerable efforts at accumulation which are rapidly displaced by superior technologies?" Now that I have thought a little more about it, "technical" is not quite the correct term, but no matter.

I think that the valuation scheme one should use in the study of capital should depend on the questions one is interested in. For example, if one is interested in the issue raised by the second question – "efforts at accumulation" – then historical cost is what you want. That is, if you are concerned with savings efforts, then the savings rate–share in income should be expressed in current prices. If you are dealing with a capital stock, however, there is an added problem. Summing up historical costs gives one a capital stock expressed in prices representing many years, and how one interprets such an aggregate is beyond me. One can still cope with the question you raise, however – or at least I think one can – by deflating the capital stock with a consumer price index. The deflation must be vintage by vintage, of course. But then one ends up with an aggregate that is expressed in the real value of the consumer goods given up to obtain the capital represented in the stock, a meaningful aggregate.

On the other hand, if one is interested in the capital stock as a factor of production, then presumably valuation should be at market price or, what should be virtually the same, net reproduction cost, expressed in constant prices. But obviously this is a very tricky area on which there is an enormous literature (including all those exchanges that make up the Cambridge controversies), and there is no full agreement as to the precise uses to which such a stock estimate may be put. It is worth noticing, however, that the two forms of deflation can result in strikingly different results, results that have analytical interest. For example, deflating the US capital stock by a consumer price index yields a rate of growth of the real capital stock across the Great Depression, World War II, and the Korean War almost twice as great as is obtained if market price deflators are used: a lot was given up in this period by way of consumer goods to get only a small increment in the productive power of the capital stock.

Next you ask, "What may we lose from our 'history' if we don't worry enough about what the GNP does not measure? That is, what have we learned about American standards of living over time?" This was an issue that I tried to deal with, at least in part, in my work on the national product in the nineteenth century. Specifically, I tried to incorporate measurements of the results of economic activity conducted beyond the reach of the market. Of course, standard GNP measures include a lot of these items; for example, the GNP is supposed to cover all agricultural output, not just output entering markets, and it also includes imputations for the rental value of owner-occupied living quarters. In addition to these items, I added estimates of the principal home manufactures, the clearing and first breaking of agricultural land, and total firewood production. I think those GNP figures are quite comprehensive. But they do not include allowances for changes in the amount of leisure enjoyed by Americans, or for the opportunity costs of the time of school children; neither do they take into account positive and negative externalities. There may be other items missing, as well.

As to the standard of living, clearly it can be affected by matters other than the volume of goods and services produced. For example, the Chicago–BYU–Ohio State project on heights has generated evidence that shows that the heights of Americans declined after the cohort of 1830. (In fact, the changes are very slight, until we get past the cohort of 1840.) This was a period in which real income was rising and nutrition levels were persistently high. Why, then, the deterioration in heights? There are many possible answers, relating to the various impacts of immigration, internal migration, work patterns, negative externalities, and changes in the disease environment. These issues have not yet been sorted out. It is not clear what the lines of causation were and, therefore, the connections – if any – between economic development and declining height are as yet unknown. This is an important area for research.

There is also the question as to how aggregate measures of material welfare, such as real national product *per capita*, may be adjusted to take into account the unfavorable events that resulted in stunting. The suggestions made by Dan Usher with respect to introducing changes in the death rate into real GNP measures need to be thought over in this context, although I think they are not problem-free (1980: 223–58).

Finally, you ask whether or not I have had second thoughts with respect to my previously-expressed views (in two papers with Lance) regarding the savings rate in the nineteenth century. Lance and I have a new paper on this subject which, with any luck, should appear in print in another year or two (Davis & Gallman 1994). I would not want to anticipate that publication, but I can at least say what will probably surprise no one: In this paper we find that we were pretty nearly right the first time around.

Bob

ROBERT W. FOGEL

Interviewed by
Samuel H. Williamson
and John S. Lyons

Robert William Fogel has been the Charles R. Walgreen Distinguished Service Professor of American Institutions, Professor of Economics, and Director of the Center for Population Economics in the Graduate School of Business, University of Chicago, all since 1981, and is a Research Associate of the National Bureau of Economic Research, as well as founding Director (1977–91) of the Bureau's program on the "Development of the American Economy." He was born in New York, New York in 1926 and was educated at Cornell University (B.A., 1948), at Columbia University (M.A., 1960) and at The Johns Hopkins University (Ph.D., 1963). He has held positions at the University of Rochester (1960–4) and at both Rochester and Chicago from 1965 to 1975 before moving to Harvard University for the years 1975–1981. He has served on the editorial boards of *Explorations in Economic History* and of *Social Science History*, was a founder in 1975 of The Social Science History Association, and was President of the Economic History Association (1978). In 1972 he was elected Fellow of The American Academy of Arts & Sciences, and Member of the National Academy of Sciences the following year. With co-author Stanley Engerman, he was awarded the 1975 Bancroft Prize in American history for *Time on the Cross*. In 1993 Robert Fogel, with Douglass North, was awarded the Nobel Memorial Prize in Economic Science. The interview was conducted by telephone on July 14, 1990 by Sam Williamson and John Lyons. Sam Williamson writes:

To me, Bob is an exemplar of the old expression "a scholar and a gentleman." I remember stopping by his office one summer in the mid 1960s to discuss a dissertation topic I was thinking about. It made no difference to him that I was only a graduate student from Purdue. He spent a couple of hours with me and insisted on taking me to lunch as well. Of course I was no exception to Bob's desire to nurture those who were finding their way into cliometrics at the time; the best testimony to his role in the field are the scores of Bob's former students who are today among the world's leading economic historians.

The first paper you presented to the "cliometricians" was on railroads at the inaugural Clio meeting at Purdue . . .

Right.

How long did it go?

I don't remember exactly how long it went. I think it went a full afternoon but, in any case, it went much longer than it was scheduled to go. People found the results of the paper (an early version of Chapter 2 of my railroad book) so astounding that they felt they had to lean all over it and they picked away in detail at all of my different estimates. They wanted me to explain in considerable detail how I had estimated this or that factor. The questions focused on the reliability of the data and of the analytical techniques I was using in the various measurements.

When the afternoon was over, were people still skeptical or did they understand what you had attempted to do?

Well, there were 20 or 30 people there. We would have to poll them on their opinions. I certainly felt that although the questions were probing and hard, and some were skeptical, they were not hostile. I had the feeling, as they pressed me, that they felt I had done a lot of work. I remember one issue that was pushed very hard. In order to estimate the social saving I had to estimate the volume of shipments from ten shipping centers in the Midwest, to about 40 receiving centers on the east coast and the south. Now, the procedure I used for estimating the volume of shipments involved estimation of the deficits in the trading areas of each of the 40 receiving centers. The first step was to estimate what was produced in each trading area, which was relatively easy, since we had a good census of agriculture. From production you had to subtract what was consumed. I estimated *per capita* consumption from budget studies. So there were lots of questions about the budget studies. You remember that I computed the social saving on four commodities: wheat, corn, pork, and beef, which represented the overwhelming majority of the interregional shipments in agriculture. The budget studies gave estimates, not of wheat, but of pounds of bread consumed. So there was an issue of how one got from pounds of bread to the wheat requirement. Lance Davis in particular, I remember, pressed me very hard on this issue. I went through different sources that I had used, including a number of formulas that reported the amount of wheat commercial bakeries used in a pound of bread. I had also examined a sizable list of cookbooks of the time, including those that were common in the rural areas. So I was able to present both household and commercial formulas. As it turned out, they weren't too far apart in the estimates of the amount of wheat needed per pound of bread. As

I said, you would have to speak to the other people because there may have been a difference between my perception and theirs, but I thought Lance was pleasantly surprised to discover how much work I had done on cookbooks.

It seems to us that the big issues, once the book was published, were not so much your detailed work, cookbooks and flour and so forth, but the kinds of issues that Don McCloskey has raised. He said that your global estimate of the social savings reduces to a simple three-line proof (1985: 116). Don analyzes the lengthy discussion in the book and your papers and argues that much of it involves a variety of rhetorical devices aimed at convincing your audience, particularly historians, of the viability of what you were doing. Does his view of your rhetorical approach sit well with you?

I have a considerable amount of sympathy for Don's approach to these issues. I agree with him that there's a lot of rhetoric in economics and the social sciences generally, and that very often points of view are shaped by arguments that lack the rigor we claim to use in settling issues. I don't fully subscribe to Don's point of view, and he was good enough to put some of my demurrers into his footnotes. I divide Don's position on my railroad book into two parts. Let me begin with his three-line proof. That's an argument you could make only after you have taken the experts through all the details of the findings. If I had gotten up at the first Clio meeting and given Don's three-line proof everyone would have said, "Who's that jerk?" What Don is willing to accept in that three-line proof (for example, that the cost of alternative transportation was twice that of railroads) is after the fact, after a long, intensive debate over the calculation. Prior to that very detailed work the prevailing estimates of the alternative cost were from exceedingly high to infinite. So I think the difficulty with Don's three-line proof is that it presumes as true what could only have been established by an enormous amount of hard work.

The second point is whether there is rhetoric in the book. Well, a lot depends on what you mean by rhetoric. The way Don uses the word, rhetoric includes tightly-knit logical arguments. And there are such arguments in the book. You have to remember that when I started this project, I never expected the result I got. So when I first obtained a low social savings, I thought I had done something wrong. After trying to discover where my error was, I gradually convinced myself that the error was not in my computational work but in my original conception of what the social saving ought to have been. I assumed that my own skepticism would be doubled, tripled or quadrupled when I presented my findings to people who had not been struggling with the problem for a couple of years. I thought about the arguments I would have to address in order to prevent readers from dismissing my work out of hand. In the first chapter I examined the traditional arguments for the indispensability of railroads, emphasizing the unverified assumptions in that analysis, and I made *prima facie* cases as to what would happen if one modified these assumptions. I also showed that some of the traditional arguments did not go to the heart of the issue of the social savings: the fact that small differences in competitive advantage can lead to very sharp shifts in the locus of transportation has no necessary implication for the size of the social saving. So Chapter 1 was designed to address the assumptions I had originally brought to the research (of course, what I had brought to the research reflected my conventional training on the role of railroads, what I and most other scholars had been led to believe were the facts) as well as lots of questions that had come up as I presented papers on my early findings. I tried to explain why the plausible traditional propositions ought to be put aside, or at least held in suspension, long enough to consider the new evidence and analysis.

I never viewed *Railroads and American Economic Growth* as a disputatious book aimed at provoking a controversy for its own sake, but as a very detailed study of the way in which a major innovation increased productivity. That was certainly the way that Kuznets viewed it. Kuznets was the last person who would have been interested in controversy for its own sake, and he would not have allowed me to write a dissertation that was speculative and disputatious, although he was willing to go along with the way I set up the opening chapter. The central objective of the book is estimation of the productivity advantage of the railroad and the allocation of that advantage among the various facets of this form of transportation. In that connection, the book looks at long-haul versus short-haul. It turns out that short-haul is more important than long-haul. And then it breaks down the overall advantage of railroads in both long- and short-haul into such components as inventory savings, wagon savings, as well as a comparison of direct payments to waterways and railroads. It turns out that the main advantage of the railroads was not that they were cheaper than waterways in direct service, but that they required much less of a very costly complementary service, namely wagon transportation. So even if one accepts Don's three-line proof, that proof would not answer the question of where the productivity gains attributable to railroads came from.

We talked before about how you went to Simon Kuznets and explained what you were going to do. He said that measuring the impact of railroads sounded like a good project. Is that right?

I got the idea from one of his lectures. Kuznets pointed out that although there had been much discussion of the economic impact of railroads, no one had yet measured the extent of their impact or analyzed the sources of the productivity gains associated with them.

Okay, we have a further question. Who came up with the idea of asking what water transportation would have cost? Who came up with the specific way you set up the counterfactual? Was that your idea or his?

Neither. It was really in the literature because people were comparing railroads to waterways all along. Let me say there is virtually nothing I did in my work on railroads that was not anticipated by some state legislator or other public figure. For example, in my book on *The Union Pacific Railroad*, I used the increase in land values to estimate the social return on the road. Well, there was hardly a session of a state legislature that dealt with a proposal to build a canal or a railroad in which the advocates didn't refer to the predicted increase in land values or use that idea to estimate the social benefit that wouldn't be covered by the income of the road. They used the expected rise in land values as an argument for subsidization. So these arguments were all over the literature. What we did was formalize the analysis; we put it in a form suitable for measurement. If you look at Al Fishlow's book on railroads, by the way, you will see that he made a lot of use of these early estimates.

Economists did not discover cost–benefit analysis. It really comes out of engineering. All the civil engineers who came before state legislatures that were considering internal improvements dealt with the relative costs and advantages of: (a) common roads or turnpikes, (b) waterways and canals, and (c) the "new" (at the time) railroads. And they provided cost estimates and benefit estimates for each of these alternative forms of transportation. So the notion of cost–benefit analysis is very old; it's a very intuitive idea, and I think a lot of what we have done in twentieth-century economic analysis is a formalization of these ideas, putting some structure on them, specifying functional relationships that make it easier to estimate both costs and benefits, interpreting various measures within the framework of partial or general equilibrium models, and so on. The fundamental ideas are not due to us. So that's my answer. It didn't come from Simon; it didn't come from me; it was just there.

You were at the first Purdue seminar in 1960. Can you tell us what the atmosphere was like?

I remember a tremendous excitement and exhilaration on the part of everybody at the meeting. I was brand new and barely a third of the way through my doctoral dissertation. I arrived at Rochester, my first teaching appointment, in August 1960, and the first cliometrics meeting was the following December. I hadn't met any of the people at the meeting except for Henry Rosovsky who had interviewed me for an appointment at Berkeley a few days before the Purdue meeting. I had read the works of many of them, and Lance Davis was very highly regarded around Johns Hopkins, as was Duncan McDougall. They were products of the school; their names often came up in the halls. From my point of view it was exciting just to meet other people who were moving in a similar direction, such as Lance [Davis], Jon [Hughes], Doug [North], Bill [Parker] and the others. I had expected to meet [Alf] Conrad and [John] Meyer, but they didn't come to the first meeting. There was a general sense that the meeting was an important occasion, that something new was happening, that we were moving in a new direction.

Since you've been to so many Clios since then, including the Second World Congress last year, do you still think there is that air of excitement, particularly among the younger people, or has it turned into just an old and blasé institution?

Well, cliometrics is now the establishment. It's not a movement of Young Turks anymore. But, I'm sure cliometrics is exciting to younger people in the same way that it would have been for me, even if cliometrics had been old. I was making my entry into the area. Moreover, I think we've remained very self-critical. By self-critical I mean we don't take our own work for granted. We're probing. I don't mean to imply that we're free of the problems that come with establishments: of thinking too highly of our own work, of believing that what we do is the only way to do it. I'm sure we suffer from some of that. But I believe we may suffer from it less than other establishments. We remain quite open to innovation, to new approaches and new problems. At the two international Clio conferences there was much of the old excitement and probing criticism. So I think the spirit has held up pretty well, despite the fact that we've moved from Young Turks challenging the establishment to being the establishment.

How did you get interested in delving into the issue of American slavery?

Well, I got interested in slavery because of the Conrad and Meyer paper, which was published in 1958 when I was a graduate student and it startled everybody. I think that I mentioned that I've written a little memoir called "History with Numbers," which describes the long and emotional debate on the use of quantitative methods in history. This essay is not focused on economic history *per se* but deals with the broader discipline of history. In it I have a paragraph describing my own reaction when the Conrad and Meyer paper was published in 1958. I didn't believe their main findings. I didn't think that a system that reprehensible could be profitable. I was one of a number of graduate students at Johns Hopkins who got into very long arguments about the paper. Most of the faculty and graduate students in the economics department at Hopkins and some in the history department were drawn into the debate over whether Conrad and Meyer were right or wrong.

So your incentive was to redo it and find out whether they were right or wrong?

No, no. Because I was working on railroads my interest in their slavery paper was tangential. It gave me confidence that this was the way to go. Beyond that, I was interested because they had posed a first-rate intellectual problem, and I played the game with them that people later played with me: Where did they go wrong? I thought I could find a major mistake that would overturn their results, but I wasn't able to find one. As I say in the memoir, the only major error that was discovered in that particular effort was the error that Yasukichi Yasuba pointed out in a paper that was originally published in Japan, and which Stan and I republished in the collection we did on *The Reinterpretation of American Economic History*. Yasuba pointed out that you needed to compute the rate of return on the cost of reproduction, not on the market price. If you use the market price, all you will discover is that the market worked reasonably well and masters were getting the average rate of return. When Yasuba recalculated the rate of return on reproduction costs, it was even higher than Conrad and Meyer had put it. And the return was increasing as the Civil War approached. Yasuba's paper convinced me that Conrad and Meyer were basically right and that I simply had to come to terms with their main finding.

Until the mid 1960s I was interested in the slavery discussions only as a fellow economic historian and as a teacher who was describing to graduate students what was interesting in the field. Then in 1962 or 1963 Stan and I decided to collaborate in writing a textbook on American economic history based on the methods and findings of the New Economic History. I have somewhere in my files sketches or outlines of about 20 chapters that represented a proposed approach to the book. We took up one problem after another, set them up formally, pointed out the issues and the key variables or effects that had to be estimated, and then we'd say: unfortunately they have not yet been estimated.

So you felt after a while that you were perhaps being a bit premature?

Yes, we were premature by about 20 years. So we talked about what we could do. We decided to edit a book that would bring together the best work in a decade of cliometric research. That led to *The Reinterpretation.* We divided the book into nine sections, and we were going to write long introductions to each of them. Our first three papers on slavery were actually part of the effort to write such introductions. There were two papers by Stan. In this connection, he did a lot of work on Dick Easterlin's regional income estimates, revising them in ways that are described in those papers, in order to get estimates that were somewhat more appropriate for the issues that we wanted to focus on, as opposed to those that Dick had been focusing on. The revised estimates indicated that the South was growing even more rapidly than Dick's figures indicated. Let me say that when Dick published his paper in 1961 in the Harris volume, we were all startled to discover that the South was growing as rapidly as the North. If the first big bombshell was the Conrad and Meyer discovery that slavery was quite profitable, the second was Dick's discovery that the South was growing quite rapidly, and Stan amended Dick's result so that the South was growing even more rapidly than the North between 1840 and 1860. The third piece was a joint paper that became too long for an introduction; we published it as a separate essay. It was an extended review of ten years of cliometric research on slavery. We looked at three issues: Was slavery profitable to the individual investor; secondly, was slavery economically viable, could it have kept going as an economic system; and thirdly, was the South growing economically?

We had originally intended a fourth issue. We raised the question of what cliometricians should look at next. In this connection we planned to have a little section on the issue of efficiency. Our aim was to illustrate, as we thought of it then, the way that cliometricians might measure how much less efficient slavery was than free labor. We were just going to have a back-of-the-envelope calculation, but that calculation showed that slave agriculture was 6 percent more efficient than free agriculture. We said, "That's screwy," and we decided not to hold up the book waiting to resolve the problem. We finished the article for *The Reinterpretation* in 1968, minus the section "What cliometricians should do next."

Meanwhile, we began probing the efficiency issue more deeply. We went from the back-of-the-envelope computation, which took perhaps a couple of weeks, to a more careful estimate that took several months as we tried to develop more reasonable numbers on key issues. One of these issues was the difference in the average weights of northern and southern livestock. We were also concerned with problems of measuring the labor input. Initially, we thought we'd find that southern agriculture was in the range of 50 to 75 percent as efficient as northern agriculture. After about two or three months of work we were beginning to think that when we got through, it would turn out that although northern agriculture was more efficient than southern agriculture, the levels were close. We just wanted to get the index to the other side of 1. We published the first two versions of our productivity calculations in *Explorations in Economic History* in 1971. The second, which we called a partially adjusted estimate, turned out to raise the southern advantage from about 6 percent to about 40 percent, instead of lowering it.

So we knew we had a problem and we did what every good economist does when they know they have a problem: we applied for an NSF grant. At the time, Stan and I were working on what we had planned as a small book on the development of the American iron industry. We settled for publishing one paper on that subject. We were so startled by the productivity results we were getting, that we shifted from the iron industry to the work on slavery. So, as Stan and I have said in the introduction to Volume 3 of *Without Consent or Contract*, we think of the project as beginning in 1965 because we date our independent involvement on the problem of slavery with the review essays we wrote. But the decision to actually get involved in digging up new data that would permit us to have better estimates was not made until 1968. I think we submitted the grant proposal late in 1968 or early in 1969, and it was approved in 1970.

Would you comment on the reception your work on slavery has received in the last twenty-some years?

Slavery was a very controversial subject. It was controversial because our generation was the generation that was raised in the new ethic on race relations. And that is an ethic which started out from the proposition that basically all races are the same, that differences between races in physical characteristics and intellectual capacity are superficial. The switch in the ethic on race was promoted by World War II, which popularized the theories of Franz Boaz. The Nazis were fighting as the pro-racist camp. They were fighting on the old anthropology and we, therefore, embraced the new anthropology. By "we" I mean the United States and the Allies generally, and we won the war. God knows what would have happened if the Axis had won the war. At the outbreak of the war my generation of scholars was in primary and secondary school or, if you take the oldest people in that intellectual generation, were graduate students or beginning teachers. So our generation, deeply influenced by the ideological issues of World War II, began to re-examine the intellectual heritage on slavery and race.

From that point of view, everything that was done was highly controversial because it was very revisionist. Kenneth Stampp's book, *The Peculiar Institution*, was certainly a very controversial book. Look at the review of it in the *American Historical Review*. *The Peculiar Institution* was not hailed as a great book there; it was treated as Mr. Stampp's opinion. It was controversial; it was challenging the dominant viewpoint (set forth by U. B. Phillips in 1918 and elaborated by Phillips and other leading historians over the next three decades). The Conrad and Meyer paper was quite consistent with Stampp. The Phillips School was the reigning school in the immediate post-World War II period, and you can find reflections of that view even in the history textbooks written by liberal Northerners such as Morison and Commager. By the way, David Brion Davis published an article in *Daedalus* in 1974 in which he says some of the same things that I am saying to you. So the new approach reflected a generational experience. Anything we did on slavery was bound to be controversial, originally because we were challenging the established scholarly views on these issues. Later on, as the black political movement unfolded (when I say black political movement, I mean to include liberal white allies), everything began to be measured against how it facilitated or hampered the fight for civil rights. Look at the storm of controversy around the work of Conrad and Meyer that erupted at the 1967 meetings of the Economic History Association. The most emotional aspects of that meeting were edited out of the printed version of the debate. Alf began the discussion by reading two letters commenting on their 1958 paper. One was from someone in Athens, Georgia, daring him to come down and make the same statements in Athens; the other was from someone in the North calling him and John Meyer racists.[1] They had simply crossed the ideological wires.

Presumably you have enjoyed working on your most recent project on heights, weights, and nutrition. How did you get started on that project?

Well, it arose partly out of the slavery project, but it also goes back to my training under Kuznets. Let me start out with that. Kuznets's main course at Johns Hopkins, a full-year course on economic growth, was divided into four segments: population growth, technological changes, long-term trends in national product and its components, and the use of national income accounts to study comparative economic growth. As a graduate student, I was most excited by the sections on technological change and that's where I did my initial work. But the other parts of the course also had a big impact on me. So in the back of my mind I recognized the importance of demographic work. One of the ablest graduate students at Johns Hopkins, Yasukichi Yasuba, did his dissertation on trends in fertility before the Civil War, which was published in 1962. He also had a major chapter on mortality in his study. So I had a good introduction to economic demography, although it was not on the front burner of my research prior to the 1970s.

When we began the slavery research I approached demographic issues mainly as they bore on our effort to improve the measure of the labor input. We collected data that would enable us to estimate how much of the available time of a woman was actually used for the production of measured output. As we got into the data, the results we obtained were so contrary to what we had initially believed that we became very interested in a variety of demographic issues we had not previously expected to pursue, and these were reflected in *Time on the Cross*.

1 Conrad (1967). See also Fogel (2003: 29), where he quotes an observation by John Meyer.

In 1974 Stan and I talked about starting work on a new project before the slavery project came to a close. We decided that we should look somewhere in the demographic area. As our talks progressed, we decided to focus on mortality. Most of the empirical work in demography at the time focused on fertility, so mortality was relatively neglected. We agreed to investigate the possibility of a project that centered on measuring mortality rates in North America before 1900, because they were basically unmeasured. We hoped to be able to produce a time series on mortality from the earliest European settlement to the time when the death registration system became widespread (about 1930). Despite our plans, we were not able to begin the mortality project in 1974. Stan went off for a year in England in August of 1974 and I was scheduled to go to Cambridge University during 1975–76. Our plan was to work ourselves into the mortality project gradually over that period, but we expected to concentrate on finishing the slavery project which, at that point, we thought we would do in two or three years. Then the controversy broke over *Time on the Cross*. We were so deeply involved in the controversy in late 1974 and most of 1975 that we didn't make any progress on the mortality project. Now, some of the controversy turned on demographic issues, particularly on the age of slave mothers at the birth of their first child and on the age at menarche.

This project on height, weight, nutrition, and mortality has been going on since the early 1970s, yet you're still working on it.

Oh, yes, and I expect it to go on after I die. I'll be disappointed if I look down (I'm assuming I'll be in heaven) and discover that the building of life cycle and intergenerational data sets has been discontinued. We finally did get going on the mortality project late in 1975. I divided my year in Cambridge mainly between teaching myself technical demography and working in the Public Record Office. Part of the mortality project involved comparing mortality trends in the US with those in the countries from which the American population was drawn. Prior to 1790 the free US population was 95 percent British in origin, so the Public Record Office was one of our most promising sources of data.

In addition to getting the mortality project off the ground, we were trying to respond to the critics on the efficiency issue. Stan and I began the work on what became the first *AER* paper on the question. We were also trying to come to grips with the demographic issues and particularly the issue that was raised first by Herb Gutman, but later also by Ned Shorter and Dick Sutch, that our estimate of the age at first birth was biased upwards by four years.[2] We were aware not only of the bias that Gutman singled out but also of downward biases that tended to cancel the upward one, so we thought our estimate of age of first birth was fairly close to the mark. We drafted a paper dealing with the various biases, which included a technique for estimating them, and sent a

2 Papers initially presented at the MSSB–University of Rochester Conference: "*Time on the Cross:* A First Appraisal," October 24–6, 1974: Gutman (1975); Edward Shorter, "Protein, Puberty and Premarital Sexuality: American Blacks *v* French Peasants [unpublished]; Sutch (1975).

copy of that paper to Ansley Coale for his comments. Ansley passed the paper on to James Trussell, who was then a young assistant professor in the Office of Population Research.

James sent me a letter saying the paper was interesting but he thought there were better ways of dealing with the biases. It turned out that he also was going to be in England and he offered to explain his procedure to me. Early in the academic year he came up to Cambridge (maybe it was October) and spent about two hours giving me a lecture on the singulate mean. It was a powerful technique, much better suited to the problem than the one I had devised. That afternoon provided a chastening lesson for me on the difference between a professional demographer and a novice. The singulate mean produced what is probably a pretty good estimate of mother's age at first birth, but in any case is a downward biased estimate of that age. James collaborated with Rick Steckel, who was developing the data needed to implement the procedure. Now the singulate mean answered the question about the average age of mothers at their first birth. We had put that age at 22 in *Time on the Cross*. Herb had said 18. The singulate mean shows it was 21. So our estimate was biased upward by about a year; Herb's was biased downward by about three years.

At that point James said to me, "You know, Bob, there is still the question of the age of menarche." He was referring to our proposition that there was considerable abstention from premarital sexual intercourse among slaves. Stan and I had accepted the opinion of Bancroft and others who reported that slaves were fecund in their mid-teens. So if slaves were fecund at 15 or 16 but did not give birth on average until 21 or 22, there must have been a lot of abstention (given the absence of contraception). Gutman, Shorter, and Sutch argued that no such inference could be made because the slave diet was so bad that slave women were over 18 when they became menarcheal. To support that proposition they cited J. M. Tanner who reported that *c.*1860 Norwegian girls became menarcheal at age 18. They contended that the age of menarche must have been at least as late for slaves as for Norwegian girls. So no inference could be made about abstention from sexual intercourse because most slave women were, after allowing for post-menarcheal subfecundity, physiologically incapable of bearing children until age 21 or so.

Trussell said, "You know, Bob, if we had data on the height by age or the weight by age of slaves, we could estimate the age at menarche very precisely." I said, "Height by age! Height by age! We have *thousands* of observations on height by age. Stan and I have been going around for years trying to figure out what to do with those data. We also have data on shoe size. What can we do with shoe size?" So that's the way I first came to learn about uses of anthropometric data. Trussell introduced me to Tanner, who looked at our data and said they indicated that menarche was probably around age 15, maybe earlier. After that it was a matter of enlarging the sample and of developing the best way of fitting the growth curve to the data so that we could estimate the peak of the growth spurt as precisely as possible. Most of the work, as you know, has been done by Rick Steckel.

I should say, by the way, that I was working in England, and Stan was in Rochester working on these height data independently, and he did a piece about the same time that has been neglected. It was published in 1976 in the British journal, *Local Population Studies*. In that paper Stan presented, not the velocity profile with which Trussell and Steckel worked, but the age profile of heights. Although his discussion was brief, Stan pointed out that the profile suggested that the physical development of slaves was reasonably good by contemporary standards.

This introduction to anthropometric data changed our approach to the mortality project. One of the key issues in the project is the contribution of improved nutrition to the secular decline in mortality. We had struggled with the question of how to get a suitable measure of nutritional status. Originally, we thought we would collect samples from probate records in order to determine the foods that were being inventoried. Of course, such samples would have told us, at best, what foods were available for consumption. They wouldn't have given us a measure of the nutrients that were actually consumed. Once I realized that the anthropometric measures were much more powerful indicators of nutritional status, I began looking at what I could get from the Public Record Office on heights, mainly from military records. The results of that survey are indicated in the long description of the mortality project ("The Economics of Mortality in North America 1650–1910") that the six original collaborators published in *Historical Methods* in 1978. So, that is how we came to integrate the work on mortality with the work on height and other anthropometric measures.

What made this new line of research possible for me was my good fortune to have made connection with Trussell and Tanner in 1975 and then with Nevin Scrimshaw in 1982. They are all exceptional teachers, with enthusiasm for their work and with great patience for the bewilderment of novices. From the moment I first met Tanner, who was then the chairman of the Department of Child Health and Growth at the Institute of Child Health in London, he generously spent numerous hours with me (and with others in our project), explaining the fundamentals of the branch of medicine called auxology (the study of human growth), looking at our data and helping us to interpret them, guiding us through basic texts, calling our attention to the latest relevant papers, and reading and criticizing our work. We received a similar education from Scrimshaw, Director of the International Nutrition Program at MIT, in epidemiology (particularly of infectious diseases), in nutrition, and in some aspects of clinical medicine.

From the perspective of 1990, what do you think are the most intriguing outcomes of your efforts so far?

Well, the original mortality project spawned two other projects. The mortality project was initially going to be based on a sample of genealogies that would eventually contain a million people in about 200,000 families linked together for up to ten generations. The genealogies contain a great deal of information on the vital events of the individuals listed in them. They also contain, less completely, such socio-economic information as occupations, places of residence at various points in the life cycle (from which one can construct migration and urbanization variables), and military service. We planned to obtain additional socio-economic information, including wealth, on the individuals in the sample by linking them to information in tax lists, probate records, the manuscript schedules of censuses, and pension records. We also planned to use data on height to measure nutritional status during developmental ages and to develop ecological variables from public health sources that would indicate the exposure to particular diseases in the localities in which the individuals lived over their life cycles.

The height data were so interesting that they became the basis for a separate project called "Secular Trends in Nutrition, Labor Welfare, and Labor Productivity." It is based on samples of height data drawn from 16 populations in the US, Europe, and the Caribbean from 1700 to 1980. We have about 500,000 observations in these samples. In 1981 we began a project aimed at tracing 40,000 white Union Army men from the cradle to the grave, looking at the impact of socio-economic factors in early life, including nutritional status during developmental ages, on waiting time to the development of specific chronic diseases in middle and late ages; and on waiting time to death from specific causes. One of the four sub-projects in the aging project deals with the factors that affected the likelihood of contracting specific diseases while in the army, as well as the determinants of the case-fatality rates of these diseases. In this connection, we treat war wounds as a class of disease. Only about 20 percent of the people who died during the Civil War died as a result of wounds. About 80 percent of all deaths were due to disease.

Now, when you get into the kinds of data sets I've been describing, you're involved in very complex problems of file management. In order to describe the whole life cycle experience of a recruit, it takes 18,000 variables, which means that there are over 700 million pieces of information that have to be managed. So a considerable amount of our time has been devoted to the development of software, both for the laptops used to retrieve the data and for the workstations and mainframes on which the data are analyzed. We have been working with subsets of the overall sample on substantive issues and have obtained some very interesting preliminary findings. But before I turn to the substantive findings, I want to underscore the importance of the advances in research technology. We are now able to create, at costs within the guidelines of funding agencies, life cycle and intergenerational data sets that will permit us to get evidence on questions we could not even dream of dealing with a few years ago, that we could, at best, only speculate about.

We have made the most progress in the publication of substantive findings in the nutrition project. Since 1979 project participants have published over 40 papers and three books. The latest is *Height, Health and History: Nutritional Status in the United Kingdom 1750–1980* by Roderick Floud, Annabel Gregory, and Kenneth Wachter. That book, by the way, is the second to appear in the NBER monograph series called *Long-Term Factors in Economic Development* (I might as well get a plug in for the series). Several papers integrating the preliminary findings of the mortality and nutrition project have been published or are in press. The most comprehensive analysis of the information in our genealogical samples is contained in papers by Clayne Pope.

We were particularly struck by the paper you gave in Santander last year.[3] Would you talk about the potential policy implications of that paper?

You have to remember that this paper is one of four that will be integrated into a little book I hope to complete in about a year-and-a-half. That book will be like *Time on the Cross*. It will be an early report on preliminary findings. I think we have now gotten to the point in our mortality and nutrition projects where we have a vision of what happened with respect to the secular trend in mortality in both Europe and America. We have a preliminary set of propositions that we think will be useful in guiding further research and that we expect to hold up reasonably well, although we also expect them to be modified in various ways as the research progresses.

Would you say that one of your propositions has to do with the efficiency of government food crisis management?

I've revised the Santander paper to put greater emphasis on policy issues. One of the major policy implications of our work so far calls into question the proposition that adults who are stunted but have a good body mass are as healthy as those whose nutrition during developmental ages permits them to attain full potential in height. Small may be beautiful, but it isn't healthy if it's due to stunted growth. That finding is evident in the iso-mortality map we included in the Santander paper. It shows that even if a stunted individual has the ideal body weight for his height, the probability of his dying is going to be significantly higher than a taller person with ideal body weight, so that malnutrition early in childhood is a major disaster throughout the life cycle. This finding argues for the importance of using whatever levers we have, which probably means some sort of government intervention, to get more nutrients to poor children. Of course, it's one thing to say that if you get nutrients to pregnant women and to children early in life, it's going to make a big difference. It's another thing to have an effective system for delivering the nutrients to them. And I don't have anything to say about delivery systems. I'm just looking at the economic–biomedical interactions. But I can't believe that effective delivery systems are beyond our capacity.

How would you relate your nutrition project to Amartya Sen's twentieth-century studies of poverty and famine?

I think he's right in his analysis of why there are famines. I believe that our work is helping to demonstrate that the real issue is not famines, but chronic malnutrition. Famines may be dramatic, but the real loss in life comes from people who are chronically malnourished all of their lives, especially during developmental ages. I hope that our findings will have some bearing on discussions of current policy. Indeed, the book

3 "Second Thoughts on the European Escape from Hunger: Famines, Price Elasticities, Entitlements, Chronic Malnutrition, and Mortality Rates." Paper presented at the Second World Congress of Cliometrics, University of Cantabria, Santander, Spain, June 24–7, 1989. Published in revised form as Fogel (1993).

I'm writing is called *The Escape From Hunger and High Mortality: Europe, America and the Third World, 1750–2050.*[4] So the book deals not only with the past and the present but with years that are yet to come. I am structuring the book in that way to emphasize its policy orientation. I also want to emphasize that even the advanced countries have not yet finished their escape from hunger, although we are much better off in 1990 than we were in 1900.

The third book in the NBER series on *Long-Term Factors in Economic Development* is by Sam Preston and Mike Haines, and it deals with the analysis of infant and childhood mortality through a study of the 1900 census. Near the beginning of the book, they make the point that when you go back to earliest times, life expectancy was probably about 25 years. In 1900 it was a bit over 47 years. So during all previous history prior to 1900 there was an increase of between 20 and 25 years in life expectancy. Between 1900 and the present there has been an increase of 27 years. During the last 90 years we have increased life expectancy by twice as much as in all previous history. It's the twentieth century that is really the century of incredible progress, especially for the lower classes. Nor has this enormous advance been confined to the West; it has also taken place in the Third World. Indeed, if you look at how rapidly death rates have been falling in the Third World, you'll see that they are declining more rapidly than they did in Europe.

Would you say that's more strongly related to the post-1935 advances in pharmaceutical knowledge or nutrition, or what?

That's the question we're trying to answer. They are both involved. With respect to scientific advances, it is not just pharmaceutical knowledge that is important. Public health measures generally have been powerful factors in reducing mortality, and you really can't separate nutrition from public health because nutrition is not just diet. Diet is what you put in your mouth. Nutrition refers to the nutrients available to the body. Diet and nutritional status often diverge. If you have severe diarrhea, no matter how much food you put in your mouth, your body is going to get very little of the nutrients you ingest. Of course, a good diet is important, but a lot of bad nutrition in the past stemmed from the fact that the body couldn't metabolize the nutrients that were consumed, or else the nutrients were siphoned off in fighting disease. Diet and public health measures are closely interrelated, and we're now trying to separate out, and to estimate, their independent contributions.

In the Santander paper I cited some evidence that suggests that improvements in nutritional status accounted for all of the improvements in mortality between 1750 and 1875 in England, France and Sweden, but only for about 50 percent of the improvement in these countries between 1875 and 1975. Sam Preston, using different data for Third World countries, found that increases in income accounted for about 50 percent

4 Published as Fogel (2004a), based in part on the Ellen MacArthur Lectures presented in November 1996 at the University of Cambridge.

of the mortality decline in the twentieth century. Those are not bad interim numbers, but I think we can do better than that. In another paper I tried to divide the contribution of nutritional status to the mortality decline before 1900 into two parts: diet and reductions in exposure to disease. I cited data that suggest that a 60/40 split might be the best interim estimate, but that is only a conjecture. Much work remains before we will have something approaching a reliable division.

The last few issues we want to deal with involve a couple of stories, and your long-run perspective on Clio: was cliometrics really a revolution?

I think we need to distinguish between the view on the spot and the view looking backward. Certainly everybody who was around at the beginning viewed it as a revolution . . . well, nearly everybody. I add the qualification because of people like David Landes, who was part of the new wave but who was a little older and a little wiser than the rest of us, who tried to emphasize the points of continuity. The same can be said of many of our teachers, including Carter Goodrich and your father, Sam [Hal Williamson], who were very encouraging to the new work but also thought very highly of the old work. They probably saw the lines of continuity better than the rest of us. But most people thought cliometrics was very revolutionary, not only those of us who were doing it, but also the critics. There were a lot of people who felt the techniques we were using – the mathematics, the statistics, the diagrams – were either irrelevant or harmful. Some of those who couldn't read our work told me of their fears that cliometrics would make them technologically obsolete. We were seen as bearers of an alien culture, and an alien language.

The language/culture shock tended to cover over the fact that we were really dealing with the same sets of issues. If you look at the issues that the cliometricians have focused on, they are largely the same issues that our teachers had been concerned with. So there was a considerable degree of continuity in the substance of the work. Some issues came more to the fore, others less, but a lot of that had to do with current public policy. What seemed interesting, what part of the past we gave the most attention to, was to a large extent a function of what society thought was important. Interest in the slavery issue has been enormous mainly because we have spent half a century struggling for the achievement of full civil rights for blacks in America on the political, social, and economic levels. Under these circumstances there was bound to be a heavy concentration on black history.

When I first tried to define what was novel about cliometrics, I mentioned the gathering of new evidence, but I made the more explicit use of theory predominant. I now think I would reverse the order. There have, of course, been important advances in theory, yet, when you get down to measurement, the theory used is usually fairly simple and much of it has been around for a long time. If you take the work on the profitability of slavery, the equation used by Conrad and Meyer is actually referred to by Phillips in *American Negro Slavery*. He cites a man by the name of Gibson who wrote a book called *Human Economics* that was published in 1909. Gibson specifically says we can take the yield equation for bonds and use it to estimate the rate of return on slaves. Conrad and Meyer didn't invent the yield equation. Nor did they choose the yield equation because they read Gibson. Once they decided to treat the economics of slavery as a problem of evaluating the return on long-lived assets, the yield equation was an obvious instrument.

The key difference between Conrad and Meyer and Gibson is that they took the measurement problems seriously. They carefully specified all the different measurements that had to be made in order to implement the yield equation. Of course, they also introduced a very interesting dichotomy between the rate of return on men and women, which plunged them into a whole series of demographic issues, which they and their critics also took very seriously. By carefully specifying all of the variables and parameters that had to be measured, and by showing that much of the information needed for these measurements was already in the secondary literature (although the reliability was open to question), they set up a long-term research program. Gibson, on the other hand, never specified the measurement issues rigorously. In his work the yield equation is largely a rhetorical device that permits him to discuss some theoretical issues. So his discussion did not touch off an empirical train of research, although in another context it might have done so.

Because the ideological implications of the Conrad and Meyer paper were disturbing to many scholars, and because the data that they culled from the secondary sources for their calculations were so questionable, critics began searching for new data that would provide more accurate estimates. Since the secondary sources did not contain the type of data required to estimate key variables, researchers turned to data locked away in the archives. Although the debate over Conrad and Meyer greatly stimulated the drawing of large samples of economic data from archives, the first historian of slavery to undertake such a task was U.B. Phillips. The large samples of slave prices that he collected before World War I are still widely used and represent an important source of information for current work. The next major effort in data retrieval was undertaken by Robert Evans, Jr. in the late 1950s. He collected new samples, not only of slave prices, but also of hire rates from various archives. Evans worked independently of Conrad and Meyer. Much of his work was undertaken before the publication of their paper. He used a somewhat more sophisticated version of the yield equation and he improved upon their procedures in some other ways. His paper, which was not published until 1962, strongly supported and extended the basic findings of Conrad and Meyer.

It was the Parker–Gallman sample, however, that really ushered in what might be called the mature phase of cliometrics. It was that sample that led many of us to recognize that the new sampling techniques and the new computer technology made it possible for us to exploit vast data collections that hitherto had been far too difficult to utilize.

That brings me to my story about Fred Lane. I was asked to prepare a paper on the difference between scientific and traditional history for the Sixth International Congress of Logic, Methodology, and Philosophy of Science which met in Hanover, Germany, in

1979. That paper was first published in the proceedings of the Congress and then, with revisions, in my book with Geoffrey Elton (*Which Road to the Past?*). At that time Fred Lane was retired and living in New Hampshire. He was working on a new book and he came down to Harvard two or three times a week to work in Widener Library. I ran into him from time to time and we set up two lunches. At one of the lunches I told him about the argument in the Hanover paper. At the other lunch he told me about the way in which medieval historians used circumstantial evidence. The second talk was particularly stimulating; it influenced the approach of my next methodological paper, which I called "Circumstantial Evidence in 'Scientific' and Traditional History."

After I told Fred about the argument of the Hanover paper, he said, "Well, Bob, what I think is really important about the cliometricians is not their use of theory but their discovery of how to utilize bodies of data that have been lying around in archives virtually untouched." I think that judgment is right. And that is another point of continuity with the past. In a sense cliometrics has restored the old emphasis on archival work. Several developments have facilitated the new archival work. We have better theory and the connection between behavioral models and statistical models is more sophisticated. We also have better theories of how to sample. All these things help. The single biggest change, however, is the computer revolution, which has reduced the cost of data retrieval incredibly. I read somewhere recently that if there had been as much increase in productivity in the production of Rolls Royce cars as there has been in information processing over the past three decades, today you could buy a Rolls Royce for $3.50.

Oh, if it were only such.

My experience confirms the point. We made our first attempt to draw a sample from the muster rolls of the Union Army in 1978. With five people working full time for about ten weeks (2,000 hours) we were able to collect 13,000 observations with about 50 characters of information per observation. At that rate we retrieved information on just 12 variables. We omitted the names of the recruits because linking the recruits to other sources was prohibitively expensive. During the summer of 1981 we drew a new and much larger sample. This time in ten weeks we retrieved a sample of 40,000 Union Army men, with more than four times as much information (including names) on each observation. Per character of information, the cost of data retrieval had declined by over 90 percent in just three years. The reduction was brought about by the use of several portable terminals with bubble memories, which could hold 100,000 characters (about as much as a fast typist could enter in 8 hours), and which had built-in modems and built-in printers. The information was entered during the day and then transmitted over the telephone to the mainframe computer at night. Since the information was recorded in strings, it had to be converted into fixed fields. That process, together with cleaning the tape of errors, required another 3,000 hours of work. Taking into account the cost of cleaning and formatting the tape, the new technology reduced the overall cost of retrieving and putting data into machine-readable form by about 80 percent per character of information.

By 1986 laptops had become so powerful and cheap that we switched to them. With the laptop we could input the data into fixed fields. As a result our cost of data cleaning and formatting declined by 90 percent over what it had been in 1981. So what have we accomplished? Are we now doing everything for a song? No . . . nonsense! We've now gone from about 200 characters per observation to 18,000 variables with an average of about five characters per variable, or about 90,000 characters per observation. What I'm saying is that our research is still very costly, but now it is costly because we're doing things nobody could have dreamed of doing, certainly not in 1978 or even in 1981. We were not nearly as ambitious then as we are in 1990. If anyone had told me in 1978 that we would be dealing with the issues that we are working on today, I would have said it was a pipe dream. Perhaps the most important thing about the new laptops is the possibilities they open up for graduate students [*e.g.*, Joe Ferrie and Ralph Galantine]. Projects that would have been out of their reach before, because they required a large NSF grant, can now be undertaken with their own resources or modest support from their departments.

Let us close with a final question. Is it true that you once said that you could open any work of history and find a Ph.D. dissertation topic in a paragraph or a few lines? Then refocus that question, directing your comments toward the young researchers in our field and tell them if you see some new or old topics that really need somebody to take a hold of, make careers out of, or just get busy on.

On the first part of the question, I think whoever told you that story conflated two things that I remember saying. I have often told friends that every lecture that Kuznets gave suggested at least one major dissertation and sometimes two, and I still feel that way. I recently wrote an essay called "Some Notes on the Scientific Methods of Simon Kuznets." In this connection I read through my old class lecture notes and there are still a lot of good dissertations there.

You ought to publish those notes.

I probably should. The other thing that I used to do involves an exercise I performed in class to demonstrate the ubiquity of implicit quantification in history books. I challenged students to pick any page at random from whatever history book they had at hand. The odds were, I said, that there'd be either an explicit or implicit quantitative statement that needed to be measured. The challenge was often taken up and I was never shown up, but I haven't tried to play that game in recent years. Anyhow, I think two things that I've said, one about Kuznets and the other about tendencies in historical literature got conflated.

On the second part of your question: There are many more good research projects than we can undertake at any point in time, because we don't have the resources to do them all. Which projects get taken up at a particular time has a lot to do with the priorities of society at that time. Certainly the funding is going to depend on what society thinks is important. I'm using society to mean not only Congress, but also administrators and peer reviewers at NSF, at the National Institutes of Health, at private foundations and, to the extent that they have resources to support faculty research, at universities.

I have never been one for proposing to students what they should do their research on. I feel that if students take my courses they will get a pretty good picture of the current interests of scholars. And that should give them a basis for picking a topic. I usually don't throw a menu before people and I rarely propose specific dissertation topics. What I usually do is to tell the students that they should propose a topic and that I'll tell them whether or not it's a feasible undertaking with the resources at their disposal. So I don't have any specific topics to single out. I'm obviously most interested in the issues that I'm working on, but they're not the only issues worth working on. I often wish I could live two lives because there are a lot of other issues that I'd love to work on. I recently became deeply involved in the statistical analysis of electoral behavior. There will be a very long paper by myself and Ralph Galantine in Volume 2 of *Without Consent or Contract* (subtitled *Evidence and Methods*) which attempts to estimate the effect of socio-economic factors on the political realignment of the 1850s. I wish I could spend ten or 15 years working on that problem. It's absolutely first rate. But, I think I like the biomedical issues even more. So that's where I'm going to spend the balance of my career.

Further reflections

Robert W. Fogel, with Mark Guglielmo

At the time of the interview in 1990, my research was focused on the Union Army project, "Early Indicators of Later Work Levels, Disease, and Death," which began in 1986 and has been funded since 1991 by the National Institute on Aging. Our aim has been to create a life-cycle sample that permits a longitudinal study of Union Army veterans as they aged. These veterans were born when life expectancy at birth was around 40. By the time the last of them died in the 1940s, life expectancy at birth had increased to around 64. By 1990, it had reached 75. As I mentioned in the interview, in all previous history prior to 1900, there had been an increase of between 20 and 25 years in life expectancy. The Union Army cohort is also significant because it was the first to turn age 65 in the twentieth century. The sample now consists of observations on more than 50,000 men; for each veteran we have collected about 15,000 items of data to describe his complete life cycle history. The sample was created by linking together information from about a dozen sources, including the manuscript schedules of censuses between 1850 and 1910; regimental, military, and medical records; public health records; Union Army pension records; surgeons' certificates giving the results of successive examinations of the veterans from first pension application until death; death certificates; daily military histories of each regiment in which the veterans served; and rejection records of men who volunteered for service but were not allowed to enlist. Currently, the data set is being expanded to take into account the public health environments in which the veterans lived throughout their lives, and the impact of these environments on morbidity and mortality throughout the life cycle.

The output of the project has been substantial: more than 80 published papers, five books, and eight Ph.D. dissertations. I have published several articles and two books drawing on our findings: *The Fourth Great Awakening and the Future of Egalitarianism* (University of Chicago Press 2000) and *The Escape from Hunger and Premature Death, 1700–2100* (2004a). I'm currently writing a third, with Roderick Floud and Bernard Harris, entitled *A Treatise on Technophysio Evolution and Consumption.*

Many other economists have been involved in the project and have utilized the data produced, including Dora Costa of MIT, Chulhee Lee of Seoul National University, Sven Wilson, Larry Wimmer and Clayne L. Pope of Brigham Young University, and Werner Troesken of the University of Pittsburgh. Dora Costa has published two important books from her participation in the project, *The Evolution of Retirement* (1998) and *Health and Labor Force Participation over the Life Cycle* (ed., 2003b). From the start, physicians have played a central role because of important interactions of biomedical with socio-economic factors. These include Dr. Nevin Scrimshaw of MIT, James M. Tanner of the Institute of Child Health (London), Dr. Louis Nguyen of Harvard University, Dr. Irwin Rosenberg of Tufts University, and Dr. Robert Mittendorf of Loyola University, Chicago. I formed the Center for Population Economics in 1981 to provide a home for scholars such as these and as a place to make our data sets available to other scholars.

One of the project's key findings is that prevalence rates for the main chronic diseases among Union Army veterans aged 65 and older in 1910 were much higher than among World War II veterans of the same ages during the middle to late 1980s. That finding was first set forth in a 1993 working paper and was elaborated and subsequently characterized as the "theory of technophysio evolution" in a series of articles (*e.g.*, Fogel & Costa 1997). This theory arose out of intense discussion among the project's senior investigators, consultants, and research assistants during 1993–4, with the physicians providing much of the intellectual leadership. The theory points to a synergy between technological and physiological improvements that has produced a new form of human evolution that is biological but not genetic, rapid, culturally transmitted, and not necessarily stable. This process is ongoing in both rich and developing countries. The theory holds that advances in technology result in improved living standards that make the human body a more efficient engine of production, causing still further advances in living standards, technology and human physiology.

This theory rests on the proposition that, over the past three centuries and particularly during the last century, humanity has gained an unprecedented degree of control over its environment, allowing for an increase in average body size of more than 50 percent and in average longevity of more than 100 percent. Further, a vast improvement in the robustness and capacity of vital organ systems has permitted a large increase in the human body's ability to withstand disease and other environmental insults. The theory appears to be relevant to forecasting likely trends over the next century in longevity, the age of onset of chronic diseases, body size, and the efficiency and durability of vital organ systems (see, *e.g.,* Costa 2003a). It also has applications to such important public policy issues as the rate of population growth, the viability of social security, and the future of health care costs. For example, it implies that by the end of the twenty-first century the average retiree will receive social security payments for many more years than current government projections suggest.[5]

In addition to my work on the "Early Indicators" project, I have studied several other policy issues. A main conclusion of *The Fourth Great Awakening* is that virtually all political parties have worked to create a more egalitarian society throughout most of American history and, as a result, both living standards and the quality of life (as reflected by longevity and body size) have increased dramatically for the poor, particularly during the twentieth century. The most pressing current problem, therefore, is an unequal distribution of spiritual resources, such as a sense of purpose and self-esteem. The government can partially alleviate this problem by providing the poor with better access to basic and higher education, but new approaches are needed to reach children in deeply impoverished families and those among the elderly who are alienated and depressed.

The Slavery Debates, 1952–1990 (2003) is a memoir of the academic debates over the profitability and efficiency of slavery and their consequences for the economic development of the United States. Readers of this volume may be interested to learn that I'm writing a book with my wife, Enid M. Fogel, on Simon Kuznets and the twentieth-century growth of economics as a discipline. In this connection, in the early 1990s we interviewed about 90 prominent economists, including nearly all the Nobel Laureates then alive.

Beginning in the late 1990s, as part of my continuing interest in technological change and other determinants of economic growth, I've studied the high performing Asian economies, especially China (2004c). Since 1999, I've visited China once or twice a year, meeting with government officials, business leaders and leading economists, and have had the honor of giving the keynote address at the annual meetings of the Chinese Economists Society (2005). Because of the Chinese government's free market reforms and rising levels of education among the population, I am extremely optimistic about China's prospects for continued economic growth.

5 For more on the "Early Indicators" project, see Wimmer (2003) and Fogel (2004b).

STANLEY L. ENGERMAN

Interviewed by
Anthony Patrick O'Brien

Stanley L. Engerman is John H. Munro Professor of Economics and professor of History at the University of Rochester, and Research Associate of the National Bureau of Economic Research. He was born in New York, New York in 1936 and was educated at New York University (B.S., 1956; M.B.A., 1958) and at The Johns Hopkins University (Ph.D., 1963). Following a year at Yale, he joined the economics faculty at the University of Rochester in 1963. He has served since 1982 as Associate Editor of *Explorations in Economic History*. Engerman was President of the Economic History Association in 1985 and of the Social Science History Association in 1992. He was elected Fellow of the American Academy of Arts & Sciences in 1985 and in 2005 was named Distinguished Fellow of the American Economic Association. With co-author Robert W. Fogel, Engerman was awarded the 1975 Bancroft Prize in American history for *Time on the Cross*. He was honored in 2004 with *Slavery in the Development of the Americas*, a *Festschrift* edited by David Eltis, Frank Lewis and Kenneth Sokoloff. The interview was conducted in March, 2000 (via email, fax and telephone) by Anthony Patrick (Tony) O'Brien of Lehigh University.

Why did you decide to become an economist and how did you become interested in economic history?

My undergraduate major was in accounting, and, while getting an M.B.A. at night, I worked for two years for a CPA in New York. I had always been interested in economics and in history, so when I found that I did not want to work as an accountant for the rest of my life, I applied to graduate schools to study economics. For my M.B.A. thesis I wrote on Henry Carey and his times, and in my first year at Johns Hopkins I gave a "journal club" presentation on the Conrad and Meyer article, one product of which was an important article on slavery by Yasukichi Yasuba, a fellow graduate student who attended this meeting. Thus, there was no single event that led me to economic history. My Ph.D. thesis in public finance, written for Richard Musgrave, was also somewhat empirical.

How did you first come to meet and work with Robert Fogel?

At Hopkins I shared an office with Bob Fogel and several other graduate students, and we had frequent discussions on topics such as the Union Pacific, the railroads, and slavery. I spent most of one summer working as a research assistant on his railroad book and, after we both graduated, he asked me if I would be willing to work as a co-author of an economic history text, which he had been planning to write.

Would you comment on that book, *The Reinterpretation of American Economic History*? What was the inspiration for bringing those articles together? Did the book have the impact on economic historians that you had expected?

Reinterpretation was intended to bring to the attention of historians the contributions made by recent work in economic history and to indicate that the work dealt with problems of interest to historians. However, the impact of this book, in bringing together many significant essays, seemed greater on economic historians. And while some essays were used by other historians, the impact overall was probably less than originally hoped for.

Do you have other reflections about the 1960s–early 1970s period?

The early cliometrics meetings were generally quite exciting and had many interesting intellectual exchanges. There was a sense of dealing with major issues in economic development and history, and the caliber of scholarship was extremely high.

Do you see the New Economic History or Cliometrics as having been a significant break with what had come before in economic history? Did you see yourself as participating in a revolutionary reorienting of the field?

Most of us saw Cliometrics as either a significant break with or, at least, a significant extension of past work in history, including economic history. The questions came both from economics and history, but the central point was in method – the use of explicit economic analysis and the attempts to get a strong empirical and quantitative base for the measures used. Some thought of themselves as revolutionaries while others regarded the work as the only reasonable way to reach important answers to long-standing historical questions. The reactions to this work often led to a hardening of positions on all sides, so the break with the past sharpened.

Would you discuss the origins of the slavery project that eventually became *Time on the Cross*? When you and Robert Fogel began the

research for the paper that was published in *Reinterpretation*, did you already intend to embark on the larger project?

The original discussions on slavery emerged in our graduate school days based on understanding Conrad and Meyer. This interest continued since slavery was an important issue in American history, and when we were putting together readings for *Reinterpretation*, we felt that it would be useful to supplement the essays chosen with one bringing the debate up to date. It was while writing that essay that we thought in detail about a more extensive project to try to answer some of the questions we felt were still open and could be answered with new data. This seemed a useful project because of the centrality of slavery to American history and the fact that many important questions were basically posed in economic terms, no matter how previously answered. It was this combination of applicability of economic and quantitative methods and the importance of the specific questions that made the study of slavery so central to discussions about the New Economic History.

You have mentioned Conrad and Meyer's article on the profitability of slavery a couple of times. Could you expand on why that article had the impact it did on you and other young economists at the time? If it had been published in the *Journal of Economic History* rather than in the *Journal of Political Economy*, would you and your colleagues have been as likely to take notice of it?

The Conrad and Meyer article was a very clearly presented piece dealing with the economic analysis of a major historical problem. It described the basic investment approach, pointed to the data needed to answer the questions raised, and examined the sensitivity of conclusions to possible alternative measures. It demonstrated how economics – both theory and data – could be used to advance the debate. I think it would have attracted about the same attention if published in any other journal, but it was interesting that the *JPE* was willing to publish it.

Obviously *Time on the Cross* was met with an extraordinary reaction. Did you expect the book would receive such a reaction?

Certainly the extent of the reaction and its duration was somewhat unexpected, although in some ways it was quite flattering. It indicated that economic and quantitative approaches could deal with questions that many people seemed to regard as important, as well as questions that did require the use of empirical data to obtain answers.

Would you say the key results of *Time on the Cross* have held up over time? Are there still important unanswered questions with respect to the economic history of slavery in the United States?

In general, I would regard the key results of *Time on the Cross* as having passed the test of time and, with the new results of studies by others, having had some influence on the study of slavery in other times and places than the United States. The issues of profitability, viability, and increasing income, as argued by numerous others as well, seemed to have some agreement, while the flexibility and dynamics of a slave economy are also noted. The economic issues with the most uncertainty are probably those of possible increased industrialization over time and a better relating of antebellum and postbellum labor behavior.

At the time, many critics of *Time on the Cross* seemed to focus on what they felt was the overly benign picture of slavery as painted in the book, at least with respect to the material standard of living of slaves. The result was an extended discussion of slave diets, housing, chances of promotion within a hierarchy of occupations, and so forth. What is your take now on the outcome of that aspect of the debate?

My reaction to the current literature is that most of the work about the material standard of living provides a view somewhat similar to that presented in *Time on the Cross* and that recent arguments of slave autonomy, which in many ways go beyond our arguments regarding slaves and masters, do provide some consistency with earlier writings.

Some critics, particularly conventional historians, have argued that cliometric literature on American slavery focuses too much on large cotton plantations in the late antebellum period to the neglect of either earlier periods or of slavery off the large plantations. Do you think that is an accurate observation?

I think that the point about focusing on a particular set of units has been useful, but I also think that any examination of the literature on southern antebellum slavery has the same concentration. When you remember the great importance of cotton plantations and the share of slaves on them, it is not obvious that for certain questions such a focus is unreasonable. For different questions, other types of agriculture and industry and other sizes of units would be necessary, but how different the answers will be from the cotton plantation case is not always clear.

When Robert Fogel eventually published his further thoughts on slavery in *Without Consent or Contract*, he acknowledges his collaboration with you on slavery research following the publication of *Time on the Cross*. Why didn't that collaboration carry through to joint authorship of *Without Consent or Contract*? Were you more content than Fogel to let *Time on the Cross* stand as your major statement on these issues?

By the time Bob was working on *Without Consent or Contract*, I had gotten interested in other related questions such as the postbellum South, slavery elsewhere in the Americas, and the re-emergence of contract labor throughout the world. I also wrote a number of essays on US slavery dealing with a variety of issues which arose. In general, there was no disagreement between Bob and me on most issues of interpretation of the US case, and there were no marked changes that I would have made.

You seem to have devoted a great deal of time in recent years to research on comparative slavery. What are the major lessons to be learned from the comparative approach to the study of history?

I think that there is so much to be gained by comparative studies, since studies of similarities and differences can highlight important aspects of each specific case. The studies of settlement patterns and of the adjustments to the ending of slavery have been quite fruitful as they provide a context for interpreting the US experience. They also remind us that comparative information was often examined by contemporaries to forecast the future and to formulate policies.

In what ways would you say our overall understanding of the economic history of slaves in the New World is distorted by a focus on American slavery?

I think that the distortions of individual studies can go two ways – misunderstanding other New World slavery by extrapolating on the basis of the US case and also misunderstanding the US case by not observing patterns of commonality with other slave societies. Recent as well as past comparisons have, for example, highlighted the demographic differences between the US and elsewhere in the Americas, including the social, cultural, and physical differences between sugar and cotton production and the similar withdrawal from plantation labor whenever possible after emancipation. Also of interest is the debate over free versus slave labor in all places and the variations in the process by which emancipation was accomplished.

You have been interested in the slave trade and, more generally, the African background to the settlement of the New World. Not much of the work done in these areas is by cliometricians (for instance, the excellent essay by John Thornton in the first volume of the *Cambridge Economic History of the United States* is a more-or-less conventional historical account). Do you have any thoughts as to why these areas do not seem to have caught the attention of cliometricians?

Probably the main reason is, thus far, the limited data that can be used to study those questions important to economic historians. Little systematic material on inputs, outputs, prices, and populations is currently available, and the range of uncertainties in any estimates remains large. Some shifts have recently taken place regarding the usefulness of the postulate of some rational economic behavior, so some questions can now be examined in more detail than before. Limited data makes economic history difficult, but it has the same effect on other types of history as well.

Do you believe a consensus has been reached from the debate touched off

many years ago by Eric Williams about the role of profits from the slave trade in financing the growth of manufacturing in England and the United States?

The Eric Williams [thesis] has its moral as well as analytical aspects, and a general consensus is difficult to achieve. Nevertheless, looking at how the question is approached, there have been some refinements in certain areas. The questions asked have included (1) the size of the shock, (2) the impacts on other parts of the economy, and (3) the nature of the economy in which the shock has been introduced. The concept of dynamic effects on other sectors has been used to argue for a large impact, presumably in lieu of large direct effects from unusually high profits. I still find the question of how Britain was able to achieve a well-functioning economy at the time to be an interesting one.

Like most other fields in economics, economic history has become more technical and quantitative. On the whole, has this been a good thing?

One big change in cliometric work was that, for obvious reasons, great attention was now being given to twentieth-century topics. Earlier, the nineteenth century and colonial period were more frequently studied. With the great abundance of qualitative as well as quantitative data prepared by the government for the twentieth century, more sophisticated analysis can be undertaken using more technical means of analysis. As long as the studies are asking useful questions and are grounded in some empirical base, they can make contributions to the field. Given the trade-offs made necessary by time limitations, technique can sometimes come at a cost. Nevertheless, we should remember what Adam Smith said about the advantages of a division of labor and not expect any one work by itself to answer all the questions.

Has anything important been lost as a result of the more technical approach? Are there any new areas or approaches to economic history, anthropometrics perhaps, that you consider particularly interesting and important?

What new approaches will prove to be interesting in the future is hard to determine now, since what seems possible to do often has surprises – as with expanded anthropometrical studies which initially emerged from the various questions related to slavery.

On the one hand, economic history has had some trouble holding its own in the economics profession, with departments dropping economic history requirements in their Ph.D. programs (and sometimes dropping economic historians as well). On the other hand, many people feel that a large gap has opened up between economists doing economic history and conventional historians. Do you have thoughts on either of these issues?

The role of economic history in both economics and history has become puzzling. In many ways, the quantitative and analytical approach has become a standard part of the historian's method, and many more studies utilize these approaches than before, even if they are not at the technological frontier. Similarly, more of the work in applied economics fits into the range of economic history, based on quantitative analysis of past data. But while applications of economic history have increased in both disciplines, there is less call for those trained specifically as economic historians. The demand among historians had dropped a few decades ago and does not seem to have made a recovery. The more recent decline in the economic history requirements in many departments does not always represent a loss of interest in economic history, since other courses may pick up that approach. Meetings of the Cliometric Society and the Economic History Association do seem to attract younger (and older) scholars and to present new research. One just wishes for a better set of job market prospects for new people in the field.

Does the economics profession at large see economic history as a legitimate subfield or simply as a tool to occasionally be made use of, as, for example, Bernanke uses the Great Depression to gain insight into macroeconomic theory?

I remember that in *Reinterpretation*, there were articles by economists and by historians, as well as by economic historians. The selections were made on the basis of questions and methods, and I still think that provides a useful approach.

When Fogel and North won the Nobel Prize, many economic historians seemed to feel that this would raise the prestige of economic history within the profession. Do you believe things have worked out that way?

The Nobel Prize did indicate that a jury of peers regarded the field of economic history as being central to the discipline. What is less clear is whether this enhanced prestige was translated into gains throughout the age distribution of economic historians.

A great deal of your work has dealt with the economic history of African Americans. It seems as if many scholars dealing with the history of African Americans have the impact of their research on current political questions firmly in mind. And certainly the reactions to such research often seem to reflect current political concerns. Has this been an issue for you?

It is difficult to do any work in African-American history – or, indeed, other fields of history – without being sensitive to possible applications to the current scene. The major difficulty is in trying to determine what we think the best or most appropriate way to see the past. During some times, the politics of seeing slaves as victims was deemed most important; more recently, it is slave autonomy that appears most frequently argued. Now, both contentions are important to understand, but emphasis on one or the other does leave any scholar open to criticism.

You have produced a great quantity of original and important research. So I wanted to take a page from Brian Lamb's interviews on C-SPAN's *Book Notes* program and ask you to describe your routine.

I usually divide my workday so that I am in my office from about 8 to 5, meeting students, talking on the phone, writing emails etc., as well as reading when there is time. In the evening, since my children are now on their own, I usually read and write for several hours at home unless there is a good basketball game or good old movie on TV. Most first drafts I write at home, usually on weekends, since there are usually fewer interruptions. As long as I still enjoy research and writing, this schedule works out well.

Do you have any observations about the age-old quandary of how to juggle teaching responsibilities with research?

The teaching quandary has never been resolved, since although I have no problem preparing lectures, it is the delivery that still poses problems. The two things I try to do, if possible, is teach courses for which there is a possible research interest and to teach early in the day so I have a block of time without worrying about class performance.

Volume I of *The Cambridge Economic History of the United States* was published several years ago. How have things gone with the second and third volumes?

With the first volume, everything worked well. Every contributor completed his or her assignment on time. With the second and third volumes, which have more contributors than did the first volume, some people dropped out along the way. Some were replaced; some were not. In the preface to the various *Cambridge Economic Histories of Europe*, published during the 1950s, the editors mention that the volumes were late in appearing because this contributor died in a concentration camp, or that contributor was killed fighting on the Finnish front. Nothing so melodramatic happened here. Volume II and Volume III should both be out this year.

Further reflections

Stanley L. Engerman

At Johns Hopkins I was most fortunate in the professors of economics and history whose classes I was able to audit or take for credit. While a graduate student in economics I did sit in on several courses in the history department that were extremely useful to me. C. Vann Woodward's courses in American history after 1865 covered a broad ground conceptually and ideologically, while Fred Lane's courses in economic history were a superb introduction to the scope and methods of medieval and modern European history. The course offerings in the economics department were quite diverse, but most usefully came together in broadening perspectives. In addition to Musgrave's course in public finance and monetary economics, which directed attention to the role of theoretical analysis in discussing real world issues and current economic policy, I took courses with Fritz Machlup, Clarence Long, and Simon Kuznets. Machlup taught what was even then considered old-fashioned microeconomics as well as a course in methodology (not the methods) of economics. Together, these theoretical discussions were quite important in teaching supply and demand analysis, but also in demonstrating the nature of assumptions made in economic and historical analysis as well as the centrality of the counterfactual approach. Clarence Long was in his last year of teaching, before going to a long and successful career in the US House of Representatives. He had just published his monumental National Bureau of Economic Research book on labor force participation in the US (1958), a work combining extremely detailed empirical analysis with broad speculations in describing changing employment patterns. Use of properly measured data was a central focus of his work, as was the need to deal with important questions and the key role of interpreting the results. I was able to take only two courses with Kuznets (my first year at Hopkins he was on leave at Harvard, and he subsequently left permanently to go there). His courses were all lecturing, on the topic of economic development, including long segments on population, innovation, and industrial change. The various measures and discussions he dealt with centered on the first few of the supplements that appeared in *Economic Development and Cultural Change*.[1] The topics were broad and sweeping in time, place, and questions with key insights generated from the immense empirical base at his command, opening up new views of many issues of historical importance.

While each of these professors made important teaching contributions in his own area, my exposure to their diversity of approaches and methods also permitted an appreciation of the value of looking at problems from different ways and to understand the importance of the many different varieties of possible questions and answers. Rather than being opposed to each other, these different methods appeared complementary and gave me a greater ability to obtain meaningful answers.

The economist's approach, of course, need not lead to a clear or simple answer to all questions that scholars might study. The complexity of people's psyches and also of events would seem to limit the possible achievement of any one single approach, but that need not be a source of disappointment. Some scholars seem to believe that there can be only one answer to a major question, and often advocate the usefulness of specific types of approach to reach the answer. Others, however, regard scholarship as more of a collective enterprise, with knowledge accumulating, and find the words of Adam Smith on the division of labour, applied to this set of problems, quite sensible. Frankly, I find the Smithian view the more reasonable one, since it provides a more realistic approach to problems of data and interpretation. My feeling is that the actual day-to-day work of economic historians is to handle rather narrow, specific questions in working towards the broader view. Defining the precise nature of the question, and

1 *E.g.*, Kuznets (1956), the first of ten substantial pieces appearing in *EDCC* through 1967, all with the main title, "Quantitative Aspects of the Economic Growth of Nations."

pointing to the types of answers desired, are vital aids in determining what methods of data gathering and analysis are most appropriate in each case. In short, much of what appears as debates on methodology are less about methods than about questions the particular scholar regards as interesting or important. It is the opportunity to ask and to answer a broad range of questions that has always made economic history such an interesting and enjoyable discipline for me to pursue.

Part VII

FROM THE WORKSHOP OF ALEXANDER GERSCHENKRON, ECONOMIC HISTORIAN

John R. Meyer

Albert Fishlow

Paul A. David

Peter Temin

In the winter of 1958, ten years after he succeeded Abbott Payson Usher in the economics faculty of Harvard University, Alexander Gerschenkron received funds from the Ford Foundation to establish a "Workshop in Economic History" for his carefully selected Ph.D. students. Those funds served for a dozen years, and in that period Gerschenkron produced what the foundation considered to be a "new generation of economic historians."[1] Unlike Kuznets's metaphorical workshop, Gerschenkron's Workshop was a pair of real office rooms in a building on Harvard Square. Albert Fishlow and Paul David were the Workshop's first tenants in the spring of 1959; Peter Temin arrived the next year. John Meyer, the first of those interviewed for this Part, was by then an Associate Professor in the Economics Department. He had benefited earlier from Gerschenkron's teaching but as a faculty member could partake neither of the Workshop nor its associated seminar. Gerschenkron's establishment of the Workshop marked a proud moment in his career, and occurred at the beginning of a decade or so when he was at the top of his game.[2]

"The Great Gerschenkron" had traversed a protracted and circuitous path to Harvard. He was born in Odessa in 1904 and died in Cambridge in 1978. Fleeing Russia with his father during the Civil War, he settled in Vienna in 1920, became a refugee again at the *Anschluss* in 1938 and emigrated to the United States the following year. Working as a research assistant and lecturer in the Economics Department at Berkeley, he spent nights and weekends writing the book that brought him immediate fame in American academia, *Bread and Democracy in Germany* (University of California Press 1943). In 1944 Gerschenkron moved to the Federal Reserve Board in Washington, D.C., as resident expert on the Soviet economy. He presented a paper on Russian industrial growth at the 1947 Economic History Association meetings, arguing that Soviet statisticians' reports of phenomenally rapid expansion in the era of central planning were most likely biased sharply upward. In a later study, *A Dollar Index of Soviet Machinery Output* (1951), he showed just how the bias arose: an index-number

1 Gerschenkron's workshop initiative is discussed in Rouvray (2005: 269–77); quotation from pp. 271–2, n. 84.

2 See Rosovsky (1979), Fishlow (2003), McCloskey (1992a; 2001) and Dawidoff (2002).

phenomenon soon named the "Gerschenkron effect."[3] "How?" may be one question to answer, but "How much?" is quite another. Assigning dollar prices to Soviet machinery required detailed information and Gerschenkron had no Soviet machinery to examine. He thus went out to visit more than 50 firms across the United States to consult with executives and engineers about the costs and qualities of American machines that might be equivalent.[4] His thorough approach to the measurement problem reflects what both impressed and inspired his students: an appetite for scholarly hard work in pursuit of knowledge for testing big ideas. Gerschenkron's continuing fascination with index numbers often bemused his students, but the work for which he is best known came to be called the "Gerschenkron hypothesis": that the pattern of economic development in nineteenth-century Europe was systematically affected by the "relative economic backwardness" of a nation when it began to industrialize. The relatively more backward, but successful, industrializing nations had found "substitutes" for institutions and actors that had played more prominent roles in previous cases of industrial expansion.[5]

Gerschenkron's students learned economic history through his lecture course and research seminar. The lectures were "little works of art, beautifully prepared and beautifully delivered" – "performances" without notes, presented to "create an impression of casual improvisation." Until 1973, when the requirement was abandoned, Gerschenkron's course in European Economic History was taken by all Ph.D. economics candidates. Henry Rosovsky remarks, "In the post-Schumpeterian era it was virtually the only course in the graduate economics curriculum that directly assaulted the provincialism of most students."[6]

The graduate seminar was something completely different; it was a forcing ground for the New Economic History, but in it the new methods brought to bear on each topic were supplied by the students. Gerschenkron seemingly believed that adversity akin to that of his own experience would strengthen the character and mind. His style as a mentor was thus to leave his students largely to their own resources but at the same time to set himself up as the ideal. Rosovsky writes, he ". . . gave us his ideas and the example of his life." Albert Fishlow says that "he never stated the standard; he embodied it. The phenomenon was 'Look at me. This is what it takes to be a first-class scholar.' " Gerschenkron's best students were invited (or allowed) to enroll in the seminar, where they became accustomed to defending themselves against fierce assault – a proper seminar "closely resembled his notions of a good dogfight." During these evening encounters he silently puffed away at his pipe; only at the conclusion would he make a comment: "Invariably it was succinct; once in a while it was also delphic." As

3 Using the relative prices of a pre-industrial output structure imparts an upward bias to measures over time of the value of production, as modern industrial outputs increase greatly in volume and their relative prices fall.

4 See Dawidoff (2002: Chs 1–4); on machinery, pp. 157–61.

5 These ideas first appeared in a 1951 conference paper, "Economic backwardness in historical perspective" (1952), an essay providing the title for his book of 1962. Fishlow (2003) is a retrospective review of the 1962 essay collection.

6 Dawidoff (2002: 250, quoting Robert Sutcliffe: 241–3), Rosovsky (1979: 1009). See also McCloskey (1992a: 242) on eliminating the history requirement.

with the seminar, so with dissertations: Gerschenkron's explicit advice to his Ph.D. students was so spare that he might have regarded the very light rein of British research supervision as rank interventionism. And as with dissertations, so with the Workshop's offices: Gerschenkron inspected them only once. Paul David says, "He came, he saw, he left – permanently."[7]

These four interviewees who engaged with Gerschenkron thus entered and occupied an intellectual environment – a scholarly environment – that he had created. Much like his friend Simon Kuznets, Alexander Gerschenkron taught his students an exacting approach to measurement and elicited in them a desire to understand the patterns of history. His erudition led students to hold him in awe; the same applied to colleagues. A regular observer of Gerschenkron's performances at the Faculty Club often thought, "This is the last man with all known knowledge."[8]

At the "Economic Growth" symposium of the EHA in 1947 Gerschenkron had mused that "history in the conditional mood" might be "an enticing pastime," one that at the time he had contemplated (but avoided) for his analysis of Russia (1947: 144). But he did not reject counterfactual thinking about the contingency of events – he encouraged it. Thus, only a few years later, as a student in Gerschenkron's European history course, John Meyer was enticed to write an explicitly counterfactual as well as quantitative paper on the economy of Victorian Britain (1955b). Thereafter, when he took up an Assistant Professorship in Harvard's Economics Department, Meyer began a couple years of teaching the undergraduate course in American Economic History. By 1959, however, he had moved on to the fields for which he is best known. Meyer has been a prime contributor to quantitative economic analysis of urban and national transport systems and is the rare scholar whose *Festschrift* serves as a textbook for an entire field of study: *Essays in Transportation Economics and Policy: A Handbook in Honor of John R. Meyer.* In many projects he led large and well-integrated research teams of students and colleagues. "By example and direction, he taught dozens of young scholars how to do research and set a standard of generosity in giving credit and coauthorship to his collaborators."[9]

Rarer still is a scholar's instigation of a strand of literature removed from his main interest. Meyer and his graduate classmate, Alfred H. Conrad, can reasonably be seen as the initial practitioners of a "Harvard wing" of the New Economic History, beginning with their teaching of the American course. Gerschenkron attended several of Meyer's classes, was excited by the discussion of the profitability of slavery that Meyer had introduced into a lecture, and urged him to produce a paper on the subject. With Conrad, who had made a similar trial run at Northwestern, Meyer did so. Given Gerschenkron's encouragement, they were the only contributors of *two* papers to the 1957 Williamstown meetings, a methodological manifesto (Meyer & Conrad 1957) and their slavery paper (Conrad & Meyer 1958). The quantitative analysis of slavery might

7 Dawidoff (2002: Ch. 10 *passim*). Quotations: Rosovsky (1979: 1010); Dawidoff (2002): quoting Fishlow, pp. 256–7; pp. 251, 253; quoting David, p. 257.

8 Dawidoff (2002: 18), quoting Martin Peretz.

9 The *Festschrift* (Brookings 1999) was edited by José A. Gómez-Ibáñez, William B. Tye and Clifford Winston. Quotation from the editors' introduction, p. 2.

not have begun as soon as it did (or perhaps at all) without that 1958 paper.[10] Although John Meyer's interests led him to a career in transport, urban and regional economics, his writings are permeated with an historical sensibility. Responding to Mark Blaug's questionnaire for *Who's Who in Economics* (1999: 772), he deliberately classified himself in the first instance as an economic historian. After all, as he told us, "All economists are historians."

Albert Fishlow, like John Meyer, is more generally recognized today for his work outside economic history than within it, although his first book, *American Railroads and the Transformation of the Ante-Bellum Economy* (1965), his Ph.D. dissertation, is a "classic" of economic history. While he has regularly published other historical pieces, the bulk of his work is in development economics, beginning with his research on Brazil in the mid-1960s. Yet Fishlow opens *American Railroads* as would an historian, and closes it as would a development economist with an understanding refined by study of historical data and past economic change. The book's contribution to "new economic history" lies between those points and, as Gerschenkron wrote (p. *viii*), also in the "statistical appendices in which the author offers a full insight into his laboratory and without which no real appreciation of the importance of the study and of the validity of its interpretative results is possible." Although Fishlow's book and Fogel's (1964) report similar estimates of the "social savings" accruing to American railroads in 1859 and 1890, respectively, their works contrast sharply: Fogel's book is a study of economic growth, Hedgehog-like, of "one big thing," while Fishlow's is, Fox-like, a study of the "many things" of economic development. As Fishlow notes in his interview, he and Fogel were focusing on different methodological questions – sufficiency versus necessity – an issue he discusses within a broader context in "The New Economic History Revisited" (1974).

Early in the 1970s Fishlow published some research demonstrating that the distribution of income in Brazil had become more unequal in the previous decade – a conclusion, as he reports, discomfiting to the Brazilian military regime, stimulating to the World Bank and involving him in a considerable hassle. Recurring international financial crises have also drawn his attention, as with the 1980s versus 1890s comparison mentioned in the interview, and more recently for the entire twentieth century with Barry Eichengreen in a paper that "reads as a history lesson on crises," "Contending with Capital Flows."[11] Over the years he has occasionally consulted for the World Bank, the United Nations, and the InterAmerican Development Bank, and has provided testimony to Congress on various topics. Since becoming Director of the Columbia Center for Brazilian Studies in 2000, he has returned to Brazil frequently, and has published much in Portuguese.[12] Fishlow says that throughout his career he has tried to maintain the intellectual independence of a scholar most interested in the longer view, from 1961, when he departed the Economic History Workshop for Berkeley, to the present.

10 On the contingency of careers, one might also say it is possible that, without the consequent debate about slavery at the Johns Hopkins Department of Political Economy, Robert Fogel and Stanley Engerman might have followed quite different paths from those they later trod.

11 Eichengreen & Fishlow (1998); comment in a review by Arvind Krishnamurthy, *JEL* 38:1 (2000: 140).

12 Likewise, a collection of his English-language papers has appeared in Portuguese translation: *Development in Brazil and Latin America: An Historical Perspective* (São Paulo: Paz e terra 2004), selected and introduced by the Brazilian economist Edmar Lisboa Bacha.

In the same year, Paul David also departed Massachusetts for California, traveling to Stanford, across San Francisco Bay from Berkeley. David took with him a partially completed Ph. D. dissertation, on industrial structure and growth in nineteenth-century Chicago, and a résumé listing but one publication, and that a joint paper of theoretical bent (Fishlow & David 1961). A dozen years later, at the invitation of Henry Rosovsky, he had returned to Harvard as visiting Taussig Professor in Economics. In the interim he had almost been denied renewal of his contract by the Provost at Stanford in 1964 for lack of higher degree and too little work in print. But by 1970 he had published many more papers, both those in the pipeline in 1964 and several others, six of them palpable "hits." With Alexander Gerschenkron's support, he had been promoted to full Professor in 1970 – but still with no doctorate. At a party in Cambridge in 1972 Rosovsky and Gerschenkron literally backed him into a corner and persuaded him that he ought to use some of his published work to complete the degree and to defend it that academic year. This Paul David did, earning his Ph.D. in 1973 and publishing the "dissertation" in 1975 as *Technical choice, innovation and economic growth.*[13] The book contains his celebrated 1966 article on the adoption of the reaping machine in America, others on American tariffs and cotton textiles, a critique of Fogel's 1964 book on railroads, and another – an early intimation of "path dependence" – on the effects of sunk costs on adoption of the reaper in Britain. Not content simply to reprint earlier work, however, he preceded these papers with two new interpretive pieces. The first is an essay on how irreversible processes, indivisible techniques and other phenomena would join so that knowing "history" would indeed matter to understanding economic dynamics. The second is an extended essay re-examining evidence and argument about the "Habakkuk hypothesis" and proposing a new explanatory framework in line with the theme of the first essay.

David's work was by then well known for its thoroughness, density of empirical detail and complexity of analysis, characteristics that prompted William Parker to open his review of *Technical choice* by asserting "This is not a book to take with you to the beach." David's ability to manipulate, reject or transform standard economic theory is so striking that Nicholas von Tunzelmann awarded him the same encomium given to Simon Kuznets two decades later; he wrote, "In this corpus of work he establishes himself as the economic historian's economist *par excellence.*" Similarly, Joel Mokyr likened this book to the "heavenly length" ("and sometimes a little longer") of a Bruckner symphony, declaring, "More than any of his colleagues, David is the economist's economic historian."[14] The essays in this book are Paul David's first steps on a path leading him to deeper study of how history matters to economic change – of path dependence and its likely, although not necessary, association with market failure, symbolized by the economics of QWERTY (see, *e.g.*, 1985; 2005). This path was neither so deep nor so narrow, however, that it kept him from stepping aside to enter the slavery debate in the 1970s (*e.g.*, David & Temin 1974), to study economic and historical demography with Warren Sanderson (*e.g.*, 1986), nor to keep him from the parallel path of his 40-year

13 See Abramovitz (2000: 3–5) and Dawidoff (2002: 265–8).

14 Parker (1976: 310); on Kuznets, Kapuria-Foreman & Perlman (1995); von Tunzelmann in *JEH* 35:4 (1975: 855); Mokyr in *EDCC* 26:1, (1977: 193, 189).

collaboration with Moses Abramovitz on American economic growth. Although in recent years he has established a firm foothold in Britain and Europe, his ties to Stanford remain strong: for example, he and Gavin Wright have compared the productivity surges of the 1920s and the 1990s resulting from the spread of electricity and of microelectronics (2003). While in Europe, David has become an advocate for a liberal interpretation of intellectual "property rights," building on the history of an "open" scientific culture that he sees as central to the emergence of modern science and technology since the sixteenth century (2004a; b).

Peter Temin's writings are remarkably diverse in subject matter, from American iron production and banking to macroeconomic crises and telephone deregulation. Over the years the issues he has investigated have proven to be among the most important of those considered by cliometrics. His interviewer, John Brown, for example, relates below how Temin's work appeared at almost every turn in the University of Michigan's graduate course in American economic history. To conclude our classical allusion, Peter Temin is perhaps the most Fox-like scholar of the lot. Nonetheless, he has brought a common approach to the "many things" he has investigated, utilizing economic models both to clarify questions and to serve as the basis for quantitative tests. Initially Temin focused his research on American (and some British) topics but he has broadened his purview geographically to Europe in the nineteenth and twentieth centuries, temporally from ancient times to the twenty-first century, and topically to the conjunction between business history and cliometrics. He has employed a variety of analytical approaches, selecting the one best suited to the problem at hand, and has expanded the range of problems he has found intriguing: from modes of behavior affecting the market for prescription drugs to the impact of culture on economic performance.

Recently Temin has begun to follow two more threads in his research, owing in one case to determination and in the other to serendipity. For years Moses Finley's view of the ancient world as a "customary economy" had nagged at him. Accordingly he set out to examine the ancient economy from an economic historian's perspective, presenting his ideas on imperial Roman markets while at a conference in Oxford. The economists at breakfast laughed; so did the ancient historians at lunch. He "decided to get serious" in response. The result was "A market economy in the early Roman empire" (2001), followed by work on prices in Babylon, Roman labor markets and on the entire ancient economy (2006). The other strand comes from chance knowledge of a private archive, which has resulted in several papers on eighteenth- and nineteenth-century British banking (*e.g.*, Temin & Voth 2005). Peter Temin is the youngest of those we have selected as members of the "first generation," although legally he is a senior citizen. Still, like many others whose conversations appear in this volume he finds it so much fun that he continues to work steadily at his chosen profession.

From the beginning Harvard was a prime center of pioneering work in the "New Economic History;" Gerschenkron's successors at Harvard have kept it so. These four interviewees are the first of a "new generation" of economic historians who have transmitted Gerschenkron's values – and their own – to further generations of scholarly descendants around the globe.

JOHN R. MEYER

Interviewed by
John C. Brown

John Robert Meyer is the James W. Harpel Professor of Capital Formation and Economic Growth, Emeritus, in the Kennedy School of Government, Harvard University, Cambridge, Massachusetts. He was born in Pasco, Washington in 1927 and was educated at the University of Washington (B.A., 1950) and at Harvard (Ph.D., 1955). He joined the Harvard economics faculty in 1955 and taught at Yale University from 1968 to 1973; he returned to Harvard as Professor of Transportation, Logistics and Distribution at Harvard Business School (1973–83), and taught in the Kennedy School until he retired in 1997. From 1967 to 1977 he was President of the National Bureau of Economic Research, a position which led to his move to New Haven to be closer to the Bureau's offices in New York. On returning to Massachusetts in 1973 he took the Bureau's headquarters with him to Cambridge, retaining the New York office as a branch. Early in his career he was awarded a Guggenheim Fellowship (1958–9) and a Ford Faculty Research Fellowship at Harvard (1962–3). He has served on the editorial boards of several economics journals and was editor of *Explorations in Entrepreneurial History* in 1957. Meyer received Harvard's David A. Wells Prize for his Ph.D. dissertation (1955a) and was elected Fellow of the American Academy of Arts and Sciences in 1968. His expertise in transportation economics and policy has led him to serve as advisor to the Canadian Pacific Railway (1974–81), the US Department of Transportation, and the World Bank. He was a board member of Conrail (1976–8) and of the Union Pacific Corporation (1978–2000), and served as UP's Vice Chairman (1981–3). On his retirement he was honored with a conference whose presentations compose the *Festschrift* noted in the Part introduction. Since his retirement he has resided both in Cambridge and in Florida and has been writing his 24th book, *Enduring Enterprise: Public Policy and the Development of North American Railroads in the 20th Century*, with Robert E. Gallamore. The interview took place in Meyer's office at the Kennedy School in September 1994 and was conducted by John Brown of Clark University, who writes:

Together with Alfred Conrad, John Meyer played a key role in the early development of Cliometrics. Two of their papers and the resulting discussion were particularly influential in the practice of economic history. One is "The Economics of Slavery in the Antebellum South," which recast the plantation economy in terms amenable to economic analysis. Their finding that the return to an investment in a slave matched the return available elsewhere is a well known contribution of the paper. It also established a long research agenda on interregional trade in slaves, the demography of slavery and other issues, within a coherent economic framework. The slavery paper also illustrated the methodological contribution presented in another piece they aimed at economic historians, "Economic Theory, Statistical Inference, and Economic History," which argued that economic historians should look for generalizations and test specific hypotheses. This second paper articulated an analytical distinction between primary literary evidence and the indirect quantitative evidence that could be used to test the implications even of qualitative hypotheses.

Let me start at the beginning. How did you and Alfred Conrad get involved in the issue of slavery? Did you approach it more from a methodological perspective, or was historical debate your primary motivation?

Alf and I were old friends; we knew each other in graduate school. In the summer of 1955, Alf went off to Northwestern University and I stayed on at Harvard as an assistant professor. Both of us, unbeknownst to the other, somehow got conscripted to teach American Economic History. In my case, the course had been orphaned by Jack Sawyer's departure to Yale. I don't know what the situation was at Northwestern. Arthur Smithies, who was the chairman of the Harvard Economics Department, made me an offer I couldn't refuse. If I taught the American economic history course in the spring, I could have half time off during the fall of 1955 for preparation. And Alf had a rather parallel experience; Harold Williamson recruited him to teach the American economic history course at Northwestern and gave him some time off from his other teaching duties to prepare. Alf, continuing some research with the Leontief Project, was in the habit of visiting Cambridge from Evanston about once every month or so. Sometime in January 1956, I believe, we were having lunch and started talking about our mutual experiences preparing to do an American economic history course. We also discovered that both of us had decided that the slavery profitability question seemed particularly suitable for illustrating the role of economics in analyzing historical issues. Both of us had sketched out a paper on the subject. We compared notes, and we found that we had almost identical outlines. I had started at the beginning, with a micro-analysis of slave profitability and Alf had started on the second part of the paper with an analysis of demographics and macro-market developments.

You were not an economic historian *per se*? Were you already working in transportation economics?

No, my thesis had been on business investment decisions, so my areas of interest were econometrics, industrial organization, and corporate finance. I became interested in transportation economics at almost the same time as I became involved in economic history.

Is it fair to say that you then had a professional interest in seeing that economic theory or econometric methods could actually be applied to historical issues?

I'm not so sure that it really wasn't the other way. Both Alf and I felt, possibly under the influence of Schumpeter, Smithies, and others, that empirical economics was quite obviously historical in nature. While today we have developed some experimental data for measuring economic behavior and phenomena, there were none back then. Even today, it seems safe to say that 98–99 percent of the relevant data that economists have for doing empirical testing is generated by historical processes.

So you saw this work as an extension of what economics was doing anyway in terms of testing hypotheses?

Yes, the Harvard graduate economics department and program were very much designed around a sort of "three-legged stool" as it was often described: theory, statistics, and history. That perhaps reflected the influence of Schumpeter, among others. Schumpeter died about six months before I arrived, so I never really had direct exposure to him. Alf, on the other hand, was probably one of the last, or the last, dissertation student that Schumpeter had. Schumpeter died before Alf finished his work. He therefore completed his thesis under Leontief, who also strongly believed in the empirical foundations of economic analysis.

How would you characterize the intellectual legacy or atmosphere that reflected Schumpeter's influence? Was it, for example, an emphasis on longer-term dynamics of development?

The Harvard department had codified into its general exam requirements the belief that you needed all three of the basic skills: theory, statistics or econometrics, and some historical perspective. Schumpeter apparently liked to stress that economists put the really important things in "*ceteris paribus*:" demographics, changes in preference functions, technological developments, all the things that often were the most important part of understanding economic phenomena.

And that will come from history?

I think historians have traditionally understood that fairly well. Very often, the role of historians in economics departments is to make people aware of things they might otherwise overlook. To broaden the agenda, so to speak.

I can see this discussion developing two branches I'd like to pursue. One is your assessment of the current role of economic history, but let's turn first to your work on slavery and the reaction it received. As economists with research interests outside economic history, you and Alfred Conrad were not insiders at the EHA meeting in 1957 where you first presented the paper on the profitability of slavery. Was the response to your work a surprise?

It was an enormous surprise, but I think it's easy to overestimate the hostility of it. The hostility was fairly limited. Most were really quite open-minded and responsive. The thing that really surprised us was how interested they were. Alf and I thought that we were doing something rather dull and pedestrian in many ways: delivering a little sermon, so to speak, on methodology and economic history.

The one on econometrics and history?

The point we were trying to make was that economic analysis is a seamless whole. Almost inevitably if you are going to do empirical work in economics, you must become involved with historical data. It might be quite recent history and be more aptly called journalism, but let's put that distinction aside. Basically, most of the data available to economists have been generated by historical happenings or circumstances. And so in order to interpret and understand the data they were using, economists inevitably have, or should, become at least somewhat familiar with historical methods and the history of the period from which their data came.

The slavery question was quite interesting because it was such an easy application of economic concepts. We also felt quite confident of the answer. All of economic theory pointed in one direction. You couldn't keep resources committed at that level without some kind of profitability in the activity. Furthermore, the rising prices for Southern farm property in the 1850s strongly suggested that there was somebody making some kind of profit out there. It was also a market with all kinds of potential rents buried in it, the most obvious being for land. Critics (*e.g.*, Doug North) pointed that out and their point was well taken, although it was also a bit more complicated than they allowed. Of course, there were other opportunities available for Southern land than slave plantation agriculture. Nevertheless, you had a market where there are lots of rents around that don't seem to be disappearing, basic factor prices were moving upward, lots of people continued to commit quite a bit of capital, energy, labor and entrepreneurial capabilities. It's difficult to imagine that such an activity didn't return something close to the average level of profits available in the economy.

You said your audience was quite receptive to both the methodology and, it seems, the conclusions.

There were some exceptions, of course. For example, Fritz Redlich (I can't remember whether he was at Williamstown or not) was quite antagonistic, again for reasons that weren't always clear to us. His major criticism seemed to be directed toward counterfactuals. In the slavery paper, we were not guilty of that. On the other hand, the paper I had done on British economic development was counterfactual in character and of course Bob Fogel's work on railroads was, and those ignited very large outbursts from Fritz.

Looking back, then, people were receptive and there was continued interest in the paper. Both Douglas Dowd and John Moes had comments published.

I think his [John Moes'] was rather more balanced, as I recall, more technical in character. I think there was a basic movement already under way in the direction that Alf and I were pointing. You had Walt Rostow's work, you had Kuznets's work, you had Gerschenkron's. Fogel, I think had already started on his thesis. You had several people in Gerschenkron's economic history workshop who were doing work of that type. I'm not quite sure that we just didn't catch the trend – or the wave, in surfer terminology.

Caught the lip of the wave . . .

Caught the moment! I never could quite understand some of the more emotional objections to the paper, because fundamentally we were not trying to take a moral stand on any of the larger developmental or political issues. We were simply trying to narrow in on the very specific question of whether slavery was a businesslike operation. Were most of the owners deriving profits from it?

Which with 20/20 hindsight looks like a very reasonable question . . .

Actually, many did ask it and many of them had the right answer. In the Lincoln–Douglas debate, if my memory is correct, Lincoln outlined most of the essentials. In particular he put his finger on why continued expansion of the system was crucial to profitability. There were several journalistic and contemporary diary accounts at the time that more or less captured the essence of how the system worked and why it was profitable. Ken Stampp's book, which appeared almost simultaneously with our work, also had the essentials developed from a more historical perspective.

But for some reason, publication of this argument in the *JPE* prompted a much larger response than it would have elsewhere.

I'm still mystified by the response.

How do you think the debate on slavery eventually played out? Did it inform historian's understanding of and economists' thinking about the past?

I'm terribly biased, obviously. I think on the whole it's been very constructive. There have been several substantial and fine contributions by Fogel, Engerman, Gallman, Parker, Goldin, Sutch, and many others. I certainly enjoyed most of what I have read, and I think we do understand the economics of slavery far better than when we started back in 1956. Some of the databases that have been developed are really very ingenious and represent very fine scholarship.

You were still pursuing research as econometrician and empirical economist. Did the economic historical research have a bearing on your other efforts?

Looking back on it, I would argue that some of the work that Alf and I did in the late 1950s and 1960s, separately and together, was from a methodological standpoint historical in character. For example, there was a paper that Ed Kuh and I did that built on some very good work done by Richard Stone on estimating consumption functions. Stone used cross-section estimates of income effects so as to conserve on degrees of freedom when doing time series analyses of price effects. What Kuh and I argued was that the processes that generate income effects across the cross-section were substantially different from those that one would have observed in a time series. Accordingly, one had to be extremely careful when blending information from these two different sources. We also got into some problems of doing price corrections using Paasche and Laspeyres indices. Almost all of that, by the way, traced back quite directly to ideas that we were exposed to in Gerschenkron's basic graduate course in economic history.

Really?

Actually, that particular paper, "How extraneous are extraneous estimates?" (Meyer & Kuh 1957), owed more to Gerschenkron than did the slavery paper. Incidentally, both Alf and I first presented the slavery paper as lectures in undergraduate classes. Watching the undergraduate reaction to it was really quite fascinating. We caught their attention to a slightly greater extent than was normal, I think. They took it as an objective exercise with none of the emotional reaction we later encountered with more senior reviewers.

From the perspective of a senior economist, do you have a sense that once the Civil Rights movement moved to the front of the national stage the work on slavery became associated with political concerns? Would the response to your work have been different in 1968 versus 1958?

Who knows? I think so, yes.

And did you encounter any of that reaction later on?

I think that the 1967 confrontation was the last time we were in the eye of the storm. From then on, Fogel and Engerman usurped that position. Alf died a few years after, and in 1967 I became involved with the National Bureau and administrative duties absorbed me. Actually, the last paper Alf worked on was one he and I were doing jointly. It was a paper on technological diffusion, a joint project among several economic research institutes around the world. Each institute took responsibility for one technology. These were all production innovations, not product innovations. The National Bureau took responsibility for the basic oxygen process. We did international comparisons of rates of diffusion of BOP technology. Alf and I were doing that collaboratively at the time of his death. Our basic finding was that the US steel industry did not adopt the basic oxygen process quite as quickly as several other countries' steel industries because of US factor prices and the US industry's existing investment in the most advanced open hearth technology. These made it less rewarding at the margin to undertake BOP investments in the US than elsewhere. Thus, it was not so much that American steel industry managements may have been misguided, but that they were confronting a different set of objective facts. Actually, if they did make a mistake, it was in not investing more in minimill or direct reduction technology using scrap metal as the raw material input.

Given the supply of scrap here in the United States?

Yes, direct reduction was the innovation that really made sense in the US context.

Subsequent discussion of entrepreneurial decline seems to have taken up exactly that point, at least in the case of cotton and steel.

Some of our European collaborators were less than fully convinced, at least in the case of BOP.

Were they more interested in looking at entrepreneurial capabilities?

In some cases, yes.

Cultures?

Cultures and attitudes. Of course, the study was also done at the time (the late 1960s and early 1970s) when finding fault with American management and institutions was somewhat in favor. But again, it is easy to overgeneralize. On the whole, I think we convinced most of our foreign collaborators.

Did you and Conrad have expectations about the impact your work would have on the practice of economic history? Were those expectations borne out?

Well, we were at least as interested in influencing economists as economic historians. In terms of convincing economists, we felt it behooves them to be aware of what economic historians are doing. I suspect that to the extent that we were preaching to economic historians, it was to suggest they spend a little more time with economists. Everyone had something to learn from each other.

And at the point when you entered the discussion the learning wasn't taking place?

Gerschenkron, Kuznets, and Rostow were certainly major figures, and they all emphasized what economists could learn from history. Much of the research program at the National Bureau of Economic Research, at that time and perhaps for two decades previously, had such an emphasis, going back to [Wesley] Mitchell.

Are we talking about different generations here? Rostow was a bridge from an earlier generation . . .

Well, they were all much younger then, especially in 1955 and 1956 when this work was done.

At what point did the interest among economists in the kind of empirical work carried out by Mitchell, collecting and then analyzing time series, really die out?

Well, I suppose that Koopmans's rather devastating review of Burns and Mitchell was one watershed. That certainly pushed back the profession's acceptance of and interest in traditional National Bureau time series analysis. On the other hand, I don't think it killed it entirely.

Has historical economic analysis maintained its position at the NBER after the key role it played during the early years? Or has its role diminished?

Perhaps in relative terms, but I'm not so sure in absolute terms. The whole scale of the NBER program has expanded quite sharply over the years. Of course the Bureau is also organized a bit differently now. Much more of its work is done in liaison or association with outside researchers and less is done exclusively as an in-house activity, so we also have to be very careful what we are measuring. When we look at the whole extended community involved in National Bureau work, my guess is that while the relative portion of historical work may have gone down, the absolute portion probably hasn't fallen that much, if at all.

So there is long-term historical continuity at the NBER?

A lot will depend again on classification. What's quantitative economic history? As I've argued earlier, much of almost anything that's empirical in economics has an historical dimension to it.

What kind of response did you get from colleagues after publishing the *JPE* piece?

Most economists were reasonably receptive. After all, we were engaging in a sort of economic imperialism for the field, trying to extend its boundaries.

Did the project you participated in at its beginning bear the kind of fruit you would have hoped it would?

Oh, that's for others to judge. My guess would be that economists' interest in economic history bottomed out a few years ago and is beginning to go up again; that is, the interest in the profession in what you might call the more historical side of the field.

What might have prompted the turnaround?

I think that there has been an increased interest, say, since the mid-1980s, in practical policy problems, and that's led in turn to some increased interest in the historical aspects of the field. The re-emergence of interest in the determinants of growth, and the questions of why some societies grow more rapidly than others, also plays a major role.

Although you don't have much professional contact with the economic history group, does the experience at Harvard suggest to you that economic history is carrying out its part of the bargain, stressing the understanding of what lies behind *ceteris paribus*?

Yes. Economic history has continued to evolve. I find that some of the work done under the heading of institutional history quite fascinating.

You've suggested that the revival of interest in economic history in the economics profession may arise from a strengthening of interest in policy issues. The young economist does not want to feel completely isolated from policy questions. What about the direct role of economic history? How can economic history inform government policy?

About the only recent experience I've had that might be relevant to answering that question is that I have been involved in some of the reform activities in Eastern Europe and the former Soviet Union. We in the West simply assume the existence of market institutions, financial institutions, legal protections for private property, bankruptcy laws, incorporation, so forth and so on. All these institutional arrangements that we take for granted have to be recreated in Eastern Europe and especially in the former Soviet Union. In the Russian case, these institutions may have been underdeveloped even prior to the revolution, in Czarist days. Of course, they are essential for developing a market economy.

The lesson is that these institutions are critical for economic development and a necessary condition for economic growth.

Yes, and I think it is significant that a good economic historian, Doug North, took a lead in identifying the problem.

In particular, your work has been in Russia itself?

Yes, Russia and the new states of Kazakhstan, Belarus, Ukraine. The work has been done for the European Bank for Reconstruction and Development.

I suppose that it's pretty clear that dusting off the laws from 1916 or 1917 is not enough to create these kinds of institutions . . .

They usually need a bit of updating! Also, people don't have experience with markets and market institutions. One reason why the market transition is somewhat easier in Eastern Europe is that predecessor commercial law is not as antiquated and not quite so many generations have gone by without any experience of modern market institutions.

Are there any other places where history may have something to say? Take, for example, economic history's thinking about the role of transport innovation and Robert Fogel's conclusions. Does that really have much resonance for you in terms of addressing current questions of transport policy or infrastructural concerns?

I really don't know. Very recently, though, Professor Gómez-Ibáñez, one of my colleagues here at Harvard, and I have been working on privatization issues in different parts of the world. One of the areas we have looked at has been highway privatization, and one of the fascinating things we discovered early on was that the US had a quite extensive program of private highway development, or turnpike development, back in the first part of the nineteenth century. They were mostly privately developed. The supplementary public investment pattern in the US in the early nineteenth century was much like that experienced with highway development in Spain and France in recent decades. The public role in all three cases became that of filling in where the private sector didn't, thereby completing the system. It worked remarkably well in the early nineteenth-century US, and the only reason it came to an end was because, of course, of the emergence of the railroad. The steam engine was apparently better designed for providing locomotion on rivers, waterways, or rails than on roads. Of course, an interest in roads re-emerged at the end of the century when the internal combustion engine appeared, apparently better adapted to highway modes. While we didn't put much of this historical background into our book (it was a matter of space), our understanding of more recent events was enhanced by reading different historical accounts of the turnpike era. Actually, the early development of the public roads movement at the end of the nineteenth century, and first part of the twentieth, is also quite fascinating and helpful in understanding today's highway development problems and prospects for privatization as an alternative.

Are countries that still need to construct a basic road network or develop highway infrastructure open to these kinds of historical examples? Or is there a presumption that the public sector should be providing these services?

No, there has been a diversity of responses in third world and other countries. Mexico has relied very heavily on private investment for development of its high performance highway network. Malaysia and Indonesia have relied less, but still have used the private sector. France and Spain used private investment for highway development in the 1970s and 1980s. The explanation of why privatization occurs some places rather than others is best attacked by taking a broad historical view, and understanding the general economic environment at the particular time highway development takes place. For example, one of the fascinating questions is why the high performance highway development that occurred in California was financed by gasoline taxes, and called "freeways." In the Eastern US, by contrast, more was done with public toll authorities and the highways were called turnpikes, parkways, or expressways. Some interesting cultural and historical explanations might be advanced to explain these differences.

Another illustration of historical issues in transport research is provided by airline deregulation, that of simply dating when deregulation began. The natural instinct is to cite October 1978, when the legislation was enacted. On the other hand, a good argument could be made that it started three or four years earlier, when John Robson was appointed chairman of the Civil Aeronautics Board by President Ford. Robson was replaced during the Carter administration by Fred Kahn, and Kahn continued, indeed accelerated, the process of deregulation that Robson had initiated. And so, how do you set up your historical comparisons, the before and after?

Is the recent emphasis on the role of infrastructure in productivity growth, by some policy makers and economists, overselling its importance? Or, is the degree to which the US infrastructure has depreciated having an adverse effect on American productivity? A believer in Fogel would be skeptical of those kinds of claims.

The truth is probably somewhere in between. You have an abundance of literature on the subject, including some very good contributions by Dale Jorgenson. Jorgenson is quite critical of the more expansive claims made for the productivity improvements, or enhancements, attributable to infrastructural investments. You really have two camps emerging, one is the macro or heavy investment solution to any infrastructure deficiencies, and the other is the micro "let us price and manage what we have better" approach. I must admit that I have more sympathy with the latter. Nevertheless, there probably are some cases where a major investment may be needed. But I believe that there are many more cases where the problem can be solved simply, with better management and pricing of facilities. Airports are a striking example of this. We had some experimentation here in Boston at Logan Airport a few years ago with pricing solutions, and they worked remarkably well. But for technical reasons, the FAA disapproved, so now the Massport [airport] authority is thinking about alternative pricing solutions, hopefully acceptable to the FAA.

You were acting editor of *Explorations in Entrepreneurial History* in 1957, and during your editorship papers by scholars such as William Parker and a new Ph.D. named Lance Davis were published. They were highly quantitative when compared with papers that appeared earlier or later in the 1950s. What kind of audience did you have an interest in reaching? Do you feel that you were successful?

I guess so. Much depends upon how you define "reach." I did have an interest in providing an outlet for what I saw as the highly interesting quantitative work that was emerging from Gerschenkron's Workshop and from other sources. Probably, though, the reason for taking the chore on had as much to do with personal relationships with Professors [Arthur] Cole and Gerschenkron as it did with any well-conceived notions of what the strategy should have been for the journal.

Do you believe that *Explorations* was helpful in opening up the overall discussion?

Well, I guess I would like to claim at least a little bit of a contribution. Of course, shortly thereafter, the more conventional and established economic history journals began to be more receptive to quantitative papers. So whatever the original motivation might have been, I think it disappeared fairly quickly.

The notion of entrepreneurship occupies a big chunk of the literature on late nineteenth-century British economic history and has reappeared in discussions of the potential for restructuring Eastern Europe and the former Soviet Union. Can we identify entrepreneurship? How much do we know about it? When does it make a difference in economic development?

I have two comments. First, I tended to be very skeptical of the importance of any intangible, such as entrepreneurship, when I was young. I even had the temerity (and the foolishness) to commit some of that skepticism to paper. As I have aged, I've become more and more convinced that I was probably somewhat misguided if not wrong in my early skepticism. What has brought that home to me recently is spending quite a bit of time in both China and Russia, worrying about development problems. There's not much doubt that the Chinese culture, both in China and overseas, produces disproportionate numbers of quite effective entrepreneurs.

But can we also identify entrepreneurship?

I suppose my reaction is like the old saying (about pornography), that "I don't know how to define it but I do know it when I see it." Entrepreneurship may come under that same sort of ephemeral classification. Some of the historical literature certainly helps, at least me, to understand better the dimensions and definitions of entrepreneurship. Historians have made a contribution there. I wish they had made more, but I'm sure they will.

The cliometric school made an attempt at deriving implications of entrepreneurial failure or "operationalizing" it. Tests of it turned to narrower discussions of whether firms were responding to relative factor prices. The discussion never truly returned to the larger question of what an entrepreneurial culture is.

I don't think that's all bad. I attempted something like this, with my early paper on British economic development in the last part of the nineteenth century. As I already indicated, I'm not sure that some of that wasn't a bit misguided. On the other hand, I think attempts to quantify entrepreneurship, to identify manifestations of it – basically what the cliometricians have done – are not mutually exclusive with the older, more qualitative approach. Another attractive development (again, I'm viewing this from afar) seems to me to be development of a new social history; that should reinvigorate some of the broader studies and attempts to conceptualize entrepreneurship.

Is entrepreneurship something that can be developed? Or does it depend strictly upon culture?

That's a very good question. I don't know the answer. We're beginning to get some interesting insights from the development literature, which is doing these comparative studies of entrepreneurial successes and failures, and national successes and failures, with economic development. Of course, the Pacific rim countries have been a particular focus for such studies, *e.g.*, the World Bank's special survey (*The East Asian Miracle*) completed about a year and a half ago. Recently, some of the people at the Harvard Institute for International Development (David Lindauer and Mike Roemer, eds) published a very interesting study comparing the development experiences of several Southeast Asian countries. They get into the contributions of Chinese entrepreneurs, since in all the countries studied (Malaysia, Singapore, Indonesia) these entrepreneurs make major contributions. The obvious next question is trying to identify what it might be in Chinese culture that produces these people. And of course Chinese culture is not the only place where such skills are produced. Many well-informed students of development would argue that Indians, when given an opportunity and government policies that don't interfere too extensively, are also quite capable of entrepreneurial spurts. It's too bad that we don't have Schumpeter to sort it all out for us. It would be interesting to have him explain why he got the relationship between capitalism and the entrepreneurial spirit right the first time, but not the second time. That would be even more fascinating.

That's one area where we have a lot to learn from historians. We are being

pushed back to fundamental questions: What prompts economic development? What accounts for successful spurts of development?

Yes, and I think that is helping revitalize the field. The new institutional and social history may eventually give us some good insights, but they're just beginning. We haven't seen their full fruition yet. Perhaps we're a bit impatient!

ALBERT FISHLOW

Interviewed by
Eugene N. White

Albert Fishlow retired in 2007 as Professor of International and Public Affairs, Director of the Center for Brazilian Studies, and Director of the Institute for Latin American Studies at Columbia University, New York, New York. He was born in Philadelphia, Pennsylvania in 1935 and was educated at the University of Pennsylvania (B.A., 1956) and at Harvard University (Ph.D., 1963). He was a member of the Economics faculty at the University of California, Berkeley (1961–77; 1983–94), at Yale University (1978–83), and was Paul A. Volcker Senior Fellow for International Economics at the Council on Foreign Relations in New York (1995–9) before moving to Columbia in 2000. He has held visiting positions at the NBER (1963–4), at the Post Graduate School of Economics of the Getulio Vargas Foundation in Rio de Janeiro (1967–8), and as a Guggenheim Fellow at All Souls College, Oxford (1972–3), and served as Deputy Assistant Secretary of State for Inter-American Affairs (1975–6). He has been honored with the David A. Wells Prize for 1963–4 and the Joseph Schumpeter Prize in 1971 by Harvard University, and with the National Order of the Southern Cross by the government of Brazil in 1999. The interview took place by telephone in October 1998 and was conducted by Eugene White of Rutgers University, who writes:

Albert Fishlow was present at the birth of cliometrics, opening the debate on the role of the railways in the growth of the American economy with Robert Fogel. After working on nineteenth-century American education and interregional trade, he turned his sights to Latin America. His work on income distribution in Brazil ignited a major controversy, and he helped to spur the growth of cliometric work in Latin America. Not content with just writing about economic change, Fishlow has long been engaged in the study of economic policy and its effects in Latin America.

How did you get interested in economic history?

Well, it was somewhat accidental. I had intended to go to Harvard Law School. With my one suit I was prepared to move up to Cambridge. Then I decided to get married and to go for a Ph.D. in economics. And I'm still married to the same woman, so obviously it was a good decision.

When I went up to Harvard, I thought of doing industrial organization or something that would combine my legal interests with the economics. I remember I also was especially interested in monetary policy – Duesenberry was there at the time – and monetary policy was a substantial issue in the United States in the late 1950s. Duesenberry had these new models he had developed, business cycle models using difference equations, and I was all eager to do that. And then I took Gerschenkron's course. In some ways, it was the sheer fascination with him and the stuff he was doing at the time that "converted" me into doing economic history. He was at his peak. He had just done the piece on the process of industrial change within Europe, and the whole question of followers, and he was writing all kinds of essays. Henry Rosovsky was finishing his dissertation on Japan and the extent to which it conformed to the Gerschenkron hypothesis. So I became intrigued. I wrote a paper for the history course (although Gerschenkron wasn't there during that spring; A. H. Imlah taught the course) on the Trustee Savings Banks in England. I tried to assess the extent to which the flow of funds into the savings banks was interest-elastic and used the new-found econometric techniques. It got published, and I got launched. When Gerschenkron came back, he had money available for the first time for fellowships for students to write dissertations in the field of economic history. There was a group of students, including Paul David and Peter Temin. We shared a little office area; it was quite an exciting experience. Out of this came the early article with Paul on the effects of imperfections in markets. I remember Gerschenkron was very angry because here was a theoretical piece we had done when we were supposed to be working on economic history. He subsequently relented when it was published in the *Journal of Political Economy*.

The group of students, in conjunction with Gerschenkron's seminar, provided independent opportunity to define an interest in the subject. Here were Paul, Peter, I – all working on the United States – and Gerschenkron knew very little about the United States. I think that's one of the reasons we all selected it! We were able to follow Gerschenkron's work with general inspiration but without being subject to applying his model, his theory or his approach. I think that was a highly useful combination.

So, you produced your dissertation . . .

While I was working on the dissertation, I had managed to get a job at Berkeley on the basis of an initial paper. I had by that time two young daughters, 15 months apart. I was working night and day during the summer before going out to Berkeley in the hope that I was going to finish. I finally produced a draft just before I left and gave it to Gerschenkron – that was the first time I had given him anything! He read it, and he said, "Well, if you want the degree, I'll give it to you, but I have to tell you, it won't win any prizes!" So I threw it away and rewrote the whole thing while I was an assistant professor in California.

That version was accepted.

Yes, that was accepted. Subsequently, it won the David Wells Prize at Harvard for the best dissertation and was published by Harvard University Press. Gerschenkron was clearly right. He helped in the sense of being sufficiently critical without being specific, indicating that somehow I could do better. One of the ways of doing better, which I have often thought of as a help to people (which doesn't happen in the market now), was going out and teaching and suddenly being an independent scholar and having regular conversations with other professors. This really upped the quality.

What led you to the railroads?

Well, I had thought I would do something about banking in the nineteenth century. Then Bray Hammond came out with his book. It seemed so substantial that I backed off, and I came up with railways, in part because of W. W. Rostow's work, summarized in "The Take-off into Self-Sustained Growth," and its emphasis on the railway as the cause of the take-off in the United States. It didn't really seem to make much sense to me. From the little that I knew of economic history at the time, the idea of the take-off in the United States seemed quite a misleading emphasis. Rostow had elaborated somewhat on the railways, and I saw that there was a chance to do something. So I selected the railways.

Any reflections on that *other* book on the railways?

Needless to say, when I selected the railways I didn't know about Mr Fogel. I read his earlier stuff on the Union Pacific, which was a master's thesis that he had done and he was obviously working away on his dissertation at the time. We first met at Harvard in 1961 before I went to Berkeley.

I had already begun work on my dissertation, and he was working on his at the time. We had some discussions about the dissertations, and it became clear to me that we were really following very different trajectories. Bob was asking the question, what kind of development would there be without any railroads? He looked at the question for 1890, asking, "What if there were no railways?" So he was busy building canals, and he was calculating his social saving based on the existence of canals, horse transport, etc. I looked at the question in 1860 and asked what was the rate of return – the social rate of return – of railways in terms of their contribution to the economy of the United States. How important were they as a factor in the process of the rapid growth that characterized the economy from the end of the 1820s down through the Civil War? I was asking a question about this very large investment. Whereas I was really interested in the sufficiency condition, namely, given that there were railways, what was the consequence of the railways, Bob was really focusing on the question of necessity. I think that difference is the characteristic that makes the two books come to different conclusions.

I think also that this difference carries through my book. When I was looking at the question of the contribution of the railway to the iron industry, I was looking at the shift initially to iron rails, and the possibility of import substitution. This occurred significantly during the 1850s with the large expansion and construction in the West and the South. I looked at the consequence of the opening of the West and the question, "Were railroads built ahead of demand *versus* in response to settlement?" I focused on what happened in New England during the 1840s when there was a different cycle, where industry was favored rather than agriculture. So I always had the sense that I was doing a history of what happened and trying to assess its consequences, whereas Bob was really asking the different question, "What if no railways had been constructed?"

The first time I heard about this debate was in 1971. I was an undergraduate at Harvard taking a history course, and scorn was ladled upon you and Bob for your efforts.

It was rather late for that to have happened, but it is a measure of the evolution of cliometrics. The reaction of people within history was, on the whole, somewhat less than enthusiastic.

What do you remember about the early Clio conferences?

Well, they were extraordinarily exciting. I remember I went to my first one in 1961. There was Robin Matthews, Paul David, Peter Temin, Dick Easterlin, Bob Fogel, Bill Parker, Doug North, Lance Davis, Jonathan Hughes, Bob Gallman, and Nate Rosenberg, among others. It was really an exceptional group of people that attended. The essential feature was the emphasis on the "metrics" – on measurement, quantification. The emphasis was clearly on being able to frame historical issues in a way that made them subject to specification as hypotheses and ultimately the application of some kind of quantitative testing that would utilize the advances that were being made in statistics at that time.

You went to subsequent Clio conferences as well.

The group stayed together, and ultimately produced the volume that was edited by Dick Easterlin, Lance Davis, and Bill Parker. The feeling was that the people at the meeting obviously had distinct and capable expertise in a variety of areas. I don't think it sold it very well, but it's a valuable measure, I think, of the activity of that decade, as well as a good book.

How did you get interested in Latin America and economic development?

I continued to do work in economic history, with pieces on trade. I did a piece at the AEA meetings that criticized Doug North's treatment of the West, the South, and the

East in terms of trade flows. I moved on to education; I did one of the first historical studies of investment in education in the US. And I wrote on railroad investment after the Civil War, in which I looked at productivity change and assessed the relative importance of the components of the productivity change. I looked at the reduction in costs that each of the components, such as heavier rails and better engines and a variety of the technological changes – heavier freight cars, for example – provided.

But what got me off to Latin America in part was President Kennedy and the Alliance for Progress. The notion was that here was a whole area of the world that had not developed satisfactorily, that the US was going to provide resources to assist. I decided that I should get involved. That was a period of time when development economics hardly existed. There were occasional courses. I never took any development economics at Harvard.

Was that a good thing?

Yes. You had various and sundry pieces written on development, classics, looking at the externalities. But, there hadn't been much history, joined with the emphasis on statistics and econometrics. And I decided to invest energy and effort into it.

I made a decision that I wasn't going to write anything on development until I had had enough experience. It was already the case that people were going down, primarily to Latin America, and on the basis of casual observation writing all kinds of stuff.

Really? People *do* that?

Yes, they really did! [laughter]. And so I got involved in a project on Brazil. Hollis Chenery at that time was the deputy director of USAID (US Agency for International Development), and Harvard had been involved in Argentina and a variety of other places, and he thought that it was smart to diversify. When this came up, I thought, why not, even though I had been studying Spanish previously. So there was a contract signed between the university and AID to help the Brazilian Ministry of Planning. I went to Brazil for the first time in 1965. I went again in 1966. In 1967, I went down there to live for a period of around a year and a half. I first worked on a long piece, which dealt with import substitution and development in Brazil from the 1880s down through the 1960s.

I took the broad perspective on development, looking at the industrialization process in Brazil and trying to get a handle on it historically, which I think was actually important since it gave rise to lots of subsequent work on the 1930s and subsequent work on the *Encilhamento* (rapid inflation) in the 1890s. I felt good about it because economic history had been a subject that people hadn't written on in Brazil. Economists hadn't participated in it, and all of a sudden it became a more active field. I then started on income distribution. One of the reasons I became involved with income distribution was that when I arrived in Brazil, I discovered that the Census of 1960 was in danger of disappearing. It had been stored in a warehouse. Since there had been the military takeover in 1964, the stuff had been left to molder. I had a student down with me at the time, and we drew a sample from the 1960 census. From this sample, it was possible to do all kinds of things. One of the questions that they had asked was about income. With some assumptions, I came up with a distribution of income for 1960.

When I went back in 1969, I ended the contract, which was not done very frequently with Brazil, because of the military takeover. But, since I had good contacts with Brazilians, I was able to go back for research purposes. When I returned again in 1971, I managed to get a sample of the 1970 census so I could make a comparison between 1960 and 1970. I concluded that the income distribution had deteriorated, in good part because of wage policies imposed after 1964. Here was this military government saying things were much better in Brazil and everybody was happy, and the economy was growing very rapidly . . . And here I came along and said, "Whoa! The data suggest a different story here." That involved me in a considerable amount of hassle. On the one side, Robert McNamara believed me, and that created problems with other people at the World Bank, as well as with the Brazilian government. McNamara threatened to stop lending to Brazil. Brazil was in a period of very rapid growth. Ironically, that period of rapid growth was something I had contributed to while down there, since I had been involved in the planning process and had made some of the early estimates suggesting that Brazilian growth could be much higher than was current. Their government did an independent study of the income distribution and utilized all the computers in the Ministry of Finance. In spite of some differences in technique, they didn't come out with very different numbers. So it really did serve as a major critique at a time when Brazil was growing rapidly and everybody was saying, in spite of it being a dictatorship, that this was really not such a bad place.

For a while I had trouble in Brazil. I had been invited to give an address at the opening of the master's program in the University of Brasilia. I was told by officials, when I got off the plane in Rio to take the connecting plane to Brasilia, that I was "sick." That made it much easier for all my Brazilian friends at the time, who would have been in great difficulty had I showed up.

I thought what was interesting and relevant about the income distribution study was that the World Bank got interested in doing work on income distribution. When one was talking about welfare change, it was always in general terms, and now one had quantified it and made it more specific. One could look at different brackets, and at how much of the income was generated from the urban sector *versus* the rural sector, and begin looking at the contribution of the various components. I think the important thing was not only the quantitative analysis but also an assessment of causality. It turns out that while education was a principal factor in explaining the distribution of income, what was equally important was what sector of the economy, what geographic area and what occupation an individual was in. As for education in Brazil, I immediately saw that kids weren't going to primary school, but some few wealthy kids were going to college. The college kids were getting a very high real return, but the rate of return was even higher in primary school; hence there was a misallocation of resources.

Isn't this still true in Brazil?

Well, the issues are still the same. Brazil has one of the highest levels of inequality in the world, and it also has one of the lowest rates of public education. It still spends too much on the university level and not enough on primary and secondary levels. It still affords a special advantage to those who have income, who can afford private schooling, because the way you get into free public higher education is by passing an examination. And the way you pass an examination, very obviously, is by having a very good secondary school background.

What was your experience like as a Deputy Assistant Secretary?

I knew the new Assistant Secretary of State in the Ford Administration, Bill Rogers. He asked me to come to Washington as Deputy Assistant Secretary of State for Inter-American Affairs. Bill Rogers was a Democrat who had been active in AID earlier.

One thing that I was able to do, which has been little noted nor long remembered, was help to resolve an expropriation case peaceably. The Marcona company had been expropriated in Peru. I suggested that, since the company was asking for much more than the government of Peru had offered, we undertake an independent study and hire SRI (Stanford Research Institute) to make the estimate. I had already made my calculations, and I was persuaded that any kind of reasonable calculations were going to come up with a number that was substantially less than what the company was asking. To my surprise and, I must say, horror, I discovered that this was first time that anybody in the State Department had done this. The previous practice had been for the company to talk to the ambassador; the ambassador complained to the country, saying, "You've violated the basic rules and regulations of international law, and now the company wants *x* dollars and you've got to pay it." I remember very well, on one occasion with an audience composed of members of the Cabinet of Peru and a blackboard, giving a lecture on calculation of valuation and talking about how one had to calculate the real value of this enterprise. The firm had been in production and distribution, and had owned the ships that were registered in Panama, which made a profit while its production didn't.

The owners got a payment that was within the realm of reasonableness and one the Peruvians lived up to. It resolved what could have been a nasty case. At the time, the whole question of foreign ownership was a matter of rather considerable discussion. I was involved in the nationalization of petroleum in Venezuela and in the North–South discussions that were current in 1975–76.

You've also done work on the debt, too.

Right. That was really the next major area because the debt became the major problem for Latin America in the 1980s. I think virtually every Latin American country, except Chile and Colombia, had gone into default and were not paying what they had owed.

In part that was a result of what had happened in the 1970s. One had a fundamental institutional change in the 1970s which had altered the relationship between creditors and debtors. Interest rates had been set on the basis of LIBOR [London Interbank Offer Rate], which changed every six months. In 1979, after Volcker had become head of the Federal Reserve, interest rates rose dramatically. The interest rates that had to be paid on the debt by these countries increased at a time when their ability to export was much reduced. I was writing on the problem of debt, as were Jeffrey Sachs and Rudi Dornbusch. It launched me into writing about the 1890s and the Brazilian and Argentine debt problems at that time and the way in which they were resolved; I wrote a piece which I enjoyed a great deal, called "Lessons of the 1890s for the 1980s."

It's another illustration, which I always like to make, between the advantage of having the broader perspective that comes from historical orientation and the more immediate view which assumes that the world began yesterday and you have to develop a policy today in order to avoid disaster. It's an interesting perspective of how people fail to really take advantage of the information that is available from the past. I continued writing on the debt problem and I tried to make some assessments of what the banks were in fact repaid as a result of the debt crisis of the 1980s. In spite of reducing the principal value at the end, through the Brady plan, banks did not emerge so badly because they had accumulated all of the interest that was due them before the reduction was made. They wound up with a rather low rate of return but it was positive.

How does economic history fit into your newest incarnation?

One of the things that I am keen on working on at the present time is the reform of the state. To some degree that is the nature of the problem in Latin America where some reform has occurred over the 1990s. In Asia, the issue is a contemporary one in terms of reforming the banking system, changing the legal system to introduce bankruptcy, providing information, and having judicial mechanisms that operate without corruption. There are a variety of institutional changes that are necessary to enable the market to function. I think that one of the things that comes out of history is that if you take a long view, you see that you can't presume that markets operate in an efficient fashion. There are a whole series of innovations and institutional changes that occur over time in order to respond to a variety of inefficiencies that lead to private wealth being accumulated, on the one hand, and public losses, on the other. To some degree that's exactly the story of what's going on in Asia today.

Is this similar to the railroads earlier in the US?

Well, to some extent. There you had a market operating, with people trying to assess whether to invest in railways. It seems to me that the whole story of economic development is precisely about externalities and the way in which they occur; markets have a tendency, even when they start out as perfect markets, to be disrupted by innovation. You create temporary circumstances in which these externalities exist. That's the process of change.

How long before the rest of us did you suspect the Asian miracle might not be?

Earlier, they had spoken about the "Brazilian Miracle," and I had written about why it wasn't quite such a miracle (1989b; see also 1994). To some degree, I think names of that sort are compelling because they show a real lack of understanding of the historical process.

To what extent are – or should be – economic history and economic development separate? What do you think is the proper role of economic history in the education of an economist these days?

In many universities economic history is now left by the side. To some extent I think that is unfortunate because I think good economic history is an essential component. If you say that economic development relates to the current process of expansion in a variety of settings and countries where the growth rate has not gone up very substantially in the past, then clearly you want to know why it hasn't gone up in the past, and you want to understand what the particular factors were that were responsible. I see the two as being substantially interrelated, and I think that in methodology, good economic history emphasizes good quantitative training, good economic history represents good theoretical knowledge, good economic history represents good institutional emphasis.

Further reflections

Albert Fishlow

Since my conversation with Eugene White in 1998, the world has changed dramatically. On the one side, the United States has been a major economic force, providing an important impetus to growth, and on the other, the emergence of China and India has had significant influence upon global economic expansion. At present, the world economy is growing about 5 percent annually, the highest continuous rate since before the first oil shock at the end of 1973. Asia as a whole – including South Korea, Thailand, Malaysia, Indonesia, Vietnam, and others – has expanded most rapidly. Until their recent recoveries both Japan and Europe had been reduced to subsidiary positions.

Latin America, too, has passed through a difficult patch. In the 1980s there was the lost decade in the aftermath of the debt crisis. In the early 1990s, many countries undertook novel stabilization measures to eliminate inflation, privatized previously nationalized activities such as public utilities of all kinds, steel, chemicals, airlines, and expanded their participation in international trade. But those, too, had only temporary effect upon the rate of growth and income inequality. Until the recent upsurge, with rising commodity prices, Latin America was again falling behind. Recent elections give an accurate sense of underlying unhappiness in many countries. Despite the export-led gains since 2003, and favorable terms of trade, more radical candidates have won a number of these electoral contests. Thereafter, they have rejected standard IMF packages, and imposed more onerous terms upon foreign investors, gaining domestic support. The case of President Chavez in Venezuela is perhaps extreme, but usefully illustrates the extent to which domestic inequality – and poverty – have become driving forces within the contemporary political scene.

What this recent Latin American development sequence underlines yet again is the relevance of economic history to the present. The great spurts of Asian growth aren't the result of the market alone, although clearly some relaxation of tight controls has made an important contribution. The limited Latin American expansion isn't solely the consequence of reliance on market forces with lesser state management and tighter control over deficits, but of various additional causes: inadequate education, inflexible labor markets, insecure property rights, excessive informality, and the like. There is no single route, no guaranteed formula, no magic equilibrium path of ascent that is valid for all countries and all times.

Alexander Gerschenkron's great insight about initial spurts in the European nineteenth-century experience provides an invaluable analytic beginning. Surely, there was a differential degree of state intervention at the beginnings of modern industrial expansions. But what happens after that initial discontinuity, and how the many different countries are now able to respond, politically as well as economically, considerably complicates the story. That continuing evolution – of new challenges and necessary responses – cannot be fully understood without an historical basis.

Within contemporary development economics, emphasis upon institutional change has become the very center of the subject. The hard part is the empirics. Everyone devises new measures. Different groups go about giving scores for the extent to which "the market" influences external trade, internal finance, entrepreneurship, the labor force, etc. Political factors also enter: type of regime, continuity, and so forth. Countless regressions are run, utilizing combinations of cross-section and time series observations. Not surprisingly, some significant coefficients eventually appear, for the most part justifying one's *a priori* hypotheses. Then comes someone else with a slightly different data set and/or definition, and the new results justify a wholly contrary view.

But rarely does this "empirical" effort go deeply enough to tell a fully persuasive story. Economics correctly tells us that continuing expansion depends upon continuing productivity growth. But an historical account can help to explain why some countries – in some periods – go off in contradictory directions. Other countries seem better able to persist, even in the midst of greater challenges. Reliance only upon a multitude of recent numbers and advanced econometrics can confuse rather than edify.

A word is also necessary about the large current account deficit of the United States. This is a truly historic novelty. For the first time since the Industrial Revolution, and even beforehand, the richest country in the world has become the principal borrower. And some of the lenders are certainly poorer countries – China, of course, with reserves now over a trillion dollars, to mention just one. Globalization is proceeding in unusual ways, quite differently from the four-fold classification of the stages of foreign investment that had become the standard pattern.

Current discussions of why the United States saves so little center on the personal accumulation of capital gains – particularly in real estate – that translate into higher levels of consumption and gross national income. But the other side, the large and increasing foreign indebtedness necessary to this process, does not much enter into discussion. Possible tariff protection to preserve a diminishing manufacturing sector does. So does the Chinese exchange rate. But how the significant adjustment from a large current account deficit will occur is much more a back-room subject, exempt from political partisanship.

We no longer live in a gold standard world, nor in one with regular, and substantial, business cycles. Those circumstances would have provided clearer indication of what was coming – as they did in the past. Yet, even in the midst of our present novel global situation, greater knowledge of the past provides an important insight: nominal wealth is not necessarily permanent.

At the end of the day, whether one is dealing with familiar issues like the international debt problem of the 1980s and early 1990s, or internal income distribution in a variety of countries, or with the current question of sustained international financial dis-equilibrium, history matters. Even more important, understanding what has happened, and how, can be immensely helpful.

PAUL A. DAVID

Interviewed by
Susan B. Carter

Paul Allan David is Professor of Economics, Emeritus, and Senior Fellow of the Stanford Institute of Economic Policy Research, at Stanford University, Stanford, California. In Europe he is Emeritus Fellow of All Souls College, Professor Emeritus of Economics and Economic History, and Senior Fellow of the Oxford Internet Institute in the University of Oxford, and Professorial Fellow of the Maastricht Economic Research Institute on Innovation and Technology (MERIT) at Universiteit Maastricht in the Netherlands. He was born in New York, New York in 1935 and was educated at Harvard University (A.B, 1956; Ph.D., 1973) and as a Fulbright Fellow at Cambridge University (1956–8). In 1961 he joined the Economics faculty at Stanford, where he was William Robertson Coe Professor of American Economic History from 1977 to 1994. He has been Taussig Professor of Economics at Harvard (1972–3), Pitt Professor of American History and Institutions at Cambridge (1977–8), and Visiting Professor of the Economics of Innovation at Université Paris Dauphine (1996–9). He was elected Fellow of the International Econometric Society in 1975, of the American Academy of Arts & Sciences in 1979, of the British Academy in 1995, Member of the American Philosophical Society in 2003, and was President of the Economic History Association in 1989. He has served on the editorial boards of several scholarly journals and is a founding Editor (since 1990) of *Economics of Innovation and New Technology*. Paul David's research in many areas of economic history and economics has been recognized in two *Festschriften*: a collection of works by former students and colleagues, *History Matters: Essays on Economic Growth, Technology, and Demographic Change*, edited by Timothy W. Guinnane, William A. Sundstrom, and Warren Whatley (Stanford UP, 2004) and a collection of works by European and American colleagues, *New Frontiers in the Economics of Innovation and New Technology: Essays in Honour of Paul A. David*, edited by Cristiano Antonelli, Dominique Foray, Bronwyn H. Hall and W. Edward Steinmueller (Elgar 2006). Paul David continues to divide his time annually between Oxford and Stanford.

The interview was conducted over two days in December 1996 by Susan B. Carter of the University of California, Riverside, and was augmented with additional queries and answers in 1999.

We might begin with a bit of biography. What brought you into the field?

Lack of preparation for something else would be the most historically accurate answer. Let me explain. I went off to college in 1952 intending to do chemistry, a subject I enjoyed greatly in high school. My Harvard freshman advisor joined me in this fantasy. After scanning my folder, he told me not to take the introductory course, but to start with stoichiometry – chemical arithmetic based on the determination of atomic weights. It was taught by a very popular chemistry professor, name of Nash. This would have been great advice for someone else. Nash's lectures and demonstrations were memorably brilliant; the labs were fun, albeit very time-consuming. But, virtually from day one I had that sensation of being in well over my head. Soon, I was drowning in "moles," balance equations and "rates of reaction" problems. With lots of help from my classmates, I managed to emerge with a shocking C+. I also emerged convinced that I had quite the wrong idea about chemistry, that I needed to take some math courses, and that I needed to find a course to replace introductory organic chemistry – which had been penciled in on my spring schedule. Econ 10, Introductory Economics, happened to be offered at a convenient hour. So, you could say that I came to economics more as a refugee than a pilgrim.

What was it about economics that intrigued you?

I should say that I was not wholly innocent of economics. From a young age I was intrigued by history, and by the time I reached high school I had been exposed to a good many economic and social issues in US and European history. But that wasn't economic analysis, which came as something of a surprise. Happily, unlike stoichiometry, this was a surprise that I could manage, and so I stayed with it long enough to become thoroughly seduced. The very idea of a unified theoretical framework for studying economic activity was a powerful one. Remember, at this time Samuelson (and Hicks) were already having a big impact on the way undergraduate economics was taught at places like Harvard – even though *The Foundations of Economic Analysis* (1948) and *Value and Capital* (1939) were not assigned until you got to the most advanced theory course.

Was there anything that was especially memorable about your introduction to theory?

I recall John Chipman's lectures as having had a big and sustained intellectual impact on me. His classroom style was the opposite of flamboyant, but the structure of the course and the classroom presentations were lucid and elegant. He took us from the formal theory of the household and the firm through to Walrasian general equilibrium analysis and its applications to real trade theory. Then he developed an interpretation of the Keynesian system as a special case of general equilibrium where some markets were characterized by price inflexibility – sticky prices, wage rate rigidities, and bond market expectations which created the liquidity trap phenomenon. This was very different from the mechanical presentation of Keynesian economics we received from Alvin Hansen's macro course. It was a revelation. I found the coherence of the whole thing exciting and wonderfully satisfying. That feeling remained even when, much later, I came to understand the serious problems that one glossed over in treating money as just another commodity whose price was determined along with those of all the other goods.

When Moe Abramovitz was interviewed, he talked about his first economics course. The way he describes it, he stumbled into it and then was just swept away by the brilliance, the coherent vision of the changes and organization of society. Was it like that for you?

Well, yes, in the analytical sense I have just described. But the idea of the economy's relationship to the organization of society wasn't a new one for me. I'd already been exposed to it, although not to its representation in a formal system that could be analyzed rigorously. You see, I had some precocious acquaintance with economic history as a field of study, more or less by accident of birth. My father, Henry David, began his academic career as a labor historian. He published *The History of the Haymarket Affair* in 1936, the year after I was born. While I was in high school, he was editing volumes in the Rinehart series on American Economic History. So, Nettles, Taylor, Kirkland, Mitchell, and Gates were "household names" to me, long before I actually read their books – also Larry Harper who, alas, wasn't able to complete the promised volume on the colonial period.

So, for you, it was the formal theory that was the new, attractive thing about economics?

Absolutely. I suppose that although it wasn't a conscious consideration for me at the time, it's not entirely coincidental that economic theory was the one aspect of the subject that seemed farthest removed from my father's areas of expertise and active interest. There was, however, another aspect of my interest in economic theory that developed very early – the intellectual history of the discipline. Why had economic theory developed in the way it did? Was it just a matter of logical progress towards "getting it right?" Or were changing external influences, including economic conditions, what had led economic thinkers to change their minds? These questions were raised by reading Heilbroner's *The Worldly Philosophers* in my introductory Econ course, but I felt that Heilbroner hadn't really answered them – that he had not even posed them.

Can I suggest that's an unusual viewpoint for a beginning student?

Perhaps, although the idea of studying the history of economic analysis was something that crystallized in my thinking only much later on – sometime towards the end of my junior year. By then I had had an opportunity to read some of Schumpeter's monumental tome on the subject. Robert Kuenne, then the resident economics tutor at Adams House, was reviewing and indexing the manuscript at the request of Schumpeter's widow, and he let me see it. What intrigued me most was Schumpeter's notion of "the vision" – the dominating conceptualization of the nature of the economy. He presented this as having shaped the way economists perceived the world around them and the directions in which they sought to extend economic analysis. Schumpeter contrasted visions of the economy as "hitchless" (Smith, Mill, Bastiat) or "hitch-bound" (Malthus, Ricardo, Keynes). But it still wasn't clear where these visions came from, or why the dominant visions changed from one generation to the next. This seemed to me a good problem to pursue.

Did you pursue it?

Well, I tried. In my senior year I took Overton Hume Taylor's course in the history of economic thought, as it was the only offering in that subject at Harvard. Unfortunately, his approach to doing intellectual history was not particularly oriented to the questions that were intriguing me; but I learned something of the literature and the craft, and that didn't discourage me from writing my honors thesis in the area. The topic I picked even now seems a peculiarly esoteric choice: neoclassical international trade theory, the Edgeworth–Loria–Bastable controversy, and the emerging critique of the doctrine of Free Trade in Britain, *c.* 1880–1906. My faculty advisor was Jim Duesenberry, and he seemed to view this proposal with somewhat perplexed bemusement. But he let me go ahead. More than that, he was of real help in straightening out some analytical tangles that I got into. Despite, or perhaps because of, the esoteric nature of its subject, my honors thesis won high marks – and I wound up knowing more than anyone I encountered at Harvard about a topic that only I seemed to find interesting, rather than a curiosity.

Was that why you didn't go on with the history of economic thought?

That would have been a good, rational reason – certainly a sufficient reason. Yet, I don't recollect having made a deliberate decision to abandon the field. What I can recall is feeling, especially while struggling to finish the wretched thesis, that this form of intellectual history really was too difficult, that it called for too many varied kinds of knowledge, none of which I really had a firm grasp of – the previous theory, the individual economist's biographies and their mental states, the times through which they were living – much less the literary skill to weave all of that into a story! I think that's why I allowed myself be deflected from the history of thought.

In what way were you "deflected?"

I came to focus more and more on the economic changes taking place in late nineteenth-century Britain. The argument of my thesis was that those changes had pushed some English economists into questioning the policy of Free Trade, and, more generally, underlay the increased appeal in Britain of the ideas associated with the German Historical School. Of course, some of the "deflecting force" was external. In the fall of my senior year I talked my way into Alexander Gerschenkron's year-long graduate course in economic history. My pitch was that I needed to study economic history for my honors thesis, and Gerschenkron's was the only [European] economic history offered at Harvard. That proved to be a potent experience for me. Gerschenkron was a man of great erudition, as probably everyone knows. His lectures ranged from the description of a Carolingian manor to subtleties of the index number problem, with lots of references to what Max Weber had said in between. He was vigorous then, and enthusiastic about infusing economic history with economic theory and statistics, and, to boot, he was personally very engaging with new students. We had to write a 20-page paper each semester and make an appointment to have him approve the topic. At my first such meeting with him, when I sketched what I thought my honors thesis was going to argue, he handed me a copy of Walt Rostow's *The British Economy of the Nineteenth Century* and said, "Well . . . why not tell me what you think about this?" So, I wrote my paper on Rostow's use of economic models to study the past, particularly the Great Depression of 1873–96. Although its explanation of the Great Depression did not leave me convinced (I had found several critical reviews), I liked the methodologically pioneering side of that book, and in my paper I tried to suggest ways of taking it further. From that point onwards, I was firmly "hooked" on what I took to be a new and more useful approach to writing economic history.

Because of its theoretical perspective?

Sure. That was a major part of its appeal for me. The idea of looking at the nineteenth-century British economy through the lens of modern economic theory was the dual of the task for my thesis – using a better understanding of the changes taking place in the economy in order to understand the evolution of contemporary economic thought. Putting the two together, I thought modern theory could be used to help understand economic thought, but in an historically contextual way. This seemed to me to be better than the conventional "internalist" approach of the scholarly literature, which was to examine each successive theory and critique it from the standpoint of how closely it had approached "the truth" – as that was manifested in modern theory.

Pretty complicated. Let me try to summarize: You were more intrigued by the historical forces that led to theoretical structures than with the elegance of a particular theoretical structure that happened to be in place?

That's a good characterization, and short! I wasn't into theory for theory's sake. My initiation into advanced economic analysis occurred before "the neoclassical system" – a self-contained axiomatized intellectual structure – was *the* form in which theoretical analysis was presented to students. When I came to trying to apply theory to understand some particular problem, I started from the premise that any bit of textbook analysis, or "off the shelf" theory taken from a journal article would, more likely than not, have some implicit empirical suppositions buried in it; and those would constitute a limitation on its range of useful application, possibly a fatal limitation. One might have to shop around for something more suitable or develop something better suited to the historical context. I still think that's so. I never felt moved by the missionary zeal that later came to characterize the proponents of studying history as a way of extending the disciplinary domain of economics, let alone the domain of neoclassical economics.

You don't consider yourself to be a neoclassical economist?

No, certainly not today. And not ever, if by that you mean believing that everything is everywhere convex, that tastes are exogenous, that agents always are maximizing well-defined objective functions, and that it's always best to start by assuming what we observe has been generated by a world of perfectly competitive markets. But, who does? To me there is an important difference between eclectically selecting some items that are in the neoclassical tool kit and buying the whole store.

So then you went off to Cambridge, England.

Okay, let's go back to 1956: that was when, after graduating from Harvard, I was very fortunate to be accepted as a Fulbright Scholar at Pembroke College, Cambridge. The people I met then, the friendships I made (indeed, a first marriage), formed the web of associations that would draw me back repeatedly to visit and live in Cambridge, and then in Oxford and elsewhere in Britain, throughout the decades that followed. They created a critical part on the path that eventually led me back to All Souls.

We'll come back to path dependence in a bit, but first, I wonder whether your primary academic interest at Cambridge was economics or economic history?

Cambridge in 1956–58 was a lively and active place for a would-be economist. D. H. Robertson was still giving wryly humorous lectures on price theory, and I went religiously to Maurice Dobb's excellent lectures on welfare analysis. But it was Kahn, Kaldor and Robinson, the once-Young Turks, who had come to dominate the scene. When I arrived, everybody was trying to figure out what Joan Robinson was saying in her recently published book, *The Accumulation of Capital*. Joan herself was not much help. She was formidable: in one seminar after another she simply stopped younger colleagues and graduate students who were brave enough to attempt expositions restating and interpreting her argument. When they would begin their talk by putting up some notation on the board, she would cut them off, saying something like: "Look. I've written it all out in my notation, so what's the point of re-writing it in some other way?" All that was amazing and entertaining. And I couldn't help but pay attention to it, because, at the end of the academic year, I would have to "sit" for the examination in five (of the eight) papers that then formed Part Two of the Economics Tripos. In addition to going to lectures and seminars, my economics tutor in Pembroke College was setting me weekly essays to write in preparation for the micro and macroeconomics examinations.

Although theory was much on my mind during that year, taking my two years at Cambridge in all it was economic history that occupied the major part of my attention. One of the fields I could choose to be examined in on the Economics Tripos was a "special subject," and that year – fortunately for me – R. C. O. Matthews was offering special subject lectures on "British Trade Cycle History, 1825 to 1850." That was my chance to do serious economic history "for credit" in the context of the Economics Diploma program in which I had enrolled. But, in addition, David Joslin, a history tutor in my college who had taken an interest in me, arranged for me to have some supervision in modern British economic history with Peter Mathias, then teaching at Queen's College. I think it was through Joslin and Mathias that I was invited to attend Postan's seminars in economic history, after when I got through the Tripos and was accepted to do a second year as a research student. My next piece of good fortune came when Robin Matthews agreed to supervise my research, which I decided to do on British economic fluctuations during the "disturbed" period from 1857 to 1869. It was an apprenticeship project, in which I tried to follow closely the model of Matthews's masterly book on the 1830s, *A Study in Trade Cycle History*.

To have worked with all those outstanding people, and through them to have been introduced to Ashton, Habakkuk, Tawney and still others, scholars who for me previously had existed only as authors on Gerschenkron's (overly ample) course bibliography, certainly was the best, and most enduringly valuable, part of my British training to become an economic historian.

Let's return to Cambridge, Massachusetts.

Well, that's what I did, as an economics graduate student, back at Harvard in the fall of 1958.

Was that a difficult decision?

No, it was an easy decision. By that time I was married, and save for the willingness of my bride to continue as an infant-school teacher in Boston, I was without visible means of support – except a fellowship offer from Harvard. So, I returned to the normal "boot camp" greeting that awaits incoming graduate students: "Never mind your undergraduate major and your two years at Cambridge; you really don't know anything; we are starting over from scratch to teach you economics." By then, however, I did have a pretty good idea of what micro and macroeconomics were about. Yet, what I had not encountered during my time at the other Cambridge, and what is both challenging and exciting for me, was econometrics, which was just beginning to be taught at Harvard. I took a year of quantitative methods from Houthhakker (who at the time was visiting, from Stanford). Apart from what I learned, there were two interesting sequels that derived from my taking that course. The teaching assistant was a second-year graduate student named Albert Fishlow, who had done well the year before in the econometrics course offered by another visitor, Johnston; that was how Al and I met and became friends, but only after he had marked my final exam and mentioned that I had done surprisingly well. The other thing was that two years later, Houthhakker was the only person who interviewed me for the job I was offered at Stanford, although by then he actually had switched to Harvard, and was asked to look me over as a favor to his former colleagues. I suppose one could say, with this tale in mind, that at least some of the roots of the Stanford–Berkeley Economic History Colloquium (which Fishlow and I organized after we got settled in California) trace right back to that econometrics course at Harvard.

You had already done Gerschenkron's course, and you had been studying economic history in Cambridge. Could you do further work in economic history back at Harvard?

Of course, although not in terms of course work. During the first part of the year I was given an assignment as a condition of my fellowship: I was to be a "research assistant" to Gerschenkron. He had had a heart attack the preceding spring, and Seymour Harris, the department chair, thought that Gerschenkron should have somebody to help him fetch stuff from the library, carry piles of books and so forth. As I was someone whom Gerschenkron already knew, and as I had hoped to work with him, it seemed logical to assign this role to me.

So you would meet with Gerschenkron?

Well, I attended his lectures again, which was good, because he was on to some new material, and I thought it would be a way to keep in touch with him on a regular basis. But he hated the idea of having a "helper" assigned to him. I think it suggested an "incapacity," and he really had no use for the services of a real research assistant. He would say: "You know, somewhere in Vico's work on vortices, there is a statement like this . . . Can you find that?" So, off I would go to Widener Library. He would have given me the citation in Italian, and my first task was to find an English translation. Then I would plow through the 435 pages of Vico trying to find something that resembled "the passage." Of course, as was not infrequently the case, it simply would not be there. In the "quotation from Vico" episode, what Gerschenkron had remembered, almost perfectly, was a half-sentence from something like page 7 and the rest from something like page 430, and he had run them together. I thought maybe he read the beginnings and ends of books first, but, when I tried out that theory on later search occasions, it didn't work.

So, like a good retriever holding a bird in my mouth, I'd return after two days and plop it down on the desk of his office in Littauer. He would look up and say, "Oh, very good! Very good! Yes! Yes! And the original Italian is . . . where? Oh. So, when you are going back to Widener to get that, so I can check this translation . . . you know, it doesn't look quite right . . . would you see, somewhere in the *Collected Works* of Freud, if you can find the essay on Michelangelo, or was it da Vinci, where he remarks . . ." It went on like that. Paper chases.

Did you *learn* anything from this?

I learned nothing from the experience, although it did broaden my education. I took it as a job that came with the fellowship: challenging, but in a way that was rather a disappointment.

But you're not angry? You're not resentful?

I think it takes a lot to make me resentful. At the time it just seemed bizarre. I felt that this wasn't serious activity, that it was a poor use of my time, given the amount of reading in economics that I had to do for my courses. I felt relieved when it came to an end. When, towards the end of that first semester, Gerschenkron said he felt he didn't need a research assistant, I agreed instantly and reported back to Seymour Harris. And for the spring semester I was assigned a really good job – being TA for the undergraduate course in American economic history taught by Alfred Conrad.

At that time, Alf Conrad had just finished a paper with John Meyer about which he was quite excited: the economics of slavery. So, I was witnessing the beginnings of that strand of the new economic history movement in the US, although at the time there were no portents of the future that I was conscious of. What I was delighted to learn was that Alf Conrad was a fine economist and a wonderfully considerate person to work with. He was enthusiastic about what he was doing in applying economic methods to the study of history, and he let me give some of the lectures on topics that interested me. Bray Hammond's interpretation of Jackson, Biddle and the struggle over the Second Bank of the US was one that I remember spending a lot of time preparing.

Conrad gave some lectures based on a new paper he was writing, dealing with structural changes in the American economy and their impact upon economic growth and stability. This was very interesting to me, as it related to model-building work that Duesenberry had recently done, and so had a connection to the research I had done in Cambridge on trade cycle history, under Matthews's supervision. I mention this because nobody looks at that paper of Conrad's today, although it's accessible in his book with Meyer. I found it stimulating for what it said about the way that the movement of the frontier, and transport innovations, were affecting investment demand; and more generally about the disequilibrium dynamics of the growth process in the nineteenth century. Anyway, it was an encouraging impetus for me to continue along my previous line of research on growth and cycles, by shifting into the US context.

What was the impetus for Conrad and Meyer? Why were they studying the economic history of slavery – was it fashionable?

It certainly wasn't fashionable in economics at the time. I think the paper on slavery came out of conversations between Meyer and Conrad on the idea of applying capital theory to historical questions, but I really can't say that with certainty. It's also possible that John Meyer had started on the subject for a term paper in Gerschenkron's course.

He subsequently did publish another economic history article that began life as a term paper for Gerschenkron, and those papers came in pairs. That was Meyer's paper applying input–output analysis to assess the effects on the British economy of the retarded growth of its staple exports in the 1880–1913 period. It's easy to imagine that the idea of applying capital theory to understanding slavery was prompted by the contemporary publication of Kenneth Stampp's *The Peculiar Institution*, which attracted a good bit of attention at the time – but, again, that's just another surmise . . .

So, it was not an entirely imperialist impulse on the part of economists. It was a conversation with historians.

Well, "imperialist" is what non-economists call the enthusiasm of economists for their way of thinking. But, really, I cannot recall either talk of disciplinary expansion or of efforts to actually engage historians in discussing economic history. The "colonizing impulse" came later and from a different quarter. At the beginning, it was more a matter of economists having conversations about history among themselves. I'm pretty certain that neither Conrad nor Meyer nor anyone else in the Harvard economics department at that time ever had any "trans-disciplinary conversations" with members of the history department, people such as Oscar Handlin and Frederick Merk (a student of Frederick Jackson Turner's), although they were teaching and writing on subjects that had a good bit of economic, as well as social and political history content.

Nor did anyone in the Harvard economics faculty seem aware that Bernard Bailyn (also in the history faculty) had recently published a pioneering piece of computer-aided quantitative economic history – on Massachusetts shipping and shipowners during the late seventeenth and eighteenth centuries. I was, but only because I sometimes had lunch with Bud Bailyn at Adams House. His work was another "straw in the wind" for quantitative economic history, but a straw that wasn't adequately noticed then, or since. Perhaps because Bailyn soon left colonial economic history to score a big hit with *The Ideological Origins of the American Revolution*, his Massachusetts shipping book has been forgotten by the annalists of "the cliometrics revolution." But, I've always thought that it was both substantively and methodologically more interesting, really far more interesting, than that much fussed-over Purdue paper on those "first 1,942 British steamships" – or however many there were.

Can you characterize the conversation among practitioners in social science disciplines at that time? Were they in closer conversation – reading one another's work more carefully and more systematically than we see today?

Although the people having those quantitative-historical conversations didn't have so clear a self-image of themselves as a discipline with a distinctive rhetoric, I would say that among the community concerned with economic and social history there was then a greater sense of unity. The impetus for the interest that economic history held for people trained in economics derived from the problems of what then were called the "less developed countries."

Economists had the sense that the tools they innately brought to discuss economic development were not adequate. Keynesian macroeconomics supposed that the problem of poverty arose from effective demand deficiencies, and, when that was found to be wrong, attention shifted to revive supply side approaches and models of capital accumulation. But they were not entirely adequate either; the resulting growth models were not taking into account some key dynamic processes of development (such as induced innovation and technology transfers), or certain aspects of the politics and culture of the developing world. Those missing elements were acknowledged as being "historical," which created an opening for economic historians. That's how I eventually got into a highly theoretically oriented economics department, as Stanford was in 1961. The graduate students all wanted to do economic development, and the faculty were persuaded – by colleagues like Moe Abramovitz and Paul Baran – that if you were going to have development as a field, you should have an economic historian to help teach it.

Are you suggesting that path dependence may have had an appeal in the 1950s in part because the economists' models left out huge areas like culture and expectations?

Not only that, they left out demography; they left out technical change. The core theory was much closer to neoclassical economics where "the givens" (*e.g.*, tastes, endowment, and technology, the institutionalized aspects of markets, and regulatory structures) are formed through essentially historical processes – as most economists today would acknowledge. Of course, economic theory would later extend itself into those areas, but in ways that preserved the ahistorical structure of the core competitive general equilibrium analysis of competitive markets.

If particular countries started with different givens, then their development paths would differ even though they faced the same current conditions?

That's right! It is relevant to understand the intellectual context in which my thinking early about "historical economics" was formed: in the late 1950s and 1960s the idea that "history mattered" had come to the fore in discussions of the developing economies. One aspect of such thought was to be seen in Paul Baran's book *The Political Economy of Growth*. If you strip away the Marxist rhetoric, the argument was that the condition of people in less-developed countries was not something that could be understood in isolation from the persisting effects of their past interactions with the now-developed world. The legacies of colonial dependency (and "exploitation," the word more often used) needed to be addressed if their future was to be different from their past; otherwise, as the argument went, the structures of dependency would go on reproducing themselves. This line of analysis had developed along with the perception that what was working in the advanced market economies of the West might not necessarily be workable in the LDCs. For one reason or another, their problems of market failure and coordination failure were more severe. The social infrastructure was different and less geared to supporting capitalist paths of growth; other, compensatory measures, institutions, and government strategies might therefore be called for.

These were the ideas with which Gerschenkron's famous 1952 article on "Economic Backwardness in Historical Perspective" had found resonance. His theme was that the "follower countries" in the spread of industrialization had not been able to actually "follow" in the footsteps of Britain. Their history had been different; they had to "substitute" new modes of organization, institutions and government action in order to overcome shortages of entrepreneurial expertise, trust and other sources of coordination failure that had permitted the channeling of investments into "industrial development blocs" characterized by mutually reinforcing positive externalities. In the absence of such concerted actions, it was suggested, those economies, too, might have remained trapped in a low-level, pre-industrialized state.

For me, and for others who came into economic history at that time, this was the real stuff of "historical economics" and, *mutatis mutandis*, it has remained so. The favorable reception and the attention stirred up in the profession at large by Conrad and Meyer's paper on the economics of slavery certainly was welcome. But it seemed to me to be orthogonal to the main reasons why economic historians should be, and were at the time being hired by economics departments. Perhaps my view was incorrect about economists' reasons for accepting the New Economic History; I always seem to be underestimating the power of disciplinary narcissism in academic life.

Okay, you're saying that when you started your career, the idea that history was important for understanding contemporary economic development issues was mixed in with the concept of market failures and government intervention? How does that relate to the current literature on path dependence?

I think that those were two separable strands of thought at the time. One strand, with a direct connection with modern views about history mattering, is that there may be multiple equilibria – as in "high-level" and "low-level equilibrium traps," the terminology then popularized by Harvey Leibenstein. Under such conditions, it was well understood (at least for the case of deterministic systems), that where you started was likely to determine where you ended up, unless some exogenous action shocked the system or altered its structure. But this hadn't been formulated as a rigorous set of propositions about the nature of dynamic stochastic processes that were "non-ergodic" – processes that would not converge to some "fixed point" defined as a limiting probability distribution. So, it could be said that it was the economic historian's task to explore and expose for economists the nature of the self-perpetuating mechanisms that would prevent economies from behaving in a convergent way, ultimately shaking free from the influence of their initial conditions.

Today, we talk about such processes as involving "positive feedbacks" and as being "self-reinforcing" and "auto-catalytic" – terms borrowed from the physical sciences. But the essential concepts and insights as to their implications certainly were quite familiar to economists and economic historians who wrote about "big push" theories of industrialization. What they added to the diagnosis was that, without intervention, the self-reinforcing mechanisms would perpetuate an unsatisfactory equilibrium; state planned investment was proposed as *the* way to escape from this. The latter prescription too often was not based on anything in the analysis, but came from somewhere else – from the philosophical traditions that shaped the style of welfare analysis, in which one was free to imagine the existence of an omniscient and benevolent public agent.

Let me bring you back to the origin of the slavery debate. Having been around Conrad and Meyer at Harvard, did you become involved in debates about the economics of slavery at this very early stage?

Not really. I was an interested spectator. As Alf Conrad lectured on the material, I felt I should study it closely enough to be able to answer questions and grade exam answers. There were some bright undergraduates in that class, who could and did give their TA a run for his money. I remember Marty Feldstein was one of them – bygone days! Of course, there was the intrinsic interest in the material, and it was exciting to be associated with doing something new and slightly daring, like talking dispassionately about slavery. But that was the limit of my involvement at that stage – and for quite a while thereafter.

When did you first attend the meetings of The Cliometric Society?

We have been talking just now about 1958–60, when there was no Cliometric Society as such, but, starting in 1960, there were the conferences held at Purdue that later came to be known as "Clio," and out of which grew the Cliometric Society. Those Purdue meetings, as almost everybody knows, played a formative role in the New Economic History movement in the States and eventually internationally. I want to say something about their importance for my personal development as an economic historian. I attended my first meeting in 1961. It was a source, a vital source, of encouragement, of reinforcement, because there were so very few of "us" at the time. We were thin on the ground and scattered across geographically separated economics departments. The formation of a network of people who one knew and with whom one could correspond casually was more crucial than you might imagine. For someone just starting out, as I was, the contacts, particularly those with the older, established people in the field were really the vital aspect of "Clio" at that stage. That had a lot to do with the very good dynamics among the group that regularly attended – they set the style. There was a sense of commitment, excitement, a wonderful openness in sharing data and helping the younger members of the group focus their research. My first conversations with Bob Gallman, Dorothy Brady, Bill Parker and Dick Easterlin on that occasion are still vivid in my memory, and it was only later that I made some connections with "the Purdue gang" proper.

You've reminded me of a comment one of my colleagues made who was attending an All-UC conference for the first time. As you know, these All-UC conferences are modeled after the Clio format. He said, "This was the strangest conference I ever attended. It wasn't *about* anything, but everyone's quite involved."

It was clear that the subtext of the Purdue meetings in the early 1960s was the emerging program for New Economic History. This was to bring more sophisticated theoretical and statistical approaches to bear on the problem of writing a quantitative history of the American economy. Other subjects were heard and discussed, but running in the background always was the creation and refinement of new estimates, and the application of analysis of new data sources to build up a picture of the development of industries and regions. There was a sense that a shared methodological approach was being forged, and there was a sense of a shared outlook. The substantive topics, of course, were distributed over quite a range, and there was no lack of criticism and disagreement on specific issues – quite the opposite!

Let me try to pin you down. Within our profession people are pigeonholed as either "empirical" or "theoretical" economists. How would you characterize this "shared outlook?" Is it theoretical? Is it empirical? Who's the audience?

First, almost all the people at those early meetings had been trained in economics, so they had a common theoretical orientation. Second, this was the beginning of the rise of econometrics, so there was a statistical orientation to much of the work, simple at first, but soon becoming more sophisticated as the recent products of graduate economics programs began to join the company. "What could you do to extract more from the numbers?" That, too, was a question to which almost everybody responded. People didn't have a common view about modeling style; it was more eclectic at that stage than it subsequently became. There was both an empirical commitment to develop new sources of information, most of them statistical, and to assemble a record. That clearly was an undertaking which was still very strongly influenced by the tradition of Mitchell, Kuznets and Burns, despite the shift that had taken economists away from the inductive legacy of the National Bureau, and towards a structural modeling approach of the sort championed by Koopmans and the Cowles Commission.

Some people felt that that unified vision and, certainly, the collegiality and camaraderie of the early days of cliometrics ended with the debate that ensued over the publication of *Time on the Cross*. You were an important participant in that debate. I wonder if you can tell us why it was so emotional, and so divisive.

Well, it's a good question, but it's not an easy question. I won't be able to give you a satisfactory short answer. I think one has to approach this with three things in mind. First, by the early 1970s, the common unifying program of research that had characterized the early days of Clio had been left behind. The field had expanded, and there were people who were working on a wider variety of topics. Also, in the early period the sense of unity flowed from interests in the problems of economic development on the part of the economics profession at large, but, by the early 1970s, new topics related to social and economic developments in the contemporary US economy – racial discrimination, labor market discrimination, urban economics, income distribution, and still other issues – had come to the fore. These caught the interest of younger economic historians, who naturally sought to work on topics that related to the current interests of their economics department colleagues. Then, too, the early program of interrelated work on American economic growth, which provided a unifying, overarching framework, had culminated with the 1963 Chapel Hill conference and the eventual publication (in 1966) of volume 30 of the NBER *Studies in Income and Wealth* (CRIW 1966). Sure, there were follow-on studies that used the estimates for growth accounting analysis, yet that too had become an increasingly specialized pursuit, rather than a unifying focal point. This all meant that when *Time on the Cross* was approaching publication, we had already left behind the initial atmosphere of there being a coherent, unifying intellectual purpose in what we "New Economic Historians" were about. Maybe it had never existed in reality, but by then even the outward semblance was hard to discern.

The second ingredient was that by that time the New Economic History had become more than just self-conscious; it had acquired a formal sense of itself as a transformative disciplinary movement that people were celebrating. It was not primarily about substantive achievement so much as having been successful in professional, academic terms. The triumph of the New Economic History was measured in terms of the NBER conference volumes, the growth of publications in the *Journal of Economic History*, sessions at AEA meetings, and articles that had made their way into the mainline economics journals. There was a sense that here was a movement that had triumphed, and we had more and more celebratory pieces about this success. So, in a sense, the organizational aspects of the sub-discipline's growth had come to replace the intellectual coherence of the early movement. Consequently, the unity of the field in terms of the degree of public consensus among the people identified with it had taken on a value in itself. Our views now were noticeable, and people had become concerned about the continued growth of funding from the NSF and other such issues. Back in the early 1960s, nobody particularly cared whether economic historians agreed or disagreed, because they were a rarity and were presenting themselves as new and developing, not as an arrived and established branch of economics. But a decade later, the people in the field who had a proselytizing impulse, a mission to convert new followers, were beginning to turn to fields beyond economics; we had filled up the readily available slots in the leading departments, and the prospects for continuing expansion and jobs for our new Ph.D.'s were looking less promising. It was time to press forward onto new terrain, the history departments. You could see this in the serious efforts that were being made at the time to have economic historians on the programs of the American Historical Society and the Organization of American Historians.

Are you suggesting that there was an externality, that people had an interest in having your colleagues do a great job, and be widely acclaimed, because that would make it easier for you?

I think it would be too strong to say that there was a political feeling resembling a call for a "united front," but a consciousness of the shared interest in "professional identity" certainly had developed. There was the idea that this was a movement that deserved to command the enthusiasm and the loyalty of a growing number of people, and that this was relevant in the larger competition for resources within academic economics.

And the third factor you mentioned?

The third factor was the intense social interest that then pervaded all issues connected with race. This made the history of slavery and history of race relations extremely loaded from the viewpoint of interpretations that people other than professional economic historians would place on the findings in this field. Hence, the subject was exciting: here was an avenue through which economic historians could reach a much larger and engaged audience. Was the current condition of Black Americans the legacy of slavery? Was it due to something that occurred after slavery – to racism in the North? What had been the role of state and federal government programs in reinforcing discrimination? These were serious and difficult issues, and the scholars who addressed them, however indirectly, through studying the historical record were sincere and not unaware of the volatile nature of public reactions to what they might say. Thus, when *Time on the Cross* appeared, it was seen to be a bold bid for attention from a wider audience, and it used that platform to make a claim on behalf of the New Economic History's power to reveal new and important truths about the history of slavery, the institution that many people saw as the root of the most pressing social issues in America. It attached to that message a still larger set of intellectual claims on behalf of cliometrics, claims that many early reviewers read as preaching a second crusade to establish this approach to doing history in history departments.

So, there are the three aspects of the scene: the effort to resume the momentum of a unified "New Economic History;" the appeal to colonize another discipline, which already had created confrontations with historians who were somewhat dubious about that proposal; and a firecracker tossed into the tinderbox of public discussion of the history of slavery and racism in America. With such mixture, it seems to me that it's a "tribute" to the way in which the debate about *Time on the Cross* was conducted *within the economic history profession* that it really didn't explode into, or degenerate into, personal animosities. Most of the serious disagreements that emerged about the book's substance were pursued at the level of "What was the historical evidence? What was the nature of the theoretical structure within which it was being interpreted?"

Contrary to what may be the perceptions of some people who were not active at the time, this was not so divisive a development within the profession. A few intemperate denunciations were flung at the critics, for "undermining the cliometric cause," and their personal motivations were questioned, but only on one or two occasions that I can recall. This was unworthy behavior, confined to a very few agitated souls, and it was far from the way in which the authors of *Time on the Cross* conducted their side of the controversy.

There were, it's true, quite a number of other academic historians (especially those outside economic history) who seemed to take delight in the fact that the folks who had only recently appeared massed on their borders in a unified invasion force, were now publicly at odds with one another. But they hadn't been reading our journals beforehand. And, furthermore, what participants from inside repeatedly pointed out was that such glee on the part of anti-cliometricians reflected a serious misperception. The strength of the new methodology was that, by comparison to many historical debates that had occurred in the past, what both sides were doing was focused on identifying and defining the set of issues about which there was disagreement *within a common disciplinary framework*. That seems to me to be a very significant, enduring accomplishment of the New Economic History. It raised up the level of the conversation, as intense as it had become on this issue, to that of disputes about quantitative methods and the ways in which economic reasoning could be used to arrive at certain kinds of interpretive statements. It was not a controversy, as so many historical controversies have been, that was animated by politics and prejudice. The spectators sometimes took a different view of what was going on; they made out of it what they wanted for purposes of their own.

Let's talk about your work on path dependence, which has attracted a lot of attention, both from economic historians and also from theorists and policy-oriented people. There have been some very spirited discussions of the concept and its implications on the EH.Res list.[1] As far as I know, however, you have not responded to the debate you've instigated, at least not in print, and I know that many people would be interested in hearing what you think about the comments your work has generated.

Well, it would be too big a task to respond here to everything that has been said on EH.Res, nor do I think I need to do that. I did post a long paper on "Path Dependence and the Quest for Historical Economics: One more chorus in the Ballad of QWERTY" back in the fall of 1997.[2] In it I tried to sort out a number of confusions that have crept into the discussion: what constitutes path dependence, the respects in which it is and is not associated with market failure, and the distinction I believe should be drawn between path dependence as a phenomenon, and the class of models that properly belong to what I'd referred to as "the economics of QWERTY." Possibly the most useful thing in it is the bibliography listing the places in which one can find the other papers that I've written since 1985, dealing with conceptual and methodological issues

1 Entry to EH.Res forum archive via URL: <http://eh.net/forums/QWERTYSu2.html>.

2 Published in revised and abridged form as David (2001). The original version, in the series *University of Oxford Discussion Papers in Economic and Social History*, remains available at URL <http://www.nuff.ox.ac.uk/economics/history/paper20/david3.pdf>.

involving path dependence in economics. These haven't appeared in the *JEH*, *EEH* or the *AER*, so they aren't under everybody's nose. But, I am still surprised that people who express a keen interest in the subject, and argue about it endlessly on the internet, don't seem to have found their way to any of them.

Are you saying indirectly that the QWERTY example is not essential to this set of ideas?

I can say that more directly. I know the thing that some people seem to be hung up on is whether QWERTY is or is not the best keyboard available today, and, if it isn't, whether that entails a big economic inefficiency. Sure, there is a rhetorical force in this illustration, and I maintain the illustration is soundly grounded in the historical evidence, but to suppose that it is substantively crucial to any of the interesting issues is plain silly. Not something I have wanted to further encourage. To be focusing so much attention on this particular question in the history of typewriter technology, as if the relevance for economics of the whole subject of multiple equilibria in stochastic processes (and the mechanisms whereby "selection" occurs among them) somehow turned upon the answer to it, seems to me a quadruple-headed mistake. Maybe I should take the time here to enumerate those heads?

I think people would like you to . . .

Okay. The first thing to notice is that you can have multiple equilibria that aren't uniquely Pareto-ranked. The issue of what is and is not "inefficient" is separable from the study of path dependence.

Second, I cannot see any justification for accepting the burden of proving empirically that the outcome of a competitive market process has been other than efficient, when you have situations in which the source of the positive feedback can be seen to be the presence of positive (network) externalities, or non-convexities such as learning effects and habituation in a dynamic process. The theoretical presumption that the market would select the most efficient option among the available alternatives no longer exists under those conditions. This isn't news; it's old hat. So, the burden of proof plainly falls on those who say that everything has turned out for the best; that QWERTY is better – in terms of social efficiency criteria – than anything that was and is available. They should try to substantiate that claim, and maybe explain whether that was just a stroke of good luck or whether something far deeper, something economic theory hasn't recognized about the workings of markets, was going on.

Third, it is not as though QWERTY were the only story of path dependence in which it has been suggested that some outcome, other than the one that people in the past lived (or with which we are still living), was not "best in the best of all possible worlds." Why obsess on this single, manifestly minor illustration? Why not look at the stories of light-water nuclear reactors (a "sub"-optimal technology if there ever was one!), or pesticide- and herbicide-intensive agriculture, and at the whole bevy of information technologies that managed to become industry standards by displacing alternatives whose adoption certainly would not have been worse, and arguably would have been more advantageous to society?

Fourth, empirical demonstrations in such cases, either way, aren't really so simple as has been suggested by those who focus on assessments of QWERTY today. Such assessments never will be easy to carry through properly when technologies and institutions have evolved along path-dependent trajectories. The notion of identifying the question of efficiency with the evaluation of just the currently observed state can't make much sense in such circumstances; you also have to consider, in the case of the QWERTY keyboard, to take a good illustration, the questions of the comparative ergonomic properties of the alternative keyboard layouts that were implemented on manual typewriters and on machines of different vintages.

Or, if you let me shift to the case of the millennium bug (another wonderful heuristic that I have tried to get people to explore analytically on EH.Res), you might need to gauge inefficiencies in terms of the path-integral of the costs of what I've called "path-constrained melioration." That's a fancy term for the process through which modifications are made in a technology, or an institution, in order to mitigate the costs of its dysfunctional properties. If you accept those dysfunctional characteristics as part of the status quo, then you look at the costs of remediation as an investment which either is or is not worth making: it's often better to throw money at the problem than to start again from scratch. But why set up an accounting system that at each point accepts the status quo as having been unavoidable; shouldn't one gauge the costs of the problems we have been handed to fix as a consequence of the poor selections made in the past? If we don't engage in research of that kind, are we likely to figure out how to avoid, or mitigate, more costly burdens that might be created for future generations to cope with?

All this seemed pretty transparent to me when I first read the attacks that were being directed at the concept of path dependence, in the form of critique of the historical evidence regarding QWERTY. I accept now that allowing nonsense to go unanswered is likely to be a mistake. Even though people eventually will figure out that it is nonsense, a lot of time and effort can be wasted in the process.

When you wrote the original QWERTY article, you presented it as an interesting example of a process that would produce a sub-optimal outcome, but you ended by backing off and saying the number of QWERTY worlds is an empirical question yet to be answered. But, as I hear you talking now, it suggests that you're thinking there are many processes that may lead to these multiple equilibrium situations, and you see this as something that's quite general.

I would certainly agree with the latter statement. At the close of my 1985 *AER* article I wrote that I believed there were "many QWERTY worlds out there." I could have said that there were certainly even more cases of path dependence in the selection of equilibria in pure coordination games. Maybe I ought to have added that, but would it have had the same rhetorical force in the profession at large? It is the prospect of something being inefficient that automatically grabs economists' attention. So, I raised the stakes by going with "QWERTY worlds." What I did want to get across was the point that the whole world is not path dependent, and, *a fortiori*, that it is not like QWERTY. There are lots of dynamical systems that, for practical purposes, we can analyze as convergent. Sorting out the ergodic from the non-ergodic economic processes, and then, among the latter, identifying those that are subject to market failures and thus belong to the economics of QWERTY still seems to me, to be a very worthwhile empirical program. It's a program that economic historians should be taking the lead in. We needn't start this "cold," for it has long been a strong prior among economic historians that, when it came to discussing technology, institutions, legal systems, culture and taste formation with economists, they should resist the incursion of ahistorical theorizing and press for a more evolutionary approach instead.

One last question. You're now spending much of your time in Europe and talking with social scientists there. Tell us about the connection between that locational shift and the development of your ideas of path dependence.

What I've found is that European economists, and social scientists more generally, are more eclectic in their thinking than their American counterparts. In no way could one say that their eclecticism reflects a casual, low-tech approach to the subject, but there still remain the effects of an intellectual tradition that is less disposed to be dogmatic about these matters. I have found that attitude rather refreshing, in that it more readily accommodates exploring new ideas in which I have a keen interest – such as the practical policy implications of path dependence. I should mention another noticeable contrast between the two intellectual environments, as it also touches on my work. History, the idea of history, and a sense of the weight of history, are thoroughly embedded in European culture and discourse, whereas Americans are much more disposed to focus upon what's new, revolutionary and going to transform the future. This is something of a truism, but the statement is no less true for being commonplace. You might be surprised at how usual it is for high-level policy conferences in Europe – whether convened by the OECD or by EC directorates, by a business association or under national government auspices – to lead off with an invited "historical benediction" on the economic topic under consideration. I suppose I may be forgiven for finding that a most congenial custom.

Yet, the most wonderful thing is that I have not been obliged to choose between extremes; All Souls College and Stanford form the best convex combination of academic environments that a historical economist could dream about. I wake up every day thankful for the reality of having been allowed to enjoy both places.

I can understand your reasons for going away, but please come back.

You can be sure of that.

Further reflections

Paul A. David

On looking back, I am struck by what I did not discuss with Susan Carter. While commenting on the conviviality of my new European colleagues, I said nothing about how I had wound up in Oxford. Readers may wonder what I was doing there, and have done subsequently, with my time away from Stanford. The opportunity to add this coda to my earlier narrative is therefore one I seize gladly.[3]

The study of evolving technological practices forms a discernible thread running through the fabric of my career; following it led me away from writing economic history and into work on contemporary science and technology policy issues, in Europe initially and later more globally. That could suffice as "the answer in a nutshell," but showing the connections requires picking up the thread in 1985, when "Clio and the Economics of QWERTY" was published and its longer sequel was written for Bill Parker's lively collection, *Economic History and the Modern Economist* (ed. 1986).

In retrospect, that pair of essays represents a significant juncture on my research path. They used a mundane illustration to point to the sources of "historicity" in economic processes, and offered a particular conceptualization of how "history matters" – and why knowing economic history therefore should matter to modern economists. Now associated with the term "path dependence," those ideas had surfaced in my wickedly subtitled 1969 review article "Transport Innovation and Economic Growth;" they found more formal expression in *Technical Choice, Innovation and Economic Growth* (1975).[4] But a newer line of thought in "QWERTY" must be traced forward in my research, rather than backward. It dealt with the role of technical and other complementarities in creating "network externalities," and the consequent strategic importance of compatibility and interoperability "standards" in market formation and network industry evolution – for modern digital information processing and telecommunications, and, in earlier times, for physical networks such as railways and electricity supply systems.

My articulation of that theme began with "Some new standards for the economics of standardization in the information age" (1987), presented the year before at an international conference in London. This offshoot from "the economics of QWERTY" attracted an interested European audience, so that soon I found myself on transoceanic flights with surprising frequency and began to think about how I could spend less time aloft and more time engaging with colleagues in Europe. That idea matured during 1992–93. Being on sabbatical as a Visiting Fellow at All Souls, I was "on the scene" when the College decided to fill a Senior Research Fellowship in economics. This improbable sequence of events led, still more improbably, to my election to the fellowship, to Stanford's agreement to my holding a joint appointment, and to my

3 Works cited by date appear in the References. See <http://siepr.stanford.edu/papers/papersautD-H.html> for other papers on topics mentioned here.

4 On path dependence, see also David (2001; 2005; 2007b), and the bibliography in the last item.

family's willingness to adapt to a lifestyle of "academic transhumance" that continues to the present.

By the mid-1990s I was thoroughly involved in the English scene, and was speaking about the economics of contemporary science policy at universities on the Continent. My further diversion into that field owed a good bit to the growing fascination with "networks" and "network externalities," and to having re-conceptualized a line of enquiry I began at Stanford in 1983–4. Prompted by the perplexity of my graduate students in a course on technological change, I tried to understand why there were two distinctive organizational modes of research – one in academic science and the other, primarily technological, in industrial R&D. The approach was to integrate insights from institutional sociology with perspectives from the economics of industrial organization – thus working toward "a new economics of science," an effort in which I was joined by Partha Dasgupta.[5]

Not surprisingly, there were some analogies between phenomena in that area and in my concurrent studies of technical networks and standards. The effective epistemological performance of peer networks in academic science (involving communications and collaboration among spatially and culturally distributed researchers) rests on a substratum of shared understandings and expectations of conformity to behavioral "norms." Two kinds of "non-engineered" standards shape the functionality of such (social) networks. First, agreed ontologies, operational definitions and standardized notations greatly facilitate precise communication of analytical and experimental procedures and results, reducing redundancy costs in information exchanges and promoting cooperation among "correspondents." Second, "standards" of cooperative disclosure and universalism – the normative core of the open science ethos – greatly augment the informational value and frequency of transactions within "invisible colleges." Both sets of norms obviously have "public goods" properties, and both may serve as salient solutions for systems of rational agents engaging in coordination games. Importantly, however, the behavioral norms of open science are not self-enforcing and consequently remain comparatively fragile; they must be renewed and reinforced by the socialization of young researchers, who learn not only the value of cooperative problem-solving, but that those who fail to reciprocate can expect to be excluded from its benefits.

Having arrived at this perspective *c.* 1990, I saw two contemporary threats to the open "Republic of Science," and hence to its continuing vital complementarity with the regime of proprietary R&D. One came from the expansion of intellectual property rights protections into frontier domains of academic science (*e.g.*, computer science, applied informatics and biotechnology). The other was the rapid growth in patenting by US universities and public research institutes encouraged by the 1980 Bayh-Dole Act (see David 2007a). These institutional policy changes created business incentives

5 See Merton, *Sociology of Science* (1973); Price (1963: 83–91) on "invisible colleges" as networks; contributions to this literature include Dasgupta & David (1994) and David (1993; 2004b).

inimical to the availability of open technical standards for scientific communications, and were encouraging publicly funded scientists to exploit patents on discoveries and inventions in ways that restricted their common use as tools for further research. By contrast with the transient welfare losses that patent monopolies might inflict until further inventive advances render them obsolete, the ethos of open science is vulnerable to more permanent and damaging ruptures. How could a new generation of bio-geneticists transmit the practical virtues of open science to future generations, when their own mentors had been rewarded and celebrated for organizing their research careers as "patent quests?"

Economists in the US (more than in Europe) tended to offer sanguine responses ("don't be alarmist") to these concerns, when they were not enthusiastically acclaiming the new, "entrepreneurial university" and urging European policy makers to follow the American system of "academic science innovation." In reaction, I committed still more time to policy-oriented research and, when opportunities arose, to advisory work for national and international agencies and private initiatives such as Science Commons, which is dedicated to "removing unnecessary legal and technical barriers to scientific collaboration and innovation."

Today I find it reassuring to note that the importance of protecting open science, and of restoring a healthier balance between sharing publicly funded scientific results and exploiting them for profit-seeking innovations, are more widely accepted. Although I continue to find the policy issues important and intellectually challenging, they do distract me from economic history, which I still regard as my proper *métier*. Therefore, looking optimistically to the future, I expect to return to historical projects perhaps too readily set aside: a book from my long collaboration with Moe Abramovitz on "two centuries of American macroeconomic development," an institutional history of "patronage, property and the pursuit of knowledge," a unified treatise on "path dependence – the past in the future of economics." There may also be time to write further chapters in that Chicago tale of the rise of "Factories at the Prairies' Edge."

An epigraph from "the Sayings of the Fathers" (*Pirkei Avos*) – chosen by Henry Rosovsky in 1966 for the *Festschrift* prepared by Alexander Gerschenkron's students – speaks of the shortness of the day, the burden of the work, the sluggishness of the workers, the greatness of the reward and the urgency of the Master. A different saying (*Pirke Avot* II: 21) now seems more appropriate to my circumstances: "It is not incumbent upon you to complete the work, but neither are you free to desist from it."

PETER TEMIN

Interviewed by
John C. Brown

Peter Temin is Elisha Gray II Professor of Economics at the Massachusetts Institute of Technology, and Research Associate of the National Bureau of Economic Research. He was born in 1937 in Philadelphia and was educated at Swarthmore College (B.A., 1959) and at the Massachusetts Institute of Technology (Ph.D., 1964). From 1962 to 1965 he was a Junior Fellow of Harvard's Society of Fellows and joined the MIT faculty in 1965. He has interrupted his tenure at MIT as Visiting Fellow at the Charles Warren Center for Studies in American History, Harvard University (1976–7), and as Pitt Professor of American History and Institutions in the University of Cambridge (1985–6). He was President of the Economic History Association in 1996 and of the Eastern Economic Association in 2001, was elected Fellow of the American Academy of Arts & Sciences in 1986 and held a Guggenheim Fellowship in 2002. The interview took place in Peter Temin's office in the MIT Economics Department on October 5, 1999, and was conducted by John Brown of Clark University, who writes:

I first became acquainted with Peter Temin's work as a graduate student at the University of Michigan, when we members of Gavin Wright's seminar in American economic history wrestled with the controversy over labor scarcity. Immediately thereafter, Peter reappeared in our discussions as a major protagonist in the battle over the "Soundness School" interpretation of the Panic of 1837, in which he contested the long-held view that Jackson's mistakes – his veto of legislation re-authorizing the Second Bank of the United States in 1832 and then his issuance of the Specie Circular in 1836 – prompted the panic and the subsequent economic downturn. We encountered Peter Temin a few weeks later as we worked our way through the debate over antebellum slavery and yet again in what, at that time, was a bold attack on the new orthodoxy of the Friedman–Schwartz perspective on the causes of the Great Depression. Peter was also at a conference on the performance of the Victorian economy that I attended in the third year or so of graduate school, so that it was clear to me that his interests extended across the Atlantic. Moving east to Clark University brought me gainful employment as well as the opportunity to attend the Economic History Workshop at Harvard. There, my appreciation grew for Peter's approach to economic history, from the give-and-take of the seminar as he probed visitors on the logic and, just as importantly, on the quality of evidence offered in support, of their arguments.

You started your career with research focusing on the American iron and steel industry, expanded to include the diffusion of steam power, banking policy, and the macroeconomic history of the Jacksonian economy. You later made an important contribution to the debate over slavery. What prompted you to go into economic history and, in particular, the study of iron and steel?

I had been interested in history before graduate school; the influence that led me into economic history was Alexander Gerschenkron. I was a student at MIT in the era of Walt Rostow, who was teaching his book, *The Stages of Economic Growth*. He wasn't doing a very good job, probably because his mind was half in Washington – this was in 1959. Gerschenkron came through and gave a smashing seminar. I went up to Harvard and took his course in the spring term. I was totally captivated by him. I wrote a paper for him, I got more interested in the subject, and he put me in contact – actually, he got me an office – with Paul David and Al Fishlow at Harvard, in the original Economic History Workshop on Harvard Square. The stimulation that I got from Alex, first of all, and then from Paul and Al, was just incredible and very attractive, so I started working. I was choosing at that time between econometrics and economic history, and this led me into economic history. I don't recall how I got interested in the steel industry, but my thesis was an attempt to write a narrative about how an important industry developed. I remember very much the process of writing it and not at all the process of beginning.

This was when you were a Junior Fellow. Did you have some teaching responsibilities as well?

No, it was just a chance to work on my dissertation, which was largely finished in the first year. I turned it into publishable form and then began to read the literature rather more seriously. That's how I got into some of the subsequent projects. *The Jacksonian Economy* was stimulated by reading Doug North's book on the antebellum period. He was giving the rather familiar cotton-cycle story of the 1830s, and it just didn't seem to have the right tone. I tell my students today, when you read something and it seems wrong, little bells go off, and you should try to figure out what happened.

What was it that "went off?" Was it perhaps intuition you had developed from course work you had done?

North argued that there were diminishing returns to cotton agriculture that led to the rise in the price of cotton in the 1830s. I did not believe that there were diminishing returns at that time or that the price rise was the result of supply factors. So I began to look in a totally different direction, which then led me into the macro area. I benefited a lot from the work of van Fenstermaker in collecting banking data. There was a lot of data available, and I was able to put together a different story. One of my disappointments in economic history is demonstrated by the questionnaire that was sent around a couple of years ago, saying "What is your view of the Jacksonian economy?" (Whaples 1995). Only about half the people seemed to have come around to this new view, which I think is now a very old view and which I would have thought would have become a standard view. I don't understand why the previous view continues to be held, or what I could have done then, what I could do now, to make this story more convincing.

That is, the old view stemming from North's focus on the cotton economy as well as the Soundness School?

The old view was that Jackson was responsible for what happened. It was loose banking rather than increase in the specie supply that led to inflation. That is not what happened.

Your 1966 paper on labor scarcity opened up another line of research and discussion quite unlike the macroeconomic analysis of the Panic of 1837 or your monograph on the iron and steel industries. It places the labor scarcity debate in the framework of a general equilibrium model, which must have set a precedent for the *Journal of Economic History*. It also is a classic of a cliometric approach to economic history.

The article about labor scarcity came of out of doing two things at once. One was reading Habakkuk's classic book, and the other was taking a reading course from Paul Samuelson. In that course, Samuelson told me about a paper that he had written about the so-called non-substitution theory, when capital is embodied labor. If everything depends on time, then the wage rate doesn't matter, only the interest rate. I was taking the theory and the Habakkuk book and putting them together – and, of course, they didn't fit. And so I wrote that up. But the idea came from knowing the economic theory, and I recommend to all students that they learn a lot of economic theory, even if it seems highly irrelevant, because you cannot tell where an idea will come from. I made this very simple-minded model to demonstrate the point, which acquired a life of its own in the trade literature.

Your comments raise an issue that I would like to pursue. In the late 1950s – before your time – the New Economic History and the cliometric conferences were starting up. When did you get involved in cliometrics? Clearly, you knew Paul David and Albert Fishlow. Were you also actually involved in the conferences?

I was not at the first conference, but I was at several of the early conferences when they were in West Lafayette at Purdue University. And they were very exciting conferences. Everybody participated. People were very concerned about where the data came from, which was a very good lesson for a young cliometrician, and there was a lot of excitement in the work being done.

Was the excitement because a new generation was taking on older problems, equipped with economic theory and econometrics?

Yes, there was a sense that we had the tools and, since we had the tools, that we were in a sense messengers of the Messiah. Fogel, of course, was the most evangelical of all, but we were all swept up in the same spirit, that there was no nut that we couldn't crack with this particular intellectual nutcracker.

Did you have a sense of conflict with more traditional economic historians?

Yes, to go from one metaphor to another, we were St George and the conventional historians were dragons, and we had to slay them. It was very definitely set up as a contest between Us and Them, very much a feeling of Them and Us. Other people have talked about the problems with the *Journal of Economic History* and how it was going to bridge these cultures. But within the cliometrics meetings, there was no feeling that we had to bridge cultures; we were the True Believers.

Would you say that people were actually choosing fights or intellectual battles by taking particular old chestnuts of economic history and subjecting them to another kind of analysis?

I think that's a very fair description of what was happening, that people would look for received wisdom and then with a flourish be able to demonstrate with a little bit of economic theory, and some new data, and so on, that in fact things were absolutely different and with any luck, exactly the reverse.

So there's a certain rhetorical expectation in terms of the work.

Absolutely.

Could we pursue this? Was there any realization among cliometricians that this approach might actually involve some tradeoffs? Clearly there was a lot to be won by doing this, but, if you focus on particular debates, are you also writing a new history? Did you believe that you had to win all this new territory for cliometric/economic history, and that it might not be necessary to fill in the gaps of a historical narrative?

Well, that's a complicated issue because most of the young cliometricians – and certainly Paul and Al and I – had appointments in economics departments. The audience that we were writing to, seeking to get tenure in our universities, was composed of economists. They wanted to see a clever use of economic theory – and then testing of economic hypotheses. The fact that this excluded – or refuted or even angered – traditional historians was just kind of a second-order issue. I think it's not really until we got a lot older and got tenure that we began to think about things, that we began to say, "Okay, it's true that these are good techniques, but they don't answer all questions," and to go back and look more at traditional history.

Your paper on labor scarcity and the Habakkuk hypothesis appeared relatively early in the intellectual history of cliometrics. It seems to me that it sparked new thinking about cliometrics, a debate with Robert Fogel, and led to subsequent iterations.

That wasn't much of a debate with Fogel. I wrote the initial paper, and then everybody jumped up and down and wrote papers saying it couldn't be so, and then, how could each of them modify my model in a different way to show this. The debate got to be kind of shapeless. I made a restatement of the theory five years later, and have come back to it periodically. But it's not been a debate like the debates on *Time on the Cross*, where the same people lined up for quite a long time. Rather, it was that there was a paper that stimulated a lot of discussion, and then there were one or two iterations. I wouldn't think of this as a struggle between me and Bob, even though Bob wrote a paper opposing me (1967). His was an isolated paper.

I guess I found it interesting because it was a kind of exchange that one would expect to see in an economics journal rather than in an economic history journal. For the time, it must actually have been unusual. The paper plowed new ground by developing a straightforward, but, nonetheless, a general equilibrium model. Someone else then comes in and argues that there is a model misspecification issue here. That's a kind of discussion I wouldn't have expected to see.

I think in retrospect you're right; it's very much within an economics mold, and so it has that kind of quality. Since we were in economics departments, that was the kind of activity to do. And it wasn't just economic historians who got into this; Larry Summers wrote an article in this debate . . . [laughter]

I didn't realize that! [laughter]

Which I think may have been a term paper in Gerschenkron's course, but still it was part of the debate (Clarke & Summers 1980). And the model got written up by Ron Jones, who worked out its characteristics, its formal properties. The model went into the economics literature, and, in a way, you're right; it stood at the edge of history and economics and went both ways. It went into the trade literature where the model got worked out and also into the historical literature, as people thought about what caused industrialization in New England.

Yes, that's kind of an unusual case.

I think actually it is.

We've mentioned Fogel, which brings to mind the extended review essay of *Time on the Cross* that you and Paul David wrote. That appeared in the *Journal of Economic History* (David & Temin 1974); it's now found in the Whaples and Betts volume of readings (1995). The essay prompts questions about the intellectual history of cliometrics, the approach followed in its critique of *Time on the Cross* and the role it might have played in your own intellectual development. So there are a couple of questions I want to ask. First of all, I'm wondering what prompted you and Paul to get involved in a critique that went to such considerable depth; the detail is impressive. What really pulled you into this debate?

Part of Bob's genius is being able to write about hot-button issues, choosing the issues that get people excited. The issue about race and slavery in America is probably the biggest issue, and the one that has the most emotion attached to it, in American history. I think we got swept into the debate for two reasons. One is that we got caught up in all of this emotion that Bob and Stan had stirred up, and, then, second, we were not convinced by the evidence that had been put forward. So partly this was a debate about the American past and an emotional issue, and partly it was a debate just like the debate over labor scarcity, which is, "Are you using the right model? Have you specified this properly? Have you taken account of other characteristics?" It is methodological in the same way, and comes a decade after the labor scarcity debate, so it is that much more technical than the earlier one was. But I think that that controversy kind of began for me a slightly different exposition, or a different trend. In the early 1960s I was part of the True Believers, very much thinking, with the economics model as my Excalibur that I would slay all dragons, could defeat all enemies ahead of me. As I began to think about slavery – and I was beginning to think about health economics, which I was getting interested in at about that time – I began to think that maybe there were issues that couldn't be explained by straight economic models. I had to think a little more about – I would say now, think about culture, but then I wouldn't have said "think about culture." It's the beginning of the strand in my work that comes out in some of the business history and modes of economic behavior and more current stuff in my Presidential address.

What did it mean for both of you to take on this kind of format: a 20–30 page review essay that offered a written critique in a published form? Was the strength of the critique at issue when you and Paul were putting it together?

There was a lot of emotion connected to this debate, and a lot of the issues were raised without ever being fully settled. I think that's probably because there was so much emotion that people couldn't resolve them. But close reading of things has been a feature of my work, not just in that case but in other cases. I think it comes partly from the way

I teach, which comes from my early training at Swarthmore as an undergraduate where we had a seminar system. We had just half a dozen or eight people together with a professor, and we discussed the work that we were doing. In my classes I still try and maintain this discussion quality, so a lot of the class – even the class that I just taught – involves looking at a paper, looking at the documentation, and saying, "Is this the right documentation? Have they actually proven their point? Have they done the tests carefully?" And so on. It's a characteristic of the way that I have approached these fields, that we make incremental progress by building on the work of others, and that one of the characteristics that I've had is taking other people seriously. When they write something, I assume they mean it. I want to learn from it . . .

The foundation should be solid . . .

And if there's a problem with it, then I go on. For example, my work on the Industrial Revolution, which is in a sense very much like this – a critique of some other work – comes directly out of teaching. There are two views of the British Industrial Revolution, and I kept inviting students to write a term paper on this because I thought that this was just the kind of thing that one could test. Since none of the students took me up on it, I did the test myself. Now it has come out, and there's getting to be a literature on it, too. But my paper came out of trying to teach this material, trying to take seriously what the people who have written on the subject have said, and trying to ask the students to think about it: does this make sense, is this consistent, have they proven their point? In the Fogel and Engerman case, I think we went into this – *Time on the Cross* was a major study, a lot of work with a lot of parts to it – and as we got into it, I think we had the sense that Bob and Stan had gotten convinced of their position and so, perhaps, had not always looked at the evidence as carefully as they should. Once we began to see their position as an ideological position, we began to look even more critically at the evidence that they had marshaled.

Your comment reminds me of a point you raised in the review essay about the methodology of economic history. You wrote that "the slant of their quantitative work [that is, Fogel's and Engerman's] reflects the economists' professional habits of mind and the methodological pull of the tradition established by Conrad and Meyer's *studiously depersonalized* approach to the history of slavery's profitability . . ." (David & Temin 1974: 779; original italics). You were particularly critical of the whole effort of Fogel and Engerman to try to compute a statement of comparative welfare from evidence on consumption and other data without addressing the fundamental question of whether it was possible to make comparisons in welfare between the well-fed, but unfree, slaves and the underfed and poorly housed, but free, white workers in the North. Does this statement offer insight into where cliometrics was at this point in its development? I mean, it seems to me that *Time on the Cross* occasioned so much controversy, primarily because of the issue of slavery, but at the same time, something else must have also been afoot.

It wasn't just this issue. You have to remember that Bob was trying to proselytize the New Economic History in America and England. I would say that the mid-1970s may be the high point of, let's call it, pure econometrics, in the sense that all you needed to know was the economic theory and that, if you just understood the competitive model, you could deal with any problem at all. I think that since then, there has been somewhat of a retreat from this. Bill Parker's Presidential Address (1971) said that maybe we've beaten this horse to death. We were trying to say, maybe you needed in *Time on the Cross* . . . maybe you needed a more expansive view of what was going on. It was not a decline in the use of economic models and evidence, but rather it was an erosion of the belief that these were the only kinds of evidence that were relevant. It was the beginning of a notion that it's not Us or Them, but maybe that it's together that we need to do this. I think it's really at that time we begin to make this approach, back and forth.

So in a way the controversy may actually have prompted a realization that cliometrics must cooperate with more traditional historians or historians rooted in other kinds of traditions?

I don't know. This reconstruction seems to have more order than I think it had as I went through it. At the same time that Paul and I were responding to *Time on the Cross*, I was also engaged at MIT in trying to encourage different approaches to economics. I had a grant for scholarships for students trying new approaches, and I was onto the pharmaceutical industry. As I got further and further into the pharmaceutical industry and into trying to understand the demand for pharmaceuticals, I got more and more convinced that a straight economic model was not explaining everything. I began to think about alternatives. The notion of satisficing was around, scarce information was just beginning to be "information as a commodity," and you had to think of people acting without having enough information. In my article on modes of economic behavior in 1980, I argued that economic behavior, "instrumental behavior," is only one of several different kinds of behavior, not the only behavior, as I think we would have said *circa* 1970. It is important to think, particularly in places where you don't expect the market to be working completely, like health or perhaps like slavery, to think about other modes of behavior that people are using.

Could you offer some background on what drew you to the pharmaceutical industry, and then to the study of the break-up of the Bell system, which offers a kind of *ex post* "inside view" of the events – certainly a methodological innovation?

Looking back on it, I have had a continuing interest in industry history, which has now molded into business history. It starts with the iron and steel industry, goes through the pharmaceutical industry, the telecommunications industry, and ends up with the business history conferences that Naomi Lamoreaux, Dan Raff, and I have been putting together. They all can be seen as continuing one from the other, but each had its own individual cause. The pharmaceutical industry was interesting to me because I was trying to think about uncertainty and lack of information, and how people act without full information. I thought briefly of trying to model this problem, and then acknowledged to myself that I was an economic historian, not an economic theorist, and said, "Let me find a place in which there is a lot of uncertainty and figure out what kind of institutions were developed to take care of it." That gave rise to my study of the pharmaceutical industry. The Bell System was an interest that follows on that, but it was stimulated by a totally different thing. I had consulted a little in the AT&T case and gathered some data for them that was not used in the trial because they wanted to argue that the government had done something in the early years of the twentieth century which I discovered the government had not done. So I was not a cooperative witness.

That's interesting; this is the work you did on the shifting regulatory regimes and the pricing, kind of the allocation of cost, and so forth.

No, no, this is before the book, work that hasn't been published. I don't think it's very interesting because it was just trying to establish priors that turned out not to be true. But I knew the people involved, and when the idea of writing the history came up, I volunteered to write it. In fact, I argued to AT&T that they wanted an economist to write this book rather than a straight historian, harking back to the earlier debate in a sense. I argued that the pricing issues, economic aspects of regulation, were critically important, that cross-subsidies were key, and that you needed an economist to understand how much of the issue revolved around prices. I did convince them, and I got the opportunity to write what I hope was a good book. It certainly was an enormous amount of fun and fascinating to write.

I can't say that I finished it, but I've certainly found it very interesting!

People in the field have given me good feedback. When you write what I call contemporary history, then there are other people who have lived through it. I have been very cheered when I get people who are in the industry who say, "Yes! That was really the way it happened!"

How did this experience differ from what you had done before, drawing on the experience of key participants, most of whom were still alive and accessible, rather than trying to reconstruct events second-hand? Did you bring a different kind of critical thinking to the process of writing this history?

It's quite different. There are lots of overlaps in the kind of logic that you bring to the issue, but I did a lot of oral history. I interviewed people like you're interviewing me. Then, of course, I had to decide how much of what they told me was reasonable, and what was unreasonable. Some of the people who had made critical decisions had very vivid memories and could tell you what happened each day. Other people had no memory at all. The question then is, does that bias the story? You have a whole new set of things to think about when you're doing contemporary history. And, of course, there are a lot of people to show it to, to get feedback.

Did you have a documentary record to draw upon to frame the discussion?

I had a long documentary record, and I had a lot of support from people: Lou Galambos, Bob Lewis, and a staff of people that included Bob Garnet, Ken Lipartito and George Smith. The paper trail, though, was only partial. We had the regulatory proceedings, which were voluminous, and we had the internal AT&T documents, which were exactly the opposite. You have to realize that AT&T had survived the anti-trust suit brought in 1949 and settled in 1956. After that, the lawyers made sure that there was nothing that was really substantive in their files. You could always find out what they were talking about, but you could only seldom find out what they said. Consequently, the paper trail within the firm was composed of some reports that were written internally, so you could see them, and a lot of speeches that were made internally, which were recorded. This was a kind of a formal communication, and I had to try to think what was behind the statements where the CEO was trying to marshal the troops. What was he trying to marshal the troops for? It turns out that deButts was a colorful character with a rather extreme view, so it was pretty easy to know what he was doing. Romney before him and Brown after him were more subtle characters, and they were a little harder to get out of the record. Of course, I could talk to Brown (and I couldn't talk to Romney), so I could get some additional information from him.

Now that you have both reconstructed the events through oral history and worked with what documentary evidence there was, did the exercise give you insight into how to treat the documentary evidence that any historian must use? Essentially, we must try to reconstruct the series of events that would have actually led to an important event such as the break-up from the fragments left to us.

I think doing a project like this has to give you a lot of humility as you approach the more distant past because it is very hard to fill in these blanks. Without the kind of evidence that you get from being able to ask people what goes on, you always have in your mind that you may just have gotten it wrong, because there was partial evidence and you put it together in a way that a contemporary just wouldn't recognize at all. I must say – if I can tell one story – that I wrote a paper about the Koreaboom in Germany, which is not contemporary history, but it is relatively recent history. I gave a seminar on in it then in England. Alec Cairncross was one of the heroes of this episode, at least as I construed it, but I was arguing against a whole intervening literature that had seen this differently. I gave the seminar, and Cairncross came to the seminar. He remembered the incident, and said, "Yes, that's what happened!" He remembered it, and gave me some more stories about it. I thought, "My!" It was an extraordinary feeling that I "passed the test," that I put the story together from the documentary evidence, and, by the grace of God, an eyewitness came back, a participant came back, and confirmed that, yes, this was the view that was accurate for that time. That was a wonderful experience for me.

Our discussion of contemporary history brings to mind the work you have done integrating business history and economic history, particularly

your work with Naomi Lamoreaux, Dan Raff and others. So far, you have organized three NBER conferences, each of which has resulted in a published volume.[1] Prompting some of the research presented at the conferences and noted in your Presidential Address is a dissatisfaction with the unwillingness in economics to account at the macro level for the evolution of, and importance of, economic cultures in shaping economic development. Economic historians are also often unwilling to abandon the economics learned in elementary classes when carrying out micro-level analyses and turn instead to more sophisticated models of economic behavior, including imperfect information, path dependence, models of learning, and so forth. The Social Science Research Council recognizes another feature of this problem with its Program in Applied Economics. Students in most economics Ph.D. programs do not receive the breadth of training that would prepare them to carry out economic history research. What could be done to train the next generation of economic historians, given the content of the Ph.D. programs they are enrolled in? How can graduate students in economics in general be made aware of the questions that the research presented at the NBER business history conferences tries to address?

Our hope in doing these conferences was that we would provide reading that could be used in a variety of courses, and in particular, that could be used in economics classes. We were hoping that even in elementary economics classes people would be willing to assign some of these stories to try and say, "You know, we have these black boxes called 'firms' and here is what firms do." You can see a firm trying to make some decision or trying to work out some problem. We were hoping that would help people understand economics and also attract people to this kind of work.

Your question about the next generation of economic historians is a very difficult one because the market for economic historians has not been a particularly buoyant one in recent years. There is a steady demand for economic historians but, while the demand for economists has been growing, the demand for economic historians has been pretty stagnant, with one or two economic historians at each school and, in fact, we like economic historians better if they're part-time economic historians who can also teach money and banking or macro or labor or econometrics or whatever. And so it has been hard to attract people into economic history as a professional activity. On the other hand, I hope that these conference volumes, and also other articles that get written, bring economic history into the range of activity of ordinary economists; that they would think that it would make sense to do an essay or do part of their thesis on an historical topic. This has been rather successful here at MIT, and there are many dissertations that have economic history chapters in them, some of which go out and become articles in the journals – Peter Berck's article on blast furnaces many years ago, Keith Head's article on learning-by-doing in the steel industry, or Matt Slaughter's article on

1 See Temin, ed. (1991), Lamoreaux & Raff, eds (1995), and Lamoreaux, Raff & Temin, eds (1999).

price convergence in the early nineteenth century. These are all papers that grew out of their economic history at MIT, done by people who are not primarily economic historians. The problem is that economic history can't survive on the isolated articles done by economists who recognize economic history as part of their activity. We have to lobby our colleagues to have some more specialists to maintain the framework from which these other people can learn, and maintain the framework that those people can hang onto as they do their individual essays and individual contributions to the field – typically quite good contributions to the field, but still episodic. None of the people that I mentioned are economic historians; they are people who have done some economic history. But let's remember Conrad and Meyer – Conrad tragically died very early, but Meyer was not an economic historian; he's a transportation economist, an industrial organization economist. Yet their foray into this debate touched off an enormous discussion. It's really very important to the field not only to have professional economic historians to identify as economic historians but also to have other people, typically economists, coming into the field because topics or questions or theorems interest them, and having an impact on the field.

What is the response from the economists at the NBER conferences? You really have three kinds of groups, the business historians, the economists, and the economic historians.

That's right. We had all these people together, and one of the wonderful things was getting them to talk with each other. The conferences have been very popular; people have wanted to come to them, and I think have enjoyed coming to them. It has not always been easy to get everybody to talk to everybody else. We had resistance to what we were doing from the traditional business historians, and we also had some resistance from the straight economists. I think that over the course of the three conferences we have swept more people into this conversation and convinced more people that this was a legitimate thing to do, but it's still only a small number of people that we could reach through the conferences. The wider group we try to reach through the volumes. I know they've been popular volumes and they get well reviewed, but I don't know how much they change people's thinking.

You only see that as time goes on. You have been so generous with your time. I'll restrict myself to one final question concerning a reference made in the most recent conference volume that you edited with Naomi [Lamoreaux] and Dan [Raff]. There was a very brief allusion to a break-up of economic and business history that took place in the depths of times past. Gerschenkron was on one side and on the other was the entrepreneurial school. It seems to me that these kinds of conferences are also efforts to overcome what has been a schism, maybe not quite of historic dimensions as is true of other schisms, but certainly an important one for the development of economic history. Are there barriers that prevent more interactions of this kind? Are they primarily the availability of tools – a barrier to working with some other kinds of historians – or does it go

deeper? Do they reflect deep methodological differences, the inductive work of the business historian *versus* the deductive approach of the economic historian: think of a model and then work from there?

We talked about the early days of cliometrics and the kinds of conflicts then between the economists and the historians. For general historians, communication with them has only become more difficult over the years, because they have gotten interested in other questions which aren't of interest to economics. It's not as much a problem of different methodologies as it is of different interests. Business historians are a different group than regular historians. Partly, they have gone to general history and corporate culture and so on. But partly they have thought about the economics and, just as history has changed, economics has changed. Economics has gotten far more subtle in its use of information and understanding of bargaining and understanding of how small groups operate, whether it be an oligopoly or a board of directors or a government agency. There has been room for a lot more discussion back and forth between economic and business history. Which goes both ways. For business historians, one can draw on a lot of economics. Maggie Levenstein is an example of that (1998). Economists also are acknowledging the importance of history. For example, the GM purchase of Fisher Body has been the classic observation in this economics-as-contracting principal–agent literature. Economists have gone back to look at the Fisher Body story, and there'll be several articles in the *Journal of Law and Economics* by Coase (2000) and others, talking about that history and arguing that, in fact, when you understand the history, it doesn't support the literature that has developed. That's an interesting kind of two-way street which I think is bringing people to those fields.

It's late in the afternoon, so I'll let you go. Do you have any other comments for the record before we conclude our discussion?

The comment is, one of the things that attracted me to economic history was that, back when I was a graduate student, it was just an enormous amount of fun to do. And now today, many, many years later, I still think it's an enormous amount of fun to do, and I wish somehow we collectively as a group could convey that to our students so that we could attract more people into economic history.

Hear, hear!

Further reflections[2]

Peter Temin

The problem with economic history today is that while it continues to be great fun for those of us working in the field, it is not attracting much attention nor many new

2 Some of this material appeared earlier in "A Hobbesian Approach to Political-Economic History," *The Journal of Interdisciplinary History*, XXXV (2005): 605–614.

scholars. Economists like the occasional reminder that history matters, but they are more concerned with current conditions than longer-run phenomena. History appears to have gone away from economic matters to other questions. And young economists and historians naturally gravitate toward the center of their disciplines. One might think that we would do better if there were separate departments of economic history, but the experience of such departments in England is not encouraging. As interest in economic history has waned there also, those departments have proven too weak to preserve their personnel and budgets.

One task of economic history that should be of great value to other social scientists is the exploration of processes that occur over long periods of time. Demographic changes of course play out over decades and longer. Economic growth also is a long-term process. My colleague Dora Costa has explored many aspects of what we might call demographic history (*e.g.*, 1998). I want to add a few words here about growth.

An insight of recent economic analyses of economic growth is that politics matters. Daron Acemoglu and co-authors have tested a variety of hypotheses on this interaction in a cross-section of different countries (*e.g.*, 2005). But where do countries come from? Charles Tilly proposed some years ago that they originated as protection rackets (1990). Powerful agents offered to protect lesser people from dangers, including prominently danger from the agent himself, for a price. We often think of this as the essence of European feudalism, but Tilly argued that it also was the model for the transition to modern states. This model carries with it the implication that the state, once established, needs to maintain a monopoly of violence. No state can rule out all violence, of course, but the state needs to make sure that there are no rivals that can erode its influence or threaten its power.

This is a very Hobbesian view of the world. Violence rules the affairs of men and women. People who are most willing, and perhaps most able, to fight and kill end up in power. There is no reason to expect this violent streak to be correlated with intelligence, and therefore no reason to think that rulers are more capable of creating good government than anyone else. In fact, one might think there is a negative correlation between violence and intelligence, implying that early rulers should have been much worse than later ones. That is, it takes time for "kleptocracies" to develop into "liberal states."

This simple model acquires weight from recent events when states have failed. The Soviet state collapsed around 1990. The state simply ceased to be. There were no effective police or courts; it was a sudden state of nature. Vadim Volkov described how commerce reemerged after the debacle in a book with the descriptive title, *Violent Entrepreneurs* (2002). He argued that criminals began to organize a protection market of fledgling businesses. He told how the criminals would take a recalcitrant businessman out to the forest and ask him to dig his own grave. This usually was enough to convince the businessman to purchase protection.

Once the merchant or producer signed on, he could not sign off again for obvious reasons. Given the large supply of aspiring criminals, it also was hard for any merchant or producer to avoid being part of one or another protection operation. In fact, it was necessary to do business. Consider a disputed bill between two merchants: how would the claimant collect his debt? There were no courts to appeal to. Instead, his protector would talk to the debtor's protector. If the two crooks decided the debt was legitimate, the debtor's protector would shake the money out of him. If not, the two crooks could appeal to a higher level of criminal for a decision. The cost of this primitive court was very high, and everyone justifiably was reluctant to appeal to it.

Further support for the Tilly model comes from even more recent events. The Iraqi state vanished after the American invasion of 2003. Institutions that lasted through the invasion were foolishly abolished by the American occupation after the war ended. In the resulting anarchy, violence again became the norm. But this violence appears to be even less economically motivated than the Russian, and it has made it difficult to restore any kind of economic activity. The result has been economic stagnation and even retrogression.

Economic historians should have been suspicious of pre-war claims of instantaneous economic progress in Iraq. The historical analysis of economic growth has described many ways in which economics and politics interact. In all of them, the transition from economic stagnation and political chaos has been neither easy nor quick. Economic history, therefore, is one element in the formulation of sound policies today. We should hope that social scientists and policy makers come to appreciate this fact and that their use of economic history will promote further support of economic history research.

AFTERWORD

The shock, achievements and disappointments of the new

Patrick Karl O'Brien

Among the present postmodern generation of historians (crippled with the *angst* of recovering meanings for a past uncontaminated by their own personalities, backgrounds, locations and preferences) autobiographical prefaces have become *de rigueur*. So, in a sense, is it also in this Afterword: to a collection of memoirs from 25 elders of an academic tribe (who I am pleased to see honoured by this prosopography) that includes (I must reveal) mentors, teachers, colleagues and friends with whom I have shared in all the fun, stimulus, intellectual acclaim and camaraderie of being part of a cycle of progress that has marked the development of our subject since it came of age after the First World War. Bliss it has been in that dawn to be in post in higher education and a privilege to be among scholars of such distinction, engaged (as they here recall) in a collective endeavour to revolutionize (or at least reconfigure) an indispensable bridge discipline for economics and history.

Alas, and for this assignment, it would have been easier and altogether more agreeable had I been instructed to write an Afterword in praise of great men and women. Instead and as one of the trio so persuasively put it, I have been chosen as a "one sympathetic with and informed about 'quantitative economic history,' but not as an enthusiastic insider;" and, he reassured me, as one "who has written critically and seriously in and about the field without having been branded a 'cliometrician'," but rather with "a perspective wider than what is thought by many historians and more traditional economic historians to be in the nature of New Economic History."

While I continue to offer plaudits to my colleagues and friends (represented in as well as absent from this volume) who carried economic history forward to higher levels of output, intellectual sophistication and acclaim during its "High Renaissance" in the 1960s and 1970s, I will also try to meet the Editors' wish for some kind of "assessment." I propose contextualizing not the achievements of 25 entirely distinctive careers, but their collective contribution to the progress of our great subject. That will not be easy, because as far as I know, no scholar has written a history of economic history on a national, let alone, an international basis.

Indeed as the Editors of this volume soon realized when they came to write their introduction, there is nothing on the shelves comparable to those multi-volume magisterial histories of physics, astronomy, chemistry, philosophy, anthropology, economics and history that help natural and social scientists as well as academics engaged with the evolution of scholarship in major humanities to comprehend from where their disciplines originated; how they developed; where to locate discontinuities and to point distant horizons towards which subjects are travelling. In short, what remains to be constructed is: a comprehensive history of the production and diffusion of knowledge that could conceivably be labelled as economic history; preferably global in scope and embracing the varieties of styles, approaches, methods, modes of organizational delivery that make up our "industry" with its multiple outputs (that continues to include economic thought, agrarian, demographic, labour, technological, business, social and institutional as well as "cliometric" history).

Once that enterprise is under way this volume will certainly become an illuminating and basic source for a key chapter, because it records the mature reflections of a remarkable group of men and women who, over a conjuncture in time that succeeded the Great Depression and Second World War, operating within a powerful, enviably resourced cultural and institutional setting and at familiar youthful moments in their lives and careers, attempted to establish hegemony for a paradigm for research, publication and teaching in economic history. They began with their own hospitable universities in the United States and then persuaded a minority of their ever amenable British cousins to follow suit. They, as their memories reveal, behaved like Greeks and announced they were already ahead of Rome. Cliometricians encountered more resistance from recalcitrant academic cultures of mainland Europe (particularly France), indifference from Germany but rejoiced in those polite, but nuanced, adaptations of their recommendations by Japanese historians and economists. Hegemony, particularly in the form of cultural transmissions, as American intellectuals realize, is never easy to achieve and almost impossible to sustain.

Yet, in academe as in other more important spheres of our ecumenical world, we all remain grateful, better informed and more educated as an outcome of their innocent impulse to persuade the worlds of higher education that "innovatory American" ways of teaching, reading, researching and representing economic history could be superior to anything accomplished by their own ancestors and predecessors, or to the established traditions of Europe, Japan, China or elsewhere in this our era of globalization.

The Gifts of Athena (as those who research into the evolution of sciences and technologies appreciate) have been the most significant force for change in the world. Outcomes flowing from innovatory knowledge are easy enough to recognize (if difficult to measure), but where that knowledge comes from, when, how and why it appears and is taken up (or resisted) is extremely difficult to analyse, let alone assess.

What can be gleaned from histories of science, art, philosophy and even economics is that historically nearly every appearance of the "New" has been contingent upon time and place, required patronage and funding to become institutionalized; was in "large" part derived from ancestors, precursors and parents; generally appropriates the label "New" and was heralded (more or less loudly and aggressively) by its "harbingers" as a salutary "departure," "discontinuity" even as a "revolution" from established traditions and paradigms for the production of knowledge in particular fields. From the times of

Socratic disputation on the Agora to the "Science Wars" of modern biology, comparable features and contexts have surrounded the appearance of nearly all claims for new and superior knowledge and which invariably promoted recurrent cycles of acrimony between "Ancients and Moderns" that litter the annals of intellectual history.

Yet, guided by the questions and agendas of their interviewers, the situated and selective memories of innovators and their enthusiastic patrons interviewed for this volume suggest that they managed (or opted) to accord entirely different degrees of *post hoc* reflection on any discontinuities or controversies that surrounded the appearance of New Economic History.

Several preferred (or were encouraged) to concentrate upon their specialized and celebrated scholarly contributions to the field. Others, in autobiographical mood, reflected in more detail upon their own family backgrounds, intellectual formations and relevant careers – often, and interestingly, in operational research for governments during and after the War. Nevertheless, the majority agreed that they had lived through and actively promoted a "movement," "discontinuity," "renaissance," "revolution" that had transformed the discipline of economic history. Of course, labels and titles bestowed upon that phase in the life of any established subject (and moment in their own lives and careers) varied from scholar to scholar, and for example became less exuberant as they grew older, even in the engaging and colourful hyperbole of Jon Hughes.

Nevertheless, there is enough and something in each and every one of these Conversations to sustain an Afterword designed to reconfigure the entire collection as a prosopographical basis for an important chapter in the history of our subject. That chapter could conceivably be preceded by several others in a book designed, as Gras recommended as long ago as 1927, to trace the origins of economic history way back to Aristotle. My sense of perspective will be satisfied, however, by a brief reference to generations of European and American economic historians writing for more than a century before "New" Economic History appeared on the scene.

Although such "disrespect" would be unthinkable in China and untenable in academic cultures where histories of thought have retained a foothold in departments of economics as well as history, with one or two conspicuous exceptions, this group pays virtually no attention to "ancestors," immediate or more distant. Yet the towering intellects of the German historical school – Marx, Schmoller, Bucher, Sombart and Weber; the English tradition of Thorold Rogers, Toynbee, Scott, Cunningham, Ashley, Lipson, Tawney, Power, Beveridge, Clapham, Postan and Ashton; Levasseur, Pirenne, Labrousse, Bloch, Simond, Vives, Heckscher from the mainland; and Gras, Day, Innes, Usher, Lane, Hamilton and Fay from North America all addressed questions and meta-narratives concerned with the technological, political, geopolitical, legal, cultural and institutional foundations for the evolution of markets and long-term economic growth. "Pioneers" from previous generations had established economic history as a separable and, for some decades, fashionable field for historical scholarship and extended its provenance to include graduate students, posts, journals and learned societies in European and North American systems of higher education. Most maintained fruitful connexions and conversations with colleagues in economics (in those days more educated and interested in history). None eschewed the use of theory, let alone quantification – think of Silberling and Hamilton! Indeed with help from the Rockefeller and Carnegie Foundations, our ancestors supported projects for research into histories of prices, wages, rates of interest, grain yields, taxes, populations and other indices of long-run change; Sombart, Heckscher, Johnson and others published pleas for more theory and asked economists to provide better tools for the job, but the corpus of economic theory accessible to them (concerned with abstract theorizing about consumer preferences, the predicted behaviour of firms under different market forms, the emerging properties of equilibrium, demonstrations of comparative advantage, even steady-state growth) did not seem immediately relevant to their interests in states, legal systems, the origins and operations of markets, institutions, cultures of enterprise, standards of living and distributions of income and wealth.

Help, still largely of a taxonomical kind, had to wait for the "second coming" of a new generation of economists interested in institutions and for the recovery and restoration of (well, yes!) "new" institutional economic history – again prone to product differentiation and repetition, disinclined to acknowledge ancestry, and predictably deferential to neoclassical economics.

Meanwhile this first wave of New Economic Historians certainly did acknowledge their contemporaries, parents and patrons, who included a group of economists linked to the National Bureau of Economic Research. Working there with Wesley Mitchell and Arthur Burns was Simon Kuznets the "Godfather" of economic quantification, recognized by everyone as a "man of surpassing virtue" and the teacher of Easterlin, Gallman, Fogel and Engerman. Along with others (including Colin Clark and Arthur Gayer and especially that famous trans-Atlantic intellectual, Walt Rostow) led by Kuznets and inspired by the Keynesian revolution in macroeconomics they became "The Force" proselytizing for the construction of national accounts and other indicators designed to measure growth and cyclical fluctuations in outputs, trade, investment, workforce participation and the pace and patterns of structural change. Kuznets never attained nor desired the celebrity status of Rostow, but his (and their) legacy consists of a renewed emphasis on quantification that led to a discontinuity in the accumulation of validated data available to economists for testing hypotheses and to historians tracing, narrating and explaining economic growth for larger and larger samples of cases (underdeveloped as well as developed countries) and for the world economy as a whole.

Parent disciplines (history and economics) maturing along different but eventually, in outcome, antagonistic trajectories played (as parents do) key roles in the childhood and adolescent intellectual formation of New Economic Historians between that early meeting in Williamstown in 1957 and the break up of "the Family" marked by the publication of *Time on the Cross* and the return, in the early 1970s, of Doug North, Lance Davis and others to the traditions of their grandparents.

For example – and as the aristocracy in economics developed a meta-theory along Copernican lines and formulated a universal paradigm for enquiry in order to sustain confidence and cohesion and to preclude controversy over fundamentals from within their imperialistic discipline – mathematical and theoretical rigour became highly impressive and seductive, if not mandatory, for young graduates. Well-trained in the latest methods for specifying and testing hypotheses and equipped with tools and techniques (with first, electro-mechanical calculators, then computers, as well as systematic sampling and regression analyses unavailable to their predecessors) with careers beckoning in departments of economics, they could hardly be expected to resist temptations to differentiate themselves and their presumably reliable knowledge as "new;" and often, with telling effect, expose the mis-specified, theoretically insecure and poorly quantified publications of older economic – let alone the pretensions of general – historians. They invaded whole territories and swathes of economic history where their modern weapons enjoyed technological leadership. Looking back, Al Fishlow recognized that their mission and "emphasis was clearly on being able to frame historical issues in a way that made them subject to specification as hypotheses and ultimately the application of some kind of testing that would utilize the advances being made in statistics at that time."

In retrospect what he, they and we (equally impressed with the power and precision of economics and econometrics) could not reasonably predict was that the quest for a universal and unifying theory to underpin all forms of enquiry in economics (theoretical and applied) would (despite the awesome mathematical achievements of a generation of Nobel Prize winners, elaborating on the properties of general equilibrium) be exposed as chimerical. Furthermore, the gains from the continued application of modern neoclassical economic theory to the meta-questions (of economic growth, concerned with technological change, the formation of states, the construction of institutions, the geographical and geopolitical bases for comparative advantage, path dependence and the play of cultures on many kinds of economic actions) ran as Gerschenkron predicted into diminishing returns; or simply generated yet another historical example of cases where markets worked, or at least worked on *ceteris paribus* assumptions.

Fortunately for our parent and premier social science, economics moved on to consider new problems and to abandon several of the key assumptions which had allowed for rigour in neoclassical theory and began to offer better tools (vocabularies, concepts, theories, new and improved econometric techniques) for tackling the intrinsically historical nature of the causes of the wealth and, more urgently, the poverty of nations.

The failure of economics to unite its proliferating and contending tribes behind something approximating to a Newtonian paradigm, the abandonment of historically contingent and mathematically convenient assumptions of neoclassical theory, the return to the theoretical subtlety and complexity as well as the "Restoration" of big and serious questions that had attracted the German Historical School and their acolytes in Britain and America for several generations before 1957, as their conversations reveal did not, however, leave the leaders of the New Economic History stranded.

Sensibly to a man or a woman they have all moved: either "sideways" (into applied economics or the history of economic thought) or forward (into biometrics) and above all "back" – and profitably – into the study of institutions, cultures and entrepreneurs. They seem to have detached themselves from dependency on "mainstream" economics. Perhaps because they realize that eclectic borrowing from a discipline that now offers (to paraphrase one of the best and brightest of the current generation of cliometricians) a dazzling array of theoretically rigorous models and refined econometric techniques will carry an argument to almost any foreordained conclusions that a historian might select? That maybe too cynical a way to regard the "new" economic geography, "new" growth theory and "new" institutional economics, which certainly do help to specify questions more cogently and to calibrate and mobilize historical data in ways that allow for the continued extension of quantification into history.

At the end, in retrospect and with hindsight, I can only speculate what a future historian of economic history might conclude about cliometrics and New Economic History. If he happens to be "British" (*pace* Feinstein, Matthews and Hartwell) he might find the "fuss" to have been unnecessary, the product of a culture lacking in respect for its elders and for tradition, with a competitive urge to differentiate discontinuities, however minor, into a revolution. If she is French and inclined to reify the achievements of the *Annales* School, she may disdain to write more than a small chapter on developments among *les Anglo-Saxons*.

Clearly "the movement" was very much more than fuss to those gathered (now more than four decades ago) at Purdue. Those few, those happy few, conveyed an enthusiasm for the subject that was contagious. "As Florentines" they taught us all working on our own sites within North American, British, Japanese and even a handful of French, German and Scandinavian universities, to think cogently, specify rigorously and quantify precisely. During that brief efflorescence they captured the attention of economists and awed historians with their capacities to stimulate excitement, claiming to settle controversies with scientific rigour and the heavy artillery of quantification. They certainly left many intellectual battlegrounds littered with disabled generalizations and dead assertions about axioms of indispensability, the necessary inefficiencies of coerced labour and the nature of the British climacteric – to take but three famous controversies.

Of course the light faded and the brotherhood (fissured by *Time on the Cross*) went their separate ways in the 1970s. Another parochial less cosmopolitan generation of economists came to power much less interested in history and reduced too many younger economic historians (when they employed them at all) to the status of serfs on their estates, labouring to recover meanings from the past, expressed in their language and congruent with the theoretical expectations of Deans and Heads of Departments.

Meanwhile the trajectory of our other parent also became considerably less hospitable to economic (indeed to all positivistic forms of) history. A minority of historians went into linguistic and semiotic spins or found literary theory sufficiently rigorous for their purposes and questions. Most (perhaps a majority) embraced cultural anthropology and researched, not into the economics but into "cultures" of thrift, consumption, risk, innovation, work, entrepreneurship – as the deeper major and moving forces (factors) behind observed variations in economic behaviour through time and across countries. History departments rarely appoint young graduates properly trained in economic history, and in some ways are more antipathetic to our field than economists, who at least recognize and distinguish important from trivial variables and significant from minor questions in narratives about economic change.

As I write these my concluding paragraphs, perhaps I am unduly afflicted by a pessimistic sense of "rejection" by both our parent disciplines, as well as a perception of the restricted appeal of too much of our work to wider intellectual readerships. Our current "plight" can have nothing to do with the intrinsic importance of our subject. Most people in most places for millennia have been concerned with obtaining the food, clothing, shelter and artefacts required to sustain first a basic, then a satisfactory and only latterly (and among a minority of the world's populations) a quite agreeable standard of living. That overwhelming historical fact justifies the field for higher education and provides us, in Stan Engerman's words, with "the opportunity to ask and to answer a broad range of questions that has always made economic history such an interesting and enjoyable discipline to pursue."

Clearly the core syllabus of the subject remains too fundamental to be virtually ignored by historians and is too complex to be left to economists with their shortcuts into cross-country multiple regressions. With evangelical fervour a previous generation of cliometricians taught us to use the tools and master the techniques and knowledge available in their day to tackle the problem of long-term growth in intellectually convincing and rhetorically exciting ways. It was salutary and good to be with them, but the subject now needs another generation of innovators: or it may be that one or other of our neglectful parents will welcome us back into their households and in the process (currently more discernible in economics than history) rejuvenate themselves.

ABBREVIATIONS

As used in the text and in the list of references.

AER	*American Economic Review*
AER: P&P	*American Economic Review: Papers and Proceedings*
AgHist	*Agricultural History*
AHA	American Historical Association
AHR	*American Historical Review*
BHR	*Business History Review*
CRIW	Conference on Research in Income and Wealth
EDCC	*Economic Development and Cultural Change*
EEH	*Explorations in Economic History*
EHA	Economic History Association
EHES	European Historical Economics Society
EHR	*Economic History Review*
EHS	Economic History Society
EJ	*Economic Journal*
EREH	*European Review of Economic History*
ESRC	Economic and Social Research Council (UK)
IEA	International Economic Association
IMF	International Monetary Fund
JEEH	*Journal of European Economic History*
JEH	*Journal of Economic History*
JEL	*Journal of Economic Literature*
LSE	London School of Economics and Political Science
NIESR	National Institute of Economic and Social Research (UK)
NBER	National Bureau of Economic Research
NCS	*Newsletter of the Cliometric Society*
n. s.	*new series*
NSF	National Science Foundation (US)
OEP	*Oxford Economic Papers*
OSS	Office of Strategic Services (US)
PFP	*Purdue Faculty Papers in Economic History*
REStat	*Review of Economics and Statistics*

REH	*Research in Economic History*
SEJ	*Southern Economic Journal*
SJE	*Scandinavian Journal of Economics*
SSRC	Social Science Research Council (US or UK)
UP	University Press

REFERENCES

URLs are correct as of October 1st, 2007.

Abramovitz, Moses (1939). "Price theory for a changing economy." Ph.D. dissertation, Columbia University.

—— (1950). *Inventories and business cycles, with special reference to manufacturers' inventories*. New York: NBER.

—— (1952). "Economics of growth." In *A survey of contemporary economics*, edited by Bernard F. Haley, pp. 132–78. Homewood, Ill.: Irwin. Reprinted in Abramovitz (1989), pp. 80–124.

—— (1956). "Resource and output trends in the United States since 1970." *AER* 46:2, 5–23. Reprinted in Abramovitz (1989), pp. 127–47.

—— (1968). "The passing of the Kuznets cycle." *Economica, n. s.* 35:140, 349–67. Reprinted in Abramovitz (1989), pp. 276–97.

—— (1979). "Rapid growth potential and its realization: the experience of the capitalist economies in the postwar period." In *Economic growth and resources*, vol. 1, *the major issues*, edited by Edmond Malinvaud, pp. 1–30. London: Macmillan; New York: St. Martin's Press. Proceedings of the Fifth World Congress of the IEA. Reprinted in Abramovitz (1989), pp. 187–219.

—— (1986a). "In memoriam: Simon Kuznets, 1901–1985." *JEH* 46:1, 241–6.

—— (1986b). "Catching up, forging ahead, and falling behind." *JEH* 46:2, 385–406. Reprinted in Abramovitz (1989), pp. 220–42.

—— (1989). *Thinking about growth and other essays on economic growth and welfare*. Cambridge: Cambridge UP.

—— (1993). "The search for the sources of growth: areas of ignorance, old and new." *JEH* 53:2, 217–43. [Presidential address, EHA, 1992.]

—— (2000). "Working with Paul. A memoir of a long collaboration." URL: <http://siepr.stanford.edu/conferences/Abramovitz.pdf>.

—— (2001). *Days gone by: a memoir for my family*. Unpublished; URL: <http://www-econ.stanford.edu/abramovitz/abramovitzm.html>.

Abramovitz, Moses, and Paul A. David (1973). "Reinterpreting economic growth: parables and realities." *AER: P&P* 63:2, 428–40.

—— (2000). "American macroeconomic growth in the era of knowledge-based progress: the long-run perspective." In Engerman & Gallman, eds (1996, 2000), vol. II, pp. 1–92. Expanded version (2001) available via URL: <http://siepr.stanford.edu/papers/pdf/01-05.html>.

Acemoglu, Daron, Simon Johnson, and James A. Robinson (2005). "The rise of Europe: Atlantic trade, institutional change, and economic growth." *AER* 95:3, 546–79.

Aitken, Hugh G. J. (1967). "Entrepreneurial research: the history of an intellectual innovation." In *Explorations in enterprise*, edited by Hugh G. J. Aitken, pp. 3–19. Cambridge, Mass.: Harvard UP.

Akerlof, George A. (2005). *Explorations in pragmatic economics: selected papers . . .* Oxford; New York: Oxford UP.

Aldcroft, D. H. (1964). "The entrepreneur and the British economy, 1870–1914." *EHR* 17:1, 113–34.

Alesina, Alberto, James Mirrlees, and Manfred J. M. Neumann (1989). "Politics and business cycles in industrial democracies." *Economic Policy* 4:8, 55–98.

Alford, B. W. E. (2004). "New frame – same picture?" *Business History* 46:4, 640–4.

Allen, Robert C., Tommy Bengtsson, and Martin Dribe, eds (2005). *Living standards in the past: new perspectives on well-being in Asia and Europe*. Oxford; New York: Oxford UP.

Ambirajan, S. (1995). "The delayed emergence of econometrics as a separate discipline." In *Measurement, quantification and economic analysis: numeracy in economics*, edited by Ingrid H. Rima, pp. 198–211. London; New York: Routledge.

Ames, Edward (1981). "On forgetting economics with Em Weiler." In Horwich & Quirk, eds (1981), pp. 355–60.

Ames, Edward, and Nathan Rosenberg (1963). "Changing technological leadership and industrial growth." *EJ* 73:289, 13–29. Reprinted in *PFP*, pp. 363–82.

—— (1968). "The Enfield Arsenal in theory and history." *EJ* 78:312, 827–42.

Anders, George (1992). *Merchants of debt: KKR and the mortgaging of American business*. New York: Basic Books.

Andreano, Ralph L., ed. (1965). *New views on American economic development*. Cambridge, Mass.: Schenkman.

——, ed. (1970). *The New Economic History: recent papers on methodology*. New York: Wiley.

Arthur, W. Brian (1989). "Competing technologies, increasing returns, and lock-in by historical small events." *EJ* 99:394, 116–31. Reprinted in *Increasing returns and path dependence in the economy*, by W. Brian Arthur, pp. 13–32. Ann Arbor, Mich.: University of Michigan Press, 1994.

Asher, Ephraim (1972). "Industrial efficiency and biased technical change in American and British manufacturing: the case of textiles in the nineteenth century." *JEH* 32:2, 431–42.

Ashley, William J. (1887). "The early history of the English woollen industry." *Publications of the American Economic Association* 2:4, 13–85.

—— (1893). "The study of economic history." *Quarterly Journal of Economics* 7:2, 115–36.

—— (1914). *The economic organisation of England, an outline history*. London; New York: Longmans, Green.

—— (1927). "The place of economic history in university studies." *EHR*, 1st series 1:1, 1–11.

Ashton, T. S. (1924). *Iron and steel in the Industrial Revolution*. Manchester: UP; New York: Longmans, Green.

—— (1934). *Economic and social investigations in Manchester, 1833–1933; a centenary history of the Manchester Statistical Society*. London: P. S. King & Son.

—— (1946). "The relation of economic history to economic theory." *Economica, n. s.* 13:50, 81–96. Reprinted in Harte, ed. (1971), pp. 163–79. [Inaugural lecture, London School of Economics, 7th February 1946.]

—— (1948). *The Industrial Revolution, 1760–1830*. London: Oxford UP.

—— (1949). "The standard of life of the workers in England, 1790–1830." *JEH* 9: supplement, 19–38. Reprinted in Hayek, ed. (1954), pp. 127–59.

—— (1955). *An economic history of England: the 18th century*. London: Methuen.

Atack, Jeremy, and Fred Bateman (1987). *To their own soil: agriculture in the antebellum North*. Ames, Iowa: Iowa State UP.

Atack, Jeremy, Fred Bateman, and Peter Passell (1994). *A new economic view of American history: from colonial times to 1940*, 2nd edition. New York: Norton.

Aydelotte, William O., Allan G. Bogue, and Robert W. Fogel, eds (1972). *The dimensions of quantitative research in history*. Princeton, N.J.: Princeton UP.

Babbage, Charles (1963 [1835]). *On the economy of machinery and manufactures*, fourth edition enlarged. London: Charles Knight. Reprinted London: Frank Cass, 1963; New York: Augustus Kelley, 1963.

Backhouse, Roger E. (2002). *The ordinary business of life. A history of economics from the ancient world to the twenty-first century*. Princeton, N.J.: Princeton UP.

Bailyn, Bernard (1967). *The ideological origins of the American Revolution*. Cambridge, Mass.: Belknap Press of Harvard UP.

Bailyn, Bernard, and Lotte Bailyn (1959). *Massachusetts shipping, 1697–1714; a statistical study*. Cambridge, Mass.: Belknap Press of Harvard UP.

Baran, Paul A. (1957). *The political economy of growth*. New York: Monthly Review Press.

Barker, T. C. (1977). "The beginnings of the Economic History Society." *EHR* 30:1, 1–19.

Basu, Kaushik, Eric Jones, and Ekkehart Schlicht (1987). "The growth and decay of custom: the role of the New Institutional Economics in economic history," *EEH* 24:1, 1–21.

Bateman, Fred, and James Foust (1974). "A sample of rural households selected from the 1860 manuscript Censuses." *AgHist* 48:1, 75–93.

Baumol, William J. (2000). "What Marshall *didn't* know: on the twentieth century's contributions to economics." *Quarterly Journal of Economics* 115:1, 1–44.

Berck, Peter (1978). "Hard driving and efficiency: iron production in 1890." *JEH* 38:4, 879–900.

Berg, Maxine (1992). "The first women economic historians." *EHR* 45:2, 308–29.

—— (1996). *A woman in history: Eileen Power, 1889–1940*. Cambridge; New York: Cambridge UP.

Berg, Maxine, and Pat Hudson (1992). "Rehabilitating the Industrial Revolution." *EHR* 45:1, 24–50.

Bernstein, Michael A. (2001). *A perilous progress: economists and public purpose in twentieth-century America*. Princeton, N. J.; Oxford: Princeton UP.

Beveridge, William (1940). "The trade cycle in Britain before 1850." *OEP* 3, 74–109.

Blaug, Mark (1978). *Economic theory in retrospect*, third edition. Cambridge; New York: Cambridge UP.

——, ed. (1999). *Who's who in economics*, third edition. Cheltenham, UK; Northampton, Mass.: Edward Elgar.

Bode, Frederick A., and Donald E. Ginter (1986). *Farm tenancy and the Census in antebellum Georgia*. Athens, Ga.: University of Georgia Press.

Bodenhorn, Howard, and Hugh Rockoff (1992). "Regional interest rates in antebellum America." In Goldin & Rockoff, eds (1992), pp. 159–87.

Bogue, Allan G. (1963). *From prairie to corn belt; farming on the Illinois and Iowa prairies in the nineteenth century*. Chicago: University of Chicago Press.

Bordo, Michael D., ed. (1989). *Money, history, and international finance: Essays in honor of Anna J. Schwartz*. Chicago; London: University of Chicago Press.

Bordo, Michael D., and Anna J. Schwartz, eds (1984). *A Retrospective on the classical gold standard, 1821–1931.* Chicago: University of Chicago Press. [NBER Conference Report.]

Bordo, Michael D., Alan M. Taylor, and Jeffrey G. Williamson, eds (2003) *Globalization in historical perspective.* Chicago: University of Chicago Press. [NBER Conference Report.]

Bridenbaugh, Carl (1963). "The great mutation." *AHR* 68:2, 315–31. [Presidential address, AHA, 1962.]

Brown, E. H. Phelps, and S. J. Handfield-Jones (1952). "The climacteric of the 1890's." *OEP n. s.* 4:3, 279–89. Reprinted in *The experience of economic growth: case studies in economic history*, edited by Barry E. Supple, pp. 204–16, with omissions. New York: Random House, 1963.

Brown, Henry Phelps, and Sheila V. Hopkins (1981). *A perspective of wages and prices.* London; New York: Methuen.

Burckhardt, Jacob (1878). *The civilization of the renaissance in Italy*; 2 vols; authorized translation by S. G. C. Middlemore. London: George Allen & Unwin; New York: Macmillan. [First edition in German, 1860; numerous later editions.]

Burns, Arthur F., and Wesley C. Mitchell (1946). *Measuring business cycles.* New York: NBER. [*Studies in business cycles*, No. 2.]

Butlin, N. G. (1962). *Australian domestic product, investment and foreign borrowing, 1861–1938/39.* Cambridge: Cambridge UP.

Byatt, I. C. R. (1979). *The British electrical industry, 1875–1914: the economic returns to a new technology.* Oxford: Clarendon Press.

Cain, Louis P. (1997). "Review" of Lebergott (1996). *JEL* 35:2, 774–5.

Cain, Louis P., and Donald G. Paterson (1981). "Factor biases and technical change in manufacturing: The American System, 1850–1919." *JEH* 41:2, 341–60.

Cain, Louis P.; with Stanley Reiter and Paul Uselding (1991). "The vital Jonathan R. T. Hughes." In *The vital one: essays in honor of Jonathan R. T. Hughes*, edited by Joel Mokyr, pp. 1–13. Greenwich, Conn.; London: JAI Press.

Cain, Louis P., and Paul J. Uselding, eds (1973). *Business enterprise and economic change: essays in honor of Harold F. Williamson.* Kent, Ohio: Kent State UP.

Cairncross, Alec (1953). *Home and foreign investment, 1870–1913; studies in capital accumulation.* Cambridge: Cambridge UP.

—— (1991). "Review" of Abramovitz (1989). *EHR* 44:2, 392–3.

Calomiris, Charles (2000). *U.S. bank deregulation in historical perspective.* New York: Cambridge UP.

Cameron, Rondo (1982). "The Industrial Revolution: a misnomer." *The History Teacher* 15:3, 377–84.

Capie, Forrest H., and Geoffrey E. Wood (1989). "Anna Schwartz's perspective on British economic history." In Bordo, ed. (1989), pp. 79–104.

Carré, J.-J., P. Dubois, and E. Malinvaud (1975). *French economic growth.* Stanford, Calif.: Stanford UP. [Trans. of *La croissance française* by J. P. Hatfield; *Studies of economic growth in industrialized countries.*]

Cassel, Gustav (1903). *The nature and necessity of interest.* London: Macmillan

Chambers, Edward J. (1966). "Review" of Urquhart & Buckley (1965). *JEH* 26:2, 270–1.

Chambers, E. J., and D. F. Gordon (1966). "Primary products and economic growth: an empirical measurement." *Journal of Political Economy* 74:4, 315–32.

Chandler, Alfred D., Jr. (1966). *Strategy and structure: chapters in the history of the industrial enterprise.* Garden City, N. Y.: Doubleday.

—— (1977). *The visible hand: the managerial revolution in American business.* Cambridge, Mass.: Belknap Press.

Chandler, Alfred D., Jr.; with the assistance of Takashi Hikino (1990). *Scale and scope: the dynamics of industrial capitalism*. Cambridge, Mass.: Belknap Press.

Chapman, Agatha L.; with R. Knight (1953). *Wages and salaries in the United Kingdom, 1920–1938*. Cambridge: Cambridge UP.

Clapham, J. H. (1922). "Of empty economic boxes." *EJ* 32:3, 305–14.

—— (1926–39). *An economic history of Modern Britain*. Cambridge: The University Press. *vol. 1, The early railway age, 1820–1850* (1926, 1930, 1939); *vol. 2, Free trade and steel, 1850–1886* (1932); *vol. 3, Machines and national rivalries (1887–1914) with an epilogue (1914–1929)* (1938).

—— (1931). "Economic history as a discipline." In *Encyclopedia of the social sciences*, edited by Edwin R. A. Seligman and Alvin Johnson, Vol. 5, pp. 327–30. New York: The Macmillan Company.

Clark, Colin (1940). *The conditions of economic progress*. London: Macmillan. Second edition, 1951; third edition, 1957.

Clarke, Richard N., and Lawrence H. Summers (1980). "The labour scarcity controversy reconsidered." *EJ* 90:357, 129–39.

Clough, Shepard B. (1981). *The life I've lived: the formation, career, and retirement of an historian*. Washington, D.C.: UP of America.

Clower, Robert (1973). "Snarks, quarks, and other fictions." In Cain & Uselding, eds (1973), pp. 3–14.

Coase, R. H. (2000). "The acquisition of Fisher Body by General Motors." *Journal of Law and Economics* 43:1, 15–31.

Coats, A. W. (1980). "The historical context of the 'New' Economic History." *JEEH* 9:1, 185–207.

Coelho, Philip R. P. (2001). "Review" of North and Thomas (1973). EH.Net Economic History Services, Dec 21, 2001, URL: <http://eh.net/bookreviews/library/coelho.shtml>.

Cole, Arthur H. (1944). "A report on research in economic history." *JEH* 4:1, 49–72.

—— (1953). "Committee on Research in Economic History: a description of its purposes, activities, and organization." *JEH* 13:1, 79–87.

—— (1968). "Economic history in the United States: formative years of a discipline." *JEH* 28:4, 556–89.

—— (1970). "The Committee on Research in Economic History: an historical sketch," *JEH* 30:4, 723–41.

Cole, Arthur H., and Ruth Crandall (1964). "The International Scientific Committee on Price History." *JEH* 24:3, 381–8.

Cole, W. A. (1955). "The Quakers and Politics, 1652–1660." Ph.D. thesis, University of Cambridge.

—— (1956). "The Quakers and the English Revolution." *Past & Present* 10, 39–54. Reprinted in *Crisis in Europe, 1560–1660: Essays from Past & Present*, edited by Trevor Aston, pp. 341–58. London: Routledge & Kegan Paul, 1965.

—— (1957). "Social origins of the early Friends." *Journal of the Friends' Historical Society* 48, 99–118.

—— (1968). *Economic history as a social science*. Swansea (Glam.): University College of Swansea, 1968. Reprinted in Harte, ed. (1971), pp. 349–65. [Inaugural lecture delivered at the college, October 24, 1967.]

—— (1974). "Changes in British industrial structure, 1850–1960." In *Fifth international conference of economic history: Leningrad, 1970*, edited by Herman van der Wee, Vladimir A.

Vinogradoff, and Grigorii G. Kotovsky, vol. VII, pp. 112–29. The Hague; New York: Mouton.
—— (1981). "Factors in demand 1700–80." In Floud & McCloskey, eds (1981), vol. 1, pp. 36–65.
—— (1982). "Long-term trends in the economy of pre-industrial England." In *Eighth international economic history congress, Budapest, 1982*, vol. 3, *The long run trends*, pp. 6–16. Budapest: Akadémiae Kiadó.
Coleman, D. C. (1987). *History and the economic past. An account of the rise and decline of economic history in Britain*. Oxford: Clarendon Press.
—— (1992). "Myth, history and the industrial revolution." In *Myth, history and the industrial revolution*, by D. C. Coleman, pp. 1–42. London; Rio Grande, Ohio: Hambledon Press.
Conrad, Alfred H. (1961). "Income growth and structural change." In *American economic history*, edited by Seymour E. Harris, pp. 29–60. New York: McGraw-Hill. Published in revised form in Conrad & Meyer (1964), pp. 115–77.
—— *et al.* (1967). "Slavery as an obstacle to economic growth: a panel discussion of Conrad and Meyer." *JEH* 27:4, 518–60.
Conrad, Alfred H., and John R. Meyer (1958). "The economics of slavery in the ante bellum South." *Journal of Political Economy*, 66:2, 95–130. Reprinted in Conrad and Meyer (1964), pp. 43–92; with revisions in Fogel & Engerman, eds (1971), pp. 342–61; and in Temin, ed. (1973), pp. 339–97.
—— (1964). *The economics of slavery and other studies in econometric history*. Chicago: Aldine.
Cootner, Paul H. (1953). "Transport innovation and economic development: the case of U.S. steam railroads." Unpublished Ph.D. dissertation, Massachusetts Institute of Technology.
—— (1963). "The role of the railroads in United States economic growth." *JEH* 23:4, 477–521.
Costa, Dora L. (1998). *The evolution of retirement: an American economic history, 1880–1990*. Chicago: University of Chicago Press.
—— (2000). "From mill town to board room: the rise of women's paid labor." *Journal of Economic Perspectives* 14: 4, 101–22.
—— (2003a). "Understanding mid-life and older age mortality declines: evidence from Union Army veterans." *Journal of Econometrics* 112:1: 175–92.
——, ed. (2003b). *Health and labor force participation over the life cycle: evidence from the past*. Chicago: University of Chicago Press.
Cottrell, P. L. (2004). "Domestic finance, 1860–1914." In Floud & Johnson, eds (2004), vol. II, pp. 253–79.
Coyle, Diane (2007). *The soulful science. What economists really do and why it matters*. Princeton, N. J.; Oxford: Princeton UP.
Crafts, Nicholas F. R. (1976). "English economic growth in the eighteenth century: a re-examination of Deane and Cole's estimates," *EHR* 29:2, 226–35.
—— (1985). *British economic growth during the industrial revolution*. Oxford: Clarendon Press; New York: Oxford UP.
—— (1987). "Cliometrics, 1971–1986: a survey." *Journal of Applied Econometrics* 2:3, 171–92.
—— (1994). "The industrial revolution." In Floud & McCloskey, eds (1994), pp. 44–59.
—— (2005). "The first industrial revolution: resolving the slow growth/rapid industrialization paradox." *Journal of the European Economic Association* 3:2–3, 525–34.

Crafts, N. F. R., and C. Knick Harley (1992). "Output growth and the Industrial Revolution: a restatement of the Crafts–Harley view." *EHR* 45:4, 703–30.

—— (2004). "Precocious British industrialization: a general equilibrium perspective." In Prados, ed. (2004), pp. 86–107.

CRIW (Conference on Research in Income and Wealth) (1960). *Trends in the American economy in the nineteenth century*. Princeton, N.J.: Princeton UP for NBER. *Studies in Income and Wealth*, vol. 24; with an introduction by William N. Parker.

—— (1966). *Output, employment, and productivity in the United States after 1800*. New York: NBER; distributed by Columbia UP. *Studies in income and wealth*, vol. 30; with an introduction by Dorothy S. Brady.

Crouzet, François, and Isabele Lescent-Gilles (1998). "French economic history for the past 20 years." *NEHA–Bulletin* 12:2, 75–101. [Nederlandsch Economisch-Historisch Archief.]

Cuenca Esteban, Javier (1994). "British textile prices, 1770–1831: are British growth rates worth revising once again?" *EHR* 47:1, 66–105.

Dacey, Douglas C., James K. Galbraith, and Bobby R. Inman (2004). "In memoriam: Walt Whitman Rostow." Documents of the General Faculty, University of Texas, pp. 3333–9. Link to "memorials" at URL: <http://www.utexas.edu/faculty/council/>.

Dasgupta, Partha, and Paul A. David (1994). "Toward a new economics of science." *Research Policy* 23:5, 487–521.

David, Henry (1936). *The history of the Haymarket affair; a study in the American social-revolutionary and labor movements*. New York: Farrar & Rinehart. Second edition, 1958.

David, Paul A. (1966). "The mechanization of reaping in the ante-bellum Midwest." In *Industrialization in two systems: essays in honor of Alexander Gerschenkron by a group of his students*, edited by Henry Rosovsky, pp. 3–39. New York: Wiley. Reprinted with revisions in Fogel & Engerman, eds (1971), pp. 214–27, and in David (1975), pp. 195–232.

—— (1969). "Transport innovation and economic growth: Professor Fogel on and off the rails." *EHR* 22:3, 506–25. Reprinted in Temin, ed. (1973), pp. 261–90, and in David (1975), pp. 291–314.

—— (1971a). "Comments by Paul A. David" [on Wright (1971)]. In Intriligator, ed. (1971), pp. 459–67.

—— (1971b). "The landscape and the machine: technical interrelatedness, land tenure and the mechanization of the corn harvest in Victorian Britain." In McCloskey, ed. (1971), pp. 145–205. Reprinted in David (1975), pp. 233–88.

—— (1975). *Technical choice, innovation and economic growth: essays on American and British experience in the nineteenth century*. Cambridge: Cambridge UP.

—— (1985). "Clio and the economics of QWERTY." *AER* 75:2, 332–7. Published in revised form as "Understanding the economics of QWERTY: the necessity of history," in Parker, ed. (1986), pp. 30–49.

—— (1987). "Some new standards for the economics of standardization in the Information Age." In *Economic Policy and Technological Performance*, edited by Partha Dasgupta and Paul Stoneman, pp. 206–39. Cambridge: Cambridge UP.

—— (1993). "Intellectual property institutions and the panda's thumb: patents, copyrights, and trade secrets in economic theory and history." In *Global dimensions of intellectual property rights in science and technology*, edited by Mitchel B. Wallerstein *et al.*, pp. 19–61. Washington, DC: National Academy Press.

—— (2001). "Path dependence, its critics and the quest for 'historical economics.' " In *Evolution and path dependence in economic ideas: past and present*, edited by Pierre Garrouste and Stavros Ionnides, pp. 15–40. London; Northampton, Mass.: Edward Elgar.

—— (2004a). "Can 'open science' be protected from the evolving regime of IPR protections?" *Journal of Institutional and Theoretical Economics* 160:1, 9–34.

—— (2004b). "Understanding the emergence of 'open science' institutions: functionalist economics in a historical context." *Industrial and Corporate Change* 13:4, 571–89.

—— (2005) "Path dependence in economic processes: implications for policy analysis in dynamical system contexts." In *The Evolutionary Foundation of Economics*, edited by Kurt Dopfer, pp. 151–94. Cambridge: Cambridge UP.

—— (2007a). "Innovation and Europe's academic institutions – second thoughts about embracing the Bayh-Dole regime." In *Perspectives on Innovation*, edited by Franco Malerba and Stefano Brusoni, pp. 251–78. Cambridge; New York: Cambridge UP.

—— (2007b). "Path dependence – a foundational concept for historical social science." *Cliometrica* 1:2, 91–114.

David, Paul A., Herbert G. Gutman, Richard Sutch, Peter Temin, and Gavin Wright (1976). *Reckoning with slavery: a critical study in the quantitative history of American Negro slavery*. New York: Oxford UP. With an introduction by Kenneth M. Stampp.

David, Paul A., and Warren C. Sanderson (1986). "Rudimentary contraceptive methods and the American transition to marital fertility control, 1855–1915." In Engerman & Gallman, eds (1986), pp. 307–79; 383–90.

David, Paul A., and Peter Temin (1974). "Slavery: the progressive institution." *JEH* 34:3, 739–83. Reprinted in Whaples & Betts, eds (1995), pp. 177–225.

David, Paul A., and Gavin Wright (2003). "General purpose technologies and surges in productivity: historical reflections on the future of the ICT revolution." In *The economic future in historical perspective*, edited by Paul A. David and Mark Thomas, pp. 135–66. Oxford; New York: Oxford UP for the British Academy.

Davis, David Brion (1974). "Slavery and the post-World War II historians." *Daedalus* 103: 1–16.

Davis, Lance E. (1957). "Sources of industrial finance: the American textile industry, a case study." *Explorations in Entrepreneurial History* 9, 189–203. Reprinted in *PFP*, pp. 625–42.

—— (1958). "Stock ownership in the early New England textile industry." *BHR* 32:2, 204–22. Reprinted in *PFP*, pp. 563–80.

—— (1960). "The New England textile mills and the capital markets: a study in industrial borrowing." *JEH* 20: 1, 1–30. Reprinted in *PFP*, pp. 596–624.

—— (1963). "Capital immobilities and finance capitalism: a study of economic evolution in the United States, 1820–1920." *Explorations in Entrepreneurial History/2nd series* 1:1, 88–105. Reprinted in *PFP*, pp. 581–95.

—— (1965). "The investment market, 1870–1914: the evolution of a national market." *JEH* 25: 3, 355–99. Reprinted in *PFP*, pp. 119–59.

—— (1966a). "The capital markets and industrial concentration: the U. S. and U. K., a comparative study." *EHR* 19: 2, 255–72. Reprinted in *PFP*, pp. 663–82.

—— (1966b). "The New Economic History. II. Professor Fogel and the New Economic History." *EHR* 19:3, 657–63.

—— (1968). " 'And it will never be literature': The New Economic History: a critique." *Explorations in Entrepreneurial History/2nd series* 6:1, 75–92. Reprinted in Andreano, ed. (1970), pp. 67–83.

—— (1980). "It's a long, long road to Tipperary, or reflections on organized violence, protection rates, and related topics: the New Political History." *JEH* 40:1, 1–16. [Presidential address, EHA, 1979.]

—— (2000). "Review" of Fogel (1964). EH.Net Economic History Services, Jul 1, 2000, URL: <http://www.eh.net/bookreviews/library/davis.shtml>.

—— (2001). "Formal estimates of personal income are really personal." In Hudson, ed. (2001), pp. 55–7.

Davis, Lance E., Richard A. Easterlin, William N. Parker *et al.* (1972). *American economic growth: an economist's history of the United States*. New York: Harper & Row.

Davis, Lance E., and Robert E. Gallman (1994). "Savings, investment and economic growth: the United States in the nineteenth century." In James & Thomas, eds (1994), pp. 202–29.

—— (1999). *Evolving financial markets and international capital flows. Britain, the Americas, and Australia, 1865–1914*. Cambridge; New York: Cambridge UP.

Davis, Lance E., Robert E. Gallman, and Karin Gleiter (1997). *In pursuit of Leviathan: technology, institutions, productivity, and profits in American whaling, 1816–1906*. Chicago: University of Chicago Press.

Davis, Lance E., and Jonathan R. T. Hughes (1960). "A dollar–sterling exchange, 1803–95." *EHR* 13:1, 52–78. Reprinted in *PFP*, pp. 235–68.

Davis, Lance E., Jonathan R. T. Hughes, and Duncan McDougall (1961). *American Economic History*. Homewood, Ill.: Richard D. Irwin. Second edition, 1965; third edition, 1969.

Davis, Lance E., Jonathan R. T. Hughes, and Stanley Reiter (1960). "Aspects of quantitative research in economic history." *JEH* 20:4, 539–47. Reprinted in *PFP*, pp. 3–10.

Davis, Lance E., and Robert A. Huttenback; with Susan Gray Davis (1987). *Mammon and the pursuit of empire: the political economy of imperialism, 1860–1912*. New York: Cambridge UP. Published in abridged form as *Mammon and the pursuit of empire: the economics of British imperialism*, Cambridge UP, 1988.

Davis, Lance E., and Douglass C. North (1971). *Institutional change and American economic growth*. New York: Cambridge UP.

Davis, Lance E., and Peter L. Payne (1958). "From benevolence to business: the story of two savings banks." *BHR* 32: 4, 386–404. Reprinted in *PFP*, pp. 643–62.

Davis, Lance E., and H. Louis Stettler III (1966). "The New England textile industry, 1825–1860: trends and fluctuations." In CRIW (1966), pp. 213–38. Reprinted in *PFP*, pp. 539–62.

Dawidoff, Nicholas (2002). *The fly swatter: how my grandfather made his way in the world*. New York: Pantheon Books.

Dawson, Doyne (2003). "The assault on Eurocentric history." *Journal of The Historical Society* 3:3–4, 403–427.

Deane, Phyllis (1948a). *The measurement of colonial national incomes, an experiment*. Cambridge: Cambridge UP. NIESR, Occasional papers, 12.

—— (1948b). "Regional variations in United Kingdom incomes from employment." *Journal of the Royal Statistical Society* 116:2, 123–35.

—— (1953). *Colonial social accounting*. Cambridge: Cambridge UP. NIESR, Economic and social studies, 11.

—— (1955). "The implications of early national income estimates for the measurement of long-term economic growth in the United Kingdom." *EDCC* 4:1 (part 1), 3–38.

—— (1956). "Contemporary estimates of national income in the first half of the nineteenth century." *EHR* 8: 3, 339–354.

—— (1965). *The first industrial revolution*. Cambridge: Cambridge UP. Second edition, Cambridge UP, 1979.

—— (1973). "The role of capital in the Industrial Revolution." *EEH* 10:4, 349–64.

—— (2001). *The life and times of J. Neville Keynes: a beacon in the tempest*. Cheltenham, UK; Northampton, Mass.: Edward Elgar.

Deane, Phyllis, and W. A. Cole (1962). *British economic growth, 1688–1959: trends and structure*.

Cambridge: Cambridge UP. Second edition, University of Cambridge, Dept. of Applied Economics Monographs, 8; with a new Preface, 1967.

Denison, Edward F. (1962). *The sources of economic growth in the United States and the alternatives before us*. New York: Committee for Economic Development.

—— (1967). *Why growth rates differ: postwar experience in nine Western countries*. Washington, D. C.: Brookings Institution.

Denzau, Arthur T., and Douglass C. North (1994). "Shared mental models: ideologies and institutions." *Kyklos* 47:1, 3–31.

Desai, Meghnad (2001). "What economic history means to me." In Hudson ed. (2001), pp. 58–61.

deVries, Jan (1974). *The Dutch rural economy in the Golden Age 1500–1700*. New Haven, Conn.; London: Yale UP.

—— (2005). "An interview with Jan deVries." *NCS* 20:1, 4–12. Interviewed by Alan Taylor.

Dimand, Robert W. (1995). "The neglect of women's contributions to economics." In *Women of value. Feminist essays on the history of women in economics*, edited by Robert W. Dimand, Mary Ann Dimand, and Evelyn L. Forget, pp. 1–24. Aldershot, UK; Brookfield, Vt.: Edward Elgar.

Dobb, Maurice (1946). *Studies in the development of capitalism*. London: George Routledge & Kegan Paul.

Drukker, J. W. (2006). *The revolution that bit its own tail: how economic history has changed our ideas about economic growth*. Amsterdam: Aksant.

Dumke, Rolf H. (1992). "The future of Cliometric history – a European view." *Scandinavian Economic History Review* 40:3, 3–28. [Presented at first EHES conference, Copenhagen, July 1991.]

Easterbrook, W. Thomas (1990). *North American patterns of growth and development: the continental context*. Edited, with an introduction, by Ian Parker. Toronto: University of Toronto Press.

Easterlin, Richard A. (1960). "Interregional differences in per capita income, population, and total income, 1840–1950." In CRIW (1960), pp. 73–140.

—— (1961). "Regional income trends, 1840–1950." In *American economic history*, edited by Seymour E. Harris, pp. 525–547. New York: McGraw-Hill. Reprinted with omissions in Fogel & Engerman, eds (1971), pp. 38–49.

—— (1962). "Review" of North (1961). *JEH* 22:1, 122–6.

—— (1974). "Does economic growth improve the human lot?" In *Nations and households in economic growth: essays in honor of Moses Abramovitz*, edited by Paul A. David and Melvin W. Reder, pp. 89–125. New York: Academic Press.

—— (1978). "Dorothy Stahl Brady, 1903–1977." *JEH* 38:1, 301–3.

—— (1980). *Birth and fortune: the impact of numbers on personal welfare*. New York: Basic Books. Second edition, Chicago: University of Chicago Press, 1987.

—— (1981). "Why isn't the whole world developed?" *JEH* 41:1, 1–19. [Presidential address, EHA, 1980.]

—— (1989). "Foreword" to Kuznets (1989), pp. 1–6.

—— (1995). "Preferences and prices in choice of career: the switch to business." *Journal of Economic Behavior and Organization* 27: 1, 1–34. Reprinted with revisions in Easterlin (2004), pp. 219–45.

—— (1997). "The story of a reluctant economist," *American Economist* 41:2, 11–21. Reprinted with revisions in Easterlin (2004), pp. 3–20.

—— (2001). "Income and happiness: towards a unified theory." *EJ* 111:473, 465–84.

—— (2004). *The reluctant economist: perspectives on economics, economic history, and demography.* Cambridge; New York: Cambridge UP.

—— (2006). "Life cycle happiness and its sources – intersections of psychology, economics, and demography." *Journal of Economic Psychology* 27:4, 463–82.

Easterlin, Richard A., and Eileen M. Crimmins (1985). *The fertility revolution: a supply–demand analysis.* Chicago: University of Chicago Press.

—— (1991). "Private materialism, personal self-fulfillment, family life and public interest: the nature, effects, and causes of recent changes in the values of American youth." *Public Opinion Quarterly* 55:4, 499–533.

Eckaus, R. S. (1955). "The factor proportions problem in underdeveloped areas." *AER* 45:4, 539–65.

Edelstein, Michael (2001). "The size of the U. S. armed forces during World War II: feasibility and war planning." *REH* 20, 47–97.

—— (2004). "Foreign investment, accumulation and Empire, 1860–1914." In Floud & Johnson, eds (2004), vol. II, pp. 190–226.

Eichengreen, Barry J. (1990). "Review" of Bordo, ed. (1989). *JEH* 50:1, 259–60.

—— (1992). *Golden fetters: the gold standard and the Great Depression, 1919–1939.* New York : Oxford UP.

—— (1994). "The contributions of Robert W. Fogel to economics and economic history." *Scandinavian Journal of Economics* 96:2, 167–79.

Eichengreen, Barry, and Albert Fishlow (1998). "Contending with capital flows: what is different about the 1990s?" In *Capital flows and financial crises*, edited by Miles Kahler, pp. 23–68. Ithaca, N. Y.: Cornell UP.

Eltis, David, Frank D. Lewis, and Kenneth L. Sokoloff, eds (2004). *Slavery in the development of the Americas.* Cambridge; New York: Cambridge UP.

Engels, Friedrich (1845 [1892]). *The condition of the working-class in England in 1844.* London: S. Sonnenschein & Co., 1892. [Translated from *Lage der arbeitende Klasse in England*, 1845.]

Engerman, Stanley L. (1967). "The effects of slavery upon the Southern economy: a review of the recent debate." *Explorations in Entrepreneurial History/2nd Series* 4:2, 71–97. Reprinted in Temin, ed. (1973), pp. 398–434.

—— (1976). "The height of slaves in the United States." *Local Population Studies* 14, 45–9.

—— (1980). "Counterfactuals and the New Economic History." *Inquiry* 23:2, 157–72.

—— (1986). "Slavery and emancipation in comparative perspective: a look at some recent debates." *JEH* 46:2, 317–39. [Presidential address, EHA, 1985.]

—— (1992). "Robert William Fogel: an appreciation by a co-author and colleague." In Goldin & Rockoff, eds (1992), 9–14.

—— (1996). "Cliometrics." In *The social science encyclopedia*, second edition, edited by Adam Kuper and Jessica Kuper, pp. 96–8. London; New York: Routledge.

Engerman, Stanley L., and Robert E. Gallman, eds (1986). *Long-term factors in American economic growth.* Chicago: University of Chicago Press. [CRIW *Studies in income and wealth*, vol. 51.]

—— eds (1996, 2000). *The Cambridge economic history of the United States.* (3 vol.) New York; Cambridge: Cambridge UP.

Engerman, Stanley L., Philip T. Hoffman, Jean-Laurent Rosenthal, and Kenneth L. Sokoloff (2003). "Afterword: about Lance Davis." In *Finance, intermediaries, and economic development*, edited by Stanley L. Engerman *et al.*, pp. 319–27. Cambridge; New York: Cambridge UP.

Erikson, Erik H. (1958). *Young man Luther; a study in psychoanalysis and history.* New York: Norton.

Evans, Robert, Jr. (1962). "The economics of American Negro slavery." In *Aspects of labor economics: a conference of the Universities – National Bureau Committee for Economic Research*, pp. 185–243. Princeton, N. J.: Princeton UP for NBER.

Fabricant, Solomon, with the assistance of Julius Shiskin (1940). *The output of manufacturing industries, 1899–1937.* New York: NBER. NBER Publications; no. 39.

—— (1984). *Toward a firmer basis of economic policy: the founding of the National Bureau of Economic Research.* Cambridge, Mass.: NBER.

Farnie, D. A. (2005). "A bio-bibliography of economic and social history, 4th edn." At URL: <http://www.ehs.org.uk/ehs/AbouttheEHS/assets/Farniebiobib4thedn.doc>.

Faulkner, Harold Underwood (1924). *American economic history.* New York; London: Harper & Brothers. [8th edition, Harper, 1960.]

Feeny, David (1989). "The decline of property rights in man in Thailand, 1800–1913." *JEH* 43:2, 285–96.

Feinstein, Charles H. (1959). "Home and foreign investment: some aspects of capital formation, finance and income in the United Kingdom, 1870–1913." Ph.D. thesis, University of Cambridge.

—— (1961). "Income and investment in the United Kingdom, 1856–1914." *EJ* 71:282, 367–85.

—— (1972). *National income, expenditure and output of the United Kingdom, 1855–1965.* Cambridge: Cambridge UP.

—— (1988). "The rise and fall of the Williamson Curve." *JEH* 48: 3, 699–729.

—— (1990). "Benefits of backwardness and costs of continuity." In *Government and economies in the postwar world: economic policies and comparative performance, 1945–1985*, edited by Andrew Graham with Anthony Seldon, pp. 284–93. London: Routledge.

—— (1997). "Technical progress and technology transfer in a centrally planned economy: the experience of the USSR, 1917–87." In *Chinese technology transfer in the 1990s: current experience, historical problems and international perspectives*, edited by Charles Feinstein and Christopher Howe, pp. 62–81. Cheltenham, UK; Lyme, N. H.: Edward Elgar.

—— (1998). "Pessimism perpetuated: real wages and the standard of living in Britain during and after the Industrial Revolution." *JEH* 58:3, 625–58.

——, ed. (1967). *Socialism, capitalism and economic growth: essays presented to Maurice Dobb.* Cambridge: Cambridge UP.

Feinstein, C. H.; with K. Maywald (1965). *Domestic capital formation in the United Kingdom, 1920–1938.* Cambridge: Cambridge UP.

Feinstein, Charles H., Peter Temin, and Gianni Toniolo (1997). *The European economy between the wars.* Oxford; New York: Oxford UP. [Revised and expanded edition, Oxford, forthcoming.]

Feinstein, Charles H., and Sidney Pollard, eds (1988). *Studies in capital formation in the United Kingdom, 1750–1920.* Oxford; New York: Clarendon Press.

Fenoaltea, Stefano (1973). "The discipline and they: notes on counterfactual methodology and the 'new' economic history." *JEEH* 2: 3, 729–46.

—— (1975). "The rise and fall of a theoretical model: the manorial system." *JEH* 35:2, 386–409.

Fenstermaker, Joseph Van (1965). *The development of American commercial banking: 1782–1837.* Kent, Ohio: Kent State UP.

Feynman, Richard P. (1999). *The pleasure of finding things out.* Edited by Jeffrey Robbins. Cambridge, Mass.: Perseus Books.

Field, Alexander J. (1981). "The problem with neoclassical institutional economics: a

critique with special reference to the North–Thomas model of pre-1500 Europe." *EEH* 18:2, 174–98.
—— (1983). "Land abundance, interest–profit rates, and 19th-century American and British technology." *JEH* 43: 2, 405–31.
—— (1987). "The future of economic history." In *The future of economic history*, edited by Alexander J. Field, pp. 1–41. Boston: Kluwer-Nijhoff.
—— (1996). "Nathan Rosenberg." In *American economists of the late twentieth century*, edited by Warren J. Samuels, 238–58. Cheltenham, UK; Brookfield, Vt.: Edward Elgar.
Field, Elizabeth B. (1988). "The relative efficiency of slavery revisited: a translog production function approach." *AER* 78:3, 543–9.
Fine, Ben, and Dimitris Milonakis (2003). "From principle of pricing to pricing of principle: rationality and irrationality in the economic history of Douglass North." *Comparative Studies in Society and History* 45:3, 546–70.
Finley, Moses I. (1973). *The ancient economy*. Berkeley, Cal.: University of California Press.
Fishback, Price V. (1986). "Did coal miners 'Owe Their Souls to the Company Store?'; theory and evidence from the early 1900s." *JEH* 46:4, 1011–29.
Fishlow, Albert (1961). "The Trustee Savings Banks, 1817–1861." *JEH* 21:1, 26–40.
—— (1964). "Antebellum interregional trade reconsidered." *AER* 54:2, 352–64. Reprinted in Andreano, ed. (1965), pp. 187–200, with a "postscript," pp. 209–12.
—— (1965). *American railroads and the transformation of the antebellum economy*. Cambridge, Mass.: Harvard UP. [Awarded the David A. Wells Prize for 1963–1964; *Harvard Economic Studies, v.* 127.]
—— (1966a). "Productivity and technological change in the railroad sector, 1840–1910." In CRIW (1966), pp. 583–646.
—— (1966b). "Levels of nineteenth-century investment in education." *JEH* 26:4, 418–36. Reprinted with omissions in Fogel & Engerman, eds (1971), pp. 265–73.
—— (1972a). "Origins and consequences of import substitution in Brazil." In *International economics and development: essays in honor of Raul Prebisch*, edited by Luis Eugenio Di Marco, pp. 311–65. New York: Academic Press.
—— (1972b). "Brazilian size distribution of income." *AER: P & P* 69:2, 391–402.
—— (1974). "The New Economic History revisited." *JEEH* 3:2, 453–67.
—— (1989a). "Lessons of the 1890s for the 1980s." In *Debt, stabilization and development: essays in memory of Carlos Diaz-Alejandro*, edited by Guillermo Calvo *et al.*, pp. 19–47. Oxford; Cambridge, Mass.: Blackwell.
—— (1989b). "A tale of two Presidents: the political economy of crisis management." In *Democratizing Brazil: problems of transition and consolidation*, edited by Alfred Stepan, pp. 83–119. New York: Oxford UP.
—— (2003). "Review essay" of Gerschenkron (1962). EH.Net Economic History Services, Feb 14, 2003, URL: <http://www.eh.net/bookreviews/library/fishlow.shtml>.
—— *et al.* (1994). *Miracle or design?: lessons from the East Asian experience*. Washington, D.C.: Overseas Development Council. [Policy Essay No. 11.]
Fishlow, Albert, and Paul A. David (1961). "Resource allocation in an imperfect market setting." *Journal of Political Economy* 69:6, 529–46.
Fishlow, Albert, and Robert W. Fogel (1971). "Quantitative economic history: an interim evaluation. Past trends and present tendencies." *JEH* 31:1, 15–42.
Fitzpatrick, Brian (1939). *British imperialism and Australia, 1789–1833: an economic history of Australasia*. Melbourne: Melbourne UP.

—— (1941). *The British Empire in Australia: an economic history, 1834–1939*. Melbourne: Melbourne UP.

Flinn, M. W. (1970). *British population growth, 1700–1850*. London: Macmillan.

Floud, Roderick (1973). *An introduction to quantitative methods for historians*. Princeton, N. J.: Princeton UP. Second edition, 1979.

—— (1976). *The British machine tool industry, 1850–1914*. Cambridge: Cambridge UP.

—— (1987). "cliometrics." In *The new Palgrave: a dictionary of economics*, edited by John Eatwell, Murray Milgate and Peter Newman, vol. 1, pp. 452–4. London: Macmillan, 1987.

—— (2001). "In at the beginning of British Cliometrics." In Hudson, ed. (2001), pp. 86–90.

——, ed. (1974). *Essays in quantitative economic history*. Oxford: Oxford UP.

Floud, Roderick, Kenneth Wachter, and Annabel Gregory (1990). *Height, health and history: nutritional status in the United Kingdom, 1750–1980*. Cambridge: Cambridge UP.

Floud, Roderick, and Paul Johnson, eds (2004). *The Cambridge economic history of Britain*. (Three vol.) Cambridge: Cambridge UP.

Floud, Roderick, and Deirdre [Donald] McCloskey, eds (1981). *The economic history of Britain since 1700*. (Two vol.) Cambridge: Cambridge UP. Second edition (Three vol.), 1994.

Fogel, Robert W. (1960). *The Union Pacific Railroad: a case in premature enterprise*. Baltimore: Johns Hopkins UP.

—— (1964). *Railroads and American economic growth: essays in econometric history*. Baltimore: Johns Hopkins UP.

—— (1965). "The reunification of economic history with economic theory." *AER: P&P* 55:2, 92–8.

—— (1967). "The specification problem in economic history." *JEH* 27:3, 283–308. Reprinted in Temin, ed. (1973), pp. 137–64.

—— (1979). "Notes on the social saving controversy." *JEH* 39:1, 1–54. [Presidential address, EHA, 1978.] Reprinted in Whaples & Betts, eds (1995), pp. 366–425.

—— (1982). "Circumstantial evidence in 'scientific' and traditional history." In *Philosophy and history and contemporary historiography*, edited by David Carr, William Dray, and Theodore Geraets, pp. 61–112. Ottawa: University of Ottawa Press.

—— (1989a). *Without consent or contract: the rise and fall of American Negro slavery*. New York: W.W. Norton.

—— (1989b). "Afterword: Some notes on the scientific methods of Simon Kuznets." In Kuznets (1989), pp. 413–38.

—— (1993). "Second thoughts on the European escape from hunger: famines, chronic malnutrition, and mortality rates." In *Nutrition and poverty*, edited by S. R. Osmani, pp. 243–86. Oxford: Clarendon Press.

—— (1994a). "Economic growth, population theory, and physiology: the bearing of long-term processes on the making of economic policy." *AER* 84:3, 369–95. [Nobel Memorial Prize lecture.]

—— (1994b). "Autobiography." From *Le Prix Nobel 1993*, as at URL: <http://nobelprize.org/nobel_prizes/economics/laureates/1993/fogel-autobio.html>.

—— (1995). "History with numbers: the American experience." In *Towards an international economic and social history: essays in honour of Paul Bairoch*, edited by Bouda Etemad, Jean Batou and Thomas David, pp. 46–56. Geneva: Editions Passé Présent.

—— (1996). *A life of learning*. New York: American Council of Learned Societies, Occasional Paper No. 34. [Charles Homer Haskins Lecture for 1996.]

—— (1997). "Douglass C. North and economic theory." In *The frontiers of the New Institutional Economics*, edited by John N. Drobak and John V. C. Nye, pp. 13–28. San Diego, Cal.: Academic Press.

—— (2000). "Simon S. Kuznets April 30, 1901–July 9, 1985." NBER Working Paper 7787.

—— (2003). *The slavery debates, 1952–1990: a retrospective*. Baton Rouge, La.: Louisiana State UP. [Walter Lynwood Fleming Lectures in Southern History, 2001.]

—— (2004a). *The escape from hunger and premature death, 1700–2100. Europe, America and the Third World*. Cambridge; New York: Cambridge UP.

—— (2004b). "Changes in the process of aging during the twentieth century: findings and procedures of the *Early Indicators* Project." *Population and Development Review* 30: supplement, 19–47.

—— (2004c). "High performing Asian economies." NBER Working Paper No. 10752.

—— (2005). "Why China is likely to achieve its growth objectives." Paper presented at the 20th Annual Meeting of the Chinese Economists Society, Chongqing City, China, June 24–26, 2005.

Fogel, Robert W., and Dora L. Costa (1997). "A theory of technophysio evolution, with some implications for forecasting population, health care costs, and pension costs." *Demography* 34:1, 49–66.

Fogel, Robert William, and G. R. Elton (1983). *Which Road to the Past? Two Views of History*. New Haven, Conn.; London: Yale UP.

Fogel, Robert William, and Stanley L. Engerman (1969). "A model for the explanation of industrial expansion during the nineteenth century: with an application to the American iron industry." *Journal of Political Economy* 77:3, 306–28. Reprinted with revisions in Fogel & Engerman, eds (1971), pp. 148–62.

—— (1971a). "The relative efficiency of slavery: a comparison of northern and southern agriculture in 1860." *EEH* 8, 353–67.

—— (1971b). "The economics of slavery." In Fogel & Engerman, eds (1971), pp. 311–41.

—— (1974). *Time on the cross: the economics of American Negro slavery*. (Two vol.) Boston: Little, Brown.

——, eds (1971). *The reinterpretation of American economic history*. New York: Harper & Row.

——, eds (1992). *Without consent or contract: technical papers on slavery*. (Two vol.) New York: W.W. Norton.

Fogel, Robert W., Stanley L. Engerman, James Trussell, Roderick Floud, Clayne L. Pope, and Larry T. Wimmer (1978). "The economics of mortality in North America, 1650–1910: a description of a research project." *Historical Methods* 11 (Spring), 75–109.

Fogel, Robert William, and Ralph A. Galantine (1992). "The change in voter alignment in the North between 1852 and 1860: an exploratory analysis." In Fogel & Engerman, eds (1992), pp. 496–585.

Fogel, Robert William, Ralph A. Galantine, and Richard L. Manning (1992). *Without consent or contract: the rise and fall of American slavery: evidence and methods*. New York: W. W. Norton

Ford, A. G. (1962). *The Gold Standard, 1880–1914: Britain and Argentina*. Oxford: Clarendon Press.

Fores, Michael (1981). "The myth of a British industrial revolution." *History* 66:217, 181–98.

Forster, Robert (1978). "Achievements of the *Annales* school." *JEH* 38:1, 58–76.

Friedman, Milton, and Simon Kuznets (1945). *Income from independent professional practice*. New York: NBER. NBER Publications; No. 45.

Friedman, Milton, and Anna Jacobson Schwartz (1963). *A monetary history of the United*

States, 1867–1960. Princeton, N.J.: Princeton UP. [NBER Studies in Business Cycles, no. 12.]

—— (1970). *Monetary statistics of the United States: estimates, sources, methods*. New York: NBER. [NBER Studies in Business Cycles, no. 20.]

—— (1982). *Monetary trends in the United States and the United Kingdom, their relation to income, prices, and interest rates, 1867–1975*. Chicago: University of Chicago Press. [NBER Research Monograph.]

Gaber, Ivor (2005a). "The origins of the ESRC." *Social Sciences* 59, 7–9.

—— (2005b). "1965–2004: Forty years of social science research." *Social Sciences* 60, 6–9.

Galambos, Louis (2003). "Identity and the boundaries of business history: an essay on consensus and creativity." In *Business history around the world*, edited by Franco Amatori and Geoffrey Jones, pp. 11–30. Cambridge: Cambridge UP.

Gallman, Robert E. (1960). "Commodity output, 1839–1899." In CRIW (1960), pp. 13–67.

—— (1966). "Gross National Product in the United States, 1834–1909." In CRIW (1966), pp. 3–76. Reprinted in Temin, ed. (1973), pp. 19–43, appendix omitted.

—— (1969). "Trends in the size distribution of wealth in the nineteenth century: some speculations." In Soltow, ed. (1969), pp. 1–25.

—— (1970). "Self-sufficiency of the cotton economy of the antebellum South." *AgHist* 44:1, 5–24. Reprinted in Parker, ed. (1970), 5–24.

—— (1977). "Some notes on the New Social History." *JEH* 37:1, 3–12. [Presidential address, EHA, 1976.]

—— (1979). "Slavery and Southern economic growth." *SEJ* 45:4, 1007–22. [Presidential address, Southern Economic Association, 1978.]

—— (1980). "Economic growth." In *Encyclopedia of American economic history, v. 1*, edited by Glenn Porter, pp. 133–50. New York: Charles Scribner's Sons.

—— (1994). "The Nobel laureates." *NCS* 9:3, 24–6.

—— (2000). "Economic growth and structural change in the long nineteenth century." In Engerman & Gallman, eds (1996, 2000), vol. 2, pp. 1–55.

Gallman, Robert E., and John Joseph Wallis, eds (1992). *American economic growth and standards of living before the Civil War*. Chicago; London: University of Chicago Press. [NBER Conference Report.]

Gayer, Arthur D. (1930). "Industrial fluctuation and unemployment in England, 1815–1850." D. Phil. dissertation, University of Oxford.

—— (1935). "The Banking Act of 1935." *Quarterly Journal of Economics* 50:4, 97–116.

——, ed. (1937). *The lessons of monetary experience; essays in honor of Irving Fisher, presented to him on the occasion of his seventieth birthday*. New York: Farrar & Rinehart.

Gayer, Arthur D., W. W. Rostow, and Anna Jacobson Schwartz; with the assistance of Isaiah Frank (1953). *The growth and fluctuation of the British economy, 1790–1850: an historical, statistical, and theoretical study of Britain's economic development*. 2 vols. Oxford: Clarendon Press. Reprinted, with a new introduction by W. W. Rostow and Anna Jacobson Schwartz; Hassocks, England: Harvester, 1975.

Genovese, Eugene D. (1962). "The significance of the slave plantation for Southern economic development." *Journal of Southern History* 28:4, 422–37.

—— (1994). "Robert W. Fogel: historian." *NCS* 9:3, 1 & 16–18.

Gerschenkron, Alexander (1947). "The rate of industrial growth in Russia since 1885." *JEH* 7:supplement, 144–74.

Gerschenkron, Alexander, assisted by Alexander Ehrlich (1951). *A dollar index of Soviet machinery output, 1927–28 to 1937*. Santa Monica, Cal.: Rand Corporation.

—— (1952). "Economic backwardness in historical perspective." In *The progress of underdeveloped areas*, edited by Bert F. Hoselitz, pp. 3–29. Chicago: University of Chicago Press. [Harris Foundation lectures, 1951.] Reprinted in Gerschenkron (1962), pp. 5–30.

—— (1962). *Economic backwardness in historical perspective*. Cambridge, Mass.: Belknap Press of Harvard UP.

—— (1967). "The discipline and I." *JEH* 27:4, 443–59. [Presidential address, EHA, 1967.]

Gilbert, Milton, and Irving B. Kravis (1954). *An international comparison of national products and the purchasing power of currencies: A study of the United States, the United Kingdom, France, Germany, and Italy*. Paris: Organisation for European Economic Cooperation.

Ginter, Donald E. (1992). *A measure of wealth: the English Land Tax in historical analysis*. Montreal; Buffalo, N. Y.: McGill–Queen's UP.

Goggin, Jacqueline (1992). "Challenging sexual discrimination in the historical profession: women historians and the American Historical Association, 1890–1940." *AHR* 97:3, 769–802.

Goldin, Claudia (1990). *Understanding the gender gap. An economic history of American women*. New York; Oxford: Oxford UP.

—— (2006). "The quiet revolution that transformed women's employment, education, and family." *AER: P&P* 96:2, 1–21. [Richard T. Ely Lecture, January 2006.]

Goldin, Claudia, and Hugh Rockoff, eds (1992). *Strategic factors in nineteenth century American economic history: a volume to honor Robert W. Fogel*. Chicago; London: University of Chicago Press. [NBER Conference Report.]

Goldstone, J. A. (1986). "The demographic revolution in England: a re-examination." *Population Studies* 40:1, 5–33.

Gómez-Ibáñez, José, and John R. Meyer (1991). *Private toll roads in the United States: the early experience of Virginia and California*. Cambridge, Mass.: Harvard UP.

—— (1992). *The political economy of transport privatization: successes, failures, and lessons from developed and developing countries*. Cambridge, Mass.: Harvard UP.

—— (1993). *Going private: the international experience with transport privatization*. Washington, D.C.: The Brookings Institution.

Goodrich, Carter (1960). "Economic history: one field or two?" *JEH* 20:4, 531–8.

Grantham, George (1989). "Agricultural supply during the Industrial Revolution: French evidence and European implications." *JEH* 49:1, 43–72.

—— (1997). "The French cliometric revolution: a survey of cliometric contributions to French economic history." *EREH* 1:3, 353–405.

Gras, Norman S. B. (1927). "The rise and development of economic history." *EHR*, 1st series 1:1, 12–34.

—— (1962). *Development of business history up to 1950. Selections from the unpublished work . . .* [Compiled and edited by Ethel C. Gras.] Ann Arbor, Mich.: Edwards Brothers.

Gray, Louis Cecil (1933). *History of agriculture in the southern United States*. Washington, D.C.: Carnegie Institution of Washington.

Greasley, David (1989). "British wages and income, 1856–1913 – a revision." *EEH* 26:2, 248–59.

Green, Alan, and Frank D. Lewis (2002). "Malcolm C. Urquhart, 1913–2002." *Proceedings of the Royal Society of Canada*, seventh ser., 1, 246–9.

Greif, Avner (2006). *Institutions and the path to the modern economy: lessons from medieval trade.* Cambridge: Cambridge UP.

Gutman, Herbert (1975). *Slavery and the numbers game: a critique of Time on the Cross.* Urbana, Ill.: University of Illinois Press.

Habakkuk, H. J. (1940a). "Free Trade and commercial expansion, 1853–70." In *The Cambridge history of the British Empire, volume II, the growth of the new Empire, 1783–1870,* edited by J. H. Rose, A. P. Newton and E. A. Benians. Cambridge: Cambridge UP.

—— (1940b). "English landownership, 1680–1740." *EHR,* 1st series 10, 2–17.

—— (1953). "English population in the eighteenth century." *EHR* 6:2, 117–33.

—— (1958). "The economic history of modern Britain." *JEH* 18:4, 486–501.

—— (1962). *American and British technology in the nineteenth century; the search for labour-saving inventions.* Cambridge: Cambridge UP.

—— (1971a). "Economic history and economic theory." *Daedalus* 100:2, 305–22. Reprinted in *Historical Studies Today,* edited by Felix Gilbert and Stephen R. Graubard, pp. 27–44. New York: W. W. Norton, 1972.

—— (1971b). *Population growth and economic development since 1750.* Leicester: Leicester UP. [Based upon the Arthur Pool Memorial Lectures, University of Leicester, 1968.]

—— (1994). *Marriage, debt, and the estates system: English landownership, 1650–1950.* Oxford: Clarendon Press; New York: Oxford UP.

Hägerstrand, Torsten (1967). *Innovation diffusion as a spatial process.* Chicago: University of Chicago Press.

Hahn, Frank (1991). "The next hundred years." *EJ* 101:1, 47–50.

Hammond, Bray (1957). *Banks and politics in America, from the Revolution to the Civil War.* Princeton, N.J.: Princeton UP.

Hammond, Claire Holton (1999). "Women in the economics profession." In *The Elgar companion to feminist economics,* edited by Janice Peterson and Margaret Lewis, pp. 757–64. Cheltenham, UK; Northampton, Mass.: Edward Elgar.

Hannah, Leslie (1999) "Marshall's 'trees' and the global 'forest': were 'giant redwoods' different?" In Lamoreaux *et al.*, eds (1999), pp. 253–86.

Harley, C. Knick (1982). "British industrialization before 1841: evidence of slower growth during the Industrial Revolution." *JEH* 42:2, 267–89.

—— (1999). "Reassessing the Industrial Revolution: a macro view." In *The British Industrial Revolution: an economic perspective,* second edition, edited by Joel Mokyr (1999), pp. 160–205. Boulder, Col.: Westview.

—— (2001). "Review" of Deane & Cole ([1962] 1967). EH.Net Economic History Services, Sept 18, 2001, URL: <http://www.eh.net/bookreviews/library/harley.shtml>.

Harley, C. K., and N. F. R. Crafts (2000). "Simulating the two views of the Industrial Revolution." *JEH* 60:4, 819–41.

Harte, N. B. (1971). "Introduction: the making of economic history." In Harte, ed. (1971), pp. *xi–xxxix.*

—— (1977). "Trends in publications on the economic and social history of Great Britain and Ireland, 1925–74." *EHR* 30:1, 20–41.

—— (2001). "The Economic History Society, 1926–2001." In Hudson, ed. (2001), pp. 1–12.

——, ed. (1971). *The study of economic history. Collected inaugural lectures, 1893–1970.* London: Frank Cass.

Hartwell, R. M. (1954). *The economic development of Van Diemen's Land 1820–1850.* Melbourne: Melbourne UP.

—— (1955). "The Yorkshire woollen and worsted industry, 1800–1850." D. Phil. thesis, University of Oxford.
—— (1959). "Interpretations of the Industrial Revolution in England: a methodological inquiry." *JEH* 19:2, 229–49.
—— (1961). "The *rising* standard of living in England, 1800–1850." *EHR* 13:3, 397–416.
—— (1971a). *The Industrial Revolution and economic growth.* London: Methuen.
—— (1971b). "Is the New Economic History an export product? A comment on J. R. T. Hughes." In McCloskey, ed. (1971), pp. 413–22.
—— (1995). *A History of the Mont Pelerin Society.* Indianapolis, Ind.: Liberty Fund.
—— (2001). "What economic history has meant to me." In Hudson, ed. (2001), pp. 123–6.
——, ed. (1970). *The industrial revolution.* Oxford: Basil Blackwell. [Nuffield College Studies in Economic History, No. 1.]
Hawke, G. R. (1970). *Railways and economic growth in England and Wales, 1840–1870.* Oxford: Clarendon Press.
Hawthorn, Geoffrey (1991). *Plausible worlds: possibility and understanding in history and the social sciences.* Cambridge; New York: Cambridge UP.
Hayek, F. A., ed. (1954). *Capitalism and the historians.* Chicago: University of Chicago Press.
Head, Keith (1994). "Infant industry protection in the steel rail industry." *Journal of International Economics* 37: 3–4, 141–65.
Heaton, Herbert (1938). "Clapham's contribution to economic history." *Political Science Quarterly* 53:4, 599–602.
—— (1941). "The early history of the Economic History Association." *JEH* Issue Supplement: The Tasks of Economic History, 107–9.
—— (1949). "The making of an economic historian." [E. F. Gay] *JEH*, Supplement 9, 1–18. [Presidential address, EHA, 1949.]
—— (1952). *A scholar in action, Edwin F. Gay.* Cambridge, Mass.: Harvard UP.
—— (1965). "Twenty-five years of the Economic History Association: a reflective evaluation." *JEH* 25:4, 465–79.
Heilbroner, Robert L. (1953). *The worldly philosophers: the lives, times, and ideas of the great economic thinkers.* New York: Simon & Schuster. Seventh edition, 1999.
Hickman, W. Braddock (1958). *Corporate bond quality and investor experience.* Princeton, N.J.: Princeton UP. [NBER Financial Research Program, Studies in Corporate Bond Financing, 2.]
Hicks, J. R. (1950). *A contribution to the theory of the trade cycle.* Oxford: Clarendon Press.
Hilton, Rodney, ed. (1976). *The transition from feudalism to capitalism.* London: New Left Books.
Hobsbawm, E. J. (1957). "The British standard of living 1790–1850." *EHR* 10:1, 46–68.
Hobsbawm, E. J., and R. M. Hartwell (1963). "The standard of living during the Industrial Revolution: a discussion." *EHR* 16:1, 119–34; 135–46.
Hodgson, Geoffrey M. (2001). *How economics forgot history. The problem of historical specificity in social science.* London; New York: Routledge.
Hoffman, Philip T. (1986). "Taxes and agrarian life in early modern France: land sales, 1550–1730." *JEH* 46:1, 37–55.
Hoffman, Philip T., and Jean-Laurent Rosenthal (2000). "New work in French economic history." *French Historical Studies* 23:3, 439–53.
Honeyman, Katrina (2000). *Women, gender and industrialisation in England, 1700–1870.* Basingstoke, UK: Macmillan; New York: St Martin's Press.

—— (2005). "Review of *The European linen industry in historical perspective*, edited by Brenda Collins and Philip Ollerenshaw (2003)." *BHR* 79:1, 175–7.

Honeyman, Katrina, and Jordan Goodman (1991). "Women's work, labour markets and gender conflict in Europe, 1500–1900." *EHR* 44:4, 608–28.

Hoppit, Julian (1990). "Counting the Industrial Revolution." *EHR* 43:2, 173–93.

Horwich, George, and James P. Quirk, eds (1981). *Essays in contemporary fields of economics: in honor of Emanuel T. Weiler (1914–1979)*. West Lafayette, Ind.: Purdue UP.

Hounshell, David (1997). "The Leonardo da Vinci Medal." *Technology and Culture* 38:3, 721–5. [Citation.]

Hudson, Pat (1994). "Review" of O'Brien & Quinault, eds (1993). *BHR* 68:4, 610–11.

—— (2000). *History by numbers: an introduction to quantitative approaches*. London: Arnold; New York: Oxford UP.

—— (2003). "Economic history." In *Writing history: theory and practice*, edited by Stefan Berger, Heiko Feldner and Kevin Passmore, pp. 223–42. London: Arnold.

——, ed. (2001). *Living Economic and Social History*. Glasgow: Economic History Society.

Hughes, Jonathan R. T. (1956). "The commercial crisis of 1857." *OEP n.s.* 8:2. Reprinted in *PFP*, pp. 207–34.

—— (1959). "Foreign trade and balanced growth: the historical framework." *AER: P&P* 49:2, 330–7. Reprinted in *PFP*, pp. 83–90.

—— (1960). *Fluctuations in trade, industry, and finance; a study of British economic development, 1850–1860*. Oxford: Clarendon Press.

—— (1966a) *The vital few: American economic progress and its protagonists*. Boston: Houghton Mifflin. Paperbound reissue, with a new introduction, Oxford UP, 1973. Expanded edn, *The vital few: the entrepreneur and American economic progress*, Oxford UP, 1986.

—— (1966b). "Fact and theory in economic history." *Explorations in Entrepreneurial History/ 2nd series* 3:2; 75–100. Reprinted in *PFP*, pp. 35–56 and in Andreano, ed. (1970), pp. 261–76.

—— (1970). *Industrialization and economic history: theses and conjectures*. New York: McGraw-Hill.

—— (1971). "Is the new economic history an export product?" In McCloskey, ed. (1971), 401–12.

—— (1976). *Social control in the colonial economy*. Charlottesville, Va.: UP of Virginia.

—— (1977). *The governmental habit: economic controls from colonial times to the present*. New York: Basic Books. Revised edn., *The governmental habit redux: economic controls from colonial times to the present*. Princeton, N. J.: Princeton UP, 1991.

—— (1981). "A note on early Cliometrica." In Horwich & Quirk, eds (1981), pp. 361–4.

—— (1982a). "The great strike at Nushagak Station, 1951: institutional gridlock." *JEH* 42:1, 1–20. [Presidential address, EHA, 1981.]

—— (1982b). "Douglass North as a teacher." In Ransom, Sutch & Walton, eds (1982), pp. 3–11.

—— (1983). *American economic history*. Glenview, Ill.: Scott Foresman. [Later edns, 1987, 1990.]

—— (1994). "A world elsewhere: the importance of starting English." In Thompson, ed. (1994), pp. 63–88.

Hughes, Jonathan, and Louis P. Cain (2007). *American economic history*, 7th edition. Boston: Addison-Wesley. [Previous edns 1994, 1998, 2003.]

Hughes, Jonathan R. T., and Stanley Reiter (1958). "The first 1,945 British steamships." *Journal of the American Statistical Association* 53:2, 453–83. Reprinted in *PFP*, pp. 453–83.

Hughes, Jonathan R. T., and Nathan Rosenberg (1963). "The United States business cycle before 1860: some problems of interpretation." *EHR* 15:3, 476–93. Reprinted in *PFP*, pp. 187–206.

Huizinga, Johan (1924). *The waning of the Middle Ages : a study of the forms of life, thought and art in France and the Netherlands in the XIVth and XVth centuries*. London: E. Arnold. [First edition in Dutch, 1919; numerous later editions.]

Hutchinson, William K., and Samuel H. Williamson (1971). "The self-sufficiency of the antebellum South: estimates of the food supply." *JEH* 31:3, 591–612.

Hutt, W. H. (1926). "The factory system of the early 19th century." *Economica* 16 (Mar.), 78–93. Reprinted in Hayek, ed. (1954), pp. 160–88.

Intriligator, Michael D., ed. (1971). *Frontiers of quantitative economics*. Amsterdam: North-Holland.

Inwood, Kris (1994). "Review" of Urquhart (1993). *Canadian Journal of Economics* 27:2, 505–8.

James, John A., and Jonathan S. Skinner (1985). "The resolution of the labor-scarcity paradox." *JEH* 45:3, 513–40.

James, John A., and Mark Thomas, eds (1994). *Capitalism in context: essays on economic development and cultural change in honor of R. M. Hartwell*. Chicago: University of Chicago Press.

Jenks, Leland H. (1944). "Railroads as an economic force in American development." *JEH* 4:1, 1–20.

John, Richard R. (1997). "Elaborations, revisions, dissents: Alfred D. Chandler, Jr.'s 'The Visible Hand' after twenty years." *BHR* 71:2, 151–200.

Jones, Eric L. (1960). "Eighteenth-century changes in Hampshire chalkland farming." *AgHistR* 8, 5–19. Reprinted in Jones (1974), pp. 23–40.

—— (1968). "Agricultural origins of industry." *Past & Present* 40, 58–71. Reprinted in Jones (1974), pp. 128–42.

—— (1974). *Agriculture and the industrial revolution*. Oxford: Blackwell; New York: Wiley.

—— (1981). *The European miracle: environments, economies and geopolitics in the history of Europe and Asia*. Cambridge; New York: Cambridge UP. Second edition 1987; third edition 2003.

—— (1988). *Growth recurring: economic change in world history*. Oxford: Oxford UP. Second edition, Ann Arbor, Mich.: University of Michigan Press, 2000.

—— (1990). "Economics in the history mirror." *Journal of Interdisciplinary Economics* 3:2, 157–72.

—— (1993). "An appreciation of Max Hartwell." In O'Brien & Quinault, eds (1993), pp. 283–7.

—— (2002). *The record of global economic development*. Cheltenham, UK; Northampton, Mass.: Elgar.

—— (2006). *Cultures merging: a historical and economic critique of culture*. Princeton, N. J.: Princeton UP.

Jones, G. T. (1933). *Increasing return: a study of the relation between the size and efficiency of industries with special reference to the history of selected British & American industries 1850–1910*. Cambridge: Cambridge UP. [Edited by Colin Clark.]

Jones, Kit (1998). *Sixty years of economic research. A brief history of the National Institute of Economic and Social Research 1938–98*. London: NIESR. [Occasional papers, 52.]

Jones, Ronald W. (1971). "A three-factor model in theory, trade and history." In *Trade, balance of payments, and growth: papers in international economics in honor of Charles P.*

Kindleberger, edited by Jagdish N. Bhagwati *et al.*, pp. 3–21. Amsterdam: North-Holland; New York: American Elsevier.

Kadish, Alon (1989). *Historians, economists, and economic history*. London; New York: Routledge.

Kantor, Shawn Everett (1991). "Razorbacks, ticky cows, and the closing of the Georgia open range: the dynamics of institutional change uncovered." *JEH* 51:4, 861–86.

Kapuria-Foreman, Vibha, and Mark Perlman (1995). "An economic historian's economist: remembering Simon Kuznets." *EJ* 105, 1524–47.

Katz, Barry M. (1989). *Foreign intelligence. Research and Analysis in the Office of Strategic Services, 1942–45*. Cambridge, Mass.; London: Harvard UP.

Keynes, John Maynard (1936). *The general theory of employment, interest and money*. London: Macmillan and Co.

Keynes, John Neville (1891). *The scope and method of political economy*. London; New York: Macmillan.

Kiewiet, D. Roderick, and Mathew D. McCubbins (1985). "Congressional appropriations and the electoral connection." *Journal of Politics* 47:1, 59–82.

Kilby, Peter (1987). "Stanley Lebergott: an appreciation." In Kilby, ed. (1987), pp. *xv–xxiii*.

——, ed. (1987). *Quantity & quiddity: essays in U.S. economic history*. Middletown, Conn.: Wesleyan UP.

Kindleberger, Charles P. (1991). *The life of an economist*. Cambridge, Mass.; Oxford: Basil Blackwell.

Kindleberger, Charles P., and Guido di Tella, eds (1982). *Economics in the long view. Essays in honour of W. W. Rostow*. 3 vol. New York; London: New York UP.

King, Willford I., Wesley C. Mitchell, Frederick R. Macaulay, and Oswald W. Knauth (1921–2). *Income in the United States, its amount and distribution: 1909–1919*. New York: Harcourt, Brace for NBER.

Kirkland, Edward C. (1932). *A history of American economic life*. New York: F. S. Crofts. [Fourth edition, 1969.]

Koepke, Nicola, and Joerg Baten (2005). "The biological standard of living in Europe during the last two millennia." *EREH* 9:1, 61–95.

Komlos, John (1987). "The height and weight of West Point cadets: dietary changes in antebellum America." *JEH* 47:4, 897–927.

—— ed. (1994). *Stature, living standards, and economic development: essays in anthropometric history*. Chicago: University of Chicago Press.

Komlos, John, and Scott Eddie, eds (1997). *Selected Cliometric studies on German economic history*. Stuttgart: Franz Steiner.

Koopmans, Tjalling C. (1947). "Measurement without theory." *REStat* 29:3, 161–72.

Koot, Gerard M. (1987). *English historical economics, 1870–1926. The rise of economic history and neomercantilism*. Cambridge; New York: Cambridge UP.

Kravis, Irving B., Alan Heston, and Robert Summers (1978). *World product and income: international comparisons of real gross product*. [Produced by the Statistical Office of the United Nations and the World Bank.] Baltimore: Published for the World Bank, Johns Hopkins UP.

Kuznets, Simon (1921). "Money wages of factory employees in Kharkov in 1920" (in Russian). In *Materials on labor statistics in Ukraine*, 2nd issue. Kharkov: Central Soviet of Trade Unions, Southern Bureau, Division of Statistics.

—— (1930). *Secular movements in production and prices; their nature and their bearing upon cyclical fluctuations*. Boston: Houghton Mifflin.

—— (1934). *National income, 1929–1932.* Senate Document No. 124, 73rd Cong. 2d sess. Washington, D.C.: Government Printing Office.

—— (1947). "Measurement of economic growth." *JEH:* supplement 7, 10–34.

—— (1956). "Quantitative aspects of the economic growth of nations. I. Levels and variability of rates of growth." *EDCC* 5:1, 5–94.

—— (1957). "Summary of discussion and postscript." *JEH* 17: 4, 545–53.

—— (1965). *Economic growth and structure: selected essays.* New York: W. W. Norton.

—— (1966). *Modern economic growth: rate, structure, and spread.* New Haven, Conn.: Yale UP.

—— (1989). *Economic development, the family, and income distribution: Selected essays.* Cambridge; New York: Cambridge UP.

Kuznets, Simon; assisted by Lillian Epstein and Elizabeth Jenks (1946). *National product since 1869.* New York: NBER.

Kuznets, Simon, and Dorothy Swaine Thomas, directors (1957–64). *Population redistribution and economic growth: United States, 1870–1950.* Philadelphia: American Philosophical Society. Memoirs of the American Philosophical Society; vols 45 (1957), 51 (1960), 61 (1964).

Lamoreaux, Naomi R. (1994). *Insider lending: banks, personal connections, and economic development in industrial New England.* Cambridge; New York: Cambridge UP for NBER.

—— (1998). "Economic history and the cliometric revolution." In Molho & Wood, eds (1998), pp. 59–84.

Lamoreaux, Naomi, Daniel M. G. Raff, and Peter Temin (2003). "Beyond markets and hierarchies: toward a new synthesis of American business history." *AHR*, 108:2, 404–33.

Lamoreaux, Naomi R., and Daniel M. G. Raff, eds (1995). *Coordination and information: historical perspectives on the organization of enterprise.* Chicago: University of Chicago Press.

Lamoreaux, Naomi R., Daniel M. G. Raff, and Peter Temin, eds (1999). *Learning by doing in markets, firms, and countries.* Chicago: University of Chicago Press.

Landau, Ralph, and Nathan Rosenberg (1992). "Successful commercialization in the chemical process industries." In *Technology and the wealth of nations*, edited by Nathan Rosenberg, Ralph Landau and David C. Mowery, pp. 73–120. Stanford, Cal.: Stanford UP.

Landes, David S. (1955). "The statistical analysis of Anglo-American economic development." *World Politics* 7:2, 326–36. [Review essay on Cairncross (1953) and Thomas (1954).]

—— (1968). *The unbound Prometheus: technological change and industrial development in Western Europe from 1750 to the present.* London: Cambridge UP.

—— (1978). "On avoiding Babel." *JEH* 38:1, 3–12. [Presidential address, EHA, 1977.]

—— (1998). *The wealth and poverty of nations: why some are so rich and some so poor.* New York: W. W. Norton.

—— (2001). "Review" of Chandler (1977). EH.Net Economic History Services, Feb 12, 2001, URL: <http://www.eh.net/bookreviews/library/landes.shtml>.

Landreth, Harry, and David C. Colander (2002). *History of economic thought*, 4th edition. Boston: Houghton Mifflin.

Lane, Frederick C. (1958). "Economic consequences of organized violence." *JEH* 18:4, 401–17. [Presidential address, EHA, 1958.]

Laslett, Peter (1965). *The world we have lost.* London: Methuen.

——, ed.; with the assistance of Richard Wall (1972). *Household and family in past time;*

comparative studies in the size and structure of the domestic group over the last three centuries . . . Cambridge: Cambridge UP.

Lazonick, William H. (1981). "Production relations, labor productivity, and choice of technique: British and U. S. cotton spinning." *JEH* 41:3, 491–516.

Lebergott, Stanley (1945a). "Shall we guarantee full employment?" *Harper's* 190 (Feb.), 193–202.

—— (1945b). "Forecasting the National Product." *AER* 35:1, 59–80.

—— (1964). *Manpower in economic growth; the American record since 1800.* New York: McGraw-Hill.

—— (1975). *The American economy: income, wealth and want.* Princeton, N. J.: Princeton UP.

—— (1981). "Through the blockade: the profitability and extent of cotton smuggling, 1861–1865." *JEH* 41:4, 867–88.

—— (1983). "Why the South lost: commercial purpose in the Confederacy." *JAH* 70:2, 58–74.

—— (1985). "The demand for land: The United States, 1820–1860." *JEH* 45:2, 181–212. [Presidential address, EHA, 1984.]

—— (1996). *Consumer expenditures: new measures & old motives.* Princeton, N. J.: Princeton UP.

Lee, C. H. (1977). *The quantitative approach to economic history.* London: Martin Robertson.

—— (1983). *Social science and history: an investigation into the application of theory and quantification in British economic and social history.* London: SSRC.

Legler, John B., Richard Sylla, and John J. Wallis (1988). "U. S. city finances and the growth of government, 1850–1902." *JEH* 48:2, 347–56.

Leunig, Timothy (2003). "A British industrial success: productivity in the Lancashire and New England cotton-spinning industries a century ago." *EHR* 56:1, 90–117.

Levenstein, Margaret (1998). *Accounting for growth: information systems and the creation of the large corporation.* Stanford, Cal.: Stanford UP.

Lewis, Frank D., and M. C. Urquhart (1999). "Growth and the standard of living in a pioneer economy: Upper Canada, 1826 to 1851." *William and Mary Quarterly*, 3rd Ser., 56:1, 151–81.

Lewis, W. Arthur (1955). *The theory of economic growth.* London: George Allen & Unwin Ltd.

Libecap, Gary D. (1989). "The political economy of crude oil cartelization in the United States, 1933–1972." *JEH* 49:4, 833–55.

—— (1992a). "Douglass C. North." In *New horizons in economic thought. Appraisals of leading economists*, edited by Warren J. Samuels, pp. 227–48. Brookfield, Vt.: Edward Elgar.

—— (1992b). "The rise of the Chicago packers and the origins of meat inspection and antitrust." *Economic Inquiry* 30:2, 242–62.

Liebowitz, Stan J., and Stephen E. Margolis (2002). *The economics of QWERTY: history, theory, and policy.* Edited, with an introduction, by Peter Lewin. New York: New York UP.

Lindauer, David L., and Michael Roemer, eds (1994). *Asia and Africa: legacies and opportunities in development.* San Francisco, Cal.: Institute for Contemporary Studies.

Lindert, Peter H. (1983). "English living standards, population growth, and Wrigley–Schofield." *EEH* 20:2, 131–55.

—— (2003). "Voice and growth: was Churchill right?" *JEH* 63:2, 315–50. [Presidential address, EHA, 2002.]

Lindert, Peter H., and Jeffrey G. Williamson (1983). "English workers' living standards during the Industrial Revolution: a new look." *EHR* 36:1, 1–25.

Long, Clarence D. (1958). *The labor force under changing income and employment.* Princeton, N. J.: Princeton UP. NBER, General series 65.

Lorwin, Val R., and Jacob M. Price, eds (1972). *The dimensions of the past. Materials, problems, and opportunities for quantitative work in history*. New Haven, Conn.: Yale UP.

Macaulay, Frederick R. (1938). *Some theoretical problems suggested by the movements of interest rates, bond yields and stock prices in the United States since 1856*. New York: NBER. Publications of the NBER, no. 33.

McClelland, Peter D. (1968). "Railroads, American growth, and the New Economic History: a critique." *JEH* 28:1, 102–23.

—— (1975). *Causal explanation and model building in history, economics, and the New Economic History*. Ithaca, N. Y.; London: Cornell UP.

McClelland, Peter D., and Alan L. Magdovitz (1981). *Crisis in the making, the political economy of New York State since 1945*. New York: Cambridge UP.

McCloskey, Deirdre (2001). "An interview with Deirdre McCloskey." *NCS* 16:2, 3–13. Interviewed by Mary Beth Combs.

McCloskey, Deirdre [Donald] N. (1970). "Did Victorian Britain fail?" *EHR* 23:3, 446–59. Reprinted in McCloskey (1981a), pp. 94–110.

—— (1976). "Does the past have useful economics?" *JEL* 14:2, 434–61. Reprinted in McCloskey (1981a), pp. 19–52, and in Whaples & Betts, eds (1995), pp. 3–37.

—— (1978). "The achievements of the Cliometric School." *JEH* 38:1, 13–28. Reprinted in McCloskey (1981a), pp. 3–18.

—— (1981a). *Enterprise and trade in Victorian Britain: essays in historical economics*. London; Boston: George Allen & Unwin.

—— (1981b). "The Industrial Revolution 1780–1860: a survey." In Floud & McCloskey, eds (1981), vol. 1, pp. 103–27.

—— (1985). *The rhetoric of economics*. Madison, Wis.: University of Wisconsin Press.

—— (1987). *Econometric history*. London: Macmillan.

—— (1992a). "Alexander Gerschenkron." *The American Scholar* 61:2, 241–6.

—— (1992b). "Robert William Fogel: an appreciation by an adopted student." In Goldin & Rockoff, eds (1992), pp. 14–25.

—— (1994). "Fogel and North: statics and dynamics in historical economics." *Scandinavian Journal of Economics* 96:2, 161–6.

——, ed. (1971). *Essays on a mature economy: Britain after 1840*. Princeton, N.J.: Princeton UP.

McCloskey, Deirdre [Donald] N., and George K. Hersh, Jr. (1990). *A bibliography of historical economics to 1980*. Cambridge; New York: Cambridge UP.

McCloskey, Deirdre [Donald] N., and Lars G. Sandberg (1971). "From damnation to redemption: judgments on the late Victorian entrepreneur." *EEH* 9:1, 89–108. Reprinted in McCloskey (1981a), pp. 55–72.

McGouldrick, Paul F. (1968). *New England textiles in the nineteenth century; profits and investment*. Cambridge, Mass.: Harvard UP.

Maddison, Angus (2001). *The world economy: a millennial perspective*. Paris: OECD.

—— (2003). *The world economy: historical statistics*. Paris: OECD.

—— (2004). "Quantifying and interpreting world development: macromeasurement before and after Colin Clark." *Australian Economic History Review* 44:1, 1–34.

Majewski, John. "Review" of Fishlow (1965). EH.Net Economic History Services, Sep 25 2006. URL: <http://eh.net/bookreviews/library/Majewski>.

Maloney, John (1976). "Marshall, Cunningham, and the emerging economics profession." *EHR* 29:3, 440–51.

Marczewski, Jean (1965). "Le produit physique de l'economie française." *Cahiers de l'Institut de Science Économique Appliquée* Serie AF, no. 4. Paris: ISÉA.

Margo, Robert A. (1990). *Race and schooling in the South, 1880–1950: an economic history.* Chicago: University of Chicago Press.
—— (2006). "Review" of Lebergott (1964). EH.Net Economic History Services, Feb 27 2006. URL: <http://eh.net/bookreviews/library/margo>.
Marshall, Alfred (1890). *Principles of economics. An introductory volume.* London; New York: Macmillan. [Eighth edition, 1920.]
Marx, Karl (1976 [1867]). *Capital: a critique of political economy, vol. 1.* Trans. from German and annotated by Ben Fowkes. London: Penguin Books, in association with New Left Review.
Mathias, Peter (2001). "Still living with the neighbours." In Hudson, ed. (2001), pp. 233–5.
Matthews, R. C. O. (1954a). "The trade cycle in Britain, 1790–1850." *OEP n.s.* 6:1, 1–32. [A review of Gayer, Rostow & Schwartz 1953.] Reprinted with a "Postscript" in *British economic fluctuations, 1790–1939*, edited by Derek H. Aldcroft and Peter Fearon, pp. 97–130. London: Macmillan; New York: St. Martin's Press, 1972.
—— (1954b). *A study in trade-cycle history; economic fluctuations in Great Britain, 1833–1842.* Cambridge: Cambridge UP.
—— (1959). *The trade cycle.* London: Nisbet. Published in the US as *The business cycle.* Chicago: University of Chicago Press, 1959. [Cambridge economic handbooks.]
—— (1971). "The new economic history in Britain: a comment on the papers by Hughes, Hartwell and Supple." In McCloskey, ed. (1971), pp. 431–3.
—— (1987). "An eclectic view from Cambridge: an interview." In *Arrow and the foundations of the theory of economic policy*, edited by George R. Feiwel, pp. 613–34. New York: New York UP. Interviewed by George Feiwel.
Matthews, R. C. O., C. H. Feinstein, and J. C. Odling-Smee (1982). *British economic growth, 1856–1973.* Oxford: Clarendon Press.
Matthews, Robin C. O., and Barry Supple (1991). "The ordeal of economic freedom: Marshall on economic history." *Quaderni di Storia dell'Economica Politica* 9:2–3, 189–213.
Meade, J. E., and Richard Stone (1941). "The construction of tables of national income, expenditure, savings and investment." *EJ* 51:202/203, 216–33.
Medawar, P. B. (1984). *The limits of science.* New York: Harper & Row.
Merton, Robert K. (1973). *The sociology of science; theoretical and empirical investigations.* Edited and with an introduction by Norman W. Storer. Chicago: University of Chicago Press.
Metzler, Lloyd A. (1941). "The nature and stability of inventory cycles." *REStat* 23:3, 113–29.
Meyer, John R. (1955a). "Business motivation and the investment decision: an econometric study of postwar investment patterns." Ph.D. dissertation, Harvard University. [Awarded the David A. Wells Prize for 1954–5, jointly with the dissertation of Edwin Kuh.] Published in revised form as *The investment decision: an empirical study*, by John R. Meyer and Edwin Kuh. Cambridge, Mass.: Harvard UP. [Harvard Economic Studies, vol. 102.]
—— (1955b). "An input-output approach to evaluating the influence of exports on British industrial production in the late 19th century." *Explorations in Entrepreneurial History* 8:1, 12–34. Reprinted in Conrad & Meyer (1964), pp. 183–220.
—— (1997). "Notes on Cliometrics' fortieth." *AER: P&P* 87:2, 409–11.
Meyer, John R., and Alfred H. Conrad (1957). "Economic theory, statistical inference, and economic history." *JEH* 17:4, 524–44. Reprinted in Conrad & Meyer (1964), pp. 3–30.
Meyer, John R., and Edwin Kuh (1957). "How extraneous are extraneous estimates?" *REStat* 39:3, 380–93.
Middleton, Roger (1998). *Charlatans or saviours? Economists and the British economy from Marshall to Meade.* Cheltenham, UK; Northampton, Mass.: Edward Elgar.

Milgrom, Paul R., Douglass C. North, and Barry R. Weingast (1990). "The role of institutions in the revival of trade: the law merchant, private judges, and the Champagne fairs." *Economics and Politics* 2: 1–23.

Mitch, David (1995). "Parker receives Hughes Prize." *NCS* 10:3, 7.

Mitchell, B. R.; with Phyllis Deane (1962). *Abstract of British historical statistics*. Cambridge: Cambridge UP.

Mitchell, Wesley Clair (1913). *Business cycles*. Berkeley: University of California Press. Reprinted, New York: B. Franklin, 1970.

—— (1927). *Business cycles: the problem and its setting*. New York: NBER.

Mokyr, Joel (1985). "The Industrial Revolution and the New Economic History." In *The economics of the Industrial Revolution*, edited by Joel Mokyr, 1–51. Totowa, N. J.: Rowman and Allenheld.

—— (1990). *The lever of riches: technological creativity and economic progress*. New York: Oxford UP.

—— (2004). "Accounting for the Industrial Revolution," in Floud & Johnson (2004), vol. 1, pp. 1–27.

——, ed. (1991). *The vital one: essays in honor of Jonathan R. T. Hughes*. Greenwich, Conn.: JAI Press. [*REH*, Supplement 6.]

Molho, Anthony, and Gordon S. Wood, eds (1998). *Imagined histories: American historians interpret the past*. Princeton, N. J.: Princeton UP.

Morison, Samuel Eliot, and Henry Steele Commager (1930). *The growth of the American republic*. New York; London: Oxford UP. [Later edns in 2 vol.; seventh edition, 1980, with William Leuchtenberg.]

Morris, Cynthia Taft (2000). "Review" of Davis & North (1971). EH.Net Economic History Services, November 4, 2000, URL: <http://www.eh.net/bookreviews/library/morris.shtml>.

Morris, Morris D. (1959). "Discussion of Kisch and Krause papers." *JEH* 19:4, 565–9.

—— (1963). "Towards a reinterpretation of nineteenth-century Indian economic history." *JEH* 23:4, 608–18.

—— (1965). *The emergence of an industrial labor force in India. A study of the Bombay cotton mills, 1854–1947*. Berkeley, Cal.: University of California Press.

Mowery, D. C., Nelson, R. R., and Steinmueller, W. E. (1994). "Introduction: in honor of Nathan Rosenberg." *Research Policy* 23:5, *iii–v*.

Myhrman, Johan, and Barry R. Weingast (1994). "Douglass C. North's contributions to economics and economic history." *Scandinavian Journal of Economics* 96:2, 185–93.

Neal, Larry (1994). "Explorations in Economic History." In *Editors as gatekeepers. Getting published in the social sciences*, edited by Rita J. Simon and James J. Fyfe, pp. 73–84. Lanham, Md.; London: Rowman and Littlefield.

Neale, R. S. (1985). "The poverty of positivism: from standard of living to quality of life, 1780–1850." In *Writing Marxist history: British society, economy & culture since 1700*, by R. S. Neale, pp. 109–40. Oxford; New York: Blackwell.

Nerlove, Marc (1966). "Railroads and American economic growth" [Review of Fogel (1964)]. *JEH* 26:1, 107–15.

Newmarch, William (1851). "An attempt to ascertain the magnitude and fluctuations of the amount of bills of exchange in circulation 1828–1847." *Journal of the Statistical Society of London* 14:2, pp. 143–83.

Nicholas, Stephen (1997). "The future of economic history in Australia." *Australian Economic History Review* 37:3, 267–74.

Nicholas, Stephen, and Deborah Oxley (1993). "The living standards of women during the Industrial Revolution, 1795–1820." *EHR* 46:4, 723–49.

Nicholas, Stephen, and Richard H. Steckel (1991). "Heights and living standards of English workers during the early years of industrialization, 1770–1815." *JEH* 51:4, 937–957.

Nicholas, Tom (2004). "Enterprise and management." In Floud & Johnson, eds (2004), vol. II, pp. 227–52.

Niebuhr, Reinhold (1941–3). *The nature and destiny of man; a Christian interpretation.* 2 vol. London: Nisbet & Co. [Gifford lectures, 1939.]

North, Douglass C. (1961). *The economic growth of the United States, 1790 to 1860.* Englewood Cliffs, N.J.: Prentice-Hall. Reprinted, New York: Norton, 1966.

—— (1963). "Quantitative research in American economic history." *AER* 53:1 (Part 1), 128–130. Reprinted in Andreano, ed. (1965), pp. 9–12.

—— (1965). "The state of economic history." *AER: P&P* 55:2, 86–91.

—— (1966). *Growth and welfare in the American past: a new economic history.* Englewood Cliffs, N. J.: Prentice-Hall. Second edition, 1974.

—— (1981). *Structure and change in economic history.* New York: W. W. Norton.

—— (1990). *Institutions, institutional change, and economic performance.* New York: Cambridge UP.

—— (1994a). "Economic performance through time," *AER* 84:3, 359–68. [Nobel Memorial Prize lecture.]

—— (1994b). "Autobiography." From *Le Prix Nobel 1993*, as at URL: <http://nobelprize.org/nobel_prizes/economics/laureates/1993/north-autobio.html>.

—— (2005). *Understanding the process of economic change.* Princeton, N. J.: Princeton UP.

North, Douglass C., and Robert Paul Thomas (1971). "The rise and fall of the manorial system: a theoretical model." *JEH* 31:4, 777–803.

—— (1973). *The rise of the Western World: a New Economic History.* Cambridge: Cambridge UP.

North, Douglass C., and Barry R. Weingast (1989). "Constitutions and commitment: the evolution of institutions governing public choice in 17th-century England." *JEH* 49:4, 803–32.

Nurkse, Ragnar (1952). "The cyclical pattern of inventory investment." *Quarterly Journal of Economics* 66:3, 385–408.

O'Brien, Patrick (1982). "In praise of new economic history." *Economia* [Lisbon] 6:1, 1–27.

O'Brien, Patrick, and Çaglar Keyder (1978). *Economic growth in Britain and France, 1780–1914: two paths to the twentieth century.* London; Boston: G. Allen & Unwin.

O'Brien, Patrick, and Roland Quinault, eds (1993). *The Industrial Revolution and British society.* Cambridge; New York: Cambridge UP.

Ohkawa, Kazushi, and Henry Rosovsky (1973). *Japanese economic growth; trend acceleration in the twentieth century.* Stanford, Cal.: Stanford UP.

Olney, Martha L. (1983). "Fertility and the standard of living in early modern England: in consideration of Wrigley and Schofield." *JEH* 43:1, 71–7.

Olson, Mancur (1985). "Review" of Kindleberger & di Tella, eds (1982). *JEL* 23:2, 622–5.

O'Rourke, Kevin H., and Jeffrey G. Williamson (1999). *Globalization and history: the evolution of a nineteenth-century Atlantic economy.* Cambridge, Mass.: MIT Press.

Parker, Richard (2005). *John Kenneth Galbraith: his life, his politics, his economics.* Chicago: University of Chicago Press.

Parker, William N. (1957). "Coal and steel output movements in western Europe, 1880–1956." *Explorations in Entrepreneurial History* 9:4, 214–30.

—— (1960). "The slave plantation in American agriculture." In *First International conference of economic history (1960: Stockholm). Contributions: . . . B. Comparative study of large-scale agricultural enterprise in post-medieval times*, pp. 321–31. Paris: Mouton and Co.

—— (1962). "Work in progress: a report to Ernst Söderlund." *Scandinavian Economic History Review* 10, 233–44.

—— (1966). "Old wine in new bottles: a review of the *Cambridge economic history, volume VI: The industrial revolutions and after*." *JEH* 26:1, 99–106. Reprinted in Parker (1984), pp. 167–75.

—— (1971). "From old to new to old in economic history." *JEH* 31:1, 3–14. [Presidential address, EHA, 1970.]

—— (1973), "Through growth and beyond: three decades in economic and business history." In Cain & Uselding, eds (1973), pp. 15–47.

—— (1978). "Review" of Rostow (1978). *JEH* 38:4, 1041–3. Reprinted in Parker (1984), pp. 186–8.

—— (1979). "Industry." In *The new Cambridge modern history XIII, companion volume*, edited by Peter Burke, pp. 43–79. Cambridge: Cambridge UP. Reprinted as "The pre-history of the nineteenth century" in Parker (1984), pp. 15–54.

—— (1980a). "The South in the national economy, 1865–1970." *SEJ* 46:4, 1019–48. Reprinted with emendations in Parker (1991a), pp. 67–86.

—— (1980b). "The historiography of American economic history." In *Encyclopedia of American Economic History: studies of the principal movements and ideas*, edited by Glenn Porter, vol. 1, pp. 3–16. New York: Charles Scribner's Sons.

—— (1982). "The American farmer." In *Our forgotten past*, edited by Jerome Blum, pp. 181–208. Reprinted as "The true history of the northern farmer" in Parker (1991a), pp. 161–80.

—— (1984). *Europe, America, and the wider world: essays on the economic history of Western Capitalism. Volume 1, Europe and the world economy*. Cambridge; New York: Cambridge UP.

—— (1987). "Historical introduction." In Kilby, ed. (1987), pp. 3–16.

—— (1991a). *Europe, America, and the wider world: essays on the economic history of Western Capitalism. Volume 2, America and the wider world.* Cambridge; New York: Cambridge UP.

—— (1991b). "The industrial civilization of the Midwest." In Parker (1991a), pp. 215–57.

—— (1991c). "The scale and scope of Alfred D. Chandler, Jr." *JEH* 51:4, 958–63.

—— (1993). "A 'new' business history? A commentary on the 1993 Nobel Prize in Economics." *BHR* 67:4, 623–36.

—— (1996). "Economic history: the teacher and the subject." *JEH* 56:2, 455–8.

——, ed. (1970). *The structure of the cotton economy of the antebellum South.* Washington: The Agricultural History Society. [Reprinted from *AgHist*, 44:1 (Jan. 1970).]

——, ed. (1986). *Economic history and the modern economist.* Oxford; New York: Basil Blackwell.

Parker, William N., and Judith L. V. Klein (1966). "Productivity growth in grain production in the United States, 1840–60 and 1900–10." In CRIW (1966), pp. 523–80. Reprinted in Temin, ed. (1973), pp. 81–109, appendix omitted.

Payne, P. L., and Lance E. Davis (1956). *The Savings Bank of Baltimore, 1818–1866: a historical and analytical study*. Baltimore: Johns Hopkins UP.

Phillips, Ulrich Bonnell (1918). *American Negro slavery; a survey of the supply, employment and control of Negro labor as determined by the plantation regime.* New York; London: D. Appleton & Co.

Pigou, A. C. (1927). *Industrial fluctuations*. London: Macmillan.

Pollard, Sidney (1990). *Britain's prime and Britain's decline: the British economy, 1870–1914.* New York: E. Arnold.

Pope, Clayne L. (1992). "Adult mortality in America before 1900: a view from family histories." In Goldin & Rockoff, eds (1992), pp. 267–96.

Postan, M. M. (1952). *British war production.* London: HMSO. [In the series History of the Second World War, United Kingdom Civil Series, edited by W. K. Hancock]

—— (1982). "Walt Rostow: a personal appreciation." In Kindleberger & di Tella (1982), vol. 1, pp. 1–14.

Prados de la Escosura, Leandro, ed. (2004). *Exceptionalism and industrialisation: Britain and its European rivals, 1688–1815.* Cambridge: Cambridge UP.

Prest, A. R. (1948). "National income of the United Kingdom, 1870–1946." *EJ* 58:229, 31–62.

Prest, A. R.; with A. A. Adams (1954). *Consumers' expenditure in the United Kingdom, 1900–1919.* Cambridge: Cambridge UP.

Preston, Samuel H., and Michael R. Haines (1991). *Fatal years: child mortality in late nineteenth-century America.* Princeton, N.J.: Princeton UP.

Price, Derek J. de Solla (1963). *Little science, big science.* New York: Columbia UP.

Purdue Faculty Papers in Economic History, 1956–1966 (1967). Homewood, Ill.: Richard D. Irwin.

Rabin, Matthew (2004). "Behavioral economics." In *New frontiers in economics*, edited by Michael Szenberg and Lall Ramrattan, pp. 68–102. New York: Cambridge UP.

Ransom, Roger L., and Richard Sutch (1977). *One kind of freedom: the economic consequences of emancipation.* Cambridge; New York: Cambridge UP. Second edn, 2001.

Ransom, Roger L., Richard Sutch, and Gary M. Walton, eds (1982). *Explorations in the New Economic History: essays in honor of Douglass C. North.* New York; London: Academic Press.

Redlich, Fritz (1962). "Approaches to business history." *BHR* 36:1, 61–86.

—— (1965). " 'New' and traditional approaches to economic history and their interdependence." *JEH* 25:4, 480–95.

Reiter, Stanley, and Jonathan Hughes (1981). "Preface to modeling the regulated economy." *Hofstra Law Review* 9, 1381–421.

Reynolds, John F. (1998). "Do historians count anymore? The status of quantitative methods in history, 1975–1995." *Historical Methods* 31:4, 141–8.

Riegel, Robert E. (1965). "Review" of Fogel (1964). *Journal of American History* 52:3, 635–6.

Robertson, Dennis H. (1915). *A study of industrial fluctuation; an enquiry into the character and causes of the so-called cyclical movements of trade.* London: P. S. King.

Robinson, Austin (1941). "Review" of Sweezy (1938). *EJ* 51:201, 101–5.

Robinson, Joan (1956). *The accumulation of capital.* Homewood, Ill.: Irwin.

Rockoff, Hugh (2000). "Review" of Friedman & Schwartz (1963). EH.Net Economic History Services, Jan 1, 2000, URL: <http://www.eh.net/bookreviews/library/rockoff.shtml>.

Rogers, James E. Thorold (1866–1902). *A history of agriculture and prices in England.* Seven vol. in eight. Oxford: Clarendon Press.

Romer, Christina D. (1994). "The end of economic history." *Journal of Economic Education* 25:1, 49–66.

Romer, Christina D., and David H. Romer (1989). "Does monetary policy matter? A new test in the spirit of Friedman and Schwartz." *NBER Macroeconomics Annual 1989*, pp. 121–76. Cambridge, Mass.: MIT Press.

Romer, Thomas, and Howard Rosenthal (1979). "Bureaucrats *vs* voters: on the political economy of resource allocation by direct democracy." *Quarterly Journal of Economics* 93:4, 563–87.

Rosenberg, Nathan (1963). "Technological change in the machine tool industry, 1840–1910." *JEH* 23:4, 414–43. Reprinted in Rosenberg (1976), pp. 9–31.

—— (1967a). "America's rise to woodworking leadership." In *America's wooden age: aspects of its early technology*, edited by Brooke Hindle. Tarrytown, N.Y.: Sleepy Hollow Restorations. Reprinted in Rosenberg (1976), pp. 32–49.

—— (1967b). "Anglo-American wage differences in the 1820's." *JEH* 27:2, 221–9. Reprinted in Rosenberg (1976), pp. 50–8.

—— (1976). *Perspectives on technology*. Cambridge: Cambridge UP.

—— (1982). *Inside the black box: technology and economics*. Cambridge; New York: Cambridge UP.

—— (1991). "Marx wasn't all wrong." *Scientific American* 265:6 (December), 158.

—— (1992). "Charles Babbage: pioneer economist." In *Charles Babbage, ein Pioneer der industrielle Organisation*, edited by Herbert Hax, Nathan Rosenberg & Karl Steinbuch. Düsseldorf: Verlag Wirtschaft und Finanzen, 1992. Reprinted in Rosenberg (1994), pp. 24–46.

—— (1994). *Exploring the black box: technology, economics, and history*. Cambridge; New York: Cambridge UP.

—— (2000). *Schumpeter and the endogeneity of technology: some American perspectives*. London; New York: Routledge. [The Graz Schumpeter Lectures, 3.]

Rosenberg, Nathan, and L. E. Birdzell, Jr. (1986). *How the West grew rich: the economic transformation of the industrial world*. New York: Basic Books.

Rosenberg, Nathan, and Walter G. Vincenti (1978). *The Britannia Bridge: the generation and diffusion of technological knowledge*. Cambridge, Mass.: MIT Press.

Rosovsky, Henry (1979). "Alexander Gerschenkron: a personal and fond recollection." *JEH* 39:4, 1009–13.

Ross, Dorothy (1998). "The new and newer histories: social theory and historiography in an American key." In Molho & Wood, eds (1998), pp. 85–106.

Rostow, W. W. (1938). "Investment and the Great Depression." *EHR* 8:2, 136–58.

—— (1940). *British trade fluctuations, 1868–1896: a chronicle and a commentary*. Ph.D. dissertation, Yale University. Published New York: Arno 1981.

—— (1948). *British economy of the nineteenth century; essays*. Oxford: Clarendon Press.

—— (1952). *The process of economic growth*. New York: Norton. Second edition: Oxford, 1960; New York, 1962.

—— (1956). "The take-off into self-sustained growth." *EJ* 66:261, 25–48.

—— (1957). "The interrelation of theory and economic history." *JEH* 17:4, 509–23. Reprinted Rostow (1990b), pp. 13–26.

—— (1960). *The stages of economic growth: a non-communist manifesto*. Cambridge: Cambridge UP. Second edition, 1971; third edition, 1990.

—— (1978). *The world economy: history & prospect*. Austin: University of Texas Press.

—— (1981). *Pre-invasion bombing strategy: General Eisenhower's Decision of March 25, 1944*. Austin: University of Texas Press, 1981. [Ideas and action series; no. 1]

—— (1986). "Professor Arrow on economic analysis and economic history." In Parker, ed. (1986), pp. 70–6. Oxford; New York: Blackwell. Reprinted in Rostow (1990b), pp. 35–40.

—— (1990a). *Theorists of economic growth from David Hume to the present: with a perspective on the next century*. New York: Oxford UP.

—— (1990b). *History, policy, and economic theory: essays in interaction by W. W. Rostow*. Boulder, Col.: Westview Press.

—— (1992). "Reflections on political economy: past, present, and future." In *Eminent economists: their life philosophies*, edited by Michael Szenberg, pp. 222–35. Cambridge: Cambridge UP.

—— (2001). "The long period is with us every day of our lives." In Hudson, ed. (2001), pp. 307–12.

—— (2003). *Concept and controversy: sixty years of taking ideas to market*. Austin: University of Texas Press.

——, ed. (1963). *The economics of take-off into sustained growth; proceedings of a conference held by the International Economic Association*. London: Macmillan; New York: St Martin's Press.

Rothbarth, E. (1946). "Causes of the superior efficiency of U.S.A. industry as compared with British industry." *EJ* 56:223, 383–90.

Rouvray, Cristel de (2004). "'Old' economic history in the United States, 1939–1954." *Journal of the History of Economic Thought* 26:2, 221–39.

—— (2005). "Economists writing history: American and French experience in the mid 20th century." Ph.D. thesis, London School of Economics and Political Science, University of London.

Rowe, J. W. F (1927). "An index of the physical volume of production." *EJ* 37:146, 173–87.

Rowney, Don Karl, and James Q. Graham, Jr., eds (1969). *Quantitative history: selected readings in the quantitative analysis of historical data*. Homewood, Ill.: Dorsey Press.

Ruggles, Richard, and Henry Brodie (1947). "An empirical approach to economic intelligence in World War II." *JASA* 42:237, 72–91.

Ruttan, Vernon W. (1980). "Bureaucratic productivity: the case of agricultural research." *Public Choice* 35:5, 529–47.

Sadler, Bryan H. (1992) "Foreword." In *Britain in the international economy*, edited by S. N. Broadberry and N. F. R. Crafts, pp. *xi–xiv*. Cambridge; New York: Cambridge UP. [*Festschrift* for A. G. Ford.]

Samuelson, Paul A. (1951). "Abstract of a theorem concerning substitutability in open Leontief models." In *Activity analysis of production and allocation*, edited by T. C. Koopmans, pp. 142–6. New York: John Wiley and Sons.

[Samuelson, Paul A., and Everett E. Hagen] United States. National Resources Planning Board (1943). *After the war, 1918–1920, military and economic demobilization of the United States. Its effect upon employment and income*. Washington, D. C.: Government Printing Office.

Sandberg, Lars G. (1974). *Lancashire in decline: a study in entrepreneurship, technology, and international trade*. Columbus, Ohio: Ohio State UP.

Sass, Steven A. (1986). *Entrepreneurial historians and history: leadership and rationality in American economic historiography, 1940–1960*. New York; London: Garland.

Saville, John (2001). "Economic history: a reminiscence." In Hudson, ed. (2001), pp. 329–32.

Saxonhouse, Gary, and Gavin Wright, eds (1984). *Technique, spirit, and form in the making of modern economies: essays in honor of William N. Parker*. Greenwich, Conn.; London: JAI Press. *REH*, Supplement 3.

Schaefer, Donald, and Mark Schmitz (1982). "Efficiency in antebellum Southern agriculture: a covariance approach." *SEJ* 49:1, 88–98.

—— (1985). "The Parker–Gallman sample and wealth distributions for the antebellum South – a comment." *EEH* 22:2, 220–6.

Schmookler, Jacob (1966). *Invention and economic growth.* Cambridge, Mass.: Harvard UP.

Schofield, Roger (1985). "English marriage patterns revisited." *Journal of Family History* 10:1, 2–20.

—— (2000). "Short-run and secular demographic response to fluctuations in the standard of living in England, 1540–1834." In *Population and economy: from hunger to modern economic growth*, edited by T. Bengtsson and O. Saito, pp. 49–71. Oxford: Oxford UP.

Schultz, T. Paul (1986). Review essay on Easterlin & Crimmins (1985). *Population and Development Review* 12:1, 127–40.

Schumpeter, Joseph A. (1934). *The theory of economic development; An inquiry into profits, capital, credit, interest, and the business cycle*. Cambridge, Mass.: Harvard UP. [First published in German, 1912.]

—— (1939). *Business cycles; a theoretical, historical, and statistical analysis of the capitalist process.* 2 vol. New York; London: McGraw-Hill.

—— (1954). *History of economic analysis*. New York: Oxford UP. [Edited from manuscript by Elizabeth Boody Schumpeter.]

Schwartz, Anna J. (1960). "Gross dividend and interest payments by corporations at selected dates in the 19th century." In CRIW (1960), pp. 407–45.

—— (1993). "Interview: Anna J. Schwartz." *The Region* [Federal Reserve Bank of Minneapolis], 4–11. Interviewed by David Fettig.

—— (1994). "Review of *International Economic Transactions*, edited by Peter Hooper and J. D. Richardson; University Chicago Press, 1991." *Journal of International and Comparative Economics* 3:2, 147–56.

—— (1996). "U. S. foreign exchange market intervention since 1962." *Scottish Journal of Political Economy* 43:4, 379–97.

—— (2002). "Anna Schwartz" [interview]. In *Reflections on the Great Depression*, by Randall E. Parker, pp. 106–29. Cheltenham, UK; Northampton, Mass.: Edward Elgar.

—— (2004). "An interview with Anna J. Schwartz." *Macroeconomic Dynamics* 8:3, 395–417. Interviewed, with an introduction, by Edward Nelson.

Scott, Joan Wallach (1987). "History and difference." *Daedalus* 116 (Fall), 93–118. As reprinted, "American women historians, 1884–1984." In *Gender and the politics of history*, revised edition, by Joan Wallach Scott, pp. 178–98; 250–4. New York: Columbia UP, 1999.

Scott, William Robert (1910–1912). *The constitution and finance of English, Scottish and Irish joint-stock companies to 1720.* 3 vol. Cambridge: Cambridge UP.

—— (1928). "Memoir: Sir William Ashley." *EHR*, 1st series 1:2, 319–21.

Seebohm, F. (1891). "French peasant proprietorship under the open field system of husbandry." *EJ* 1:1, 59–72.

Semmell, Bernard (1957). "Sir William Ashley as 'Socialist of the Chair'." *Economica n.s.* 24:96, 343–53.

Sen, Amartya Kumar (1960). *Choice of techniques; an aspect of the theory of planned economic development.* Oxford: B. Blackwell.

Sewell, William H., Jr. (2001). "Whatever happened to the 'social' in social history?" In *Schools of thought: twenty-five years of interpretive social science*, edited by Joan W. Scott and Debra Keates, pp. 209–26. Princeton, N.J.: Princeton UP.

Shannon, Fred A. (1934). *Economic history of the people of the United States*. New York: Macmillan. Later editions, *America's economic growth* [Macmillan, 1940, 1951].

—— (1945). *The farmer's last frontier, agriculture, 1860–1897*. New York; Toronto: Farrar & Rinehart. [*Economic history of the United States*, vol. 5]

Shannon, H. A. (1934). "Bricks – a trade index, 1785–1849." *Economica* 1:3, 300–18. Reprinted in *Essays in economic history*, vol. three, edited by E. M. Carus-Wilson, pp. 188–201. London: Arnold, 1962.

[Sinclair, W. A.] Forster, Colin, ed. (1970). *Australian economic development in the twentieth century; essays by W. A. Sinclair*. London: Allen & Unwin; New York: Praeger, 1971.

Slaughter, Matthew J. (1995). "The antebellum transportation revolution and factor-price convergence." NBER Working Paper 5303.

Smith, Robert Worthington (1946). "Was slavery unprofitable in the ante-bellum South?" *AgHist* 20:1, 62–4.

Smith, Vernon (1981). "Experimental economics at Purdue." In Horwich & Quirk, eds (1981), pp. 369–73.

Smith, Walter Buckingham, and Arthur H. Cole (1935). *Fluctuations in American business, 1790–1860*. Cambridge, Mass.: Harvard UP.

Snowden, Kenneth A. (1987). "Mortgage rates and American capital market development in the late nineteenth century." *JEH* 47:3, 771–91.

Sokoloff, Kenneth L. (1988). "Inventive activity in early industrial America: evidence from patent records, 1790–1846." *JEH* 48:4, 813–50.

Solow, Robert M. (1957). "Technical change and the aggregate production function." *REStat* 39:3, 312–20.

—— (1986). "Economics: is something missing?" In Parker, ed. (1986), pp. 21–9.

—— (1998). "How did economics get that way and what way did it get?" In *American academic culture in transformation: fifty years, four disciplines*, edited by Thomas Bender and Carl E. Schorske, pp. 57–76. Princeton, N.J.: Princeton UP., 1998.

Soltow, Lee, ed. (1969) *Six papers on the size distribution of wealth and income*. New York: Columbia UP for NBER. *Studies in income and wealth*, vol. 33.

Stampp, Kenneth M. (1956). *The peculiar institution: slavery in the ante-bellum South*. New York: Alfred A. Knopf.

Steckel, Richard H. (1979). "Slave height profiles from coastwise manifests." *EEH* 16:4, 363–80.

—— (1986). "A peculiar population: the nutrition, health, and mortality of American slaves from childhood to maturity." *JEH* 46:3, 721–41.

—— (1995). "Stature and the standard of living." *JEL* 33:4 1903–40.

—— (2005). "Health and nutrition in pre-Columbian America: the skeletal evidence." *Journal of Interdisciplinary History* 36:1, 1–32.

Steckel, Richard H., and Roderick Floud, eds (1997). *Health and welfare during industrialization*. Chicago, Ill.: University of Chicago Press.

Steckel, Richard H., and Jerome C. Rose, eds (2002). *The backbone of history: health and nutrition in the Western Hemisphere*. Cambridge; New York: Cambridge UP.

Stone, Richard; with D. A. Rowe (1954). *The measurement of consumers' expenditure and behaviour in the United Kingdom, 1920–1938*. Cambridge: Cambridge UP.

Strachey, John (1936). *The theory and practice of socialism*. London: Victor Gollancz. [Left Book Club.]

Summerhill, William R. (2003). *Order against progress: government, foreign investment, and railroads in Brazil, 1854–1913*. Stanford, Cal.: Stanford UP.

Supple, Barry (1971). "Can the new economic history become an import substitute?" In McCloskey, ed. (1971), pp. 423–30.

—— (1989). "Review" of Jones (1988). *EHR* 42:2, 303–4.

Sutch, Richard (1975). "The treatment received by American slaves: a critical review of the evidence presented in *Time on the Cross*." *EEH* 12:4, 335–438.

—— (1982). "Douglass North and the New Economic History." In Ransom, Sutch & Walton, eds (1982), pp. 13–38.

Svennilson, Ingvar (1954). *Growth and stagnation in the European economy*. Geneva: United Nations Economic Commission for Europe.

Sweezy, Paul M. (1938). *Monopoly and competition in the English coal trade, 1550–1850*. Cambridge, Mass.: Harvard UP. [Awarded the David A. Wells Prize for 1937–8; Harvard Economic Studies, No. 63.]

—— (1942). *The theory of capitalist development; principles of Marxian political economy*. New York: Oxford UP.

Swierenga, Robert P., ed. (1970). *Quantification in American history: theory and research*. New York: Atheneum, 1970.

Sylla, Richard (1969). "Federal policy, banking market structure, and capital mobilization in the United States, 1863–1913." *JEH* 29:4, 657–86. Reprinted in Whaples & Betts, eds (1995), pp. 482–508.

—— (2002). "An interview with Richard Sylla." *NCS* 17:1, 3–10. Interviewed by Howard Bodenhorn.

Taylor, Arthur J. (1975). "Editor's introduction." In *The standard of living in Britain in the Industrial Revolution*, edited by Arthur J. Taylor, pp. *x–lv*. London: Methuen.

Taylor, George Rogers (1951). *The transportation revolution, 1815–1860*. New York: Rinehart.

Taylor, K. W., and H. Michell (1931). *Statistical contributions to Canadian economic history, vol. 2*. Toronto: Macmillan of Canada.

Taylor, Miles (1997). "The beginnings of modern British social history?" *History Workshop Journal* 43, 155–76.

Temin, Peter (1964). *Iron and steel in nineteenth century America: an economic inquiry*. Cambridge, Mass.: MIT Press.

—— (1966a). "Labor scarcity and the problem of American industrial efficiency in the 1850s." *JEH* 26, 277–98. Reprinted in Temin, ed. (1973), pp. 113–36.

—— (1966b). "Steam and waterpower in the early nineteenth century." *JEH* 26:2, 187–205. Reprinted with omissions in Fogel & Engerman, eds (1971), pp. 228–37.

—— (1969). *The Jacksonian economy*. New York: W.W. Norton.

—— (1971). "Notes on labor scarcity in America." *Journal of Interdisciplinary History* 1:2, 251–64. Reprinted in Temin, ed. (1973), pp. 165–80.

—— (1976). *Did monetary forces cause the Great Depression?* New York: W.W. Norton.

—— (1980a). "Modes of behavior." *Journal of Economic Behavior and Organization* 1:1, 175–95.

—— (1980b). *Taking your medicine: drug regulation in the United States*. Cambridge, Mass.: Harvard UP.

—— (1987). *The fall of the Bell System: a study in prices and politics*. Cambridge; New York: Cambridge UP.

—— (1989). *Lessons from the Great Depression*. Cambridge, Mass.: MIT Press.

—— (1994). "Labour scarcity and capital markets in America." In Thompson, ed. (1994), pp. 257–73.

—— (1995). "The 'Koreaboom' in West Germany: fact or fiction?" *EHR* 48:4, 737–53. Translated into German in RWI-Mitteilungen (1996), 207–24. Reprinted in Komlos & Eddie (1997), pp. 351–69.

—— (1997a). "Two views of the British Industrial Revolution." *JEH* 57:1, 63–82.

—— (1997b). "Is it Kosher to talk about culture?" *JEH* 57:2, 267–87. [Presidential address, EHA, 1996.]

—— (2001). "A market economy in the early Roman Empire." *Journal of Roman Studies* 91, 169–81.

—— (2006). "The economy of the early Roman Empire." *Journal of Economic Perspectives* 20:1, 133–51.

——, ed. (1973). *New Economic History: selected readings*. Harmondsworth, UK: Penguin.

——, ed. (1991). *Inside the business enterprise: historical perspectives on the use of information*. Chicago; London: University of Chicago Press. [NBER Research Conference Report.]

Temin, Peter, and Hans-Joachim Voth (2005). "Credit rationing and crowding out during the industrial revolution: evidence from Hoare's Bank, 1702–1862." *EEH* 42:3, 325–48.

Thomas, Brinley (1954). *Migration and economic growth; a study of Great Britain and the Atlantic economy*. Cambridge; New York: Cambridge UP. Second edition, 1973.

Thompson, E. P. (1963). *The making of the English working class*. London: Victor Gollancz; New York: Vintage Books.

Thompson, F. M. L. (1994). "Introduction." In Thompson, ed. (1994), pp. 1–22.

——, ed. (1994). *Landowners, capitalists, and entrepreneurs: essays for Sir John Habakkuk*. Oxford: Clarendon Press; New York: Oxford UP.

Thornton, John K. (1996). "The African background to American colonization." In Engerman & Gallman, eds (1996, 2000), vol. I, pp. 53–94.

Tilly, Charles (1990). *Coercion, capital and European states: AD 990–1990*. Cambridge, Mass.: Blackwell.

Tilly, Richard (1997). "Cliometrics in Germany: an introductory essay." In Komlos and Eddie, eds (1997), pp. 17–33.

—— (2001). "German economic history and Cliometrics: a selective survey of recent tendencies." *EREH* 5:2, 151–87.

Tooke, Thomas (1838–57). *A history of prices, and of the state of the circulation, from 1793 to 1837; preceded by a brief sketch of the state of corn trade in the last two centuries*. Six vol. London: Longman, Orme, Brown, Green, & Longmans. Reprinted, with an introduction by T. E. Gregory, New York: Adelphi Co., 1928.

Toutain, J.-C. (1961). "Le produit brut de l'agriculture française de 1700 à 1958." *Cahiers de l'Institut de Science Économique Appliquée* Serie AF, nos. 1–2. Paris: ISÉA.

Tribe, Keith (1995). *Strategies of economic order: German economic discourse, 1750–1950*. Cambridge; New York: Cambridge UP.

—— (1997). "Introduction." In *Economic careers: economics and economists in Britain, 1930–1970*, edited by Keith Tribe, 1–12. London; New York: Routledge.

—— (2000). "The Cambridge Economics Tripos 1903–55 and the training of economists." *Manchester School* 68:2, 222–48.

Unger, Irwin (1964). *The Greenback era: a social and political history of American finance, 1865–1879*. Princeton, N.J.: Princeton UP. [Awarded the Pulitzer Prize for History, 1965.]

—— (1967). "The 'New Left' and American history: some recent trends in United States historiography." *AHR* 72:4, 1237–63.

Ure, Andrew (1835). *The philosophy of manufactures; or, an exposition of the scientific, moral, and commercial economy of the factory system of Great Britain*. London: Charles Knight. Reprinted London: Cass; New York: A. M. Kelley, 1967.

Urquhart, M. C. (1959). "Capital accumulation, technological change, and economic growth." *Canadian Journal of Economics and Political Science* 25:4, 411–30.

—— (1986). "New estimates of Gross National Product, Canada, 1870–1926: some implications for Canadian development." In Engerman & Gallman, eds (1986), pp. 9–88.

—— (1993). *Gross National Product, Canada, 1870–1926. The derivation of the estimates.* Montreal; Buffalo: McGill–Queen's UP. [With chapters by A. G. Green; Thomas Rymes; Marion Steele; A. M. Sinclair; D. M. McDougall; R. M. McInnis.]

Urquhart, M. C., and K. A. H. Buckley (1965). *Historical statistics of Canada.* Toronto: Macmillan of Canada and Cambridge UP.

Usher, Abbott Payson (1929). *A history of mechanical inventions.* Cambridge, Mass.: Harvard UP. Revised and expanded edition, 1954.

—— (1932). "The application of the quantitative method to economic history." *Journal of Political Economy* 40:2, 186–209.

Usher, Dan (1980). *The measurement of economic growth.* New York: Columbia UP.

van Ark, Bart (1994). "Review" of Urquhart (1993). *JEL* 32:4, 1927–8.

Volkov, Vadim (2002). *Violent entrepreneurs: the use of force in the making of Russian capitalism.* Ithaca, N.Y.: Cornell UP.

von Tunzelmann, G. N. (1978). *Steam power and British industrialization to 1860.* Oxford: Clarendon Press.

—— (1980). "Conference reports: Cliometrics at Warwick (GB)." *JEEH* 9:1, 219–32.

—— (2003). "Sir John Habakkuk, 1915–2002." *The Eagle 2003*, 74–6. [St John's College, Cambridge.]

Voth, Hans-Joachim (2004). "Living standards and the urban environment." In Floud & Johnson, eds (2004), pp. 268–94.

Ward-Perkins, C. N. (1950). "The commercial crisis of 1847." *OEP, n.s.* 1:3, 300–18. Reprinted in *Essays in economic history, vol. three*, edited by E. M. Carus-Wilson, pp. 263–79. London: Arnold, 1962.

Webb, Walter Prescott (1931). *The great plains.* New York: Grosset & Dunlap.

Weintraub, E. Roy (2007). "Economists talking with economists, an historian's perspective." In *Inside the economist's mind: conversations with eminent economists*, edited by Paul A. Samuelson and William A. Barnett, pp. 1–11. Malden, Mass.; Oxford: Blackwell.

Weir, David R. (1984). "Life under pressure: France and England, 1670–1870." *JEH* 44:1, 27–47.

Weiss, Thomas (1998). "Remarks made in accepting the Hughes Prize for Bob Gallman." *NCS* 13:3, 7–8.

—— (2001). "Review" of Fogel & Engerman (1974). EH.Net Economic History Services, Nov 16, 2001, URL: <http://www.eh.net/bookreviews/library/weiss.shtml>.

Weiss, Thomas, and Donald Schaefer, eds (1994). *American economic development in historical perspective.* Stanford, Cal.: Stanford UP.

Whaples, Robert (1991). "A quantitative history of the *Journal of Economic History* and the Cliometric revolution." *JEH* 51:2, 289–301.

—— (1995). "Where is there consensus among American economic historians?" *JEH* 55:1, 139–54.

Whaples, Robert, and Dianne C. Betts, eds (1995). *Historical perspectives on the American economy: selected readings.* Cambridge; New York: Cambridge UP.

White, Eugene Nelson (1984). "A reinterpretation of the banking crisis of 1930." *JEH* 44:1, 119–38.

Williamson, Harold F., ed. (1944). *The growth of the American economy.* Englewood Cliffs, N.J.: Prentice-Hall. Second edition, 1951.

—— (1966). "Business history and economic history." *JEH* 26:4, 407–417. [Presidential address, EHA, 1966.]

Williamson, Jeffrey G. (1985). *Did British capitalism breed inequality?* Boston: Allen & Unwin.

—— (1996). "Globalization, convergence, and history." *JEH* 56:2, 277–306. [Presidential address, EHA, 1995.]

Williamson, Samuel H. (1991). "The history of Cliometrics." In Mokyr, ed. (1991), pp. 15–31.

Williamson, Samuel H., and Robert Whaples (2003). "Cliometrics." In *The Oxford encyclopedia of economic history, vol. 1*, edited by Joel Mokyr, pp. 446–7. Oxford; New York: Oxford UP.

Wilson, Charles (1954; 1968). *The history of Unilever; a study in economic growth and social change.* London: Cassel. [vols 1 & 2, 1954; vol. 3, 1968.]

—— (1965). *England's apprenticeship, 1603–1763.* London: Longman; New York: St Martin's Press. Second edn, Longman, 1984.

Wimmer, Larry T. (2003). "Reflections on the *Early Indicators* project: a partial history." In Costa, ed. (2003), pp. 1–10.

Woodman, Harold D. (1976). "A Cliometric key for a historical lock." [Review article on David (1975).] *Reviews in American History* 4:2, 230–6.

Worcester, Kenton W. (2001). *Social Science Research Council, 1923–1998.* New York: SSRC.

World Bank (1993). *The East Asian miracle: economic growth and public policy.* New York: Oxford UP.

Wright, Gavin (1970). " 'Economic democracy' and the concentration of agricultural wealth in the cotton South, 1850–1860." In Parker, ed. (1970), pp. 63–94.

—— (1971). "Econometric studies of history." In Intriligator, ed. (1971), 413–59.

—— (1978). *The political economy of the cotton South: households, markets, and wealth in the nineteenth century.* New York: Norton.

—— (1986). *Old South, new South: revolutions in the southern economy since the Civil War.* New York: Basic Books.

—— (1989). "Parker retirement conference." *NCS* 4:3, 5–6.

—— (2000). "In memoriam: William Nelson Parker, 1919–2000." *JEH* 60:2, 542.

—— (2006a). "An interview with Gavin Wright." *NCS* 21:1, 4–13. Interviewed by Susan Wolcott.

—— (2006b). *Slavery and American economic development.* Baton Rouge, La.: Louisiana State UP. [Walter Lynwood Fleming Lectures in Southern History, 1997.]

Wrigley, E. A. (1967). "A simple model of London's importance in changing English society and economy 1650–1750." *Past & Present* 37, 44–70.

—— (1983). "The growth of population in eighteenth-century England: a conundrum resolved." *Past & Present* 98, 121–50.

—— (2002). "Population history." In *History and historians in the twentieth century*, edited by Peter Burke, pp. 141–64. Published for The British Academy. Oxford: Oxford UP.

—— (2004). "British population during the 'long' eighteenth century, 1680–1840." In Floud & Johnson, eds (2004), pp. 57–95.

Wrigley, E. A., and R. S. Schofield; with contributions by Ronald Lee and Jim Oeppen (1981). *The population history of England 1541–1871. A reconstruction.* London: Edward Arnold.

Wrigley, E. A., R. S. Davies, J. E. Oeppen, and R. S. Schofield (1997). *English population history from family reconstitution 1580–1837.* Cambridge: Cambridge UP.

Yasuba, Yasukichi (1961). "The profitability and viability of plantation slavery in the United States." *The Economic Studies Quarterly [Kikan riron–keizaigaku*, Tokyo] 12, 60–7. Reprinted in Fogel & Engerman, eds (1971), pp. 362–8.

—— (1962). *Birth rates of the white population in the United States, 1800–1860, an economic study.* Baltimore: Johns Hopkins UP.

—— (2005). "An interview with Yasukichi Yasuba." *NCS* 21:2, 4–9. Interviewed by A. J. H. Latham.

CREDITS

Photograph of Moses Abramovitz taken at Stanford University, early 1990s; courtesy of Gavin Wright and Department of Economics, Stanford University

Photograph of Mac Urquhart taken at Queen's University, 1988; photographer Martin Prachowny; courtesy of Frank Lewis

Photo of Anna Schwartz taken at New York office of the NBER, about 2000; courtesy of the photographer, Marinella Moscheni

Photo of Walt Rostow taken at Austin, Texas, about 1978; courtesy of Martha Harrison and Elspeth Davies Rostow

Photo of Stanley Lebergott taken at Wesleyan University, 1993; courtesy of Bill Burkhart, Wesleyan University Photographer

Photo of Hrothgar Habakkuk taken at Oxford, early 1970s; photographer B. J. Harris (Oxford) Ltd; courtesy of Alison Hoddell

Photo of Phyllis Deane taken at Cambridge, mid-1980s; courtesy of the photographer, Dorothy Hahn

Photo of Max Cole taken at Swansea, Wales, April 1998; courtesy of the photographer, John Latham

Photo of Robin Matthews taken at Cambridge, early 1990s; courtesy of Robin Matthews

Photo of Bill Parker taken in Connecticut, mid-1980s; courtesy of Jarrett Parker

Photo of Doug North taken at Washington University, early 2000s; photographer Herb Whiteman; courtesy of Doug North

Photo of Lance Davis taken at Pasadena, California, summer 2004; courtesy of Lance Davis

Photo of Jon Hughes taken at Northwestern University, mid-1980s; courtesy of Northwestern University Archives

Photo of Nate Rosenberg taken at Stanford University, early 1980s; courtesy of Nate Rosenberg

Photo of Charles Feinstein taken at Oxford, July 1996; courtesy of Anne Digby

Photo of Max Hartwell taken at Oxford, August 2004; courtesy of the photographer, Mark Thomas

Photo of Eric Jones taken at Melbourne, Australia, November 2003; courtesy of the photographer, Christopher Jones

Photo of Dick Easterlin taken at the University of Southern California, August 2004; courtesy of the photographer, Pouyan Mashayekh-Ahangarani

Photo of Bob Gallman taken at Baltimore, Maryland, September 1990; courtesy of the photographer, Matthew Gallman

Photo of Bob Fogel taken at Center for Population Economics, July 2006; photographer Dan Dry; courtesy of The Graduate School of Business, University of Chicago

Photo of Stan Engerman taken at Rochester, New York, April 2004; photographer J. Engerman; courtesy of Stan Engerman

Photo of John Meyer taken at Harvard Business School, 1980; courtesy of Lauren Marshall and Office of News and Public Affairs, Harvard University

Photo of Albert Fishlow taken at Columbia University, 2000; courtesy of Teresa Aguayo and The Center for Brazilian Studies, Columbia University

Photo of Paul David taken at Point Lobos Reserve State Park, Monterey, California, October 2003; courtesy of the photographer, Matthew David <matt@navigate9.com>

Photo of Peter Temin taken at MIT, 2004; courtesy of Peter Temin

CONTRIBUTORS

John C. Brown, Department of Economics, Clark University, Worcester, Massachusetts

Louis P. Cain, Department of Economics, Loyola University Chicago, Illinois and Department of Economics, Northwestern University, Evanston, Illinois

Charles W. Calomiris, Graduate School of Business and School of International and Public Affairs, Columbia University, New York, New York

Fred Carstensen, Department of Economics, University of Connecticut, Storrs, Connecticut

Susan B. Carter, Department of Economics, University of California, Riverside, California

Nicholas F. R. Crafts, Department of Economics, University of Warwick, Coventry, Warwickshire

Alexander J. Field, Department of Economics, Santa Clara University, Santa Clara, California

Nancy Folbre, Department of Economics, University of Massachusetts, Amherst, Massachusetts

Mark Guglielmo, Center for Population Economics, University of Chicago, Chicago, Illinois

Michael Huberman, Department of Economics, Université de Montréal, Montréal, Quebec

William K. Hutchinson, Department of Economics, Vanderbilt University, Nashville, Tennessee

A. J. H. (John) Latham, School of Humanities, University of Wales, Swansea, Wales

Gary D. Libecap, Bren School of Environmental Science and Management and Department of Economics, University of California, Santa Barbara, California

John S. Lyons, Department of Economics, Miami University, Oxford, Ohio

R. Marvin McInnis, Department of Economics, Queen's University, Kingston, Ontario

John V. C. Nye, Department of Economics, Washington University, St Louis, Missouri and Department of Economics, George Mason University, Fairfax, Virginia

Anthony Patrick O'Brien, Department of Economics, Lehigh University, Bethlehem, Pennsylvania

Patrick Karl O'Brien, Department of Economic History, London School of Economics and Political Science, London

Paul Rhode, Department of Economics, University of Arizona, Tucson, Arizona

Kenneth L. Sokoloff, Department of Economics, University of California, Los Angeles, California

William A. Sundstrom, Department of Economics, Santa Clara University, Santa Clara, California

Mark Thomas, Department of History, University of Virginia, Charlottesville, Virginia

G. Nicholas von Tunzelmann, Science Policy Research Unit, University of Sussex, Brighton, Sussex

Eugene N. White, Department of Economics, Rutgers University, New Brunswick, New Jersey

Samuel H. Williamson, Department of Economics, Miami University, Oxford, Ohio

INDEX OF NAMES

For Product Safety Concerns and Information please contact our EU representative GPSR@taylorandfrancis.com
Taylor & Francis Verlag GmbH, Kaufingerstraße 24, 80331 München, Germany

www.ingramcontent.com/pod-product-compliance
Lightning Source LLC
LaVergne TN
LVHW011102300926
849160LV00008B/258
* 9 7 8 0 4 1 5 7 4 8 3 8 4 *